The Mindful Interview Method

The Mindful Interview Method: Retrieving Cognitive Evidence provides investigators with a proven methodology to gather authentic, reliable information from eyewitnesses to help identify potential suspects. The book offers police, and non-law enforcement readers, step-by-step techniques to improve gathering reliable evidence through a "mindful" interview process. The author also provides an assessment component that can measure the reliability of previous interviews performed, and further help to improve the interview process, the skills of the investigator, and thus the reliability of cognitive evidence gathered from future interviews.

It is notable that there is minimal to no instruction or training currently offered to those individuals most-often tasked with interviewing an eyewitness about a crime as part of criminal investigations. Despite the lack of training and certification, we allow interviewers to conduct questioning in the face of well-established research as to the malleability of human memory. The assumption is that officials, trained in the rules of evidence, will innately ask the right questions—and in the proper manner—without the proper understanding of the fragility of human memory or the proper training. That assumption is false, and the reality is quite the opposite. In fact, we learn of cases commonplace in the media, that frequently involve questionable interview tactics, misidentifications, and wrongful convictions of innocent people.

The Mindful Interview Method uses cognitive research to inform the methods and principles for a mindful approach to gathering only the information the subject remembers. This is the best way to use evidence-based lines of questioning, to perform interviews that elicit the most reliable accounts and information for investigative purposes. Considering current reforms on best practices throughout the criminal justice system, the book provides a path forward for professional interviewers to adopt interview methodologies that guide the practitioner to question anyone in a mindful manner.

Gil Zamora retired as the police artist at the San Jose Police Department (SJPD) in 2011. During his time there, he interviewed well over 3,000 eyewitnesses to crimes ranging from indecent exposure to murder. He was certified in the FBI Composite Art technique in 1993 and apprenticed with renowned police artist, Tom Macris, from 1992 to 1995. He developed his own interview methodology, Compositure (1998), based on the cognitive interview technique and focused on the elimination of post-event information to stimulate eyewitness memory. His interview technique led him to help solve several hundred investigations in the Bay Area and testify as an expert forensic artist in various criminal court cases. Mr. Zamora was a senior instructor (from 2000 to 2014) in the cognitive interview technique and trained investigators throughout the state of California in advanced interview techniques certified by Commission on Peace Officer Standards and Training (POST). He provided annual training for SJPD investigators coming into the bureau to inform them about forensic art resources to help in their investigations. Mr. Zamora is a frequent speaker at local universities, victim advocacy groups, and law enforcement agencies. Since 2017, Mr. Zamora has been a lecturer at San Jose State University, and has taught criminal justice students the art of mindful interviewing while supporting the justice studies department in lecturing other topics.

The Mindful Interview Method
Retrieving Cognitive Evidence

Gil Zamora

CRC Press
Taylor & Francis Group
Boca Raton London New York

CRC Press is an imprint of the
Taylor & Francis Group, an **informa** business

First edition published 2023
by CRC Press
6000 Broken Sound Parkway NW, Suite 300, Boca Raton, FL 33487-2742

and by CRC Press
4 Park Square, Milton Park, Abingdon, Oxon, OX14 4RN
CRC Press is an imprint of Taylor & Francis Group, LLC

© 2023 Gil Zamora

Reasonable efforts have been made to publish reliable data and information, but the author and publisher cannot assume responsibility for the validity of all materials or the consequences of their use. The authors and publishers have attempted to trace the copyright holders of all material reproduced in this publication and apologize to copyright holders if permission to publish in this form has not been obtained. If any copyright material has not been acknowledged, please write and let us know so we may rectify in any future reprint.

Except as permitted under US Copyright Law, no part of this book may be reprinted, reproduced, transmitted, or utilized in any form by any electronic, mechanical, or other means, now known or hereafter invented, including photocopying, microfilming, and recording, or in any information storage or retrieval system, without written permission from the publishers.

For permission to photocopy or use material electronically from this work, access www.copyright.com or contact the Copyright Clearance Center, Inc. (CCC), 222 Rosewood Drive, Danvers, MA 01923, 978-750-8400. For works that are not available on CCC please contact mpkbookspermissions@tandf.co.uk

Trademark notice: Product or corporate names may be trademarks or registered trademarks and are used only for identification and explanation without intent to infringe.

Library of Congress Cataloging-in-Publication Data

Names: Zamora, Gil, author. Title: The mindful interview method: retrieving cognitive evidence / Gil Zamora. Identifiers: LCCN 2023001015 (print) | LCCN 2023001016 (ebook) | ISBN 9781032203102 (hardback) | ISBN 9781032200798 (paperback) | ISBN 9781003263173 (ebook) Subjects: LCSH: Interviewing in law enforcement. | Criminology—Methodology. | Memory. | Forensic psychology.
Classification: LCC HV8073.3 .Z36 2023 (print) | LCC HV8073.3 (ebook) | DDC 363.25/4—dc23/eng/20230216 LC record available at https://lccn.loc.gov/2023001015LC ebook record available at https://lccn.loc.gov/2023001016

ISBN: 9781032203102 (hbk)
ISBN: 9781032200798 (pbk)
ISBN: 9781003263173 (ebk)

DOI: 10.4324/9781003263173

Typeset in Palatino
by Deanta Global Publishing Services, Chennai, India

This book is dedicated to Isabel and Inocente Zamora.

CONTENTS

Preface … xv

SECTION I Perspectives

1 Introduction … 3

2 A Different Path … 7
- The Art of Policing … 7
- Enhancing the Investigative Process … 9
- Eyewitness Interviews Take Center Stage … 10
- Real Beauty … 11
- Students and Eyewitness Interviews … 11
- Understanding Cognitive Evidence … 12
- For Your Consideration … 13

SECTION II Establishing Principles

3 Cognitive Evidence … 17
- Guidance on Eyewitness Interviews … 18
- Cognitive Evidence … 20
- Considering Confidence of Recollection … 21
- The Discretion to Search for More … 22
- Understanding How Eyewitness Memory Works … 24
- Reliable Not Accurate … 24
- Estimator Variables and Cognitive Evidence … 25
- System Variables in Eyewitness Interviews … 25
- How Precise Can Eyewitnesses Be? … 26
- Did He Have a Beard? … 27
- Tell Me Exactly Where This Feature Goes on the Face … 28
- Experiments and Practitioners … 30

CONTENTS

Accountability for Cognitive Evidence	32
For Your Consideration	33

4 The Detective Mind — 35

Eyewitness: Systems 1 and 2	36
Where's the Drug Money?	37
Focus on the Bounce	37
Serial Robbery Case	40
Be Mindful of the Detective Mind	42
For Your Consideration	42

5 Heuristics of Interviewing Eyewitnesses — 43

Similarities in Interviews and Interrogations	43
The Heuristics for Investigations	44
Heuristics in Forensic Art	44
Qualitative Research and Eyewitness Interviews	46
Semi-Structured Interview	47
Breaking Habits	48
For Your Consideration	50

6 Investigating Mindfulness — 51

Mindfulness	51
The Spiritual Laws of Success	52
Mindful Opportunities	53
Driving Mindfully	54
Practicing Being Present	54
We've Heard It Before	56
That Is All There Is	57
Are You Really Present?	57
Attention to Detail	57
Being Mindful before the Interview	58
Awareness	59
Try It before You Knock It	61
For Your Consideration	61

SECTION III How We Interview Eyewitnesses

7 Mindful of the Innocent — 65

Mindful of DNA	65

Innocence Project	67
Reforms	68
Transparency and Adherence to the *Guide*	71
Excerpt from Case Study #1	72
Excerpt from Case Study #2	72
For Your Consideration	74

8 Mindful of Interrogations — 75

Interviewing Eyewitness and Not Interrogating Them	75
We Should Treat Eyewitness Memory Like Trace Evidence	77
Don't Be Suspicious of Your Eyewitness	78
Objective Perspective	79
The Unreliable Eyewitness	80
Stay with the Interview Process	82
For Your Consideration	83

9 Empathetic Strategy — 85

Establishing Rapport	85
Integrating Empathy and Compassion	87
For Your Consideration	89

SECTION IV *Mindful Interview Method*

10 Principles behind The Mindful Interview Method — 93

Behind the Mindful Interview Method	93
The Mindful Interview Method Principles	94
The Mindful Interview Method Standards	95
Mindful Reset	95
Mindful Interview Method Probing Framework Standard	97
Intentional Listening Standard	98
Practicing Mirror Probe Questions (MP)	100
Mindful of Cognitive Evidence Standard	102
Mindful Interview Method Conclusion Standard	103
For Your Consideration	104

11 How to Perform the Mindful Interview Method — 105

Practicing the Mindful Interview Method	105
Topic 1	107
Topic 2	108

Mindful Interview Method Analysis   112
For Your Consideration   114

SECTION V   Meta-Eyewitness Interviews

12   Eyewitness Interview Paradigm   117

A Framework for Interviewing Eyewitnesses   117
Special Note   118
Investigating the Eyewitness Interview Paradigm   118
The Cognitive Interview in Brief   118
Cognitive Interview Introduction and Mindful Interview Method Mindful Reset   119
Rapport Building   120
A Cognitive Interview Framework   121
Open-Ended Narration Phase and Narrative Recall versus Suspect Description and Element of the Crime   122
Probing Images and Concept Codes Phase versus Accessing Topic 2   122
Review and Closing Phases   126
The Conversation Management Approach in Brief   127
Respect for the Eyewitness   129
Looking for Triggers or Being Mindful of *That Is All There Is*   129
Expecting Too Much from Investigators When They Aren't Trained?   130
The Approach Can Be Judgmental   131
Preparing for a Certain Type of Interview   132
Embracing the Positives   133
For Your Consideration   133

13   Eyewitness Interview Training   135

Eyewitness Interview Training   136
Forensic Art and Eyewitness Interview Training   139
Eyewitness Interview Training Is Optional   141
Why Aren't All Law Enforcement Personnel Receiving Eyewitness Interview Training?   141
Lack of Understanding   143
Supplemental Training for Certain Officers   144
Scrutinizing Eyewitness Interviews   145
For Your Consideration   147

14   Measuring the Noise   149

We Didn't Hear the Noise at the Forensic Art Workshop   149
Shadow Sketching   150
Measuring Noise Excerpt   152

Studies Focused on Eyewitness Performance	153
Measuring Noise and Cognitive Evidence	153
Performance Focused on the Interviewer, Not the Eyewitness	154
Anatomy of Establishing a Benchmark for a Mindful Interview	155
Method	156
Data Collection for Benchmark	157
Applying the Efficacy of Eyewitness Interview Assessment to the Interview Session	162
Obtaining Actual Eyewitness Interview Transcripts from Law Enforcement	162
Reviewing the Transcript and Coding Exchanges	163
Entering the Data into the Question Category Matrix	164
Confirming the Topic Sequence	166
Interpretation of Data and the Reliability of Cognitive Evidence	167
Summary Report for Efficacy of Eyewitness Interview Assessments	168
The Efficacy of Eyewitness Interview Assessment Summary Report and Mindful Interview Method Standards	170
Reliability Scale Changes	170
Efficacy of Eyewitness Interview Assessment Narrative Report	170
Assessing the System Variables	171
For Your Consideration	172

SECTION VI   Analyzing Case Studies

15 Case Study #1	175
Looking at Noise in an Eyewitness Interview	175
Case Study #1	176
Topic 1	176
Topic 1	177
Topic 1	178
Topic 3	182
Topic 5	187
Efficacy of Eyewitness Interview Assessment[SM]	189
Narrative Report for Case Study #1	189
16 Case Study #2	193
The Cooperative Eyewitness	193
Topic 3	193
Efficacy of Eyewitness Interview Assessment[SM] Narrative Report for Case Study #2	195
17 Case Study #3	199
Our First Mindful Interview	199

CONTENTS

Case Study #3	200
Topic 1	200
Topic 2	202
Topic 3	204
Topic 4	207
Topic 5	207
Efficacy of Eyewitness Interview Assessment[SM]	208
Narrative Report for Case Study #3	208
18 Case Study #4	**211**
An Interview of Complexity	211
Topic 1	212
Topic 2	213
Topic 3	219
Topic 4	224
Topic 5	227
Efficacy of Eyewitness Interview Assessment[SM]	229
Narrative Report for Case Study #4	229
19 Case Study #5	**231**
A Mock Interview	231
Topic 1	233
Topic 2	234
Topic 3	235
Topic 2	235
Topic 3	237
Topic 4	238
Topic 3	239
Topic 4	240
Topic 4	242
Topic 3	244
Topic 4 (Narrative Summary)	245
Topic 3	246
Topic 4	248
Topic 2	249
Topic 4 (Narrative Summary)	249
Topic 5	251
Efficacy of Eyewitness Interview Assessment[SM]	254
Narrative Report for Case Study #5	254

SECTION VII Expectations

20 Expectations and Future Research	259
Appendix A: Category of Comments and Questions	263
Appendix B: Sample Mindful Interview Method Script	267
Appendix C: Forensic Art Indexing	269
Appendix D: List of All Case Studies	277
Appendix E: Case Study Transcripts and Efficacy of Eyewitness Interview Assessment Reports	279
Bibliography	501
Index	507

PREFACE

However innumerable sentient beings are, I vow to save them all;
However inexhaustible the passions are, I vow to extinguish them;
However immeasurable the Dharmas are, I vow to master them;
However incomparable the Buddha-truth is, I vow to attain it.

The Four Great Vows

Since 2000, I have been interested in the psychology of human memory and how we as interviewers gather information from our eyewitness interviews. The setting in which I was accustomed to interviewing eyewitnesses was often described as therapeutic and cathartic by some victims of heinous crimes. Yet, most of the eyewitnesses I interviewed were everyday people who happened to see something and were brave enough to offer their assistance in helping police locate and identify the culprit. It was these interactions with real people that helped me to incorporate my mindful qualities for gathering the most reliable information.

When I began to accept speaking engagements about my forensic art discipline, I noticed that people were interested in how I retrieved the information. I also noticed that many people had ideas for how I might have come up with the features of the subject, only to be surprised at my uncomplicated process. I would often speak to large audiences and demonstrate my interview technique by going around and asking audience members to describe a certain feature – it was a game of "telephone" with more than 200 people, and I was sketching the features of this subject that had been created from the collective consciousness of the audience. While most audience members were impressed with my ability to draw the features they described, I was more interested in showing them how certain benign questions could lead to unreliable information.

Following up their response with a leading question was one way I demonstrated how eyewitnesses were open to accepting my suggestions. The act of drilling down and getting to the root of what they meant by "short hair" and finally settling on a crew cut that was evenly cut about 1.5 inches from the top of the head and down to a fade on the sides – that kind of detail was always within their perception – or so they thought. Having the audience understand that our memories are not so precise was always a challenge.

Over the years I had learned to accept that sometimes *That Is All There Is* (TIATI) when interviewing an eyewitness. It was a premise that I was able to adopt because of the number of interviews I was conducting on a weekly basis, and because of the reams of research material I had read on human memory throughout my career. Because my interview questions were structured, they became automatic, and I was able to listen to the eyewitness more intently. Because I knew the next question was the same question I had asked several hundred times, I didn't have to think about the eyewitness response and ask a different question because of their response. Because I was so in tune with the retrieval process, I was able to focus on the details and interpret them to come up with more realistic-looking sketches (which helped my eyewitness recall the suspect).

PREFACE

Testifying in court and explaining my interview process to the jury was always something defense attorneys would cringe at having to cross-examine my process. Because my interview technique was so structured and mindful of not asking suggestive questions or showing images to stimulate memory recall, there was very little to scrutinize. The jury would see the process for what it was, a reasonable interpretation of eyewitness statements obtained by asking a majority of open-ended questions, where the eyewitness is able to confirm the features as being remarkable to what they remembered of the suspect. Many times, the sketches lacked detail and were very generic – that often was something that could be gleaned as similar to the mugshots that were shown side by side as being remarkable. The sketch represented the essence of the fragile nature of the eyewitness's memory.

Sometimes the sketches had more intensity in the eyes, and other times they showed more detail in the hair or a certain scar along the cheek. In each sketch there was something the eyewitness remembered more than the other features and it was very clear to me as I sketched them. An interviewer who may not be sketching along as the eyewitness describes the face is also imagining what the suspect looked like, and what they were wearing, and what they said, and how they said it. Detailing this information is important for the reliability of the crime report.

In one of the case studies in this book an investigator happens to be present in the interview room and I allow them to ask questions near the end of my sketch interview. The contrast in interview styles is an eye-opening experience. At the time of that interview, I remember I was amazed at the number of questions posed to the eyewitness that returned unreliable information. It was these types of experiences, throughout my career, that lead me to consider writing this book.

When I began teaching in the Justice Studies Department at San Jose State University in 2017, I was hoping that I would have an opportunity to expose criminal justice majors to the complexities of gathering eyewitness information and relying on it for solving investigations. What I learned very quickly is that students could see the differences in asking questions that led to unreliable information and were willing to practice asking more mindful questions that led to more reliable information. While not all of the students were hoping to become police investigators, they did express their satisfaction in learning how to interview people to gather important information. Gathering information from people is happening all the time, whether it's your waiter asking you about your order, the expert at the hardware store asking about your remodel ideas, or your doctor asking about your health, they all have the opportunity to listen and understand what you are saying.

My mother asked me to join my father as he met with his primary care doctor. She was concerned my father wasn't receiving accurate information from the doctor and she was concerned the doctor wasn't getting the real truth about how my father was feeling – I was asked to get the story straight. As the doctor came in and greeted us both he began to question my father about some of his complaints. I couldn't help but see the similarities in my interview sessions where I was gathering reliable information from eyewitnesses who had experienced something in their day. The doctor was patient as my father sometimes struggled to say specifically what he was experiencing. The doctor could have easily fallen into a practice of completing my dad's thoughts and offered him a reason for his complaints. I was impressed with the doctor's demeanor as he gathered only what my father was saying – nothing more, and nothing that the doctor had suggested. I hadn't seen this type of information-gathering from other doctors, but I assumed they must have been trained to do this in medical school.

A few months later I was speaking with a law school student, and they asked about my background and what I was working on. I told them I was thinking about writing a book about eyewitness interviewing and they were very interested in hearing more. They said they had been conducting mock interviews with people and they felt a little lost at how to go about gathering important information. They said their training for conducting interviews with non-suspects was almost non-existent. As I offered some ideas, I remembered years earlier when working with prosecutors and how they would interview eyewitnesses in post-interview sessions. Many of them lacked the discipline to gather reliable information and yet, here they were, managing the case.

A few months later I was fortunate enough to have an actual university police officer conduct a mock interview in my university eyewitness interview class, I didn't know what to expect from the officer regarding the interview technique he might have learned in becoming an officer. All I knew was the officer had recently graduated from the police academy and was a highly regarded officer on the force. The students and I debriefed after the interview session, and they were amazed at how the officer conducted the interview. You can read about this case study in chapter 15. Many of my criminal justice students commented on the number of leading questions the officer asked, others asked about the topic sequence and why the officer might have jumped around certain topics and missed information, and still others asked whether all officers were trained this way. After our debrief, I was more inspired to complete this book and share my experiences and my technique with others who have to gather important information about an event or background about someone.

In 2013 I was a part of an amazing social experiment where real women were asked how they felt about themselves and I interviewed them to come up with a sketch of their comments. I interviewed random people who shared some time with these real women and then I interviewed them about who they saw. The sketches were placed side by side in an emotional reveal that demonstrated how real women were often too hard on themselves about their appearance and that most people don't see them in the same way. My interview technique allowed me to interview these women, with confidence, without using reference materials and without having them review the sketch for likeness. I had to rely on their statements alone to come up with a sketch that best represented their statements. I had to accept what they told me and not infer anything more. It was a real test for my TIATI (That Is All There Is) premise and for being mindful of how I interpreted their statements. This book is my attempt to convince you to consider interviewing subjects in a way that only retrieves the most reliable information. Whether you are a veteran investigator, patrol officer, dispatcher, law student, nurse, doctor, human resources administrator, or someone interested in being a better interviewer, this book will help you become better at the art of analyzing what is and isn't reliable information.

Section I

Perspectives

If you seek, how is that different from pursuing sound and form? If you don't seek, how are you different from earth, wood or stone? You must seek without seeking.

Wu-Men Wenyan

1

Introduction

In the beginner's mind there are many possibilities, but in the expert's mind there are few.

Shunryu Suzuki

Do you know why you are here (DYKWYAH)? I've asked eyewitnesses that question in some form or fashion since 1998 to learn about their perspective in being labeled an eyewitness to a crime. These regular people are living their lives, and because of the crime, society sees them as victims, innocent bystanders, or reluctant witnesses with fears of retaliation. The DYKWYAH question forces the eyewitness to acknowledge how self-aware they are about an event that has now brought them into the investigative machine charged with identifying the suspect, arresting them, and bringing them to justice. Understanding the mindsets that Dr Ellen Langer wrote about in her book *Mindfulness* (2014) can offer us some perspective on how our minds may work without concern for certain events. These "premature cognitive commitments" can give us a clue as to how eyewitnesses perceive certain aspects of the scene itself; for example, if the eyewitness says the suspect was wearing some sort of cap but is unsure. Then later, when they are interviewed by the investigator, they accept the suggestion that it was a baseball cap – maybe the Giants' logo – because that makes more sense and other possibilities were "not explored" like not having a strong recollection (Langer, 2014). The investigator can fall prey to this mindless premature routine by assuming the dark cap was a "baseball cap with the Giants' logo" because they learned that another victim was assaulted by a similar looking suspect a few weeks earlier. Because the investigator has relied on hunches that led to many arrests, they follow this heuristic for making suggestions to the eyewitness to solve this case. When we layer the variables of eyewitness perceptions and judgments over the confidence they exhibit about their recollections, it becomes a web of memories the investigator must unravel and decipher to identify the reasons for the assault and the identity of the suspect.

The entertainment industry has enjoyed unraveling criminal investigations for over 70 years with shows like *Dragnet* (1951), *The FBI* (1965), and *Law and Order* (1990), and they all approached the eyewitness with a sense of utility to find the suspect and close the case. When we hear Sgt Joe Friday ask the eyewitness to give him "just the facts," do we understand why he had to clarify receiving facts versus other information? Were we exposed to Sgt. Friday's bias under the umbrella of solving the case no matter what? Crime dramas accelerate the investigative process on film which can lead to a false sense of how crimes are solved in the real world. Unfortunately, that may be true for both sides of the crime drama equation when investigators assume eyewitnesses know more and should offer more detailed information. Recently, the advent of DNA exonerations has shed light on the interview and interrogation processes involved in many investigations. Many of these cases revealed the bias investigators had about certain theories and their acceptance of post-event information by eyewitnesses to derail many of these cases from the truth and identifying the real culprit. The problem with many of these cases is that they may represent only a tip of a more convoluted issue of gathering unreliable eyewitness evidence.

In 2018, I was asked to speak at Harvard University about the impact of forensic art on criminal investigations. The main theme of the program asked each of the speakers to consider whether we were wrong about something in our process and to explain how we might correct it. Interestingly enough, Dr Langer was there to speak to the audience about her work on how we experience our mindless activities. I had found her book insightful as I studied about my mindful work as an interviewer. In retrospect, reflecting on my interview process reignited my desire to cast a spotlight on the specific act of interviewing eyewitnesses. This presentation was an opportunity to educate the public about my perspective on interviewing thousands of eyewitnesses in a manner that was respectful of their limitations for revealing details of the crime. I spent 17 years asking eyewitnesses about what they saw even though science was telling me how unreliable it was for me to count on their memories for accuracy. The success I was having at recovering important details of their memory about the suspect was a testament to the process I was employing every time I met with an eyewitness. Nevertheless, millions of interviews are conducted every year whereby law enforcement personnel, judicial agents, human resource officers, and medical personnel ask people to reveal information that is important and sometimes life-changing without regard for the limitations of their memory. Many of these interviews are documented by officials interpreting eyewitness statements destined for processing in our justice system; these sessions showcase the investigator's quest for finding the culprit and following their expectations instead of accepting limited eyewitness information. In this book, we will be focused on the eyewitness interview, which can be an informal conversation with a citizen about issues in the neighborhood, a caller reporting a crime, a victim, a bystander, or someone with information to share. The interview framework in the *Mindful Interview Method* will be well suited for both criminal investigations and non-law enforcement professionals looking for reliable information that can be used in furtherance of understanding an issue.

Because eyewitness memory and testimony have drawn so much attention from psychologists over the last 50 years, we have to begin to consider the efficacy of how our investigators are retrieving reliable cognitive evidence. For years, researchers have studied the accuracy of eyewitnesses under certain laboratory conditions and used the found results to make recommendations that shaped system variables associated with interviews. The focus on eyewitness accuracy has left little room for others to contemplate mandating interview protocols that could improve the evidence-gathering process. The few comprehensive studies engineered by respected collaborative groups have resulted in positive recommendations for all agencies to consider, yet the complicated budgetary priority systems in place for law enforcement administrators makes it difficult to formulate changes to a ubiquitous interview process that appears unobtrusive. The perspective I take in this book is to inform the public as well as investigators about how complex the act of gathering reliable eyewitness cognitive evidence is. If we focus on the proficiency of interviewers to retrieve reliable cognitive evidence instead of the inaccurate choices eyewitnesses make to accept information from their interviewers, we can begin to reduce the effects of estimator variables that negatively impact cognitive evidence.

This book is laid out in six parts. In Part I, we briefly go over my experience at interviewing eyewitnesses and introduce you to my more mindful technique of interviewing eyewitnesses. In Part II, we focus on the principles that led me to establish the idea of cognitive evidence and highlight the obvious pitfalls of unreliable cognitive evidence. We'll consider how the "detective mind" is influenced by the psychology of mindsets that seem to operate without concern for proper evidence collection. In Chapter 5, we contemplate how investigators engage in heuristics that affect the reliability of cognitive evidence. In the following chapter, we investigate mindfulness and learn how I used it to improve my interview technique. In Part III, we discuss how interview questions may contribute to misidentifications and wrongful convictions only to be exonerated by DNA evidence. In Chapter 8, we examine interviewing an eyewitness with interview techniques that are more interrogative and compare that to interviewing someone mindfully. We then compare the tactics used by US and UK investigators who have been trained in the cognitive interview technique and ask why they are not more proficient. In Chapter 9, we focus on the role of empathy and compassion in implementing the *Mindful Interview Method* (MIM), and we see how we can include them to maintain rapport. In Part IV, we look at the principles behind MIM and investigate further how and why we employ them in this fashion. In Chapter 11, we go through the MIM process step by step and offer you sample scripts to consider when practicing MIM. In Part V, we compare the Cognitive Interview technique and the Conversation Management Approach to MIM and discover similarities and differences that showcase the positive aspects of MIM. In Chapter 13, we look at the state of eyewitness interview training and see how efforts to change this training from the UK has led to troublesome proficiency results in the US. In Chapter 14, we look at the Efficacy of Eyewitness Interview Assessment (EEIA) and look at our process for measuring the reliability of cognitive evidence. We review the components of EEIA and analyze the decisions made by investigators to ask certain questions. Finally in Part VI, Chapters 15 through 19, we look at case studies of actual eyewitness interviews and show you how they fared in preserving the reliability of cognitive evidence. In Chapter 20, we discuss my opinions on future research for eyewitness interview best practices and look to academic researchers to embrace collaborations with investigators who conduct actual interviews.

Conducting a sketch interview with an eyewitness about a violent crime is one of the most complicated interviews to master when you consider the nature of human memory, the skill of the artist, and the ability for the eyewitness to recall sufficient details of the face to create a sketch that resembles the suspect. As the police artist, I interviewed every conceivable eyewitness to a prolific or mundane case where my interview process was always the same and successful at gathering reliable evidence. This book will lean into my experiences at interviewing all of these eyewitnesses and present novice and veteran investigators with an opportunity to adopt my interview technique for gathering reliable cognitive evidence.

For more information about the Mindful Interview Method go to www.mindfulinterviews.com

2
A Different Path

The only Zen you find on the tops of mountains is the Zen you bring up there.

Robert M. Pirsig

When I joined the San Jose Police Department in 1985, I attended the police academy and participated in the rigors of becoming a police officer. Standing at attention in lines wearing khaki suits and a blue baseball cap while wearing a leather duty belt around my waist became my routine for the next four months. Before being selected to join the police force, I had been a draftsman and electrical designer in the electrical engineering field for five years, designing electrical systems for commercial buildings in Silicon Valley. Being a draftsman and a designer was very rewarding; even so, I would often spend time sketching faces and caricatures of people in humorous situations. Marching on the asphalt at 6AM with my fellow recruits was a major departure from working comfortably at a drafting table and meeting with architects and mechanical engineers. During the class time at the police academy, I would spend my free time sketching the instructors in the class and challenging myself to capture the essence of their faces and demeanor as they lectured on department philosophy. Little did I know that years later my caricatures would lead me to meet my mentor, Tom Macris, the department's first police artist.

THE ART OF POLICING

During the end of my time at the academy, many of the instructors and trainers would tell me that I should consider becoming the next police artist. At the time I had no idea the department had a position called the Police Artist, and I had no idea it involved working with the investigative bureau. After the academy, the Field Training Officer (FTO) program, a few years on patrol, and being selected to be an FTO, I found myself looking for a new position after experiencing an on-duty vehicle accident with a drunk driver. As I contemplated my return to duty, I began to consider the police artist position. I began to submit crudely drawn cartoons for the department newsletter and the editor was kind enough to consider placing them near the back without fanfare. It paled in comparison to the professionalism of the *Cops a Field* cartoons Tom Macris and Bill Mattos would produce for the newsletter. I was too naïve to see the lack of quality and humor my illustrations contained, so I continued submitting them every month. Sometimes I would receive rare praise from one or two colleagues about the humor they found in one of my panels which gave me the courage to keep going. A few years later, I found myself getting up the courage to visit Tom in his office. Tom had been a police artist since 1976, and when I met him in 1991, I had no idea he was nearing retirement. Fortunately, I had the opportunity to be his apprentice from 1992 to 1995, and in May 1995 I was officially appointed the police artist.

Tom had been a founding member of the forensic art group of the International Association for Identification as they formalized the forensic art discipline. Tom was an exceptional artist and attributed his success to his training sessions with renowned Bay Area pastel artist, Bob Gerbracht. After my first year with Tom, he suggested I train with Mr. Gerbracht and receive the one-on-one guidance he gave him. To ready myself for the intensity of sketching, I began drawing four to eight faces every day from magazines, newspapers, and mugshots, for six to eight hours a day – and more on the weekends. Throughout my time with Tom, he never suggested I sketch a certain way or demand that I conduct my interviews in a certain manner. Instead, his mentoring sessions consisted of occasional conversations about his philosophy for interviewing eyewitnesses and sketching alongside his interview sessions. At this point in my law enforcement career, I had already interviewed hundreds of people about routine crimes like auto accidents, burglaries, and simple assaults, and I felt I was prepared to do a good job of interviewing eyewitnesses of violent felony crimes. In the police academy we would conduct mock interviews with eyewitnesses about crimes and go about asking Who, What, When, and Why? The focus of my inquiries was to document victim statements in a crime report and establish the elements of the crime. We were expected to ask basic questions about the suspect's race, height, weight, hair, and eye color, and list the clothing along with any unusual scars or marks. My apprenticeship in composite art expanded on this basic inquiry and led to more detailed questions about the head, nose, chin, and cheeks. When I attended the FBI Composite Art Course in 1993, I learned how forensic artists were being trained to interview eyewitnesses about the face and realized Tom and I were more concerned about how we might contaminate someone's memory.

When I decided to seek out the position of Police Artist in 1992, I had no idea how enamored I would become with eyewitness evidence. At first, I thought eyewitness evidence was about sketching the human face as realistically as possible, but after a few hundred sketch interviews I started to believe it was about how well I interpreted eyewitness statements. After another thousand sketch interviews, I began to realize that it was about how well I could ask the eyewitness questions in a way that would not affect their authentic recollections. I hadn't formed the complete cognitive evidence idea by this point, but I started to consider the information I was gathering from the eyewitness to be an integral part of our collaboration for the sketch evidence. I had already mastered the quality of the sketch to help the eyewitness compare it to their recollection of the suspect, but now I had to master the interpretation of eyewitness statements to the sketch I was creating. I was becoming aware of the tendency of the eyewitness to be impressed by the realistic quality of the sketch in the recognition phase of the sketch interview and losing sight of the wealth of information in the recollection phase. In other words, I needed to compare the statements I heard from the eyewitness when their eyes were closed and recalling the suspect's face, to their recognition of the sketch compared and the changes they would make to the sketch. It was as if I was manifesting the recollection of the suspect in the sketch and revealing the tenuous nature of their precision. During my apprenticeship, I had heard thousands of descriptions of features that in the end turned out to be eyewitness perceptions that were never formally confirmed and yet they still resulted in legitimate identifications. By the time I was appointed as the police artist, I began having reservations about how I was interviewing eyewitnesses. I questioned why it mattered whether I showed the eyewitness images before, during, or after the interview session and found some answers in the books Tom had suggested I read.

ENHANCING THE INVESTIGATIVE PROCESS

Near the end of my forensic art apprenticeship with Tom, he suggested three books I should read: *Memory-Enhancing Techniques for Investigative Interviewing* by Ronald P. Fisher and R. Edward Geisleman (1992), *Eyewitness Testimony* by Elizabeth Loftus (1979), and another book by Deepak Chopra called *The Seven Spiritual Laws of Success* (1994). He said I should read them and that they would help me understand the psychology of human memory and give me a perspective on interviewing eyewitnesses. One of Tom's sketches was featured in Loftus's book as she offered a case study on the process for obtaining eyewitness information about a robbery suspect. I read her book several times since my training, and I must admit I never appreciated the experiments or the basis for certain theories she had developed until much later. Theories like unconscious transference or post-event information would become very prominent in future interview sessions and eventually contributed to my fascination with eyewitness evidence.

The idea that you can convince yourself that you saw someone in one place but later realize you were actually confusing that person with someone you say you saw at or near the same place is almost impossible to grasp unless you conduct an investigative interview with an eyewitness or experience the phenomenon yourself. Interviewing an eyewitness who describes someone who was not the suspect can create a crisis of confidence for the eyewitness and the investigator. Their confidence in believing it was the same person (that they were correct) is something that can be difficult to separate from the evaluation of eyewitness evidence. In Chapter 8, we review a case where the victim describes the suspect who happens to resemble the person she saw at the store she frequents. Her confidence in reporting every feature of the face was exemplary and yet later proved unreliable.

Looking back on the Advanced Methodology Tom and I were using to interview eyewitnesses, I imagined Dr. Loftus would consider the reference images we used to refine the sketch to be post-event information. By exposing the eyewitness to these images with the suggestion that some may look like the suspect, we were actually contaminating their memory every time we showed them. We were challenging their ability to keep their initial memory of the suspect in their mind while showing them similar images of men that might alter their recollection. Just as Loftus, in some experiments, had convinced her eyewitnesses of the fact that they saw a stop sign versus a yield sign, we were using reference images to force the eyewitness to distinguish between the type of facial features the suspect actually had in their memory to what they were seeing in the photographs. I remember watching eyewitnesses go through the mug book and sometimes struggling to select three images they found similar to what they remembered. Then there were times when I think I subconsciously influenced their choices by asking, "Are you sure?" and watching them put the photo back and turn the page. The act of the eyewitness choosing these photos and making a decision about their likeness to their memory was intense at times and meant that any slight gesture, word, pause, or reaction on my part, might change the recollection of the eyewitness.

When law enforcement professionals, early in their career, train for a specific task, they often don't have the luxury or the wherewithal to question certain operations. When Tom shared his process for interviewing an eyewitness as a police artist it was much different from when I interviewed someone about a crime as a patrol officer. The need for specific information about the suspect's face was more complex than determining the elements of the crime and obtaining a basic description of the suspect based on the face sheet of a crime report. Soon after being appointed the police artist, I began to question the interview process and realized I was reflecting on my interview role as a facilitator for the recollection of memory. The idea of interviewing a person who had seen someone for a few seconds, and then creating a sketch that oftentimes looked remarkably like the suspect, left many considering the whole process mystical.

EYEWITNESS INTERVIEWS TAKE CENTER STAGE

Three years after I was appointed the police artist at San Jose Police Department, I appeared on the Oprah Winfrey show in a segment that featured how eyewitness memory can be unreliable and how people react to realizing it. I was one of three forensic artists they asked to be on the show, and they did a very good job of demonstrating the unreliability of human memory. This television appearance put me on a trajectory to reflect on my interview technique more fully and to scrutinize my methodology for processing eyewitness memory as cognitive evidence. Even though I had a great time on the show, I have to admit that in the real world I would not have thought my eyewitness was reliable and I would have advised the investigator not to publish the sketch. Because the producers asked me to conduct the interview as I would in any real-world investigation, I told them that for entertainment purposes I would reluctantly go along.

From the moment I met the eyewitness she kept saying, "I can't believe I'm on the Oprah Winfrey Show" I tried to stay in character (as the forensic artist) and asked her if she saw the "suspect" again would she recognize him and she said, "I think so, I didn't get a very good look." I went ahead and suggested my calming techniques and we proceeded with the interview. Her responses were less than specific (more generic), but typical for someone who was not that sure about remembering the face of the suspect. As I sketched parts of the nose, mouth, and eyes, I sensed that the suspect looked like me, so I asked her if I reminded her of the suspect's face, she said, "Oh no, he didn't have a beard!" I was wearing a light beard at the time, and she found that feature distinguishable in the suspect. Near the end of our interview, there was a knock at the door. It was a production staff member, and they said they needed to speak with my eyewitness. They left for a few minutes and when she came back, I was putting the final touches on the sketch when she said, "I think he had a mustache! Yeah, it was dark – he had a mustache!" Needless to say, I wasn't going to challenge her at this point and I didn't want to embarrass anyone. While I had her acknowledge that she hadn't mentioned the mustache during our initial review of facial features, she demurred and said that she remembered the mustache later. I added the mustache to the sketch, and we finished up the interview with her saying the sketch reminded her of the suspect.

As we settled into our seats in front of the audience, Oprah began to describe what had occurred a few minutes before; the monitors played a scene where a clean-shaven Caucasian male made his way to the front of the audience, grabbed a woman's purse and then ran away. As the video played my eyewitness tugged at my arm and said, "I'm sorry" because she realized she had not given me what she thought was a good description of the suspect. This instant feedback was a unique opportunity for me as a forensic artist. I had long believed that eyewitness memory was unreliable, and I often struggled to separate their displayed confidence with their lackluster articulation of specific details. This feedback experience left me more confident in my interview process and in retrospect reinforced my initial reaction not to accept the new information from the eyewitness. Instead, I began to rely on my perceptions of authentic recollections to create sketches that represented actual descriptions from eyewitness statements.

REAL BEAUTY

Perception from the eyewitness is what I've been dealing with all of my career, and in December 2012, I was hired to be a part of a media campaign to showcase how real women saw themselves versus how other people actually saw them. *The Dove Real Beauty Sketches* garnered well over 150 million views worldwide after it debuted in April 2013. The company had collected data from around the world on this perception issue and decided to use a forensic artist to bring about their results in a creative way. Sketching behind a curtain while asking the person about the facial features of the "real woman" was reminiscent of my apprenticeship days with Tom. In those interview sessions with victims and witnesses, I had to listen intently to their descriptions of the suspect while sketching, a few feet away, my impressions of what they were saying without their input to change the sketch. I was being asked to do the same thing for this project, without actual feedback from the random person about their impressions of the real woman. My 20 interviews for this project bolstered my belief that my interview technique was an authentic retrieval of perceptions and that not using reference images to stimulate their memory had been the best practice all along.

STUDENTS AND EYEWITNESS INTERVIEWS

In 2017, I began teaching an elective college course I called *Forensic Art and Eyewitness Interviews* at San Jose State University. Over the previous five years, I had been invited to speak to the Justice Studies Department by the venerable Professor Steven Lee about my experience as a forensic artist. I even participated in the Forensic Science Camp held annually where local high school students would come for a week to learn about forensic science. A few years later, Dr. Lee asked me if I would be interested in joining the faculty as a lecturer and I said yes. I was thrilled with the opportunity to teach criminal justice majors about forensic art and the process of interviewing eyewitnesses. When I prepared to teach this eyewitness interview course to students, I had to reflect on my practice and identify investigative stories I could present to students in order to inspire them to learn more. As I went about setting up my learning modules and formulating my syllabus, I realized that while I had gathered reams of research on human memory, I had very little information on drawing composite sketches. Since I was in the Justice Studies Department, there was no prerequisite for artistic abilities to take the course. Regardless, I decided to keep the sketching element in the course and let it assist students in asking questions about the face. In my lectures I explained to students how gathering reliable information from the eyewitness was the most important part of the interview session and not to get hung up on the quality of the sketch. I showed them pictures of sketches that were done by professional forensic artists around the country, and they soon realized the quality of realism in these sketches varied widely. We discussed how sketching the face proficiently was something that was expected but that understanding the limitations of what people remembered was more important.

Eventually, I changed the title of the course to ease the minds of students reluctant to tackle sketching faces. I settled on naming the course *Forensic Eyewitness Interviews*. The Justice Studies Department was very receptive to offering the elective course and I've been fortunate to teach the course a few times over the years. The name change helped to get more students to take the course and while some students felt they had to sketch while interviewing their fellow students (mock eyewitnesses), most understood that gathering the information was key and they would be evaluated on this process versus the quality of their sketches. One thing the students taught me is that when you present them with the foundational knowledge of the malleability of human memory and you describe the techniques to gather reliable information from an eyewitness, they tend to understand the pitfalls of not adhering to the process and stay away from it. Conducting mock interviews will never replace the real thing, but what it *does* do is show students how even well-rehearsed portrayals can seem real when the investigator is following a script. That script can lead to some amazing results and reveal the issues of mis-identification to some aspiring criminal justice majors.

UNDERSTANDING COGNITIVE EVIDENCE

For years I had been asked my opinion on whether the eyewitness was telling the truth after interviewing them; at first it was empowering to believe that the investigators were relying on my interaction with the eyewitness to provide them this crucial bit of information, but I soon realized that I might have been contributing to an already biased investigation. Interestingly enough when we are experiencing an unconscious bias act, we don't consider it a tragedy in justice; instead, when we debrief we chalk it up to being a tenacious investigator. The intimate nature of the interview session lends itself to an opportunity for the investigator to direct the eyewitness in a way that may not rely on their recollection statements alone; instead, eyewitnesses may attempt to fill in the parts of their statements with information that they perceived happened versus what they actually saw.

Years later I became interested in neuropsychology and read how scientists study the parts of the brain that handle these functions of perception. From the frontal cortex to the amygdala, I began to find the mechanics of creating and accessing memory, an exploration of how people behaved, how they reacted to certain stimuli, and the limitations of their recall. I found myself learning about how I could prepare myself to be a better investigator and be a skilled illustrator to generate quality sketches. I would reflect on my interview experiences with the articles and books I was reading and begin to formulate my own theories and best practices. As the police artist, I had complete autonomy over how I conducted my sketch interviews and was relied on to offer expert analysis of facial descriptions and insight into eyewitness statements. I had the opportunity to set aside time to meditate and prepare for my eyewitness interviews as well as read about how our brains make decisions and why that might be important for me as an investigator.

I have used parts of the enhanced cognitive interview technique in my sketch interviews since 1993 and modified certain aspects of it as I've progressed through thousands of interview sessions. Throughout the early years, I considered research articles and books on psychology, human memory, and human behavior. Conducting a mindful interview is not easy, and deciding to adhere to an interview process can also be difficult if you don't practice it. Nevertheless, would you rather continue interviewing eyewitnesses knowing full well that the information you may be gathering is unreliable? Or do you think your investigations aren't serious enough to warrant an evaluation of your process?

We should not assume that because we passed the police academy or received our criminal justice or forensic science degree that there is nothing more to learn about interviewing an eyewitness. Fortunately, we are beginning to learn about interview errors that have led to misidentifications and wrongful convictions because of misleading or inappropriate interview techniques that have gone unchecked. These recent reports have sounded alarms in the criminal justice system about the way our investigators are practicing their interview techniques, and now law enforcement institutions are considering changing norms to reflect the evolution of eyewitness memory research. When Tom was trained in the standard methodology (FBI), he eventually realized he needed to make a change to address issues he found to be problematic, so he developed his advanced methodology. I was trained in the advanced methodology and eventually realized that utilizing reference images in *any* form was troublesome for what I learned about human memory, so I developed my own interview technique that was mindful of memory contamination. In each iteration, we both considered the science behind eyewitness memory and the psychology associated with retrieving it. I expect that one day my methodology will be improved upon, and someone will build on what we know today and come up with a better method to gather the most reliable cognitive evidence from the eyewitness.

FOR YOUR CONSIDERATION

- Sometimes your path to your calling is not clear and you have to insist on it.
- Interviewing thousands of eyewitnesses in a mindful manner gives you credibility and confidence to retrieve reliable cognitive evidence.
- Applying eyewitness research to your interview techniques will improve cognitive evidence.
- Being mindful is just paying attention, and some of us do that every day.

Section II
Establishing Principles

In walking, just walk. In sitting, just sit. Above all, don't wobble.

Yun-Men Wenya

3
Cognitive Evidence

Things are entirely what they appear to be and behind them ... there is nothing.

Jean-Paul Sartre

Law enforcement practitioners and forensic scientists are accustomed to considering and collecting evidence from a crime scene, and they are cognizant of that evidence being protected from contamination. Criminal justice professionals are also encouraged to consider labeling eyewitness memory as "trace evidence" so that law enforcement personnel might consider "utilizing best practices to collect and preserve eyewitness evidence" (Loftus et al., 2019). The potential for trace evidence to play a major role in criminal investigations was first recognized in the early twentieth century by Edmond Locard, a French lawyer and medical doctor, who believed that the examination of trace materials could link places, people, and objects to a crime. Locard's exchange principle, often quoted as "every contact leaves a trace," soon became a maxim of forensic science (Trejos et al., 2020). Figure 3.1 illustrates the culprit entering the consciousness of the victim, thereby leaving a memory of their presence in their mind for post retrieval.

During court testimony an eyewitness might recall certain aspects of the crime and attest to their authenticity. This recollection of events is trace evidence that is located in the brain synapses of the witness (Jaquet-Chiffelle & Casey, 2021). Psychologists label the eyewitness the "observation instrument" in considering trace evidence and investigators are cautioned to be mindful of the unreliability of these eyewitness statements (Jaquet-Chiffelle & Casey, 2021). Acknowledging the lack of precision and quality of eyewitness observations magnifies the influences investigators have over the interview process. The questions investigators ask have a distinct bearing on how eyewitness recollection is considered reliable or not.

In *Memory-Enhancing Techniques for Investigative Interviewing* (1992), Fisher and Geiselman write about the complexities of eyewitness memory and refer to the "importance of E/W evidence" for the investigation (p. 11). They refer to eyewitness evidence as being critical to the investigation, and that the information (eyewitness evidence) should be "extensive and accurate" (Fisher & Geiselman, 1992). In the *Conversation Management Approach* (2013), Shepherd and Griffiths highlight the vestiges of the "trace" in their "nature of investigation," but do not assign it the label of evidence. Nevertheless, they make valid distinctions in regard to the investigation of information that needs to be validated, facts

THE MINDFUL INTERVIEW METHOD

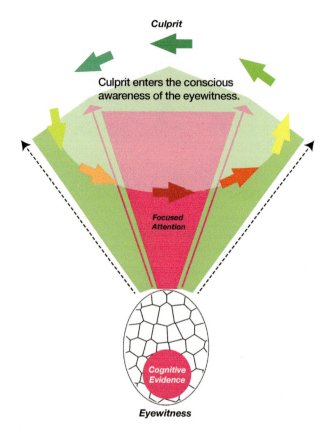

Figure 3.1 Cognitive evidence of the culprit and the eyewitness. Diagram of the culprit entering the consciousness of the eyewitness and leaving cognitive evidence of their appearance for the eyewitness to process. The interviewer should be mindful of how the cognitive evidence may reside in the mind of the eyewitness.

that are hard or soft, and evidence that points to the individual who committed the crime. *The Approach* (2013) offers an extensive overview of how investigators share commonality on how to "use information to protect the wellbeing of individuals … by solving … a problematic occurrence" (p. 4). While they don't focus on the description of eyewitness evidence, they do explain how the relationship developed for this interview will facilitate: (i) maximum spontaneous disclosure, (ii) maximum capture of fine-grain detail, and (iii) rapid, timely identification of issues and anomalies requiring probing – questioning to obtain expansion and explanation (Shepherd & Griffiths, 2013).

GUIDANCE ON EYEWITNESS INTERVIEWS

In the police academy, police cadets are trained to collect fingerprint evidence from various materials that may have been touched by the suspect. While many agencies have begun to leave the collection of evidence to highly trained Crime Scene Investigators (CSIs), some law enforcement personnel must have a working knowledge of gathering this type of trace evidence. The officers are trained to collect fingerprint evidence and process it for examination. Many times, officers do not know whether the partial fingerprint found at the crime scene was of the suspect, the victim, or someone else. They only know that they found something and booked it into evidence. Regardless, many officers and forensic practitioners are trained to be careful not to contaminate the trace evidence and send it in for evaluation by an expert fingerprint examiner.

Interestingly, when you apply evidence collection procedures that employ powders and chemicals to latent fingerprints, they may degrade the integrity of the evidence. Researchers (2005) showed that latent fingerprint brushes used to gather fingerprint evidence had been cross contaminated from use in the prior collection of evidence. Fortunately, law enforcement disciplines have evolved to employ new technology to recover trace evidence, and recent advancements in the collection of trace evidence by non-disruptive processes have relied on advanced photography, digital enhancement methods, and laser technology to visualize the latent print outside of the crime scene. Established forensic practitioners like Foster and Freeman of Australia follow the *Golden Rule* for retrieving trace evidence in that, "Whenever possible, non-destructive investigations should be performed first." If we insist that our law enforcement personnel treat eyewitness memory like trace evidence, we may find that they will be more mindful of how they conduct interviews.

In a friend-of-the-court brief filed by the Innocence Network in *Oregon v. Lawson* (2010), they write how eyewitness memory should also be considered trace evidence:

> Because of the alterations to memory that suggestiveness can cause, it is incumbent on courts and law enforcement personnel to treat eyewitness memory just as carefully as they would other forms of trace evidence, like DNA, bloodstains, or fingerprints, the evidentiary value of which can be impaired or destroyed by contamination.
>
> (p. 27)

Since eyewitness testimony has a significant impact on jurors' perceived reliability for accurate recollection, Dr. Gary Wells and his colleagues contributed to the creation of rules that can reduce misidentification errors; rules which have now become part of the material found in the *Eyewitness Evidence Guide for Law Enforcement* (Technical Working Group on Eyewitness Evidence, 1999, 2003). The *Guide* covers interview techniques such as those discussed in Part IV of this book and recommends procedures for the collection of eyewitness evidence from the use of line-ups and photospreads. As a forensic artist, I was conducting eyewitness interviews long before the *Guide* was developed, and I based my interviews on the cognitive interview technique; however, after reading the *Guide* (1999), I began to consider eyewitness statements I gathered about the suspect as trace evidence. Since I was creating these sketches after interviewing the eyewitness about how they were interpreting their memory, I soon referred to my sketch interviews as *cognitive sketch interviews* and called the sketches created from my eyewitness interviews *cognitive sketches*. Ten years later I began referring to eyewitness statements related to the crime as *cognitive evidence*. By reframing the collection of eyewitness statements as *cognitive evidence*, I created a structure where my process for retrieving cognitive evidence surpassed the collection of eyewitness evidence featured in the *Guide*.

COGNITIVE EVIDENCE

Eyewitness memory is cognitive evidence. When we interview someone about an event that happened to them (whether it has been hours, days, or months), we must be mindful of how we go about gathering evidence. The trace evidence (memory of the event) is fragile and can be manipulated (disturbed), so great care must be taken when facilitating the retrieval (interview) of it. After all, the eyewitness will surely begin recalling the event as soon as the event is over. They will be making decisions about certain aspects of the event, and their biases will be compounded by their discussions with a loved one, a friend, a passerby, or the 9-1-1 dispatcher. Just as the fingerprint technician must be mindful of the surfaces of where the latent print is located, so must the investigator be mindful of where the memory of the event is located. The cognitive evidence *is* located in the mind of the eyewitness and great care should be employed when collecting and preserving the evidence.

Since cognitive evidence is trace evidence of the event left in the memory of the eyewitness, we should not insist on manipulating the evidence to our liking. The same goes for physical evidence: If there is partial evidence at the scene, we must not make it whole by adding our own information, artifact, or lines. It wasn't there to begin with, so why *fill in the blanks*? When CSI technicians gather fingerprints at a crime scene, they lift only the print(s) that are there; they don't add their own ridges to make the fingerprint(s) whole (see Figure 3.2). Tampering with the collection of fingerprints would cause them to be deemed unreliable and would be rejected later by the fingerprint examiner. The same can be said for the investigators who fill in the blanks of eyewitness statements during eyewitness interviews.

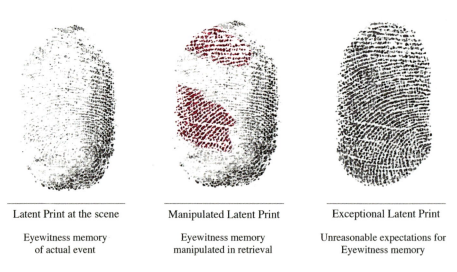

Latent Fingerprints representing Cognitive Evidence

Latent Print at the scene — Eyewitness memory of actual event

Manipulated Latent Print — Eyewitness memory manipulated in retrieval

Exceptional Latent Print — Unreasonable expectations for Eyewitness memory

Figure 3.2 Latent prints and cognitive evidence. The latent print (left) shows areas that are unclear or missing information while the manipulated latent print (center) shows new lines drawn in red.

When investigators choose to accept that an eyewitness may have seen something from the crime scene even though they may have not, they risk relying on cognitive evidence that has not been deemed reliable. Investigators enjoy professional autonomy in their investigations and are rarely concerned with scrutinizing their evidence-gathering tactics. Their quest for the truth usually outweighs any concern for the credibility of eyewitness statements. While the veracity of these statements may be evaluated by investigators at some point in the investigation, their cognitive evidence collection process is not – which should be factored in analyzing the reliability of cognitive evidence.

CONSIDERING CONFIDENCE OF RECOLLECTION

In a mindful interview you always consider the Confidence of Recollection (COR) for the eyewitness. This usually takes place in Topic 1 (Welcome, Introduction, Assessment) where the interviewer is building rapport and should be assessing whether they can proceed with the interview. In the Mindful Interview Method we do this by asking the Qualifying Question: "If you saw the suspect would you recognize them?" How the eyewitness answers this question should be considered on whether to move forward with the interview, or not. Listing every possible response to this question will not be beneficial for readers of this book; however, describing the essence of responses may be useful in utilizing the discretion to move forward. If the eyewitness responds with "I think so, it really happened pretty fast" you should consider following up with another open question. For instance you might ask, "Ok, I understand. Do you know why you are here? If they say that something happened to them and that they told the patrol officer that they didn't remember much–you should consider asking another question. You could ask, "Well, we find that when eyewitnesses close their eyes and take a few deep breaths, they tend to become relaxed and more focused. Can you try that for me and think about what happened and tell me what you see?"

At this point, if the eyewitness follows your direction and closes their eyes and begins to tell you details about the suspect or the event you can accept this brief recap as being satisfactory to move forward. For example, if the eyewitness says, "I see the guy coming up to me–it was dark, but the light from the ATM machine lit him up. I think he was wearing a blue hoodie and some jeans. I think he was white, he had some facial hair, and he had a big nose. That's all I can remember. He ran away after that!" With this type of response, we can move forward with confidence that the eyewitness has some recollection of the suspect and the event.

If, however, the eyewitness claims (after closing their eyes), "I just don't see him–it was dark, and I really wasn't paying attention. It happened so fast and when he ran away, I started dialing 9-1-1. I didn't want to see where he ran to!" In this situation, you should show some empathy for what happened and thank them for coming in to speak with you. You should remind them that it is very common for victims to recall information about the crime–days later, and that they should call and tell you anything that they remember.

There are instances where the eyewitness seems to have confidence in their recollection, but then as you begin to conduct your interview their answers are less specific and may be considered generic. Asking more open-ended questions should allow the eyewitness to elaborate on generic information if there is something there, otherwise you adhere to That Is All There Is (TIATI) and move on. These generic or less confident answers in topics 2 through 4 will affect the COR rating that is factored into the Efficacy of Eyewitness Interview Assessment (see chapter 14).

THE DISCRETION TO SEARCH FOR MORE

I know that some experienced interviewers might be saying, "But sometimes our eyewitnesses need some help in recalling details, and just like CSI technicians dust surfaces to locate fingerprints, we're using certain questions or reference images to help them recall the event." There's a difference between locating and collecting the evidence, versus locating and then *shaping* the evidence to conform to what you *believe* is evidence that can lead to an identification. We should be mindful of the evidence and collect it as is – with all the uncertainty that comes with recalling memory events. That doesn't mean we leave it unanalyzed, but if we collect cognitive evidence mindful of the complexities of memory recall then we can ensure the process of analysis will be unbiased.

The act of remembering is a complicated process and sometimes under the best of circumstances, we fail to remember something that is important. A few years ago on vacation, I remember returning from an errand, and I failed to make a left turn down the street where I was staying and I went out of my way for about three blocks until I realized I had made the mistake. I had driven down this road at least two dozen times at different times of the day and night so I was familiar with the street. After turning around, I became more focused on making it home and wondered why I had missed the turn. While I was heading home, I started noticing the signs I had missed as I got closer to the turn I should have taken earlier. In my focused review I saw the sign for the "Bath Inn." That's where I should have made a left turn, and across the street (at a diagonal) there was a small child's bike with pink striping and what appeared to be a note taped to the frame that read, "Free." It was very obvious now where I should have made my turn, and trying to figure out why I missed the turn was less obvious. My attention on driving itself was good enough, but my attention for *turning* at the proper location was not focused, and instead I proceeded down the road not realizing I had missed the sign to make the left turn. The information about how I traveled from the errand to the house was in my mind and eventually I made it home. So what does that mean for someone conducting an interview with an eyewitness?

It can mean that, potentially, an eyewitness's focus – in recall – is on something else, not necessarily on the thing they or the interviewer thought, which is why it is important not to influence in any way or to otherwise enter an interview with preconceived notions. As in my example, I may have been focused on driving but not on the turn. So, I remembered some details of the event, only to recall other details after reflection. Many times, our eyewitnesses recall events in ways that are not necessarily as we anticipated, and allowing them to give an account of how it really happened may offer more details of the event.

In one example, an eyewitness recounted details about an event but seemed to introduce information that was not necessarily what was expected. She had been involved in an accident that seemed to be instigated by the suspect in order to attack her. The details of the accident seemed to conflict with statements about what she saw before the accident. In one exchange I asked the eyewitness to tell me what had happened, and she mentioned pulling out of a store parking lot and then seeing the suspect vehicle with a "dim light." Later on in the interview, she mentioned the suspect "hit" her truck from behind, so she pulled over to view the damage and said that "one of his lights was all the way in so [she] thought that [it] happened when he crashed [her] truck because [she] obviously (sic) [saw] the dim light." Earlier she had mentioned going past an intersection ("I went past the light") and seeing him (or his vehicle) and then saying, "one of the lights didn't work" before the assault occurred. Seeing the dim light before the accident means that she thought his truck may have been damaged before the incident which contradicted her statements – later from the accident. It was important to allow her to retell her narrative of what she felt happened and to be mindful of how memory works.

Since we know that memory is an act of re-creation, we can assume that the dim light became something of a signpost for her to remember the details of the event. The eyewitness decided to create a logical reason for believing it was the same vehicle that collided with her. Whether the headlight was damaged before or after the incident does not diminish the fact that the suspect collided with her vehicle. We have physical evidence at the scene of the suspect vehicle, and witnesses that saw the suspect vehicle. We also have her cellphone that the suspect used to speak with her boyfriend (possible DNA evidence). We have a lot of evidence to corroborate details of the event, and determining whether the suspect vehicle had a damaged headlight before the incident or not is irrelevant at the time of this interview. Being mindful of how this information should be treated is vital to ensure the questions asked are pertinent and lead to more reliable information. Instead of latching on to the inconsistency of their recollections and deciding what is significant (we show our bias), we should be more mindful of how our mind works in recalling events. We need to be patient and allow the recollection process to flow as a discovery process for the witness.

Let's go back to the scene at the Bath Inn sign and imagine I was an eyewitness you had to interview about an incident that occurred just before. When you ask, "Tell me what happened before you got home?" you should listen intently and imagine the event as they retell it. You'll use the mindful interview techniques to slow the eyewitness down and allow them to experience the realization that they may have seen more than they said they did. For example, say the eyewitness recalls having missed the turn and arrived late. If you allow them to expand on this "missed turn," you might allow them to be more mindful of what happened. You can probe further and learn details of the Bath Inn sign or the small bike on the corner with the "free" sign taped across the bars. Are those details significant to the case? We don't really know at this time, and why should *we* be the judge of what is or isn't important? Why change our mindset from investigator to arbiter within the retrieval process? The difference in conducting a more mindful interview and one that is not, is that you are allowing the eyewitness to recall the events as they happened organically and not influencing the outcome with your bias. There will be more time (after the interview) to decide what is and isn't important about what the eyewitness said – or how they said it. There will be more time for follow-up interviews and talking to other witnesses to confirm old or new information. If we treat the recollection of events as cognitive evidence, we'll be more careful to leave it intact and resist contaminating it or worse – altering it to fit our perception of the event.

UNDERSTANDING HOW EYEWITNESS MEMORY WORKS

The day-in and day-out process of meeting with an eyewitness can seem rather mundane until you are faced with working on an investigation that involves a serial case (rapes, robberies, homicides), and then all bets are off. We expect our investigators to consider how important eyewitness statements are and whether we can rely on them to develop leads and eventually apprehend the culprit. When Wells (2011) commented on the *Perry v. New Hampshire* case, he articulated why "eyewitness evidence [was] special" and how it should be treated with importance. Wells (2011) detailed the effects of misidentifications from the tireless work of the Innocence Project and the hundreds of exonerations gained in finding the truth. Unfortunately, not all cases include the collection of DNA evidence, and we are left with police procedures that seek the truth in conjunction with eyewitnesses that may or may not have reliable information to offer our investigators. Wells (2011) challenges the premise that eyewitnesses can be relied on to offer reliable evidence even though investigators don't "understand how perception and memory work." If we understand cognitive evidence, we can ensure viability for relying on it to help us find and apprehend the culprit. The problem with preparing our first responders with education about eyewitness memory and how to conduct interviews is that very little is done to prepare our most specialized investigators.

When I asked my mentor, Tom Macris, about the training he received about eyewitness memory, he recalls it as being "predominately done in the style of observer … *On the job training* at New York PD" where the "dissemination of knowledge was informal." I can attest to that same fact that when I apprenticed under Macris, I never received any formal written documentation about eyewitness memory, although I insisted on sketching alongside Macris as he interviewed the eyewitness so I might gain some insight into the sketching process. The same might be said for most law enforcement personnel when they think back on their formal training about human memory and eyewitness testimony. It took me five years into my position as police artist to begin understanding how eyewitness memory research could improve my success at interviewing eyewitnesses.

RELIABLE NOT ACCURATE

We all now know that eyewitness memory is unreliable. Regardless, we insist on retrieving it in sometimes extraordinary circumstances to solve crimes. Because eyewitness memory is relied on by jurors in criminal and civil court cases, to determine the guilt or innocence of a person, it is imperative that the professionals that gather this cognitive evidence be mindful of the quality of it. Because cognitive evidence is susceptible to contamination, we should not refer to eyewitness statements as being *accurate* or *correct*, especially when the recollection may be affected by event and witness factors. We should stay away from terms like *right* or *wrong*, *exact* or *precise*, when discussing cognitive evidence, and instead rely on the idea that these statements may be *reliable* or *unreliable*. Investigators passing judgment on the veracity of eyewitness statements without considering whether they are consistent with or inconsistent with estimator and system variables can affect the perceived value of those statements and impact the reliability of cognitive evidence.

ESTIMATOR VARIABLES AND COGNITIVE EVIDENCE

An estimator variable is often divided into categories that focus on the retrieval of memory and the confidence of memory stated or exhibited in court while testifying (see Table 3.1). Being mindful of these variables does not mean we should memorize each variable, but we should have a working knowledge of how they might affect the interview. For instance, in Case Study #10, the eyewitness's first language was not English, but she had a good look at the suspect. Because I was mindful of this witness factor (estimator variable) I was careful to ask more probing, multiple-choice, and force-choice questions to elicit as much information as possible. Instead of correcting the eyewitness when she used the word "small" for short hair, I accepted her word and adapted my understanding of it as she was using it. By being mindful of this witness factor (Witness Characteristics and Conditions) I ensured the cognitive evidence was not negatively impacted.

SYSTEM VARIABLES IN EYEWITNESS INTERVIEWS

System variables are conditions or methodologies that can be controlled by the criminal justice system. While most research studies about system variables focus on eyewitness misidentifications and photo line-ups, there are some that have been instrumental in creating lesson plans that focus on standard eyewitness interviews (Table 3.1). The National

Table 3.1 Estimator and System Variables for Line-Ups and Eyewitness Identifications Were Originally Developed by Dr. Gary Wells (1978)

Estimator and System Variables for Line-Ups and Eyewitness Interviews		
Estimator Variables for All Eyewitness Identifications	**System Variables for Line-Ups**	**System Variables for Eyewitness Interviews**[a]
Stress	Pre-identification instructions	Instructions
Witness attention	Blind administration	Qualifying question
Duration of exposure	Line-up construction	Limit leading questions
Environmental viewing conditions	Simultaneous vs sequential line-ups	Suggestive feedback
Witness characteristics and condition	Show-ups	Post-event information
Description	Multiple viewings	Use of cognitive sketch
Perpetrator characteristics	Suggestive questioning	Recording interview
Speed of identification	Suggestive feedback/recording confidence	
Level of certainty	Retention intervals	
Memory decay	Use of composite sketches	

[a] The System Variables for Eyewitness Interviews were based on the Mindful Interview Method originally employed under the Compositure™ technique in 1999.

Institute of Justice (NIJ) booklet on Eyewitness Evidence offers law enforcement personnel basic information about interviewing eyewitnesses as they follow up an investigation. Even though they emphasize the importance of retrieving eyewitness evidence, their guidance is limited and lacks widespread adoption by agencies across the country (*Eyewitness Evidence, A Trainer's Manual for Law Enforcement*, USDOJ, NIJ, 2003, Working Group, TWGEYE; NCJ 188678). Many studies have found that asking more open-ended questions can improve recall of eyewitnesses. Being mindful of how the eyewitness is remembering events can make it easier to decide when to engage in more probing questions that enhance memory. The words we use can influence the outcome of their statements, so we must understand the power of our influence. We know that leading questions can change the outcome of initial eyewitness statements, so we need to avoid them to preserve the integrity of cognitive evidence. Let's look at how being mindful of both estimator and system variables is practiced when illustrating features of a suspect.

HOW PRECISE CAN EYEWITNESSES BE?

Forensic artists ask the eyewitness about the suspect's face so they can sketch each feature. Sometimes if you ask about the suspect's ears, they might say that they don't remember. In this case, you should follow up and ask them if the suspect *had* ears? This may sound like a silly question, but since we are mindful of estimator variables, we should be considering the time, distance, and lighting of the event to see how these variables might have affected their attention to detail. When we ask whether the suspect might have had ears, we are also mindful of the system variables, so we ask the question in an open-ended format. After receiving the response from the eyewitness, we probe further to understand their perspective. For instance, if the eyewitness said the suspect *did not* have ears, then the suspect's appearance would be more distinctive, and our investigation would have us look into databases of suspects *without* ears. Nevertheless, when we ask this question (about the ears), we're looking to distinguish what the eyewitness saw and what they assumed was present at the time of the crime event. When they respond with, "Yes, he had ears," without any detailed description of the ears, we can be sure they observed the person without unusual characteristics, so the sketch artist can draw typical ears for the suspect archetype.

Being mindful of event factors allows us to interpret eyewitness statements carefully. We know that eyewitness memory research has shown that people recall events or faces by interpreting what they saw together with past experiences to shape their final perception. Because of this, we cannot expect the eyewitness to recall events exactly as they experienced them but rather under the cloud of re-creation shaped by the questions we ask. When we are mindful of system variables, we understand that eyewitnesses may recreate their recollection of events or descriptions of persons based on a multitude of information, so we shouldn't rely on their statements to be precise. For example, if we ignore the idea that *That Is All There Is* (TIATI) and we ask the victim of an assault about the face of the suspect and rely on our bias to structure our questions, we may affect the quality of their responses. Let's say we've reviewed the crime report and read the statements from other eyewitnesses that say the suspect had a beard, so we figure the suspect in this case has a beard. Now, when we conduct our interview with the eyewitness, we decide to probe further (about whether he had facial hair) when they say, "I'm not sure." The decision we make to probe further may affect the reliability of our eyewitness statement. Let's see how this decision to probe further might transpire in the excerpt: Did He Have a Beard?

DID HE HAVE A BEARD?

INV: Did the suspect have any facial hair?
EW: I'm not sure, maybe.
INV: Was it a beard or stubble?
EW: I don't know, maybe a light beard?
INV: Could it have been a week-old beard or more like two weeks?
EW: Maybe ten days, I don't know.
INV: Okay, and the color of his beard?
EW: Probably dark brown.

Let's consider the information the eyewitness actually offered about the facial hair of the suspect. First, we know that facial hair can be changed easily, so we should not consider it as important as other features like height, eye color, weight, etc. Second, if we adhere to TIATI, we accept the information and move on to the next feature. In this case the investigator does not adhere to TIATI and is determined to probe further and get the eyewitness to agree that the suspect had a beard even though they were unsure at the outset. When we are mindful of this facial hair feature not being critical in the overall description of the suspect, we should not engage in asking multiple probing questions when the eyewitness is unsure to begin with.

When we analyze what the eyewitness said in this brief exchange, we can see how their statements were altered to accept the investigator's view. In every response the eyewitness was unsure and answered the question with another question or framed their reply in ambivalence. When the investigator asked about the suspect having facial hair, they replied: "I'm not sure." When the investigator followed with a force-choice question, they responded with, "I don't know, maybe a light beard?" And finally, when the investigator asks an open-ended question about the color of the beard, the eyewitness reluctantly says, "Probably dark brown." Not once was the eyewitness allowed to offer a genuine response that was accepted by the investigator as being satisfactory. If the Confidence of Recollection (COR) is considered at the start of the interview, the investigator will be more mindful to either not continue with the interview or accept *That Is All There Is* (TIATI) in eyewitness responses. Throughout this book, we'll look at these benign exchanges and challenge ourselves to accept the TIATI premise when we engage in eyewitness interviewing.

When we participate in real-world eyewitness interviews, we don't have the luxury of pristine lab experiments to shield us from outcomes that may change the lives of real people. We don't have the outcome predetermined and can test the accuracy of the eyewitness after the interview is complete. Our real-world interview process places the unknown identity of the suspect at the forefront of the investigation, so the outcome of eyewitness statements cannot be measured for accuracy until the case has matured and a suspect has been identified. By that time, it may too late to persuade the lead investigator to change course or to reevaluate the cognitive evidence. In our *Beard* example, the investigator pursued the line of questioning mindlessly, and when we read in the crime report that the suspect had a ten-day old dark brown beard, we now know, because of our analysis, that this statement was aided by the investigator to satisfy a bias they had about the description of the suspect and not from eyewitness recollection. We can see from this example how easy it can be to alter eyewitness memory and how the investigator's simple inquiries can shape the outcomes. Eyewitnesses will often relinquish control over their limited recollection when the investigator reinforces their authority to assist the eyewitness in offering more details, and disregard the COR at the start of the interview session.

TELL ME EXACTLY WHERE THIS FEATURE GOES ON THE FACE

We see this type of harmless manipulation when forensic artists work with eyewitnesses to determine where the exact location of a facial feature lies on the face. For example, some forensic artists looking to place the suspect's nose on the rough sketch of the face will use a straight edge to ask the eyewitness to choose where the bottom of the nose will reside (see Figure 3.3). Their desire to have the eyewitness *accurately* place the tip of the nose on the

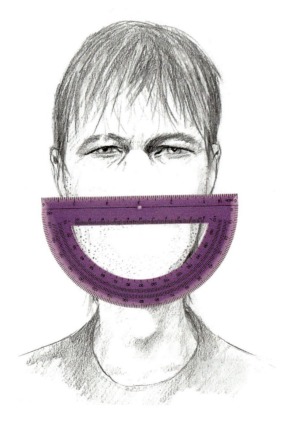

Figure 3.3 Simple manipulation with straight edge. Example of simple manipulation using a protractor to force the eyewitness to choose the location of the nose on the sketch. © 2022 Gil Zamora.

paper is highly problematic for a few reasons. Since we know that eyewitness memory is malleable, we shouldn't be relying on it to place a feature on a sketch that is based on their perceived recollection. The estimator variables like distance to the suspect or lighting for the event should caution us on not relying on the eyewitness for precise placement of features. We can certainly count on them to let us know whether the suspect had a nose and whether the size was distinct, but the placement of the nose should be left to the expertise of the sketch artist.

The forensic artist should be skilled enough to place an average nose on the plane of the face relative to the overall size of the head and the initial descriptions of the nose. For example, if the eyewitness describes the nose as being "normal" or "nothing unique," then the sketch artist can draw a typical nose and place it in between the eyes and the base of the jaw; or if the mouth is already sketched in, between the mouth opening and the brow of the eyes (see Figure 3.4). The overall size of the head will dictate the perceived size of the nose being too large, average, or too small. When the eyewitness views the sketch

Figure 3.4 Sketch of suspect without simple manipulation. Example of a sketch created without simple manipulation. © 2022 Gil Zamora.

holistically, they can utilize their recognition skills to guide the artist to make changes or leave it as is. Their placement of the nose says nothing about their accuracy or clear recollection of the suspect; it's more about the expectations the forensic artist has for eyewitness accuracy, which research has proven to be unreliable. As an investigator, we must have a basic understanding of how eyewitness memory works in order to properly evaluate eyewitness statements, so being mindful of all estimator and system variables will lead to cognitive evidence we can rely on for the investigation.

EXPERIMENTS AND PRACTITIONERS

In the book *Eyewitness Testimony* (1996), Dr. Loftus conducted many experiments where they purposely introduced new information to see if the eyewitness would accept it and include it as their own memory. These experiments demonstrated the power of the words used by interviewees as well as the authority to introduce new information to be considered by the eyewitness. Many of the innocuous statements made by interviewers showed how benign actions of inquiry could influence someone to change their perception of what they saw.

In one experiment I share in my Eyewitness Interviews college course, students read about the experimenter asking would-be eyewitnesses about a traffic accident they observed and learning that when investigators used certain words the eyewitness would alter their recollection. After watching a film of an auto accident, eyewitnesses were asked whether there was glass present at the scene. In one group, the experimenters asked how fast the cars were going when they *smashed* into each other, while the other group was asked how fast they were going when they *hit* each other (Loftus, 1996). The post-event information (glass present at the scene) resulted in 43% more accounts of glass in the *smashed* group versus the *hit* group. The findings in this research show how much influence interviewers have in affecting eyewitness memory and Loftus makes an important plea to investigators to "avoid the introduction of 'external' information into the witness's memory" (p. 78).

In many of these experiments we know the facts that are being tested for eyewitness accuracy: The vehicle accident is staged; the questions are generated and scripted; and the results are clear. We can see how the eyewitness was manipulated by suggesting the pace of the vehicle at the accident by the use of the words *smashed* or *hit*, which generated impressions for the speed of the car that either they accepted or rejected. In the real world of investigations, we are often working with the unknown. We have no idea what the eyewitness saw and the extent of their attention during the event. If the investigator begins to assume certain facts about the investigation and shapes their questions based on these presumptions, their questions may in fact alter the cognitive evidence. In actual criminal investigations, we don't know the impact of the words used by law enforcement investigators until the reality of the event is revealed post investigation. By then, it may be too late to correct statements or alter the chain of events that may have resulted in an innocent person being identified as a suspect.

Investigators interviewing eyewitnesses ask people what they saw and ask them to describe what happened every day. Because most investigators don't rely on eyewitness memory research to dictate their strategy for gathering information, we have to bring the science to the practitioners. One exercise that I use to demonstrate the suggestibility of the investigator on the eyewitness is the Deese, Roediger, and McDermott (DRM) experiment (Roediger & McDermott, 1995). The DRM task is an exercise that demonstrates the false memory paradigm in which subjects are presented with lists of semantically related words and later tested on their recall while being exposed to post-event information. It exemplifies how easily we can manipulate people into thinking they saw something. In this exercise the investigator can see how easily this can happen and can appreciate the fragility of eyewitness memory. In future exercises I will add some form of the Confidence of Recollection (COR) statement so investigators can be mindful of how it may affect the recollection performance of the eyewitness – at least consider it. For example, in this exercise I use words that focus on the theme of an airport (see Table 3.2), but I don't initially use the word "airport" in the list of 12 words. I ask the audience to study the words for 90 seconds, then I give them another two minutes to write all the words they remember (a self-report). At this point I would ask them to indicate on a scale of 1 to 3 (three being very confident, and 1 not confident at all) how well they think they remembered the words from the list. After they complete this task, I expose them to another activity for a few minutes and then show them each word – one by one (on a large screen) and ask them to raise their hands if they have the word on their list. Inevitably the audience sees the word "airport" and some hands go up. There is an uneasy moment in the audience when some people realize they didn't see the word. The people with their hands up seem confident that they saw the word *airport* even though the rest of the group is shaking their heads that they didn't. I've done this experiment in my university classes, and I find that students were more concerned about their accuracy of recall and not the acceptability of false information by their colleagues.

Many students described trying to remember so many words and some creating word palaces to help them remember. Some only remembered ten words while others only kept seven to memory. Some of them told me they accepted *airport* when they figured it must have been a word they couldn't remember. In this exercise we know that the word we are offering as post-event information is *not there*, and when we see that some people accept it as being there, we can surmise that they chose to accept it as their own recollection. It was easy for them to decide that many of the words reminded them of an airport, and when they saw the word on the screen, they decided to accept it as being there. This exercise demonstrates how post-event information can be offered and accepted with relative ease

Table 3.2 Inspired from Deese, Roediger, and McDermott Experiments

DRM Exercise for Post-Event Information: "Airport"		
Chairs	Planes	Taxis
Luggage	Restaurant	Terminal
Passports	Runway	Tickets
Pilots	Security	Travelers

Used in Presentations for Forensic Art Audiences and Criminal Justice Students.

when it is being presented by someone of authority. When we show eyewitness images that are similar to the suspect to stimulate memory recall, we can also expect that they may accept the image as their memory. Unfortunately, we never know the impact of this suggestion unless post-investigation analysis is completed well after the event.

Many times, investigators ask a question and expect a certain answer because they have a theory about what happened. Understanding what may be happening in the eyewitness's mind might be helpful in determining whether investigators can rely on this statement or not. When we look back at the audience members in the DRM exercise who raised their hands in confidence, investigators should consider these findings when they interact with their eyewitnesses and exercise their own theories. If we study the confidence level of the audience member and hear their comments, we can hear some common threads. Some might say, "I'm positive it was there!" or, "I'm sure I'm right." Are investigators willing to stake their reputations on whether they know the eyewitness is remembering a false memory? What about interviewing an eyewitness that was reluctant to offer details about the suspect and the crime event? Is the investigator willing to engage in a process of filling gaps of unclear information from the eyewitness to settle on a perfunctory suspect description or elements of the crime? While investigators may not rely on source monitoring framework to decipher how the eyewitness determined where they saw that word (Johnson et al., 1993), they should be mindful of how acceptable our minds can be when confronted with similar words, images, or items related to the crime.

ACCOUNTABILITY FOR COGNITIVE EVIDENCE

Measuring the credibility of eyewitness statements is a subjective exercise practiced by investigative bureaus throughout the country, and the need to determine the veracity of eyewitness statements often determines the path the investigation follows. When there is no standard for interviewing eyewitnesses in a way to elicit reliable information, it is futile to contemplate the accuracy of eyewitness statements. Fisher and Schreiber (2019) challenge law enforcement administrators to scrutinize their interview strategies and consider the value of a more thoughtful interview process which may offer unreliable information. The point of conducting a more mindful eyewitness interview session is to be *present* for all information and acknowledge the role the investigator has in generating the information. Unfortunately, we may not be holding our *first-time interviewers* to the same level of scrutiny that we subject our more experienced detectives even though these first statements may have a significant impact on the direction of the investigation or the focus of the alleged suspect.

Because our law enforcement investigators are responsible for asking questions, they should be held to the same level of scrutiny that eyewitnesses are held in offering credible and reliable information for the investigation. We should be more transparent in how we develop statements and allow others (in the bureau) to gain insight into the process of gathering reliable cognitive evidence. Field studies have been conducted that show promise for gathering this information; however, since it is not mandated throughout all law enforcement agencies, we cannot benefit from their results. Still, small studies found police interviews were lacking uniformity in retrieval methods and thus limited the valuable cognitive evidence obtained for certain encounters.

While we can imagine the reluctance of police agencies to scrutinize their methods for gathering cognitive evidence, we have to realize that their interview methods are eventually scrutinized when DNA exonerations are featured on the national stage. Instead of being oblivious about the lack of comprehensive training for interviewing eyewitnesses, we should embrace the limited findings and invest in commonsense approaches to enhance our eyewitness interviews so we can reduce the number of misidentifications and wrongful convictions. Wells (2011) cited the fact that only a fraction of exoneration cases was solved using DNA evidence and that many other crimes lacked this physical evidence to exonerate the innocent. For example, most robbery cases involve very little DNA evidence and instead rely on eyewitness statements to develop leads in identifying the culprit. We cannot ignore the fact that there may be errors in gathering eyewitness statements which may lead to misidentifications and arrests that lead to the prosecution of innocent people. While we can appreciate the goals of the investigation is to find the culprit or learn what happened, we must insist on ensuring the process for gathering cognitive evidence is proper and mindful of post-event manipulations.

FOR YOUR CONSIDERATION

- When we are mindful of estimator and system variables, we respect the interview process.
- If we value the quality of cognitive evidence, we'll be mindful of the types of questions we ask.
- Before proceeding with the interview the investigator must evaluate the Confidence of Recollection.
- When we acknowledge TIATI, there is no reason to probe further.
- Having the perspective that eyewitness memory is a process of re-creation should heighten the objectivity for accepting cognitive evidence.
- Eyewitness memory can be considered reliable after it has been objectively evaluated.

4

The Detective Mind

The fundamental delusion of humanity is to suppose that I am here and you are out there.

Yasutani Roshi

When I read the introduction to the characters of the story in *Thinking Fast and Slow* (Kahneman, 2011), it reminded me of the intuitive impulse officers have in recognizing danger as they take preventative steps to ensure their safety and the safety of others. Kahneman described these characters as being agents of a system that helps us make decisions. Kahneman defined these systems as follows (Kahneman, 2011, pp. 20–21):

- System 1 operates automatically and quickly, with little or no effort and no sense of voluntary control.
- System 2 allocates attention to the effortful mental activities that demand it, including complex computations. The operations of System 2 are often associated with the subjective experience of agency, choice, and concentration.

Kahneman described how System 1 makes decisions based on viewing an image of an angry woman and then makes predictions of what will happen next. He followed that up by showing us a problem "17 × 24" and asked us to multiply the numbers knowing full well that we would have to slowly run through the process of calculating and come up with the proper answer (408) to demonstrate how System 2 operates. This example of taking specific steps to figure out a problem is very reminiscent of how we think our law enforcement officers operate when trying to figure out what happened at a crime scene. What psychologists have studied about these two systems is that System 1 operates automatically and System 2 requires attention. Understanding these "systems as agents with their individual abilities, limitations, and functions" in the law enforcement context will create a detective mind that will be more open to processing cognitive evidence (Kahneman et al., 2021). Just as Kahneman labeled Systems 1 and 2 as agents in his book, we can frame our discussion for this topic by calling them Detective 1 and Detective 2 mindsets. Before we examine our detective mindsets, let's look at our partial list for Detective 1:

- Depth of perception for objects (speeding cars).
- Loud noises associated with weapons (move to the location and assess).

- Complete the phrase "Code …" when all is safe (ten code).
- Detect aggressive behavior in a person (mindful of words, volume, and tone).
- Understand the words "2 John Adam X-Ray 456" (license plate).
- Drive patrol car while observing traffic laws while listening for call sign.
- Detecting furtive movements (where are the hands?).

All of these mental activities happen automatically and require very little mental effort for the officer. Because law enforcement personnel are trained in certain activities and understanding certain conditions, they've "learned associations between ideas" to process them innately (Kahneman, 2011). Most of the skills on this list were developed specifically for the law enforcement official at the police academy or the field training program, so they can be prepared for any eventuality. Many of these activities start with Detective 1 and then require the focus of Detective 2. Now let's look at our specially curated list for Detective 2 mindset:

- Focus on the gun sights before pulling trigger (range qualifications).
- While on perimeter of crime scene observing subjects in an out of area.
- Recent Be on the Lookout (BOL) for a robbery suspect driving a vehicle (red Toyota Camry).
- Being mindful of speaking with citizens on walking beat.
- Offering an explanation for a certain penal or vehicle code violation.
- Completing the crime report.
- Focus on the movements of the car after failing to yield to your emergency lights and siren.
- Summarizing eyewitness statements.

In every one of these situations, the officer must pay attention or else they will not meet a high degree of proficiency. Detective 2 mindset has limited capabilities when they are taxed with figuring a problem, so they are usually focused on an important task.

EYEWITNESS: SYSTEMS 1 AND 2

When we are mindful of the eyewitness interview, we should also consider the Systems 1 and 2 responses from their perspective as well. According to Kahneman et al. (2021) the job of System 1 is to "maintain and update a model of your personal world." Because we know that something happened to the eyewitness, we are now going to interview them about an event that happened to them or to someone else. The event was something out of the norm and not expected. Since our System 1 is looking for patterns for what makes up our lives and our "expectations of the future" (Kahneman et al., 2021), we have to be ready for the eyewitness to fill in sections of the event with what they believe actually happened. System 1 is looking for causes for this event or will try and make sense of it. For instance, when we interview an eyewitness to a robbery, they might associate the suspect with a gang or consider his desperate situation in looking to rob someone for money for drug use. These *connections* must be accepted as their statements but should not influence the investigation in that particular direction. We have not corroborated their perceptions of the suspect with other independent evidence (statements from other eyewitnesses, surveillance video at the scene, etc.), so we shouldn't move with these impressions as being investigated.

When we look at our robbery victim and we ask about the incident and they say the suspect was looking for "drug money," we don't have to investigate this impression any more than asking another open-ended question:

WHERE'S THE DRUG MONEY?

INV: So then what happened?
EW: Well, I know he was a drug addict looking to get money for drugs, and he was holding the knife out in front like this and said, "Give me your fucking shit!"
INV: Drug addict?
EW: Yeah, he looked like he was strung out on dope and needed a fix.
INV: A fix?
EW: Yeah, like meth or heroin or something like that.
INV: What kind of knife was it?
EW: I don't know, but it was long, and he kept waving it at me.

When we examine the questions asked in this excerpt, we can see that our questions about the drug addict offer us no significant information related to the crime of robbery but rather provide us with more impressions of the suspect and is rather reflective of the interviewee's perception of only the individual. Their System 1 is looking for reasons why the robbery took place and the type of person that would do this to them. Unless the eyewitness said that they had been using drugs with this guy before and had a history of drug use, we cannot rely on their impressions to be factual – they are just a perception of why something happened to them, and we should be mindful of their memory trying to make sense of what happened.

FOCUS ON THE BOUNCE

Many have heard of the experiment by Christopher Chabris and Daniel Simons in their book *The Invisible Gorilla* (2010) where a group of people are bouncing a basketball, and you're tasked with concentrating on the number of times the basketball is passed to each person. There are two teams, and one is wearing white shirts while the other wears black shirts. We have to focus on how many times the white team passes the ball to each other and ignore the black team. In the middle of the scene a person wearing a gorilla costume walks into the scene, thumps their chest and walks through the group of players. The gorilla walks through the group in less than ten seconds and more than half of the people that watch this scene do not see the gorilla. The instructions to ignore the black shirts and to count the number of ball bounces the team makes is what is causing the gorilla to disappear for some people. Kahneman reiterates there are two key takeaways from this study: "we can be blind to the obvious, and we are also blind to our blindness" (p. 24).

The essence of the *Mindful Interview Method* is that we are mindful of everything that is presented to us in the eyewitness interview session. Being mindful of our Detective 1 and 2 mindsets can help us return to a proper interview framework or understand why the eyewitness might have responded in a certain manner. We can see examples of Detective 1 and 2 mindsets controlling our process for investigation at our discretion for asking questions. A simple example would be not asking certain questions because we want to save time.

Say we relied on the initial robbery crime report to inform us about the race, age, and body build of the suspect. We intend to interview the eyewitness from the crime report to follow up, but because we found the information from previous eyewitness interview sessions to be consistent with the crime reports we create a heuristic for bypassing this initial inquiry with our eyewitness. Instead of asking them about their race, age range, and body build when we begin the interview to learn first-hand of their perceptions of the suspect, we move past this inquiry and instead ask the eyewitness only about the crime event. The problem with engaging in this heuristic is that we may find the eyewitness was not sure about the race, age, or body build of the suspect to begin with or was offered information by the initial officer that changed their recollection of the event. For instance, if the patrol officer asked the eyewitness about the race of the suspect and the eyewitness said, "I'm not sure, it was dark and he was wearing a hood," the officer might insist on relying on their belief that the suspect was Hispanic or Black by asking, "Well, was he Black or Hispanic?" The eyewitness might feel pressure to accept and affirm one of these choices and say, "Well, maybe Hispanic." And the officer would document the race of the suspect as being Hispanic even though the eyewitness did not actually recall the suspect being Hispanic.

Our Detective 1 mindset is engaged at this juncture when they try to create a complete picture of the suspect. When the eyewitness is unsure whether the suspect is Hispanic, Detective 1 mindset automatically suggests the suspect was either Hispanic or Black because of their historical perspective of the area or other information unrelated to the case but may in fact be associated. The eyewitness's System 1 agent accepts the officer's suggestion of Hispanic and completes their logical assumptions.

Later during the follow-up interview, we assume the suspect is Hispanic because it is listed in the crime report, and when we begin asking about the suspect's facial description, we soon realize the eyewitness is offering descriptions that are more consistent with a Black individual which lead us to believe the eyewitness may be misleading us. The reality is that the eyewitness was unsure when they were first interviewed by patrol officers and now, under more mindful questioning, is revealing more authentic recollections about the suspect's face. If we were to assume the content from the crime report was accurate, we wouldn't gain any new information about the race from the eyewitness interview session. Instead, we might receive conflicting information which may lead us to believe the eyewitness is unreliable. Because we're relying on the initial officers' inquiries to support the follow-up interview session, we may be diminishing the reliability of the cognitive evidence. While we might be efficient with our time in the follow-up interview, we would not be taking into account the initial officer's Detective 1 mindset inquiry (about race, age, and body type) in a way that allowed for eyewitness uncertainty.

When we conduct eyewitness interviews, we should limit our Detective 1 thinking and instead be more mindful of the effects our assumptions may have on eyewitness statements. Since investigators are considered the experts when they ask questions, eyewitnesses are not expected to caution or question the investigator about their inquiries altering their memory. Most eyewitnesses want to help us solve the case, and their desire to collaborate with us should not be left to investigative heuristics that welcome bias and allow assumptions to settle in our analysis. A more mindful interview would limit the heuristics of Detective 1 thinking and instead allow for a more methodical Detective 2 mindset approach to our inquiries.

In her book, *The Scout Mindset*, Julia Galef describes the soldier mindset as having been already hard wired into the way we deal with things in our life (2021). She describes our subconscious as having many soldiers "defending our beliefs against threatening evidence" (Galef, 2021). Many investigators consider themselves as having all the answers to getting to the truth of the matter when it comes to interviewing an eyewitness. Their interview techniques become "entrenched" and safe from objective scrutiny. She challenges us to make an incremental change and have more of a scout mindset. In her recommendations for scout habits to consider she asks,

> The next time you're making a decision, ask yourself what kind of bias could be affecting your judgment in that situation, and then do the relevant thought experiment.

This scout mindset can be achieved when we are mindful of our role as investigators. Being mindful and self-reflective can allow us to identify what Julia called "motivated reason" (Galef, 2021). Motivated reasoning can manifest in many forms for someone responsible with gathering information about an event. Whether you're motivated by accepting your Detective I mindset to see the victim as being unreliable, without any viable leads, or whether your suggestion for the race of the suspect is better than listing unknown on the crime report; in both cases you are ignoring the motivated reasoning to accept your bias and post event information. Being mindful of "motivated reasoning is an essential step on the way to reducing it" (Galef, 2021). When we are more mindful, we can be honest about how we make decisions for the next question or the lead we will follow in the investigation.

Since 1999, I have asked my eyewitnesses this question before I start the interview session: "Do you know why you are here?" You'd be surprised to hear the responses I get from some eyewitnesses. Some would look at me and say, "No, I told the officer I didn't see anything!" or "I think something happened and I may have seen the guy?" or "The guy robbed me, and he got away!" I'm purposely leaving nothing to chance when I ask this question, and I'm allowing for the possibility that I may have a reluctant victim, a hostile witness, or an oblivious bystander. Asking this question before starting the interview session can settle some nerves for the eyewitness and clarify issues before proceeding with the interview.

If we look at eyewitness interview sessions through the lens of neuropsychology, we can begin to understand our influence over eyewitness responses. In the book: *Noise, A Flaw in Human Judgment*, we see how people make judgments without knowing whether they were correct in their prediction (Kahneman et al., 2021). For instance, a patrol officer in a robbery case is making a calculated judgment that they know what questions to ask based on the crime, where it happened, the time it happened, the stereotype of the eyewitness, and the initial descriptions of the suspect. Yet, we never truly realize the accuracy of this judgment and learn from it. We don't know whether the patrol officer asked a force-choice question and whether the eyewitness was reluctant to choose one option or if they asked an open-ended question and the eyewitness offered a robust account of the event. When an investigator completes their preliminary interview with an eyewitness and comes away with an impression of veracity and sequence of events, they can set their course for how they value the cognitive evidence and ignore other information that may be just as significant. For example, if we interview an eyewitness and ask about the race of the person and they respond, "I'm not sure," if we then inquire further by asking if they could have been Asian or Black, we've just offered our prediction of what ethnicity we might have expected for this case. Instead, we should leave the ambiguity of their recollection in place and move on to the next area of inquiry. This may appear to be counterintuitive to the idea that the investigator needs to be probing the memory of the eyewitness in order to help them come up with the most *accurate* recollection of the event, but if we are mindful of our influence on the statements made by the eyewitness, we should be confident in accepting the reality that they are not sure. The investigator should accept the ambiguity in statements and resist the heuristics of asking more questions to gather more detailed information.

SERIAL ROBBERY CASE

Sometimes the System 1 agent for an eyewitness is right and we can rely on it to get us closer to the truth of the event. In 2007, I interviewed an eyewitness about a serial robbery case and asked them about the suspect's clothing, and they said it was a "surfer-type" jacket. I remember sketching the jacket and hearing the skepticism of their initial description. In the end the "surfer-type" jacket turned out to be very instrumental to the patrol officer on the street. While the eyewitness had only seen the suspect for five seconds as he passed by, tucking his motorcycle helmet under his arm, it was the first time anyone had seen his face after robbing more than ten convenience stores with his helmet on. It turned out the eyewitness had frequented this store to buy cigarettes every week. A few days later when they went to buy cigarettes, they had no idea the store had been robbed, and detectives canvassing the area looking for possible witnesses asked them to come in for a sketch interview. A week after my sketch interview, officers working the beat from the Field Training Officer (FTO) program had the sketch in their back pockets as they responded to a loud music call. After several minutes of good investigative work, one of the young officers asked their training officer if the guy resembled the serial robbery sketch. It turns out one of the officers was very familiar with the "surfer-type" clothing because he had grown up in a beach community in southern California, so for him, one of the subjects at the loud music call fitted the description of the suspect in the sketch. The subject was brought to the station for questioning and eventually confessed to all the robberies.

Because of my interview method, I wasn't biased to showing pictures (post-event information) of "surfer-type" clothing to help them recall the distinct pattern on the jacket. I knew that they had only seen the suspect for seconds, and I shouldn't expect them to offer accurate details about the face and clothing. I had to rely on my interview process to work with their impressions and gather only the information they had available to them. We can see both System 1 and Detective 1 working positively in this particular case. The eyewitness, thinking back on the suspect's clothing, believed they were seeing a "surfer-type" jacket, even though they couldn't describe it in detail they had a pretty good idea. Their System 1 agent latched on to the characterization of the suspect's clothing and completed their memory of that segment of the event. The recruit officer's Detective 1 mindset made a connection with the subject at the scene and the sketch he had viewed hours before. The "surfer-type" label in the BOL triggered something in both of them to see that in the subject. Even though the subject wasn't wearing the jacket, there were other factors that Detective 1 concluded were important, like the motorcycle nearby and the subject's resemblance to the sketch. It was enough for him to pull out a copy of the sketch and compare it to the subject. After several minutes of investigating and finding other incriminating items like a jacket, a weapon, a motorcycle helmet, and money, they decided to arrest the subject for unrelated items and bring him to the station for questioning. He subsequently confessed to all the robberies and said that he had dyed his hair dark because he had seen the sketch on TV and thought it looked like him. The officer's Detective 1 mindset made the connection that the subject was the wanted serial robber and activated his Detective 2 mindset to proceed methodically to gather physical evidence and consult with fellow officers before deciding to bring him to the station for questioning.

I had the pleasure of interviewing officers Austin Grogan, Jesse Ashe, and Sgt. Jim Overstreet about this case in 2014 and found their insights about their involvement in the investigation to be examples of their Detective 1 and 2 mindsets in action. Sgt. Overstreet had been a veteran of investigations and knew that canvassing robbery scenes for possible eyewitnesses might lead to important information that could lead to an arrest, so a few days after the latest robbery, he met the eyewitness and asked them to meet with me for a sketch interview. Because Sgt. Overstreet was methodical in his process, he presented the sketch to officers in patrol briefings so they would have the latest information about the case. Officers Grogan and Ashe were in the audience at one of these briefings and saw Sgt. Overstreet's presentation about the "Artus Bandit" case. Officer Ashe mentioned in our interview that he had not had many arrests during the FTO program and was hoping things would turn around for him. This case changed his impression of BOL notices and the unrelated calls that may lead to a once-in-a-lifetime arrest.

Officer Grogan found this case to be *surreal* and he was amazed at how the information had led them to this loud music call and then to the arrest of this serial robber. He remembers the calls that night were slow, and when the loud music call came out, he figured the beat sergeant would send them on it because he felt they needed the experience as new recruits. Officer Grogan said after this case he would be more mindful at gathering BOLs and review the details of every event. This arrest experience was an example of Grogan's Detective 1 mindset making the connection with the sketch and triggering the Detective 2 mindset to look at the subject, jacket, motorcycle, helmet, and weapon at the scene and consult with colleagues to make the arrest. Had they not been mindful of the possibility that the subject might be associated with the serial robber, they might have just arrested the suspect for possession of drugs and a weapon; instead, they were engaged with the possibilities and acted upon them in an unbiased manner.

BE MINDFUL OF THE DETECTIVE MIND

The Detective Mind we discuss in this chapter, like Kahneman's System 1 and 2 agents, is a metaphor for us to consider how our minds work and how we process information. The mental processes are seamless and oftentimes generate an internal dialogue that you may or may not acknowledge. When we are mindful of our role in the investigation, mindful of the tactics we'll take to question the eyewitness, and mindful of the responses we receive from the eyewitness, we'll be more suited to process the information in a way that will not diminish cognitive evidence.

Because the pace of interacting with eyewitnesses in determining what is or isn't important for elements of the crime, it may be easy for Detective 1 to make decisions that set the course for the investigation on a path that has not been fully inspected. When we recognize this early in our conversation with the eyewitness, we can begin to engage our Detective 2 mindset and figure out the problem in an intentional manner instead of relying on heuristics to latch onto unreliable cognitive evidence.

FOR YOUR CONSIDERATION

- Knowing my Detective 1 mindset can be biased, I should pay attention to what I'm thinking.
- It is easier to allow Detective 1 to handle the investigation until interesting details are revealed that Detective 1 cannot process.
- Having the Detective 2 mindset engaged at the start of the eyewitness interview session will ensure you gather the most reliable cognitive evidence.

5
Heuristics of Interviewing Eyewitnesses

Our life is frittered away by detail … Simplify, simplify.

Henry David Thoreau

Investigators rely on their keen sense of experience and interaction with witnesses and victims of crimes to ask the right questions and eventually come up with the identity of the assailant. While many of these cases are solved without fanfare every day, we sometimes read about wrongful conviction cases where investigators make suggestions to victims that allow them to believe they had selected the correct suspect while prosecutors ignore the unreliability of eyewitness statements and move to convict an innocent person. If we allow our investigators to rely heavily on heuristics that ignore mindful principles for collecting reliable evidence, then we ignore the accountability for administrators to ensure the evidence is being collected with the highest of integrity. If we reject the possibility that cognitive evidence may not be reliable because the tactics used were based on the assumption the eyewitness may be untruthful, then we risk jeopardizing the investigation. While we understand that when we interrogate, we "…ask questions of, to question (a person) esp. closely, or in a formal manner; to examine by questions" (Oxford Dictionary of English, 2021), we will see that both interview disciplines use similar tactics to retrieve information from the eyewitness. Having this heuristic for asking questions that result in unreliable information available to investigators can be catastrophic when we consider the outcomes.

SIMILARITIES IN INTERVIEWS AND INTERROGATIONS

Hostage negotiator Chris Voss writes about the goal of the interrogation being a "process with a mindset of discovery" (Voss, 2016). When we have this mindset, we can look at the information from the interview and analyze it for what it is. Unfortunately, many investigators rely on their experience alone to guide them through most eyewitness interview sessions which may include biases that infect their questions or their evaluation of eyewitness statements. The aphorism Voss uses to tell us that *until you know something you don't*, aligns very well with *That Is All There Is* (TIATI) in Chapter 3. Another common attribute of interviews and interrogations is the idea that when you are asking questions, your eyewitness is listening and coming up with their answer while you are thinking of your next question. If you are coming up with your next question while they are responding, you aren't actually listening. Even interrogators are taught to make their sole purpose an "all-encompassing focus" of the person they are interviewing (Voss, 2016). Aside from accusing someone of lying or asking questions to confuse or catch them in a fabrication of their recollection, elite investigators practice more mindful tactics and insist on nurturing trust so their interviewees can talk more and reveal as much information as they know. The main distinction between the *Mindful Interview Method* (MIM) and interrogations is that we do not expect to interview a deceitful eyewitness. Instead, we are looking to mindfully retrieve the most reliable cognitive evidence from the eyewitness. There is no room for cutting corners or making assumptions because of our experience. When we are dealing with cognitive evidence, we must be mindful of preserving the integrity of statements and allow for inconsistencies to be resolved with other corroborating evidence.

THE HEURISTICS FOR INVESTIGATIONS

In Chapter 4 we were introduced to the psychology behind System 1 and System 2 thinking and how we should be mindful of the effects on our *Detective Mind*. Because many investigators rely on a priori to shape their style of investigation, many of them embrace their assumptions and rely on them to solve their cases. The idea of gaining experience by allowing the investigator to discover the pitfalls of their investigation in a hands-on approach to learning is rather problematic. Even so, law enforcement investigators are given great latitude to follow these heuristics in the spirit of catching the culprit. These heuristics for the *Detective Mind* are easily accepted by our Detective 1 mindset because it is effortless. These mental short-cuts are often based on previous training investigators received or the experiences they've had being mentored by veteran officers. They trust them because it has worked for them in the past and they have a pretty good idea of what happened, so they move forward and go about identifying the culprit. If their investigative techniques are presumptive why would they change?

This investigative heuristic has led to numerous instances where our law enforcement personnel resort to practices that lead to someone being wrongfully convicted or dies in custody. In the 1984 case of Ronald Cotton, investigators practiced showing the victim a line-up where they knew the position of the presumed suspect in the photo array. The investigators in this case allowed the victim to take an unusually long time at deciding whether she recognized any of the photos to be the suspect. When she finally settled on one picture, they praised her for picking the same person from the in-field line-up they had done before. This type of identification process has been in practice for decades and, only now, because of the advent of DNA science, has been deemed problematic because innocent people have been identified as assailants. We'll learn more in Part III, Chapter 7 in Mindful of the Innocent.

HEURISTICS IN FORENSIC ART

When I started my career as a forensic artist, the eyewitness interviews were conducted in a manner that was questionable. At the time, the process for interviewing eyewitnesses

HEURISTICS OF INTERVIEWING EYEWITNESSES

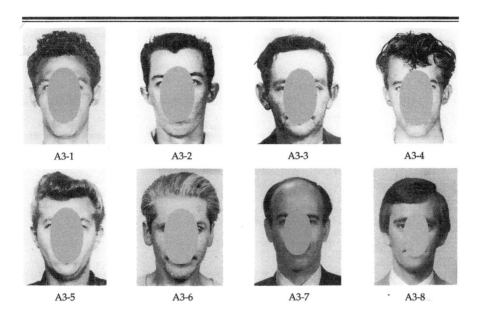

Figure 5.1 Reference images for creating composite sketches. Page 3 of FBI Facial Identification Catalog, November 1988, upper quadrant of facial features "Triangle Head."

was built on heuristics that did not consider the limitations of eyewitness memory. For instance, when I was trained at the FBI in composite art, we were trained to have the eyewitness review a small catalog of men's faces and asked them to choose the label associated with the different features. We would later review their choices and create a rough draft of the sketch based on these selections (see Figure 5.1).

The heuristic we employed to create the sketch of the culprit involved the aid of the facial identification catalog of features. We would have the eyewitness tell us what the person looked like and have them use their recognition skills to distinguish an unknown person from their memory of the suspect. We were in fact showing post-event information without consideration for memory contamination. This heuristic had been in practice by sketch artists since 1984 and had been a great exercise in developing the skill for creating realistic-looking suspects. However, the shortcuts for creating the composite sketch suffered at the hands of making it easier for the sketch artist to draw a human face. Unfortunately, the training for interviewing eyewitnesses by forensic artists is steeped in familial trial and error that diminishes a more authentic experience. Because most forensic artists utilize reference images to either stimulate memory or refine the sketch, their illustrations cannot always be relied on to be mindful of preserving the reliability of cognitive evidence. The same can be said for criminal interviewers (police, attorneys, corrections, probation officer, and dispatchers) whereby their practice for gathering information from an eyewitness is rooted in asking Who, What, Where, When, and Why?

Because asking questions rooted in these "5-Ws" is easier, most investigators frequently rely on it and underestimate the negative impact it can have on an investigation. Sometimes asking Who and Why can be complicated when the eyewitness has no idea who the suspect is. If we look at other disciplines that involve interviewing people, we'll find they require more structure in formulating their inquiries instead of assuming they know best. If we look at the academic field, we find that qualitative researchers are well prepared to ask questions in a way that preserves information so they can categorize and analyze data without bias. While most qualitative researchers have a research question in mind, criminal investigators are often subjected to *"whodunnit"* cases that limit the variety and number of questions asked of their eyewitness.

QUALITATIVE RESEARCH AND EYEWITNESS INTERVIEWS

We know that qualitative research is focused on field research that intends to document, investigate, and describe how people have experienced something (Bailey, 2018). Police officers, dispatchers, and investigators spend most of their time documenting and investigating events relayed to them via eyewitness accounts of a significant experience. While the dispatcher is not specifically conducting research to support a "clear statement of purpose" from the eyewitness, they are documenting and describing events as they are recounted to them (Bailey, 2018). The investigator, in essence, is conducting research on an event that happened and is tasked with gathering reliable cognitive evidence from the eyewitness to understand what happened. This broad interest in discovery by the investigator transforms the inquiry into a narrow perspective focused on finding the truth. Just as the qualitative researcher utilizes certain types of interview styles to gather their statements, the criminal investigator should also have a plan for conducting their interviews with the eyewitness.

We know the qualitative field researcher uses certain types of interview styles like unstructured, structured, and semi-structured formats to get the respondent to reveal details about their experiences (Bailey, 2018). We also expect that criminal investigators will oscillate between all three styles depending on the crime and the eyewitness. For instance, an officer on patrol might be on a walking beat and strike up a conversation with a civilian in front of a business. The dialogue between the officer and citizen might encompass many topics and lead to "fruitful caches of information" (Bailey, 2018). This unstructured interaction between the officer and citizen is an opportunity for the officer to practice mindful interview techniques. We know that officers must practice officer safety at all times, especially when they are exposed to the public in unfamiliar surroundings. So their training in the police academy and the Field Training Officer (FTO) program transforms these mundane encounters into heightened awareness for their position: Gun-side away, balanced positioning, looking for places of cover, observing the hands of the person in front of them, all while listening to the hum of radio traffic for their call sign. If we consider another layer of focused attention onto these *unstructured* conversations, we may find it to be a challenge at first, but with enough practice it will become easier.

Just as the officer is mindful of the subject's hands, so too can they be mindful of what the person is saying, how they are saying it, and what expressions they make when they say it. In this benign encounter, the officer can be mindful of the response of the eyewitness to their questions and listen to their concerns about their neighborhood.

Practicing active listening and asking open-ended questions are important principles in establishing a mindful interview practice with an eyewitness. While we currently don't specifically train our officers and dispatchers to be conversationalists with the people they encounter, a recent California law (SB494) will soon require California Commission on Peace Officer Standards and Training (POST) to create a course that focuses on "advanced interpersonal communication skills" (CA POST, 2021). Our law enforcement personnel will likely be trained on how to have simple conversations with people that do not lead to an arrest, and they'll be expected to engage mindfully with people in a respectful manner.

Being more mindful in our conversations with people will enhance our cognitive evidence-retrieval skills and improve the quality of eyewitness statements. Being *present* and focused on listening to every word the eyewitness says should become effortless. Just as the qualitative researcher is prepared with certain questions and understands their order and pace, the officer on the beat might have standard opening and follow-up questions that are comfortable and genuine. For instance, if the officer on patrol is aware of certain troublesome issues in the neighborhood, they can have a plan for their encounters with citizens. A qualitative semi-structured interview format would be best in this instance. It might go something like this:

SEMI-STRUCTURED INTERVIEW

Officer: How are you doing today?
Citizen: (smiles) Fine, and you?
Officer: I'm pretty good. We're just walking the beat today and making sure we address any issues neighbors might have.
Citizen: That's good to know. Last week my neighbor's car got stolen.
Officer: I'm sorry to hear that. We were informed of the theft, and it turns out it was found a couple days later with very little damage. We haven't found the suspect, but we're working on it.
Citizen: Oh, they found it? That's great, yeah, I park my car in my … and make sure I lock it.
Officer: That's excellent advice. We also ask people not to leave valuables in their cars. We've been asking neighbors to share their security video with us so we might find the suspects.
Citizen: Yeah, we don't have a RING camera – we just have a dog.
Officer: I understand. Luckily there are a lot of neighbors that do, although I do enjoy my dog and he's pretty good at alerting me when there's someone suspicious out front. Anyway, if you see a suspicious person, don't hesitate to call 9-1-1 and we'll be sure to check it out.
Citizen: Ok, sure will. Have a good day officer!
Officer: You too! Take care.

In this brief exchange, we see the officer gather important information about the neighborhood. While the officer may not be categorizing certain topics for their report (no written report is necessary for a citizen contact), they can become keenly aware of the information they're receiving and practice being more mindful. We know from this conversation that neighbors talk to each other about crime issues. We can see from speaking to this person that crime prevention tips are adhered to. Instead of being brief with the citizen and offering a perfunctory greeting, the officer stopped, listened, and informed the neighbor. This innocuous communication is good practice for mindfully interviewing an eyewitness and denies a more common heuristic most patrol officers might take.

This mindful conversation had the basic elements of the qualitative research interview and was very much law enforcement specific. We see that the conversation starts with an open-ended question (broad focus) and then moves on to the topic of auto theft (narrow focus). Since this individual is not the victim, there is no need to question (probe) them in a fashion that seeks more information and changes the tone of the conversation. When the officer informs the neighbor that they were aware of the incident, the neighbor has an impression that the police were doing their job; there is no need for the officer to offer specifics. Generalities will do in this case. The genuine interest of the officer to ask about the neighborhood and respond with concern and interest in making life better is an intangible we call rapport. Bailey (2018) says, "Rapport is an important ingredient" for the qualitative field researcher, and I propose it is vital to the patrol officer to make an impression that results in goodwill for themselves, and the next officer.

BREAKING HABITS

I had the pleasure of training investigators from all over the state of California about the cognitive interview technique, and what's important to understand about teaching adults how to establish rapport is that it's not an easy task. Bailey (2018) characterizes the interviews law enforcement conduct as "utilitarian" with the understanding that we (police) need something from you (eyewitness). While that may be the case, we can certainly leverage our position as crime solvers and be more like facilitators. Establishing an authentic rapport at the outset of the interview can certainly enhance the communication process between the officer and the eyewitness. During our training exercises, the investigator, even in these mock exercises, had to rely on the eyewitness to cooperate and offer as much information as they could regarding the incident. However, after observing the investigators go through their initial rapport-building segment, I often had to stop the exercise and reset the mock interview because of the heuristics many would engage in. Many detectives were reciting scripts (depending on the case) and lacking genuine empathy in their demeanor. They would ask how the person was doing, ask if they wanted some water, and then move on to asking for details about the event. It was as if they were going through the motions placating the administration to show they cared. During our time-out, I would demonstrate my process for establishing rapport (at the start) and ask them to imagine the eyewitness was a loved one.

Just imagining the eyewitness was someone they cared about changed the tone in the room; the investigator became more attentive, spoke less hurriedly, made more eye contact, and seemed genuinely concerned. I believe we all have it inside ourselves to be empathetic and more mindful of how we interact with the eyewitness. If we are mindful *before* we start the interview process, we understand our task more clearly. We see the elements of the crime; the eyewitness is someone who has gone through an ordeal, and we're present for every nuance of the details and every pause in reflection by the eyewitness. Establishing rapport throughout the interview process is something we must integrate into every encounter with an eyewitness. When I interviewed a rape victim, a robbery witness, or an attempted murder victim, I didn't change my approach to the interview; it was always the same semi-structured interview style focused on gathering details about the suspect's face and documenting their statements in the form of the sketch. Investigators must resist the availability heuristic associated with establishing rapport and instead be authentically available to hear them and respond to their concerns (Tversky & Kahneman, 1973). Do we truly believe the eyewitness needs some attention, or are we asking because we've been told that this is what victims need at the start of the interview?

Just as the qualitative researcher reviews their report of statements, the investigator should review statements made by the eyewitness to confirm and correct details. Investigators should always record their interview sessions (at the minimum an audio recording) so the report is documented with accuracy. While investigators may not be identifying topics and themes like a qualitative researcher, they must have a good idea of what happened and understand the gaps in information so they can follow up with more interviews. Their report of eyewitness statements is their qualitative analysis of what happened, without tables to show common themes being recited by multiple eyewitnesses, or without a conclusion about the event. What investigators need is an accurate record of what was told to them by the eyewitness, without manipulation of memory and without bias.

If we are mindful of the limitations of human memory, we will see that most eyewitness statements will consistently lack the specificity of details in their recall of events and descriptions of suspects. Investigators must accept this reality and resist attempts to be more *accurate* and complete in their documentation. If the eyewitness is unsure about a certain detail of the event, then it must be documented in this fashion. Just as the integrity of the report for a qualitative researcher would be questioned if reviewers found the researcher asking leading questions using words that the eyewitness did not actually say, we might question the veracity of the crime report if we learned the investigator did the same thing.

Both the academic researcher and the criminal investigator can learn a lot from each other. While the academic researcher might have a hypothesis to challenge before they select the group interview, the patrol officer (investigator) is faced with a never-ending rush of unique encounters with people who need their help and many others who would rather not engage with them. Conducting a mindful eyewitness interview encompasses all facets of the interview process, from planning the strategy to asking certain types of questions to documenting the veridical account of the event. We know that conducting an eyewitness interview with the heuristics of trial and error can result in devastating consequences for innocent people. By randomly collecting actual interview data of actual eyewitness interviews, we can evaluate the retrieval process and begin to improve eyewitness interview training to benefit all members of the department.

FOR YOUR CONSIDERATION

- Since investigators are engaged in a process that is often repetitive, they should not give in to heuristics that reduce the quality of cognitive evidence.
- When investigators rely on their experience alone, they can resort to tactics that can affect the reliability of cognitive evidence.
- When we compare the process of gathering information from interviews with qualitative and investigative frameworks, we realize the similarities in their outcomes.

6
Investigating Mindfulness

Act without doing; work without effort.

Tao Te Ching

A group of research scientists found that when investigators commit to a theory early in the investigation (without actual evidence), it can result in a waste of time in identifying someone who is not the culprit (O'Brien, 2009). They believed that unless you are open to different scenarios for the crime, your mindset may lead to a cognitive bias about what you are pursuing. This confirmation bias may color the questions you plan to ask eyewitnesses and reduce your opportunity to gather reliable cognitive evidence. If we are honest about our role as investigators, we must reflect on what may be clouding our judgments and pursue avenues to clear them. If we do not pursue a path of objectivity and ethical principles, we contribute to the pattern of working with unreliable cognitive evidence that supports the misidentifications of innocent people.

MINDFULNESS

Mindfulness for an investigator is being open to monitoring and accepting what is happening in the moment. Monitoring and acceptance "are common to almost all definitions of mindfulness" (Creswell & Lindsay, 2014). Being mindful of what we are doing and how we are doing it is an excellent way to be more *present* about the facts *today* and help identify issues with evidence so we can evaluate leads with objectivity. Being mindful of how we investigate the crime before us is critical to how strong the case is at the time of prosecution and ultimately benefits everyone involved in the investigation. Because most law enforcement personnel engage in many more mundane tasks like interviewing eyewitnesses as victims or witnesses to a crime, their agencies should demonstrate the efficacy of their performance for these interview sessions.

When we pursue a path towards changing our mindset to be more mindful, we effectively seek wisdom about the situation we are in and attempt to locate evidence to support our intended path. Cognitive scientists have defined rational wisdom as having the "ability to view experiences and changes in the environment in proportion to one another"

(Tirch, et al., 2016). As investigators, we make decisions about how much to value certain perceptions of eyewitnesses and weigh them against the physical evidence we've identified as being relevant. The eyewitness relies on the wisdom we've gained through training and experience to be investigators that look at an issue under the light of objectivity. The idea of a mindset that is *awakened* has been referred to "as the perfection of transcendent wisdom ... through training in mindfulness, acceptance, compassion, and concentration" that we create in ourselves (Tirch et al., 2016). As investigators, we are attracted to the idea of solving problems and locating the truth in a maze of complex statements and physical evidence that may not offer all the clues. This drive to seek out and learn new information is a powerful element in enhancing our Detective Mind.

In the book *The Seven Spiritual Laws of Success* by Deepak Chopra (1994), I found the transcendent topic resonated with my yearning for a mindful process. The idea of practicing meditation and quieting my thoughts was appealing to me and helped me forge a new path for discovery. I began to look at the process of interviewing eyewitnesses in a different light, and I was becoming more mindful of my attention to detail even though I wasn't describing it in this manner. I began to purposely monitor my actions as the police artist and looked to these laws to guide me on a successful path towards helping victims identify their assailants and assist our detectives in identifying the culprit. I found the *Laws of Success* to be a blueprint I could follow to support my journey as the new police artist.

THE SPIRITUAL LAWS OF SUCCESS

- Pure Potentiality.
- Law of Karma.
- Law of Least Effort.
- Law of Detachment.
- Law of Dharma.

I practiced the law of *Pure Potentiality* by setting aside time to remain present for the upcoming interview session. I practiced the *Law of Giving* by being respectful of the interview process and accepting whatever the eyewitness could offer. Giving the eyewitness this safe space to recall events made it easier for them to offer me reliable information. Because I made the choice to respect the interview process, the *Law of Karma* provided an interview session that would result in more reliable information. Because I made the choice to not engage in a practice of memory contamination, I caused the retrieval of cognitive evidence to be more reliable. When I accepted the premise that eyewitnesses may not have specific information about the suspect, I was applying the *Law of Least Effort* which allowed me to be open to all possibilities and descriptions. Since my intentions for the interview were unbiased and open to any information, I was adhering to the *Law of Intention* and remained unattached to the outcome. I started the interview with the intent of being present for whatever comes from the interview, and because I was mindful of the *Law of Detachment*, I refrained from conducting eyewitness interviews from a biased perspective. I allowed the eyewitness to recall details as they experienced them and not fill in gaps to satisfy my theories. I accepted the fact that eyewitnesses may not offer complete and accurate information. And finally, I applied the *Law of Dharma* by accepting my position as a police artist and utilized my artistic and investigative talents to help victims and witnesses confronted with a crime. By expressing my talents to help eyewitnesses I was joining my fellow law enforcement officers in serving our community.

MINDFUL OPPORTUNITIES

Since 2016 the Southern California Intergovernmental Training and Development Center (ITDC) operating under the name of Government Training Agency (GTA) began offering wellness programs that offer mindfulness practices that "[C]an be immediately implemented to enhance all aspects of [law enforcement] personal lives and work performance." These wellness programs are grant funded and cover the following topics for law enforcement, including professional staff and dispatchers:

Course Topics

- Emergency services unique stressors.
- Individual stress ratings and analysis.
- Effectively managing the pace of modern times.
- Self-care time management – family and friends.
- Stress inoculation techniques.
- Restoration techniques and improving sleep.
- Mindfulness.
- Autogenic breath control.
- Rediscovering purpose, meaning, and legacy.
- Training your brain for happiness.
- Physiology of stress.
- Transference – caring for friends and family.
- Balancing body, mind, and spirit.

The number of programs related to mindfulness training in 2016 was 22 sessions offered by the GTA. While this number pales in comparison to the hundreds of investigative courses offered by law enforcement training agencies throughout the US, it does signal that mindfulness is being considered an option for law enforcement practitioners looking to improve their interactions with citizens.

Some studies have documented that mindfulness has been attributed to improving cognitive skills and "has been shown to make practitioners more likely to respond compassionately," which is vital to investigators interviewing traumatized victims of violent crimes (Drigas & Karyotaki, 2018). Not only does practicing mindfulness improve the cognitive skills of the practitioner, but it is a "valuable tool [for] individuals looking for personal and professional development" to improve their overall performance goals. Because many investigators have high self-efficacy expectation, they believe they are ready to confront any challenge placed in front of them. This internal drive to achieve excellence makes any individual looking to improve their interviewing skills a great candidate for practicing mindfulness. As more investigators choose to practice mindfulness, the opportunities to improve empirical research and investigate "the models of mindfulness and the cognitive mechanisms they propose" will be greatly enhanced to meet their expectations (Chiesa et al., 2011).

DRIVING MINDFULLY

Working at being more mindful reminded me of the narrative driving exercises we practiced in the Field Training program when I first started as a police officer, after the police academy. Our Field Training Officers (FTOs) would evaluate us on how well we described what we were seeing as we were driving around in our beat. The narrative driving exercise forced us to be mindful of the weather, the speed of the car, the sounds of the road, and the people walking by with rifles on their shoulder – yes, I missed that one! While my FTO and I were riding near the fairgrounds in San Jose (early afternoon), I was busy reciting my narrative driving exercise when my FTO asked me if I had seen the man with the gun on the street. I cringed and said no. He told me to turn the car around and make contact with the man. As I made the U-turn I could see a man (about 30 yards away), dressed in camouflage holding a rifle on his right shoulder, carrying a rectangular black case in his left hand, and walking alongside a woman on the sidewalk. I stopped my patrol car (facing him, about 20 feet away), got out and walked up to him and calmly asked for his identification and registration for the rifle. It turned out he was on his way to a gun show event at the fairgrounds (about 50 yards away). Looking back on this event proved one thing to me, that even though I was narrating what I was seeing, I obviously wasn't focused on what I was seeing. How could I miss a man walking down the street with a rifle in broad daylight? From that day forward, I challenged myself to be more mindful as a patrol officer of what I was seeing – driving just below the speed limit, glancing at my mirrors several times in a minute, anticipating what might happen, and deciding what I would do should an event turn violent.

PRACTICING BEING PRESENT

In *Wherever You Go There You Are* by Jon Kabat-Zinn (1994), the chapter on *Patience* describes cultivating your own reasons for pursuing your meditation practice and how you couldn't have "harmony without commitment to ethical behavior." It reminded me of my unique position in being the police artist for the largest law enforcement agency in Silicon Valley. After my appointment to the position of police artist, I was struggling with the idea of continuing to interview eyewitnesses by using reference images even though I had begun to accept the findings by psychologists on the malleability of eyewitness memory. If showing eyewitnesses reference images was a form of *post-event information*, then why continue interviewing eyewitnesses in this manner? I found myself focused on the idea that my interview sessions would be more ethical if I relied on the memory of the eyewitness and not on my ability to manipulate and influence their statements by using reference images.

Paying close attention to our role as investigators will enhance our abilities for retrieving more reliable information from the eyewitness, and being more mindful about how we plan and do things can greatly enhance our interview sessions. When we start to pay attention in this way, our relationship to things changes and we see more deeply and clearly; we start seeing a connectedness between things that were not apparent before (Kabat-Zinn, 1990). When we take the time to prepare for the interview even for five minutes, we realize afterwards how clearly we imagined what the eyewitness was telling us and that capturing all relevant eyewitness statements is not fully appreciated until the session is evaluated for reliability.

Kabat-Zinn (1990) wrote in *Full Catastrophe Living*, "Knowing what you are doing while you are doing it is the essence of mindfulness practice," and as investigators we are supposed to be the experts ready with the right questions and responses for the eyewitness. With intentional focus we do this more clearly and are mindful of the limitations of eyewitness memory, which allows us to gather more reliable cognitive evidence that is valuable to the investigation. When we are "present on purpose," we tend to see things in statements that might not have been relevant before, and because we are more aware, we can analyze them with confidence (p. 17).

For instance, when we begin our interview and we ask our eyewitness to close their eyes and take a few deep breaths and they don't, we should recognize it. If we ask our next question without acknowledging their reluctance to comply with our request, we are establishing an investigator–eyewitness dyad that can be construed as being mindless. When we ask a question or give guidance to the eyewitness, we should see a positive response or at least a query about why we've made the request. Pema Chodron writes in *The Places That Scare You* (2002) that sometimes when we train in being mindful "we see that we've been pretty ignorant about what we're doing" (p. 34). If we let our request for compliance from the eyewitness go without acknowledging their reluctance, we may miss important facts about the investigation. Instead, we should take the time to find out why this is happening and show some empathy and understanding for what they are experiencing. The reluctance in complying with our request for focus may be due to our inability to explain the reasons why closing their eyes will benefit them in the end.

When Jessica Nordell wrote in the *End of Bias* (2021) about investigating the idea of training police officers to become more mindful to help them become healthier and more present for their roles on the streets, it would follow that these investigators might be more receptive to these principles of introspection and quality of being. Investigators have always been singled out as being successful at identifying the culprit by being tenacious and dedicated to their inquisitive nature. Their confidence in being in charge and open to new information makes them successful investigators, and while their success may not have been purposely aligned with a *mindful* approach, it was surely done in a thoughtful manner. Being more mindful will help to acknowledge certain biases that may come up as we meet eyewitnesses, and acknowledging our bias we can move past the negative perception and focus on the mechanics of the interview. Being mindful of every step and every word used for each question will ensure that whatever the eyewitness says in response to our questions will be reliable for the investigation and ensure cognitive evidence will be preserved for scrutiny and follow-up later in the prosecution of the case.

Nordell (2021) highlights the work of Richard Goerling and Cheryll Ann Maples in her book as they ponder how they might change the way police officers engage with the public. Goerling asked about a way to "systematically change officers' behavior" through mind and body exercises, while Maples found her path in practicing meditation and applied a kinder manner in her enforcement of people to change their perception of her. Instead of relying on officers, dispatchers, and investigators to meet every situation unprepared, we should inspire them to treat these benign encounters as important exercises in developing cognitive evidence. Thich Nhat Hahn writes in the book, *Keeping the Peace: Mindfulness and Public Service* (2005) that everyone should walk "with mindfulness" and suggests that police officers walking the beat should consider being more aware of their surroundings and see everything in front of them and appreciate every step and every sound and every smell as they conduct foot patrols. He suggests that since *you* have to "pay attention and do your job," why not enjoy it more fully and notice the good as well as the bad (Hahn, 2005).

When we *practice awareness* during our interviews, we will be more prepared to deal with any issue that may present itself, and when we conduct a mindful interview, we reinforce our *cognitive control* and react with a purpose of gathering reliable cognitive evidence. Because we are mindful of what the eyewitness is presenting before us, we can react specifically to the information related to the question. Because we are not distracted, we can observe and interpret every exchange of communication from within the interview setting. Regardless of whether the dispatcher is taking the call, the first officer on the scene, the first investigator being exposed to the evidence, the loss prevention officer conducting the preliminary interview, or the attorney reviewing the case for the first time, developing the mindset to slow things down is a skillset that should be practiced. Sometimes the reality of the influences of day-to-day operations can reduce the time to investigate and cause our minds to take on a heuristic to solve the case. While it may appear that seasoned investigators rely on actual factual evidence to get truthful answers, some may conduct the investigations in a manner that leads them to gather unreliable information, and we don't see that outcome until it is too late. If we are truly seeking the truth of the matter, then we must abandon all efforts to shape the narrative of the eyewitness, and "pay attention and see things as they are" (Kabat-Zinn, 1990). Just because we have heard it before doesn't mean we know what happened, even though the circumstances sound similar, it doesn't mean they are.

WE'VE HEARD IT BEFORE

An investigator may work with a specific unit and hear the same types of descriptions from eyewitnesses as they attempt to describe the face of the suspect or the weapon used. When we challenge ourselves to be a mindful detective, we can listen more intently and resist completing eyewitness thoughts when they struggle in providing more specific information. Our documentation for the interview session will be more credible when we list only what they said and not our clarified or altered version. When we collect the cognitive evidence with integrity, everyone sees the true event as it was relayed.

For instance, say we interview the eyewitness about a scam, and the eyewitness said the suspect drove a small compact car. We ask the eyewitness about the make and model of the car, and the eyewitness says they don't know. "I'm terrible at distinguishing cars." If the investigator then asks, "Well, was it a Kia or a Toyota?" the eyewitness might say, "Do they make small cars? Can you show me some models?" There are two issues with this mindless suggestion: (1) The auto maker suggestions are post-event information, and (2) if the eyewitness chooses one of the suggested automakers, the choice is not from authentic memory, which means showing images of Toyota and Kia compact cars is post-event information that has altered the memory of the eyewitness. Acknowledging this alteration at this critical point of the interview session is something that rarely gets noticed and instead becomes a part of documented witness statements. A more mindful tactic would be to document the "small compact car" and quote the eyewitness saying, "I'm terrible at distinguishing cars."

We know it is important to get to the truth, but we should not sacrifice the integrity of eyewitness statements by insisting on clarifying each detail because we assume proper phrasing. If we are mindful of the margins of eyewitness memory, then our reports should reflect these limitations. If we are truly seeking the truth of the matter, then we must abandon all efforts to shape the narrative of the eyewitness. Just because investigators have "heard it before" doesn't mean they know what happened.

THAT IS ALL THERE IS

Being mindful means that our "Awareness requires only that we pay attention and see things as they are. It doesn't require that we change anything" (Kabat-Zinn, 1990). If we can challenge ourselves to be mindful of our role as investigators, we will *listen* and document authentic eyewitness details without insisting on offering suggestions. Even though an eyewitness might say the weapon was a "black gun," we shouldn't insist on clarifying that it was a semi-automatic pistol by showing them our weapon or finding online pictures that force them to choose. Subsequently at trial, the defense attorney might cross-examine the witness and learn that they were not familiar with weapons and that the investigator assisted them to identify the type of weapon used in the assault. This *assistance* may create some concern for the jury and cast doubt on the veracity of other statements gathered from the eyewitness.

When we are being mindful, we are "Being grounded in present-moment awareness" and an investigator that incorporates a mindset that allows them to observe what is happening at each moment instead of tangled in different theories will allow them better opportunities to realize "the interconnectedness of things" (Kabat-Zinn, 1990).

ARE YOU REALLY PRESENT?

As you read this sentence, ask yourself: Am I present?
Am I aware of everything around me as I read these words?

ATTENTION TO DETAIL

When we decide to pay attention to our breath "in an awareness of breathing, even for one or two breaths," we notice that we pay attention to our mind as it meanders in thought

(Kabat-Zinn, 1990). The idea that we may experience something *special* when we engage in being present may be a letdown when we first sit in silence and imagine the intentional breath and the exaggerated exhale. When we participate in being mindful at each moment, we may find that being in that moment is nothing more than experiencing it as it comes. We may not realize the changes we've made in being present with each moment, but we may eventually reflect on the decisions or choices we've made and see how mindful or mindless we've been.

Being present in the eyewitness interview session means that we're prepared to deal with an eyewitness that recalls very little but may hold the key to solving the case. Being present in the eyewitness interview means that we're aware of our influence on the eyewitness, and we must control it to reduce any negative impact on the outcome. Being present means we're able to gather detailed information from the eyewitness by being mindful of our process. We can gather this important information when we prepare for the interview by being mindful of what we say and how we say it.

Being mindful of our influence on the eyewitness is important to understand, so we should be considerate of our preparation. The eyewitness wants to trust us and believe that we know what we are doing and rely on our questions to solve the case. Being mindful of our responsibility can ensure we focus on cognitive evidence that is deemed reliable. For example, psychologists have found that eyewitnesses can be convinced they saw something just by using certain words or showing them images (Loftus, 1979). So when we ask the eyewitness what the hair was like and they say, "It was short, kind of wavy, pretty neat," we shouldn't follow-up with, "Was it a crew cut?" or "Was it a fade cut?" Either question might influence the eyewitness to respond with, "I guess so, yeah it was like a crew cut." When we offer the eyewitness these clarifying choices, we may convince them into thinking *we* know something about the description of the suspect. This less mindful attempt at clarifying details has changed their memory of the hair because of *our* post-event information. Because we've offered *our* clarification of details in our position of authority, the eyewitness, in their willingness to please us, has accepted our post-event information without hesitation. When we are present and aware of the dynamics of the interview session, we can be prepared to move away from this situation before it happens.

BEING MINDFUL BEFORE THE INTERVIEW

The mindful reset in the *Mindful Interview Method* (MIM) prepares us to be present and aware of what we are about to do in interviewing the eyewitness. If we think back on our last workday at the office (or home office), we can imagine various morning rituals that we go through in preparation for the day. As we go through these activities, we may not be fully aware of what we are doing even though we are *doing* things to get ready for our day. When we are in the act of "not knowing, we take actions and say things, carried along by the momentum of the sense of habit and doing" (Weisman & Smith, 2010). Enabling a mindful ritual to prepare for our next interview can enhance our wellbeing by cultivating the "skillful qualities of mind" (Weisman & Smith, 2010).

AWARENESS

As a forensic artist, I had many opportunities to practice meditation and cultivate an awareness that benefited my interview techniques. I found that being present and aware of what was being said and how it was being said (without judgment) allowed me to draw the features in a way that resonated more closely with what the eyewitness remembered. Many victims would gasp when they viewed the sketch for the first time and realized their simple statements had resulted in a sketch that resembled their assailant. They couldn't believe I was able to sketch the features based on their limited recollections; however, what they didn't know is that their limited recall was enough to present them with a sketch that represented everything they remembered. Seeing this in front of them instead of in their mind was sometimes a shock to their reality (see Figure 6.1). Even though the eyewitness made changes to the sketch many times (during the refinement process), they knew that the sketch looked enough like the suspect that they could rely on it to confirm their recollections. Interviewing an eyewitness about the face of the suspect is a complicated task and being more mindful gave me confidence in relying on their memory of details to create a sketch that resembled their suspect.

Investigators are expected to focus on the details of the case and the information gathered in support of the investigation and can be "a cornerstone [for a] mindfulness practice" (Kabat-Zinn, 1994). We all do it every day when we decide to pay attention and engage in a specific task. Our concentration can result in positive outcomes, or it can be diluted and

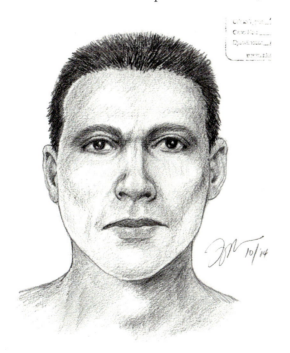

Figure 6.1 Cognitive sketch from recollection. © 2014, Gil Zamora.

lead to negative consequences. When we take a moment to check in on our ability to concentrate, we can begin to understand the idea, refocusing ourselves before the interview session. We prepare for our mindful interview by practicing the *mindful reset* before we meet the eyewitness. The mindful reset is part of the MIM and is vital to ensuring we are prepared for the complexities of the interview session. Planning for every eventuality is key for the successful investigator.

Being an investigator requires understanding the laws surrounding the crime, the policies imposed by the agency to react in a professional manner, and officer safety considerations to make sure we take care of ourselves and others around us. These tasks are not simple unless they're practiced several hundred times, so they reside in our Detective Mind. The mindful reset allows us to simplify our attention so that we can take advantage of our experience and focus on eyewitness statements and the evidence surrounding the event. When we simplify our process to attend to active listening and accept the limited availability of eyewitness memory, we can identify strategies to inquire further and look for new information in new locations.

If we think about our mindful reset as giving our Detective 1 mindset a rest and prepare our Detective 2 mindset for intentional work, we can begin to understand how valuable our attention to detail is. We should do everything in our power to be successful at conducting the interview in a setting that keeps our Detective 1 mindset in check by diminishing bias in interpreting eyewitness statements and allow our Detective 2 mindset to evaluate statements made without undue influence. Since we learned that our Detective 1 mindset is automatic and considers its intuitive insight as a superpower for an investigator, we should prepare ourselves to "recognize situations in which mistakes are likely and try harder to avoid [them] when the stakes are high" (Kahneman, 2011). Every day, investigators meet with eyewitnesses about a crime event that may have changed the lives of many people; the stakes are often high, and the margin for error should be minimized at all costs. Since we know that our Detective 1 mindset cannot be turned off, we must find ways to remind our Detective 2 mindset of the effort we plan to use in our next interview session. Taking a few minutes to focus our minds before we interview the eyewitness is a good start.

I practiced sitting meditation, and while it was difficult at first, I acclimated to the premise of being more present and saw the benefits it could bring to my interview process. If I became more self-aware, I could be a better listener and allow my imagination to interpret eyewitness statements about the suspect's face more clearly. I would be able to understand the benefit and utility of the natural pause in between my questions and the response I would get from the victim that seemed to add more detail to the event. Because of becoming more present, I could be more empathetic to the plight of the eyewitness which would enhance overall rapport. It would take me 20 years to realize I had been striving to be mindful all along and that eyewitnesses were benefiting from the open nature of our exchanges. In 2008, a *Mercury News* article described one interview session like this:

> Zamora softly tells his clients to close their eyes. The ambient music throbs. Now centered, he sits at his easel, and begins to speak in the voice and tone of a therapist–trying to visualize the scene, feel the trauma from the event.

(Webb, 2008)

TRY IT BEFORE YOU KNOCK IT

Until you practice a mindful interview, you should not discount the benefits of practicing this method. There had been many times in my first two years of interviewing eyewitnesses where I found myself trying to finish their sentence when they couldn't find the right word to describe a feature or a place. Luckily, I became more mindful of my intentions and instead waited in silence until they came up with their own word(s). I had to manage my eagerness to fill in the blanks of descriptions and settle for a more realistic representation of their memory. The process of being patient and accepting of their limited recollections gives me a post-interview evaluation I can count on for reliability. Later, when I testify in court and the defense is looking for events of memory manipulation, they are left empty handed. When I describe my process for interviewing an eyewitness to the jury and say my sketch represents my best interpretation of their statements, there is very little to cross-examine. The interview process is made simple for the jury to understand, and they accept the sketch represents the cognitive evidence gathered from the eyewitness utilizing the mindful interview process. The same is true for non-forensic artists and interviewers that practice the MIM. The cognitive evidence gathered is reliable and leads to credible apprehensions that withstand the scrutiny of examination.

FOR YOUR CONSIDERATION

- A Detective Mind that is mindful is prepared to follow the evidence wherever it leads.
- Being present for the interview means you see everything and understand how the statements flow.
- Most interviewers practice focused attention to plan their interview sessions, so being mindful strengthens their focus.
- Employing the mindful reset will generate a reliable eyewitness interview session.

Section III
How We Interview Eyewitnesses

Easy is right. Begin right and you are easy. Continue easy and you are right. The right way to go easy

Is to forget the right way and that the going is easy.

Zhuang Zi

7
Mindful of the Innocent

If you cannot find the truth right where you are, where else do you expect to find it?

Dogen

In 2009, the *60 Minutes* episode about the North Carolina wrongful conviction case of Ronald Cotton accused of raping Jennifer Thompson in her apartment in 1984 aired, and as a forensic artist, I was intrigued by the issues surrounding eyewitness memory. The two-part episode included Dr. Elizabeth Loftus and Dr. Gary L. Wells explaining the issues pertaining to eyewitness recall and the system variables that contribute to misidentifications. The episode made me reflect on my interview process and consider whether I might be contributing to misidentifications. Since I was interviewing over 250 eyewitnesses of felony crimes a year, I wondered how many more eyewitnesses across the country were being interviewed by investigators oblivious to the issues of misidentifications.

MINDFUL OF DNA

Over the years, the criminal justice system has relied on scientists and psychologists to help them identify culprits, and through their discoveries they have been instrumental in proving beyond a shadow of doubt that someone committed the crime. In 1987, law enforcement relied on deoxyribonucleic acid (DNA) to convict Robert Melias in the UK and Tommy Lee Andrews in the US (Panneerchelvam & Norazmi, 2003). Years later, attorneys for many of the persons wrongfully convicted looked to this novel scientific process to help them clear their clients of their convictions and get them out of prison. In 1989, Gary Dotson became the first person to be exonerated after serving time for rape in Illinois. In 1993, Kirk Noble Bloodsworth was the first person on death row in Maryland to be exonerated after being convicted of the rape and murder of nine-year-old Dawn Hamilton in 1984 (The National Registry of Exonerations, 2022).

According to the FBI Crime Data Explorer, there were less than 3.5 million crime events in 2021 (that number is low considering 56% of law enforcement agencies submitted data to the FBI in 2021, https://crime:data:explorer.app.cloud.gov/pages/explorer/crime/quarterly). A small number of these crime events involve an innocent person being misidentified or wrongfully accused of committing a crime. The misidentification problem has highlighted the fact that even though the numbers are small compared to the number of actual contacts and excellent investigations, systematic issues related to investigations remain that contribute to these miscarriages of justice. Innocent incarcerated people have pleaded with the judicial system to only hear their pleas to give up on revealing the truth about their wrongful conviction. After several years of organizations highlighting the miscarriages of justice, Congress created the Justice for All Act of 2004 which authorized the establishment of the *Kirk Bloodsworth Postconviction DNA Testing Grant Program*. This program, supported by the National Institute of Justice (NIJ), funds programs like the *Postconviction Testing of DNA Evidence*, to help states defray the costs associated with post-conviction DNA testing (see Table 7.1). States use the funds in cases that involve violent felony offenses where it is believed that an innocent person may be involved. The NIJ website touts the great work of the grantees by listing 51 exonerations supported by the programs to date (https://nij.ojp.gov/topics/articles/exonerations:resulting:nij:postconviction:dna:testing:funding#list:of:exonerations).

These figures coincide with the great work The National Registry for Exonerations is doing to list cases and support the creation of groups that look to free innocent people from incarceration. The registry is a project of the University of California Irvine Newkirk Center for Science & Society, University of Michigan Law School, and Michigan State University College of Law. Their 2021 annual report showed that 68% of the 161 exonerations were for violent crimes like murder and rape, while factors leading to conviction involved 70% Official Misconduct and 29% Mistaken Eyewitness Identification. The exonerations were from 26 states, including 18 cases from New York; California and Michigan each had 11. The registry website (https://www.law.umich.edu/special/exoneration/Pages/about.aspx) articulates the magnitude of the problem by focusing on the number of years innocent people have spent behind bars.

> Defendants exonerated in 2021 spent 1,849 years incarcerated for crimes they did not commit, an average of 11.5 years per exoneree. These figures underestimate the actual amount

Table 7.1 National Institute of Justice Information about Their Post-Conviction DNA Testing Program (51 Cases Were Listed)

	Exonerations Supported by NIJ Programs – Crimes		
Crime Type	Percentage of Exonerations	Issue	Percentage of Exonerations
Homicide	47	Misidentification	57
Rape	39	False Accusation	35
Robbery	6	False Confession	25
Child Exploitation	4	Official Misconduct	25
Sexual Assault	2	Misleading Forensic Evidence	25
Burglary	2	Perjury	4

of time they lost ... Anthony Mazza, was exonerated of a murder in 2021, for which he served 47 years and two months—the longest period of incarceration of any exoneree in the Registry.

(NRE, 2022)

Since 2012, the registry has reported on the number of exonerations in the US and in their inaugural report, "Exonerations in the United States, 1989–2012," they listed 873 exonerations where innocent people "were convicted of vicious crimes in which other innocent victims were killed or brutalized" (Gross & Shaffer, 2012). Sadly, many of these victims had to endure more trauma years afterwards when the fact of their mistaken identification was revealed. They had to come to grips with the idea that the actual suspect had not been caught and the realization that they had sent an innocent person to jail. Not only were the victims affected, but we can't ignore the honest investigators who felt they were doing their job to make society safer.

INNOCENCE PROJECT

Since 1992, the Innocence Project has helped wrongfully convicted persons get their cases reviewed and eventually exonerated using DNA science. Their *Fast Facts* website report on DNA exonerations in the US found that of the 375 DNA exonerated cases they worked on, 69% involved eyewitness misidentification, and 29% involved a misidentification through some other procedure (e.g., mistakenly "recognizing" someone on the street and reporting them to law enforcement), and were the leading cause of wrongful convictions (https://innocenceproject.org/dna:exonerations:in:the:united:states/). Their advocacy in highlighting the research of eyewitness processing of information led to reforms that changed the way many agencies across the US conduct photo line-ups to identify suspects. They insist investigators must be acutely aware that "Inaccurate eyewitness identifications" can derail the investigation from identifying the real suspect and thus allow them the ability to assault more victims (Innocence Project, 2022a).

One case of mistaken identity focused on a 1985 murder involving a 16-year-old girl from Marcy, New York. She was last seen walking from home to meet a high school friend. The next day, police officers found her body had been raped and strangled and left near the side of a dirt road. Several eyewitnesses were interviewed and told police that they had seen the young girl walking along a busy street between 5:30PM and 6PM. More eyewitnesses said they saw a distinctive truck on the road around the same time the victim was walking home, and the owner of the truck, Steven Barnes, soon became a suspect based on these statements. Another eyewitness, in police custody for an unrelated incident, testified that while riding in a police vehicle, he saw the victim walking on the road and saw a truck similar to the suspect's nearby. Even a police officer said he saw a young man matching Barnes's description parked alongside the street that night, while the suspect's brother-in-law testified that he saw a young woman getting into a truck along the road that was clearly not the suspect's truck. Even more eyewitnesses said they saw Barnes at a local bowling alley through the evening of the murder. While we don't have the transcripts to analyze each eyewitness statement, we can imagine how these sightings may have led police to believe that Barnes could be responsible. We know now that Barnes did not commit this crime because DNA evidence proved he was not with the victim at the time of her death; however, the interview statements retrieved from eyewitnesses led investigators to focus on Barnes and so they collected evidence to confirm their suspicions. In the end their suspicions were not confirmed, and the *real* suspect remained at large (Innocence Project, 2022b).

In 2003, another case of mistaken eyewitness identification and police misconduct happened in Gilbert, Arizona. A 48-year-old woman was attacked as she walked on a street, dragged into some bushes, and raped. Eight days later police began questioning John Watkins because he resembled the description given by the victim. During an interrogation, Watkins was coerced into confessing by police and they made him wear a white t-shirt – the type of shirt described by the victim – and took his photograph which was then placed in a photo line-up with five other photos of suspects who were all wearing black t-shirts. The victim then identified Watkins as her attacker. In 2009 Watkins asked for his DNA to be tested against the rape kit and he was later exonerated for the crime he did not commit (The National Registry of Exonerations, 2022).

The common thread in these misidentifications is that eyewitness statements were obtained and then resulted in questioning of a subject who later would be arrested or coerced to confess to committing a crime they had not committed. In both cases the real suspect was not apprehended and committed more crimes. In many of these cases we do not have access to actual transcripts of these eyewitness interviews, so we can only surmise from the misidentification that questionable tactics were used and may have not been ethical in proper police procedures. Fortunately for the cases mentioned, their investigations included biological evidence that had been collected. Unfortunately, there are many other arrests where biological evidence is *not* collected, and eyewitness statements have led investigators down the wrong path.

REFORMS

By late 1999, the district attorney in Santa Clara County offered local law enforcement agencies in Silicon Valley guidelines for showing photo line-ups. Even though I wasn't showing photo line-ups to eyewitnesses, I understood that the research they were citing pertained to engaging with an eyewitness as they proceeded through the identification process. Years later when Professor Brandon Garrett of Duke University School of Law studied misidentifications, they found suggestive police practices in 80% of the cases (https://innocenceproject.org/how:eyewitness:misidentification:can:send:innocent:people:to:prison/). They also found the same concerns I could see in the mindset of my colleagues when they believed their eyewitnesses were trying to deceive them. As Dr. Garrett learned:

> When eyewitnesses are mistaken, they are not lying–they sincerely believe that they have identified the right person and have often been led to that belief by poor or biased investigations. Therefore, it is incumbent on the criminal justice system itself to embrace reforms that help to avoid these tragedies.
>
> (Innocence Project, 2022)

Many of the reforms created to reduce misidentifications and wrongful convictions focus on basic interview considerations and the administration of photo line-ups. A technical group of experts convened and produced a report called, *Eyewitness Evidence: A Guide for Law Enforcement* (1999) that incorporated many of the psychological research findings about eyewitness memory. Dr. Gary Wells and his colleagues (Wells & Seelau, 1995; Wells et al., 1998) from the University of Iowa suggested rules that were included in the *Guide*. Dr. Wells is an experimental social psychologist who has focused his academic studies on the reliability of eyewitness identification. His work on the pitfalls of showing photo lineups in suggestive ways led to many of these reforms. Because the *Guide* was a recommendation and not a mandate, we find many jurisdictions across the country unable or unwilling to employ the guidance from this manual. In Attorney General Reno's message, she hoped the *Guide* would be "invaluable to a jurisdiction shaping its own protocols" and indeed it was for my agency (San Jose Police) as they rolled out the procedures to the entire bureau of investigations. The Technical Working Group for Eyewitness Evidence (TWGEYEE) consisted of the names I had followed in regard to eyewitness memory research. Names like: James Doyle, Attorney, Ronald P. Fisher, Ph.D., Gary L. Wells, Ph.D., and Roy S. Malpass, Ph.D. I had read their many papers as they recommended procedures that would improve system variables and improve eyewitness evidence. The information from this report was very straightforward and acknowledged the fallibility of eyewitness memory in regard to misidentifications and wrongful convictions. It also provided a forum for a variety of perspectives on how to interview eyewitnesses in a way that maintained integrity for their statements. Just as Dr. Garrett explained that eyewitnesses are not necessarily lying, the *Guide* suggests investigators are not necessarily pursuing practices that "Undermine eyewitness reliability and accuracy" and therefore consider the importance of eyewitness evidence (p. 2):

> Eyewitness evidence is often viewed as a critical piece of the investigative puzzle, the utility of which can be further enhanced by the pursuit of other corroborative evidence. Sometimes, even after a thorough investigation, an eyewitness identification is the sole piece of evidence. It is in those cases in particular where careful use of this *Guide* may be most important.
>
> (p. 3)

The *Guide* presents each topic area with procedures that focus on preserving eyewitness evidence. Since this book is focused on eyewitness interviews, we look at the sections that are primarily concerned with interacting with eyewitnesses. These areas include: (i) initial report of the crime, (ii) investigating the crime scene, interviewing the eyewitness, and (iii) creating a composite sketch of the perpetrator. Because this book embraces the notion that showing any reference images for stimulating eyewitness memory is considered post-event information, we don't include Sections 2 (Mug Books and Composites), 4 (Field Identification Procedures), and 5 (Eyewitness Identification of Suspects). In two of the four sections listed in Table 7.2, we see that asking open-ended questions and avoiding asking leading questions are important to preserving eyewitness evidence. Although the composite images section is limited, they do stress avoiding showing photos before the development of the composite unless it is part of the procedure. The irony in the composite images section is rather amusing if it wasn't so important; nevertheless, it would have been

Table 7.2 Partial List of Topics from the *Guide* (1999) Focused on Retrieving Reliable Eyewitness Evidence

Sections of Eyewitness Evidence: A Guide for Law Enforcement		
Section	Principle	Procedure (Main Takeaway)
Initial Report of Crime (Preliminary Investigator)	9-1-1 dispatcher must obtain and disseminate, in a non-suggestive manner, complete and accurate information from the caller.	Ask open-ended questions and avoid asking suggestive or leading questions.
Investigating the Scene (Preliminary Investigating Officer)	Preservation and documentation of the scene, including information from the witnesses and physical evidence.	Identify perpetrator(s), determine the crime, broadcast description of the incident and perpetrator. Verify identity of eyewitnesses.
Obtain information from witness(es)	The manner in which the preliminary officer obtains information from the witness has a direct impact on the amount and accuracy of that information.	Establish rapport, ask open-ended questions, and avoid asking leading questions. Clarify information received from the witness and document in the crime report.
Developing and using composite images	Composite sketches may be used to develop investigative leads.	Assess the ability of the eyewitness to provide description of the perpetrator. Select procedure for creating composite image (identikit-type, artist, or computer-generated images). Unless part of the procedure, avoid showing photos immediately prior to development of composite.

interesting to learn why the *Guide* felt it necessary to include the statement, "Unless part of the procedure" when concluding that you should "avoid showing photos immediately prior to development of composite."

In 2014, the National Academy of Sciences published a report called *Identifying the Culprit* where it amplified the prior calls for reform in how investigators conduct eyewitness interviews and recommendations for agencies to improve eyewitness identifications. They include the calls for training for "all law enforcement agencies [to] provide their officers and agents with training on vision and memory and the variables that affect them, on practices for minimizing contamination, and on effective eyewitness identification protocols." Even the *Guide* suggests that prosecutors consider all the issues before charging someone in regard to eyewitness identifications, and they also make a case for evaluating the cognitive evidence recovered from eyewitness statements. When we decide to tailor our interview process to be mindful of bias, increase transparency, and offer an objective analysis of eyewitness statements, our interview process will be much improved. While some administrators may look at these recommendations as focused on administering photo line-ups, I look at them more broadly and apply them to interviewing eyewitnesses. We should not look at these recommendations with a narrow focus and ignore the overlap in the number of eyewitness interviews that are conducted every day that lack the basic considerations for improving eyewitness evidence.

TRANSPARENCY AND ADHERENCE TO THE *GUIDE*

If more than three quarters of the wrongful convictions include some form of suggestive practice by investigators, how many more eyewitness interviews being conducted every day might be affected by the benign practices of well-intentioned interviewers? We don't know the number, because law enforcement agencies don't record all their eyewitness interviews. A 2018 bill in California called SB1421 may begin to ensure that thousands of hours of recordings and transcripts from eyewitness interviews with witnesses and suspects are made available for scrutiny. The new bill currently allows access to three categories of law enforcement records targeting: Use of Force, Sexual Assault, and Official Dishonesty. The California Reporting Project is one organization that has sought these records to analyze how police agencies hold themselves accountable. The podcast *On Our Watch* (2021), hosted by Sukie Lewis and produced by NPR and KQED, features nine episodes focused on officer misconduct from the cases obtained from the California Reporting Project. Two particular excerpts involve the suspect (officer) and the eyewitness (victim) for the same case. We analyzed one of the cases from this episode and focused on the interview process to broaden our survey of 15 law enforcement interviews for this book. In this chapter, we briefly focus on the adherence to the principles from the *Guide* and how it can lead to misidentifications or official misconduct. Later in Part VI, we analyze the complete transcripts for comparison to the *Mindful Interview Method*.

In this first interview (interrogation) the police officer is interrogated about the claims being made by the victim. When you interview a police officer, there are certain rights they have, and you must acknowledge them or you'll jeopardize the investigation. In the US, police officers who are under investigation must be interviewed under the rules of the Police Officer Bill of Rights. In California, some of these rights include the right to know why they're being investigated, questioned by no more than two interrogators at a time, the interview session must be free of offensive language and threats towards the officer, and the choice to be interviewed while on duty or at another convenient time (Public Safety Officers Procedural Bill of Right Act, 1976). While the officer in our case study is not an eyewitness, we can still rely on the interview transcript to analyze how the investigator asks questions and determine whether they are adhering to system variables that mitigate misidentifications, featured in the *Guide*. The point we're trying to make here is that because of SB1421, these interviews are now being released and we can see how investigators ask questions and gather cognitive evidence against the officer. Let's look at the brief excerpt from Case Study #1:

THE MINDFUL INTERVIEW METHOD

EXCERPT FROM CASE STUDY #1

SUSP: I tried to explain to her several times that she needed to get the light fixed. She kept on saying that she didn't understand. ... Or we could get a hotel room or a motel room, something like that. I don't remember the exact words.
INV: What did you mean when you asked her – when you told – suggested to her to get a motel room? What does that mean?
SUSP: To be intimate.
INV: So, you were proposing to her a motel room for the purpose of having sexual relations with her?
SUSP: Yes
INV: Why would you ask her that question?

In the first part of this interview the investigator asks an open-ended question concerning the "motel room." When the suspect responds with being "intimate" the investigator asks a leading question about whether he wanted to have "sexual relations with her?" Even though the suspect responds with "yes," we know his original answer was to be "intimate" – *not* to have sexual relations. We have to keep in mind that when we analyze these interview exchanges throughout the book, we are not specifically concerned with the outcome of the questioning (aggregate of responses that point to the subject being truthful or not); we are only paying attention to the decisions made by the interviewer to ask certain questions. The questions determine the preservation (being mindful) of cognitive evidence, and the response by the eyewitness (suspect in this case) from these questions dictates the effects they had on the overall reliability of cognitive evidence collected. The second excerpt focuses on the victim of Case Study #1.

EXCERPT FROM CASE STUDY #2

EW: Then he started saying to me, well, you know what? You want me to get one motel room for me and you? I said, what?
EW: A motel room for me and you?
INV #1: Is there any way that she could ... Is there any way that you misunderstood what [the officer] was saying?
EW: No, I understand everything.
INV #2: You don't need anybody to speak in Spanish. You understand English?
EW: I understand English, but ...
INV #3: Just to tell you, this is highly unusual for a citizen to tell me this with this officer. I just; I'm not saying I don't believe you. I was just thinking it's very out there, you know? It's very out in left field for this exchange to happen, so ...
EW: No, but I don't lie. I tell you exactly what he's saying.
INV #3: I don't believe you're lying to me, but understand that this is very unusual.

In this excerpt, we notice very quickly how the investigator is not mindful of the alleged crime and lacks any empathy for what the victim is telling him. He soon begins to question her understanding of the English language and infers that she may be exaggerating the incident. The tone is very accusatory and diminishes the reliability of cognitive evidence.

In the first interview excerpt, the investigator is leading the suspect to accept his version for his intentions for the motel room. In the second interview, the investigator is not asking many open-ended questions that generate reliable information; instead, he makes statements and accusations that consequently leave the victim uncertain that her complaint will be investigated thoroughly. While we may not have a specific issue of misidentification in these two cases, we do see that investigators are not adhering to the basic recommendations of the *Guide* and thus jeopardizing the quality of evidence collected in both interview sessions. We can only speculate on why the investigator chose to lead the suspect to accept that he got the motel room for "sexual relations" instead of just being "intimate." If the investigator wanted clarity about the meaning of intimate, he could have asked, "What do mean by intimate?" If the suspect revealed more information about his intentions for intimacy then it would be germane to the line of questioning. Unfortunately, the practice of asking an open-ended question with a leading question is counterintuitive to "the collection and preservation of eyewitness evidence" (NIJ, 1999). Because our access to recorded eyewitness interview sessions from law enforcement interviewers is limited, we can expect that thousands of eyewitness interviews are conducted in this (less than reliable) manner without careful examination.

Eyewitness interviews are conducted every day, and because first responders are given discretion for how they question them we cannot always rely on the information from these encounters to be reliable. In 2017, the FBI reported there were at least 142 robberies and aggravated assaults committed every hour in the US, and each of those crimes required a dispatcher to gather initial details and officers to respond and interview eyewitnesses (https://ucr.fbi.gov/crime:in:the:u.s/2017/crime:in:the:u.s.:2017/topic:pages/offenses:known:browse:by:national:data). Law enforcement officers meet with eyewitnesses at least 3,400 times every hour and yet they are not mandated to show proficiency for conducting these interviews. While some agencies require supervisor approval for crime reports involving felony crimes and use of force, many others are reviewed for proper content, establishment of proper elements of the crime, and processing of evidence. Supervisors can suggest more follow-up or ask for clarifications for statements made in order to improve the quality of the report.

The misidentifications and wrongful convictions are just a symptom of a widespread systematic problem law enforcement has not addressed regarding eyewitness interviews. The recent reforms related to misidentifications are specific to creating non-biased photo line-ups because they resulted in a small number of wrongfully convicted persons, comparatively speaking. The same can be said for the reforms focused on questioning eyewitnesses in interviews because some of them led to misidentifying an innocent person who was later convicted of a crime they did not commit. In both circumstances, the numbers are significantly small, about 13 exonerations a month in 2021, compared to the number of police interactions with suspects and eyewitnesses (over 300 robberies a day), but because they resulted in undue harm to innocent people, these reforms have become a priority for some agencies (Statista, 2023). In 2021, there were 161 exonerations; 86 for crimes of murder and sexual assault, 47 cases involved misidentification, and 33 cases involved forensic evidence that was either false or misleading (National Registry, 2021). The reforms for administering photo line-ups in an unbiased manner did not come from within the law enforcement community until it was faced with unprecedented pressure about the miscarriages of justice.

When I decided to not show reference images to the hundreds of eyewitnesses I interviewed every year, I understood that showing these images might contaminate their memory. I did not ask administrators whether it was the proper procedure or not – I was the expert in this field, and they granted me the autonomy to perform my job at the highest levels. Even though it was well known that showing reference images might contaminate eyewitness memory, many of my forensic art colleagues (about 100 in the US) would continue using reference images to either stimulate memory or refine the sketch. That meant that at least 1,000 eyewitness interviews were being conducted showing reference images every year, and administrators were not asking why or whether this interview process needed to change. Because a majority of eyewitness interviews do not end up misidentifying an innocent person, the problem for gathering unreliable cognitive evidence may seem unimportant to law enforcement administrators in light of all the issues surrounding use of force and misconduct. However, if we are asking law enforcement agencies to change the way they show photo line-ups because a number of misidentifications are happening in spite of the millions that go on without a problem, then why would we not consider evaluating eyewitness interview sessions to elevate their level of proficiency and subsequently lower the risk of contributing to misidentifications and wrongful convictions?

Every year we expect our officers to be proficient in firing their duty weapons even though they rarely fire them in the course of their careers. According to a recent survey conducted by the Pew Research Center they asked recently retired police officers how many times they had fired their weapon during the course of their career, and about a quarter of all officers in 2016 said they had fired their weapon on duty (Morin & Mercer, 2017). That means a majority of over 675,000 sworn officers will never fire their weapon on duty while patrolling the streets. And yet we mandate that they all show proficiency at firing their weapon on duty every year. Why not expect this type of accountability for what more than 900,000 officers encounter almost every day of their careers: interviewing an eyewitness and gathering eyewitness statements of the crime?

FOR YOUR CONSIDERATION

- Eyewitness misidentifications are an issue that should be considered when preparing to interview an eyewitness.
- Being mindful of eyewitness memory research and the guidelines regarding eyewitness evidence from the Department of Justice should be implemented at every law enforcement agency in the US.
- Recording eyewitness interviews for analysis will improve the preservation of cognitive evidence and mitigate misidentifications.
- On average there are about 3,400 robberies and aggravated assaults being investigated every hour in the US, and these crimes require an officer to gather reliable eyewitness evidence to identify the assailant. How do we measure the proficiency of these eyewitness interviews if we don't conduct annual audits on these important interactions?

8
Mindful of Interrogations

We think in generalities, but we live in detail.

Alfred North Whitehead

Many investigators often rely on interview tactics that consider the eyewitness mendacious in their recollections. While they don't necessarily teach officers in the academy that eyewitnesses may be prone to fabricating details of the crime or facial descriptions of the suspect, it may be that many law enforcement officers are uninformed about the fundamental principles of eyewitness memory. Officers may become frustrated when they believe eyewitnesses are having trouble recalling details and seem to be unwilling to try harder. After all, if we believe the eyewitness has seen everything there is to see at the crime, then why shouldn't they tell us everything we need to know? This narrow mindset often leads to investigators assessing some witness and event factors as being signs of deceit about an event.

INTERVIEWING EYEWITNESS AND NOT INTERROGATING THEM

When I refer to a cooperative eyewitness in this book, I mean victims and witnesses to crimes who agreed to meet to meet me for a sketch interview. They all had seen something – whether it was the suspect's face, or the criminal event – and their vantage point to the event gave me and the initial officers on the scene reason to believe they would be a good candidate for a sketch interview. After a few years as the police artist our department had a standing policy, for the investigative bureau, that if an officer on the scene interviewed an eyewitness (victim/witness) without a known suspect, they should refer that person for a sketch interview. When I would meet them, I assumed they were victims and had nothing to do with the assault; I figured that their lives would be turned upside down because of this event, and I needed to be mindful of that to ensure they would be willing to speak to me. They were unaware of the complexities of the investigative interview and could not imagine how their minds would work through the process of recalling what happened to them.

In Santa Clara County between 1994 and 2011, most eyewitnesses that had to sit with me to recall a heinous event were considered authentic eyewitnesses that would be given the benefit of the doubt no matter their lack of recollection. My process for gathering cognitive evidence was the same in every case, and the steps I took to ensure the reliability of the sketch and my evaluation of their statements gave investigators confidence about the credible leads they could rely on. One of the first steps I took to decide whether they were a good candidate for the sketch interview was to ask them the *Qualifying Question*. Their answer to *"If you saw him again would you recognize him?"* would give me confidence on whether I would be able to create a sketch of the suspect or not (the evaluation of their answer to this question is a component called Confidence or Recollection (COR) that is factored in the Efficacy of Eyewitness Interview Assessment in Chapter 14). The variety of personalities and aptitude for understanding my questions was always an adventure during many interview sessions, but the one constant throughout each encounter was my process for interviewing them. I felt the interview process had to be consistent in every session, and I had to be flexible to accommodate their situation. I was mindful of the variables but mindful about the principle behind my interview technique, and I had no bias in believing they might be lying or associated with the crime. I was focused on gathering the cognitive evidence residing in their minds.

While most police personnel (dispatchers and officers) receive some training in conducting eyewitness interviews, they spend most of the time determining whether the facts relate to whether someone is lying or not. Professor Richard Leo, Associate Professor of Law at the University of San Francisco and an expert on false confession said in an interview about the Norfolk Four investigation (1997) that most police officers are trained in the psychological methods of interrogating someone, which is one of the reasons why it is puzzling that they are not accepting of the latest psychological research about eyewitness memory (Bikel, 2010). The Norfolk Four case in Virginia exemplified the lack of integrity the investigation had in searching for the truth. Leo further explained the role of police as being "investigators" to determine the facts of the case and write reports that lead to the prosecution determining whether to charge them or not (Bikel, 2010). Unfortunately, there is bias in some investigations, and sometimes police are "not neutral investigators" and perceive that someone is not telling them the truth (Bikel, 2010).

As Jay Salpeter, a former NYPD detective and hostage negotiator, mentioned in his interview about the Norfolk Four case, sometimes police are "just interviewing witnesses to a crime ... You're more or less trying to get information from them." It's this type of mindset that leads many patrol officers and call-takers to resort to a heuristic that arrives at details regardless of what the eyewitness may say (Bikel, 2010). This mindset can lead to misleading information and contaminate the memory of the eyewitness. For instance, say the arriving police officer asks the eyewitness about the robbery suspect's car and the eyewitness says, "I'm not sure, but I think it was an American car" and the officer suggests, "Was it a Ford or a Chevy?" The eyewitness might respond with, "I guess it was a Ford, but I'm not sure." Because the officer assumes the American car is a Ford or a Chevy, they instead employ a heuristic in putting out more detailed information that may be related to the crime. Officers may do this all the time because they feel they know more about car descriptions better than the average eyewitness. When the officer then broadcasts this vehicle information to the entire beat or division, they are establishing facts that were not specifically uttered by the eyewitness. If and when another officer initiates an emergency high risk vehicle stop on a Ford vehicle, they may be putting innocent people in jeopardy because of the tenuous information retrieved form the eyewitness. We cannot minimize the amazing hunches many police officers have made from scant details offered by reluctant eyewitnesses that resulted in apprehensions that took dangerous individuals off the streets. I have experienced amazing stories related to me regarding sketches I made that led to violent suspects arrested for serious crimes. While they are not hunches, the investigators following the leads from the cognitive evidence collected can sometimes locate people that should be found and brought to justice.

In one case, a detective working a child sexual assault canvassed an area near the crime scene and found another suspect that resembled the sketch I had created after interviewing the child. He was a wanted felon for prior sexual assaults and had been in hiding for several months and evading arrest. The detective's tenacity and her teams' willingness to go out and walk the beat (sketch in hand) led to another child predator being arrested and brought to justice. Unfortunately, the great work of the sexual assault unit was never recognized in the media, but internally we knew we had placed a dangerous felon behind bars. While the suspect in this case looked like the predator they found instead, the cognitive evidence collected from the victim was reliable and led to the apprehension of this wanted person. They eventually located the suspect on this sexual assault and, indeed, he looked like the arrested felon. While many of these legitimate arrests go on without media attention, we have to also acknowledge that many times errors are made in the collection of cognitive evidence where innocent people have been hurt or killed because of misleading information.

While Salpeter focuses on the interrogation of the Norfolk Four in his interview, it's interesting to hear him describe the detective as "putting you into that state." A state of compliance? A state of accepting the authority in the room? *I am the investigator, and you must provide me with the answers that I expect. You cannot give me information about the suspect without specific details and you must be highly descriptive.* The transcripts show how skilled Salpeter was at denying the accusations – it was a master class in psychological manipulation. Sadly, these types of interviews take place every day in police stations and correctional facilities all across the US. We only hear about them when an injustice has been revealed through enormous efforts of the accused or their advocates that support their innocence. When you participate in an interview of an eyewitness, you should distinguish the difference and be mindful of when the eyewitness is doing their best to recall an event and when you may be "bringing in subjects who are potential perpetrators" (Bikel, 2010). In an interview setting, you must cast aside the idea that you are an officer that is, as Salpeter said, "arrest-oriented," and instead be mindful of gathering reliable evidence for the investigation (Bikel, 2010). Walsh and Bull (2013) found that such biases may lead investigators to be overly confident about the suspect's guilt and influence their behavior, thereby contributing to confirmation bias. When interviewers presuppose something that may be relevant to the crime event, they can miss out on important details that may lead to better information.

WE SHOULD TREAT EYEWITNESS MEMORY LIKE TRACE EVIDENCE

For most investigators the eyewitness is someone that saw something, and they need to ask the eyewitness what happened so they can go out and arrest the suspect. It sounds simple if the eyewitness could be relied on to remember everything in great detail – but they can't, and that's why it's not that simple. If we accept my premise that cognitive evidence is the trace evidence of eyewitness memory, we can look at the process for gathering this evidence under the same principles as gathering physical evidence.

For example, when law enforcement officers process a physical crime scene that requires intense follow-up and gathering of evidence, they string yellow crime scene tape out about 50 to 200 feet from their perceived actual crime event perimeter; they have an officer document who comes and goes from the space (I was tasked with that job on a few homicide cases while I was on patrol). Crime scene technicians sometimes come in white plastic suits (covered head to toe) to walk in the same space as the suspect and victim; they take hundreds of photos of every angle of the crime scene, place numbered markers on the ground, sometimes collect latent fingerprints and possible DNA from discarded items the suspect may or may not have touched. They arrive in these white suits to ensure the scene is not contaminated or cross-contaminated with other evidence. Detectives arrive later and look over the scene, discuss theories for what happened, and determine strategies for the next steps. They are methodical and comprehensive on what needs to be done to ensure they understand what happened. Why not have that same kind of attention to detail when it comes to interviewing the eyewitness?

I don't suggest that we isolate the eyewitness and have an officer assigned to them to document who they talk to and when they leave to go to the bathroom – that would be unrealistic. I have interviewed multiple eyewitnesses who were taken to the police station (kept in separate rooms) in the middle of the night and had to wait until I arrived several hours later to be interviewed by me for a sketch because the homicide detectives wanted to control their ability to share information. While that is an extreme case (and very appropriate for high-profile cases), most of the time the conditions for a cooperative eyewitness to retain everything they remembered are less than optimal and the opportunities for memory contamination are very high. Instead, what I suggest is that we treat the eyewitness with care and factor in the limitations of human memory when determining our strategy for conducting the interview. If the officer is mindful of the witness and event factors that may affect the cooperative eyewitness, then they'll move to a place that is quieter (if possible), more comfortable, with fewer distractions to conduct the interviews. They'll check in with the eyewitness and ask how they feel and if they need something (water, something to eat) before they start their interview. The investigator will make sure they are *present* and allow themselves to be *empathetic* when appropriate. They'll be prepared to ask questions in a manner that does not suggest bias for the incident nor rush the eyewitness to offer specific details. They can even imagine themselves in a plastic suit and tread lightly, being mindful of contaminating evidence.

DON'T BE SUSPICIOUS OF YOUR EYEWITNESS

When we interview a cooperative eyewitness, we shouldn't include a level of suspicion in our tools for inquiry. In other words, don't come into the interview with the impression the eyewitness may be lying about the event or descriptions of the suspect. We should limit our bias and reduce the *noise* (see Part V for more information about Measuring the

Noise) for conducting the interview. So, what do we do when we believe the eyewitness may be lying? First, we ask ourselves why we might be making that determination? What do we know about the crime event that leads us to believe that the cooperative eyewitness is offering us unreliable information? If the eyewitness begins to offer us statements that seem inconsistent or bring us concern, we should acknowledge it internally and refrain from challenging the veracity of the eyewitness. Remember, this eyewitness interview is *not* an interrogation, and we should not consider the eyewitness to be unreliable after a few responses. If our eyewitness, after completing our interview, is deemed to be making unreliable statements, then the cognitive evidence collected will be unreliable as well. We can certainly set up a follow-up interview or corroborate details of their statements with other eyewitnesses before contemplating interrogating this eyewitness. The mindset of the investigator should be to interview the cooperative eyewitness and gather the most reliable statements possible without contaminating their memory.

OBJECTIVE PERSPECTIVE

A forensic artist has a unique position in law enforcement; more specifically *sworn* forensic artists enjoy a certain level of regard when trying to solve a crime. The sworn forensic artist is at the intersection of law, psychology, and art, and in this space they can offer the lead investigator a perspective that is quite unique. Veteran investigators will tell you that there's a lot of speculation that goes on in a standard criminal investigation, and most of the time it revolves around whether an eyewitness is telling the truth or not. This may be one reason why many eyewitness and forensic art interview training programs spend a lot of time searching for eyewitnesses that may be lying. Sadly, the line between eyewitnesses that are trying to deceive you and ones that have faulty memories is very thin, and relying on novice investigators to shift gears and confront an eyewitness they consider is lying can be a difficult line to come back from when it turns out they were experiencing normal faulty recall. One way investigators can be confident in challenging that line is using the forensic artist to offer an objective opinion on how reliable eyewitness statements are.

Over the years, many detectives have asked me whether the eyewitness I had just interviewed was telling the truth and that led me to develop an evaluation form that factored the estimator variables in Table 8.1 and focused on how reliable I found the eyewitness to be in my sketch interviews (see Figure 8.1). Since 2006, I have conducted a post evaluation of all my sketch interview sessions and settled on a reliability score that I share with investigators. While the reliability score does not offer my opinion on whether the eyewitness is lying, it does offer my opinion on whether I believe their information is reliable. I know that my sketch interview with the eyewitness is contributing to the predictive process of figuring out who committed the crime, and I want to ensure the investigator has all the facts to determine who might be the assailant.

To be mindful of our role in the investigation, we must acknowledge that we do not know everything that happened. If we come into this interview session with that in mind, we will be better prepared to retrieve the cognitive evidence and analyze the information with an objectivity that will offer us reliable leads to pursue. If we are honest about the investigation and consider that we are speaking to the cooperative eyewitness for the first

THE MINDFUL INTERVIEW METHOD

Table 8.1 Estimator Variables Were Derived from Over 2,000 Sketch Artist Interviews between 1993 and 2002

Estimator Variables for Cognitive Sketch Analysis Evaluation	
Estimator Variable Observed	What Are We Measuring?
Recall	Their recall of information is critical to how reliable their information is to the investigation
Articulation	How well they articulate their thoughts and descriptions is vital to how well we gain the same perspective
Confidence before and after	Understanding their confidence before and after the interview session is important to understand how much influence they gained from the interview session
Lighting	Being mindful of the lighting conditions will determine how well we can rely on their descriptions
Duration	Knowing how much time they spent with the suspect will give us an idea on their perspectives
Unique features	Understanding what was remarkable for the eyewitness about the suspect's face will be important for the description of the suspect
Emotion	The effects of emotion at the scene and exhibiting them during the interview gives us a perspective on the impact of the event
Conversation	The level of conversation about the event and during the interview contributes to many aspects of understanding the state of mind of the eyewitness
Body language	Being mindful of acknowledging involuntary body movements during the interview is important to observe and take into consideration based on the questions asked
Likeness	When the eyewitness is satisfied they find the likeness to be remarkable and thus the task of creating a sketch that resembles the suspect is achieved
Changes to sketch	Changes to the initial sketch are expected and allow the eyewitness to have ownership of the outcome

time about the event, we should not assume facts that have not been offered to us by the eyewitness. Investigators often confuse the lack of specific recall by the eyewitness to be an attempt to thwart the investigation or to sabotage it to save face for an embarrassing situation, and sometimes these seemingly cooperative eyewitnesses can lead us astray.

THE UNRELIABLE EYEWITNESS

Years ago, I interviewed a victim of a sexual assault and before investigators told me about their theories about the case, I asked them not to share their opinions before my interview.

Cognitive Sketch Analysis			Case Information	
Recall	4		Date	March 22, 2019
Articulation	5		Interview Date	3/22/19
Confidence Before	3		Sketch time	1210 - 1300
Confidence After	4			
Lighting	5		Event date	3/6/2019
Duration	4		Detective	Garcia
Unique Features	4		Agency	Mountain View Police
Emotion	3		Case Number	19-0119356
Conversation	5			
Body Language	3		Crime	211
Likeness	4		Race	Black
Changes to sketch	4			
			Age range	40 - 45
Reliability Score	48		Body type	Scrawny
			Eyewitness	F.S.

Cognitive Sketch Analysis Reliability Scoring Range

1. Unfavorable condition or response; 2. Slightly less than optimal condition or response; 3. Optimal condition or response; 4. More than optimal condition or response; 5. Exceptional condition or response

Reliability Total Score Range

Unreliable: < 17 ; Questionable: 18 - 29; Less than Reliable: 30 - 43; Reliable: 43 - 53; More than Reliable: > 54

The Cognitive Sketch Analysis (CSA) is for reference only and may be used to determine the reliability of an eyewitness when participating in a sketch interview. Sketch-Artist, LLC, © 2022.

Figure 8.1 Cognitive Sketch Analysis form. The CSA form is used to offer post analysis of the cognitive sketch interview.

I had been trying to discourage investigators from sharing their opinions about the case, especially since many of them would later ask me whether the victim was lying or not. I advised investigators that allowing me to interview the eyewitness without their bias would provide them with an objective evaluation of their statements. Later they could use my sketch and the sketch interview analysis form to either build on their investigation or discount their assumptions and locate other corroborating evidence. After completing my interview with the eyewitness, I presented the sketch and the Cognitive Sketch Analysis form to the investigators with the following caveat: While we were able to create the sketch, I didn't believe the information the eyewitness recalled was from the actual event and I felt the sketch was *unreliable*. Even though I had reservations about her responses (during the interview) I continued my interview process – acknowledging my concern internally, and completed the interview session in the same fashion as I completed thousands of others before. We'll go over this in specific detail later on when I discuss handling questionable responses from the eyewitness in Part IV. After the interview I made my subjective evaluation of our session and the Reliability Score came back "Less Than Reliable."

Weeks later, investigators informed me that the eyewitness had lied about the sexual assault. It turned out the investigators canvassed the areas near the victim's home and knocked on doors asking people if they had seen the person in the sketch. At one door, the man looking at the sketch exclaimed "Why do you have a sketch of my face?" After a few minutes of explanation for the sketch, investigators brought him down to the station and interviewed him about his whereabouts during the crime. Investigators later learned that he worked at the local grocery store the victim had frequented. When they informed the victim of the identification (showing a photo with the sketch) the victim broke down emotionally and revealed that she had been having an affair with another person, and when her spouse came home unexpectedly, she panicked and told him that she had been assaulted by a stranger. As police investigated the incident, she felt she had to come up with a suspect for the police and remembered the guy at the grocery store. She relied on his face to imagine what the suspect might look like and figured detectives would never find him, and the interest in finding the suspect would just fade away. When police initially asked for her to come in and meet with me for a sketch interview, she delayed, hoping they would give up; but they didn't, and she eventually came in for the interview over seven months later.

The investigators in this case were under the impression, early on, that the victim might be lying but they couldn't figure out why, so they followed department protocol and asked for a sketch to develop leads for the case. Since the investigators did not share their biases about the case they could rely on an independent source (my sketch interview) to offer them more information. Even though portions of the interview demonstrated uncharacteristic clarity of detail considering the length of time since the assault, I did not challenge the victim's veracity and instead documented her descriptions. It was only later, after my evaluation of the sketch interview, that I found the information she had offered me was unreliable. The interview process worked, and the eyewitness answered questions about the suspect's face that allowed me to create the sketch. Even the grocery man agreed the sketch looked remarkably like him.

The investigators did a great job at canvassing the immediate area for possible witnesses despite their reservations for the truthfulness of the victim. Even though I advised them the sketch was unreliable, they still published the sketch and used it to corroborate eyewitness statements. Their willingness to be methodical in all aspects of the investigation paid off, and they were able to resolve the case as being a fabrication. While their initial suspicions about the victim were eventually realized, they didn't let that cloud their judgments about the victim's delay tactics (over six months from the time of the assault), and they pursued the case like every other case and requested the composite sketch for the investigation. That one step, in a long line of steps, got them to the result: Learning that the victim had decided to lie to their spouse and police in order to cover up an illicit affair. Instead of resorting to interrogation tactics *during* the interview session, I relied on a more mindful interview process to reveal whatever was present – in this case, an unreliable eyewitness (victim).

STAY WITH THE INTERVIEW PROCESS

When we conduct a mindful eyewitness interview with a cooperative eyewitness, we must acknowledge our bias and reduce our tendency to question the motives of the eyewitness.

In other words, there'll be a time to accuse a person of their fabrication or unsubstantiated details of the crime *after* the initial interview and follow-up interviews. I'm reminded of the true crime documentary series called *24 Hours in Police Custody* (The Garden, 2014) and how UK law enforcement officers conduct their interviews with suspects. The detectives ask the suspect (arrested person) questions about the crime and the suspect responds with, "No comment" repeatedly. It's an interesting dichotomy in interview tactics compared to US interrogators portrayed on TV yelling, threatening, and coercing the suspect, as the suspect tries to challenge the detective with their own comments, lies of their own, or silence. In one episode of *Police Custody*, a female officer closes the interview by smiling and telling the suspect that she was happy he offered her "No comment" because it was better than the last suspect who sat there in silence for over 20 minutes as they went over case details. The suspect demurred (without handcuffs) and smiled back, saying it wasn't personal. Even after all the "No comments," the officer was able to establish the evidence and clarify the details of the crime to subsequently charge the suspect for the crime(s) and remand him to custody with his future court date. I found the exchanges between the investigators and the accused to be very civil and somewhat mindful of their roles. The officers had their perspective about the crime and they asked questions, and the suspect would choose to offer or not offer a response. It didn't matter that the suspect must have known or otherwise knew of certain details about the questions asked – it was up to the investigator(s) to find the evidence that proves the suspect committed the deed. Remember, just because our eyewitness saw the suspect commit the crime doesn't mean they will remember every detail about the event that satisfies the elements of the crime or offer a description that leads officers to the suspect. Sometimes all we have is *That Is All There Is* (TIATI), and we might have to look elsewhere to find the answers.

FOR YOUR CONSIDERATION

- Even though you may have theories about the case, keep them to yourself and let the eyewitness tell you what actually happened.
- Abandon the interview strategy that allows you to consider the eyewitness a suspect.
- Allow the mindful interview process to generate objective outcomes regarding cognitive evidence.

9
Empathetic Strategy

The notes I handle no better than many pianists. But the pauses between the notes–ah, that is where the art resides.

Arthur Schnabel

I've been an instructor teaching detectives and patrol officers the Cognitive Interview (CI) technique since 2002 and recently to criminal justice college students. The CI developed by Fisher and Geiselman (1992) has been considered an advanced interview course that detectives take in order to prepare for their new positions in their investigative bureaus. I have the book in my library, and I refer to it when I teach students and detectives the fundamentals of the CI technique for basic interviewing sessions. I studied the same techniques when I was developing my own methodology for interviewing eyewitnesses, even though I only used the narrative portion and found the reverse order and other perspectives to be too cumbersome for everyday eyewitness interviews. As I began to develop my own style, I learned that rapport-building wasn't something you just checked off at the start of the interview. For instance, the CI technique specifically instructs the student to take the time to gather basic information and check in on their eyewitness before moving onto the interview (gathering details of the event). I had already completed well over 1,000 interview sessions in the Advanced Methodology (AM) before I was formally introduced to the CI technique, and while there was some rapport building in the AM, it wasn't as structured.

ESTABLISHING RAPPORT

In my instruction to CI students, I reminded them that rapport with the eyewitness should be nurtured from the moment we meet with them. Some important issues we considered in regard to rapport were (a) being mindful of the fact that we might never meet the eyewitness again; (b) that we would have a limited time to gather cognitive evidence; and (c) that our empathy was required to allow the eyewitness to feel safe. I also encouraged detectives to imagine that they were going to talk with someone they loved dearly. I knew that most of the students had families and loved ones, and I figured that somewhere deep inside their hearts there was a place of genuine concern that they could bring up to frame their affect for the eyewitness. When we think about establishing rapport, we should give ourselves an opportunity to consider imagining the eyewitness is someone who is truly special and is relying on us to help them.

When we employ a mindful empathetic strategy, we become cognizant of what the eyewitness says, and we tend to address it appropriately. For example, if the eyewitness was traumatized by a robbery, we should be patient as they recall details of the ordeal. If the eyewitness expresses themselves as being fearful of the suspect, we should acknowledge it and show our empathy for what must have been a life-changing experience. Being aware of their willingness to stay in the moment and allowing them to describe the event fully without interruption is best before we decide to move on to the next topic. We know that people become more interested in us if we show interest in them, so as investigators we should be more aware of this fact and approach the development of rapport with a strategy for employing empathy.

When we are aware of establishing rapport to enhance the interview session, it is important to understand authenticity is crucial to building trust; i.e., when I meet with a sexual assault victim, I know how difficult it must be for them to agree to the interview and to be expected to reveal intimate details of the assault. I must not assume any facts, and I need to be sensitive to how comfortable the victim is about talking about the ordeal. Checking in with them is vital; that means checking on their needs for comfort or understanding during the interview process. Asking how they're doing would be appropriate, and listening intently to what they say is critical to establishing trust. Just as important is explaining the interview process in a way that is professional and open to questions. For instance, in the *Mindful Interview Method* we explain that the first part of the interview will require the eyewitness to close their eyes for about ten minutes as we ask them about the suspect's face. Of course, this is after we have evaluated their COR and decided to proceed with the interview session. After directing them on calming techniques we explain that we'll ask them to open their eyes and then ask about the crime event. Then we tell them we'll review their statements and make sure they are satisfied. They should have a pretty good idea of what is going to happen and so we ask them if they understand. They can see that there are three parts to the interview and that we are taking our time to make it as unobtrusive as possible. During the interview we check in between each phase for comfort and their understanding of what is coming next.

When we are mindful of the eyewitness, we acknowledge the crime event, and we acknowledge whether they may or may not have been injured, scared, reluctant to talk to police officials, or fearful of offering to help authorities to identify the culprit. We acknowledge that they experienced something unique and that because we're the investigator, we can be there with them as they move through the investigation process. We are their confidant, their guide, and the person they can trust with intimate details of the event. The empathetic engagement we nurture throughout the interview session must be assessed and curated at all times, and we can only do this if we are present and mindful of our interactions with the eyewitness. We know now that establishing rapport is more than just checking in at the front end of the interview session. It's about being mindful of the eyewitness, our goals and their goals, and being open to anything that may come up. Having an empathetic mindset does not mean we spend 15 minutes on every emotional trigger or reaction to every disturbing recollection by the eyewitness, but we should be authentic in the empathy we express.

INTEGRATING EMPATHY AND COMPASSION

I participated in the Compassion Cultivation Training (CCT) program in 2017 at Stanford University after completing a Mindfulness-Based Stress Reduction (MBSR) course in 2016. I wanted to enhance my meditation practice and found these two programs to be worthwhile. As a forensic artist working with eyewitnesses, I found the exercises with my partners in these groups to be reminiscent of my one-on-one sketch interview sessions. When we broke out into small groups and revealed our experiences, I was very comfortable speaking in a group and sharing my thoughts for the exercise. Many of the people in the group were looking for ways to deal with personal stress or to develop more empathetic strategies to help them with their personal relationships. I found myself to be a practitioner in search of ways to formalize my interview techniques and enhance my mindfulness practice. My interview technique had always been characterized as being therapeutic and cathartic for the eyewitnesses, and I wanted to learn how being more mindful and practicing meditation could enhance my interview method. What I learned was that my interview methodology had been conducive to being mindful of the eyewitness and their limitations for providing accurate and complete information. I also learned that being more empathetic and understanding compassion for myself and others would strengthen my interactions with eyewitnesses and enhance the underlying principles I practiced in gathering reliable cognitive evidence.

Since interviewers are exposed to various details about the crime from eyewitnesses, we can expect that the information may contain negative and sometimes disturbing content. When we practice self-compassion, we can mitigate our reactions to these negative details and respond appropriately (Neff & Germer, 2017). My experience in interviewing over 3,000 eyewitnesses was that when some witnesses would reveal their stories in vulnerable detail, I would treat them as if I were hearing it from someone I cared for deeply. If their mood changed to recall something personal, I would be patient and guide them through the process. I was always mindful of the role I had in gathering cognitive evidence, but my authentic empathetic response to their pain and emotion was always present. The most important thing I could do during these moments was to give them time to collect themselves and express their fears. At that moment, I was the only person they could trust with the information, and they had to believe that I would handle it with great care. While I experienced only a few hundred of these types of emotional cases, they were memorable.

I recall a case where I interviewed an elderly man (victim) who had been tricked into giving the suspect all of his life savings in the hope he would double his *investment*. He told me he was approached by a person as he walked out of the grocery store and after listening to him for about five minutes decided to help him. As he engaged with Suspect #1, another confederate joined him and collaborated on their new-found luck. Suspect #1 had said he had a winning lotto ticket and was trying to find the lawyer's office he was referred to by a friend in order to secure the winnings; however, because he was not a US citizen, he could not reap the rewards. So, he was willing to part with the ticket for a large sum of cash in return. Suspect #2 happened to be walking by and heard part of the story and said he would be willing to help Suspect #1 take him to the attorney's office with the victim. The scam included Suspect #2 calling the number from the printed document and handing the phone to the victim in order to prove the legitimacy of the scheme. The person on the phone confirmed their story and the scam was in full swing.

The suspects persuaded the victim to help them retrieve the lottery money by suggesting they each offer good faith money from their bank accounts. The second suspect just so happened to have a large wad of cash and showed his money to the victim and Suspect #1 to prove he was all in. As they drove to the victim's bank, the suspects praised the victim's generosity in helping Suspect #1 and mentioned how lucky they were to have found the one person to help Suspect #1. As the victim parked the car, the suspects said they would wait for him. The victim withdrew all his savings from his account as the bank teller expressed concern about the withdrawal. The victim assured the teller he was fine and that he just wanted his money. The victim walked out of the bank with his cash withdrawal and returned to the suspects huddled in his car. The victim sat in the driver's seat as Suspect #2 opened the envelope with his cash already inside and asked the victim to add his money and close the envelope. The victim took the envelope from Suspect #2 and stuffed his cash and closed it. Everything was happening as they had planned, and even though he said he had some reservations early on, they seemed to fade as he found himself imagining the large lotto winnings he would bring home to his loving wife and family.

They were now on their way to the attorney's office to complete the transaction and turn the lotto ticket over to the victim so he could collect the winnings. On their way to the attorney's office, Suspect #1 said he was beginning to feel sick and needed the victim to drive them to a drug store so they could get something to settle his stomach. They stopped nearby and both suspects got out of the car and said they would be back in a few minutes. The victim waited in the car with the envelope of cash next to him on the passenger seat. Fifteen minutes passed by, and the victim began to worry and wonder whether something happened to his new compatriots. He knew his wife was waiting for him at home, and she was going to be worried if he didn't come home soon. He got out of the car and walked to the store entrance and noticed no one was at the cashier counter. He rushed back to the car and agonized over opening the envelope. He told himself they'd be back soon and to be patient, but more time passed and another person left the store and they were not coming out. He remembered the suspects praising him for his honesty, and they thanked God they found him to solve their problem. He grabbed the envelope and slowly tore the seal open. The envelope burst with strips of white paper stuffed to reveal his misfortune. Tears ran down his cheeks as he tried to explain how embarrassed he was telling his wife and son what had happened. He was a proud man who had worked hard all his life and for a moment he thought his fortunes had changed. He didn't want to call the police – he wanted to forget it, but his son insisted he call the police so that other people might be spared the same experience.

Throughout his recollection, I did not interrupt and ask about what the suspects were wearing and whether they spoke English or what names they gave him. I didn't ask about tattoos or distinguishing marks on the faces of the suspects, and I didn't ask about facial hair or the name of the attorney on the document. I listened and let him talk. I let him tell his story as he had told it before to his wife and son, only this time I'm sure it was with more detail and more trepidation about the reality of this fraud. I acknowledged his pain and told him that coming forward would help other victims and maybe help us find the suspects. I handed him a tissue box and he thanked me as he wiped away the tears. He was my father's age and I imagined how my father would have felt had this happened to him; just imagining that helped me be more patient and allowed me to be more empathetic. He thanked me again and said he wanted to finish the interview to complete the sketches of the two suspects.

When we engage in a mindfulness practice as investigators, we become compassionate about ourselves and others. We engage with the eyewitness empathetically and allow the eyewitness to express themselves without reservation and become more resilient in our eyewitness encounters (Neff & Germer, 2017). When we practice *loving kindness* with the eyewitness, we create an environment whereby the eyewitness is more apt to trust the exchange of information and allow for their vulnerability to manifest in the interview setting. I practice this compassion exercise before every interview session, and I find that my interactions with eyewitnesses are more meaningful, which results in a robust quality of information from the eyewitness. Before each interview session I would picture an eyewitness before me and say, "May you be happy, may you be well. May you be free from harm." I do this before my Mindful Reset and let the feeling of loving kindness take hold (see Chapter 11).

Engaging in this practice of compassion and focused attention involves a non-judgmental reflection (Neff & Germer, 2017). As an investigator, it is imperative that our integrity is in place before, during, and after the interview session. As we conduct our interview, we must be mindful of the details of the event and how the eyewitness experienced them. Showing empathy at appropriate times is critical to demonstrating authentic emotions that the eyewitness will receive and appreciate as they recall events. Developing this authentic empathy under these circumstances is vital to the success of the interview session – at least to the satisfaction of the eyewitness. When we express empathetic feelings, we can counteract the rough interactions (Davis, 2017). If we look at these eyewitness sessions as mini relationships, we can apply empathetic strategies that have been found to enhance social relationships.

As investigators, we are placed in situations where we are expected to accept the thoughts and experiences of our eyewitnesses as they recall the crime event. Being mindful of this fact can prepare us to be more open-minded and available to connect with the eyewitness. When we employ this empathetic strategy, we create a "social bridge that allows us to connect with one another" and we ensure a temporary bond that can reveal details to help us solve the case (Weisz & Zaki, 2017). Embracing an empathetic strategy in the interview session establishes a safe place where the eyewitness can be vulnerable to express themselves without judgment and offer as much information about the crime as possible.

FOR YOUR CONSIDERATION

- Establishing rapport throughout the interview session is essential for building trust between the investigator and the eyewitness.
- Being authentic in our responses to comments made by the eyewitness is vital to the empathetic strategy.
- Understanding empathy and compassion as an investigator will improve your interview sessions.
- When investigators are mindful of being good listeners and showing empathy, it allows the eyewitness the freedom to express themselves about the crime.

Section IV
Mindful Interview Method

Anything more than the truth would be too much.

Robert Frost

10
Principles behind The Mindful Interview Method

The map is not the territory.

Alfred Korzbyski

Let us assume that we all want the same result: To gather reliable statements from someone so we can learn more about an event. Being mindful on how we gather these statements is the foundation for the *Mindful Interview Method*.

BEHIND THE MINDFUL INTERVIEW METHOD

The philosophy I rely on for interviewing any cooperative eyewitness is based on my commitment to treating cognitive evidence like trace evidence left at a crime scene. I do that by adhering to the principles and standards that support the *Mindful Interview Method* (MIM), and I've employed these essential elements to interviewing eyewitnesses in some fashion since 1996. The MIM Principles remind me to keep my focus simple so that when I deal with complicated investigations, I can maneuver through the maze of memory recall (Figure 10.1). The MIM Standards ensure I follow proper procedures in every interview session by engaging in the Probing Framework which includes five topics that are recommended for a comprehensive interview session. These topics include (1) Welcome, (2) Suspect Description, (3) Elements of the Crime, (4) Confirmation of Details, and (5) Conclusion.

Because I was practicing my interview technique autonomously since 1995, I was able to develop my interview process based on a legacy of success from Macris (Advanced Methodology), certification by the FBI, and my own pursuit of evidence-based research about eyewitness memory. In order to explain my interview process for this book, I had to investigate the principles behind my process; and while I knew them instinctually, I had never been asked to explain them for instructional purposes. This book is my attempt to offer concepts, principles, and specific guidelines to help novice and experienced

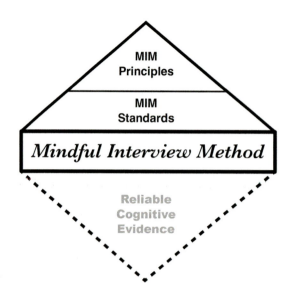

Figure 10.1 The discipline of the Mindful Interview Method system for retrieving reliable cognitive evidence.

investigators learn how to conduct interviews using my mindful technique. I believe the mindfulness and compassionate training I received after my years at San Jose Police Department helped me to rediscover certain aspects of my interview sessions with eyewitnesses that allowed me to define key elements of the success I had in helping to identify suspects of crimes.

I hope you'll come back to this chapter again and again and meditate on these MIM Principles before you embark on your own mindful interview. In Chapter 11, we see how the MIM works and in Parts V and VI we compare other eyewitness interview techniques on their preservation of cognitive evidence.

THE MINDFUL INTERVIEW METHOD PRINCIPLES

The MIM Principles are the foundation of the MIM, and just as law enforcement officers learn the procedures of weapon safety before handling, and engaging in target practice to measure proficiency, they must also learn the principles behind when, where, and why they can engage in using deadly force. I adopt the same ideas for handling eyewitness interviews, and so I created these principles to shape the mindset for interviewing eyewitnesses.

The MIM Principles are rather simplistic to ensure the integrity of each eyewitness interview session is reliable.

- Respect the Eyewitness: Respecting the eyewitness includes acknowledging the crime, any injuries or loss, mindful of their limitations for recollection, and refraining from accusations of deceit.

- Accept *That Is All There Is* (TIATI): Being mindful of eyewitness memory issues and accept that the eyewitness may not remember specific details of the event or the suspect.
- Limit Suggestive Questions: A mindful interview will always limit the use of multiple-choice, leading, and force-choice questions.

The MIM Principles fortify each of the MIM standards by reminding the investigator to protect and preserve their cognitive evidence.

The first two MIM principles are applied before the interview begins. When we ask the eyewitness DYKWYAH (Do You Know Why You Are Here), and the Qualifying Question ("If you saw the suspect again would you recognize them?") we are evaluating their Confidence of Recognition (COR) and deciding whether to continue with the interview session, or not. If they respond with a remark that signals their reluctance to continue, or they are unsure of their memory we must address it before starting the Probing Framework. If the eyewitness does not respond to these questions in the affirmative the interview must not proceed. In Part VI, all the forensic art case studies are examples of interviews that were conducted after the eyewitness affirmed their COR of the suspect's face.

THE MINDFUL INTERVIEW METHOD STANDARDS

It's important to adhere to the MIM Standards and be mindful of the order of preparation and then engagement. When we listen intentionally and are mindful of cognitive evidence our framework for probing each topic will produce more reliable evidence that can lead to righteous identifications.

1. Mindful Reset.
2. Probing Framework.
3. Intentional Listening.
4. Mindful of Cognitive Evidence.
5. Mindful Closing.

MINDFUL RESET

The mindful reset is about preparing the investigator for an important task that requires the full attention of the Detective Mind. We learned in Chapter 4 how our Detective Mind can rely on systems that don't necessarily function in an objective manner. To reduce the heuristics for jumping to conclusions, we should give ourselves the chance to be present as an objective investigator. What if practicing this mindful reset benefits the many other important roles we perform at our agency? Jon Kabat-Zinn, creator of the *Mindfulness-Based Stress Reduction* course, believes that:

> when you start to pay attention in this way, your relationship to things changes. You see more, and you see more deeply and clearly. You may start seeing an intrinsic order and connectedness between things that were not apparent before.

(Kabat-Zinn, 1990, p. 16, pg. 2)

THE MINDFUL INTERVIEW METHOD

When we schedule this time before interviews, we signal to our body and our mind that *this* interview will be different. It will be a mindful conversation that will require our full attention to determine the elements of the crime and to gather details of the suspect's features. At first, this practice will be difficult to achieve, but as we challenge ourselves to make the time, we'll see there is time, and when we experience more success in the interviews, we'll appreciate the effort we took to make it happen. When we begin to rest "in an awareness of breathing," we become aware of how we are feeling at that moment and focus on the "feeling of each in-breath and each out-breath" (Kabat-Zinn, 1990).

Before we start the Mindful Reset, we should set our timer for ten minutes so we don't worry about missing our appointment (see Figure 10.2). When we employ the Mindful Reset, we should start in a seated position, feet on the floor and our back straight upright. We begin by taking at least three full breaths and exhale with full attention to the sound we make as the breath passes our lips. When we take in the breaths, we breathe through our nose and imagine the air drawing in each nostril. One might draw more than the other and so we acknowledge it. When we exhale, we sense the flow of our breath at the back of our front teeth moving past them against our lips. We notice how our chest moves and our belly reacts to taking in our breath. We realize for a second that we notice we have only the thought of our breath in our mind as we draw our next breath. We begin to count (in our mind) as we draw another deep breath: 1, 2, 3, 4; hold our breath for 1, 2, 3, 4; and then push our breath slowly, counting 1, 2, 3, 4, 5, 6, 7, 8. We start again with a purposeful inhalation through our nostrils (we notice our belly rising): 1, 2, 3, 4, hold, 1, 2, 3, 4, and then release slowly and with intention, 1, 2, 3, 4, 5, 6, 7, 8. We repeat one more time before allowing our

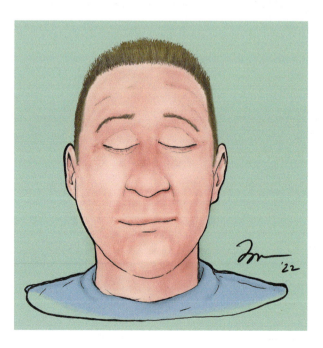

Figure 10.2 The Mindful Reset is part of the Mindful Interview Method. © 2022 Gil Zamora.

breath to settle in a steady rhythm. As we stay in this place of awareness, we realize that we are able to focus on our breath without distraction until we find thoughts in our mind we cannot ignore.

Our mind may wander a little (this is normal), so we guide it back to paying full attention to our breath as we notice our breath again and then exhale. When we acknowledge our wandering, we are paying attention to what is happening and bring ourselves back to focus on our breath until the next time we wander again, and then we focus on our breath again. We can label our wandering mind by saying, "thoughts" so we can be present with what we are doing that very moment. When we practice this Mindful Reset, we can also speak with confidence when we suggest to our eyewitness that closing their eyes can bring them more focus and help them recall events without distraction. When we take the time to prepare for our mindful interview, we'll have more confidence in analyzing the cognitive evidence in an objective manner.

After ten minutes of the Mindful Reset, we should begin to notice every sound and every color more intensely (if you don't, that's okay), and our focus will be enhanced (if it's not, that's okay too). You may have to practice a few more times before you begin to be more present and ready to acknowledge each moment (this is a practice and may take some time to master). After my Mindful Reset for my sketch interviews, I would look for the first name of the detective and the penal code associated with the crime. I would grab my 2B leaded pencil and head to the electric sharpener while glancing at the date and the time of the event. Did this event happen during the day or at night? What was the weather like that day? As I push my pencil into the sharpener, the grinding sound lets me know I'm ready to meet the eyewitness – this act of sharpening my pencil is a trigger to my conscious mind that I am about to conduct an important eyewitness interview. I check my demeanor. Am I at peace? Am I ready to meet this person? Right now, this is the most important person I am going to meet in my day. It may take a few Mindful Resets to appreciate the clarity of focus for your interview, but when you experience it for the first time, you may never look back and you may decide to increase the practice for your own wellbeing.

Because we're absorbed in a Mindful Reset before the interview session, we have acknowledged our bias and understand the importance of first impressions with the eyewitness. Since we are *present* and aware of our role in the investigation, we are more prepared and ready to gather cognitive evidence. Because of our focused attention we are more prepared to offer empathetic engagement when appropriate. Since we are more *present*, we are better listeners and will be more prepared to listen first and commit to probing questions later.

MINDFUL INTERVIEW METHOD PROBING FRAMEWORK STANDARD

In the Mindful Interview Method we ask the Qualifying Question: If you saw the suspect again would you recognize them? If they say, "Yes" or any unequivocal comment that affirms their confidence about the suspect, then you can accept their answer and proceed with in the interview. If, however, the eyewitness makes any comments that signal their lack of confidence about the suspect or the crime event, then *you must* address this issue

Table 10.1 Mindful Interview Method Probing Framework of Five Topics

Topics
1. Welcome
2. Suspect Description
3. Crime Elements
4. Confirmation of Details
5. Conclusion

before you start the Probing Framework. Addressing this issue is critical to ensuring your interview session starts with the highest of integrity. It may involve you determining the eyewitness is not reliable enough to offer information for the investigation and you'll have to end the interview and ask them to contact you later should they recall more details. If, however, you decide to move forward with a reluctant eyewitness that uses words like, "I don't remember," "I'm not sure," "I think so," (to name a few) in response to your open-ended questions (in Topics 2 through 4) then you risk diminishing the reliability of your cognitive evidence.

Having a structured format for the interview session does not mean we lose the discretion to ask questions outside of the framework. Understanding why we are adhering to the probing framework is more important than being rigid about its application. If the initial questions inspire the eyewitness to provide information about another topic, this does not mean we stop the eyewitness from recalling information and demand they return to the previous topic. There is a reason they may be focused on this topic, and we must be mindful of the reasons why. Not only that, we must find a way to get back on track without sabotaging the flow of their recollection. Because we are mindful of the MIM Principles, we ask questions that preserve the cognitive evidence retrieved and we engage in a conversation that allows the eyewitness to speak freely without concern for time. When investigators are guided by these topics, they can presume all aspects of the crime will be investigated (see Table 10.1).

INTENTIONAL LISTENING STANDARD

Investigators of all stripes believe their goal is to get to the truth of the matter, and when they question the victim, witness, bystander, or potential suspect, they just want to know what happened and who caused it. More importantly, they want to know whether someone broke the law and how this person can be brought to justice. In our quest for justice, we tend to reside in a "cognitive bias for consistency instead of truth," so when things don't add up, we tend to believe someone may be lying to us (Voss & Raz, 2016). We seem to think we have a better idea of what happened because, as experienced law enforcement officers, we've seen this or heard that before. If we apply John Sweller's Cognitive Load

Theory (CLT) (1988) to the task of interviewing someone, we can expect that the interviewers would have foundational knowledge for gathering cognitive evidence. The interviewer would then apply their knowledge to interviewing the eyewitness and try and solve the crime. The CLT expects that learning materials which contain many elements of interaction are more difficult than learning materials with less interaction (Skulmowski & Xu, 2022). Thus, I would say that interviewing an eyewitness requires a "substantial cognitive capacity to process information." Depending on the experience level of the interviewer, the cognitive load for conducting the interview may be too high which may affect their capacity for learning what happened. If the interview technique is too complicated to employ (for example, looking for signs of deception, tracking inconsistencies, tracking long pauses, etc.), it might interfere with the main goal of gathering reliable cognitive evidence. This cognitive load can create a disconnect with gathering evidence. FBI negotiator Voss (2016) argues that when we're not listening intently, "we're thinking about their arguments, and when [the investigators] are talking they're making their arguments," when we should have an "all-encompassing focus" on what the eyewitness is saying. This intentional strategy to hear *every* word and to let it resonate within our consciousness should be our focus in every interview session.

When we engage in *intentional listening*, we can practice the communication tools that have been successful in supporting the eyewitness in their recollection of events. Not interrupting them when they are recalling details is a prime example of one of the communication tools that enhance memory. When the eyewitness senses that you are truly listening, they will begin to feel safe and trust your questions to be sincere and your responses to be thoughtful. One specific way to listen intentionally is to offer words that show you are following along like an occasional "uh huh," or "okay, or "mhm" at natural pauses or near the end of their sentence.

Another way to show you are listening intently is to reflect their words back to them or have them elaborate on a topic. This technique is difficult to master, so you should practice it outside of an actual eyewitness interview session. I have been practicing this technique since 1999 and I had called it "echo-words" when I trained investigators and later taught criminal justice students how to gather more information from an eyewitness interview. This *isopraxism* technique has been used by FBI hostage negotiators for years and they call it "mirroring" as they use it to get the suspect to feel comfortable and feel somewhat safe with their new relationship (Voss & Raz, 2016). This mirroring of body language, phrases, or words, begins to develop a sense of familiarity with the eyewitness and the investigator which reinforces the synchrony of their goals. While the FBI suggests you mirror the last three words of what the person said, I've always relied on repeating a word (could be the last or a previous significant word) to create what I call "stickiness." I want the eyewitness to begin to *stick around* certain parts of their recollection and elaborate on items or scenes where the suspect is present – or near present – so they slow down and clarify details. I want them to become familiar with my Mirror Probe questions (MP) and get into a routine of going back to a phrase or word they said and explain it further, so they enhance their recall and stay on track.

For example, say you interview an eyewitness about a robbery, and you know the suspect robbed the victim at the ATM and as they begin to describe getting close to the bank, you try and create some "stickiness."

PRACTICING MIRROR PROBE QUESTIONS (MP)

EW: So, I remembered I needed to get some cash for the party and so I saw the bank and I decided to pull into the parking lot.
Inv: The bank?
EW: Yeah, I usually go to the bank on Willow Street, but I wasn't on that street, so I saw the logo of my bank and I decided to turn in.
Inv: Mhm.
EW: Anyway, I pull in and I can see this car backed into the lot across from the ATM.
Inv: Backed in?
EW: Yeah, you know it was facing forward toward the ATM. It was weird I didn't think about it …
Inv: Weird?
EW: I didn't want to assume anything bad, but I just got a bad feeling about it. I could see there was someone in the driver's seat …
Inv: Driver's seat?
EW: Yeah, I think it was a man – he was smoking with the window open. The parking lot light was on, but he was parked away so I couldn't get a good look.
Inv: Smoking?
EW: Yeah, I could see the glow of the cigarette and the smoke as it came out of the car window.
Inv: And then what happened?

From this interview example, we can see how the MP were used to create "stickiness" and allow the eyewitness to offer more information and details that they recalled, to investigate further. For instance, if we are the patrol officer or the follow-up investigator on the scene conducting this interview, we might consider viewing the bank security video footage to see if we can see the suspect vehicle parked in the lot. We can also go to the parking spot where the suspect may have parked and look for physical evidence for DNA processing. The point is, if we get the eyewitness to slow down their explanation of events, we can keep them *in the moment*, which allows them the opportunity to provide details with some confidence.

Because we are listening with intention, we also offer non-verbal reactions to their statements while they are speaking. Whether we believe it or not, the eyewitness is paying attention to our non-verbal reactions and our gestures occurring within the interview session. Be mindful of these non-verbal cues and acknowledge their effects. For example, if the eyewitness says something and you begin to write something down or you look through some papers, they might be under the impression that you are not listening or considering another question (still not listening). Acknowledge it and let them know why you did what you did. By intentionally cultivating our active listening approach, we create an environment for the eyewitness to trust us and provide the most reliable information to use in the investigation.

Being prepared for this interaction does not mean we pierce the personal space of the eyewitness and extract their feelings about the event. Nevertheless, being mindful of expressing our empathy, when appropriate, is vital to establishing genuine rapport and creating a safe place for the eyewitness to express themselves. Meeting someone for the first time, knowing full well that they may not be comfortable is something we should consider before we greet them. Eyewitnesses come to the interview with their own bias and understanding of the investigative process, and we must take that into consideration before the interview session begins. One way to establish a clear objective for the interview is to gauge the perspective of the eyewitness. Is the eyewitness reluctant to come in and assist us with the investigation? Are they worried about retaliation? Do they know the suspect? Are they associates of the suspect? Are they worried they won't be able to describe the features of the suspect? There is any number of perspectives the eyewitness can have about their role in the investigation, and we have to be ready for any of them.

For example, when I meet an eyewitness for the first time, I reach out my hand and greet them with a smile and say, "Hello, I'm Gil." We walk to the interview room and along the way I might ask them how they're doing. I don't expect much, but I look for words they use to describe how they are feeling at this moment. I'm taking glances at their facial expressions, being mindful of their body language and their pace at which they take their steps. I'm doing this while listening intently to their response. I try not to use their name again unless I need to make a point or get their attention. I've used their name once, in my initial greeting, and I've told them mine – that should be good enough for a while as I move mindfully through the first phase of the interview session.

As the eyewitness settles down in their seat, I ask them if they know why they are here (DYKWYAH). Their answer gives me an idea about their cooperation with and perspective on the investigation so far. At this point of the interview, I have no idea of the effects of their initial interview with officials at the crime scene (or from the 9-1-1 dispatcher). Instead of assuming that they are cooperative and willing to offer details about the event, I'd like to hear it for myself; and while most of the time the answer I get is perfunctory, sometimes the responses are surprising.

Being genuinely interested in the eyewitness is something that should not fade into the background of the interview session. If you are mindful of their wellbeing, their limitations in memory, their struggles with articulation, and their anxiousness for the time in the interview (to name a few items that may be at the top of the eyewitness's mind), they should feel your empathetic engagement instilling trust in the interview process. For example, they may describe the moment in the crime where they became scared; they pause as they gather themselves and then softly describe what the suspect said at that moment. You might acknowledge their fear (within the pause or when appropriate) that it must have been frightening to be confronted that way. You can also show your empathy by being mindful of your tone of voice, your use of words and the pace at which you say them. Stay quiet (pause with them); no need to remind them to continue – they will. Give them the space to tell you what happened. As Chris Voss, FBI negotiator, says, "It's not that easy to listen well" and when you're conducting an eyewitness interview that you consider uncomplicated, it is more difficult to focus (Voss & Raz, 2016).

If we consider our interaction with the eyewitness as a form of *instrumental support*, we can engage with the eyewitness to learn what happened and guide them along the path of authentic recollection (Davis, 2017). When we acknowledge the eyewitness being hurt or expressing fear, we can express sorrow for what happened or acknowledge their bravery to overcome the situation. Our ability to imagine the event from their perspective gives us license to express our empathy. Our authentic loving kindness will signal to the eyewitness that we are present, listening to every word, and understand what they are feeling.

MINDFUL OF COGNITIVE EVIDENCE STANDARD

When the investigator is more mindful of their biases and how their questions can manipulate responses from the eyewitness, they become more aware of their power to influence the statements derived from the interview session. As we discussed earlier, when we choose to treat eyewitness memory like cognitive evidence, we begin to understand the delicate nature of the evidence-collection process. This mindset will be a major shift for most investigators and will require some practice before they understand how they can do both: Gather reliable cognitive evidence and follow up on certain details. The difference between asking more leading probing questions and asking more open-ended questions in an interview session can lead to an increased number of unreliable details not initially anticipated.

Understanding how we ask questions and the responses we get from these questions is vital to having confidence in acknowledging TIATI. Most interviewers do not have the confidence in applying this maxim without making the argument that the eyewitness just needs to be coaxed into recalling every detail. This coaxing is often manifested in the number of leading questions: Multiple-choice, force-choice, and probing questions (to name a few) within the interview topic and question sequence. Since most eyewitness interview sessions are not measured for reliability, the bad practice is nullified when crime reports are signed into evidence.

One of the reasons I don't use reference images in my sketch interviews is because I know that eyewitness memory can be manipulated in the most benign ways – even under the best of intentions. Because reference images are considered post-event information, I know that showing them to an eyewitness can alter their memory. Because I'm mindful of eyewitness statements being cognitive evidence, I treat them like trace evidence left at a crime scene. Eyewitness memory researchers like Dr. Gary Wells of Iowa State University have found that placing an innocent person's photo in a photo line-up with poor fillers can result in misidentification of that innocent person. So, we have to consider the fact that showing reference images that may be similar to the suspect's description may influence the eyewitness to accept certain facial features to be like their memory of the suspect. What we never know is when the new information alters or replaces the memory.

If we are mindful of the malleability of human memory, we should consider the number of times someone may have recalled the incident and others who may have questioned them about it. While investigators cannot control what happens to the eyewitness after the crime event, they can ensure they are well prepared to understand the confidence level of the eyewitness, their articulation of the event, and what factors may have influenced their recollection (estimator variables). This does not mean we discount their statements, nor eliminate them as credible eyewitnesses; however, we should be cautious in how we label their reliability for the investigation.

One such eyewitness described a suspect who had assaulted another person, and as he was describing certain features with precision, I asked him if the sketch reminded him of the suspect. He exclaimed, "Oh, yes! You did a great job! I just want to make the sketch perfect!" During the interview, he was very confident in describing the suspect's features, and he provided extraordinary details that I found to be highly unusual for the event factors established at the crime scene. When he saw the sketch for the first time to refine it and make changes, he began to ask for minute changes that did nothing for the overall appearance of the suspect image but satisfied his confidence in having a photographic mind. The cognitive evidence in this case was not improving in reliability; it was only achieving an exceptional quality for the eyewitness.

Just as the latent print examiner determines whether the print is usable (reliable), we should make an evaluation of whether the cognitive evidence is reliable and usable. We should be evaluating the cognitive evidence for its reliability to offer the investigation valuable leads or to eliminate them as unreliable. We can only do this by ensuring we are not manipulating the cognitive evidence. For instance, we do not expect the crime scene technician to "look at a partial print and fill in the blank spaces with their own lines. They must maintain integrity about the prints they found" and we should do the same with cognitive evidence (Zamora, 2018).

How can we identify manipulated cognitive evidence when we are not scrutinizing the eyewitness evidence collection procedures? There is a quandary here for prosecutors, defense counsel, judges, and juries, whereby investigators diligently gather cognitive evidence while ignoring the possibility that their eyewitness statements are unreliable. Do we know what the eyewitness said when asked whether they could recall the suspect's face if the saw them again (Qualifying Question)? Did the investigator start the interview even though they rated negatively on COR? Should we ask if eyewitness statements are reliable when law enforcement officials are relied upon to assure the criminal justice system that they are? Should we ask if the eyewitness initially was not sure about specific details but then was convinced by the police and now is more certain about their recollection? Even the courts find suggestive procedures to be highly problematic as they tend to allow for "greater [...] chance eyewitnesses will seem confident and report better viewing conditions," even though the confidence in their eyewitness is misplaced by investigators (Doyle et al., 2019, §3:4[a][2], p. 42). Investigators must be trained to treat eyewitness statements like cognitive evidence so they will be mindful of how they handle it – just as they do with other physical and biological evidence.

MINDFUL INTERVIEW METHOD CONCLUSION STANDARD

After gathering cognitive evidence, investigators may offer a summary of what they have heard (not necessary if the interview session is recorded). The conclusion section should include some check-in on how the eyewitness is feeling and cover the next steps after the interview session is over. We should make sure they understand that they can contact us with more information and that it is normal for them to recall more details after leaving the interview. Many times, they may have a question about the investigation or what services they can receive as a victim, and we should do our very best to answer each question. This may be our final impression we leave with the eyewitness, and it may have repercussions for follow-up investigations and court appearances, so we should be mindful of the potential requests that may come later to the eyewitness from our colleagues.

While we may not ask the eyewitness to complete a survey about their satisfaction with the interview itself, we can have an understanding of how the interview succeeded in retrieving cognitive evidence. When we conduct a mindful interview, we imagine the events of the crime, we might have a mental picture of the suspect, and we get a sense of the emotional energy expressed in the event. When we can document all of these elements, we can be assured we have been a mindful listener and know all there is to know about the event. When the eyewitness leaves the interview session, they should be satisfied they told us all that they know and more.

When we rely on the MIM Principles and Standards, we can ensure our interviews will generate reliable cognitive evidence and give us confidence in evaluating the reliability of our eyewitness statements. When we adhere to the MIM, we can be sure the eyewitness evidence is more reliable and can lead to presumptive outcomes.

FOR YOUR CONSIDERATION

- Understanding MIM Principles will make it possible to achieve the MIM Standard.
- Being respectful of the eyewitness and the evidence collected from the interview will ensure the investigative leads are reliable. Respecting the eyewitness may not be confident about their memory of the suspect or elements of the crime must be considered before starting the interview.
- Interviewing eyewitnesses in the MIM Standards will improve your current interview technique.

11
How to Perform the Mindful Interview Method

As is the human body, so is the cosmic body. As is the human mind, so is the cosmic mind.

As is the microcosm, so is the macrocosm. As is the atom, so is the universe.

The Upanishads

I believe the *Mindful Interview Method* (MIM) can be used to interview *any* person about *any* type of incident regardless of the magnitude of the event. When you understand the MIM Principles and Standards, you can apply the MIM with confidence, knowing you retrieved the most reliable information from the eyewitness. Over the years I have heard investigators, after sitting in on my sketch interviews, astonished that I had gathered so much information from what seemed an innocuous conversation. The fact that the interview session resulted in a realistic illustration of the suspect's face was another element that mystified the interview process for them.

So how do we practice the MIM? Instead of presenting you with a sanitized example of an eyewitness interview, we examine an actual interview session I conducted, and review the steps I took for conducting this interview (the excerpt has been anonymized for instructional purposes). Keep in mind that every interview session is unique and each one may challenge the adherence to the MIM practice. Let's be mindful of the topic sequence (Table 11.1) for this interview session and understand how it affects the reliability of cognitive evidence. Finally, we must evaluate the Confidence of Recollection (COR) from the eyewitness and decide whether we need to ask more questions, or end the interview altogether.

PRACTICING THE MINDFUL INTERVIEW METHOD

In this 2005 investigation, I interviewed an eyewitness who was a yard-duty volunteer at a school who confronted a woman who had tried to come on to the school grounds to

THE MINDFUL INTERVIEW METHOD

Table 11.1 Mindful Format and Focus of Topic Sequence from the Mindful Interview Method

Topic	Focus of Topic	Description
1	Welcome, introduction, and assessment	A professional welcome that is mindful of the crime and witness factors. The welcome should include an explanation of the interview process and a brief introduction to the limitations of eyewitness memory. The Qualifying Question should be asked and the COR should be evaluated before proceeding with the formal interview. The welcome should include a confirmation of understanding the interview process. Rapport should be established and maintained throughout the entire interview session.
2	Suspect description	The suspect description section will include any and all information related to the suspect (descriptors, clothing, ethnicity, associates, associated vehicles, and last known location).
3	Elements of the crime	The focus of these questions will be to establish the elements of the crime based on the initial information from the report and the information from the eyewitness.
4	Confirmation of details	Clarification of information is important to establish reliability of cognitive evidence. Summary of narrative may be employed if the interview is not recorded. Adherence to TIATI is expected and probing questions are relevant to establishing elements of the crime.
5	Conclusion	A professional closing of the interview is mindful of the rapport established throughout the interview and the witness is offered an opportunity to ask questions related to the investigation. Information related to follow-up interviews and instruction to contact investigators if they remember something post interview.

The topic sequence is the preferred method for conducting a mindful interview. Investigator discretion to change the sequence can be problematic and can diminish the reliability of cognitive evidence and should be avoided at all times. Mindful Interview Method © 2022.

kidnap a young middle school student. Once the eyewitness challenged her for her reason for being on site, she left the grounds. A police report was generated, and the investigator requested a sketch be made of the female suspect. The yard-duty volunteer comes to the interview, and I realize that English is not her first language. The interview begins with the eyewitness seated in a comfortable chair to my right as we're both seated parallel to each other at about a foot a part – I'm facing in her direction and she's facing in mine. Before our dialogue begins, I want you to know that I have already met her and introduced myself as we walked to my office for the interview (Topic 1). I had already asked her about her day, and I'd also asked the *Qualifying Question*, and she said yes. My transcript comments are in *italics* in between sections I believe may need explanation or at significant points of the interview.

TOPIC 1

INV: Okay, the way this works is I'm going to ask you some general questions about the person's face and what I'd like you to do is go ahead and answer to the best of your knowledge.

I already know that English is not her first language by her thick accent. I also had to repeat myself a couple of times when I initially met her, so that tells me she may not understand every word I use. Because of this I want to be mindful of using specific words and allow her to express herself without concern for her lack of understanding. I'm being mindful of estimator and system variables from the moment the interview starts.

EW: Okay.
INV: Most people don't remember everything in great detail …

I begin my monologue about eyewitness memory and my interview process. It's important to explain to the eyewitness the expectations we have for the amount of information they may offer. We have to expect that the eyewitness will have certain expectations as well. Making sure we are on the same page is important. Because I want to make sure they understand, I intentionally pause my monologue when I hear her say something (active listening).

EW: Yeah.
INV: But a lot of people do remember a lot of information when they're here and they're focused on the questions. You're going to have your eyes closed for about five minutes and then I'm going to ask some questions about her face and then after I'll have you open your eyes, I'll have you tell me what happened, what you saw, and I'll show you the sketch and if we need to we'll make some changes.

At this point of my monologue some eyewitnesses tend to close their eyes. This tells me they are listening, trusting the interview process, and expect me to move forward.

EW: Okay.
INV: All right; do you have any questions for me?
EW: No questions.
INV: Okay, good; we're just going to do the gal that you saw with short hair. So all of my questions are going to be about her. Okay?

I had initially asked her why she was here (DYKWYAH), and she began to tell me everything that had happened in the brief encounter with the suspect. She mentioned that the suspect had short hair, so I refer to it in this excerpt. There happened to be two suspects involved in this case, and one was driving the car and the other she confronted on the school grounds. It's important to establish the parameters of the questions, so I make sure she understands I'm going to be asking her about the one suspect.

EW: Okay.

TOPIC 2

INV: So, go ahead and close your eyes. Give me a nice deep breath, let me know you're relaxed, and we'll begin. First of all, what would you say is the race of this person?

It's important to have the eyewitness focused on the questions and give them the opportunity to imagine and recall what the suspect looked like. Closing their eyes does this very well and it also reinforces the rapport we've built to this point of the interview. When I ask someone to give me a nice deep breath, I demonstrate the action by breathing in deeply with them and then exhale gently. Most eyewitnesses will follow my lead or do it on their own. I look for their shoulders and hands to be relaxed and their feet on the floor as they settle back and embrace the comfort of the chair. I take a short pause and then I make sure the tone of my voice is professional and appropriate for our distance. I begin by asking an open-ended question about the race of the suspect.

INV: Her race? White? Caucasian? Black? Mexican?

Because English is not her first language, I expect that I'll have to ask more multiple-choice questions or force-choice questions to help her understand. Unfortunately, these questions are known to diminish the reliability of cognitive evidence, but you'll see that I use them sparingly and allow the eyewitness to express herself without interruptions.

EW: Black
INV: She's black? Okay. Age range?

I use the Mirror Probe (MP) when she says the race of the suspect was black. I normally don't ask these MPs at this early stage of the interview session, however, since her ability to understand my questions is compromised somewhat, I want to get her accustomed to my questioning style. As she accepts my MP, she begins adding more information as we establish a synchronistic pattern that will be extremely useful when we get to other parts of the interview.

EW: 22–24.
INV: Her body? What was that like?
EW: Small, like physical body.
INV: Small?

At this point I continue using MPs to create familiarity, but I don't acknowledge her phrase "physical body" because I don't want the eyewitness to feel uncomfortable for using phrases that may not be familiar to me. I know that I'll be asking more questions about the crime (topic 3) and thus I can ask about the suspect's body later. At this point, I want to make sure I maintain rapport and allow her to gain confidence in speaking without my concern for her descriptive nomenclature ("physical body" versus athletic or fit).

EW: Yeah.
INV: Okay, when you think of the shape of her face, what kind of shape does it make?
EW: Ah, small eyes …

Instead of wondering what word she did not understand I wanted to make sure that I rephrased the focus of my question and offered her generic answers to understand what I was asking. I'm mindful of asking multiple-choice questions, and I know that asking too many of these types of questions will diminish the reliability of cognitive evidence, so I offer more than three choices (distractors) to force her to choose one or offer her own answer.

INV: No, no, no, the shape of her face, just the face. Is it a round face? A square face? A long face? A small face?
EW: Small.
INV: Small? Okay, tell me about her hair. What is that like?
EW: Small.
INV: No, her hair.
EW: Hair? Short hair like a little bit more than me, but short.

I notice she used the word "small" to describe the length of hair. I'll be mindful of this later. You'll notice that once I used the MP after she used the word "small" that she offered more information without prompting.

INV: A little bit more than you?
EW: Yeah.
INV: Aha, and how does she comb her hair?
EW: Ah very little.
INV: Very little? And what's the color of her hair?

Once again, I allow her unique phrasing to settle into the conversation and refrain from asking for clarification of the word "small" because I understand it to be another form of describing length. Since I know I will be showing her the sketch, I don't need to ask more questions about how the suspect combs her hair because when she sees the sketch, I'll ask her about the hair. If there is anything in the hair that needs changing (length, style, volume, or color), she can direct me. If her hair is short, the suspect would have very little to comb.

EW: Ah, brown.
INV: Brown? Okay, and are there any parts in her hair? Does she part it down the middle, or side or anything like that?
EW: No.
INV: What does the hair do around the ears?
EW: Um a little bit closer.

The eyewitness has used words like "small," "very little," and a "bit closer" to describe what I believe is short hair. I have to learn the limits of her articulation of facial features in order to gain insight into what she saw. I must allow her the freedom to use the words that are comfortable and not frustrate her with my lack of understanding. Because I will show her the sketch, I know that she'll have the opportunity to use her recognition skills to offer more clarifying information if needed.

INV: A little bit closer, okay. And tell me about her ears. What are they like?
EW: Very little.
INV: Very little? Are there any earrings? Does she wear earrings?
EW: Yes.

INV: And what are they like?
EW: Little.
INV: Small earrings?
EW: Yes.
INV: Are they studs or are they hoops?
EW: They're studs.
INV: Studs?
EW: Yeah.

Because the eyewitness is able to describe the earrings it means my belief that her hair was short is probably correct. Once again, she uses the word "little" to describe small, so I understand her better – she also is able to distinguish between studs and hoop earrings. I don't clarify it further by asking about the metal, color, or stone – she's going to see the sketch; I leave that detail for later. I want to continue accessing her mental image of the face and keep going over the face so she's familiar with the task.

INV: Okay. Tell me about her nose. What was that like?
EW: A little bit bigger.
INV: What do you mean by that?
EW: Like a little bit like mine but a little more. More down.

It is common for someone to refer to their face when trying to describe another person's features. Their ability to compare and contrast makes it easier for them not to articulate their descriptions. They often motion to their face and make gestures to enhance their words. There is no need to get exact measurements or determine the overall size of the nose because we know their precision is unreliable.

INV: More down, okay. What about her lips? What are her lips like?
EW: Ah very, not too big but normal. Normal lips.
INV: Did she wear any lipstick?
EW: Yeah
INV: What color?
EW: Brown
INV: What was her attitude like?

When I ask about the lipstick I'm not concerned about the specific color because I'm sketching the face in black and white, however I am interested in how much detail she picked up from seeing her. I'm getting a sense of the description of the suspect, and I want to compare that to my own impressions. My next question about her attitude is about getting an overall sense of the suspect and her interaction with her. What type of information will she offer me that reveals her perceptions of the suspect? Will she say a word to describe her attitude, or will she offer more details?

EW: Um she was very like, you know, yelling at me.
INV: Yelling?
EW: Yeah. Because she said, "I'm going pick up my kids." And I said, "I never see you at this school. Why don't you go to the office?" And that's the time the (inaudible)

started and I see her take a phone and I think maybe she call the other lady and the other lady call and say, "Oh security, security, security, excuse me, I need to go to the office" and when they go inside the car, they just go straight to the street.

The MP after she says, "Yelling at me?" generates a lot of information related to the incident (topic 3). I can tell from the exchange that she was close enough to the suspect to speak to her and confront her about being on school grounds. We also learn that she believes the suspect is associated with "the other lady" and that they get into their car and leave the area.

INV: Mhm. Tell me about her chin? What was that like?
EW: You're talking about …
INV: Her chin and her cheeks on her face.
EW: She's got some dark …
INV: What?
EW: She's got some dark things like maybe she put something on her face.
INV: Some dark things?
EW: No like to make her like, you know, more clearly.
INV: So, she was wearing makeup?
EW: Yeah.

Even though she ventures into topic 3 I wait until she completes her thoughts about the suspect leaving in their car and come back to the topic we were discussing–the suspect description. At first she doesn't understand my question about the chin and so I ask it again by adding more details like the cheeks on her face. Even though I ask about a certain part of the face (cheeks and chin), she focuses on "dark things" the suspect had on "her face." Instead of directing her back to the cheeks and chin I allow her to go where she wants to go. Later in the interview this will become important because the makeup is covering something on her face. I didn't know it at this stage of the interview (you have to be open to anything), but once I felt she was fine with the makeup clarification I moved on to the next feature.

INV: What about her cheeks? What are they like? Her cheeks? Chubby cheeks? Skinny cheeks? Medium cheeks?
EW: Skinny.
INV: What about her neck?
EW: Not too big.
INV: What kind of clothes was she wearing?
EW: She wore like a small things right here but all of this out. (Inaudible) you know, very tight.

The eyewitness again gestures around her shoulder area about the type of shirt the suspect was wearing. I know she will see the sketch, so I don't investigate further and leave it for later.

INV: Mhm. What color was the shirt?
EW: Um, like a little bit brown.
INV: Mhm. Did it have sleeves and a collar?
EW: No sleeve.

INV: No sleeves?

What we can't experience from the transcript is the time between questions and answers. The pace of my delivery of questions in response to her answers is not clear from the text; however, when she made the gestures around her shoulders, I wondered if she meant the shirt was sleeveless, so I wanted to ask the question in another point of my inquiry to not disturb the flow of the interview.

EW: Yeah, no sleeves. She dressed like she was going to go to fitness and just (inaudible) and she got the white sneaker.

Once again the MP generates more information from the eyewitness. She gives me more information about the type of shirt the suspect was wearing without actually offering the specific type of shirt. She says the suspect was "dressed like she was going to fitness" and then adds that she was wearing "white sneaker[s]." My impression is that the suspect was wearing athletic clothing and the shirt is a type of tank-top. I sketch the clothing with this mind and expect the eyewitness may accept it when she eventually views it.

INV: Mhm. Does she have any tattoos, scars, or marks on her face?
EW: No, I don't see any.
INV: And what about the color of her skin?
EW: Light skin almost like me, you know my hand.
INV: Mhm. Tell me about her eyes?
EW: Eyes a little bit round.
INV: What about the look in her eyes?
EW: Look in eyes?
INV: Mhm. What is that like?
EW: A little bit brown, like dark inside.
INV: Dark inside?
EW: Yeah.
INV: Okay.

By the end of this topic (Topic 2: Suspect Description) I'm not concerned about the lack of answers to every question. For instance when I ask about the "look in her eyes" and she repeats my question only to offer me the color I don't go back and ask again. Instead I move forward and end this portion of the interview session.

MINDFUL INTERVIEW METHOD ANALYSIS

We end the MIM interview demonstration here and analyze how I addressed certain issues along the way. Even though we covered Topic 2 extensively, we did get some information about Topics 3 and 4. I eventually covered Topics 3, 4, and 5 as I do with all eyewitness interviews, but for this analysis we just focus on Topics 1 and 2. Keep this in mind when you view the Reliability of Cognitive Evidence (RCE). As I have mentioned before, eyewitness interviews can be very complicated and even though we try and adhere to a certain standard, we have to be open to being flexible and focus on the

HOW TO PERFORM THE MINDFUL INTERVIEW METHOD

Figure 11.1 Cognitive sketch for Case Study #10. Cognitive sketch of suspect from sketch interview. Copyright 2005, Gil Zamora.

end result. In this case, the eyewitness gave enough information about the suspect to generate a sketch (see Figure 11.1) even though she struggled with articulating common facial description terms.

When we review this interview session for adherence to the MIM Principles, we can see that I respected the eyewitness by being patient, being accommodating to the words she used to describe the suspect, and I did not interrupt her recollection or make her feel less adequate. I was empathetic for her role as the yard-duty monitor and relied on her statements to generate the sketch. I was respectful of the elements of the crime and allowed the eyewitness to only offer the details she remembered and not suggest more nefarious intentions of the suspect. I listened intently and made sure I used MP questions to enhance her recall of events, and I limited my suggestive questions. Remember, I did that only to help the eyewitness understand my inquiry and not to satisfy a bias or theory I had about the case. I adhered to the maxim of *That Is All There Is* (TIATI) and allowed her responses to remain part of the record. For the complete Efficacy of Eyewitness Interview Assessment report, see Case Study #10 in Appendix E.

The eyewitness reviewed the sketch and was satisfied with the likeness. Regardless of her level of articulation, she was able to offer enough information to create a cognitive sketch to generate reliable leads for the investigation. Keep in mind that in each MIM example, the principles and standards were employed to preserve cognitive evidence. In Part VI, you'll see these principles applied to forensic art interviews and to other interview sessions for comparison which will allow you to make your own conclusions from our analysis.

For those of you reading this and asking yourself, "I'm not a sketch artist and I won't be creating a sketch for the crime report. How does this mindful interview benefit me?" We can certainly document the results of this interview in written form. The cognitive sketch is a representation of the cognitive evidence gathered from the mindful interview. Even though most crime reports have boxes related to the description of the suspect (hair color, height, weight, etc.) there is no policy that inhibits the report writer to include a supplementary report and include more information. For example, we could list the information from the interview as follows:

Additional Suspect #1 information:

In addition to suspect descriptors listed above the eyewitness recalled the following: Suspect #1 was athletic and wore clothing commonly worn to a gym. The dark shirt she was wearing was tight-fitting and sleeveless and she wore white sneakers. The suspect's face was thin and she wore makeup to cover blemishes. She wore small studded earings and her dark hair was too short to comb. When confronted by the eyewitness the suspect used a cell phone to make a call asking for security and then left with suspect #2 in an unknown make vehicle.

This supplemental information will enhance the standard crime report suspect boxes that ask for race, age, DOB, eye color, hair color, etc. Instead of ticking off the routine boxes why not include a more comprehensive description from the eyewitness? The additional suspect description will be more representative of the mindful interview you conducted and compliment the information you included about topic 3 (Crime Elements). Keep in mind, this crime was just a trespassing (misdemeanor) investigation, nevertheless, it could have been a felony kidnapping of a child had the security guard not intervened. When we interview every eyewitness to the highest standards the crime type makes no difference in how we gather and document cognitive evidence. Adhering to the MIM Standards will ensure every eyewitness interview will gather the most reliable cognitive evidence possible.

FOR YOUR CONSIDERATION

- When you adhere to the MIM Principles and Standards, you practice the MIM with integrity.
- The MIM can be used by anyone tasked with interviewing a cooperative eyewitness.
- The MIM Standards allow a comparative analysis of other interview techniques against the MIM.
- Measuring the reliability of cognitive evidence for interview sessions will give law enforcement administrators quantifiable results they can utilize to prioritize eyewitness interview training for their personnel.

Section V
Meta-Eyewitness Interviews

There is nothing either good or bad but thinking makes it so.

William Shakespeare

12
Eyewitness Interview Paradigm

There is nothing worth thinking but it has been thought before; we must only try to think it again.

Johann Wolfgang von Goethe

Instead of just presenting you the *Mindful Interview Method* (MIM) as the interview technique you should practice for all of your eyewitness interviews, I decided to introduce you to examine the theoretical framework around gathering cognitive evidence. The two structured interview techniques I feature in this book, for comparison, are the *Cognitive Interview Technique* (CI), and the *Conversation Management Approach* (CMA, or *The Approach*). These two interview techniques have been employed in law enforcement agencies around the world and continue to be the foundation for inspiring other interview strategies.

A FRAMEWORK FOR INTERVIEWING EYEWITNESSES

The CI was developed by Ronald P. Fisher, Ph.D., and R. Edward Geiselman, Ph.D., and presented in the book *Memory-Enhancing Techniques for Investigative Interviewing: The Cognitive Interview* (1992). Since 1992, I've conducted or participated in employing major elements of the CI technique in thousands of eyewitness interviews with victims as the police artist. From 2000 to 2012, I was also one of the instructors for training law enforcement officers on using the CI technique to interview eyewitnesses. The CI focuses on having the eyewitness access memory codes by encouraging the investigator to facilitate the process through enhanced communication techniques. The CI book offers the investigator a step-by-step process for conducting the interview with an eyewitness.

The Conversation Management Approach (CMA) is part of the Preparation and Planning; Engage and Explain; Account; Clarification, Challenge Closure; Evaluation (PEACE) police training package that was delivered to uniformed personnel in England and Wales after 1981. It was Dr. Eric Shepherd who referred to the interview technique as "conversation management" while training officers in the City of London police in 1983 (Milne & Bull, 2008). The CMA or the *Approach* (as it is often referred to in this book) offers an array of options for conducting interviews with eyewitnesses and suspects alike. The second edition by Shepherd and Griffiths (2013) includes helpful mnemonics and specific scripts that offer new investigators a wealth of foundational knowledge. The *Approach* insists that it is more of a framework for managing conversations with eyewitnesses and suspects.

In the MIM, we consider the eyewitness to be cooperative, and our interview is an exercise in retrieving the most reliable cognitive evidence we can find under the circumstances. After the interview, we evaluate the cognitive evidence and decide whether it is reliable or not, and only then we will offer the information to the case administrator to decide the next steps (follow-up interviews, corroboration of evidence, more interviews with other eyewitnesses). In this chapter, we cover each technique briefly and highlight certain similarities and differences in the techniques to retrieve the most reliable information from the eyewitness. If you utilize either the CI or the CMA interview techniques in actual interviews, you'll have practical experience for the comparisons we make throughout this chapter.

SPECIAL NOTE

As the forensic artist for one of the largest law enforcement agencies in California, I interviewed victims of felony crimes like rape, robbery, violent assaults, sexual assaults, burglaries, and witnesses to murders. I mention this so you'll take my analysis into consideration when you examine your own perspective and compare it to the recommendations of other non-practicing authorities.

INVESTIGATING THE EYEWITNESS INTERVIEW PARADIGM

When we compare the MIM for interviewing eyewitnesses to the CI and CMA interview techniques, we focus our attention on how they manage the cooperative eyewitness. While the MIM was inspired by the CI technique, the MIM only relies on certain aspects of the systematic process to ensure the effectiveness of gathering statements made by eyewitnesses. Interestingly enough, when we review the CMA technique and compare it to MIM (see Table 12.1), we also find common references to mindful considerations embedded in MIM.

THE COGNITIVE INTERVIEW IN BRIEF

The systematic approach suggested in performing the CI technique is valuable in that it is clear to the practitioner that the intention of the interview is to meet with an eyewitness who is a victim or witness to an event that is being investigated. The CI begins with the idea that the "goal of the interview is: (a) to guide the E/W to those memory codes that are richest in relevant information, and (b) to facilitate communication when these codes have been activated" (Fisher & Geiselman, 1992). You are instructed to conduct the interview with the premise that the eyewitness only needs to be directed to *memory codes* to reveal

Table 12.1 Similarities and Differences between Mindful Interview Method and Both Cognitive Interview & Conversation Management Approach

Interview Technique	Similarities*	Significant Differences[a]
Cognitive Interview	• Preparation • Professional welcome and introduction • Establishing rapport • Confirmation of details Formal closing	• QQ and COR evaluation; Mindful Reset • Calming techniques for eyewitness • Systematic topic query • Limited suggestive queries No accusations or interrogation
Conversation Management Approach	• Preparation • Engage/explain • Free recall Closing/evaluation	• QQ and COR evaluation; Mindful Reset • Calming techniques for eyewitness • Systematic topic query • Limited suggestive queries No accusations or interrogation

[a] The similarities and differences are based on my personal experience of employing the Cognitive Interview in interview sessions and my analysis of the Conversation Management Approach for his book.

what happened. Although the CI expects that the investigator will engage in active listening throughout the narrative portion of the interview, they do so by identifying images to clarify in the memory-probing phase. When the investigator listens to the eyewitness with the intent of deciding what images (topics) are important and what needs to be reviewed later, are they really listening and examining what the eyewitness recalled?

COGNITIVE INTERVIEW INTRODUCTION AND MINDFUL INTERVIEW METHOD MINDFUL RESET

We know that the CI technique expects that you prepare for your interview and expects that you'll "develop in the E/W the appropriate psychological mood and to promote effective social dynamics" so, making sure you're mindful of the eyewitness's state of mind will be key (Fisher & Geiselman, 1992). The CI expects that your first impression will be positive and that to be successful you'll keep this in mind before you rush and begin collecting demographic data.

In the MIM, we expect you to be present with the eyewitness in whatever condition they are in (see Table 12.2 for the different phases of MIM). The Mindful Reset establishes your focused state of mind before the interview begins, and you are aware of the magnitude of the eyewitness's role in the investigation. When you come out of your Mindful Reset, you are ready to greet the eyewitness and begin developing rapport to build trust

Table 12.2 Different Phases of the Cognitive Interview and the Mindful Interview Method

Cognitive Interview	Mindful Interview Method
Introduction	Mindful Reset
Open-ended narration	Welcome, introduction, and assessment*
Probing memory codes	Probing framework: Topics 1 through 5
	Intentional listening
Review	Confirmation of details
Closing	Conclusion

* Moving beyond topic 1 is acceptable only after reviewing eyewitness responses to QQ and COR.

in this brief relationship. Because of our Mindful Reset, we've ensured our psychological mood is mindful of the eyewitness, and therefore we can model this social dynamic for the eyewitness.

The CI does an excellent job of breaking down the mindset the investigator should have for the interview. They discuss managing the anxiety of the eyewitness, developing rapport, making sure the eyewitness is the focus of the interview, and reminding us of our role in asking questions. In controlling the eyewitness's anxiety, the CI insists on the investigator "spend[ing] time at the very outset of the interview to calm the E/W and to build up their confidence. Failure to do so […] results in spending the remainder of the interview very inefficiently" (Fisher & Geiselman, 1992).

To be mindful of the eyewitness's psychological mood, we must be open to empathy and express ourselves in kindness to others. The MIM suggests listening intentionally to every nuance of the eyewitness's recall of events. Because of our Mindful Reset, we are well prepared to recognize the emotional and psychological needs of the eyewitness.

RAPPORT BUILDING

In the CI, establishing rapport early on is essential to the interview, while making sure the eyewitness is central to the conversation. While the CI offers strategies like sharing "common experiences," it relies on your specific personality to find common ground in specific topics to be used later to maintain rapport (Fisher & Geiselman, 1992). Establishing a central role for the eyewitness is the guidance Fisher & Geiselman give for discouraging "passive responding" to create a space where the eyewitness is encouraged to reveal more information (1992).

The MIM instead employs a mindful introduction whereby the eyewitness is placed front and center for the interview. When we ask, "Do you know why you are here?" (DYKWYAH) the eyewitness is expected to give their brief perspective of how much detail they may have to offer the investigation. When we ask the *Qualifying Question*: "If you saw the suspect again would you recognize them?" We are evaluating their COR of the suspect and details of the event. If the eyewitness is not confident enough to recall the suspect's face or details of the event, then we must ask clarifying questions that may offer more information. We can ask the eyewitness to imagine the crime scene or the suspect's face and ask an open question about what they see. If they are still unable to offer any substantive information about the suspect or the event, then the interview must not continue. However, if they do recall the suspect's face enough to remember them, then we can begin to establish their perspective and explain our expectations for their memory and encourage them to do the best they can. We offer the eyewitness an overview of the different phases of the interview so they can be comfortable in understanding the timeline for the interview session. If we are respectful of their time and role in the investigation, it will go a long way to ensuring they believe they are at the center of the inquiry.

A COGNITIVE INTERVIEW FRAMEWORK

In the next CI phase, the investigator is directed to be explicit in dictating how the eyewitness should offer their statements. They advise the investigator to remind the eyewitness not to "edit any of her thoughts" and to be careful that they don't take this advisement as "license to fabricate answers" (Fisher & Geiselman, 1992). This last part of the introduction section involves the investigator explaining how difficult the interview will be and to be successful the eyewitness must participate with intense concentration.

In the MIM introduction (Topic 1, Welcome, Introduction, Assessment), we're mindful of certain psychological effects like associative coherence, priming, and the anchoring effect (Kahneman, 2011). As we learned earlier about our *Detective Mind*, we know our mind can make automatic associations based on the ideas our brain receives. Because we are mindful of these effects, we are mindful of what we say and how we say it to our eyewitness. We know the eyewitness is coming into the interview with their own theories about how the investigation will proceed. If we give them the idea the interview will be difficult or complex, they may build on these associations and prepare themselves for a difficult time. Instead, we establish a positive professional tone that improves the start of the interview session.

The other effects we consider in MIM are *priming* and *anchoring* the eyewitness for success. We understand the science behind the belief that our System 1 agent will create impressions that often become our choices for our actions. So, we *prime* the eyewitness to accept their role as the competent eyewitness. For instance, when we go through the MIM monologue we say that "Most people don't remember everything in great detail." When we say this, we *prime* the eyewitness to lower their expectations for what they *think* they remember – their articulable thoughts, and their ability to offer specific details about the suspect description or the crime event. We know that some eyewitnesses believe they have photographic memories while others believe they can't describe their partner's face. If we help the eyewitness reside in a space where they can accept their unreliable recollections, we can spend more time gathering the cognitive evidence that *is* there. When we prime the eyewitness for the reality of their recollection, we also anchor them in strategies for success. After we acknowledge the malleability of eyewitness memory, we suggest that to help them focus and remember the details of the event they should close their eyes and take three deep breaths. Their minds will immediately associate this request to meditation or New Age thinking. Our suggestion for success in improving their recollection is what is important in this anchoring mechanism.

OPEN-ENDED NARRATION PHASE AND NARRATIVE RECALL VERSUS SUSPECT DESCRIPTION AND ELEMENT OF THE CRIME

The CI says the "goal of the narrative phase is to develop a strategy for the remainder of the interview, not to collect specific details" (Fisher & Geiselman, 1992). The CI expects the investigator to create a general context of the event before asking the eyewitness to offer their narrative. While the eyewitness is recalling the event, the investigator must pay attention to certain items that are important to developing their strategy for probing for more details. The investigator must consider how the eyewitness is recalling the event and whether they are offering details of the suspect's physical appearance, which the CI considers unusual for most eyewitnesses.

Since the MIM Probing Framework is structured with five topics, the investigator is well aware of each topic focused on certain aspects of the crime: For example, after the welcome there is Topic 2: Suspect Description; Topic 3: Elements of the Crime; Topic 4: Confirmation of Details; and Topic 5: Conclusion. There is no need to formulate a strategy to decipher what perspective is best for the eyewitness to offer details about the suspect. In MIM the eyewitness has already been asked the *Qualifying Question*, their COR has been evaluated to proceed with the interview, and they've been primed to be relaxed and focused (eyes closed) as they begin to answer the guided questions, all in Topic 1.

Interestingly enough, these guided inquiries through each topic are aligned with the CI's *Principle of Detail and The Principle of Momentum*. We don't have to worry about what image is "presently in consciousness" since we are asking about the *one image* that should be front and center to the eyewitness: The suspect's face (Topic 2). And since we have the suspect's face in their mind, we can satisfy the Principle of Momentum and continue to ask questions related to the facial features (Fisher & Geiselman, 1992). In the MIM script (see Appendix B) we first ask about the age, ethnicity, and body build of the suspect to begin to get the image of the suspect in their mind. With the suspect's face in their present awareness, we then ask about the features starting with the face shape, hair, ears, etc. Since we are focused on the face, the Principle of Momentum is achieved because the eyewitness is continuously responding to questions about the face – in a specific order – requiring them to look at it (in their mind) and bring about the context for the crime event. Once we gather all the information about the face, we move on to asking the eyewitness about the crime event (Topic 3).

PROBING IMAGES AND CONCEPT CODES PHASE VERSUS ACCESSING TOPIC 2

The CI technique expects the investigator to identify key elements of the narration from the eyewitness as prime images to probe further. The investigator must identify these images (of the suspect) from the details of their narration. For example, they saw the suspect as he came into the store, then they saw him again as he pulled her purse, then again as he turned and left running out of the store. Each of these key points in her narration is taken as still images to be reviewed later to gather detailed information about the suspect's face. The investigator must probe each still image, continue with a follow-up probe, probe remaining images, re-probe images activated earlier, and then probe concept codes. This comprehensive exercise in probing for details from the eyewitness is highly problematic for most investigators inexperienced with eyewitness memory concepts.

For example, in the book *Memory-Enhancing Techniques for Investigative Interviewing* (1992) their sample interview and analysis asks the investigator to ask the eyewitness to "focus on the 'man with the gun'" and asks the eyewitness to close their eyes to develop a mental picture of the suspect (pp. 155–174); this is after the eyewitness has already recited details of the crime. While the directions are excellent at advising the eyewitness to "concentrate" and offer "as much detail" as they can, this example relies on the eyewitness to offer a lot of detail without much prompting. And that is highly unusual with most eyewitnesses. The CI expects the investigator to be skilled at using appropriate pauses and change topics without concern for missing details.

To illustrate the information gathered from the interview I've taken the liberty of sketching my interpretation of the details from the interview for this book. As you can see from Illustration 12.1, the suspect image is lacking eyebrows and a nose. One of the last questions asked about the face is the skin tone and then one very good question (that I often ask) about the "most distinctive feature" of the suspect's face. The eyewitness says the suspect had a "crazy

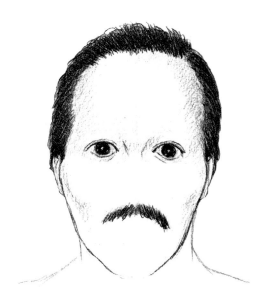

Illustration 12.1 Sketch of robbery suspect #2.1. Sketch of robbery suspect #2 from CI sample interview, *Cognitive Interview* book, pp. 164–165. Investigator did not ask about eyebrows, nose, or neck and upper clothing at this stage of the interview. © 2022 Gil Zamora.

look" in his eyes, which is excellent information if a composite sketch were produced. Then the investigator abruptly makes a "clear break" and moves on to another topic (pp. 164–165). The instruction comments in the sample interview are very helpful in understanding the reasons for asking questions, and we see the investigator move on to the sound of the voice of the suspect and ask the eyewitness to concentrate on the "voice only."

In MIM you are expected to stay on topic and allow the eyewitness to exhaust all descriptions related to it. Since we are focused on the suspect's face, it would be reasonable to have the eyewitness access the mental picture of the suspect over and over as they describe each feature. Another interesting aspect of the CI is the reminder to ask the eyewitness to "close your eyes" over and over again as the investigator encourages the eyewitness to move into another topic or describe another element of the crime.

In MIM we instruct the eyewitness that closing their eyes will help them concentrate and help them answer questions about the crime, and they are expected to have them closed during Topic 2. In the CI sample interview script, we see the investigator remind the eyewitness to close their eyes twice, once when the questions focused on the suspect yelling and then the second time to help them focus on the gun. It is not clear from the sample script whether the eyewitness inadvertently opened their eyes and they had to be instructed to close them again, but I have found that when you ask the eyewitness to close their eyes at the start of the interview, they rarely open their eyes until they are done with their statements, or I ask them to open them.

Returning to the robbery interview from the CI book, I continue interpreting the dialogue between the investigator and the witness and work on Illustration 12.2. The investigator returns to asking about the suspect's description and retrieves enough information to seemingly complete the suspect's face. Even though the line of questioning is not necessarily focused on the suspect's face, I was able to sketch features about the face from the questioning centered on the weapon, the clothing, and his arm. The questions directed at her interpretation of what her husband remembered about what the "leader" experienced in this event are problematic. The premise behind asking the eyewitness to consider the event from another perspective might be helpful in some cases; however, in other cases like sexual assaults, asking a victim to presume to think like the suspect to gain their perspective would not be a recommendation I would make.

In MIM you are supposed to stay on topic and allow for some off-topic discussions (eyewitness driven), while still focused on gathering as much reliable information about the topic as possible before you move on to the next topic. In MIM we exhaust every detail of the suspect's face in Topic 2, and we rely on the eyewitness to decide the best views and allow them to rotate and highlight the image of the suspect in their mind as they access it when we ask our questions about each facial feature. If the eyewitness offers a less-than-detailed response, we ask the eyewitness to clarify their answer. For example, if we ask the eyewitness, "Tell me about his hair?" and they say, "I think it was black and short," we might ask them to clarify their answer by asking, "How did he comb his hair?" or "What about the texture of his hair?" If the eyewitness has more information about the hair, we might expect that they will offer it – if not, then *That Is All There Is* (TIATI). So what would this robbery suspect have looked like had I interviewed the eyewitness? See my example in Illustration 12.3.

Most of the MIM *probing* is done with intentional listening techniques. One mindful exercise, One mindful exercise, *Mirror Probe* (MP), creates a rhythm of pauses by mirroring

Illustration 12.2 Sketch of robbery suspect #2.2. Sketch of robbery suspect #2 from CI sample interview, *Cognitive Interview* book, pp. 169–173. Investigator never asked about eyebrows and mouth. © 2022 Gil Zamora.

their word(s) at specific times in their recollection which allows for more information to be revealed in greater detail without generating unreliable elaboration. Since facial features are gathered in Topic 2, the remaining topics will cover other aspects of the crime. In MIM, the recollection of the crime event (Topic 3) can offer information that may be used to measure the value of the cognitive evidence gathered.

Let's say an eyewitness to a shooting event says they would recognize the suspect if they saw them again (Response to QQ in Topic 1). We decide to interview them (after evaluating their COR), and during Topic 2, they describe a small scar above the suspect's right eye. When we get to Topic 3, we learn that they were outside after dark, obscured somewhat by some bushes, and about 20 feet away when they saw the suspect shoot at the victim. We can surmise from the information gathered from Topic 3 that the scar they described in Topic 2 could have been seen in another setting or may be exaggerated from the features they saw (*cognitive interference*). There will have to be some follow-up regarding their account, but there is no need to confront them now until we corroborate other details of the event. Allowing the eyewitness to describe the suspect first (in Topic 2) gives us important information we can use when they then describe the circumstances from their perspective. Since we gather cognitive evidence from each topic, we can evaluate the results of our findings with objectivity and make decisions for follow-up interviews.

THE MINDFUL INTERVIEW METHOD

Illustration 12.3 Sketch of robbery #2.3. Reimagined sketch of robbery suspect #2 utilizing MIM. Copyright 2022 Gil Zamora.

REVIEW AND CLOSING PHASES

The CI and MIM are very much aligned in summarizing details of the interview and making sure the eyewitness is encouraged to contact the investigator for any future questions. Since we know that memory can be triggered by other events, now that the eyewitness has gone through this process of recollection, they may remember more information or offer clarifications to statements they made. Regardless, they should feel welcome to contact the investigator and the investigator should be able to contact them for follow-up. Being mindful of the rapport established in the interview session ensures a positive follow-up contact.

The initial mindset of the CI assumes the eyewitness knows *everything* and that "All relevant information is stored in the E/W's mind" (Fisher & Geiselman, 1992). The interviewer practicing the CI may believe the eyewitness only needs to be guided through their memory to recall accurate details for the crime event, while the goal of the MIM is to facilitate authentic eyewitness memory recall through a mindful process. While the CI is very systematic, the next interview technique is touted as being a framework for managing conversations that provide investigators a wealth of information to consider when preparing for an eyewitness interview.

THE CONVERSATION MANAGEMENT APPROACH IN BRIEF

The comprehensive *Conversation Management Approach*, 2nd edition (2013), by forensic psychologist Eric Shepherd and Dr. Andy Griffiths, is an interview program adopted by UK law enforcement after the Police and Criminal Evidence Act of 1984 (PACE) was enacted to centralize police powers to unify police practices and hold them accountable when considering the rights of citizens. This *Approach* (Conversation Management Approach) technique was included in the framework called PEACE, which was instituted in agencies in the UK and eventually around the world (except the US) ten years later. The PEACE framework stands for: Planning and preparation; Engage and explain; Account; Closure; and Evaluate. The PEACE framework was established further in a directive by the National Police Improvement Agency (NPIA, 2009) that states:

  i. The aim of investigative interviewing is to obtain accurate and reliable accounts from victims, or suspects about matters under police investigation.
  ii. Investigation must act fairly when questioning victims, witnesses, or suspects. Vulnerable people must be treated with particular consideration at all times.
  iii. Investigative interviewing should be approached with an investigative mindset. Accounts obtained from the person who is being interviewed should always be tested against what the investigator already knows or what can reasonably be established.
  iv. When conducting an interview, investigators are free to ask a wide range of questions in order to obtain material which may assist an investigation.
  v. Investigators should recognize the positive impact of an early admission in the context of the criminal justice system.
  vi. Investigators are not bound to accept the first answer given. Questioning is not unfair merely because it is persistent.
  vii. Even when the right of silence is exercised by a suspect, investigators have a responsibility to put questions to them.

The directives from the NPIA are excellent and put officials on notice when interviewing a suspect of a crime; however, I would also like to see directives that are distinguished for interviewing cooperative eyewitnesses. I believe there should be another set of principles that are solely focused on the cooperative eyewitness. They might reflect the MIM principles and standards and be listed in this fashion:

The aim of a mindful investigative interview is to obtain reliable accounts from cooperative victims or witnesses about matters under police investigation.

  i. The investigation must act mindfully when questioning victims, or witnesses, and all people must be treated with respect at all times.

ii. A mindful investigation should be approached with an unbiased mindset, and the accounts obtained from the person who is being interviewed should always be retrieved with the idea of preserving the integrity of cognitive evidence.
iii. When conducting a mindful interview, investigators are free to ask a wide range of mindful questions to obtain cognitive evidence which may assist an investigation.
iv. Investigators should recognize their positive impact in the context of the criminal justice system and strive to enhance it throughout the session.
v. Investigators should not ask leading questions or offer post event information to probe eyewitnesses that may not have sufficient recall of an event.
vi. Investigators should employ intentional listening techniques that focus on recall and understand eyewitness memory limitations.

Notice the change in emphasis on gathering cognitive evidence mindfully from the eyewitness instead of the option for interviewing a possible suspect. We can do this when we expect to interview eyewitnesses and not interrogate suspects.

The section on planning and preparation covered in the *Approach* manual is outstanding information and should be reviewed by *all investigators* seeking to refine their systematic approach to eyewitness interviews. The *Approach* manual offers the investigator a reference index of every conceivable interview scenario and provides the investigator specific scripts for solving the issue. Nevertheless, when we compare the *Approach* to the MIM, we find some distinctions in the process of interviewing eyewitnesses that center on mindfulness and the reliance on the investigator to be diligent when applying mindful principles. In the following sections, we examine some areas of the *Approach* that are different and similar to the MIM by focusing on the framework for interviewing eyewitnesses (see Table 12.3). Every investigator should have a copy of this book to supplement their interview instruction and refer to it when planning first-time interviews with eyewitnesses.

Since the *Approach* presented the argument of practicing psychotherapists having "difficult conversations" with their patients as being equal to criminal investigators interviewing eyewitnesses and suspects, we can assume highly trained forensic artists would be included in this category (Shepherd & Griffiths, 2013). As a forensic artist, I interviewed eyewitnesses that were victims of violent crimes and witnesses that viewed suspects either

Table 12.3 The Conversation Management Approach and the Mindful Interview Method

Conversation Management Approach	**Mindful Interview Method**
Planning and preparation	Welcome, introduction, and assessment
Engage and explain	Probing framework: Topics 1 through 5*
Free recall	Mindful of cognitive evidence
Questioning	
Closing/evaluation	Conclusion

* Moving beyond topic 1 is acceptable only after reviewing eyewitness responses to QQ and COR. For Complete Enhanced Interview Technique, see Shepherd & Griffiths, 2013, p. 307.

Table 12.4 Mnemonic for the Approach Interview Process

	Mindful Behaviors for Relationship Building
R	Respect
E	Empathy
S	Supportiveness
P	Positiveness
O	Openness
N	Non-judgmental attitude
S	Straightforward talk
E	Equals talking "across" to each other

Investigative Interviewing, Shepherd & Griffiths, 2013, p. 19

specifically or inadvertently. While many forensic artists focus only on the description of the face and body of the suspect, the MIM asks the eyewitness to describe the details of the event to enhance their description of the suspect and gain more insight about the elements of the crime to enhance their recollection.

RESPECT FOR THE EYEWITNESS

The RESPONSE mnemonic in Table 12.4 is an excellent example of an interview process that is centered on making sure the interaction with the eyewitness results in a positive outcome. When we are mindful of our role as an investigator, we should consider these behaviors to create an environment that is conducive to gathering reliable cognitive evidence. The many references to being mindful may have not been the intention of the mnemonic, but the *Approach* reinforces mindful principles for conducting more focused interviews. The MIM Principles are aligned with RESPONSE as they Respect the Eyewitness; Accept the limited information that might be revealed (non-judgment); and Limit Suggestive Questions (which is supportive of maintaining integrity for eyewitness statements). As we mentioned in our comparison to the Cognitive Interview, we must first assess the confidence the eyewitness has in their recollection (QQ and COR) of the suspect and details of the event before we move past topic 1. *The Approach* does not consider this issue of confidence before starting their interview. They instead rely on techniques to aid the eyewitness in remembering details of the event regardless of their initial reluctance.

LOOKING FOR TRIGGERS OR BEING MINDFUL OF *THAT IS ALL THERE IS*

While the *Approach* offers the investigator a comprehensive overview of retrieval methods for eyewitness memory, the MIM relies on the eyewitness to access the environmental context from their memory alone to reduce the effects of post-event information contaminating their memory during retrieval. The triggers mentioned in the *Approach* are centered on accusing the eyewitness or suspect during an interview. They focus on a question regarding guilt, a "trailer question" that could be considered leading, and the productive question that is focused on a specific topic or detail previously recalled (Shepherd & Griffiths, 2013, p. 430).

The *triggers* that the *Approach* supports in gathering cognitive evidence have been widely expressed in the CI technique developed by Fisher and Geiselman (1992); however, when we practice the MIM we are wary of exposing the eyewitness to these triggers and consider the impact of these types of questions to be too extreme to utilize in a standard eyewitness interview session. Since the MIM is based on the premise of TIATI, any effort to influence the production of eyewitness memory, outside of open-ended questions and mindful tactics, may call into question the reliability of the cognitive evidence retrieved.

The *Approach* offers insightful information about questioning the eyewitness; however, it leaves many opportunities for the novice practitioner to engage in interrogation tactics that are not appropriate when working with cooperative eyewitnesses. For example, the *Approach* authors offer examples of inappropriate questioning and caution the practitioner for the harmful effects of this procedure (Shepherd & Griffiths, 2013). In MIM we are *not* expected to offer leading questions that suggest an answer to the eyewitness, so we confidently proceed without concern for unreliable cognitive evidence. Some investigators struggle with this concept of just relying on the eyewitness to offer limited information about a criminal event. Unfortunately, the idea that the investigator is expected to know whether the eyewitness is revealing all that they know is a cognitive bias that should be eliminated when conducting a reliable eyewitness interview.

EXPECTING TOO MUCH FROM INVESTIGATORS WHEN THEY AREN'T TRAINED?

We can certainly assume the confidence in investigators expecting more from their eyewitness may be a result of not understanding the basic tenets of human memory. Many believe that our law enforcement investigators are more qualified to recall events and that they are the experts in questioning people about every detail. In other words, they are experts at asking questions and interacting with the eyewitness to orchestrate a valuable recollection of statements related to a past event. The truth is law enforcement personnel are just as prone to recalling unreliable information as the average person (Ainsworth, 1981).

When we review the *Approach* manual, we notice it is filled with an abundance of practical considerations for preparing, conducting, and evaluating an interview session. While the authors advise us that the information should be taken as a framework, it can be rather daunting for an investigator attempting to apply the techniques to a routine investigation. We know that the *Approach* considers the RESPONSE as a precursor to practicing a more empathetic strategy, while Greeting, Explanation, Mutual Activity, and Closing (GEMAC) plays a role in eyewitness engagement through the end of the interview session. When we compare these valuable mnemonics to MIM, we see that they are relatable to the same mindful practices, except when they are not (see Table 12.5).

In fact, when we look over the "A" section in GEMAC for Assertion, we find that it requires the investigator to ask questions to "maximize spontaneous initial disclosure." What is not clear from the text is whether the disclosure is related to a suspect confessing

Table 12.5 GEMAC Mnemonic from the Approach

GEMAC	Expectations
Greeting	The investigator sends signals to the eyewitness about the relationship they wish to establish. This is all done within the first few minutes of the interview. Creating mutual trust is very important.
Explanation	The explanation occurs within or soon after the greeting. The investigator explains their role, outlines what is about to happen, and offers explanations throughout the interview session to improve understanding.
Monitoring	The investigator is expected to engage in active listening tactics to capture key elements from eyewitness recollection of events and analyze any issues that may require more follow-up.
Assertion	The investigator assists the eyewitness in remembering more details of the crime event and engages in ethical persuasion when appropriate.
Closing	The investigator presents a professional closing for the interview session and reinforces the rapport established with the eyewitness by making sure they understand next steps and all questions are answered.

See Conversation Management Approach, Shepherd, & Griffiths, 2013, pp. 20–25.

about a crime or whether it is an eyewitness revealing details about the crime (Shepherd & Griffiths, 2013). While the GEMAC framework may enhance most interviews, presenting the elements in this fashion is highly problematic for communicating with cooperative eyewitnesses. Nevertheless, when the Assertion (in GEMAC) mentions that we need to engage in "ethical persuasion" when receiving unusual disclosures, this tactic can lead to manipulating cooperative eyewitness statements which results in unreliable cognitive evidence. The *Approach* infers the interview session might cast a shadow of doubt on the information recovered from the inquiry which challenges the investigator to determine whether they have an eyewitness or a suspect in front of them.

The MIM encourages the evaluation of cognitive evidence post interview but not under the shadow of suspicion or expectation of deception for the eyewitness. While an investigator can review the cognitive evidence after the MIM interview, they do so to evaluate the reliability of the evidence and decide whether to follow up, search for corroborating evidence, or identify new eyewitnesses. There is no need to challenge the eyewitness about the investigator's lack of perceived inaccuracy or deceit. We can be confident in understanding that sometimes an inaccurate account by the eyewitness may have been the result of human error which is always a factor in eyewitness memory recollection.

THE APPROACH CAN BE JUDGMENTAL

The *Approach* does a masterful job of presenting the experienced investigator with many alternatives to managing the interview from a cooperative eyewitness to a criminal suspect. There is a wealth of information regarding planning and preparing for the interview that goes well above the requirement for a routine petty theft, automobile accident, or an indecent exposure investigation.

In an analysis by Milne and Bull (2008), they conclude that the *Approach* insists on preparing plans for the interview that rely on schemata to "form judgments about the event in question" (p. 56). This cognitive bias for generating certain questions based on the crime event can be troublesome for an inexperienced investigator. After all, if the investigator assumes the victim of a robbery must have seen the face of the suspect because they approached them at the ATM, they might assume certain facts like they must have been aware of their surroundings as they walked up to the ATM machine; viewing the suspect's face because they turned around and they pointed the gun at their face; or that they saw their car parked in the stall before they entered the lot. These assumptions in judgment, beforehand, can lead to biased questions that diminish the opportunity for the investigator to be open to what the eyewitness actually remembers.

The MIM requires the investigator to focus on the task of interviewing the eyewitness in a non-judgmental fashion which resonates with the UK Home Office guidelines that suggest the investigator should begin the interview with "an open mind" to ensure the best practice is used to enhance the reliability of the statements received (Milne & Bull, 2008). On the other hand, the *Approach* presents the investigator with strategies to conduct interviews and interrogations to confront suspects. This pre-interview mindset of interviewing a potential suspect can result in less effective interviewing techniques when interviewing cooperative eyewitnesses. These negative perceptions may resonate throughout the interview session and lessen any rapport-building efforts.

As Milne and Bull (2008) describe the GEMAC process for building rapport, they remind the investigator to be mindful of the interviewee's personal space and advise the reader of earlier police interrogations where this tactic of invading personal space was used to "create pressure in the interview room" (p. 66). While the intersection between interviewing an eyewitness and interrogating a suspect may be dubious for some investigators, it may be undeniable in maintaining the integrity of the investigation. In MIM we are mindful that we are speaking with an eyewitness who observed something, and we are relying on their recollection to gather the most reliable cognitive evidence. There is no question that if the eyewitness is unreliable, it may be because of other factors other than being responsible for the crime. More importantly, even before starting the interview session, if the eyewitness does not answer the *Qualifying Question* in an affirmative fashion, the interviewer is expected to consider the COR response and ask another question (or two) to confirm their lack of confidence.

PREPARING FOR A CERTAIN TYPE OF INTERVIEW

The PEACE framework (1992) suggests to investigators that they should conduct their interviews in a fashion that should bring them more information, and that they do this by following a specific set of guidelines to ensure completeness. For example, when we hear that the suspect is described as violent and aggressive in the robbery, biased investigators may assume certain characteristics about the suspect's face that may not be present in the eyewitness's statements. Facial hair, certain build, language used in demanding property, etc., may invade the interviewer's mind and create an expectation to hear some of these details from the cooperative eyewitness (victim). Unfortunately, the PEACE framework can find investigators following a linear model that anticipates challenging the recollection of the eyewitness about events when the investigator may not be satisfied with their answers.

There is no doubt that the *Approach* offers the investigator a library full of interview strategies like Achieving Best Evidence (ABE), GEMAC, and PEACE to use in conversations with a person who may or may not be involved with a crime. These approaches offer the investigator many options to consider when conducting the eyewitness interview; however, they all seem to have a component that often shifts to confronting the suspect. We can assume most investigators are above-average conversationalists and are comfortable speaking with unknown persons who have suffered a life-changing event. We also know there is limited training for the average officer about the knowledge base to handle "difficult conversations" (Shepherd & Griffiths, 2013). Still, law enforcement personnel are often given the benefit of the doubt by citizens and potential eyewitnesses as they take on the roles of protector and problem-solver. If we begin to offer all future investigators mindfulness strategies to embrace and add to their inquisitive nature, we have an opportunity to develop more empiricists who can distinguish between a cooperative eyewitness and a potential suspect that needs to be interrogated.

EMBRACING THE POSITIVES

In this chapter we identified portions of the CI technique and the CMA that are similar and significantly different from the MIM procedure. The ambiguity from both the *CI* and the *Approach* surrounding the detection of whether you are interviewing an eyewitness or a potential suspect is complicated when the investigator has not been properly trained. In the next chapter, we discuss the training associated with interviewing cooperative eyewitnesses and consider the lack of adoption by agencies that were either selected or sought to implement the advanced instruction only to find their officers' proficiency unacceptable. There is too much discretion in both the *CI* and the *Approach* about how the investigator should consider perceived conditions of deception when in fact the eyewitness may be unable to recall enough details accurately to satisfy the investigator's expectations. In both interview techniques, there is no consideration for these outcomes, and it leaves the investigator with the impression that the eyewitness will (and should) be able to recall every detail because of the interview technique used. The Mindful Interview Method considers the fact that the eyewitness may not have seen enough of the suspect's face to remember specific details, so we ask them the Qualifying Question to gauge their confidence and evaluate their COR. If they are unable to remember details of the suspect (without suggestive questions by the interviewer) then we do not continue the interview.

FOR YOUR CONSIDERATION

- The MIM is similar to the CI technique in the attention to professionalism and how the investigator may influence the eyewitness by their demeanor and level of interaction.

- The MIM is similar to the *Approach* as both profess being mindful of how questions can affect eyewitness statements.
- Both the CI technique and the *Approach* caution the investigator to consider the eyewitness misleading at times which creates issues for maintaining rapport and relying on the credibility of eyewitness statements.
- One major distinction between the Mindful Interview Method and both the Cognitive Interview and the Conversation Management Approach is that an interview will not proceed when the eyewitness cannot recall details about the suspect or the crime event.

13
Eyewitness Interview Training

One sees great things from the valley, only small things from the peak.

G.K. Chesterton

According to the FBI's Uniform Crime Reporting (UCR) Program, in 2019 there were over 1.2 million violent crimes in the US. These crimes ranged from murder, assault with a deadly weapon, to rape and robbery. We know that there are over 18,000 law enforcement agencies in the US, and not all of them report to UCR because not all of them have agencies large enough to conduct in-depth investigations or have crimes listed in the UCR. Many of these agencies have fewer than 25 officers, and sometimes they are the patrol officer and lead investigator on the case. When they aren't investigating violent crime, they are interviewing eyewitnesses about property crimes, which accounted for more than 6.9 million crimes in 2019 (see Figure 13.1). That's at least 8 million eyewitnesses being interviewed about violent and non-violent crimes every year. In 2009, the rate of robbery cases reported in the US was 133.1 per 100,000 people, compared to 81.8 per 100,000 people in 2019, *Trend of Violent Crime from 2009 to 2019* (FBI, 2019). I chose the FBI UCR for 2019 because it was the last year before the pandemic, and these numbers were representative of what I had experienced as a sworn police officer and police artist from 1985 to 2011. The fact that so many eyewitness interviews are being conducted may not surprise most people; however, what is revealing is the lack of dedicated instruction focused on eyewitness interviews. The inadequacy of eyewitness interview instruction may be due to the impression of administrators that interviewing someone should be pretty easy to master.

Research about the confidence of law enforcement professionals in interviewing eyewitnesses says a lot about their own idea of proficiency. Walsh and Bull (2013) "found that almost all untrained investigators believed that they were already skilled at interviewing" (p. 45). I found that to be true when I trained veteran investigators on the Cognitive Interview (CI) technique to interview victims of sexual assault. Many of the investigators were highly professional in their approach to the interview, but many more resorted to tactics that would not be conducive to gathering reliable evidence. In fact, many investigators would latch on to certain details of the narrative recall by the eyewitness and would interrupt them several times to focus on salient characteristics of the suspect instead of allowing the narrative to take its course. The overconfidence in interrupting the interview was

THE MINDFUL INTERVIEW METHOD

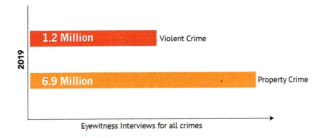

Figure 13.1 Crime reported by the FBI in 2019. Source: FBI's Uniform Crime Reporting (UCR) Program.

practiced time and time again, and in each instance I had to pause the interview and offer them strategies to be more mindful and listen and allow the eyewitness to recall more information. Persuading experienced patrol officers to change their ways can be a daunting task when they know their interviews are never scrutinized. With every crime report they turn in without evaluation, it creates a false sense of exceptionalism about securing reliable statements. Prosecutors or investigators brought in to complete the investigation know too well the paucity of credible information from these reports which creates more work and additional re-interviews that may frustrate potential eyewitnesses and reflect negatively on the initial investigation.

EYEWITNESS INTERVIEW TRAINING

When you consider the amount of law enforcement training available at the California Commission on Peace Officers Standards and Training (POST) and the New York State Standards and Compliance Verification Manual (NY Standards and Compliance), you might expect an abundance of instruction on conducting eyewitness interviews (see Table 13.1). These certifying bodies offer police officer training for two states that employ nearly 21% of all police officers in the country, of which, in 2020, there were 79,000 in California and 58,000 in New York (FBIa, 2020). While you won't find eyewitness interview training at the top of the list of courses offered at these agencies, you do find the instruction is focused on procedural duties and certain methodologies related to investigations and patrol. When you search the NY Standards and Compliance website for the topic of eyewitness interviews, you see there is no specific mention of eyewitness interviews; however, we do find "interviews and interrogations" under the Criminal Investigations section 50.1(C).

The POST offers some courses that brush up against the topic of eyewitness interviewing and are hyper-focused on specific types of cases like child abuse or sexual assault, which are very important. A recent review of amendments, for this book, in the POST Learning Domains found only nine mentions for the words, interview, interviews, interviewing, and questioning in the following topics: Child Abuse Reports, Sex Crimes,

Table 13.1 Eyewitness Interview Training Course at CA POST, NYSSCV, and Government Training Agency

State Training Agency for Law Enforcement	Eyewitness Interview-Specific Training?	Information Related to Eyewitnesses or Interviews
California Police Officers Standards and Training (POST)	None	Some interview training for special cases like Child Abuse, Sex Crimes, Disputes, Crime Scene, and Hate Crimes
New York State Standards and Compliance Verification Manual (NYSSCVM)	None	Offer guidance to agencies to establish guidelines that specify the elements to be included in the report.
Government Training Agency (GTA)	None	Some interview training for special cases like Sexual Assault, Domestic Violence, Specialty topics, and Dispatchers. From 2016 through 2021: 53 DV, 30 SA, 83 SP, and dispatchers: 13 DV, 8 SA, 4: SP.

Courses were searched based on the keywords "eyewitness interview training" July 2022.

Disputes, Crime Scene, and Hate Crimes. The amendments are basically updating certain regulation changes approved by the Office of Administrative Law for POST and become the latest version of the training standards offered to all California law enforcement personnel.

The POST learning domains discuss aspects of interviewing eyewitnesses in non-specific sections that are usually part of an overall framework for engaging with a particular eyewitness. The workbook learning activities are armed with excellent examples of victims needing officers to employ empathetic strategies that are mindful of the circumstances. They encourage officers to ask more open-ended questions, and address the issue with genuine concern and attention to identifying the suspect. Finally, the POST Glossary for Victimology/Crisis Intervention is very useful for promoting a more mindful eyewitness interview with tasks like active listening, empathy, and sympathy which are included alongside more specific terms related to defining the victim. Many of the core principles for interviewing an eyewitness mindfully are presented in various portions of the instruction; however, a standalone comprehensive course for conducting eyewitness interviews is not offered in their course catalog.

The Government Training Agency website (https://www.govtraining.com) which offers training to law enforcement across California and is based in San Diego, offers open-source access to their courses but does not provide their syllabus or course materials for review. Like POST and NY Standards and Compliance, there were no specific courses listed for eyewitness interviews. Their course offerings were focused on offering supplemental instruction to the investigator for interviewing an eyewitness who may have witnessed a crime event instead of being an actual victim of a crime. These topics

THE MINDFUL INTERVIEW METHOD

Table 13.2 List of Prominent Police Academy Agencies in California

Police Academy	Response for course materials request?
Alameda County Sheriffs' Office: Police Academy	No reply
California Highway Patrol: Personnel and Training Division	No reply
College of the Siskiyous: Police Academy	No reply
College of the Redwoods: Administration of Justice	No reply
Contra Costa County Sheriff: Police Academy	No reply
Fresno City College: Police Academy	No reply
McClellan Public Safety Center: Police Academy	No reply
Napa Valley College: Criminal Justice Training Center	No reply
Oakland Police Academy	No reply
Sacramento Police	No reply
San Diego Miramar College: Administration of Justice	No reply
San Francisco Police Academy	No reply
San Joaquin Delta College	No reply
The Academy: South Bay Regional Public Safety Training Consortium	No reply
Yuba College: Administration of Justice	No reply

In December of 2021 I sent out emails and letters to each police academy agency listed with the introduction: "I am currently conducting research on the learning domains of various police academies in the country. My research focuses on Eyewitness Interviews and how they are presented to law enforcement personnel."

are important and should be considered when training law enforcement personnel on conducting these interviews, but without access to the syllabus, we have no idea whether they offered foundational knowledge for eyewitness memory and how their interactions may influence statements. In preparation for this book I sent letters to 15 agencies that were listed as police academies in California (see Table 13.2). I asked them for their syllabus or any materials related to Eyewitness Interviews. In my letter I advised them of my research on learning more about how they instructed police personnel on interviewing eyewitnesses. The letters were sent in December 2021 and to date I have not received a reply from any of these agencies.

When we consider that in 2020 California had over 740 law enforcement agencies and New York over 595 agencies (FBIa, 2020), and none of them published any comprehensive training titles related to eyewitness interviewing practices, we can begin to understand why academics in the field of eyewitness memory are underwhelmed by the level of proficiency from law enforcement officers in interviewing eyewitnesses (see Table 13.3). In spite of eyewitness interview training a recent statute vetoed by California Governor Gavin Newsom directed POST to develop a communications course that will be available to

Table 13.3 The Five Largest Municipal and County Law Enforcement Agencies by Number of Full-Time Sworn Officers

Agency	Full-Time Sworn Personnel
New York City Police (NY)	36,563
Chicago Police (IL)	13,160
Los Angeles Police (CA)	10,002
Los Angeles County Sheriff (CA)	9,565
Philadelphia Police (PA)	6,584

Census of State and Local Law Enforcement Agencies, 2008, Bureau of Justice Statistics, Department of Justice, Office of Justice Programs, July 2011, NCJ 233982.

agencies across the state instead of making it mandatory. This gives agencies more flexibility on who can attend and when. Even so, this course is expected to be incorporated into the core courses of instruction for regular officers and investigators interested in "ethical science-based interviewing." It would be a specific course that officers would have to find in the POST catalog instead of taking it as part of their annual continuing professional training.

Nevertheless, the statute defined advanced interpersonal communications skills as the skills involved in establishing rapport, active listening, reflection, non-judgmental approaches, and empathy. They expect the officer to determine the communication style that is best to gather reliable statements and to adapt accordingly. They cautioned the investigator to seek the truth and offer the "best evidence in the interest of justice" (SB494, 2021). This directive to engage with the eyewitness in a more mindful way should make it easier for investigators to begin to accept more thoughtful and reliable tactics for interviewing eyewitnesses.

In the book *Investigative Interviewing, Psychology and Practice* (2000), authors Rebecca Milne and Ray Bull echo my sentiments about the lack of eyewitness interview training. They recognize, as I do, how important the eyewitness interview is to all investigations and found that "throughout the world police training in [eyewitness interviews] has been relatively minimal and such training for other professionals ... non-existent." In the paper titled *Interviewing Protocols to Improve Eyewitness Memory* (2007), Dr. Ronald Fisher and Dr. Nadja Schreiber of Florida International University offer their disappointment that, "not much has changed about police interviewing procedures." Before writing their paper, they conducted a survey with a local police agency in Florida and found that "police interviewing behaviors were disappointingly similar" to what they found 20 years ago.

FORENSIC ART AND EYEWITNESS INTERVIEW TRAINING

I recall the same lack of specific training for interviewing eyewitnesses when I think about my apprenticeship in becoming the police artist. Tom Macris was the San Jose police artist from 1978 to 1995, and part of his training to become the police artist involved traveling to New York and Los Angeles to learn from some of the storied names in the field of composite art: Frank Domingo from NYPD, and Fernando Ponce from LAPD. These forensic art pioneers were already aware of the intersection between law and psychology and did their best to filter through the maze of eyewitness memory research to enhance their sketch interviews. Frank Domingo posited that "it [was] necessary for the composite artist to balance common-sense practical experience with relevant theories about memory," as he wrote to fellow sketch artists about conducting composite sketch interviews (Taylor, 2001). The instruction Tom received from Ponce and Domingo was predominately done in an informal style of being an observer where there were no officially prepared instructional materials or dissemination of knowledge. When I asked Tom whether he thought he was prepared to conduct eyewitness interviews he said:

> Absolutely not! The idea had never crossed my mind. I wasn't even trained in basic police interview or interrogation principles beyond the basic academy level. My police experience at that time consisted of 3-1/2 years in patrol, 3-1/2 years in traffic motorcycle traffic enforcement duty and an overlapping year and a half or so with the riot control group. The specialty of doing police drawings with witnesses was presented to me due to my graphic support of teaching materials for advanced training programs.
>
> (T. Macris, personal communications, April 6, 2022)

Tom eventually trained with the FBI in 1984 and completed the first-ever composite art training course with Horace Heffner, developer of the program and lead instructor. I attended the same FBI course in 1993 and completed the Age Progression course at Quantico in 1994, a year before I was appointed the police artist.

When I arrived at the FBI to learn the art of composite sketching, I found myself singled out for conducting sketch interviews in what Horace referred to as "more advanced." Horace announced that I was from San Jose Police and that Tom and I were conducting our sketch interviews in a more advanced technique and that students should pick my brain for how we were creating our composite sketches. Several days into the training session, I began to realize the disconnect between accepted eyewitness memory research and the best practices for interviewing eyewitnesses by forensic artists. Days later I remember asking Horace why the FBI composite sketch system had not evolved (like we did) over the years and changed their interview methods to adopt the latest in human memory research. He said that they had to create a composite art system that could be utilized by all types of law enforcement agencies, and they had to consider the proficiency and experience of the police artist while adopting the relatability of the science about human memory. He added that the sophistication of eyewitness memory research at the time was not sufficient, in his opinion, to alter their guidance across the board to forensic artists.

I spent the remainder of my time during the composite art course working on mock sketch interviews and practicing parts of the CI technique that Tom and I adopted. The lack of concern for how we might be contaminating eyewitness memory in our interview process was never a major topic, and instead we focused on how similar our sketches resembled the target image. Even though I did my best to explain our interview technique to all of the composite artists in attendance, they all returned to their agencies utilizing the FBI model and never looked back. Seventeen years later I was still trying to convince new forensic art colleagues about the problematic nature of using reference images to stimulate eyewitness memory.

The limited opportunities for eyewitness interview training were inconsistent for me as an aspiring forensic artist in 1992. Sadly, it has not changed much since my entry into this field, and while we now have a well-established organization that offers certificates to forensic artists for attending workshops and certifications for composite imaging, postmortem reconstruction, and age progression, the disconnect between eyewitness memory research and how the discipline of forensic art performs eyewitness interviews remains unchanged (IAI, 2023). The same can be said for law enforcement personnel and their lack of specific training to conduct interviews with cooperative eyewitnesses.

EYEWITNESS INTERVIEW TRAINING IS OPTIONAL

Just as forensic artists should be trained in the best practices for interviewing eyewitnesses, so should *all* law enforcement personnel. Sadly, researchers have found "relatively little time is spent on explaining the scientific principles" of eyewitness memory nor participation in practical exercises to become familiar with the technique (Fisher & Schreiber, 2007). They suspect that the "quality of American police interviews may reflect the training they receive," and since they are not getting the basic eyewitness interview training at the academy or at the station, their access to this information is limited (Fisher & Schreiber, 2007). Interestingly, the FBI offers about 25 hours of interviewing cooperative eyewitnesses in its 17-week standard training program and relies on the CI technique to gather reliable statements from eyewitnesses (Fisher & Schreiber, 2007). In the UK, officers and civilian staff receive training on interviewing eyewitnesses based on their needs. There are five levels which are at least categorized instead of the enigmatic process US agencies offer their officers. The UK offers a Tier One basic course on eyewitness interviewing that all officers *must* attend. Tiers Two and Three are more like the US model where investigators are testing to join specific investigative bureaus and seek out more advanced eyewitness interview training to bolster their chances of being selected. Suspect interrogation is part of Tiers Four and Five and is more advisory – especially for major cases (Fisher & Schreiber, 2007). In my experience over the years, I have found lead investigators at Bay Area police agencies were often officers with advanced training in specific types of investigations. In the US the requirement for receiving basic eyewitness interview training that includes eyewitness memory research and practical exercises with formative assessments is rare to find.

WHY AREN'T ALL LAW ENFORCEMENT PERSONNEL RECEIVING EYEWITNESS INTERVIEW TRAINING?

The number of dedicated hours of training law enforcement personnel receive from the police academy (see Table 13.4) in interviewing eyewitnesses is almost non-existent. I can speak from experience in that I received only cursory instruction at the police academy (1986) and the field training program (1987), and none during annual continuing professional training mandated by the state.

Table 13.4 Partial List of US Law Enforcement Academies in 2016

Type of academy	Number	Percentage
Private	245	36
Municipal	132	19.9
2-year college	221	33.3
Sheriff	66	9.9

Source: BJS bulletin, July 2016, NCJ 249784.

According to the Bureau of Justice Statistics (2016) the average length of instruction in the classroom for police recruits was 843 hours per student.

- Municipal agencies: 936 hours.
- Sheriff: 706 hours.
- 2-year colleges: 882 hours.
- More than 80% of all agencies required some field training program after the academy with an average of another 521 hours of training.
- Municipal agencies: 71% offered Field Training Officer (FTO) program with additional 630 hours of training.
- Sheriffs' offices: 37% offered FTO program with additional 506 hours of training.
- 2-year college: 14% offered FTO program with additional 332 hours of training.

Major subject areas offered in certain sections for police academies were Operations, Weapons, Self-Improvement, and Legal Education (see Table 13.5). We can infer from the topics in Operations and Legal Education that there might be some instruction on conducting interviews with witnesses and victims. For instance, they cover topics like report writing, investigations, traffic accident investigations, criminal and constitutional law, traffic law, and juvenile justice law/procedures in legal education. On average, most

Table 13.5 Major Subject Areas Included in Basic Academy Training for State and Local Law Enforcement

Training Areas	Average Number of Hours Required per Recruit
Investigations	42
Ethics and Integrity	8
Communications	15
Sexual Assault[a]	6
Crimes Against Children[a]	6
Victim Response[a]	5

[a] Special topics were offered at certain academies: 92% for Sexual Assault, 90% for Crimes Against Children, and 80% for Victim Response. BJS Bulletin, July 2016, NCJ 249784.

police academies allotted 42 hours for investigations and 53 hours for legal education. The Bureau of Justice Statistics (BJS) report highlighted many police academies that offered special topics related to domestic violence, mental illness, sexual assault, crimes against children, gangs, victim response, and others. The special topic most offered was domestic violence, with 98% of academies offering the topic (13 hours of instruction), while victim response was offered at 80% of the academies (five hours of instruction). There were no reality-based mock scenarios of interviewing eyewitnesses offered at any of the police academies based on this report.

LACK OF UNDERSTANDING

Even though many officers are trained in advanced interview techniques, many do not retain the information or understand the acquisition and retrieval process involved when interviewing an eyewitness. I remember completing a sketch interview for a sexual assault several years back, and as the eyewitness and I walked out of my office the detective on the case met us outside. I said my goodbyes to the victim and left her with him, and as I turned to walk back to my office, I could hear him ask the eyewitness, "Does he look like that? Was his hair that style? Did he have a mustache?" (The sketch showed only stubble, not a full mustache.) I walked back and politely advised the investigator that the sketch represented the results of the interview and that the eyewitness had confirmed *every* feature as being like the suspect. I could see the eyewitness becoming uneasy (as if they had done something wrong); it was unprofessional of the detective and demonstrated his bias for the suspect description. It was as if *he* didn't understand the sketch interview process. I invited him to sit in on my next interview session so he could experience the interview himself and understand how I gathered the information for the sketch, but he did not take me up on my offer. Many investigators and patrol officers believe that they *know* what they *need* to identify the culprit, and they *expect* the eyewitness to *deliver* the answer, as if it's there in their eyewitness's mind and they just don't know they have it (the answer).

To draw an analogy, it would be like the CSI technician going to a crime scene and insisting that there should be a fingerprint on the backdoor because that's where burglars enter homes. Since the CSI technician in this example has a biased perspective, they neglect all other possibilities and resort to finding what they believe is a partial fingerprint on the backdoor, not realizing that it was their *own* fingerprint left there when they opened the back door. At the risk of being too simplistic, most interviewers are under the impression that they know what happened before meeting with the eyewitness and rely on them to be a vehicle for solving the case. It's this type of mindset that hinders many eyewitness interviews.

Police officers, dispatchers, and law professionals should understand that to ensure the reliability of eyewitness information they must acknowledge certain truths:

- Eyewitnesses may not know everything about the crime.
- Eyewitnesses may have not seen every detail.
- Eyewitnesses may have not been focused on the face of the suspect.

- Eyewitnesses may have not been aware of the danger.
And
- Eyewitnesses are willing to answer your questions to help you find the suspect.

These facts must be top of mind before eyewitness interviews are considered. Even so, the reality for most eyewitness interviews is that minimal reliable information will be retrieved. and the investigator will struggle to find enough information to identify the suspect. Many crimes go unsolved as we see from the 50% clearance rate for most police agencies in the US, as reported by the Marshal Project, https://www.themarshallproject.org/2022/01/12/as-murders-spiked-police-solved-about-half-in-2020. The clearance rates in 2020 were lower for other crimes: Rape: 30%; Assault: 47%; Robbery: 27%; Burglary 14%; Theft: 15%. The data is based on FBI's UCR program which covers all Part I offenses (except arson). Nevertheless, many investigators will rely on physical evidence at the scene, scientific processes to lead them to identify the suspect, and/or use of corroborating statements from eyewitnesses to confirm the presence of the suspect.

SUPPLEMENTAL TRAINING FOR CERTAIN OFFICERS

From 2000 to 2017, I was part of a team of experienced investigators who trained police officers throughout the state of California on the *memory-enhancing techniques* of the CI (Fisher & Geiselman, 1992). The interview and interrogation workshops were intense, and our instruction included some of the best actors who gave the attendees an authentic interview experience. I thoroughly enjoyed coaching these actors (eyewitnesses) in challenging the empathetic strategies of the officers. Many of these officers attending the workshop were preparing to join their detective bureaus or add more training for their collateral duties as patrol officers. I was given a lot of latitude by the administrators of the program to offer my unique perspective on applying the CI technique because of my experience as a forensic artist. I spent most of my time in these sessions explaining to the officers that rapport was not just a portion of the interview session but should be considered throughout the entire interview. Because I knew how important it was, I would often suggest to the officers that they should treat the eyewitness like a family member in order to find that empathy inside of them.

As Fisher and Schreiber (2007) noted, learning to employ the CI properly will improve the information retrieved from eyewitness interview sessions and they challenge US law enforcement agencies to keep "pace" with their "theoretical advances in psychology of memory" and make sure more officers have the opportunity to learn this technique (p. 57, pr. 2). In our workshop, many times, officers were successful in gathering all the pertinent statements from the eyewitness during the mock interviews, but sometimes we would run into difficulties that found officers reverting to their standard question-and-answer routines. We had limited time to run through the major phases of the CI, so we often focused on the narrative and reverse-order sections to enhance the actor's engagement. What I learned from these training sessions is that many of the detectives I worked with wanted to learn, and they wanted to employ this new way of interviewing people. They knew this type of interaction could be used to gather reliable information, and that it might lead to quality crime reports and result in the arrests of legitimate suspects.

The advanced training group I was a part of was only one of many throughout California that were highly regarded and established like Third Degree Communications, a Bay Area company that provides comprehensive in-person and online police training courses related to eyewitness interviewing and interrogation. While many of these classes were not specifically labeled "eyewitness interview," we can infer from the topics that they involved some instruction about interviewing victims of certain crimes (see Table 13.6). Out of the 15 groups listed, only one offered specific eyewitness interview considerations. The others focused on a blended approach that left open the possibility that the eyewitness might be withholding information and thus be treated as a suspect. All these accomplished courses had one thing in common though; they were all supported by dedicated and well-experienced practitioners in the field of interviewing. While we can assume that many law enforcement personnel are attending these courses, we may wonder why the interview strategies and principles for gathering reliable cognitive evidence may not be taking hold.

SCRUTINIZING EYEWITNESS INTERVIEWS

Walsh and Bull (2013) found UK officers who participated in these interview training programs "enabled a culture change [among investigators] so that unethical practices" were found to be non-existent in the recorded interviews they observed. When law enforcement agencies decide to scrutinize their eyewitness interview sessions, they will be able to identify generally accepted interview practices that may generate unreliable cognitive evidence. Because the PEACE models were instituted as universal training for all UK law enforcement, they received basic eyewitness interview instruction that was mindful of tactics that diminish reliability. They insisted on these interviews being recorded and all officers were instructed to adhere to the training principles. Menmon et al. (1994) conducted a study where they examined the effects of training experienced officers in the CI technique. Their study found that these officers did not maintain their level of proficiency for CI because of the "ingrained habits of the officers" and felt the CI training should be delivered over time in a phased approach with opportunities for self-reporting and reflection on their progress, including constructive feedback from their trainers. Criminal justice professionals, police officers, and dispatchers should receive foundational and theoretical knowledge at the university level to prepare them for any advanced training they receive later for advanced investigations. If they all receive the same basic instruction in eyewitness interviewing, they will be better prepared to conduct interviews with reporting parties and gather reliable information to assist their colleagues as they follow up to manage the case.

Walsh and Bull (2013) found that half of the investigators they surveyed in their study received minimal training in the PEACE model of interviewing, even though their 2008 study revealed investigators receiving advanced training improved their performance when compared to untrained investigators. It may be that the perceived benign task of asking an eyewitness what happened about a crime event may sound elementary to the

Table 13.6 List of Private Companies Offering Eyewitness Interview-Type Courses

Training Company	Eyewitness Interview Specific Course	Interview and Interrogations	Name of Course Referencing Interview
Argus Research Group	No	Yes	Trauma-Informed Incident Response & Interviewing
Behavioral Analysis Training Institute	No	Yes	Investigative Interview & Interrogation
Center for Innovation and Resources	No	Yes	Child Forensic Interviewing
College of Extended Learning	No	Yes	Fact Finding and Investigative Interviewing
eCornell	No	Yes	Employee Relations and Investigations
Forensic Interview Solutions	Yes	Yes	Cognitive Interviewing: Investigative Interviewing of Witnesses and Victims
Investigative Academy	No	Yes	Interviewing Skills for Investigators
Investigative Solutions Network	No	Yes	Investigative Interviewing
John E. Reid and Associates	No	Yes	Reid Technique for Patrol Officers. Interviewing and Interrogations for Investigators
Justice Institute of British Columbia	No	Yes	Introduction to Investigative Skills & Procedures
National Children's Advocacy Center	No	Yes	Forensic Interviewing of Children
Savage Training Group	No	Yes	Modern Interview and Interrogation Course
Third Degree Communications	No	Yes	Interview & Interrogation
Threat Assessment Group	No	Yes	Investigative Interviewing
Wicklander-Zulawski & Associates	No	Yes	Criminal Interview & Interrogation

Information was accessed in July 2022.

law enforcement administrator prioritizing training budgets, but the task of asking questions in a way that recovers the most reliable cognitive evidence is more complex and multi-faceted. Because our memories are not capturing events before us like video cameras which we can rewind and replay whenever we like, we have to rely on what we actually pay attention to. Because we can't pay attention to everything, we can only "remember some aspects of what is happening" and not everything in great detail (Genova, 2021). Every single person who intends to conduct any type of investigation should be trained in evidence-based techniques to gather cognitive evidence. Anything less may result in biased interview techniques that may lead to misidentifications or unreliable information about an event.

We know there are many more eyewitness interviews being conducted every day than there are interrogations, and because they are happening every day, we should be more mindful of how we conduct them. In 2016 there were over 17 million victimizations reported to national surveyors in the US (Vera, 2022). Prioritizing the availability of educational training concerning eyewitness interviews for law enforcement personnel will go a long way to improving eyewitness statements documented in these crime reports.

FOR YOUR CONSIDERATION

- We should insist on comprehensive eyewitness interview training in our police academies.
- State certifying agencies should consider adding comprehensive eyewitness interview training to their annual perishable skills offerings.
- Since officers meet with citizens every day, why shouldn't they be trained in better communication?
- Just because we don't evaluate all of our eyewitness interviews doesn't mean they're done properly.

14
Measuring the Noise

Even if our efforts of attention seem for years to be producing no result,
one day a light that is in exact proportion to them will flood the soul.

Simone Weil

Do you ever stop and think that the way investigators interview eyewitnesses may not be the same as other investigators? You would expect that most investigators would adhere to certain national guidelines to ensure eyewitness statements were reliable and consistent no matter who interviewed them. In this chapter we'll see how measuring the types of questions asked in an interview can get us closer to learning why decisions were made to ask these types of questions; all we need to do is "measure [the] noise" to see whether investigators are adhering to the expected norm or not (Kahneman et al., 2021).

WE DIDN'T HEAR THE NOISE AT THE FORENSIC ART WORKSHOP

In 2010 I had the opportunity to speak to a large group of esteemed forensic artists from around the country at the annual International Association for Identification conference, held in Washington state. The workshop was called *Liberating Your Sketches* because I wanted to introduce my interview technique for creating composite sketches to the artists who all used reference images to create their sketches. In retrospect, I was embarking on an experiment that would bring me closer to understanding the differences in how forensic art interviews were managed to develop sketches. My method for the exercise involved an audio recording of an interview I had conducted a few years back. I included it in a slideshow with the original copy of the sketch on the last slide.

I asked the artists attending to keep only their drawing tools and their pad of paper in front of them. My hypothesis focused on whether sketch artists who listened to the audio recording and sketched along in response to my questions and the answers from the eyewitness, would result in sketches that looked similar to mine. I was taking a gamble that some artists would not go along or that others would struggle to complete the sketch within the timeframe of the class. Luckily everyone in the room went along and surprised themselves. Looking back on the workshop I can now say that I was measuring the *noise* in how the forensic artists developed their sketches.

All the forensic artists attending the workshop were experienced, and developed composite sketches using reference images to stimulate eyewitness memory or to refine and clarify details about the suspect's face. I, on the other hand, did not use reference images to conduct my interviews and relied only on eyewitness statements in response to my guided questions to produce the sketch. My recorded interview was the established norm, and I would be measuring how well these artists could adhere to the retrieval process I presented to them. Instead of having them interview an eyewitness that saw the same person, with their interview technique, they would have to acquiesce and follow along as I interviewed the one eyewitness and produced the one sketch for comparison.

I was convinced that if the sketch artists eliminated their suggestion tools (reference photos, leading questions, multiple choice questions, etc.) and focused on the process of gathering reliable cognitive evidence that it would result in sketches that offered a more consistent representation of eyewitness statements. As I prepared to start the audio recording, I asked the artists to put away their reference materials used to create their sketches. Some artists came prepared with their forensic sketch artist tools as they planned to attend other drawing classes and mock interview sessions later in the conference. The room filled with the chatter of how they had never completed a sketch interview without all their tools. I explained that they would be listening to an actual interview session I had conducted years ago and that their task would be to sketch along to the statements of the eyewitness. I had completed the original sketch interview session within 45 minutes and many of the sketch artists in the room were filled with anxiety at the prospect of having to complete the sketch in this time frame – many forensic artists often spend over 90 minutes on an average case. After the audio ended, I showed my sketch to the artists and many of them were surprised at the remarkable likeness in their sketches. When the artists were forced to adhere to a specific process for creating the composite sketch, without reference images, and mindful of eyewitness statements, their sketches were like all the sketches in the room. We had reduced the *noise* in their judgment to use reference images and all the questions associated with them to create a sketch that was more representative of what the eyewitness actually said versus how the sketch artists often shaped eyewitness statements.

SHADOW SKETCHING

I got the idea for asking the sketch artists to sketch along with the interview recording from my self-imposed training exercise during my apprenticeship as the police artist. Part of my training would be to sit nearby, with my sketch pad and pencil, as the police artist Tom Macris, would interview the witness about the crime; I would later call this training exercise *shadow sketching*. After each sketch interview we would compare my shadow sketch to Tom's sketch and critique it for proportions, overall shading, and resemblance to Tom's sketch. I realize now that when Tom and I were looking at my sketch we were not only looking for similarities, but the inconsistencies we did find were actually the *noise* in my interpretations of eyewitness statements.

MEASURING THE NOISE

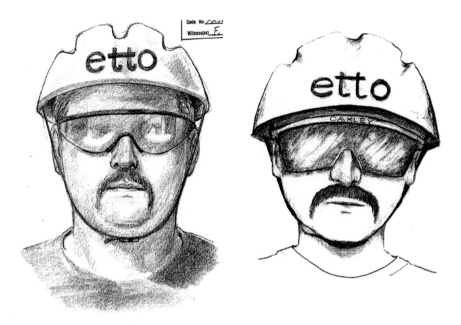

Figure 14.1 Shadow sketch comparison. Copy of sketch created by Tom Macris (left) next to *shadow sketch* made by Gil Zamora (right), August 1992 (same eyewitness interview session). Copyright © 1992, used with permission.

In Figure 14.1 we can see my shadow sketch (on the right) next to Tom's sketch and scrutinize the following differences: Overall proportions and age of subject are distinguishable, helmet is over-sized, glasses are larger and labeled, the nose is more distinctive, and the mustache is wider and darker. Even though the sketch on the right appears to be dissimilar we can accept that it may be of the same person, since that was my intention. The fact that the major differences in the sketches were about proportion and realistic quality and not about content means we can assume that my interpretive skills were acceptable. At this point of my apprenticeship, I had been sketching with Tom for about four months. Had my sketch not included a mustache we could have easily surmised that I was not paying attention to eyewitness statements.

We don't need to know the crime or the eyewitness to see the differences in the sketches. We can still learn a lot from comparing the sketch outcomes to determine whether there was consistency in how information was gathered. Each feature or item on both sketches confirms our perception of eyewitness statements. The quality of our renderings is a variable we can accept; however, any deviation from displaying features or items on the sketch would be problematic and would need to be corrected. Comparing the sketch outcomes can give us a lot of information about how each artist interpreted eyewitness statements and that interpretation can manifest as *noise* in their outcomes. Reviewing interview transcripts from eyewitness interviews would give us more insight into what questions were asked and how they responded so that we could see the deviations from the norm. We probably couldn't gather a room full of investigators and have them listen to an interview

I conducted and have them document the statements to see the differences in questioning and outcomes from the eyewitness. After all, I would be modeling the desired interview technique without actually learning how each investigator might have deviated from my process.

Instead, if we analyze a standard eyewitness interview session, we might be able to identify what Kahneman et al. described as a "systematic deviation and random scatter" [of] "bias and noise" (2021). We don't need to know the crime or the circumstances surrounding the investigator and the eyewitness. If we understand the investigative format, we can see how the investigator deviates from the norm and where we might consider adopting new strategies to bring about more reliable information. Any deviation from this norm will give us the information we need to refine the interview process and correct issues to ensure the best possible outcome for gathering reliable cognitive evidence. For example, when we review a transcript of a fictitious eyewitness interview session, we can read how the interviewer asked questions to gather certain information:

MEASURING NOISE EXCERPT [QUESTION TYPES IN BRACKETS]

[FC] Inv/Officer:	Was the suspect black or white?
EW:	I guess white …
[MLQ] Inv/Officer:	What about his age? 20–30?
EW:	Yeah, I think so …
[LQ] Inv/Officer:	Was he pretty athletic, like a runner?
EW:	I don't know if he was a runner, but he looked pretty strong.
[FC] Inv/Officer:	Was he bigger than me?
EW:	He might have been – he was in the driver's seat.

We can identify some *noise* in this interview excerpt by the type of questions asked by the officer. We can conclude that they were pretty sure of the ethnicity of the suspect when they gave the eyewitness a binary choice between "black or white," even though they could have just asked an open-ended question about the race. When the investigator asks about the age range, the eyewitness must infer from the choices offered that they could not deviate from the range – the eyewitness offers a demure response, and the officer does not acknowledge it. When the investigator decides to ask a force-choice question they create an "unwanted variability [in their] judgments" that can be revealed in a noise audit (Kahneman et al., 2021). In this case the investigator *primed* the eyewitness about the age of the suspect (question 2) even though the eyewitness may not have had a good idea about the age. We will never know what age the eyewitness would have chosen because they were never given the chance to offer their perception. The suggestion of an age range by the investigator gave System 1 of the eyewitness an opportunity to "make [the information] true" and accept the suggestion as their own memory (Kahneman et al., 2021). Finally, when the investigator asks whether the suspect is "bigger than me?" we don't get a true response for the size of the suspect – instead the eyewitness reminds the officer that the suspect was seated. These initial four lines of inquiry by the investigator can tell us a lot about their interview style and what they believe is important. They also show us the investigator is biased towards not offering open-ended questions, lack of attention to details from eyewitness statements, and a tendency to ask leading questions. In these four lines the investigator chose to ask two force-choice, one multiple-choice leading, and one leading question to start the interview. These questions produce *noise* for the investigation because they are biased, and the eyewitness responses are unreliable. The issue here is not about finding fault with the interview process, but to identify the operations in interview tactics that increase the *noise* and reduce the amount of reliable cognitive evidence that can be used to identify the culprit and solve the case.

STUDIES FOCUSED ON EYEWITNESS PERFORMANCE

The lack of empirical research studies that measure the effectiveness or performance of investigators interviewing eyewitnesses is concerning when compared to the many experimental studies that focus on the accuracy of eyewitnesses. In one meta-analysis that focused on the accuracy of information gathered from eyewitness interviews, they found the Cognitive Interview (CI) technique was successful in generating accurate information even though they also found the enhanced version of the CI technique also generated more incorrect information (Kohnken et al., 1999). These studies were focused on how well the mock eyewitnesses did on recalling information and ignored the questions asked by investigators. In another study by MacDonald et al. (2016) they examined whether there was a difference in how veteran law enforcement officers interviewed eyewitnesses after they received eyewitness interview training. The training involved teaching law enforcement officers the CI techniques by Fisher and Geiselman (1992), *Investigative Interviewing* by Milne and Bull (2008), practical investigative interviewing by the National Centre for Policing Excellence (2004), and Shepherd & Griffith's (2007) *Investigative Interviewing: The Conversation Management Approach*. The training introduced questions that were deemed appropriate or inappropriate to ask the eyewitness and are similar to the questions we focus on in this book (see Table 14.1). Our examination relies on interview transcripts that must be operationalized to measure the reliability of cognitive evidence.

MEASURING NOISE AND COGNITIVE EVIDENCE

In this book we accept the challenge of Kahneman, Sibony, and Sunstein, to generate *noise audits* to identify the different strategies used to gather cognitive evidence (2021). While we expect the experienced investigator will rely on their intuitive insight for the investigation their empiricism should be "informed, disciplined, and delayed" (Kahneman et al., 2021).

Table 14.1 Question Types That Were Deemed Appropriate or Inappropriate

Appropriate	Inappropriate
Probing	Leading
Open-ended	Force-choice
Closed Yes or No	Multiple-choice

When we break down the complex judgments of eyewitness interviews into a series of "mediated assessments" we can begin to evaluate each one independently and focus on the results (Kahneman et al., 2021). We can do this by identifying guidelines for asking questions and begin to see how much *noise* there really is in our eyewitness interviews. In other words, since we know that structuring our interview results in reliable cognitive evidence, we can decide to ask certain questions in a systematic way knowing full well we will be able to clarify and investigate further in a subsequent phase. When we agree to interview an eyewitness in a structured format, we can begin to develop diagnostic guidelines to evaluate outcomes and improve our process to enhance our cognitive evidence.

While Kahneman et al. (2021) remind us of the abundance of noise research in the medical field we can only expect that the criminal justice field will expand their empirical research to areas in police investigations and procedures. Law enforcement agencies rely on our patrol officers to make life-and-death decisions every day and they collect data on incidents more broadly to scrutinize training that is mandated for all officers. Police Strategies is a company that uses "Data Science to Drive Police Reform" and helps law enforcement agencies to scrutinize their policies and training programs to hold themselves accountable. Bob Scales, the owner of the company, frequently posts informative essays on social media outlets about the use of force or police accountability in the US. His data collection strategies are a clarion call for law enforcement administrators to share their "existing police incident reports to identify patterns and trends" to contrast the mainstream reporting on calls for justice reform. They currently offer their analysis to nine police agencies which utilize their data collection into web-based interactive dashboards that the public can review, you can view them all from their website at www.policestrategies.com.

Even so, data collection for less benign tasks, like how officers interview eyewitnesses, is non-existent. Even though we know the officer's documentation of eyewitness statements can turn into a life-changing event for an innocent person, we have no idea how these interviews might have relied on unreliable cognitive evidence until it is too late. The judgments made in asking certain questions, along with decisions not to employ memory-enhancing techniques, loom large for many cases – without proper evaluation these uninformed judgments may never be realized.

It turns out we can measure the noise without revealing the interviewer which may be important for law enforcement agencies concerned about alienating their personnel or identifying deficiencies in their specific training (Kahneman et al., 2021). Because our investigators are making judgments about when and how to ask certain questions based on the response of the eyewitness, we can focus on the exchange of information regardless of the accuracy of the eyewitness. Measuring the systematic deviation from these interviews will bring us closer to understanding the cognitive evidence gained from them.

PERFORMANCE FOCUSED ON THE INTERVIEWER, NOT THE EYEWITNESS

Most of the previous eyewitness interview studies concentrated on the accuracy of the eyewitness (mostly mock eyewitnesses from experiments) and how interviewing them with certain interview techniques resulted in more truthful answers. I have conducted eyewitness interviews with actual eyewitnesses to crimes, and I know that eyewitness memory is highly susceptible to manipulation and can result in unreliable information; that is why I ask my questions in a mindful way. Before I interview them, I have no idea whether the person is accurate or not, and my interview technique is not biased towards finding the eyewitness may be fabricating details of the event. I do know that asking the eyewitness certain questions can lead them to guessing the answer or offering information that was not in their memory. I also know that asking certain questions, in a certain cadence or structure, can confuse the eyewitness or have them recall less than they know. I know that when I am more mindful, I am more open to what is being said, and when I listen to the eyewitness intently, I can formulate questions that are pertinent to what they are saying and not focused on another topic. I understand how important the interview is for gathering reliable cognitive evidence; therefore I focus my practice on enhancing the process of gathering eyewitness statements.

In the next section we look at how I designed a diagnostic instrument to analyze my interview sessions to come up with a normative baseline for conducting mindful eyewitness interviews. I walk you through my data-gathering process and show you what I'm looking at when I measure the reliability of cognitive evidence. I use this diagnostic instrument to measure the reliability of cognitive evidence for all the interview sessions.

ANATOMY OF ESTABLISHING A BENCHMARK FOR A MINDFUL INTERVIEW

Before I could measure the reliability of cognitive evidence from eyewitness interview sessions, I had to examine my interview process and determine what was important in recovering statements from the eyewitness. One of the first areas I determined to be important was the topic areas consistent with credible eyewitness interviews. I determined that five topics were consistently accessed for routine eyewitness interviews where I was gathering evidence to identify the culprit (see Table 14.2). A total of 11 randomly selected forensic sketch interviews, from hundreds of video or audio recordings, were transcribed using traditional content analysis techniques and anonymized for this book (see Table 14.3). The small sample size was processed several times over a period of three months in the diagnostic instrument to check validity. All the sketch interviews were conducted in the Compositure® interview technique, which I developed in 1996. The Compositure®

Table 14.2 Routine Eyewitness Interview Topics

Topic	Description
1	Welcome, Introduction, Assessment
2	Suspect Description
3	Elements of Crime
4	Confirmation, Clarification, Review
5	Conclusion, Follow-up, Q&A

Table 14.3 List of Forensic Sketch Interviews for Benchmark

Crime Type	Year
Suspicious Person	2005
Indecent Exposure	2006
Indecent Exposure	2006
Suspicious Person	2010
Assault with Deadly Weapon	2012
Home Invasion	2013
Robbery	2013
Indecent Exposure	2017
Attempted Kidnapping	2018
Attempted Kidnapping	2019
Robbery	2019

technique was a technique I used from 1998 through 2012 and was the precursor to the *Mindful Interview Method* (MIM) established for this book.

Each interview transcript was analyzed in order to determine:

A. Topic inquiry.
B. Type of question or comment made by the interviewer.
C. Response, if any, made by the eyewitness.
D. Empathetic strategies used.

METHOD

My strategy was to come up with a baseline for my interview sessions – a self-evaluation – and focus on key performance indicators adhering to cognitive evidence. I had to gather the data from my interview sessions and look closely at how I inquired about each topic and interacted with the eyewitness after their response. Refer to Appendix C for all information related to creating the baseline index for forensic art eyewitness interviews.

I had practiced a version of my mindful interview technique for over 12 years with over 2,000 eyewitnesses, so I was very comfortable in documenting my process step by step. I had recited my process to several juries over the years when prosecutors asked me to describe my process. It was so simple that defense attorneys looking for suggestive practices were left wondering how I was able to create a sketch that looked so remarkable to their client. I always attributed my success to my practice of only retrieving the statements the eyewitness remembered – not altering or paraphrasing but using their words to imagine what the suspect looked like. In Chapter 10 we covered the principles behind the mindful interview that were the foundation for the interviews I conducted several hundred times every year since 1999. Those principles led to the MIM Standards I created for this book. The diagnostic elements I chose to collect data are based on those interview domains.

DATA COLLECTION FOR BENCHMARK

I had made copies of several hundred interview sessions for training purposes before I retired from the San Jose Police Department and then continued recording my interview sessions in audio format thereafter. I had never reviewed my sessions until I wrote this book. The majority of the interview sessions are over five years old, and when I selected the cases for this book, I chose a couple I had used in previous instructional sessions with law enforcement. The majority of the other cases were cases from other Bay Area agencies and were only audio recordings. I began recording the sessions initially to ensure credibility in my process and to memorialize others for my frequent court appearances. None of the recordings identified the witness, and other than an occasional case number I had no idea the date of the recordings. When I selected the recordings files, I chose one video (used in previous law enforcement training), and the remaining ten were audio recordings. Each of the cases was associated with a sketch I had completed for the investigation. I chose to use only some of the sketches for certain cases to demonstrate the reliability of the eyewitness to answer enough questions to create the sketch. Since I picked the cases at random, I had no idea about the length of time of the interviews, the crime type, the gender of the victim, or the agency. I only realized the specific agency once I located the sketch (see Appendix D for a complete list of all cases).

Each recording was transcribed by a trained stenographer who was instructed to use a template I created for each case study. The template was created in a word processing application where the first line listed Topic 1 and displayed numbers for every line of text anticipated (see Figure 14.2). The stenographer was instructed to use the designation INV for the interviewer, and EW for the eyewitness. When there were more than one in each group, they were instructed to number them (INV1, INV2; EW1, EW2). The stenographer completed each transcript, and I reviewed the final document for clarity of content.

In my first review of the 11 transcripts, I examined each line of questioning and assigned them a topic based on the questions and responses. I completed the review in one sitting and then moved on to another task. After a day or two, I reviewed the transcript again and coded another copy (Figure 14.3). I then compared each copy and resolved any differences in question coding. This final review would be the copy I would use to input data into the Forensic Art Index (see Table 14.4).

The Forensic Art Index Table established the standard deviation for this small sample size and identified the mean scores for each of the specific interview domains. The totals from the Forensic Art Index determined the parameters of the highest proficiency scores for each of the interview domains (Table 14.5). These parameters were used to create the Benchmark Scale table to measure the effects of the interview tactics on the cognitive evidence collected. The Benchmark Scale for interview domains in Table 14.6 covers the areas I believe are vital to ensuring the reliability of cognitive evidence.

I divided each column based on a Likert scale that focused on the acceptability of each interview domain aligned on the Y-axis. Each of the percentages was derived by taking

Eyewitness Interview Analysis (EIA)

TRANSCRIPT REVIEW - CRIMINAL, FORENSIC ARTIST

Topic 1

1. INV: Ok, the way this works is I'm going to ask you some general questions about the person's face and what I'd like you to do is go ahead and answer to the best of your knowledge.
2. EW: Ok.
3. INV: Most people don't remember everything in great detail...
4. EW: Yeah.
5. INV: but a lot of people do remember a lot of information when they're here and they're concentrating on the sketch. You're going to have your eyes closed for about 5 minutes and then I'm going to ask some questions about her face and then after I'll have you open your eyes, I'll have you tell me what happened, what you saw, and I'll show you the sketch and if we need to we'll some changes.

Figure 14.2 Sample Eyewitness Interview Analysis with a clean transcript. The transcript dialogue is entered into the EIA template for review. Partial sample is shown.

Eyewitness Interview Analysis (EIA)

TRANSCRIPT REVIEW - CRIMINAL, FORENSIC ARTIST
CSIO

Topic 1

1. *ARC* INV: Ok, the way this works is I'm going to ask you some general questions about the person's face and what I'd like you to do is go ahead and answer to the best of your knowledge.
2. EW: Ok.
3. *ARC* INV: Most people don't remember everything in great detail...
4. EW: Yeah.
5. *ARC* INV: but a lot of people do remember a lot of information when they're here and they're concentrating on the sketch. You're going to have your eyes closed for about 5 minutes and then I'm going to ask some questions about her face and then after I'll have you open your eyes, I'll have you tell me what happened, what you saw, and I'll show you the sketch and if we need to we'll some changes.

Figure 14.3 Sample Eyewitness Interview Analysis from the second review. The transcript is reviewed twice to determine the question type and eyewitness response. The total number of questions and responses were entered into the table for operationalizing questions to determine the baseline for a mindful interview. The sample shows coded marks and tally marks for entry into the forensic art index.

Table 14.4 Operationalizing Questions for Cognitive Evidence Reliability - Forensic art interview sessions; Percentages used to quantify each interview domain, confirmed March 25, 2023

	DRCE	SD	M	IRCE	SD	M	MR	SD	M	EWR	SD	M	T2	SD	M	T3	SD	M	TSQ	SD	M
CS3	4		10	68		10	61		10	20		50	51		84	91		88	60	0	2
CS4	4		10	55		34	62		49	24		50	88		81	98		70	0		2
CS6	8		2	76		9	83		9	50		-1	51		89	96		88	116	5	7
CS8	3		9	60		25	67		50	15		49	92		85	98		70	0		2
CS9	1		7	63		16	56		48	6		49	95		88	96		68	0		2
CS10	18		12	71		2	64		50	12		49	80		87	0		28	3		5
CS11	6		12	63		10	56		50	20		49	91		84	90		62	0		2
CS12	11		17	57		11	64		50	21		49	78		85	80		52	2		0
CS13	14		8	66		9	59		50	19		49	83		90	85		57	0		2
CS14	11		17	66		10	59		50	20		51	85		78	83		55	0		2
CS15	16		10	76		1	69		51	11		50	73		80	89		61	2		0
AVG.	9	6	10	66	7	64	12	10	15	50	1	50	85	7	86	81	28	64	1	2	2

DRCE: Diminish Reliability of Cognitive Evidence, IRCE: Improve Reliability of Cognitive Evidence, MR: Mindful Rapport, EWR: Eyewitness Responses, T2: Topic 2, T3: Topic 3, TSQ: Topic Sequence, SD: Standard Deviation, M: Mean.

Table 14.5 Acceptable Proficiency Scores for each domain – Confirmed March 25, 2023

DRCE	IRCE	MR	EWR	T2	T3	TSQ
10	65	14	50	86	73	2

Figures derived from eleven forensic art sketch interviews randomly selected. Proficiency ranges: The acceptable proficiency scores (APS) were derived by taking 50% of the average mean scores for each cognitive evidence domain. The proficiency range was based on the APS minus 50% of the (SD) for each level: APS - SD/2 = Acceptable Proficiency Score

Table 14.6 Proficiency Range for each interview domain - confirmed March 25, 2023

Cognitive Evidence Effect	More than Acceptable = 3	Acceptable = 2	Less than Acceptable = 1
Diminish Reliability (DRCE)	< 7%	7% - 10%	> 10%
Improve Reliability (IRCE)	> 61%	61% - 57%	< 57%
Mindful Rapport (MR)	> 9%	9% - 4%	< 4%
Eyewitness Response (EWR)	> 49%	49% - 48%	< 48%
Topic 2 (T2)	> 82%	82% - 78%	< 78%
Topic 3 (T3)	> 59%	59% - 45%	< 45%
Topic Sequence (TSQ)	< 1	1 - 2	> 2
Reliability of Cognitive Evidence scores	**Highly Reliable** 21 - 18	**Reliable** 17 - 14	**Less Than Reliable** 13 - 7

Mean scores derived from forensic art sketch interviews (n=11)

the maximum proficiency scores for each interview domain and subtracting that number by 50% of the standard deviation for each level. For example, the Diminish Reliability of Cognitive Evidence (DRCE) interview domain was calculated in this fashion: 10% (maximum proficiency level) – (SD/2) = 7% which is now the **More Than Acceptable** score of 3. The DRCE middle range increased by (SD/2); 7 + 3 = 10% to represent a range of 7–10% as the **Acceptable** range. The **Less Than Acceptable** percentage was set at >10%. I expect that this benchmark scale will change over time as more assessments are completed. Once the Forensic Art Index was set, I was able to establish a reliability score that focused on these seven areas (Table 14.6, Cognitive Evidence Effect row) that were important for a mindful interview. I then created the **Reliability of Cognitive Evidence** (RCE) scores after cycling all possible outcomes. The RCE range for measuring the effectiveness of the interview session is: **21–18: Highly Reliable; 17–14: Reliable; and 13–7: Less Than Reliable.** This RCE score will be an important factor when considering the effectiveness of the eyewitness interview session and give administrators reliable assessment tools to evaluate their interviewers. Since I was establishing the baseline using my eyewitness interviews, I realized that all my mindful sketch interviews had something in common: an evaluation of the Confidence of Recollection. Each of my interview sessions started with what I call an evaluation of Confidence of Recollection (COR) (I covered the mechanics for evaluating the COR in chapters 3 and 10). In this section of the book, I'll explain why I believe the confidence of the eyewitness should factor in the overall reliability score. The Reliability of Cognitive Evidence (RCE) score is made up of the seven domains of the mindful interview (DRCE, IRCE, MR, EWR, T2, T3, and TSQ. In examining other interview transcripts, I was able to track all these domains and categorize the questions. I soon realized that some of these interviews were being conducted with eyewitnesses that were reluctant to offer authentic recall when asked about a specific condition, and I had not considered that in the overall RCE. In order to capture these conditions, I created the Confidence of Recollection (COR) rating (see Table 14.7). The RCE now includes an evaluation of the confidence of the eyewitness before they begin the interview. If the transcript includes verbiage that signals the COR as being positive the rating will be "0." If the transcript does not include any verbiage about a COR, then an evaluation of topics 2 through 4 will be reviewed for unauthentic recollection statements, which may result in "-1" or "-2" (depending on the number of reluctant statements. The transcript will be marked with "COR" on statements that were deemed to be less confident about their answer. Please keep in mind that all the forensic sketch interviews offered for this book included a COR rating of "0."

Table 14.7 Confidence of Recollection (COR) evaluation

Qualifying Question	Eyewitness Response	Follow-up required?	Eyewitness Response	COR Rating
If you saw the suspect again, would you recognize them?	Yes	None. Post event information is limited.	N/A	0
If you saw the suspect again, would you recognize them?	Maybe	Yes. What do you remember? Post event information is limited.	Offers some information that allows the interviewer to imagine what the suspect looks like	-1
If you saw the suspect again, would you recognize them?	No	Yes. Can you tell me anything about the suspect?	No, I can't remember anything!	-2
Asks questions about the suspect or crime event	I don't remember, I don't know, …	Asks leading questions to clarify lack of details	Agrees with suggestion offered	-1 (15% – 25% of responses); -2 (over 25% of responses)

The Qualifying Question (QQ) should be asked either before the interview begins or within topic1. Some transcripts are unclear about whether a QQ was asked. In this case, any questions about the suspect or the crime event that result in the eyewitness offering less confident information or that inspire the interviewer to suggest post event information, within topics 2 thru 4, should result in a negative COR rating.

THE MINDFUL INTERVIEW METHOD

APPLYING THE EFFICACY OF EYEWITNESS INTERVIEW ASSESSMENT TO THE INTERVIEW SESSION

The diagram in Figure 14.4 shows the Efficacy of Eyewitness Interview Assessment (EEIA) process to evaluating interview transcripts and generate a reliability score that focuses on the effectiveness of retrieving eyewitness statements (cognitive evidence).

Now that the benchmark has been established for a mindful interview, we can measure the effectiveness of *any* eyewitness interview session by taking the following steps:

1. Obtain audio or video transcript of eyewitness interview.
2. Review transcript twice and assign each line of communication by labeling the topic, COR, and question type.
3. Enter data from the final transcript review into the Question Category matrix.
4. Confirm Topic Sequence.
5. Determine the Reliability of Cognitive Evidence score.
6. Review EEIA Summary Report and report on findings (if necessary).
7. Generate EEIA Narrative Report on project findings and make recommendations.

OBTAINING ACTUAL EYEWITNESS INTERVIEW TRANSCRIPTS FROM LAW ENFORCEMENT

We know that confidentiality is paramount in any criminal investigation; however, we also expect that law enforcement agencies will see the benefit of assessing their eyewitness interview sessions. By conducting these assessments, they can be assured their personnel

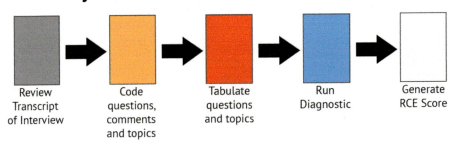

Figure 14.4 Efficacy of Eyewitness Interview Assessment Process. Efficacy of Eyewitness Interview Assessment was inspired by elements in the book, *Noise* by Kahneman, Sunstein, Sibony (2021).

are retrieving the most reliable cognitive evidence on a day-to-day basis. They can also be certain that the statements they collect from eyewitnesses will result in credible leads and more reliable apprehensions of suspects. Many departments in the US are now equipping their officers with body-worn cameras (BWC), and their policies for releasing video evidence vary from state to state.

While most departments have a policy that requires permission from the Chief of Police to release their video outside the department, even fewer agencies have a policy that offers clear guidance on when they can share the video evidence with other departments. According to the Brennan Center for Justice at the New York University of Law, the policies that affect when officers must record using their BWC is varied and focused on "adversarial encounters" likely resulting from potential criminal activity (2019). Yet, many of these encounters usually involve a reporting parting or witnesses that may have seen something before or during the criminal act. Departments may add to their list and encourage their officers to activate their BWC when they begin to interview an eyewitness about a crime. Retaining these interview recordings past the current retention policies can serve two purposes: 1) Assist officers in report writing in recalling specific details or statements made by the eyewitness about the event, and 2) Assist agencies in developing evidence-based eyewitness interview training that meets their specific needs. While these policies are directed at BWCs, many veteran officers already carry recording devices with them and have utilized similar devices for years. Many of the veteran officers I worked with on patrol carried a portable recording device and used them when they interviewed their witness or victim of a crime. We know that detectives utilize official hidden recording devices in their interview rooms to interview key witnesses and suspects about important investigations, and these recordings are later analyzed for reporting and case strategy sessions with investigators. If agencies decide to add eyewitness interview sessions to this list of when to activate BWCs, they can begin to collect valuable data and improve their collection of cognitive evidence.

Once the video or audio data is collected from the eyewitness interview session, the agency can anonymize the transcripts and have them available for evaluation. The anonymized transcripts should be delivered in secure password-protected devices or offered via electronic link to a secure cloud-based system. In either case, the recipient must be approved for analyzing the data in lieu of the assessment.

REVIEWING THE TRANSCRIPT AND CODING EXCHANGES

Once the transcripts are delivered, they will be evaluated for clarity and completeness. The transcript should be reviewed by an experienced interviewer from start to finish to determine whether the interview is complete and identify any omissions or anomalies present. It is important for the reviewer to locate where the interviewer establishes the Confidence of Recollection (COR) from the eyewitness about the suspect(s), and crime event. The Reliability of Cognitive Evidence (RCE) score *can* be affected if the eyewitness is not confident of their recollection. More importantly, the mindful interview should not continue if the eyewitness does not recall information about the suspect(s) or the crime event. If the eyewitness does not mention their confidence of recollection, then the reviewer must look for instances, throughout the transcript, that signal the eyewitness may not be comfortable in declaring their statements as being confident in their recall. Once the transcripts are reviewed for completeness the examination process begins.

The reviewer assigns topics (1 through 5), and every line is evaluated to determine the question type (coding). In this first examination, the reviewer should assign the question type based on their initial assessment and move through the interview session without hesitation. While some exchanges may involve some internal debate on the question type that most represents the line, the reviewer should be confident in assigning the question type knowing it will be reviewed another time. The review process should be conducted in a Portable Document Format (PDF) so that the original document is not altered and annotations can be retained for final processing. The second and final transcript review copy should be retained and labeled: TR_(case number or other identifying number) and stored in an electronic folder for cataloging and input into the Question Category matrix of the EEIA program.

ENTERING THE DATA INTO THE QUESTION CATEGORY MATRIX

Once the final transcript review is complete, the data from the interview session is entered into the Question Category matrix from the EEIA program. The Question Category matrix (Table 14.8) lists all 14 question types in the top row while all five topics are listed in the first column. The transcript is reviewed page by page, and tally marks are placed on the transcript PDF to signify the entry of the data. As the data is entered into the Question Category matrix, the units are tabulated and distributed throughout the EEIA into various tables and graphs for analysis.

The header row of the Question Category matrix includes every question type that was present in every one of the 11 forensic sketch interviews. The number of questions was eventually updated after reviewing the other five law enforcement cases for this book, and more question types were added to be more comprehensive. The question types used for the Efficacy of Eyewitness Interview Assessment are as follows:

- AQC – Administrative Question or Comment
- ACQ – Accusatory Comment or Question
- EC – Empathetic Comment
- FC – Force-choice question
- LQ – Leading Question
- MCQ – Multiple choice questions
- MP – Mirror Probe question
- MQ – Multiple questions
- MLQ – Multiple leading questions
- NR – Narrative review
- OEQ – Open-ended question
- PQ – Probing question
- PLQ – Probing leading question
- AL – Active listening

Table 14.8 Example of Question Category Matrix

Topic	AQC	ACQ	EC	FC	LQ	MCQ	MP	MQ	MLQ	NR	OEQ	PQ	PLQ	AL	Questions Only	Topic Totals	EWR
1	2		1								3	2		3	8	11	10
2	1						11				17	12		15	41	56	39
3	1						10				14	8		7	33	40	33
4	1									4	2	2		3	9	12	9
5	1		2							2	2	2		2	9	11	9
Totals	6	0	3	0	0	0	21	0	0	6	38	26	0	30	100	130	100

Question Category Matrix from Efficacy of Eyewitness Interview Assessment[SM]

The following questions or comments were included after non mindful interview transcripts were examined: Accusatory Comment or Question (ACQ), Multiple Leading Question (MLQ), Narrative Review (NR), and Probing Leading Question (PLQ).

CONFIRMING THE TOPIC SEQUENCE

Once the data is entered into the Question Category matrix, several tables are populated with important information that describes, in figures and graphs, the interaction between the interviewer and the eyewitness. For instance, the Topic Access section in Table 14.9 displays an accounting of every question related to each topic. It also lists the proportions of questions to eyewitness responses as they relate to the overall interview session. This is important information especially when you find a disturbing pattern in how certain topics are accessed more than others. When you conduct the EEIA bi-annually, you can begin to see a practice of how your personnel handle the retrieval of cognitive evidence.

Quantifying the access of topics by interviewers is important, but examining how they access these topics is also important. In Figure 14.5 we see an example of an eyewitness interview session where the topics were accessed in a peculiar fashion. We know that accessing information about the crime is important and that guiding the eyewitness to focus on a certain timeframe is always best to ensure they recall as much information as they can about a certain topic. When the investigator deviates from this strategy, they may jeopardize the collection of reliable information.

When we consider the number of questions per topic and how they were sequenced, we have a better idea of why something may have been missed or why the eyewitness may have responded in a certain way. For example, say the interviewer asked whether the suspect had facial hair at question number 26 (Figure 14.5), and the eyewitness described the fact that it was dark, and they couldn't see the face that well. The interviewer then shifts to the crime scene and asks whether there was any lighting nearby (Topic 3). The eyewitness replies that there was a light nearby, but it was dim and about 20 feet away. The

Table 14.9 Sample Topics Accessed per Interview

Topic	Questions per Topic	Questions per Interview	Eyewitness Responses	Responses per Interview
1	7	11%	9	13%
2	38	58%	38	54%
3	12	18%	15	21%
4	6	9%	6	9%
5	3	5%	2	3%
Total	66	Total	70	
Average Questions	13	Average Responses	14	

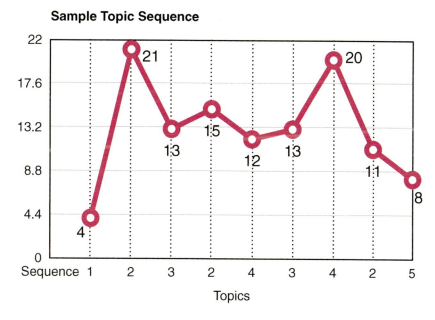

Figure 14.5 Sample topic sequence. The questions are tallied within the topic to give an illustration of how the questions were sequenced in the interview session.

interviewer continues down this line of questioning for another 13 questions only to come back to Topic 2 and ask about the suspect's eyes. In this example, we don't know whether this practice of disjointed questioning affected the eyewitness's recall of the face, but when we review the transcript we may see that the facial hair was not completely reviewed and important information was never recovered. Unfortunately, we may never know whether the eyewitness remembered more information about the face. We do know that because the interviewer changed topics before exhausting all questions related to that topic, they may have missed opportunities to retrieve a complete picture of the face.

Knowing whether your investigators are practicing this type of topic sequencing is important to understand should the reliability of their statements come into question. Understanding the potential negative impact on eyewitness statements when this topic sequence strategy is employed can allow the department to address this issue and employ better training concepts so that investigators are more confident in practicing a more structured format.

INTERPRETATION OF DATA AND THE RELIABILITY OF COGNITIVE EVIDENCE

After examining the Topic Access and Topic Sequence data, we turn our attention to the reliability of cognitive evidence. As I mentioned earlier in the chapter, I established benchmarks for each of the interview domains and categorized their proficiency as being

More Than Acceptable, **Acceptable**, or **Less Than Acceptable**. The scores from each of these interview domains, and the COR rating, are totaled to come up with the RCE score which informs us whether the information from the interview session is **Highly Reliable**, **Reliable**, or **Less Than Reliable**.

The proportion of questions that Diminish RCE or Improve RCE are key to the overall impact of the reliability of cognitive evidence. Many of these DRCE questions are biased and can be used to confuse the eyewitness. Many times, the responses to these questions give the investigator the impression the eyewitness may be less than truthful without considering that the question may have caused the unreliable information.

When we adhere to the MIM Standards, these types of questions are not used, and instead more mindful (IRCE) questions are asked. For example, in a MIM interview session, we might ask Force-Choice (FC) and Multiple-Choice Question (MCQ) inquiries in response to an open-ended question where the investigator asked about the suspect's clothing and the eyewitness responded with, "I think he wore a black or blue t-shirt with dark pants." The investigator would follow up with, "Was the shirt black or blue?" Even though this question is categorized as DRCE the effects of this question, asked at this particular time, will not significantly affect the reliability of the cognitive evidence gathered from this segment because the proportion overall is not significant. As we can see, anything less than 7% is More Than Acceptable in a mindful interview whereas anything more than 12% of DRCE questions would be Less Than Acceptable. As long as the investigator is mindful of the type of question they are asking, and why they are asking it, it can and should be considered.

SUMMARY REPORT FOR EFFICACY OF EYEWITNESS INTERVIEW ASSESSMENT

In addition to the narrative summary each interview session will include the EEIA[SM] Summary Report which highlights different aspects of the eyewitness interview session (see Figure 14.6). The summary report focuses on the data that affect the reliability of cognitive evidence. For instance, Section A lists the topic descriptions used throughout the transcript. Section B looks at the way the investigator proceeded through each topic and whether their sequence for questioning was reasonable and enhanced the recollection process. Section C looks at each topic and the number of questions asked by the interviewer along with the eyewitness responses. We expect the exchanges to be fairly even, so when they aren't we can begin to ask why and look at the type of questions asked in Section D. The type of questions asked is key to ensuring the reliability of cognitive evidence, and in this section we can see the distribution of Type I through Type IV questions that impact cognitive evidence. While we may not know why certain questions were asked, we can go back to the transcript and see what the eyewitness may have said to generate this line of questioning.

Since we are concerned with solving the crime, Section E reports on the number of Types III and IV questions used in inquiring about Topics 2 and 3. This section not only highlights the questions related to the suspect and the crime, but it also reports on whether

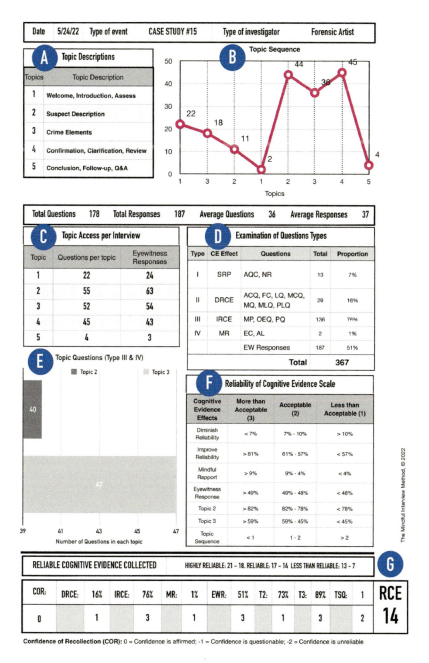

Figure 14.6 Example of Efficacy of Eyewitness Interview Assessment Summary Report.

the interviewer utilized questions that enhanced cognitive evidence. Finally, Section G reports on all of the diagnostic data collected to give us the RCE score. This RCE score tells us how well the interviewer did in gathering reliable cognitive evidence.

THE EFFICACY OF EYEWITNESS INTERVIEW ASSESSMENT SUMMARY REPORT AND MINDFUL INTERVIEW METHOD STANDARDS

While the EEIA relies on the transcript data to generate the RCE score, we can examine the effectiveness of the decision-making process for the investigator by referring to the MIM Standards to give us some insight into why certain elements were more mindful than others. For instance, we understand that establishing an empathetic strategy with the eyewitness early in the interview will build trust and result in more reliable information retrieved for the interview. The EEIA examines the interview exchanges between the eyewitness and the investigator, question types, and topics covered, to effectively measure the *noise* in the interview session in the Examination of Question types (Section D, Figure 14.6). While we may not identify questions as productive, risky, or non-productive (as the *Conversation Management Approach* does), we will insist that some questions are more mindful and lead to more reliable cognitive evidence from the eyewitness. Because each topic is presented separately, we can measure the level of engagement for each topic and advise investigators when they are not spending enough time on an important topic.

RELIABILITY SCALE CHANGES

We expect the RCE scale to change over time as we conduct more EEIA reports and include more types of cases. Nevertheless, we can begin to understand the effectiveness of our interview sessions and identify areas to develop better eyewitness interview training.

EFFICACY OF EYEWITNESS INTERVIEW ASSESSMENT NARRATIVE REPORT

The narrative report will be a comprehensive report on the entire assessment project and will define the parameters of the examination and report on findings. The report may include specific dialogue from the transcripts that highlight a more mindful interview experience, key moments when cognitive evidence was preserved, and strategies to consider when planning eyewitness interview curriculum training. The report will be a proposal defining the assessment procedures and ensuring the confidentiality of the documents accessed for evaluation. The narrative report should be generated at least 90 days after the final assessment is completed.

ASSESSING THE SYSTEM VARIABLES

When psychologists confronted the misidentification issue in relation to photo line-ups conducted by law enforcement personnel, they focused on reducing the ability for eyewitnesses to make erroneous selections of suspects from photo arrays. They focused on what Wells et al. (1998), called system variables that could be changed to improve the outcomes of these photo line-ups. When the Guide (1999) was published with recommendations on how to conduct eyewitness interviews, it also looked at the system variables agencies could alter to mitigate the misidentification phenomena. In each circumstance we see institutions urging first responders to change their ways to mitigate injustices on the citizenry because if we don't find a way to convince "law officers and others to adopt eyewitness reforms," we may end up losing the battle and find more cases of wrongful convictions that started with an eyewitness interview (Wise et al., 2014).

In the following chapters, we'll see the proficiency results of five cases (two internal affairs, two sketch interviews, and one mock interview) to distinguish the effectiveness of the MIM versus other contemporary law enforcement interview techniques. While we don't have information about the interview techniques used in three of the five cases (most agencies do not document the interview techniques used by their officers in their reports), we can still examine how the interviews were structured and evaluate the *noise* associated with them.

An EEIA summary report will be generated for each case study and offer the reader an important overview of the areas that affect the reliability of cognitive evidence. Each case study will delve into the particulars and provide an opportunity to understand how questions were asked and how they influenced eyewitness responses or degraded the cognitive evidence. Since the EEIA measures the deviation of the interview process for gathering reliable cognitive evidence, I imagined how that reliability score would fall on a target of proficiency. And just like the bull's eye figure in Kahneman's opening chapter of *Noise* (2021), we will illustrate how an interviewer may be on-target, biased, noisy, or both, at the end of each case study (see Figure 14.7).

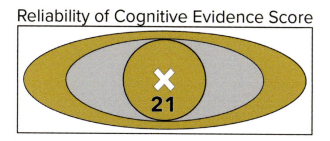

Figure 14.7 Reliability of Cognitive Evidence target, EEIA^SM, 2022; on target with RCE score of 21.

FOR YOUR CONSIDERATION

- The Efficacy of Eyewitness Interview Assessment[SM] (EEIA) will reveal interview tactics employed by the investigator in an objective manner.
- The EEIA[SM] should be applied to eyewitness interview transcripts to ensure reliability of the cognitive evidence retrieved from eyewitness interviews.
- When the EEIA[SM] is randomly applied annually it can reveal eyewitness interview practices that may or may not be adhering to policy.

Section VI
Analyzing Case Studies

In addition to providing the Efficacy of Eyewitness Interview Assessment (EEIA) Narrative and Summary Reports for each case study, I include additional insights (*in italics*) about the interview exchanges as they relate to a more mindful interview process. My *commentary* of the interview process is not part of the EEIA and is provided as bonus material for you to consider.

The EEIA offers the requesting agency an idea of whether their interviewer is adhering to their norms for interviewing important subjects. Any scrutiny about interview tactics used in these conversations is intended for educational purposes so that all interview practitioners can benefit from the analysis and discussion.

15
Case Study #1

LOOKING AT NOISE IN AN EYEWITNESS INTERVIEW

In 2021, a fascinating podcast called *On Our Watch* (Dirks & Lewis, 2021) featured investigative audio recordings of interviews that gave true crime audiences amazing access to interrogations that were centered on misconduct by law enforcement officers. In Chapter 8 we discussed how interviewing people mindfully would lead to gathering evidence with integrity instead of considering them deceitful and switching to a format of interrogation. The idea of conducting the interview with a suspicious mind is counterintuitive to a mindful interview session and so we ask practitioners to consider abandoning this option. When we can take advantage of a more mindful process for conducting interviews we can focus on the integrity of cognitive evidence. Because of the unprecedented access to these interviews, we can now assess the interview exchanges for these internal investigations and see how the effects of questioning affected the reliability of cognitive evidence. Because the interview is between internal affairs investigators and the accused officer, the demeanor of the investigators is much less confrontational, which is due to the legal protections officers have when being investigated for misconduct. Nevertheless, we can still view the retrieval of cognitive evidence from the officer (suspect) in an objective manner and evaluate the reliability of their statements using Efficacy of Eyewitness Interview Assessment (EEIA). The cognitive evidence in this case is the assessed officer's recollection of misconduct. The interviewer is probing Topic 3 to determine whether they can gather enough cognitive evidence to properly arrest the accused officer.

The excerpt we examine in this case study does not include questions about Topic 2 (Suspect Description) because they are interviewing the suspect, and so we included one administrative comment and response for that section to complete the analysis without error. In our analysis for this transcript, we look for conditions that may or may not deviate from a mindful interview process. Historically, most interrogations are somewhat confrontational, but because police officers have certain rights that investigators must abide by we don't see the same type of exchanges; nevertheless, because of the access to these interview transcripts we can evaluate the retrieval of cognitive evidence under this type of interview setting.

THE MINDFUL INTERVIEW METHOD

You should listen to the interview, beforehand, so you'll appreciate the production value of the story. The transcript is edited to focus on the exchanges between the investigator and the interviewees and so some portions were edited because of their length. See Appendix E for the complete EEIA and summary report.

CASE STUDY #1

You should refer to the glossary of evaluation terms for any annotation. As you read each case study, they will become easier to remember.

This transcript excerpt has been edited from the podcast episode called *Conduct Unbecoming*, (May 27, 2021, URL: https://www.npr.org/transcripts/1000175441). Complete transcripts were provided to the author for this book.

Topic 1

1.	INV:	Okay Officer McGrew, have you spoken to anyone besides your representative regarding the nature of this investigation?
2.	SUSP:	No.
3.	INV:	How long have you been employed as a peace officer with the California Highway Patrol?
4.	SUSP:	Over 13 years.
5.	INV:	Okay. And when did you first begin your training at the California Highway Patrol Academy?
6.	SUSP:	December of 2002.
7.	INV:	Okay. When did you graduate from the academy?
8.	SUSP:	June of 2003.
9.	INV:	Can you give us an explanation as to why you wanted a career in law enforcement?
10.	SUSP:	It was a good career. I wanted to help the public and have a good retirement, make a difference.
11.	INV:	Okay. Where have you been assigned since you've graduated from the CHP Academy?
12.	SUSP:	West Valley CHP.
13.	INV:	Okay. So for the duration of the 13 and a half years that you've indicated, you've been at West Valley the whole time?
14.	SUSP:	Yes.
15.	INV:	Okay. And what is your current assignment?
16.	SUSP:	At the West Valley Area? I was the VIN. VIN inspection officer.
17.	INV:	Okay. And is this considered a special duty position?
18.	SUSP:	Yes.
19.	INV:	How long have you been assigned to this position?

The investigator does a great job at asking open-ended questions. Had the investigator utilized some mirror probe (MP) queries the suspect might have offered more information later when he moved to

CASE STUDY #1

Topic 3. When we listen intently, we can engage the suspect to offer more information. For example, had the investigator asked a mirror probe at line 10 instead of moving right past the answer he might have revealed more information. 9. INV: Can you give us an explanation as to why you wanted a career in law enforcement? SUSP: It was a good career. I wanted to help the public and have a good retirement, make a difference; INV: Retirement? SUSP: Yeah, I figured I could work for 25 years and then retire and do something else. I've employed Mirror Probes for years and it works! When you apply it early in the interview, before reaching the point where you want them to elaborate, it can be very powerful and now the suspect/eyewitness is familiar with your questioning style.

Topic 1

20.	INV:	Okay. Please describe your duties and responsibilities as the West Valley Area VIN Officer?
21.	SUSP:	Primary duty is locating stolen vehicle components and verifying safety standards are met with the vehicles.
22.	INV:	Such as air bags and seat belts?
23.	SUSP:	Yes.
24.	INV:	Okay. And is there any part of the process that you do that has to do with verifying information through the Department of Motor Vehicles?
25.	SUSP:	Yes.
26.	INV:	Or CLETS?
27.	SUSP:	Yes.
28.	SUSP:	And what is that?
29.	SUSP:	Making sure the vehicle's not stolen, running vehicle components, mainly the VIN to make sure the vehicle's not stolen.
30.	INV:	Okay. As part of your duties, do you have any requirement to do any monthly or quarterly paperwork?
31.	SUSP:	Yes.
33.	INV:	And what does that entail?
33.	SUSP:	I do two forms for any blue tags that were issued, unnumbered blue tags as well as numbered blue tags.
34.	INV:	Do you know? I'm sorry ...
35.	SUSP:	I also complete a 136 form which is a vehicle, vehicles that were stolen or recovered in our area reported by our officers.
36.	INV:	Okay. And the two forms that you reference with regard to the blue tag, do you know what those form numbers are and what they're called?
37.	SUSP:	36 and number 97A.
38.	INV:	Okay.

At line 20 the investigator begins this section with a good open question. Instead of building on the suspect's answers and allowing him to elaborate further the investigator asks more than 50% closed-ended questions that encourage the suspect to reply with one-word answers. We can assume that the investigator wants to establish access to law enforcement databases that were used improperly, but instead of being patient and allowing the suspect to reveal that on his own he decides to lead the suspect with the information on lines 22, 24, and 26. A simple, "And what else?" or "What else?"

177

THE MINDFUL INTERVIEW METHOD

Could have encouraged the suspect to reveal more information. Unfortunately, this pattern of suggestions continues throughout this interview excerpt and the cognitive evidence retrieved becomes less reliable.

Topic 1

39. INV:	Okay.	
40. SUSP:	Then I make sure that they've already been to the DMV. And if they haven't been to the DMV, then I'll refer them to the DMV, and then I go about getting their name, phone number, year and make of the vehicle, and make sure they have the appropriate documentation.	
41. INV:	Okay. So then the information that you take from them, the information you just described, what do you then do with that information to keep track of who's coming and going for your appointments?	
42. SUSP:	I put it into a computer. Name and phone number.	
43. INV:	Okay.	
44. SUSP:	And the year of the vehicle and the make?	
45. INV:	Okay. And …	
46. SUSP:	In an appointment block to document what time their appointment is, day and time.	
47. INV:	And you indicate you put it into a computer. You're referring to Microsoft Outlook calendar where you keep track of your appointments there?	
48. SUSP:	Yes.	
49. INV:	Okay. And nobody besides you makes those entries? You're the only one that has access to that and keeps track of your own appointments and enters that information?	
50. SUSP:	Yes.	
51. INV:	Okay. So let's say a clerical person couldn't accept a phone call for you and has access to your calendar and schedules an appointment for you, you're responsible for scheduling your own appointments?	
52. SUSP:	Correct.	
53. INV:	Okay. With regard to the Microsoft Outlook program and your familiarity with it, when you enter an appointment in an … let's say an hour block of time just to allow for an appointment. There's the ability to classify each appointment, and by classify, I mean, it allows you to make it urgent, a low priority, follow-up, or personal. Can you explain how these appointments get classified by you?	
54. SUSP:	You're talking about changing the color in the block?	
55. INV:	Yes.	
56. SUSP:	Okay. I just, for me, I just selected green for a VIN appointment that was completed and there's no further follow-up to be done.	
57. INV:	Okay.	
58. SUSP:	I would use red for VIN appointments that did not show up and blue for blue tag.	
59. INV:	Okay.	

60.	SUSP:	And I think it was a salmon color, light orange, that was a VIN appointment that needed to be followed through. So if their air bag system wasn't working right or usually it's air bags. So if the air bag system wasn't working right, then they would have to come back after they fixed the air bag system …
61.	INV:	Uh-huh.
62.	SUSP:	…come back for a follow-up appointment, no appointment needed. I would write information on their copy of what they got from DMV and give it back to them, tell them that they needed to fix the air bag system at any … any place, bring back that documentation as well as calling first to make sure that I was there that day, that I didn't have court, that I wasn't at training, to make sure, talk to me and ask to make sure that I was there that day that they could come in and finish their appointment.
63.	INV:	Okay.
64.	INV2:	Can I ask a question real quick?
65.	INV:	Yes.
66.	INV2:	Green was just for a VIN inspection that went A-okay?
67.	SUSP:	Right.
68.	INV2:	Okay.
69.	INV:	So when I asked you that question, I listed four items that are attached to each one of the appointments. Do you use or were you the one who entered or classified those appointments under those headings or were those already a preset on the Microsoft program – you're using colors?
70.	SUSP:	They were preset in the Microsoft program.
71.	INV:	Okay.
72.	SUSP:	I just used the colors.
73.	INV:	Okay. So when somebody comes in for a VIN appointment, can you just explain the normal process for how you proceed with that appointment with the …
74.	SUSP:	To make a VIN appointment? Or …
75.	INV:	No – No. When somebody comes in for a VIN appointment. What's the normal process for you?
76.	SUSP:	I'll meet them at the front desk, make sure that they have the paperwork for the vehicle. If they don't have – I've had in the past they came in with no paperwork for the vehicle. So then I would tell them they had to return, bring in the paperwork, because when I made the appointment on the phone, I told them to bring driver's license, current valid California driver's license, DMV papers, the title, and anything else that they had paperwork for the vehicle as well as the vehicle itself.
77.	INV:	And with regard to other paperwork, are you talking receipts? Or …
78.	SUSP:	Right. If they don't have the title, then a Bill of Sale or receipts for components that were replaced, yes.
79.	INV:	Okay. And if they don't have the paperwork you've requested, what happens next?
80.	SUSP:	Then they would have to come back and reschedule, because it's not just a quick air bag system check. They would have to reschedule whenever my

		next free block was or if I had a cancellation the next day, then I could fit them in the next day.
81.	INV:	So if they didn't bring their required documents, you wouldn't be able to conduct the inspection properly?
82.	SUSP:	Correct. Because I need the DMV documents showing, you know, telling me the reason for the VIN inspection as well as the title to make sure that they have the title for the vehicle or a Bill of Sale or some type of ownership documentation for the vehicle.
83.	INV:	Okay. Are there times when your inspection takes place in the front parking lot versus in the auto bay in the back of the West Valley Area?
84.	SUSP:	Yes
85.	INV:	Okay. Can you describe what the difference is or what the circumstances are?
86.	SUSP:	Usually, if it's just an air bag re-inspection, I can complete that in the front parking lot. Motorcycles, I would usually do in the front parking lot, and pretty much I can't think of any exception. All of the other inspections would be completed in the back parking lot because I'm looking at confidential VIN locations and crawling underneath the vehicle so …
87.	INV:	Okay. So … when you're taking these people's documents, you don't make copies of everything that they bring necessarily? You said you make a copy of the title or the salvage certificate and their driver's license.
88.	SUSP:	Yes.
89.	INV:	The purpose of copying their driver's license on to the piece of paper is for what?
90.	SUSP:	Just if there's a later date when the vehicle does come back stolen, or I have just the documentation of the actual individual that brought the vehicle in.
91.	INV:	Okay. And as far as your records go with regard to your completed VIN appointments, how do you maintain your records and where do you keep those?
92.	SUSP:	The completed records were in a file cabinet above my desk.
93.	INV:	Okay. And how do you … how do you maintain those? Do you keep them in monthly folders together?
94.	SUSP:	Yes, monthly folders.
95.	INV:	In a chronological order? How you completed the inspection? Is that how you had them organized?
95.	SUSP:	Yes.
97.	INV:	Okay. Can you explain the reasons why a vehicle, outside of not having the paperwork, why a vehicle might be passed on an inspection as opposed to, I think refused is the terminology that's used if it's … if it doesn't pass that day or you can't sign off?
98.	SUSP:	Say that again.
99.	INV:	When you're conducting a VIN inspection, a vehicle either passes or fails? Essentially …
100.	SUSP:	Right.
101.	INV:	So, under the circumstances when a vehicle would fail, what are some of the reasons?

102.	SUSP:	Usually air bags. If they have multiple components that do not have VIN numbers, then I can refuse them and have them bring in receipts where they got those components from.
103.	INV:	Okay.
104.	SUSP:	Those are the two main reasons that I can think of ...
105.	INV:	And in your Microsoft Outlook calendar, do you make notes to yourself when somebody fails?
106.	SUSP:	Yes.
107.	INV:	What do you put there?
108.	SUSP:	Usually I'll block it red that they failed, indicating if I look at a weekly calendar, I can see fail, fail really quickly.
109.	INV:	Okay.
110.	SUSP:	And then I'll put usually the reason for it, air bag, you know, if it's a – if I turn them away, no paperwork.
111.	INV:	And ...
112.	SUSP:	Or if they're late to the appointment.
113.	INV:	Okay. Do you also make notes on the copied notes sheet that you referred to earlier with the title and their driver's license? Do you make notes on there as well as to what their ... the status of their appointment was?
114.	SUSP:	Yes.

In this segment the investigator is establishing the fact the suspect has control over the Microsoft Outlook program and that he is the only person that can make changes to the program. Instead of asking questions that will allow the suspect to elaborate on their own he asks more closed-ended questions that garner one-word responses from the suspect (questions 47, 51). At question #53 the investigator makes a statement about classifying appointments and then ends with asking the suspect how "these appointments get classified by you?" Once the suspect asks for clarification (#54) he begins to give a response that allows the investigator to employ active listening techniques in lines 55 through 68. At line #73 the investigator asks a very good Open-Ended Question (OEQ) even though he had to clarified once more. The suspect elaborates on his answer at line #76, but the investigator then follows up with a PLQ that asks about "receipts." The investigator continues down the path of the VIN inspection process and now asks about other situations instead of allowing the suspect to reveal it on his own with Mirror Probe Questions (MPs) and other OEQs. At line #81 he offers the suspect another reason for not conducting the inspection: The driver not bringing in "required documents." The investigator then insists the suspect said that "You said you make a copy of the title or the salvage certificate and their driver's (sic) license" at line #87 and the suspect responds with "Yes," even though he had not said that specific statement. Then at line #89 the investigator asks the suspect to explain the reason for "copying" their documents? At this point the suspect responds with a reason by saying in case the "vehicle does come back stolen" or at least a record of them coming in. The investigator then asks a very good OEQ at line #91, after the suspect answers that he keeps the files above his desk he asks MLQ with how he maintains them (again), but then leads the suspect by saying, "in monthly folders together?" Which the suspect then agrees at line #94. At line #97 he makes a confusing statement about how a vehicle might not pass inspection and then makes a more succinct inquiry at line #99 at which time the suspect then agrees by offering a one-word answer: "Right." The investigator does a better job of asking the same question at line #101 and the suspect responds with more information at line #102. After another leading question at line #105 the investigator asks an OEQ at line #107 and the suspect responds with more information. The investigator shows his active listening skills through line #111. Unfortunately, the investigator then refers to the previous suggestion about making copies of title and salvage documents at line #113 and mentions the suspect had said, "the copied sheet that you referred to earlier" and the suspect replies, "Yes."

There is an issue we must address in these transcripts and that is we do not have all of the information – which is obvious. But for those of you that may be building arguments for how questions were asked, keep this in mind: We are only concerned about preserving the cognitive evidence from the statements made by the suspect (in this case). Regardless of the strategies employed by the investigator (previous search warrants uncovered information; statements made by other witnesses; statements made by fellow colleagues, etc.) the information that these questions are retrieving can be deemed unreliable just because of the fact that these types of questions are known to elicit unreliable statements.

115. INV:	Okay. So once a vehicle does not pass, you give these individuals direction on what they need to do to satisfy the requirements for you to sign off your paperwork, their paperwork?
116. SUSP:	Yes.
117. INV:	Okay. During a VIN inspection, is it necessary or do you find yourself needing to question the person who brought the vehicle in about the vehicle or the components or the paperwork?
118. SUSP:	Sometimes, yes.
119. INV:	Okay. During a VIN inspection – I'm sorry. Why would you question them about what's the purpose of it if you have any question about it?
120. SUSP:	If they're missing NHTSA labels I would just ask them if that component was purchased from a salvage yard or if the NHTSA label is missing, if there was. they purchased it that way; just clarification.
121. INV:	Okay.

Topic 3

122. INV:	During a VIN inspection, does your conversation with members of the public ever deviate from the questions which are necessary to conduct the inspection?
123. SUSP:	Questions? Not at the beginning – no.
124. INV:	Okay. I'll repeat the question. During a VIN inspection, does your conversation with members of the public ever deviate from the questions which are necessary to complete the inspection?
125. SUSP:	Ever? Yes.
126. INV:	And can you elaborate on that?
127. SUSP:	The reason for this investigation, inappropriate comments.
128. INV:	And what do you mean by that?
129. SUSP:	Making comments to the public that don't have anything to do with the inspection.
130. INV:	Are you referring to a specific comment that you make? Or are you referring to a conversation that takes place? Or what specifically are you referring to when you say making inappropriate comments?
131. SUSP:	Conversations that have taken place in the past.

132. INV:	Okay.	
133. SUSP:	Some of the people that came in for VIN inspections.	
134. INV:	Is there anything that you specifically remember?	
135. SUSP:	Specifically, the last – the appointment that she complained, I was trying to explain to her that she had to get the air bag system fixed, she could either bring the vehicle back to the office or get a hotel room.	
136. INV:	Okay. So you had a VIN appointment with somebody. Do you remember when this was? The specific person you're just referring to?	
137. SUSP:	It was the beginning of (redacted).	
138. INV:	Do you remember this person's name?	
139. SUSP:	No.	
140. INV:	Was it a man or a woman?	
141. SUSP:	A woman.	
142. INV:	Okay. You explained that she needed to get her air bag system fixed, and you gave her two options it sounds like.	
143. SUSP:	No – I gave her one option, to fix the air bag system.	
144. INV:	Okay. But after the air bag system was fixed, you gave her two options as to what to do next. You said you can either come back for an inspection at the office? Yes?	
145. SUSP:	That I would complete the VIN inspection – that I would complete the air bag inspection either way, yes.	
146. INV:	Okay. So she needed to have an air bag system fixed, you meaning you weren't going to pass her like you had just previously described? You suggested to her that she come back for a re-inspection at the West Valley office?	
147. SUSP:	Yes.	
148. INV:	Okay. Which is normal for you, right? And then the other option you just said was to get a motel room?	
149. SUSP:	To get the air bag system fixed, yes.	
150. INV:	What do you …	
151. SUSP:	I mean, I could.	
152. INV:	I – what did you mean when you asked her – when you told – suggested to her to get a motel room? What does that mean?	
153. SUSP:	To be intimate.	
154. INV:	Did you tell her that?	
155. SUSP:	No.	
156. INV:	What did you tell her?	
157. SUSP:	What I said, to fix the air bag system and then either come back to the West Valley office or to get a motel room.	
158. INV:	Okay. So you were proposing to her a motel room for the purpose of having sexual relations with her?	
159. SUSP:	Yes.	
160. INV:	How long into this appointment did this conversation take?	
161. SUSP:	It was at the end of the appointment after I had completed the inspection.	
162. INV:	Okay. So when I asked you earlier does your conversation with members of the public ever deviate from questions which are necessary to complete the inspection, and you said yes, is this normal for you?	

163. SUSP:	No.	
164. INV:	Why did it happen that day?	
165. SUSP:	I don't know.	
166. INV:	Was is it something that she said to you that prompted you to ask her this?	
167. SUSP:	I had to … I think she didn't speak very good English, and I didn't – I was trying to explain to her what to do, and I kept explaining it to her, explaining it to her, and she didn't understand.	
168. INV:	Okay. Did she, in any way, infer that that's what she wanted – was to go to a motel room?	
169. SUSP:	Not to a motel room, no.	
170. INV:	Did she do anything to make it appear that she was attracted to you?	
171. SUSP:	I don't remember.	
172. INV:	Was this your idea? The motel room.	
173. SUSP:	Yes.	
174. INV:	Yes? That was a yes?	
175. SUSP:	Yes.	
176. INV:	When you suggested the motel room, did you suggest a time?	
177. SUSP:	No.	
178. INV:	Did you suggest a location?	
179. SUSP:	No.	
180. INV:	How, in your mind, did you anticipate that playing out?	
181. SUSP:	I didn't think she would understand me because she – I couldn't explain to her that she needed to get the air bag system fixed.	
182. INV:	You didn't think that she would understand the fact that you had asked her to a motel room?	
183. SUSP:	I didn't think she would understand.	
184. INV:	So if you didn't think she would understand what you were saying, why did you say it to begin with?	
185. SUSP:	I don't know.	
186. INV:	So if you asked this woman, who you'd only met that day for her VIN appointment, is that a yes?	
187. SUSP:	Yes.	
188. INV:	So you asked this woman that you only met that day if she wanted to go to a motel room with you to have sexual relations, how did you anticipate or expect that to work out? When was this going to happen?	
189. SUSP:	I didn't expect it to happen.	
190. INV:	Okay. Was it – you just expressed the intent of being intimate with her. So was there – did you have a plan in place?	
191. SUSP:	No.	
192. INV:	No?	
193. INV:	How many times has this happened?	
194. SUSP:	I don't know.	
195. INV:	More than once?	
196. SUSP:	Yes.	

CASE STUDY #1

197. INV:	Twice?
198. SUSP:	More than twice.
199. INV:	So since you've been a VIN officer, since (redacted) has this happened on numerous occasions during that period of time?
200. SUSP:	More than twice – I don't know how many times.
201. INV:	Ten?
202. SUSP:	I don't know.
203. INV:	20?
204. SUSP:	I don't know.
205. INV:	Is it possible that you've done this 20 times?
206. SUSP:	In two years, I don't – that – not 20.
207. INV:	How many?
208. SUSP:	I don't know – I'd have to – I don't – I don't know.
209. INV:	Has anybody, with regard to CHP employees ever been present when you've done this?
210. SUSP:	No
211. INV:	Does anybody know that you do this?
212. SUSP:	No
213. INV:	So you're the only one who's been there when this has occurred – along with the individual who's having the VIN inspection?
214. SUSP:	Yes.
215. INV:	So nobody else would know how many times this has occurred other than you?
216. SUSP:	Yes.
217. INV:	You've indicated you don't know how many times, but I'm going to – I'm going to ask you, how many times – and I'll give you time to think about it. How many times do you think that you have asked somebody to go to a motel during a VIN appointment?
218. SUSP:	REP: Okay. You're asking him for an estimation now or a guess? Because he stated that he can't remember. He said that it's more than two, but not more than 20.
219. INV:	Okay. Yes – so I'm asking for a clarifying number.
220. SUSP:	REP: Okay. If he can't remember an exact number, as we stated at the beginning of this, he's not supposed to speculate or guess, and he's narrowed it down from two to 20. So I don't know – if you don't want – if he's not to guess, how's he supposed to narrow it down more than that?
221. INV:	Given the fact that he's the only one who's been present at these appointments, I'm going to give him an opportunity to think about it and to think back as to how many times he thinks this has occurred. So it's somewhere between two and 20. Can you think back to any other specific occasions when this has occurred?
222. SUSP:	Not specific occasions – no.
223. INV:	Okay. Is there – you said it's happened twice?
224. SUSP:	More than twice.
225. INV:	Okay. Can you think of one other occasion when it's occurred?
226. SUSP:	Not specifically, no.

THE MINDFUL INTERVIEW METHOD

227.	INV:	Okay. The woman you were just talking about that you said you gave her the option of coming back to the office for the inspection or going to a motel room, who was with her that day?
228.	SUSP:	I think her son was with her.
229.	INV:	Her son? How old was her son?
230.	SUSP:	I don't remember.
231.	INV:	Was it an infant?
232.	SUSP:	I don't remember.
233.	INV:	Was this son a baby?
234.	SUSP:	No.
235.	INV:	Okay. So this was a child that was walking around with her, right?
236.	SUSP:	Yes.
237.	INV:	A child that presumably can carry on a conversation and understand what's being said?
238.	SUSP:	Yes.
239.	INV:	So did you make that comment to this woman in front of her son?
240.	SUSP:	No.
241.	INV:	Where was her son when you asked?
242.	SUSP:	He was outside of the car.
243.	INV:	And where were you when this happened?
244.	SUSP:	I was – I think I was sitting in the driver's seat showing her the air bag light.
245.	INV:	And she was in the car as well?
246.	SUSP:	She was standing beside the car.
247.	INV:	In the front parking lot?
248.	SUSP:	Yes.
249.	INV:	You don't remember her name?
250.	SUSP:	No, sir.
251.	INV:	Would you recognize her if you saw her again?
252.	SUSP:	No.
253.	INV:	Why does that particular appointment or that particular woman stick out in your mind and you're unable to remember the others?
254.	SUSP:	Because she went into the office to complain.
255.	INV:	Has this happened so many times that you can't keep track of it?
256.	SUSP:	No, I just don't remember because some of them were possibly a year ago. I don't …
257.	INV:	Okay. So going back during your assignment as the VIN officer, (redacted) of (redacted) to (redacted) of (redacted) you think that it's possible that this happened as long ago as a year ago?
258.	SUSP:	Possibly.
259.	INV:	Okay. Is it ever necessary for you, when you're doing a VIN appointment, to contact the individual after they've left?
260.	SUSP:	No.
261.	INV:	Okay. And I'll clarify that, after you've passed somebody for their VIN appointment, is it necessary for you to ever contact them?

262.	SUSP:	Sometimes, yes, to follow up on the appointment if I refuse them. In the past I've contacted people to do follow-up to make sure that they're going to come back to complete their inspection, yes.
263.	INV:	Okay. So the question was – for VIN inspections where you've passed them, when they've passed, is it necessary for you to contact them after they've left?
264.	SUSP:	Passed – no.
265.	INV:	Okay.
266.	INV2:	Yeah.
267.	INV:	Go ahead.
268.	INV2:	Morgan, you mentioned that – you mentioned a motel room to her?
269.	SUSP:	Yes.
270.	INV2:	What motel were you going to? What one did you have in mind specifically?
271.	SUSP:	I didn't have any hotel room in mind.
272.	INV:	And did she seem happy about the comment?
273.	SUSP:	She was confused and then unhappy.
274.	INV:	Did she repeat the question to you for verification once you mentioned motel? Did she ask you what or ask you to specify what you meant?
275.	SUSP:	I don't remember.
276.	INV:	Okay. Okay.
277.	INV:	When you said somebody fails an appointment that you needed to re-contact them for – or if there was a need to re-contact them, how do you normally do that?
278.	SUSP:	By phone.
279.	INV:	Okay, the office phone?
280.	SUSP:	Yes.
281.	INV:	Have you ever had occasion to contact them on your cell phone?
282.	SUSP:	I don't think so.
283.	INV:	Okay. And how long does a typical VIN appointment take to complete?
284.	SUSP:	About an hour.
285.	INV:	Is that the average or is that kind of – is it maximum of an hour and some take less than that?
286.	SUSP:	For a newer vehicle, up to an hour. For an older vehicle, it could take more than – more than two hours.
287.	INV:	And about how long does a re-inspection take if you've already seen this vehicle?
288.	SUSP:	That takes less than 30 minutes.

Topic 5

289.	INV:	Okay. Okay We're going to move on from the topics we just talked about. We need to move into some policy stuff and discuss that with you right now. Okay. So we're just going to go through some documents, and I think before we do that, we're going to take a ten-minute break. Okay? So it's, by my clock it's 8:45 right now, and we'll come back . . .
290.	SUSP:	Okay.

Starting at line 122 the questions begin to focus on the suspect's misconduct. After asking a Leading Question (LQ) the suspect replies with a question of his own and then offers a clarification. The investigator asks the same question again in accusatory fashion. The suspect again replies with a question (line 125) and then says "Yes." The INV then asks an OEQ and the suspect responds with the "reason for this investigation" at line 127. He asks another good OEQ at line 128 that results in the suspect admitting to making "comments to the public that don't have anything to do with the inspection." At line 130 the INV follows up his very good OEQ with a MLQ which leaves the suspect choosing one of three questions to answer. The INV does a good job at employing AL techniques at line 132 which allows the suspect to elaborate then helps the INV to ask an OEQ which leads to more reliable information at line 135.

At this point the INV is trying to establish recollection of the complainant and the suspect is not providing specific details. At line 142 the INV suggests the suspect "gave her two options" regarding her air bag system, but the suspect denies it and says he gave her "one option to fix the air bag system" even though in fact he did say, "she had to get the air bag system was (sic) fixed she could either bring the vehicle back to the office or get a hotel room." At line 146 the investigator then asks a LQ about not "pass[ing] her like you had previously described?" And he asked another question about the "re-inspection" and the suspect says, "Yes." At line 148 the INV suggests that getting the air bag fixed was normal, but then adds the "other option" for getting a "motel room." The suspect qualifies his response by saying yes to getting the "air bag fixed" but doesn't address the motel room comment. At this point they talk over each other briefly and the INV restates his question about the motel room. The suspect replies at line 152 the reason for the motel room was to be "intimate." The INV asks for clarification on whether he told the woman that specifically and he said he hadn't, so the INV ask for the specific comment he made to her. At 157 the suspect restates the previous comment about fixing the air bag but now adds "to get motel room." When we review the transcript closely, we see that the suspect actually used the words "hotel room" at line 135 and then 13 lines later the INV suggests the "motel room." By the time we get to line 157 the suspect has accepted the "motel room" as his recollection.

Throughout the interview the INV used the words "motel room" 11 times (after line 148) and twice used by another investigator at lines 268 and 270. The suspect used "hotel room" at line 135, then accepted "motel room" at line 153 when he made the intimate comment. Then at line 157 the suspect includes the motel room comment as he describes asking the women to come back to the office, but then at line 169 in response to the INV asking about the motel room he says, "Not to a motel room." Finally, at line 173 he acknowledges it was his idea for the "motel room" and then reaffirms it by line 175. We can see how easy it is for the INV to suggest the type of room involved in the misconduct and how the inconsistencies in the suspect's responses can lead to unreliable information.

At lines 181 and 183 the suspect explains that he didn't think she would understand about getting the motel room, but only says, "I didn't think she would understand." The INV then asks if she didn't understand why "did you say it to begin with?" The suspect replied at line 185, "I don't know." By line 188 the INV is trying to understand how the meeting would take place and the suspect says he "didn't expect it to happen." The INV asks at line 190 if he had a "plan I place?" And the suspect said, "No." At line 193 the INV begins to inquire about how many times this had happened. Although the INV is not explicit we can infer from the question (as did the suspect) that he meant how many times he had asked a person to be "intimate" while performing his duties as an officer. From lines 193 to 207 the INV is trying to figure out how many times the suspect has committed this misconduct. The suspect never admits to the number of times and the INV pivots to asking whether anyone else was present during his misconduct and the suspect said he did not know. At line 217 the INV asks again about the number of times, and it sounds as if another party (representative for the suspect?) steps in and advises the INV that the suspect could not remember the number and asked him if he wanted the suspect to "guess" and the INV says he was only "asking for a clarifying number" (line 220). By line 221 the INV settles on the number being between two and 20 times and asks the suspect if he remembers another time "when this has occurred?" The suspect responds with, "Not specific occasions – no." By line 223 the INV tries again and says, "You said it happened twice." The suspect demurs and replies that it happened "more than twice." The INV asks if he can remember another time at line 225 and the suspect says, "Not specifically, no."

The INV then moves on and asks a POQ about who might be with the woman during this visit (line 227) and then the INV tried to establish the age of the "son" that was with the woman. The INV was certainly looking for another witness to the comments made by the suspect but when he asks whether the son was nearby when he asked to be "intimate" the suspect said, "No" (240). Between lines 241 and 247 the INV tries to clarify the location of all parties when he made the comment. At line 249 the INV asks the suspect whether he remembered her name even though he had asked him the same question at line 138. He then asks the suspect if he would be able to recognize her if he saw her again at line 251 and the suspect said, "No." The INV asks why he seems to remember this woman and the suspect replies, "because she went into office to complain." The INV ignores his response and instead accuses the suspect of not recalling her because his misconduct happens "so many times that you can't keep track of it?" The suspect then responds with "some of them" happened over a year ago.

At line 259 the INV asks the suspect a general question about contacting a person after the VIN inspection appointment and the suspect says, "No." The INV clarifies his question by adding that the contact was made after they "passed" the VIN appointment. The suspect says, "yes ... if I refused them" (line 262). The INV now asked whether the VIN inspection had "passed" would it be necessary for him to contact the vehicle owner? The suspect says, "Passed – no" at line 264.

At line 268 another investigator changes the topic and asks about the "motel room" and then asks whether he had a certain motel room in mind. The suspect responds that "I didn't have any hotel room in mind" at line 271. The first INV then asks about her demeanor after the suspect made the inappropriate comment and the suspect said she "seemed confused and then unhappy." At line 274 the INV asks a LQ about whether she asked him to repeat his comment or to clarify it. The INV then shifts to asking about how the suspect contacts people after their appointment. At line 278 the suspect says, "By phone" and the INV asks a LQ by suggesting he uses the "office phone" and the suspect agrees. After a couple more questions about the length of an average appointment the INV says he needs to move to "policy stuff" and suggests taking a ten-minute break.

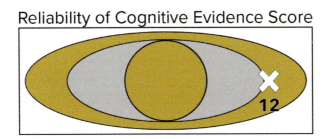

Figure 15.1   Reliability of Cognitive Evidence Target (RCE) score "12."

EFFICACY OF EYEWITNESS INTERVIEW ASSESSMENT[SM]
Narrative Report for Case Study #1

The Reliability of Cognitive Evidence (RCE) score for this interview session (Figure 15.1) was "12" which means we can consider the cognitive evidence retrieved from this interview to be **Less Than Reliable**. The efficacy of this interview is questionable when we consider the proportion of diminished reliability questions being asked at a pace of nearly half the time a question was asked. Because of this unreliable rating, we would expect some follow-up interviews with the subject and decide whether there is an opportunity to recover more reliable cognitive evidence from other eyewitnesses.

The transcript shows the investigator is well capable of asking more mindful questions by the number of combined improved and mindful questions and comments (52%) overall. The investigator does a great job at addressing Topic 3, however, 39% of the questions asked were less mindful and diminished the reliability of the suspect's comments. Had the investigator considered asking more open-ended type questions they would have improved the reliability of statements and contributed to the mindful rapport previously established.

We can see from this case study that the investigator is doing more assessing than listening which is a contributing factor to the overall unreliability of cognitive evidence retrieved. We can observe in the transcript that every time the investigator ignores a response from the suspect and instead makes a suggestion, the suspect often accepts the suggestion as theirs, which is a glaring example of accepting unreliable cognitive evidence.

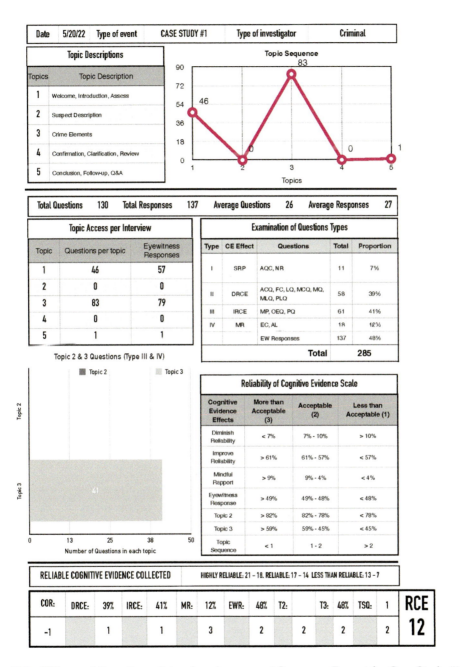

Figure 15.2 Efficacy of Eyewitness Interview Assessment Summary Report for Case Study #1.

16
Case Study #2

THE COOPERATIVE EYEWITNESS

When we conduct investigative interviews, we must be sure we are mindful of the bias and the noise associated with the judgments we make in deciding how we are going to interview the eyewitness, otherwise we jeopardize the value of the cognitive evidence we gather. If we do not acknowledge the bias we have in planning the interview, we may find our interview deemed unreliable in a post-evaluation for assessing best practices. We continue reviewing the excerpts from the podcast *On Our Watch* (2021) by reporter Suki Lewis as her team uncovers astonishing audio recordings from internal investigations conducted by law enforcement agencies in California considering the Right to Know Act, or Senate Bill 1421. In this excerpt we read about the exchange between the investigator and the cooperative eyewitness (the victim) from Case Study #1. Listen to this episode of the podcast here: https://www.npr.org/transcripts/1000175441.

The transcript begins with an interview already in progress, so we won't evaluate Topics 1, 2, 4, and 5. Our focus for this evaluation will be on Topic 3 and how the investigator attempts to retrieve reliable cognitive evidence. The COR rating we'll assign this interview will be "0" and assume she has valuable information about the suspect.

Topic 3

1. EW: Then he started saying to me, well, you know what? You want me get one motel room for me and you? I said, what?
2. EW: A motel room for me and you?
3. INV #1: Is there any way that they could – is there any way they misunderstood? Is there any way that you misunderstood what [the officer] was saying?
4. EW: No, I understand everything.
5. INV #2: You don't need anybody to speak in Spanish? You understand English?
6. EW: I understand English, but …
7. INV #3: Just to tell you, this is highly unusual for a citizen to tell me this with this officer. I just – I'm not saying I don't believe you. I was just thinking it's very out there, you know? It's very out in left field for this exchange to happen, so …

THE MINDFUL INTERVIEW METHOD

8. EW: No, but I don't lie. I tell you exactly what he's saying.
9. INV #3: I don't believe you're lying to me, but understand that this is very unusual.

We can assume that the investigator asked an Open-Ended Question (OEQ) that sparked her shocking response to the suspect's inappropriate comments. Instead of expressing empathy the investigator engages in manipulation and accusations. We can apply neutralization theory to the strategies employed by the investigator at lines 3, 7, and 9. In line 3 we can see the investigator Distorting the Facts of the complaint by suggesting that she may have misunderstood what the officer was asking her. The Denial of Circumstances at line 7 when the investigator insinuates the complaint is far-fetched and very uncharacteristic for the officer, and then Hiding Behind Imperfect Knowledge of the Norm at line 9 by characterizing his investigation so far has not revealed anything illegal. All four of the questions or comments made by the investigator in this section diminished the reliability of cognitive evidence.

10. INV #1: Ma'am, did you have any alcohol to drink last night? Nothing that would …
11. EW: No, sir. I don't drink alcohol. I don't do drugs. I don't smoke.
12. INV #1: Okay.
13. EW: I have four kids. I'm mother to four kids.
14. INV #1: Okay.
15. INV #1: I just – I feel like I smell some alcohol in here, and I mean no disrespect or anything, but I just – that's why I asked.
16. EW: No, no.
17. INV #3: You haven't had something to drink in the last 12 hours?
18. EW: Nothing.
19. INV #1: Can I – I'm just going to walk over there. I'm going to have you follow my finger.
20. EW: Yeah, yes, sure. We can leave my son here?
21. INV #1: Oh, no, this will just be right here. I was just going to have you follow my finger with your eyes. Try not to move your head, Okay? Okay, thank you, ma'am. I just sometimes – I don't know if it's this room, but I felt like I was smelling alcohol. Maybe it's from that breath machine right there, so I apologize.

In this section the investigator engages in what could be considered highly questionable tactics when interviewing a victim of a complaint. We do not have all the information from the interview setting and we have to consider the investigator's investigative skills to be professional, but we do not read any objective characteristics of someone under the influence from the initial lines in this transcript. Regardless, the accusations of being under the influence are at best suspect considering the investigator mentions there was a "breath machine right there." Once again, the pattern of asking questions that diminish the retrieval of cognitive evidence are very intentional and three of the four questions asked were accusatory.

22. INV #3: Is there any reason why you think he would say this to you? Is it maybe to help you get a certificate or help you pass to get registration for your vehicle?
23. INV #3: Why do you think he was asking for a motel room for you and him?
24. EW: Because he no respect the ladies.
25. INV #3: What does that mean?
26. EW: He no respect the ladies because …

CASE STUDY #2

27.	*Investigator and Eyewitness speak Spanish …*
28. INV#3:	Okay. They said, well, it's disrespect to her. And I go, what does that mean to you? And they says, sex between him and – her and the officer.
29. INV:	Okay.
30. INV:	In Spanish.
31. INV:	Do you have any questions for us?
32. EW:	No. (Speaking Spanish.)
33. INV #3:	They's describing that they's scared, confused, and they doesn't understand this department, that they's worried that we're going to protect him. And they – there wasn't a reason for this to happen.
34. INV#1:	Well, ma'am, we take complaints seriously, and we will fully investigate this incident. So just know that we're not going to dismiss this and think that it's no big deal. It's a big deal to us.

The final 11 lines of investigator engagement are more in line with being more mindful of the complaint. The only question that is counterproductive is at line 22 when the investigator asks the victim to consider the reason why the officer might have made the comments and then suggests maybe to "help you get a certificate or help you pass …?" The remaining questions show the investigator is able to ask OEQs and finally reassure her that they will follow up and investigate the complaint "seriously." We have no idea whether the victim in this case was satisfied with the interview; however, we can surmise from the excerpt that most people would be disturbed by what has just taken place in light of the initial complaint.

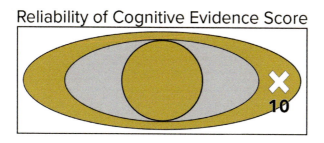

Figure 16.1 Reliability of Cognitive Evidence Target (RCE) score "10."

EFFICACY OF EYEWITNESS INTERVIEW ASSESSMENT℠ NARRATIVE REPORT FOR CASE STUDY #2

The Reliability of Cognitive Evidence (RCE) for this interview session is off the mark at a score of "10" which means we can consider the cognitive evidence **Less Than Reliable** (Figure 16.1). The efficacy of this interview is questionable when we consider 17% of the questions asked were based on diminishing the reliability of cognitive evidence (Figure 16.2). Because of this unreliable rating we would expect some follow-up interviews with the victim and decide whether there is an opportunity to recover more reliable cognitive evidence from this and other eyewitnesses.

The transcript demonstrates the investigator was biased for not accepting the victim's accusations as factual and the overall lack of mindful questions demonstrates this. The investigator does not address Topic 3 in an acceptable manner and instead resorts to accusing the victim of being under the influence which influences the lack of reliable cognitive evidence collected for this topic. Our assessment of this interview shows unwanted judgments made by the investigators that did nothing to collect reliable cognitive evidence. We can see from this case study that the investigator is using neutralization techniques that contribute to the unreliability of the cognitive evidence collected.

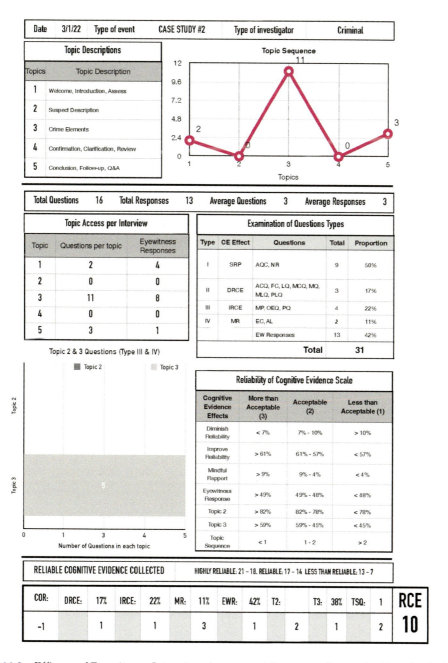

Figure 16.2 Efficacy of Eyewitness Interview Assessment Summary Report for Case Study #2.

17
Case Study #3

OUR FIRST MINDFUL INTERVIEW

In the previous two case studies we looked at transcripts from internal investigations that focused on the interrogation of the suspect and the interview of the victim. In this case study we take a look at our first classic eyewitness interview session to give you some perspective on how the *Mindful Interview Method* (MIM) is applied and how it fares when evaluated by our *Efficacy in Eyewitness Interview Assessment* instrument. It is important for the interview practitioners, experienced and novice, to begin to see how the MIM is applied in real-world situations. The transcripts provide you with extraordinary access to the question strategies, and insight comments offer you more information to consider related to the mindful qualities of interviewing. While we cover the MIM principles and standards and explain the differences between interview techniques, in previous chapters, it is important for you to see how questions are used to gather the most reliable cognitive evidence from the eyewitness. Keep in mind that when this interview was conducted, I had not formally developed the MIM; nevertheless, I was confidently practicing mindful techniques and concerned about the reliability of eyewitness statements.

Even though most forensic artist interview sessions only focus on the facial features of the suspect, you'll see how I gather all relevant crime event information to develop a comprehensive account of what happened. The MIM can easily be used by non-forensic artists to interview *any* eyewitness. In either case, the investigator and the forensic artist are interviewing an eyewitness to gather cognitive evidence. In the case studies that follow we may find that transcripts start at different points of the welcome (Topic 1) portion of the interview. These varied starts are not intended to minimize the importance of the welcome portion or the establishment of rapport – it is merely what was saved in the original audio version. We can still measure the reliability of eyewitness evidence by focusing on how the cognitive evidence is retrieved and maintained throughout the interview process.

Finally, the Confidence of Recollection (COR) is not revealed clearly in this excerpt. Because I have two eyewitnesses I must evaluate who may be the more confident witness and decide whether to leave them both in the room or ask one of them to remain outside while I interview them separately. Because of their parental relationship I decide to leave them in the room (since they may have discussed the circumstances of the case many

THE MINDFUL INTERVIEW METHOD

times before meeting me). While we do not see the Qualifying Question (QQ) being asked in Topic 1 we can assume I had asked it before I started recording the interview, since I have asked the QQ on every interview session I have conducted since 1995. More importantly, to the COR rating, I wanted to evaluate the confidence in offering details about the suspect's face and the circumstances of the crime. You'll notice the eyewitness does not offer any statements that cast any doubts about her confidence in her memory of the event, and because of this I have assigned a COR of "0."

CASE STUDY #3

In the interview room there are two eyewitnesses, mother and daughter, and I'm trying to decide which of the two had a better recollection of the suspect. I'll make my decision after a brief inquiry. I'm looking at each eyewitness to see if there is disagreement on what is being said. Most of the time when there are two eyewitnesses to the same event, one of the eyewitnesses will dominate the conversation while the other sits by in support. I expected the same in this situation. After a few responses I decided to focus my questions on the mother and have the daughter sit nearby and listen. I would eventually have both mother and daughter view the sketch – separately – and allow them to make changes to the sketch. In the end they both were satisfied with the resemblance of the sketch.

Topic 1

1. INV: Okay, the way this works is that I'm going to ask you about the person's face.
2. EW: Okay.
3. INV: And was it one suspect?
4. EW: Yeah.
5. INV: I'd like you to go ahead and answer to the best of your knowledge.
6. EW: Okay.
7. INV: Most people don't remember everything in great detail; however, a lot of folks tend to remember a lot of information especially when they're here and focused on the questions.
8. EW: Okay.
9. INV: You're going to have your eyes closed for about five minutes – that's going to help you relax and focus on the questions. It makes it a little easier to describe. Then after that I'm going to ask you to open your eyes and I'm going to ask you to tell me what happened and then I'll show you the sketch and if we need to, we'll make some changes. Do you understand?
10. EW: Mhmm.
11. INV: Now, so there's two of you, so um. Can you give me an idea of the location where you were? You were together when this happened?
12. EW: Ah no, she was playing in the playground like maybe a block away from our apartment.
13. INV: Okay.
14. EW: It's inside our apartment.
15. INV: Okay.

200

CASE STUDY #3

16. EW: There were a group of kids – like maybe ten or 12 kids playing together and in that, four were girls ranging from six to 12 years of age and my daughter she was playing and I think a couple of more kids were doing the same thing and she tells me that this guy ... like a little bit away from them was taking pictures and he had a cellphone and then she could notice that he was videotaping when he came closer to them. And I asked her like how you suspect that he's videotaping you and she says she's had a cellphone since seven years of age so knows how to take a picture and how to take a video recording and he was holding the camera horizontally pointing it towards them and especially toward the body part.
17. INV: Okay, so when did you see him?
18. EW: Umm, then what happened she suspected that and said to her friend, "hurry up, let's go home" so all of them came home and she described the situation. My husband was at home, so I told him around 7:15 in the evening and I was explaining to him suddenly that person appeared in front of my apartment looking for them. And I had the idea that something was wrong, and I was about to go out and you know this guy just ... and I ask him, "why are you following them?" and he said, "no I'm not following." I said, "you are taking picture" and he said, "no. I'm not taking picture." I was talking on my cellphone, and he started walking very fast. And I think he suspected something so his car was parked right in front of my apartment – a little bit on the left side, but it was ... so he just went and sat in his car. That's how my husband went inside to get the camera to take a picture but by the time I go there he was sitting in his car ...

What you don't glean from the transcript is that I had spent a few minutes before the interview meditating (five minutes) on meeting the next eyewitnesses (Mindful Reset). When I meet them, I greet them in the lobby, and we walk to the office where we will conduct the interview. In lines 1 through 9 I'm explaining the interview process as well as my expectations for their recollection of details. As I've discussed previously it's important to prime the eyewitness to have reasonable expectations for what we expect from them and what they should expect from us. Asking whether they understand at this point allows them to feel that this will be a collaboration and that I will be facilitating the interview moving forward. It's important to understand that even though the first part of the interview (Topic 1) is about clarifying who would be interviewed and who would stand by and listen, we must be mindful of establishing rapport and showing empathy throughout the interview. At line 11 I try to determine which eyewitness believes they had a good look at the suspect. This self-report does two things: (a) it gives me an idea of the interest the eyewitness has in speaking about the event, and (b) their vantage point to the viewing of the suspect. Since we are mindful of eyewitness memory limitations, we know that interviewing multiple eyewitnesses at the same time can be problematic, so determining who is the best first eyewitness to interview will be key. As it turns out, the parent eyewitness saw enough to sit for the entire interview and the child offered confirmation of the resemblance of the sketch afterwards. As we learn during the complete interview there are more eyewitnesses to interview, but these two eyewitnesses were deemed the best candidates by patrol officers at the scene. Question 17 sparked a long answer whereby the eyewitness talks about the entire event without being asked (covering multiple topics). It is vital that you do not interrupt the eyewitness if this happens. This is important to them, and they want to tell you what happened. You must be mindful of the details they offer but stay true to the framework. In other words, after they are done telling you the initial details, you get back on track, "OK, that gives me a better idea ..." and you proceed to the next topic (in this case we were at Topic 1 so now we move to Topic 2). Since we know we are following a certain topic format we are not concerned about the information the eyewitness has already revealed. If we are confident in the interview process, we won't be concerned with topic hopping or getting frustrated with how the cognitive evidence is being revealed.

Topic 2

19.	INV:	Okay, that gives me a better idea because I'm going to ask you (speaking to Victim #2) the same questions – I'm going to ask all of my questions to your mom, okay? So, you both have cellphones. You want to make sure they're on silent, so we don't get interrupted. So, all of my questions are going to be to you.
20.	EW:	Okay.
21.	INV:	So you go ahead and answer to the best of your knowledge. Just tell me everything, okay. And then, umm, after when I show you the sketch, then you'll have an opportunity to make comments if you need to, okay? So, all of my questions will be to her. You just sit back and relax. You'll also need to close your eyes and relax as well. Okay? Do you have any questions for me?
22.	EW:	No.
23.	INV:	Okay, go ahead and close your eyes and give me a nice deep breath and we'll begin. First of all, what would you say is the race of this person?
24.	EW:	White.
25.	INV:	Age range?
26.	EW:	40–45.
27.	INV:	Body build?
28.	EW:	Skinny.
29.	INV:	When you think about the shape of this guy's face, what shape are we talking about?
30.	EW:	Umm, a little bit on the longer side.
31.	INV:	Tell me about his hair.
32.	EW:	No hair. Totally bald.
33.	INV:	He was bald?
34.	EW:	Mm.
35.	INV:	Some men when they have a bald head their shape is a little distinctive. Anything unusual about the shape?
36.	EW:	It was totally round and nicely shaped.
37.	INV:	Okay, perfect. Tell me about his ears.
38.	EW:	Um, the ears I couldn't notice. Since he was white it was obvious, I could see his ears nicely.
39.	INV:	Okay, any earrings on this guy?
40.	EW:	No.
41.	INV:	Tell me about his nose.
42.	EW:	Straight nose.
43.	INV:	His mouth and his lips?
44.	EW:	Lips were kind of thin?
45.	INV:	Thin?

46.	EW:	Yeah.
47.	INV:	U-huh. What was his attitude?
48.	EW:	Ah, he was pretty arrogant.
49.	INV:	Okay. Any facial hair?
50.	EW:	Ah, no.
51.	INV:	Tell me about his chin.
52.	EW:	His chin was kind of pointy.
53.	INV:	Any hair on the chin?
54.	EW:	No.
55.	INV:	And his cheeks? What were they like?
56.	EW:	They were kind of flat.
57.	INV:	Skin color?
58.	EW:	White.
59.	INV:	The texture of his skin?
60.	EW:	Kind of shiny.
61.	INV:	Any scars or marks on his face and neck?
62.	EW:	No.
63.	INV:	And tell me about his neck.
64.	EW:	Um, his neck was like kind of normal. He was wearing a white t-shirt.
65.	INV:	A white t-shirt?
66.	EW:	Mm.
67.	INV:	Have you ever seen this guy before?
68.	EW:	No.
69.	INV:	Tell me about his eyes?
70.	EW:	His eyes were like cat eyes, um, maybe a little bit of greenish blue.
71.	INV:	Okay. And what do you mean by cat eyes?
72.	EW:	Um, it's like – it's not totally black it's a mixture of green and blue.
73.	INV	Okay. I see what you mean – the color.
74.	EW:	Yeah.
75.	INV:	Tell me about the overall look in his eyes – the size of his eyes – things like that.
76.	EW:	Could you explain?
77.	INV:	Um, the size of his eyes?
78.	EW:	They were kind of normal. Not too big, not too small.
79.	INV:	Okay. And then the look in his eyes.
80.	EW:	Scared.
81.	INV:	Okay. And eyebrows?
82.	EW:	Eyebrows are normal.
83.	INV:	When you saw this guy, was it daytime or nighttime?
84.	EW:	It was evening and light.
85.	INV:	And this happened indoors or outdoors?
86.	EW:	It was outdoors.
87.	INV:	And what do you remember the most about this guy's face?
88.	EW:	His nose.
89.	INV:	And why do you remember the nose most?
90.	EW:	Sharp nose like straight.

91. INV: Does this guy have a mannish face or a boyish face?
92. EW: A mannish face.
93. INV: How close did you get to him?
94. EW: Mm, like a couple of feet.

Topic 2 is focused on the description of the suspect's face. In this part of the interview we must be mindful of how the description of the suspect is being recalled and not interrupt the eyewitness. The investigator must allow the eyewitness to complete their recall of details and pause before asking the next question. The questions should be focused on a natural progression from the face shape (broad area to a specific area) to the eyes. There are a couple of questions that are more esoteric to refining the sketch and displaying a more realistic illustration, but they can offer the investigator some insight into the perspective the eyewitness had about the suspect. For instance, when we ask forced choice questions like if the suspect had a "mannish or a boyish face" and the eyewitness says, "mannish" we can feel confident that the 40–45-year-old figure they gave us initially was in line with the rest of the description. The same goes for the question about the "attitude" of the suspect (line 47), while the artist can sketch some of the emotion onto the illustration that resembles an "arrogant" person, a non-artist investigator can have an impression of the suspect that will help them understand the description better. The arrogance comment may be a personality trait the suspect may have, and other witnesses may offer the same opinion which might enhance our opinion of the suspect. It also allows the eyewitness to describe the suspect in other terms not related to specific facial features.

The use of Mirror Probe(s) (MP) after an Open-Ended-Question (OEQ) is important and should be practiced before being confident to employ it in an actual eyewitness interview session. Since interviewing an eyewitness is a brief social interaction, we can leverage neuroscience and utilize the mirror neurons in our brains to predict the behavior of others by modeling the same behavior and creating familiarity. As we discussed in Chapters 10 through 12, when we probe for more information in this manner, we create a space where the eyewitness gets comfortable with you listening and repeating the last word(s) that are interesting, or that you need more information about. When you employ this MP technique early (line 33) it becomes familiar to the eyewitness, which is what you want to create early in the interview session so when it is critical, they will be more open to reveal more information. You want them to trust you and using this tactic will establish rapport throughout the interview.

In Topic 2 we focus on the suspect's facial description and it is easy to establish our MP here as the eyewitness offers descriptions in response to our questions. We also use this tactic to probe further and use our discretion to accept the limited information. For example, at line 43 we ask about the mouth and lips of the suspect and the eyewitness responds with, "Lips were kind of thin?" The MP we use (line 45) is "Thin?" And they say, "Yeah." We won't always get more details after we ask this type of question, but when we ask it early in the interview it won't be as odd when we ask it when we actually need more information. In this case, the lips are thin and That Is All There Is (TIATI). We ask another MP at question 65 after the eyewitness describes the suspect wearing a "white t-shirt." We ask that question to see if they remember more details about the shirt. Maybe there is a logo, a name, or an illustration that might come to memory – if not, then TIATI. We don't need to probe further because there is nothing more to gather.

Topic 3

95. INV: All right, you can open your eyes. Now what I want you to do is I want you to tell me what happened. I want you to tell me what you were doing just prior to running into this guy and then take me through the incident up until the police get involved.
96. EW: Okay, so, um, I explained to you that I confronted him then I followed him, and I saw he was sitting in his car. By the time I go there he was taking a …

97.	INV:	He was taking what?
98.	EW:	He was about to leave.
99.	INV:	Mm.
100.	EW:	So I could read his number plate and I was repeating it loudly and starting with the 2FP. And there were some numbers, and I was repeating that loudly so by the time he just went away, and I get inside and I told that number to my husband and he immediately called 911. And they transferred us to another dispatch – police officer – so he showed up between 3–4 minutes and he came there and he asked what happened and I told him and he talked to my daughter and the kids and asked them if what he was wearing, how tall he was, if he touched them or did he talk to them – all those kinds of questions and he asked us if we saw this man before and then somebody told us – the neighbors told us: that we have a video camera near our apartment and I told him and he went to the manager's apartment.
101.	INV:	Who went to the manager's apartment?
102.	EW:	The police officer.
103.	INV:	Oh, okay.
104.	EW:	But she said the cameras were off. It was not on.
105.	INV:	Okay.
106.	EW:	So he came back, and he said, "do you remember the make of the car?" and I couldn't. I just gave him the 2FP and the numbers and he took down my driver's license and my phone number and said he would call if he needed you there and "how good is your memory – would you recognize him?" and we said, "yeah, we could recognize him" and after that he left. And around 10:30 he called again, and he said, "do you know the make of the car – do you suspect it can be some car?" and I said, "umm I don't really remember because I was totally concentrating on the number plate." And the detective called, and he gave me the number to call you.
107.	INV:	Did they stop anybody for you to look at that night?
108.	EW:	Repeat that.
109.	INV:	Did they stop anybody for you to look at that night?
110.	EW:	No. The police officer said he will roll through the database, um, you know to look for the car, just to see whether there is anybody who lives nearby and need to make sure that's not and I couldn't find anybody. No. Not like that person.
111.	INV:	Right. Did your husband see the car?
112.	EW:	No, he just went inside. Actually, he was inside when this guy came and we were near our door about to leave, but since he showed up and he started running, my husband went in to just get a camera to take a picture, but this guy was next to our apartment, and he just ran by – But he saw that person.
113.	INV:	He did see him?
114.	EW:	Yes.
115.	INV:	How did he see him?
116.	EW:	Because we were standing near our door about to go out just to see what happening …
117.	INV:	Oh.

118.	EW:	At the park and immediately this guy showed up just to see where the kids are basically following them all over to our apartment.
119.	INV:	How many other kids were there?
120.	EW:	Because there were kids, the younger one was six, and one was 6 1/2 and the other was 12 years old.
121.	INV:	And do you know them all?
122.	EW:	Yes.
123.	INV:	And what area was this?
124.	EW:	Umm it's in … off … near the …
125.	INV:	Oh, okay. All right, I'm going to show you the sketch.

(*The sketch is shown to EW#1 and then EW#2: This portion has been edited to focus on the retrieval of cognitive evidence and not on the forensic art process.*)

At line 95 we come out of Topic 2 and ask the eyewitness to open their eyes and focus on the following queries about the elements of the crime (Topic 3). I could have checked in with the eyewitnesses, to see how they were doing and whether they needed something to drink or needed a break to reinforce the rapport we have so far. I could have also made sure I confirmed her understanding of what I expected from her in the next phase of the interview session. Instead of coding this part as being an Administrative Question or Comment (AQC) it would have been coded as Empathetic Concern (EC) which would have increased the overall reliability of the cognitive evidence score.

While the majority of the questions asked in Topic 3 Improve the Reliability of Cognitive Evidence (IRCE) there are a few times when I ask force-choice questions that tend to diminish RCE. For instance, at line 83 I ask about whether it was "daytime or nighttime" when she saw the suspect. I could have asked a more open question like, "When did this happen?" And see if I get an idea of the time of day or night this happened. If you recall from previous chapters, I don't rely on the information from the crime report, I would rather get it straight from the eyewitness and learn new information if possible. Because I'm mindful of not asking too many of these types of questions they have very little effect on the overall reliability of cognitive evidence.

Because we employed the MP in Topic 2 to create "stickiness" when we employ it here in Topic 3 it becomes more important to decide when to use it and at the best times. For instance, when the eyewitness begins to recall details of the event after our OEQ we must find the word or phrases that they say near the end of their natural pause to repeat. For example, at lines 97 and 101 we repeat the last words that were spoken by the eyewitness to see if we can get her to elaborate further. At line 98 she gives us a brief answer, but at line 102 through 106 we see how the MP triggered more information that led to more inquiries. I only included Active Listening (AL) to keep her on track. At line 109 I'm trying to see if I should be concerned for memory contamination from post-event information. When we conduct these interviews, we must accept the fact that estimator variables like witness and event factors may happen, and we have no control over them. We should be aware of them and make allowances for them if needed. For instance, say the eyewitness had been exposed to in-field show-up of a possible suspect and he was not identified as the perpetrator I would want to know about her experience with it. I would ask open questions about what she saw and how she felt. Getting her impressions of her ability to distinguish between post-event information and her memory of the event will enhance our interview session because of what we learn about how the in-field show-up may have added to her memory of the event.

At line 111 I ask the eyewitness if her husband saw the suspect because she had mentioned him being there when she came in the apartment repeating the first characters of the license plate. She offers more information about his location and gives us an idea for interviewing more people (the husband and the other children). By line 122 I've established that there were three children ages six through 12 and her husband was near the doorway and may have seen the suspect as well as other *neighbors who reside next to her apartment. You'll also notice that I adhere to TIATI by not probing more than is needed. For example, when she says that she was repeating the license plate number "2FP" and she mentioned telling the initial officer, I didn't probe further about the color of the plate or about the make and model of the car. She was obviously doing her best to recall what she saw, and she was describing it very well – no need to frustrate her by confirming that she did not remember more. We can investigate further with security camera footage (if any) and see what a database search from the partial plate produces for possible vehicle registrations that match the description of the suspect.*

Topic 4

126.	INV:	And what kind of camera did he have?
127.	EW2:	Um, it was a cellphone that had a camera in it?
128.	INV:	So what kind of cellphone?
129.	EW2:	It looked very much like mine.
130.	INV:	And what kind do you have?
131.	EW2:	Mine is a …
132.	INV:	Have you ever seen this guy before?
133.	EW2:	No.
134.	INV:	No? How about your friends?
135.	EW2:	No, none of us had ever seen him.
136.	INV:	Have you guys been talking about it?
137.	EW2:	Sometimes.

Topic 5

138.	INV:	Mm. And … the initials to your name?
139.	INV:	… Got it. Okay. Here's my card. If you have any questions, you can give me a call.
140.	EW:	Sure.
141.	INV:	And I will give this to the detective.
142.	EW:	Okay, sounds good. Thank you.

Part of Topic 4, for the forensic artist, is going through each facial feature and making sure the eyewitness is satisfied with the outcome. This often takes more than 15 minutes to complete and may lead to new changes that can alter the reliability of cognitive evidence. In this case study the eyewitness was satisfied, and I moved on to other information that would require some follow-up. For instance, when I asked about the cellphone, I'm trying to establish whether we should be downloading the images from the cellphone. At this point the investigators have not asked for the phone so there may be some follow-up to come. Asking about the suspect at line 132 is something I do because I want to know if the suspect reminds them of someone or (and this has happened before) they recognize him because they have seen him before this incident and they did not inform the initial patrol officer. Asking whether her friends have been discussing the incident also gives me an idea about the post-event information we should consider when settling on the reliability of the interview session.

My closing could have been more comprehensive and asked her if she had any questions for me. A lot of the conformation of details (from the sketch review) included remarks about what comes next and her satisfaction with the interview process.

For the complete EEIA see Appendix E, Case Study #3.

THE MINDFUL INTERVIEW METHOD

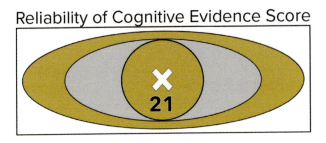

Figure 17.1 Reliability of Cognitive Evidence Target (RCE) score "21."

EFFICACY OF EYEWITNESS INTERVIEW ASSESSMENT[SM]

Narrative Report for Case Study #3

The RCE for this interview session is a score of "21" which means we can consider the cognitive evidence **Highly Reliable** (Figure 17.1) The efficacy of this interview is impressive when we consider the proportion of questions asked that enhance cognitive evidence retrieval (Figure 17.2). The transcript shows the interview was unbiased by the number of questions asked (78%) that improve the reliability of cognitive evidence and enhance mindful rapport. The questions that focused on the suspect description (84%) and crime elements (88%) gathered reliable information and were more than acceptable overall. The number of Diminish Reliability of Cognitive Evidence (DRCE) questions was less than 5% which improved the overall score and the reliability of the evidence collected.

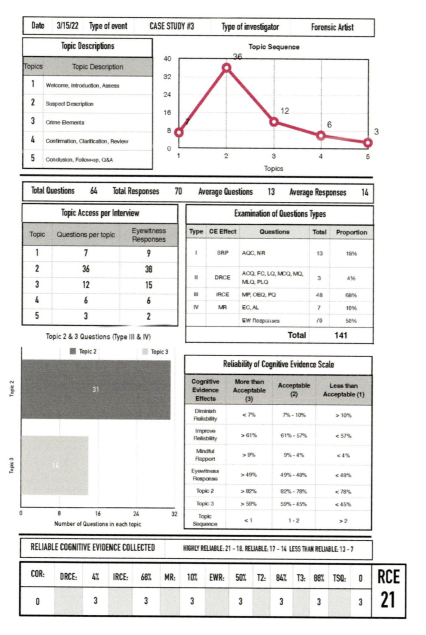

Figure 17.2 Efficacy of Eyewitness Interview Assessment Summary Report for Case Study #3.

18
Case Study #4

AN INTERVIEW OF COMPLEXITY

In this case study we see what I call the *traps of wanting more information*. It's where investigators add information to eyewitness statements because they are impatient or feel they know the right words to use to complete eyewitness thoughts. One of the main differences in the *Mindful Interview Method* (MIM) from other interview techniques is that in MIM we are confident in receiving partial information and therefore we don't try and augment the lack of complete cognitive evidence from eyewitness statements. We are confident because we understand how eyewitness memory works and we adhere to *That Is All There Is* (TIATI). The eyewitness in this case had been a victim of an assault and appeared injured.

    Before the interview starts, we advise the eyewitness what to expect and it settles their insecurities and comforts their concern for life's timetables. We can only imagine what is going on in their life and how this crime event has jolted their life in many ways. We are a part of that reality, and we must do our part to not contribute negatively to the event. We can accept that they have an idea that they will be interviewed, but their ignorance of the process and how their memories contribute to the investigation must be acknowledged professionally and empathetically. We do this by explaining the process and confirming their understanding of our guidance. Our explanation (monologue) is also a way for us to present our demeanor, our voice, and tone, the pace at which we'll be speaking, and the confidence in our role in gathering cognitive evidence. We are the experts in interviewing the eyewitness and while they acquiesce to our professional standing, we must be mindful of earning it throughout the interview process. Our explanation should dissuade any preconceived notions about how the interview will proceed and diminish the CSI effect of solving the case within 45 minutes.

    Since the MIM process is eyewitness-centered, it should be obvious from the start that the eyewitness will be in control of what they remember and how they offer the information. The investigator must be mindful of the type of words the eyewitness uses to describe certain items, conditions, events, or elements of the crime. The mindful quality of being present for their every word should enable the investigator to understand what the eyewitness means and use appropriate questions to get clarification without altering their memory. We're also looking for compliance and willingness to accept the calming and focus techniques.

Because I have limited time with the eyewitness to build trust and help them recall the events of the crime, I'm present and my demeanor is intentionally calm and confident as I assure them we will not do anything unless they were comfortable doing it. I want to convey the feeling that we have all the time in the world to discuss this crime event. I want them to understand that their responsibility for recalling every detail of the event will not place undue pressure on them and that I'm there to guide them and make sure they are safe to respond.

I explain the process to the eyewitness as being three phases: Suspect description, crime event details, and confirmation of details. I know that if they understand there are three main parts to the interview session their concerns about the time for the interview session will be alleviated. After each phase, I acknowledge their progress and then describe the next phase – each time getting their confirmation of understanding. When I explain the process and get their approval, I am building rapport as we venture into the interview. The manner and pace of my instruction reassures them that I am patient and willing to listen. Sometimes an eyewitness relying on their expectations for the investigation might say, "Aren't you going to show me some pictures?" or, "I thought I was going to look at some pictures and you were going to sketch the guy from the photos I picked?" When I tell them I'm only going to ask them questions that rely on their memory alone and if they don't remember something it'll be fine, they seem to pay attention more about their role in the process.

When I start to explain how we can imagine the event better if we have our eyes closed, I see many eyewitnesses slowly close their eyes and settle in before I complete my sentence. As I continue explaining that being calmer will help them focus better, the details on their faces seem more relaxed and they settle deeper in their chair. By the time I ask them to take three deep breaths, many are starting their second breath before I complete my demonstration of taking one deep breath. Their body language is telling me they trust me. Their attention to my every word tells me they are compliant, and they want to do whatever they can to do their part in this interview session.

We begin the interview …

Topic 1

1. INV: Hi…, I'm…Nice to meet you.
2. INV: Alright. Do you know why you're here today?
3. EW: Yeah …
4. INV: Okay, what happened to you? I just want to know what was the crime. I don't need to know the story right now.
5. EW: Okay. Well he hit my truck.
6. INV: Uh huh.
7. EW: Like bumped it a little bit. So I pulled over obviously.
8. INV: Mhm.

9.	EW:	I got out of the truck and he said that he didn't have …..(inaudible) So I told him to give me money. And he said he didn't have it so he went to the truck to supposedly to get it and he came back ……. (inaudible).
10.	INV:	Oh I'm sorry. It was like a robbery?
11.	EW:	Yeah he took all the stuff from my truck.
12.	INV:	Okay. And you're Okay right now?
13.	EW:	Yeah I had a CT scan because I was swollen and I was bleeding like crazy.
14.	INV:	Oh I'm sorry. Okay. And you're feeling better?
15.	EW:	Mhm. I still feel like paranoid.
16.	INV:	Oh yeah.
17.	EW:	Like whenever I drive.
18.	INV:	Oh I can imagine. When did this happen?
19.	EW:	The day before yesterday.
20.	INV:	Okay. And how's your memory about this guy?
21.	EW:	Pretty good.
22.	INV:	Okay. And if you saw him again would you recognize him?
23.	EW:	Yeah.

In this segment, her response after line #2 is "Yeah" which trailed off into inaudible sounds. The next question was meant to clarify her state of mind and to evaluate her Confidence of Recollection (COR). Since the eyewitness was present in an injured state it is important to understand how this might affect the quality of recollection or her ability to focus on the questions. We should be listening intently and being mindful of how they sequence the significant events. Since we are mindful of diminishing the bias in our interview, we do not have specific details about the event, nor do we entertain any theoretical influences from anyone outside of the case.

As the eyewitness describes the event it is important to be empathetic about the violent assault they experienced. Our authentic concern enhances our rapport with the eyewitness and strengthens the trust that is being forged in our new relationship. As we share our concern for her injuries the eyewitness continues to offer details of crime elements that will be important later in categorizing the specific crime (this can be important when charging the suspect and or determining the charges to add or reduce when prosecuting). We would want to retrieve the records from the emergency hospital visit and gather the doctor's notes about the injuries and their prognosis for full recovery. There may be photographs that were taken from hospital personnel that could be added to the case folder to bolster the physical evidence about her physical injuries. With each empathetic comment we see how the eyewitness continues to offer information about her state of mind and post event issues she may deal with moving forward. We get her back on track (line 18) by asking when the event happened (even though we know the case number, the day, and time of the event from the initial request by the detective for the sketch interview) and make sure she is fully present. We then end the segment (line 22) with the Qualifying Question – if she saw him again, would she recognize him – she says "Yeah," and we move on to the next topic.

Topic 2

24.	INV:	Okay. Very good. I'm going to move a little closer so you can hear me. The way this works is I'm going to ask you some general questions about the person's face. I'd like you to go ahead and answer to the best of your knowledge. Most people don't remember everything in great detail however a lot

of folks tend to remember a lot of information especially when they're here and they focus on the questions. You're going to have your eyes closed for about 5 minutes to help you relax. It helps you to focus on the questions and it makes it a little easier to describe. Then after that I'm going to ask you to open your eyes and ask you to tell me what happened and then I'll show you the sketch and if we need to we'll make some changes. Do you understand that? Do you have any questions for me?

25. EW: No.
26. INV: All right go ahead and close your eyes. Give me a nice deep breath. I want you nice and relaxed. Very good. Okay? First of all, what would you say is the race of this person?
27. EW: I would say Chicano.
28. INV: Okay. Age range?
29. EW: Around 28–35.
30. INV: Very good. Body build. What would you say his body is like?
31. EW: He was slim but not super slim.
32. INV: Okay. Tell me about his face shape. What was that like?
33. EW: It was round.
34. INV: Okay. Tell me about his hair. What was that like?
35. EW: His hair – um it was like a guys haircut. The ones that go like – I don't know how to explain it.
36. INV: It's Okay. Go ahead.
37. EW: It was like – oh what's it called – they told me – those haircuts that were all one size but they go like…do you know what I'm talking about?
38. INV: Was it short?
39. EW: No it wasn't. It was like grown out.
40. INV: Okay and the color of his hair?
41. EW: It was black.
42. INV: Okay and is it long enough to comb?
43. EW: No, it was probably like an inch or a little shorter.
44. INV: All right and um does he have any parts in his hair?
45. EW: No.
46. INV: Okay and – what were you going to say?
47. EW: Um it wasn't like a – I don't know what it's called.
48. INV: You said somebody told you something?
49. EW: Yeah, my boyfriend told me the haircut…
50. INV: Was he there?
51. EW: No but I told him how and he told me what it was.
52. INV: Hmm
53. EW: I'm trying to remember what it's called…
54. INV: Is it a unique look?
55. EW: No. A lot of guys get it.
56. INV: Mhm.
57. EW: Those when they get faded.
58. INV: Mhm.
59. EW: It goes like this and it goes like that. You know it was all one size.

60.	INV:	All one length?
61.	EW:	Yeah.
62.	INV:	Okay.
63.	EW:	And some get it long at the top and short at the bottom.
64.	INV:	Not him?
65.	EW:	Not like that, no. It was all one size.
66.	INV:	Okay and the color of the hair again?
67.	EW:	It was black.

Some interviewers may find themselves with the need to clarify and suggest information that would jeopardize the cognitive evidence, or what I call the traps of filling the gaps. In MIM we consider the cognitive evidence as it is and preserve it as best as we can. When we ask the eyewitness questions (looking for evidence) we are mindful of where we find the cognitive evidence, how it presents itself, and what we can do to recover it without contaminating it. If we have to clarify eyewitness statements to understand the meaning (or quality of evidence) we do it without introducing new information that may alter their memory.

After asking about the hair at line 34, the eyewitness struggles to describe the hair to her satisfaction. We can sense her frustration when she says, "I don't know how to explain it." And "It was like – oh what's it called – they told me – those haircuts that were all one size, but they go like … do you know what I'm talking about?" You'll notice that I don't offer my opinion on the hairstyle. Too often investigators fall into assisting the eyewitness to come up with an answer they believe is the correct one based on what they believe the eyewitness saw, however, if we are mindful of the interview process, we must let the eyewitness offer whatever it is that they remember. If the investigator probes the eyewitness with multiple-choice and force-choice questions the eyewitness may become discouraged at their lack of recall, or worse – decide to accept the suggestion made by the investigator. This suggestion would be considered post-event information since it was introduced after the event and is being used to clarify cognitive evidence. The MIM strategy is to continue asking about the hair; about the color and the manner of combing the hair to keep the eyewitness focused on the hair. No matter how unspecific the information may be for the investigator, they should strive to keep her there and let her settle the description as she sees fit.

We continue letting her try and figure out the hairstyle when we learn that she had spoken to her boyfriend about the event and he offered her a name for the hairstyle of the suspect. We confirm he wasn't there at the crime scene, but we do learn they discussed the suspect description (good information for follow-up and corroboration). By question 54 we ask if the hairstyle is unique, and she says no. Because the suspect's hair is unremarkable, we can accept that her struggle with articulating the hairstyle may be more about her inability to recall the name of the style her boyfriend told her instead of it being an unusual haircut. We have to consider the fact that when she described the suspect to her boyfriend, she didn't know how to describe the hair, so the boyfriend offered her a description that the eyewitness accepted – even though the boyfriend was only guessing based on the description he had heard. Had we offered our own opinion of the hairstyle during the interview we might have complicated the description further and created another layer of detail she might have accepted as her own. Our new information might have contradicted the boyfriend's description, thus diminishing the integrity of her initial recollection.

In MIM we patiently wait, and we accept the lack of specificity and understand that sometimes TIATI. Since we know the eyewitness will view the sketch in preliminary form (for feedback and refinement) we can exhaust her recollection of the description of his face now and focus on her recognition of the sketch to her memory later, to learn if she accepts the hairstyle. It will also be easier for her to distinguish between what she has in her mind about the hair and what she sees in front of her (the sketch represents the interpretation of her statements). By the time we get to question 123 we've covered the majority of the face except the eyes. We ask the eyewitness a question about the suspect's attitude to get another perspective about his demeanor and how the eyewitness saw him. This question often leads to more information that may have not been revealed initially.

68.	INV:	Okay. Tell me about his ears. What were they like?
69.	EW:	They were not big or….they were just normal size.
70.	INV:	Okay and was he wearing any earrings?
71.	EW:	No.
72.	INV:	Okay and what about his forehead? What was that like?
73.	EW:	Um it wasn't too big because he had bushy eyebrows.
74.	INV:	Okay.
75.	EW:	It was just like perfect.
76.	INV:	Okay. Tell me about his nose.
77.	EW:	His nose was like…it wasn't wide but it wasn't closed, you know what I mean? It wasn't narrow. It was like a medium size.
78.	INV:	Okay very good. His mouth and his lips?
79.	EW:	Um, his lips, they were pretty small I think. (inaudible) His mouth – cuz he was covering it a lot of the time.
80.	INV:	With what?
81.	EW:	His hand.
82.	INV:	Okay.
83.	EW:	He was also smoking, so…
84.	INV:	What's his attitude like?
85.	EW:	It was like really relaxed but nervous. Like he would hardly speak but he didn't seem like panicked. He was just nervous, I'm guessing, that's why he didn't speak much but I didn't think (inaudible).
86.	INV:	Any facial hair on this guy?
87.	EW:	Um not that I remember because I told them he did but I believe that he didn't because at first I thought he had like something here… (holding her chin).
88.	INV:	Mhm.
89.	EW:	but then I don't think he did.
90.	INV:	And when you say you told them he did, who were you talking about?
91.	EW:	I told the sheriff.
92.	INV:	Oh Okay.
93.	EW:	I thought I saw a goat tee but then I thought about it and remembered.
94.	INV:	So now you're saying probably not?
95.	EW:	No.
96.	INV:	Okay. And um what's the chin like?
97.	EW:	It was round. Everything came along with his face you know how some chins stick out? His fit.
98.	INV:	Does he have a mannish face or a boyish face?
99.	EW:	I think he had a boy face. Like a little kids face.
100.	INV:	Mhm. Tell me about his skin.
101.	EW:	His skin was very light. Maybe a little lighter than me but the reason I said he was Chicano was that I was speaking to him in English but some of the words came out in Spanish…

102.	INV:	For you?
103.	EW:	Yeah for me. And I was like, "Do you speak Spanish?" And he was like, "Kind of. I understand it." (inaudible)
104.	INV:	And he told you in English?
105.	EW:	Yeah.
106.	INV:	Okay.
107.	EW:	(inaudible)
108.	INV:	Mhm. Tell me about his neck. What was that like?
109.	EW:	I didn't see his neck because he was wearing a hoodie – a dark hoodie – and it went pretty high.
110.	INV:	Mhm.
111.	EW:	But I think it was short because he covered it.
112.	INV:	And go ahead and tell me how he was dressed.
113.	EW:	He was wearing a dark hoodie, just like this, With no zipper and I believe he had a white tee on the bottom and long jean shorts down to his knee, maybe a little bit longer. I didn't see his (inaudible). And they were light – they weren't dark.
114.	INV:	What was light?
115.	EW:	The pants.
116.	INV:	Okay.
117.	EW:	They were light blue.
118.	INV:	Mhm.
119.	EW:	His shoes I didn't see. I didn't pay attention.
120.	INV:	Any scars, marks or tattoos?
121.	EW:	No, not that I saw.
122.	INV:	Mhm.
123.	INV:	Tell me about his eyes.
124.	EW:	His eyes were kind of round but stretched out. Kind of like Asian but not too Asian. They were like oval but stretched out a little. (inaudible)
125.	INV:	And the color of his eyes?
126.	EW:	Black/brown. Dark.
127.	INV:	And tell me about his eyebrows.
128.	EW:	They looked kind of bushy.
129.	INV:	Mmm
130.	EW:	Not super bushy, but a little bit.
131.	INV:	Did you ever see this guy before?
132.	EW:	That guy looked like a guy I went to high school with but the guy I went to high school with was like more taller….more (inaudible) basically the same thing but the guy I met in high school had facial hair.
133.	INV:	When did you see that guy?
134.	EW:	Back in high school.
135.	INV:	So you haven't seen him since?
136.	EW:	No.
137.	INV:	Oh Okay. But you're saying he kind of reminded you of him?
138.	EW:	Yeah that was my first impression when I saw him. That he looked like him.
139.	INV	Mhm.

In this segment we get the sense the eyewitness had a very good look at the suspect and was close enough to gather very specific impressions of him. Our "attitude" question (line 84) is more about keeping her focused on the suspect's face and understanding her judgment about his attitude. When we ask about facial hair, we learn that she spoke to a law enforcement officer about the description of the suspect, and we see that she decides he doesn't have a "goatee" after she recalls her conversation with the deputy. This might be critical information later and we might ask for the supplemental report (if there is one) about the preliminary interview that was conducted between the deputy and the eyewitness at the scene. We eventually learn that she believes the suspect might be "Chicano" because he spoke with a Spanish accent. We can tell from her comments her bias regarding people of color, and this may be important when the suspect is eventually identified and we learn more about his ethnicity. After we exhaust the questions about the face, we pivot to eyewitness factors that may contribute to her recall.

We ask her whether she has ever seen the suspect before (131). This question can generate interesting answers even though most of the time the answer is no. In this case the eyewitness recalls a boy she knew in high school. It was important to understand the context of her recollection, so we ask when she might have seen the boy from high school. She clarifies not since high school, but says it was her "first impression when she saw [the suspect]" that makes her think the suspect "looked like him." If we want to conduct more extensive background on her statements about the suspect, we might obtain the high school yearbook and ask her to locate the boy she remembered. It might be useful to compare the image to the eventual suspect identification and confirm the details of the suspect to evaluate the reliability of her recollection.

140.	EW:	His color. Just his face.
141.	INV:	Mmm. Did this happen during the day or at night?
142.	EW:	At night. It was like 10 or 9:50.
143.	INV:	Oh really. What was the lighting like?
144.	EW:	I think there was just one light there on the street. The ones on the big pole. And my truck lights. But I could see his face.
145.	INV:	And he was in front of you or behind you?
146.	EW:	He wasn't…we were standing side to side.
147.	INV:	Mhm.
148.	EW:	And I would sometimes face him but he was always to the side.
149.	INV:	Mmm. Anything else you can tell me about his face?
150.	EW:	… (inaudible) looked like – not a baby you know – a young person, you know? Like he didn't have no acne. Nothing like that.

We then move to Topic 3 (Elements of the Crime). When we move into the crime event we engage with more active listening and mirror-probing tactics which encourages the eyewitness to offer more cognitive evidence. When we interview an eyewitness who is comfortable speaking about the incident, we may have to apply the Mirror Probe (MP) tactics sooner and make our decision rather early to ensure the MP works. Sometimes when we employ the MP we don't get the eyewitness to elaborate, but we need to continue engaging in this delicate process so we eventually get more information.

Out of the ten questions in this next segment we engaged in five MPs to allow the eyewitness to elaborate on more details (151 – 179). As you read the exchanges it may appear to be disjointed but in person it flows quite naturally as I mimic her tone of voice and her pacing. She is quite comfortable hearing me repeat her own words (and phrases) and resetting herself to offer me just a bit more information every time we use the MP. For example, even though I advise her to tell me what she was doing "just prior to running into this guy" we don't know how far back in the event, before the suspect enters, that she'll start describing what she remembers. As she begins retelling the incident, she begins at a point already on the road and it sounds like the suspect will come into the picture very soon. While it might have been better for her to start her narrative from before her getting into the vehicle, we should manage the narrative as she presents it and use our active listening skills to focus on cognitive evidence. We don't need to interrupt her as she begins to tell us how she ran into the suspect and then make her feel like she failed my instructions. Instead, we should be flexible enough to engage in MPs to slow her down and get her to reveal more information.

Topic 3

151.	INV:	Nothing like that. All right you can open your eyes. Now what I want you to do is tell me what happened. I want you to tell me what you were doing just prior to running into this guy and then take me through the incident up until the police got involved.
152.	EW:	Okay. So I was actually going to Savemart right here to go get milk and I pulled out and…
153.	INV:	You pulled out?
154.	EW:	Yeah I pulled out of Savemart And I went to the strip mall by Oak.
155.	INV:	Savemart?
156.	EW:	Yeah. And think I went past the light and I saw him.
157.	INV:	You saw him?
158.	EW:	Yeah. Not him. I saw the truck. The way I recognized the truck is the lights were dim cuz one of the lights didn't work. (inaudible)
159.	INV:	One of the lights?
160.	EW:	Huh?
161.	INV:	One of the lights, you said?
162.	EW:	Yeah and um Okay whatever and he was still (inaudible). And I went to Texaco I think it's called – the gas station on Oak Street.
163.	INV:	Mhm.
164.	EW:	And I put gas in but there wasn't too many people. There was just like a little bit so I could see everyone around cuz it was small and I could see everything so I put gas in and I pulled out and I was already coming back towards Oak.
165.	INV:	Okay.
166.	EW:	Because I didn't… (inaudible).
167.	INV:	Towards Oak?
168.	EW:	Yeah and (inaudible) once I hit the light on Oak towards (inaudible) he was coming. The truck.
169.	INV:	He was coming so you knew it was him?
170.	EW:	Yeah I knew it was him cuz of the light.
171.	INV:	Got it.
172.	EW:	So like, that's weird, you know. So I saw the light (inaudible) so um how do I explain it to you… the light..was red.
173.	INV:	Oh the signal light?
174.	EW:	Yeah. I stopped there and he was coming in the same lane I was going to turn. I was going to turn left and he came right behind me and he just like hit my truck. Like bumped it not even hard.

175.	INV:	He bumped your truck?
176.	EW:	Yeah. I was like great. What are you doing? So I looked out my window (inaudible) the mirror
177.	INV:	Oh okay, you looked at the mirror?
178.	EW:	Yeah and he was looking at me cuz he told me to pull over. He told me to pull over. I was like okay, but I wasn't going to pull over to there because there was no space. So I turned to watch the road but the bridge was really narrow so I couldn't pull over there so I went to the first block and I wasn't even to the edge so he pulled over to the edge…
179.	INV:	He pulled over to the edge?
180.	EW:	Yeah and I was like inside the lane like whatever and I tried to look in my mirror to see if I could see the truck – my truck or his truck but I couldn't so I pulled down my window but I couldn't so I just go out to see the truck – the back of my truck. So one of his lights – remember his light?
181.	INV:	Yes.
182.	EW:	So one of his lights was all the way in so I thought that happened when he crashed my truck because I saw obviously the dim light but I wasn't that close so I could see it was pushed in so I was like ohhh. So I got out and my truck was just scratched and he got out too and I was like, "What were you thinking? You're not going to tell me you didn't see me because I was right there stopped at the light. Obviously you could see me."
183.	INV:	Mhm.

The MPs help to describe more information like where she "pulled out" from and how she went "past the light and saw him." She then corrects herself by saying she "saw the truck" (158) and clarifies the reason she recognized it was because "one of the lights didn't work." She eventually offers a lot of detail about being at the gas station and describes the scene fairly well. She leaves the gas station and then goes past a certain light and realizes it is him because she remembers the "light." This segment gives us a lot of information about her state of mind and how she was suspicious of him. We can also imagine how she might have been on guard for something to happen.

184.	EW:	And he was like, "Oh I'm sorry." And he was like, "I was trying to light up my cigarette." So when he told me that he actually started to light up his cigarette and I was just like oh my god. And he said, "So what are you trying to do about it?" And I was like, "I have full insurance. I have everything. Do you have insurance?" And he was like, "No I don't have nothing." And I was like, "Oh my god I don't know what to do." And I was like, "I want to call the cops." And he was like, "No no no no. Let's try to fix something."
185.	INV:	He said, "Let's try to fix something?"
186.	EW:	Yeah and I was like okay cuz you know I've never been in an accident you know and I just got the truck so…
187.	INV:	Okay.
188.	EW:	So I called my boyfriend and I told him what happened and I was like I don't know what to do.
189.	INV:	You called your boyfriend?
190.	EW:	Yeah.

191.	INV:	While you were there?
192.	EW:	Yeah. I was like, "I don't know what to do. What should I do?" And he was like, "Well ask him for money or something." And I was like okay, (inaudible) for money and so he said, "Let me talk to him." But the guy wouldn't say many words. He was like, "Yeah. No." Like he wasn't… (inaudible) I guess he told him his name and he told him some phone numbers.
193.	INV:	He told your boyfriend his name?
194.	EW:	Yeah.
195.	INV:	Okay.
196.	EW:	He told him phone numbers. Obviously it wasn't… (inaudible) And um so he just passed him to me and he was like, "Talk to him." And I was like – talk to my boyfriend. And I told him like what did you guys say? And he was like, "Well he's gonna give you $200. He said he has it in his truck." So I was like, "Okay. So what's going to happen with the incident?" And he was like, "Just report that somebody hit you or something else." And I was like Okay. So I was like, I told the guy, but I was on the telephone with him, "So do you have the money with you?" And he was like, "Yeah." And I'm like, "Okay." But I was expecting him to pull it out or go get it or something.
197.	INV:	Right.
198.	EW:	And my boyfriend was like, "What is he doing?" And (inaudible) he was like, "Ask him for the money." And I was like, "So do you have the money with you or do you have it in the bank. Do we have to go somewhere?" And he was like, "No (inaudible)." And I was like, "Give it to me."
199.	INV:	Right.
200.	EW:	And he wouldn't do it. He was just standing there thinking about what to do – I don't know. So umm he actually got – I guess he was just standing there and I wasn't saying anything and so he got impatient (boyfriend) and he was like, "Tell him. Tell him to give you the money." And I was like, "Okay, well take it out. Take out the money." And he was like, "Okay." He said Okay again and I was like, "Okay I'll wait for you right here. Go get it." Cuz I was like, "Is it in your truck? He was like, "Yeah." So he went to his truck.
201.	INV:	Okay.
202.	EW:	And he went to his passenger seat and he bent down and he like got something. And he went to the side he was driving. I don't know why but he did. And he was walking towards me slowly (inaudible) but he was looking around and I was like Okay this is weird and so was walking toward me and he pretended to put something under his sweater maybe to make me think he was putting the money in there cuz as he was coming up to me he had his sweater like this…
203.	INV:	Mhm.
204.	EW:	He was pretty close to me already and I still had the phone on my ear…
205.	INV:	Okay.
206.	EW:	and whenever – he was going to get the money…
207.	INV:	Okay.
208.	EW:	I was writing down his plate number.

209.	INV:	Okay.
210.	EW:	And um once he was right next to me – actually he pulled out his hand and I pulled out my hand so he would like give it to me and he hit me, like right there (inaudible) he hit me right here and my glasses fell off my ear and he kept hitting me and hitting me in the face and all over my head.
211.	INV:	He just kept hitting you.
212.	EW:	Yeah my face, my head, my nose. And probably like three times and I fell to the ground.
213.	INV:	Okay.
214.	EW:	And he hit me one more time and I was screaming (inaudible) so he could get the point and once I didn't say anything, he stopped. So he basically thought he had knocked me out. I wasn't right. And he reached down to the floor and grabbed my phone and went inside my truck and took my bag and I think he took the milk because it (inaudible) the milk was on top of the (inaudible) It was on top of my purse. It was a little carton. It wasn't big. He grabbed it and took it and my purse was wide open. It was really open
215.	INV:	Mmm.
216.	EW:	and it's big so anything could have fallen out. So he got the purse and he went in the truck and he (inaudible). And I looked if he was fully gone, I just got in the truck and I just turned on the truck and pressed the gas and I pulled into this driveway
217.	INV:	Mhm
218.	EW:	Because this truck was pulling out and I got out of the truck. I put it in park and I got out of the truck and I was bleeding like a lot and my nose and (inaudible) and I told these guys – there were two young guys – they were like 20 something almost 30 and I told them, "Can you guys help me? Can you call the police?" And they were like, "No!" They were like scared.
219.	INV:	Oh were they?
220.	EW:	Yeah and I was like, "Can you please at least call them." "What happened to you?" And then when I told them that the truck had been robbed they were like, "Well Okay." Because they were scared: I don't know what they were afraid of.
221.	INV:	Mhm. And what did they do?
222.	EW:	They got out of the truck and they were standing right there and I was like, calm down and the other guy was like, "Calm down!" telling me to calm down because I was freaking out and – the dad I guess got out of the house and he was like, "What happened?" And I told him. And he was like, "You need to just breathe. You're Okay." He was trying to calm me down. He was like, "You're in one piece. You don't have to fight still." And I was like Okay. So he went to call (inaudible) back for me and (inaudible) my glasses and I kept seeing him (inaudible) so um I told the guy I was like, "Will you go see if my glasses are over there? I don't know if he ran them over or if he took them or…" And he was like, "Yeah, yeah." And he was looking for them on the floor and he got them but he didn't want to pick them up because (inaudible)
223.	INV:	Evidence. Right.

224.	EW:	He was like, "They're right here." But cars are coming and he had to pick them up.
225.	INV:	Oh. It was on the street.
226.	EW:	Yeah it was in the middle of the street. And so he picked them up and I put them on because I couldn't see, you know.
227.	INV:	Right.
228.	EW:	But I was bleeding so I just took them off. (inaudible)
229.	INV:	Mmm.
230.	EW:	And so first the paramedics came- no, no, the ambulance and then the paramedics came. So I'm guessing, I'm not sure cuz my boyfriend called the cops, too (inaudible). So two cops came. First one, and then another one. I don't know if they came together.
231.	INV:	Okay. Got it.
232.	EW:	The other guy. First the paramedics sat me down and took my blood pressure and (inaudible). I was sitting down and (inaudible) he took me to the ambulance. (inaudible) And then my boyfriend arrived and he go there and he was (inaudible) because he didn't know what happened and they were like hold on, hold on, and they were like, "We need to have the police." Oh and after that they were like, "Are you sure you don't want us to take you to the hospital." And I was like, "No because I don't have insurance."
233.	INV:	Mhm.
234.	EW:	And I went to the side to speak to the cop.
235.	INV:	Mhm.
236.	EW:	(inaudible) And after that they took me to my truck and so the cops went to my truck (inaudible) and after that Okay, I gave them all the information and the other cop, he came back because I guess he found my wallet…
237.	INV:	Oh, Okay.
238.	EW:	So what the cop thought that since my bag was open that probably when he (inaudible) he got it, my wallet fell out cuz he found it I guess on the edge…
239.	INV:	Nearby?
240.	EW:	Yeah nearby I don't know if he threw it out or…So then they gave it to me and everything was in there. Everything not even my money was gone.
241.	INV:	Oh.
242.	EW:	That's why I don't know.
243.	INV:	Mhm.
244.	EW:	(inaudible) That's when he told me what he thought happened. So he gave me his card.
245.	INV:	Mhm.
246.	EW:	And he's like,"I'm gonna be gone until Sunday." So maybe another cop will take the case. I was like, Okay…take her home.So (inaudible) cuz I live in Watsonville.
247.	INV:	Right.
248.	EW:	My cousin I live with…
249.	INV:	Mhm.

250.		She and her husband always go to bed super early cuz they work really early so (inaudible) they're not going to be able to take care of me.
251.	INV:	Right.
252.	EW:	And I'm like – so they took me to their house and I started calling my checking..
253.	INV:	Right.
254.	EW:	and all those places.
255.	INV:	Right. So did the police show you any pictures of possible suspects?
256.	EW:	They said they didn't want to confuse me cuz the picture was fresh in my head of my head.

At this point we move on to Topic 4 and confirm details of the suspect description. We remind her that we just want her to tell us whether each drawn feature resembles what she remembers about the suspect. We also remind her that our memories are not "exact" and that the sketch will reflect the same condition (261). Nevertheless, we want to be as close as possible to what she remembers and that the sketch might help her remember. We move on to a series of open-ended questions that look for her impressions and welcome her scrutiny for changes to the sketch. If this interview did not involve a sketch this section would confirm details already stated by the eyewitness.

Topic 4

257.	INV:	Right. All right, I'm going to show you the sketch. When you look at the sketch, I don't need you to tell me whether or not it looks like him just yet. What I want you to do is just look at the sketch, see what I'm doing. After you look at it for a few seconds, we're going to go over the same questions again, but this time you'll be looking at the sketch. As I ask you about each feature, I want you to tell me whether we're in the ball park or whether you want me to make changes.
258.	EW:	Okay.
259.	INV:	Do you understand that?
260.	EW:	Yes.
261.	INV:	We're never gonna be exact because your memory isn't exact.
262.	EW:	Yeah.
263.	INV:	But we want to be very, very close. So when you look at it, it helps you to remember. Alright? This is what I have so far… First of all, just the shape of the face. How's the shape of the face?
264.	EW:	Pretty good.
265.	INV:	Okay. The hair on his head?
266.	EW:	Yeah.
267.	INV:	Something like that? And dark? His hair?
268.	EW:	Yeah.
269.	INV:	Okay. The ears I gave him?
270.	EW:	Yeah. Oh maybe a little bigger.
271.	INV:	In what way?
272.	EW:	Like…
273.	INV:	Okay…Tell me about his nose.
274.	EW:	His nose looks about right.

275.	INV:	His mouth and his lips?
276.	EW:	Yeah.
277.	INV:	Yep. His chin and his cheeks?
278.	EW:	His cheeks may be a little thinner.
279.	INV:	A little thinner. Mhm. (drawing…) So it looks like um…so did he end up taking anything after all? I mean, I don't remember now.
280.	EW:	(inaudible)
281.	INV:	Oh, he did get the bag. Got it. (drawing) So did you end up going to the doctor or hospital?
282.	EW:	Yesterday.
283.	INV:	What did they say?
284.	EW:	They took a CT scan and they said everything was Okay.
285.	INV:	Okay. Just headaches or something like that?
286.	EW:	Yeah it hurts. My face.
287.	INV:	Yeah I can imagine.
288.	EW:	(inaudible)
289.	INV	Yeah I know. Okay. Umm the eyes?
290.	EW:	The eyes need to be a little more open.
291.	INV:	Okay. More open?
292.	EW:	Yeah they were like kinda stretched out but big.
293.	INV:	Alright I can do that (drawing). I don't remember but did he take your truck?
294.	EW:	No. Thank God.
295.	INV:	Okay.
296.	EW:	The cops said he stole the truck he was in.
297.	INV:	Oh really? Oh yeah, that's right because you wrote down the license plate. They have that?
298.	EW:	Yeah.
299.	INV:	Good. That was pretty smart of you. And he didn't see you doing that, huh?
300.	EW:	I guess not cuz then he would have (inaudible)…

After question 293 the interview continues with more feature confirmation. We resume at the part of the interview where she begins to offer more information about the elements of the crime. We now learn that this crime was not a carjacking, but in fact more of an assault with a deadly weapon.

When we think about her struggle to describe the hair style of the suspect we welcome the fact that the hair style illustrated in the sketch met her expectations. We can be assured we didn't offer our own interpretation of the hair style and that what is represented was the best interpretation of her statements. She has the authority to make any changes at this point, and she is well positioned to feel in control of her narrative and making changes to the sketch and approving them. During the back and forth of confirming features we have some time to question her for more information that may need some clarification. For instance at this point we need to confirm whether the crime was a carjacking (as the report was delivered to us) or whether it was something else. We know the suspect did not take her car, but do we know if he tried or whether he committed another crime besides trying to attack her?

301.	INV:	Yeah. (drawing…) So what about the name he gave your boyfriend?
302.	EW:	It was Emilio (inaudible).
303.	INV:	And you guys already told the police that, right?
304.	EW:	Yeah. (inaudible)
305.	INV:	Did your boyfriend recognize the name or anything?

306. EW: No.
307. INV: (drawing) How's that on the eyes?
308. EW: Yeah.
309. INV: Better?
310. EW: Yeah.
311. INV: The eyebrows?
312. EW: Um they weren't that long.
313. INV: Mhm. How about the thickness?
314. EW: I think it's about (inaudible)
315. INV: So I made one thicker than the other. Which one is it more like? This one on the right or the one on the left? On the right? When you say longer you mean take it away from here?
316. EW: Yeah...You're good.
317. INV: Oh, thank you. Well you have a good memory, too, so that's good.
318. EW: Not really. (inaudible)
319. INV: How's that?
320. EW: Yeah.
321. INV: How about his age? How are we doing on his age?
322. EW: He kinda looks younger but he did still look young.
323. INV: Yeah, how old does this guy look here?
324. EW: I don't know. Like 18?
325. INV: It's up to you. So you want him a little older or are we Okay?
326. EW: Maybe a little bit older. I don't know.
327. INV: Okay, what about the sweatshirt?
328. EW: Yeah that's fine.
329. INV: Okay. And no scars or marks?
330. EW: (inaudible)
331. INV: Okay. I'm just going to finish him up a little bit. (drawing) So were you able to cancel everything?
332. EW: Yeah.
333. INV: Good. (drawing) The next time you see this sketch, you might see the sweatshirt. The hoodie. You might see it black, like really dark. So I'm not gonna have you sit here to fill it all in. So I'm just letting you know if you ever see it again, you'll notice that it's considerably darker than what it is today. I just worked on his age a little bit. What I want you to do is ask yourself, "Does it remind me of him." If there's something else that you want me to change or adjust, just let me know and I'll take care of it, Okay?
334. INV: Does that remind you of him?
335. EW: Yeah.
336. INV: Do you want to make any changes?
337. EW: I don't get the hair.
338. INV: How do YOU want it? I just filled it in.
339. EW: Is it slicked back, or how is that?
340. INV: If you want it slicked back, I can make it slicked back. I don't have it slicked back.

341. EW: It was like normal.
342. INV: Yeah. Standing up. That's the way I had it. If you look at the edges here – watch – (drawing).
343. EW: It was just like normal. (inaudible) Yeah.
344. INV: Something like that? Good. Anything else?
345. EW: I don't think so.
346. INV: Okay. About as close as we're gonna get?
347. EW: Yeah.

Topic 5

348. INV: Good job! Okay. (drawing) The initials to your name are AU? And this happened around noon? If you have any questions, you can always call. They wanted you to talk to somebody? Did you know who that was?
349. EW: (inaudible)
350. INV: Okay. I'll walk you out. Take care of yourself, all right?

We learned a lot from this segment of the interview. When we investigate further about other eyewitness event factors like the proximity to the suspect and environmental conditions, her answers help to clarify her statements about the investigation. We learned: (a) the suspect took a bag of hers; (b) the license plate information she gave police allowed them to determine the vehicle the suspect was driving was stolen; (c) we know she went to the doctor to get treatment the next day; (d) we also know that the suspect didn't take her car; and (e) that the name he gave her boyfriend was "Emilio" and she did not recognize it.

As we ask about confirming each feature, we limit our multiple-choice questions, or exact measurements, or specific details. When we are mindful of eyewitness memory, we know that asking questions like this can lead to unreliable statements from the eyewitness, so we try and curb the opportunities for her memory to "recreate" something that wasn't there.

For example, when we ask her about the eyes and she says they need to be "a little more open," we don't expect her to offer a number or a specific length or ask her to demonstrate the opening on her eyes. We accept the fact that when she sees the sketch the eyes are not as open as she remembers and opening the eyes (in the sketch) is something we (as forensic artists) can do without much effort from the eyewitness. The eyewitness only needs to react to the likeness of the sketch features to their memory of the suspect. We also must be cognizant of the fact that every time they see the sketch it becomes more familiar which becomes more acceptable to what they remember.

Just as the eyewitness becomes confident that the suspect they picked from a photo line-up is the same person they saw at the scene, we must expect that they will find their confidence heightened as they view the sketch multiple times. Regardless, the difference in the photo line-up process and the MIM sketch interview is that the sketch was derived totally from memory while the photo line-up was created from images of similar looking alleged suspects. When we consider the fact that initially the eyewitness struggled with describing the hair and that she was specific about the eyes, we are mindful of this and make sure these two areas meet her satisfaction. It doesn't mean we make sure the sketch is "exact;" we already told her we know her memory will not be great and that the sketch will never match her memory precisely, we only want the sketch to resemble the suspect enough for her to say that it reminds her of him.

THE MINDFUL INTERVIEW METHOD

Figure 18.1 Cognitive sketch of subject created from eyewitness interview, Gil Zamora © 2012.

The sketch interview in this case study exemplified the MIM technique for creating a sketch (see Figure 18.1). Not only did this sketch interview gather robust information about the face, it also allowed the eyewitness to place her memory in the context of the crime event in an eyewitness-centered format.

While I am not suggesting that every "whodunnit case" requires a cognitive sketch to support eyewitness statements, we can see how interviewing an eyewitness in this mindful manner will result in valuable information that can be used to create the illustration that will enhance the investigation. Regardless, this case study also exemplifies the comprehensive nature of the MIM and allows the non-forensic artist interviewer to gather the same amount of information that can lead to promising leads and reliable identifications.

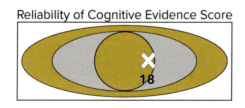

Figure 18.2 Reliability of Cognitive Evidence Target (RCE) score "18."

EFFICACY OF EYEWITNESS INTERVIEW ASSESSMENT℠
Narrative Report for Case Study #4

The Reliability of Cognitive Evidence (RCE) for this interview session is "18" which means we can consider the cognitive evidence **Highly Reliable** (Figure 18.2). The efficacy of this interview is outstanding when we consider the use of interview tactics that enhance cognitive evidence retrieval (Figure 18.3). The interview is impressive when we consider the proportion of questions asked that enhance cognitive evidence retrieval. The transcript shows the interview was unbiased by the number of questions asked (89%) that improve the reliability of cognitive evidence and enhance mindful rapport. The questions that focused on the suspect description (88%) and crime elements (98%) gathered reliable information and were more than acceptable overall. The number of Diminish Reliability of Cognitive Evidence (DRCE) questions was less than 5% which improved the overall score and the reliability of the evidence collected.

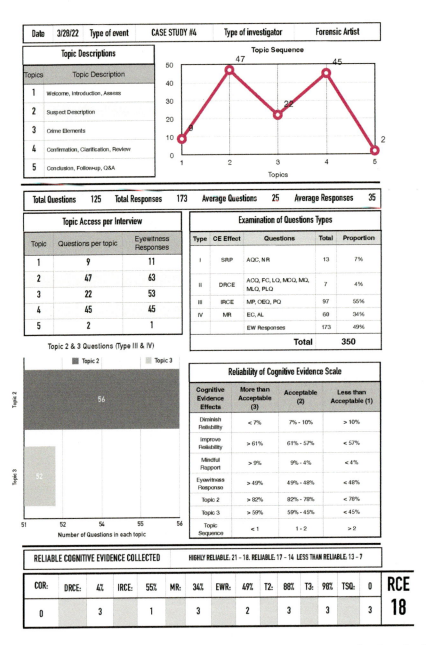

Figure 18.3 Efficacy of Eyewitness Interview Assessment Summary Report for Case Study #4.

19
Case Study #5

A MOCK INTERVIEW

This is our last case study, and it features what I consider two main areas of concern for eyewitness interviews: (a) the lack of efficacy in preserving cognitive evidence, and (b) the lack of awareness at retrieving unreliable cognitive evidence. Because we do not evaluate the performance of law enforcement in interviewing eyewitnesses, we have no idea about the magnitude of this issue: Relying on unreliable cognitive evidence to generate leads and identify culprits for arrest.

I wanted to see how eyewitness interviews were being conducted by newly trained police officers, so I enlisted the help of a wonderful university police officer to showcase their interview skills in front of a class of Eyewitness Interview students. I invited a San Jose State University (SJSU) police officer to join my Eyewitness Interview course to interview a student who portrayed a robbery victim in our mock interview demonstrations. I had conducted a few eyewitness interviews with students so they could compare my interview technique with others that we either viewed online or within class from their peers. All students had been prepared to conduct an analysis of the interview based on my Composite Sketch Analysis form that I altered for students in this class. I provided them with background knowledge on eyewitness memory research findings and the role witness and event factors play in analyzing the effectiveness of the gathering eyewitness statements.

During the semester students were given a script to follow based on my *Mindful Interview Method* (MIM) technique and were encouraged to use it when they interviewed each other. Each student was expected to evaluate each other on how they applied the interview technique and adhered to the script. Many students became very comfortable following the script and understood how to limit their contributions to contaminating eyewitness memory. None of the students mastered the MP questions and many were proficient at asserting OEQ to drive the interview session. They could see how asking these questions and allowing the eyewitness (fellow students) to recall the event as they remembered was better than interjecting and directing them to answer certain questions. Asking a sworn police officer to conduct the mock interview in class, in my opinion, was an amazing coup that enhanced the education of students in class.

THE MINDFUL INTERVIEW METHOD

While I agree that eyewitness memory may be unreliable to use as the single source for identifying the culprit and pushing prosecution, I do believe we must consider the interview technique that gathers cognitive evidence to confidently pursue the suspect identification. Until we agree on the best practices for conducting eyewitness interviews that are mindful of eyewitness memory issues, we can never be comfortable with the result of eyewitness interviews. This mock interview session was my attempt to educate future criminal justice professionals on how questionable our process for gathering cognitive evidence was, and how we use that evidence to sometimes pursue innocent people and change their lives forever. I had no idea what to expect and I made sure not to bias the interview session.

I had been lecturing criminal justice students on the aspects of the cognitive interview technique and my own mindful interview technique that I had demonstrated a few times over the last month. I introduced the students to assessment forms and asked them to use them when evaluating their own interview sessions. While the students were not skilled interviewers, they had been exposed to basic eyewitness memory research and had some formative evaluations about their knowledge of conducting reliable eyewitness interviews. This eyewitness interview session would be conducted remotely because of COVID protocols, but the students had an exclusive opportunity to watch the interview live and experience the back-and-forth process of retrieving cognitive evidence.

The male student (eyewitness) would be playing the role of a robbery victim who was robbed by suspects while at campus. I told the officer that the student would be "in character" the entire time and would only come out of character at my direction (Figure 19.1). I wanted to create as much authenticity as possible for the officer so they could proceed in the interview as any other investigation. In my email to the officer I told him that I would announce the specific details of the crime at the time of class and that I would turn it over

Figure 19.1 Mock robbery victim from online eyewitness interview demonstration. Eyewitness is wearing a large bandage on his head. Used by permission. © Gil Zamora, 2021.

to him after that. I also asked the officer to email me with any questions or concerns prior to the interview date, and I ended my email by asking him to "handle your interview like you do and take all of the time you need. It should be straightforward." The officer did not ask any questions and showed up on time to conduct the interview. The officer was as professional as would be expected and certainly represented the department well. I did not suggest the details of the assault to the student eyewitness (prior to the interview session) and relied on his creativity to offer an authentic experience for the officer.

The interview lasted 38 minutes and the class, the officer, and the victim heard my description of the crime event all at once – before I turned over the interview to the officer. It's important to note that I did not coach the officer to be prepared for anything other than to interview the victim as they would any other victim on campus. I am utterly grateful for the opportunity to be in a position to ask police administrators to allow members of their department to participate in these types of demonstrations in order to further the academic study of eyewitness interviews and criminal justice students.

This case study offers us some important information to review because the officer was an experienced patrol officer, well aware of the demonstration parameters, and was expected to conduct the interview based on the latest techniques employed by law enforcement at this time. Just as Fisher and Schrieber conducted their study on 23 experienced detectives before contributing their work on *The Handbook of Eyewitness Psychology, Vol. 1, Memory for Events* (Ed. Toglia et al., 2007) we ask you to consider this specific demonstration to see how far we've come since their publication.

Here are the details I announced to the officer and students about the mock robbery event: *The Reporting Party (RP) called the police about the robbery attack and left his contact information. The RP says he didn't get a good look at the suspects but knew that they were beating up the victim. The RP saw the suspects run away. One suspect is described as a white male and the RP says he couldn't get a look at the other one. The suspects have not been located.*

Topic 1

1. INV: All right so, I'm very sorry this happened to you Mr. Greg – I'm just trying to figure out what happened exactly, so where were you at?
2. EW: It happened right in front of the Seventh Street garage, I was walking to MacQuarrie Hall but I was on San Fernando.
3. INV: Okay, were you on the campus side? Or were you on the other side of the 7-Eleven in that area?
4. EW: I was on SJSU.
5. INV: Okay, so did you know these two guys at all?
6. EW: No, I was just walking to class
7. INV: And how long ago did this happen?
8. EW: Well, mm. It happened around my lunchtime so probably about 12:30.
9. INV: 12:30, so about it's about 1:40 right now, so about an hour ago?
10. EW: Yeah.

Even though this interview was a demonstration we made it clear to the officer and the student eyewitness that we were looking for authenticity: (a) from the eyewitness to remain in character; and (b) for the officer to proceed like any other investigation or call for service. In the first line of the transcript, we read that the officer acknowledges that something had happened, but we don't get the sense that the officer is really aware of the condition of his eyewitness (see the image of eyewitness, Figure 19.1). We can only imagine that because it was being held remotely, via web video, that the officer wanted the students to experience the inquiry and the less perfunctory greetings. Nevertheless, we know that it is important to establish the welcome and be present for whatever is in front of you. In this case, the eyewitness (victim) arrived with a large bandage covering his head. He was slow in speech and appeared to be speaking in a weak tone. We would expect the officer to acknowledge the condition of the eyewitness and employ an empathetic strategy right from the start. Not only is the welcome and authentic concern valuable for the interview but it transcends this interview and projects a professional and caring quality that the agency would welcome. A simple, "How are you doing?" from the officer, might start an exchange of information that will be based on trust and cooperation. Even though the lack of acknowledging the condition of the eyewitness may never result in a definitive negative impact on the reliability of cognitive evidence we can decide that we want our officers to be mindful of the eyewitness (in every aspect) and acknowledge what is before them. As we discussed earlier, we do not need to know anything about the crime or the eyewitness to see the noise that may be contributing to unwanted judgments. Determining why the officer made the judgment not to acknowledge the bandage on the head of the injured eyewitness, at the start of the interview, is important to identify in considering deficits in training.

Early in the interview it is important to establish a rhythm between the investigator and the eyewitness. After the initial welcome and explanation of the process, the questions asked by the investigator will decide how the interview flows and what role the eyewitness will play. We can see from the transcript that there is no introduction of calming or memory-enhancing techniques to help the eyewitness prepare for the inquiry. We can only imagine that the eyewitness is under the impression that offering the investigator the answer as briefly as possible is the best policy – we know that is not.

Investigators are well aware that many eyewitness interviews come with some preliminary information that is provided by dispatch, another patrol officer, or the crime report itself. When we ask questions of the eyewitness that should be known by the investigator, we risk losing some credibility if we continue down the same path. For example, in the MIM we may ask the eyewitness "Do you know why you are here?" in order to establish a baseline for context and compliance for participating in the interview. If the eyewitness expresses a concern for their involvement because they assured the officers (at the scene) that they did not see anything – then we would ask more questions about what they did recall. Only then would we determine whether the eyewitness would be a good candidate for an interview (COR).

In this case the investigator asks an OEQ which is always preferred but then follows up with a force-choice question that stifles the narrative quality we seek in the interview. We should ask OEQs and follow up with active listening and MPs to encourage the eyewitness to continue talking and telling us as much as possible. We should have the mindset that we know nothing of the event nor where it happened and allow the eyewitness to reveal as much details as possible.

Topic 2

11. INV: Okay, and you said it was two males?
12. EW: Yeah, was definitely two guys.
13. INV: What color clothing did you notice on one or the other?
14. EW: Yeah, some, there is one guy who was wearing a blue sweater with the bear I think it was Cal Berkeley bears sweater. He was a white guy and then I think he was wearing some like basketball shorts or something and then …
15. INV: Do you, do you know what color the basketball shorts were?

16.	EW:	I dunno.
17.	INV:	Okay, did you notice anything about the shoes by chance?
18.	EW:	I don't know, sorry.
19.	INV:	Okay, was he, did he have black hair, red hair, blonde hair?
20.	EW:	I think he had blonde hair, but it was more like it was if it was covered by the hoodie he was wearing and so I only got to look at his skin color which is why his face kinda had acne on it.
21.	INV:	Okay. Do you think you'd recognize this guy again if you saw him?
22.	EW:	Yeah.
23.	INV:	Okay, all right.

Topic 3

24.	INV:	What direction did he head off in? 'Cause you said you were walking by the Seventh Street garage so you're walking (EW: Yeah) you're walking westbound on the north sidewalk right?
25.	EW:	I was walking towards MacQuarrie Hall, yeah.
26.	INV:	Okay, so what direction did this guy head off after that?
27.	EW:	Honestly, I am a little disoriented because I fell to the floor after being hit by something
28.	INV:	Okay. When did the white guy hit you or did the other guy hit you?
29.	EW:	They both kinda hit me it's just (INV: Okay) the one who hit me on the head was the white guy and he's the one who stopped me in my tracks in the first place.
30.	INV:	What did he say to make you stop in your tracks?
31.	EW:	Well, that's not what he said I mean he stood right in front of me as I was walking and then I told them I was listening to my headphones, I took them, I took out my AirPods and then I asked him what's up how can I help you he's that just like we're taking your backpack and it kinda happened from there.
32.	INV:	Okay, so did he brandish a weapon? Did he did physically like stop you like this? Or did he grab you? Or did he just stand there and block your way?
33.	EW:	He, he stood in front of me, I don't know what he pulled or what he hit me with – I don't know what he had, but it was hard as hell because it left a big hole cut right here in my forehead.
34.	INV:	Okay. Who put the bandage on you and where did you go to get that fixed outa curiosity?
35.	EW:	Actually, there was a kid who helped me afterwards, his name's Alan.
36.	INV:	Alan. (EW: Yeah.)
37.	INV:	Okay, all right, so now I got a decent description of the first guy.

Topic 2

38.	INV:	What did the second guy look like?
39.	EW:	He was kind of tanned I want to say maybe Hispanic. I'm Mexican. I want to say Mexican. He was – he had kind of long hair; I don't know.

THE MINDFUL INTERVIEW METHOD

40.	INV:	Okay. Um, what type of clothing was he wearing?
41.	EW:	What was he wearing? He was wearing a white hoodie with some pants, I wanna say jeans.
42.	INV:	Okay. Did you notice anything about shoes or tattoos or anything?
43.	EW:	No, well he was covered. I didn't get a look at the shoes, he came from behind – that one.
44.	INV:	So he came from behind?
45.	EW:	Yeah.
46.	INV:	Um, these guys, were they – the white guy, was he tall? Short? Fat? Skinny?
47.	EW:	He was kind of skinny.
48.	INV:	Skinny?
49.	EW:	Yeah. The white guy was kinda skinny; the other guy was kind of bulky.
50.	INV:	Bulky?
51.	EW:	Yeah.
52.	INV:	Um, about how tall? How tall are you outa curiosity?
53.	EW:	I'm six feet tall.
54.	INV:	You're six feet tall. Okay was the white guy – was he taller or shorter than you?
55.	EW:	Yeah, he was a little bit shorter.
56.	INV:	Okay was he like five-five or was he a lot shorter? I'm five-nine so would you say hypothetically he was about my height?
57.	EW:	Yeah, I just, I mean he wasn't too much shorter than me.
58.	INV:	Okay, so what about the other guy?
59.	EW:	I, I honestly, I couldn't tell you because he came from behind me and then the next thing I know I was on the floor.
60.	INV:	Okay, so did you see a hat? Was he wearing a hat or a backpack, or anything of that nature?
61.	EW:	Um, no, they wanted my backpack. They kept on saying just take it off or just give it to us, and then they just kept on hitting me, so.

When we conduct our analysis of the interview, we expect to see a structure that is reasonable and allows for the eyewitness to express themselves in the sequence that is more familiar to them – as it happened to them. Interviewers can initiate the start of the eyewitness's recollection by anchoring their recall – when we ask the OEQ, we should let the eyewitness narrative carry the load so we can create a pathway that allows them to go over areas to help them remember more. When the interview feels disjointed and unstructured it can cause important information to be missed and cause the eyewitness to pull back and offer less important information. What we see in this interview, beginning at line 24, is a tendency for the interviewer to go back and forth between topics that seem out of sequence. When we pursue the cognitive evidence in this manner, we run the risk of orchestrating how the information will come to us and diminish the opportunity for the eyewitness to reveal something that they remember as they remember it. At this point of the interview the investigator has not allowed the eyewitness to offer a free narrative recall of the event so we can begin to delve into the particulars (later) in a way that allows for their memory to be enhanced. Instead, we see the topics covered and the victim begins to offer brief answers to specific questions that may or may not offer more details of the event.

Another item we should discuss at this point in our analysis of the interview session is how the investigator asked a rather casual opening question like "what happened exactly" and then fell into a pattern of a basic police interview that researchers have known is unreliable for recovering information from eyewitnesses. Just as Fisher et al. (2007) found in their research on police interviews, most of them started with an open narrative question but soon interrupted them with a question that stymied the free recall by the eyewitness. We see something similar happening in our mock interview at question 1 when the investigator asks, "what happened exactly" followed by "where were you at?"(Coded AQC because it was the start of the interview, but could easily have been coded MQ) which complicated the eyewitness's attempt to deliver a free narrative recall for details of the crime event. When we ask multiple questions in this fashion the eyewitness must choose one of them, and in this case we can see the eyewitness chose the second question and focused on the location. The officer allowed the eyewitness to continue down this road and left the opportunity to find out what happened, as the eyewitness recalled it. In Fisher et al.'s (2007) research they found on average the interruption, after the open question, came in at 7.5 seconds into the interview. In our excerpt we can see on line 2 the eyewitness was only able to start their answer when the investigator jumped in and followed up with clarifying questions. The idea of a free narrative was lost, and the interview moved on to Topic 2 at question 11.

The interview moves through the suspect description (Topic 2) and shifts to the crime event (Topic 3) pretty quickly without an eyewitness narrative recall (24). We get to line 36 and the officer asks who "put the bandage on you?" which is an opportunity to offer some empathy for the injuries the victim sustained. Unfortunately, the officer shifts back to Topic 2 and on line 40 leads the eyewitness to believe he received adequate information about the first suspect and moves on to asking about the second suspect. Had the investigator stayed on the injury topic to offer concern and build rapport he might have learned more about the location of the event, the number of people nearby and more information about the Good Samaritan.

When the officer asks about the suspect's hair color (in the first Topic 2 inquiry) and offers suggestions of "black hair, red hair, blonde hair" (line 19) he is essentially encouraging the eyewitness to make selections based on his offerings. At line 24 the officer moves on to Topic 3 and tries to establish where the suspect ran to after the attack. At one point the victim says he's confused because of his current condition and the officer misses another opportunity to show empathy and establish rapport. The tone of the interview setting is shaping up as a forgone conclusion that the investigator has a pretty good idea of what happened and the eyewitness need only confirm the details, like where he was (so they can view the video), what direction the suspects came from and left the scene, and what items they took so they can be entered into the database. This is all-important information that needs to be gathered, however, when we establish the interview format in this fashion, we encourage the eyewitness to answer briefly and wait for the next question. In this next segment the topic returns to the injury to the victim and the investigator shows more empathy and builds some rapport, however, his tendency to lead the eyewitness continues.

Topic 3

62. INV: Okay, so what when they hit you where did they hit you at?
63. EW: Well, I have a bruised rib right here I can feel it. Um, the guy who hit me in the head and struck me made my forehead right here so it's bleeding all on the front of my forehead but it hurts like in the back of my head.
64. INV: Okay.
65. EW: Um, and then when they took my backpack I was also holding on because they pulled it over my head and my right arm got caught in it because I didn't want to let it go and so one of them kicked me in the shoulder and now I'm kind of, I'm I feel like I'm bruising around this area.

THE MINDFUL INTERVIEW METHOD

66. INV: Okay, so is it your collar bone? Does it feel like it, so you got kicked basically in your collar bone area?
67. EW: Yeah, it's more it's more like the shoulder area
68. INV: Shoulder area? Okay, so with that you wanna have somebody pick you up and have you, do you want me to call an ambulance to get you checked out and that type of stuff? (EW: No) because your head injuries, those can be with head injuries especially. I'm not a doctor I mean I've had some little medical training (EW: Yeah) probably you need to get your head checked out because you could have a concussion and it just to be safer on that side, okay?
69. EW: That's okay, I'll go on my own.
70. INV: You sure?
71. EW: Yeah, that's fine.

We see the officer inquire about the injury only to introduce information that is not authentic to the eyewitness's recollection of the event. When the eyewitness says one of the suspects hit him in the head while the other kicked him in the shoulder the officer proceeds to suggest he was actually kicked in the "collar bone" even though the eyewitness says it was "more like the shoulder area." The officer does a great job at using a MP like "shoulder area?" But doesn't pause enough to allow the eyewitness to elaborate further. Instead, he moves on to suggesting they seek medical treatment for the injuries, which is a very good thing, however, we are now at the quarter mark of the interview session and the concern for the victim's wellbeing is now being suggested and offered as an option. What do we say about all of the information the officer gathered previously? Has the concussion diminished the recall of details? Will the defense attorneys find this advantageous for their clients?

While this portion of the interview suggests great empathy and concern by the officer, for the eyewitness's injuries, it might have been a better strategy to engage with this line of questioning at the start of the interview when we see the eyewitness come into view with a large bandage covering the majority of his head. The officer suggests the eyewitness seek medical attention for what may be "a concussion" and humbly suggests he's "not a doctor" but has some experience with people with head injuries. The tone of this portion of the interview is positive and shows the officer is genuinely concerned which feeds the rapport-building aspect of the interview. Unfortunately, it contrasts with the proceeding inquiry into the stolen items, back to the injury, and then back to establishing the location of the crime event.

Topic 4

72. INV: Okay, that's all right. So, then I'm going to ask you some more questions here (EW: Okay), and so this is just to establish like what exactly was taken. So you had your backpack, what's your backpack look like?
73. EW: It's a black Michael Kors backpack and inside that I had my stuff for my project that I was gonna go work on which included my laptop, a textbook, some pens and pencils, and my notebook.
74. INV: Okay, so with the Michael Kors backpack, and those are pretty expensive, about how much would you say that's worth roughly?
75. EW: It was a gift for Christmas, but I think it was like $600.
76. INV: Okay it's 600 bucks on that (EW: Yeah) with the laptop what type of laptop is it?
77. EW: Macbook pro.

78. INV: Macbook pro?
79. EW: Yeah.
80. INV: Okay about how much is that one worth?
81. EW: Well, I enhanced it so about two grand.
82. INV: So $2,000?
83. EW: Yeah.
84. INV: Okay. Now do you know the serial number for that?
85. EW: I couldn't tell you.
86. INV: Okay, well outa curiosity do you have the box back at home?
87. EW: I do, I do.
88. INV: Okay, that'll be perfect because what we do is we can get that serial number and put it into our APS which is our stolen items stuff and if another officer runs across it, we can find it that way.
89. EW: Okay. Thank you.

Topic 3

90. INV: So we definitely want to get some follow-up stuff you'll probably need to get checked out by the doctor first and we can get back to that later.
91. EW: Okay.

Once again, the officer returns to Topic 3 with a great OEQ, but then follows up with a benign leading question about the value of the stolen backpack. What is important to understand is the pattern of suggestibility by the officer; while it may appear to the lay person that the officer is delving into the particulars of the case, they are actually creating an interviewee–investigator dyad where the eyewitness is allowing the officer to fill in the blanks and accept their suggestions.

In this scenario the officer's quest to find the truth outweighs their negative impact on the cognitive evidence retrieved. For instance, when the officer asks the eyewitness to offer an estimate for the cost of the backpack instead of just asking the eyewitness the value, they frame the question with a suggestion that the backpack was very expensive, thus suggesting to the eyewitness that they should offer a number that is expensive. When the officer makes the decision to suggest an expensive outcome, they are engaging in a biased inquiry that may result in an inflated value by the eyewitness, or an anchoring effect that forces the eyewitness to consider the value when they have no idea of the true value (Kahneman, 2011). At line 77 the eyewitness was unsure of the price because it was a gift but then offers a $600 value for the backpack. When we Google (www.google.com) "Michael Kors backpack" we find a list of backpacks that are priced at a range of $329 to $395, and when we go to the Michael Kors website (https://www.michaelkors.com/hudson:pebbled:leather:backpack/_/R:US_33S0LHDB2L) we find others that are priced between $298 and $498. The point is the eyewitness may have been encouraged to offer the higher value because of the suggestion by the investigator. We'll never know because we don't conduct a post-interview evaluation of the eyewitness to learn whether certain question tactics affected their responses. We must keep in mind that sometimes That Is All There Is (TIATI) and we should gather the information as reported in the initial interview. If and when we conduct a follow-up interview, we might inquire further about the price and learn the actual price paid for the item instead of guessing along with the eyewitness. For crime report purposes we can always indicate a range of value, so we understand the level of crime involved (misdemeanor versus felony). The officer does a great job at asking an OEQ about the "type of laptop" and uses MPs with probing questions to encourage the eyewitness to elaborate, however, the officer *did not maintain this line of inquiry throughout the interview session and resorted to combining MPs with leading questions which lessened the reliability of the cognitive evidence.*

Topic 4

92. INV: Anything else? You said a textbook, what type of textbook?
93. EW: It was just a school textbook for my justice studies course.
94. INV: Okay, it's kind of a weird thing so if we stop somebody, what kind of book was it exactly? Just because if we find somebody and then you have your name in it or anything …
95. EW: Well, I checked it out from the library, but financial aid paid for it so I couldn't tell you how much it costs.
96. INV: Okay, did you have any identifying markings on the laptop?
97. EW: Yeah, there's a Nike logo on it – it's like a sticker.
98. INV: Okay. Awesome. Where was it located on the laptop?
99. EW: It was in the front upper – well if you close the laptop, it's in the front upper right.
100. INV: Okay, upper right?
101. EW: Yeah.
102. INV: With the backpack, you said it was a Michael Kors, did it have anything on the outside? Did it have your name on it anywhere? Or like a luggage tag something of that nature?
103. EW: No, I was going for the more minimal things so I didn't customize it or anything like that.
104. INV: Okay, anything else in the backpack that got taken?
105. EW: I think I had my SJSU hoodie.
105. INV: SJSU hoodie?
107. EW: Yeah.

At line 96, the officer begins a line of inquiry with "kind of a weird thing" in that if police stop someone and they find certain items that have been specifically documented as belonging to the eyewitness it might make it easier for them to make a proper arrest of suspects. When we are mindful of our role as an investigator, we must be cognizant of what we say and how we say it. When the officer begins the sentence by labeling something as "weird" they create an expectation for the eyewitness that they should consider what the officer is offering as weird – without explanation. In the transcript we never understand why having your book with your name or the kind of book title might be "weird," we just read that if "[they] find somebody …" and the book has their name on it, it's implied that it might be a good thing? We see from the exchange that even though the officer asked about the textbook and whether it was marked with his name, the eyewitness focused on the book cost instead of the "name in it." Could it be that the questions in lines 75 through 85 focused on the cost of items that the eyewitness was mindless and offered the cost of the item instead of being mindful of the actual question? We'll never know; however, we do know that the officer did not acknowledge the fact the eyewitness did not answer the question completely and instead moved on to the markings on the laptop discussed in lines 99 through 103.

The questions about the laptop are a great example of asking an OEQ followed by a MP and a follow-up probing question. The eyewitness is able to offer the investigator exactly what they remember. Unfortunately, the OEQs are short lived. For example, at line 107 the officer asks a very good OEQ about what else might have been taken followed by a MP after the eyewitness says he thought his "hoodie" had been taken. Instead of pausing to allow the eyewitness to elaborate further, after using the MP, the officer suggests the colors of the hoodie (blue or yellow) and the eyewitness has to consider these choices when in fact it was another color (gray). When we continue in this manner of asking leading questions, we jeopardize our ability to gather reliable information and instead convince the eyewitness that they only need to offer information based on what the officer asks and not what the eyewitness actually remembers. Learning to be patient after asking the MP is a skill that takes time to learn. When we pause for a response, we allow the eyewitness to acknowledge our repeating of their own words and also get them to think about it and offer whatever more information they might remember about it. Sometimes, it's more, sometimes it isn't, however, we never know until we employ the mirror question and the pause properly whether we've succeeded in gathering reliable information. Chris Voss, former FBI hostage negotiator, says that "A mirror needs some silence to be effective" and we shouldn't interrupt the pause by "asking another question" (Voss, 2016).

108.	INV:	Okay, all right. Was it a blue one a yellow one?
109.	EW:	It was gray.
110.	INV:	Gray one. Okay, did it have your name in it or anything?
111.	EW:	No, it didn't, but it did kind of have a little tear in the stomach pot pouch.
112.	INV:	Um, did you have a notebook in the backpack like papers with your handwriting or anything?
113.	EW:	Yeah, I was working on a project, that's why I was going to MacQuarrie Hall.
114.	INV:	What, what color was the notebook?
115.	EW:	It was purple.
116.	INV:	Purple, any other like distinguishing stuff with that?
117.	EW:	Um, in sharpie I wrote my class on it I think it's like JS 1-85 or something
118.	INV:	All right, right. Estimated cost for the hoodie and the notebook?
119.	EW:	I think the hoodie was somewhere around $60 and then my notebook was like a dollar.
120.	INV:	A dollar, okay.

At question 114 the officer suggests more information under the guise of getting to the truth of what was inside the backpack. Instead of asking another OEQ like "What else was in the backpack?" and waiting to hear what the eyewitness might remember, he suggests there might be "papers with your handwriting." The officer is obviously looking for more evidence of stolen items to add to the list and advise other officers of the evidence that may be found when they locate the suspects. This is very conscientious investigative work, however, it's best to allow the eyewitness to tell us all that was stolen and not suggest items that might be stolen. When we employ this tactic of suggesting items, paraphrasing statements, or forcing the eyewitness to choose from two distinct items we may offer post-event information that may turn into new eyewitness memory. While the suggestion of papers with handwriting may not result in tragic outcomes in this case, when we practice these types of post event suggestions in benign settings, we become accustomed to the practice and employ them throughout our interviews without concern for the negative impact on future investigations.

At this point of the interview the topic shifts back to the location of the crime. While we can agree it is important to establish the scene of the crime, we know from eyewitness memory research that our memory is not as reliable as we think and the accuracy for times, distances, and locations may be susceptible to suggestion or error. When we have the opportunity to corroborate eyewitness details, independent of their recollection, it is always best to rely on the eyewitness for an overview of what happened. For instance, if we know we have security cameras throughout an area we believe the victim was present, we should expect to review the video footage and pinpoint the exact location and time of the incident at a later time. When we gather the main points of the crime event from the eyewitness, we do not need to rely on their specific information to determine whether it is accurate. When we employ this strategy, we risk having the eyewitness agree to something they are unsure of and then later we may find their indecision, or incorrect information, to be a cause for questioning their veracity. We must be mindful that we may cause the indecision with our questioning, and we should instead adhere to TIATI and gather the most reliable information as part of the recollection of details and focus on areas that the eyewitness can provide specific details about, like facial features, clothing of the suspects, and what the suspect(s) might have said.

Topic 4

121.	INV:	So now this is just to narrow down the area that you're at. You said you were at San Salvador, right?
122.	EW:	Um. I think so.
123.	INV:	Okay, so you say you're in the Seventh Street garage area, right?
124.	INV:	Well, the reason why I asked is we have some cameras in that area so I'm gonna try to see if we can really narrow down the area. So you know where the police department is?
125.	EW:	Um, I like on campus?
126.	INV:	Yeah, yeah.
127.	EW:	Er, is that ...
128.	INV:	It's at the Seventh Street garage area you could actually cut through the building when you when you pull into the garage.
129.	EW:	Okay.
130.	INV:	Okay, so we're on both sides of the that area. So you said you're on San Salvador right there right on that street, okay. Well, do you, were you closer to where you got hit; you were you going to MacQuarrie so you're going around the garage and then over to the MacQuarrie Hall?
131.	EW:	Well, I had gone to an ATM right before that because I know campus has an ATM ...
132.	INV:	Okay. So are you over at over at like lot four? Where we have the four ATMs?
133.	EW:	Um, I think so.
134.	INV:	All right, is it by the Student Union?
135.	EW:	Yeah, is that where the Wells Fargo is on?
136.	INV:	I think that's where the Wells Fargo is, yes ...
137.	EW:	... probably over there.
138.	INV:	Okay so were you there before? Didn't you say that's where you started off before you went over to MacQuarrie Hall?
139.	EW:	Yeah, so I was walking through the campus, but it happened kind of around there.
140.	INV:	Oh, it happened over there over by the ATMs?
141.	EW:	No. So I, I had gone to the ATM for a little bit, and I don't know if they were following me since then but (INV: okay) it happened around the Seventh Street garage area.
142.	INV:	So, okay you were you on the north side of the garage or were you on the street side?

143.	EW:	No, I was I was on campus.
144.	INV:	You're on campus. Okay, so you weren't on the road whatsoever there; by the sidewalk when I asked you if you were on the actual north side of the garage where there's not that street.
145.	EW:	I think, I think my problem is that because I could see it; it's I'm just kind of identifying where it's at but I, I was on campus for sure.
146.	INV:	Okay, so do you know if you were by the building right next to MacQuarrie?
147.	EW:	Um …
148.	INV:	Sweeney Hall. It's got like an open courtyard area.
149.	EW:	I was in an open courtyard area but I, I couldn't tell you. I'm a justice studies major so the only building I need to go to is MacQuarrie Hall.
150.	INV:	Okay, okay so you just weren't at MacQuarrie?
151.	EW:	Yeah.
152.	INV:	But you're by the Seventh Street garage?
153.	EW:	Yeah.
154.	INV:	And you come from the ATMs?
155.	EW:	Yeah.
156.	INV:	Um, okay all right, when you think you're – so, what were you – if you were over by the ATM did you walk back towards MacQuarrie and if so like what route did you take? Did you go through the south of the Student Union or south of the event center? Do you know?
157.	EW:	Um, I think I went south of Student Union (INV: Okay), I, I took the most direct route because this route is from my time at SJSU, it's been the fastest.
158.	INV:	Okay so, so you kind of went if you were at – from the ATM went south of the student union and then over onto Seventh Street Plaza, right, okay, and then walking towards MacQuarrie did you then walk through like the San Carlos Plaza area?
159.	EW:	Um, I don't think so. I think I could have very briefly, yeah, I was listening to my headphones so … (INV: Okay) I wasn't exactly paying attention to where …
160.	INV:	Gotcha, so could you see MacQuarrie from where these guys beat you up at?
161.	EW:	Yeah, it was, it was within my sight but like it would take me about a minute to get there walking.
162.	INV:	Okay, okay, so you were kind of in that courtyard area between Sweeney and MacQuarrie and the Seventh Street garage. There's that kind of like courtyard area between those three (EW: Yeah, I was about …) and you got to San Carlos Plaza like just to the north of you there …
163.	EW:	Yeah, well the plaza, yeah, I mean I could see I know what area you're talking about I can't say where exactly it took place because it was kind of like they stop me in one area and then the actual area where I got hit happened in like a little bit more towards another area.
164.	INV:	Okay, okay, so just for your – if it happened in that area of that plaza between Sweeney and MacQuarrie we have – or we used to have at least have a camera up there so I can go and check that footage for you.
165.	EW:	Okay.

At line 134 the officer begins to try and narrow down the place where the crime event took place. Once again, if we are mindful of what we ask and what the eyewitness says in response we'll be more inclined not to ask this type of question because we know the eyewitness is unsure (to this point) and their response confirms it. When the eyewitness begins to respond, the officer interrupts their answer and mentions "Sweeney Hall" (line 150) as the place near where this might have taken place. The eyewitness is reluctant to accept the Sweeney Hall location and instead says, "I was in an open courtyard area, but I couldn't tell you." The officer seems to move past this piece of information and tries to settle on another place: San Carlos Plaza. By line 160 the investigator once again tries to convince the eyewitness into saying he was at a certain place, but the eyewitness again demurs with, "Um, I don't think so. I think I could have very briefly …" and said he wasn't really paying attention. So by question 164 the officer reframes their exchange to state that the eyewitness had been "in that courtyard area between Sweeney and MacQuarrie and the Seventh Street garage" and the eyewitness in response says, "Yeah, well the plaza, yeah, … I know what area you're talking about I can't say where exactly it took place" and the officer reassures the eyewitness that they may have a security camera in that area and he would check it to make sure.

Let's think about that for a bit here and consider the fact that the eyewitness was not sure of the location of the assault and tried, in his responses, to let the officer know that he was not sure. Now the eyewitness knows the officer will check the video to confirm the location. What if the eyewitness is not seen in that particular part of the security video coverage area? Will this lack of corroboration be seen as a negative outcome of statements made by the eyewitness, or will it be attributed to the suggestion by the officer?

Unfortunately, in many cases we do not know the outcome of the corroboration, nor do we have access to the interview context so we can see the deviation in what was said and how it was interpreted. When we are mindful of our interview process, we ensure this is not a possibility because we don't offer post-event information and we adhere to TIATI. When we rely on this type of questioning and confirmation of corroboration to eyewitness statements, we expect the investigator to be mindful of gathering the most reliable cognitive evidence – who is corroborating the reliability of cognitive evidence?

In the next excerpt the officer moves back to the Topic 3. While the eyewitness may not understand the nuance of asking about how and where the suspects struck the victim or what and how much they took, it is obvious to the officer so they can be sure the suspects are charged appropriately. As you may recall back at line 28 where the officer asked six leading questions about whether a weapon was used, whether the eyewitness was stopped in a certain manner, and how he was stopped "in [his] tracks" the eyewitness corrected the investigator's inference of what actually happened. The decision the officer makes to suggest specifically where the assault took place is the noise we're trying to locate or identify when we conduct these noise audits.

Topic 3

166.	INV:	Back to how they hit you. So you said you got hit in the head first right?
167.	EW:	Yeah, so some guy stood in front of me – the white kid – and then he told me we're taking your backpack and I kind of felt somebody behind me feeling my backpack up and then that's when I kind of lunged forward to get the person behind me to stop feeling my backpack and then that's when I got hit in the head I don't know by what.
168.	INV:	Okay, gotcha.
169.	EW:	… and then I kind of curled up and then as I was curling up because you know my forehead hurt, the guy behind me who already had my backpack in his hand started pulling my backpack above me like up from me, like that kinda, and then almost took it off and that's when my arm got hooked in to one of the

		straps on my backpack, um … and then after that I kept on getting kicked in the legs. I, I think they wanted like to put me to the ground or something …
170.	INV:	So when you're curled up, were you like curled up in a ball but not on the ground like kinda hunched over?
171.	EW:	Yeah, I'm like in fetal but standing (INV: Okay). Like it's kinda like that because I didn't know how I don't want to be blushing gut – gushing blood (INV: Okay) but I didn't know, you know, I've never been through something like this. It's never happened to me before, so I don't know how to react …
172.	INV:	Okay, so you got hit in the head, when you went down they tried pulling it off your arm and it got hooked. How many times did they kick you in the – was it your right leg or left leg?
173.	EW:	So I got kicked on my right leg for sure, um, in the back of the knee and that's kind of where my knee pain comes from (INV: Okay) because that one kind of – that one fucked me up and dropped me to the ground. And then, sorry …
174.	INV:	No, no about how many times did you get kicked in the right leg?
175.	EW:	Probably maybe two really good kicks.
176.	INV:	Okay, now you get kicked anywhere else?
177.	EW:	Yeah, my shoulder (INV: Okay) it was when I was trying I was holding on to my backpack because I didn't want them to take it and then the guy who hit me – the white kid who hit me in the head – he ended up kicking the shit out of my shoulder and that's when I lost my grip on my back.
178.	INV:	Okay did the other guy – did he just pull the backpack off, or did he kick you also?
179.	EW:	So the guy who was behind me, and I think I, I'm pretty sure he's the one who kicked me in the back of my knee so that's why my knee is like throbbing right now, but I can't say if he hit me any more, because after that I was pretty much was like I wanted it to stop while I was in the fetal position.

At this point of the interview the investigator has traversed the topics in an unconventional manner. The topics were being accessed in sequence for 22 questions into the interview when the officer changes strategy and moves from Topic 3 back to 2, 3, and 4. There were 87 questions asked between Topics 1 and 4 (lines 1 through 181) and 45% focused on Topic 3 (40 questions). Overall, there were seven deviations in sequence which made for inconsistent retrieval of information which can lead to unreliable cognitive evidence.

At line 182 the officer moves to Topic 4 and begins one of three attempts at summarizing events. We categorized this summary as Narrative Review (NR) to distinguish it from other specific questions focused on gathering cognitive evidence. The officer was using this NR to clarify details he had documented and make statements about what he believed happened. The eyewitness had to correct the officer's summary details which convoluted the process. If we focus on Topic 4 (Confirmation of Details) and misrepresent the details with the eyewitness, we risk alienating them and discourage them to participate in the investigative outcome.

Topic 4 (Narrative Summary)

180.	INV:	Okay, all right. So that's so I can – just for simplification – just so I can get an idea, you're somewhere in that courtyard area. I'm just gonna summarize real quick what I got so far.

THE MINDFUL INTERVIEW METHOD

181.	INV:	You're in a courtyard area walking from class. You just come from the ATMs, you don't notice the guys beforehand (EW: Okay), but the white guy stands in front of you, stops ya and then they're taking your backpack. You feel the other guy come up behind you – grab it, right?
182.	EW:	Right.
183.	INV:	Um, then you get hit on the head, but you don't know by who or with what, but you think it's the white guy, but you don't know for sure and you don't know if he had a weapon or anything. Or you just think it's just – do you think it was a fist or hand slap or …?
184.	EW:	No, so this has never happened to me before, but I've kinda been and kind of like – because I have brothers, so I know what a punch feels like and it didn't feel like a …
185.	INV:	Not like a punch. Okay. Gotcha, but you got hit with something though.
186.	EW:	Yeah.
187.	INV:	… and you kind of go down to the ground. You're in kind of a standing fetal position.
188.	EW:	Yeah.
189.	INV:	… and then they try to pull the backpack off you, and you get kicked in the shoulder because it gets stuck there and then they keep kicking you in your right knee a couple times – one time really hard that drops you to the ground, okay?
190.	EW:	So, I think I got hit and then I kind of bent over, and then as I was going to go to the ground, after I got hit in the head, I got kicked in the knee and that's what took me to the ground.
191.	INV:	Okay.
192.	EW:	As I was going to the ground they pulled my backpack off and then my arm got stuck (INV: Okay) so this is as I'm going to the ground.
193.	INV:	Okay – so head, so you get hit in the head first, then the knee, then they're pulling the backpack, shoulder gets kicked, and then you go down to the ground. Did you get kicked or hit any time after that?
194.	EW:	Um, I think after that they must've been running by then because my backpack was gone. I guess that's all they wanted because I looked up and they were both running in different directions.
195.	INV:	Okay, gotcha, so they were running in separate directions from you?
196.	EW:	Yeah. I couldn't tell you which specific one was running where.

Topic 3

197.	INV:	Okay. Gotcha. Do you know, can you give me just a general idea of which – I don't know – a general idea of which way each of them went? It doesn't have to be exactly specific about whether the white guy went this way, or the other guy went that way I just need a general idea.
198.	EW:	One was running towards MacQuarrie Hall and then the other one was running towards in a diverted direction not towards MacQuarrie Hall. I don't know where he was running …

199.	INV:	Gotcha. Okay. So you said the person that bandaged you up – did they see all this by chance?
200.	EW:	Yeah, Alan.
201.	INV:	Alan?
202.	EW:	Yeah.
203.	INV:	Do you have – do you know how I can get a hold of Alan by chance? Did you get a phone number? Do you know him from something else?
204.	EW:	Honestly Alan is just some Asian student at SJSU who kind of saw the whole thing and he told me, he's like, "Tony, I saw" – well, he didn't say "Tony" he told me, he was like, "hey, I saw the whole thing …"
205.	INV:	Okay.
206.	EW:	… but there were people starting to crowd around and he's the one who helped me.
207.	INV:	Okay, was there anybody else in the area that might have seen these guys?
208.	EW:	Yeah, yeah, for sure there were other people in the area, but I don't know if they were paying attention to it.
209.	INV:	Okay, um, with that I just have to decide did you fear at all that you were gonna get hurt? Or that they – that they were going to hurt you during this whole process?
210.	EW:	Honestly, because okay, I've usually kind of been able to avoid situations like this because I'm six feet. Well, when it's two against one you kind of start, you know, I don't want to say that I was like a little bitch or anything, but it definitely humbled me in the sense that I, I didn't want it to continue for sure.
211.	INV:	Okay, gotcha, and then they obviously – they didn't have permission to take your stuff?
212.	EW:	Of course not.
213.	INV:	And you were fearful that they were going to beat you up a little more, right?
214.	EW:	Right, I don't know what they wanted and okay, I kind of was just hoping that I wasn't going to die.
215.	INV:	Okay, um. Okay, yeah. You were hoping that you're not gonna die that's definitely (EW: Yeah), that's definitely good, I mean glad you're glad – you're not in the best situation which you could obviously be in and you're a little beat up, but you're here and you're safe right now and you're okay, and um, the reality is, well the thing is that these are just items that were taken and they can be replaced – yes it's a pain in the butt, and no it's not – it's a violation of you – of them taking all your stuff, but for the most part it's, we – they can be replaced, you can't …
216.	EW:	Yeah, but I had so much data on that laptop – so much data.

Many of the NR segments (starting with line 183) offer more suggestion than confirmation of what was actually said. In this summary segment the investigator suggests the eyewitness didn't know whether the suspect used a weapon to strike him or whether it might have been a "fist or hand slap." The eyewitness is quick to correct the assertion by saying, "No" and he knew what a punch felt like because he had brothers. At line 187 the officer acknowledges the lack of "a punch" but then ignores the fact that it may have been something more. Had the officer employed OEQ and MP tactics in this segment he might have learned more about the type of weapon the suspects used – or at least what the eyewitness might have thought it to be. Instead, the officer proceeds to list the events as he remembered them and gets the sequence wrong.

The eyewitness corrects the summary sequence at line 192. Even after clarifying his statements, he asked the eyewitness whether he was "kicked or hit any time after that?" The problem with this question is that based on the previous eyewitness statements about the struggle for the backpack back at line 28 he started asking again about who hit him and how many times. We must be careful repeating questions about areas we've covered already. When we are not mindful of the questions and the responses we've received, we can create a sense of not listening for the eyewitness and they may become reluctant to offer more information. Had Topic 3 (Elements of the Crime) been thoroughly investigated earlier we would have learned about how the assault took place and how it ended, instead, because this topic previously ended after six leading questions and the eyewitness described how he was hit on the head with something that was "hard as hell" the officer shifted the focus of the topic to who had placed the bandage on the eyewitness's head.

In this next excerpt the officer specifically looks for statements that fulfill the elements of the crime (Topic 3). This information can be considered questionable in light of gathering reliable cognitive evidence. The three leading questions and one empathetic concern comment creates an unusual point in the interview, whereby the investigator is trying to make sure he has a particular crime juxtaposed with the eyewitness concerned for his life, and the data he may have lost in the robbery. Because the officer did not start the interview from the beginning – by asking the eyewitness to offer a narrative recall of events that led to the assault, the officer is trying to backtrack and ensure the elements of the crime are included in the interview. Even though the officer inquired about the elements of the crime at Topic 3 (11 questions into the interview) we know now that more suggestions were made and eventually was diverted to asking about the bandage on his head (line 36). Our Efficacy of Eyewitness Interview Assessment (EEIA) sees this and asks why?

Topic 4

217. INV: So, do you track your laptop at all with like, find my phone app sort of application or anything of that nature?
218. EW: Well, I have an iPhone so I know my account. Ahh, my phone account is logged in my apple account.
219. INV: Okay, well I believe we can use it if you have the find my iPhone app. Does it connect up to the computer? We could possibly find out where it's at.
220. EW: Yeah, I can – my, my main concern is what if they smash it? I have a whole lot of stuff on that computer.
221. INV: Okay well, well, well, we can – do you have your phone with you right now? We can just pull it up real quick to see if it's, if it's showing up anywhere.
222. EW: I don't. I don't have my phone on me (INV: Okay) I don't want to say it's with my backpack, but it could be in my sweater I don't know where it's at right now (INV: Okay) I could have left it in my car.
223. INV: Okay. Gotcha. Do you have your keys to your car?
224. EW: Yeah, they're in my pocket.
225. INV: Okay, was there anything that had like your address on it in your backpack?
226. EW: Um, like I, I know that my – my wallet was in my backpack and my wallet's got my ID and then, so yeah.
227. INV: But there weren't keys to your house in there, were there?
228. EW: Not to my house, no because I have all my keys on the same link as my car keys.

Topic 2

229.	INV:	Okay, um did you ever – have you never seen these guys before whatsoever or seen them around campus at all?
230.	EW:	No, I, I could recognize them, but I couldn't tell you anything about them all.
231.	INV:	Okay, you would you recognize both of them, or just the one guy?
232.	EW:	Well, definitely the white kid with acne who stood in front of me because he kind of had this grin on his face before he said, "We're taking your back" but the other guy, all I know is that he had longer hair and he was kind of like darker complexion.
233.	INV:	Okay, um, they weren't wearing sun – and this is gonna sound odd, especially in COVID times, were they wearing a mask or not?
234.	EW:	Yeah, well yeah, they were wearing a mask for sure.
235.	INV:	What color masks were they wearing do you know?
236.	EW:	Well, the one in the white sweater was wearing a white mask, probably to blend in more, and the other one was with the one in the blue sweater, he was wearing blue.
237.	INV:	Was it a hoodie? Was it a zip-up, anything like that?
238.	EW:	It was, it was a hoodie as well. It was just white, and I couldn't – I, I didn't get a clear look at any logos on it but it looked like a plain white sweater to me.
239.	INV:	Okay, gotcha – gotcha – gotcha – so nothing with his jeans? Um, did you notice any jewelry? Did they have any watches? Or rings? Or earrings?
240.	EW:	Nothing immediate, um, I couldn't see earrings, they were covered by hoods.
241.	INV:	Okay, um, no tattoos? You didn't see them on a bike? Or anything of that nature either?
242.	INV:	Or did you see anybody else with them beforehand?
243.	EW:	No, honestly, I didn't notice them until what was happening happened.
244.	INV:	Okay.
245.	INV:	Um, but it was just them for sure? There wasn't anybody else?
246.	EW:	No.
247.	INV:	All right, so these two guys – the white guy and you think he's Hispanic or would you say Asian or …?
248.	EW:	Well, all I know is that is hair was kind of wavy (INV: Okay) I don't know if that matters at all but …
249.	INV:	It just helps sometimes just to – with that stuff.

Topic 4 (Narrative Summary)

250.	INV:	Um, so, all right, so two males, the skinny, skinny white guy he's about five nine-ish around there with the blue sweater and basketball pants, blue Cal Bears sweater, basketball pants, and he had blonde hair – he's the one that um stopped you originally and said, "we're taking your backpack," right? And then you have the possibly Hispanic male with longer hair with a white hoodie and jeans it was, he was shorter than you, also. And he was a little heavier right?

251.	EW:	He was. He was definitely bulkier, but he was taller than me.
252.	INV:	He was taller than you?
253.	EW:	In the white sweater, yeah, I would say he's about easily six-two.
254.	INV:	Six-two, okay, so six-two long-haired Hispanic, white hoodie, with jeans, no backpack or anything like that?
255.	EW:	No, well they have my back – they didn't have a backpack.
256.	INV:	But, but no backpack?
257.	INV:	So both of them showing up with no weapons or anything seen of that nature right?
258.	EW:	I didn't see a weapon no, but, okay like I said, I got hit over the head with something and then I can take a punch, but whatever that was they – yeah got me.
259.	INV:	Gotcha, okay, and they take your Michael Kors black backpack worth about 600 bucks with your MacBook pro which was upgraded and worth about $2,000, a SJSU gray hoodie with a tear in the stomach that was about 60 bucks, your notebook which is about a dollar and you think your phone might be in there but you're not sure.
260.	EW:	Well, it could be in my backpack, it could be in my car. I'd have right now but I'm in, I'm in the office at SJSU.
261.	INV:	Okay, and your wallet was also in your backpack right?
262.	EW:	My wallet was in my backpack.
263.	INV:	Um. Have you checked to see if there's, I know it's a little early but we need to check to make sure the cards aren't being used – that they've been canceled too on that end, okay?
264.	EW:	Okay, um, I don't have my phone on me so I can't really – I don't have access to them right now and I'm in the nurse's office – they're just letting me use this to talk to you guys.
265.	INV:	Okay, um, what type of debit or credit cards did you have there?
266.	EW:	I have, let's see I have about two credit cards and one debit card – my debit card is Wells Fargo.
267.	INV:	Debit is Wells Fargo?
268.	EW:	Yeah.
269.	INV:	Okay, what are the two credit cards?
270.	EW:	Um, one is Capital One for sure and then the other one might be American Express.
271.	INV:	Okay, what was your last purchase – obviously I'm guessing your debit card was the last time you used – it was at the ATM?
272.	EW:	Yeah, I took out 40 bucks.
273.	INV:	Okay. So you take out $40. So that was the last time you used that card, do you know the last time you used the Capital One or the Amex card?
274.	EW:	I don't know specifically, I couldn't tell you – probably something on Amazon, I don't know.
275.	INV:	Okay, Amazon. So another thing that we really want. A lot of times we can get really good surveillance footage of who uses these, so after the fact, so if you can give me those credit card numbers and if they've been used at

276. EW: another place a lot of times – they usually have only a couple weeks of window to where we can actually get footage. But if you can give me those, if they're used at all then we can go get surveillance footage and hopefully identify these guys that did this, okay?
Oh, okay, I don't have that information right now.

Topic 5

277. INV: And I understand that. I'm just saying when you get home, well, I'd love to say, hey go home and rest, but it's kind of helpful for solving this – if we can get the serial numbers from your computer and credit card and debit card numbers so that way we can get it all entered in and then if it's used we can go and find out who's using that and kind of track it back.
278. EW: Yeah. Okay.

In this segment we find ourselves on the topic of suspect description for the fourth time. At this point the officer has already asked 18 questions about this topic and will ask another 10 more for a total of 29 times during the same period where the officer asks about Topics 3 and 4 with more than 84 questions. The officer continues with a pattern of offering post-event information, in this case (line 239) whether the "blue sweater" was a hoodie, "zip-up, or anything like that." We must understand the magnitude of this practice of offering suggestions in our questions and leading the eyewitness to accept something that may or may not have been present at the time of the crime event. We cannot absolve the practice because it turns out the officer was right. We have to place this suggestion into perspective. This biased interview technique can only lead to questionable results in future investigations and our EEIA identifies it as an issue that needs to be addressed.

The next concerning inquiry focuses on the number of suspects at the scene. At question 244 the officer asks whether the eyewitness saw anyone else "beforehand?" The eyewitness candidly replied that he didn't notice the suspects until they were accosting him. The officer then asks whether he was "sure?" And could there be "anybody else?" Memory researchers have done numerous studies where eyewitnesses are asked suggestive questions like this and change their recollections to resemble the inferred information (Loftus, 1979). In this case we know that we have access to security camera footage, and we review the footage to determine who might have been involved when the robbery took place. Some people might have an unsettled feeling about "Alan" and that he might have been involved and only offered to help because he felt remorse after the incident – we'll never know.

The last concerning issue for this Topic 2 inquiry was the question about the race of suspect number two. The officer asked about the race of the suspect and suggested he might be Hispanic or Asian. When we look back at the transcript (line 41) the eyewitness says the second suspect was "maybe Hispanic" and he adds that because he was also "Mexican" that he wanted "to say Mexican." We have to assume from the exchanges after this response that the officer was satisfied with the answer, however, when we get to this portion (line 249) of the interview it is disconcerting that the race of suspect number two comes into question without any explanation. When the eyewitness replies that the suspect's hair was wavy (line 250) and whether that mattered, the officer says that it often "helps sometimes ... with that stuff." We have no idea what the officer means by this comment and whether we should be concerned about confirmation bias throughout the interview session. In this case the eyewitness did not offer any more information and we don't know how the officer documented the results of this inquiry.

279. INV: All right, um where, how did you get to campus? Do you have any more questions or anything right now?

THE MINDFUL INTERVIEW METHOD

280. EW: Um, well, not really, what should I do now?
281. INV: Okay, so what I'm gonna give you is, I'm gonna give you a report receipt with your case number here, okay. It's gonna have my name, my phone number, and my badge number. Um, I'm probably going to follow up with you – will later today to –.
282. INV: Well one, are you sure you don't go to hospital for one? (EW: No, I'm okay.) At least get checked out?
283. INV: I would suggest going to at least your primary care doctor or over to the wellness center here at least to get checked out by them, okay?
284. EW: Okay.
285. INV: I'm gonna give you this report receipt. It's got my name on it, case number, all the stuff. That's just to identify your case number and what not. Hold on to that. I got some victim assistance stuff that I can give you too and I'm gonna give you that tell you like what's what and things that are available to you on campus here you know. We do have our escort program – you're a big guy you might not want to at times, I get that, but at nighttime, it's dark, you can call the police department and either our cadets or officers will escort you back and forth to and from your car, or however you get on campus at night.
286. EW: Ah, okay.
287. INV: Um, and that's kind of where we're at here as of this point. Um, did you drive to campus?
288. EW: I did, yeah.
289. INV: Okay Are you gonna be okay to drive with your head injury?
290. EW: Um, well I don't know, can a person drive? I mean I feel fine but ...
291. INV: I'm just saying you might not want to drive. You may want to call somebody to come pick you up especially since you said you're feeling in the back of your head, you got hit in the front. Sometimes it's kind of a sign of a concussion so the last thing I want you to do is pass out behind the wheel after this whole thing, so you might just want to get somebody to pick you up and then take you to your primary care doctor, okay? Just to get checked out – if you're saying got hit up front and then you're hurting on the back of your head that usually means it's kind of a sign of a concussion. So, you either need to go get you checked out by an adult – I mean you're – how old are you?
292. EW: I'm 25.
293. INV: Yes, so you're an adult you got the rights to do whatever you want to do on that end, but I would suggest you to go on an ambulance, or at least have a buddy take you to the doctor to go get that checked out because I don't want you to drive. I personally, then this is me being a person, I want you getting medical care because that might be a concussion and the last thing you want to do is pass out behind the wheel, okay?
294. EW: That makes sense.
295. INV: So let's, let's go and see if you got a buddy that we can call to come pick you up and drive you to the doctor. That sounds like a good idea to me.
296. EW: Okay.
297. INV: Okay, so we'll get that taken care, I'll stand by with you here until he shows up and you can go off and get checked out by them.

CASE STUDY #5

298. EW: Yeah, I am. I gonna get my stuff back?
299. INV: I'll be honest um, you might not. That is, the quicker you can give me some of that information the more likelihood it is that we will get – we can hopefully recover it, but I'm not gonna tell you everything's all great and gravy and that you were going to get this stuff back, okay?
300. EW: That's fair.
301. INV: I will say that the more likelihood of getting things back is a lot better when we have serial numbers, and that type of stuff, and the credit card numbers, because we can track back and at that point it's easier for us also to find people and prosecute them for it so it's kind of like, I, I'd love to say it's my job now – I can go find and do the stuff but I need your help by getting me this information so that we can find these people and arrest them for the robbery here, okay?
302. EW: So I should just get home as soon as possible then?
303. INV: Well, I'd say go to the doctor first – get that checked out and then give me that information, okay? Your health and wellbeing is more important to us than finding these guys right now, okay?
304. EW: Okay, okay all right so I can call somebody then I'll be good.
305. INV: Yep ... I'll stand by here with you 'til they get here – to make sure you get to the car and head off, okay?
306. EW: Okay.
307. INV: Um, you got the report receipt, you got my phone number, if anything else comes up. I might call you in a day or two just to follow up, um, this has kind of been a traumatic experience for you. We also have counseling services available here on campus if you feel like you need to talk to somebody and I'll probably call you in a day or two to see if you remember anything else about this – to see if, um, like you know maybe over time thinking about things if you remember something else and that type of stuff okay?
308. EW: Is it, is it possible that I could use your phone to call Gil Zamora right now?
309. INV: That's no problem.
310. EW: Okay.
311. INV: All right.
312. EW: Okay, yeah, I'll call Gil right now.
313. INV: All right, I'll stand by here and wait for him till he gets here and then we can head off from there. So any other questions or concerns?
314. EW: No, I just kinda want my stuff back. I wish this never happened to me. I'm kind of mad. I'm kind of sad and I don't know how to handle this but ...
315. INV: Those are all kinda normal responses to this – um, they violated, and you feel like you should be able to walk across the street here and on campus and feel safe. Yeah, and this unfortunately happened to you, and there are pain-in-the-butt people everywhere around and unfortunately you got kind of picked on today to meet one, two of them in this situation.
316. EW: My luck.
317. INV: Yeah.
318. EW: Okay, so, well thank you.

THE MINDFUL INTERVIEW METHOD

At this point of the interview session we can see the officer wrapping up the inquiry and employing plenty of empathy about the health of the eyewitness. The officer does an outstanding job at ensuring the eyewitness was well aware of what needed to be done, what was going to happen with the investigation, and that getting the eyewitness home safe was the investigator's first priority. The officer represented the agency as being compassionate and considerate for the eyewitness's wellbeing and seeking closure for the investigation. At line 295 the officer offers plenty of empathy by suggesting that "I personally … being a person" would want the eyewitness to get medical attention because it might be a concussion. While the officer's choice of words may have not been the most elegant the genuine concern at this point was quite clear and we can expect this surely left a positive impression on the eyewitness.

Why does one officer make noise in their interview session and another not? It's one of the main reasons to conduct a Efficacy of Eyewitness Interview Assessment and use the information to inform the officer and the agency about their tendency to create unwanted decisions that gather unreliable cognitive evidence. Had the officer been more mindful and asked the eyewitness an OEQ (back at line 28) like "tell me how they hurt you?" instead of asking a leading multiple-choice question like "When did the white guy hit you or did the other guy hit you?" he might have offered more reliable information. Or had the officer started the interview, from the outset, with, "tell me what happened?" and had been willing to listen and allow the eyewitness to offer their authentic free recall of the event while using MPs and probing questions to help the eyewitness elaborate, the officer might have gained much more reliable cognitive evidence. We might have learned what happened right from the start of the interview and been able to clarify statements later. We could consider medical records from the hospital (if the victim receives treatment) that might generate important information about what the physician found in their expert opinion on the type of injuries the eyewitness received and what type of instrument (or weapon) may have caused the injury. When we are mindful in our strategy and our presence of mind to be present with what is being said and how we are listening we can be assured we will be open to all possibilities of investigating the matter properly.

For the complete EEIA see Appendix E, Case Study #5.

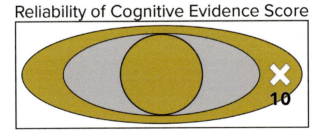

Figure 19.2 Reliability of Cognitive Evidence Target (RCE) score "10."

EFFICACY OF EYEWITNESS INTERVIEW ASSESSMENT[SM]

Narrative Report for Case Study #5

The Reliability of Cognitive Evidence (RCE) for this interview session is "10" which means we can consider the cognitive evidence **Less Than Reliable** (Figure 19.2). The efficacy of this interview is problematic when we consider the use of interview tactics that diminish cognitive evidence retrieval (Figure 19.3). The transcript shows the interviewer was biased

CASE STUDY #5

towards asking questions that bounced from topic to topic and represented seven topic sequence changes.

The summary report shows the interviewer asked more than 32% of questions that diminished the reliability of cognitive evidence and less than 52% of the questions focused on the suspect descriptions. Fifty-six percent of the questions focused on the elements of the crime which was above the acceptable standard and eyewitness responses were 49% which was more than exceptional. The number of Diminish Reliability of Cognitive Evidence (DRCE) questions was 25% more than is expected for an exceptional interview session, while the interviewer displayed an exceptional mindful rapport tactic (19%) throughout the interview session.

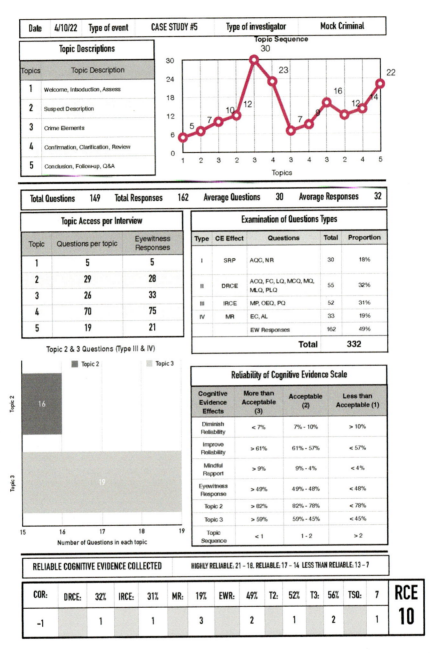

Figure 19.3 Efficacy of Eyewitness Interview Assessment Summary Report for Case Study #5.

Section VII

Expectations

20
Expectations and Future Research

When I thought about the expectations for this book, I wanted to make sure I was as concise as I could be at the risk of being too simplistic, and what I came up with is this: The information we obtain from eyewitness interviews should be treated like cognitive evidence. Since 1999, the institutions overseeing the justice system have been encouraging local law enforcement agencies to take a look at their research and consider changing their ways (Figure 20.1). The focus on the reliability of eyewitness evidence and the preservation of its integrity to assist law enforcement in convicting righteous criminals was front and center. Years later the National Academy of Sciences published a report on the state of eyewitness memory research and amplified the previous Department of Justice (DOJ) report in encouraging more collaboration and effective research designs that would admittedly inspire law enforcement agencies to consider adopting less problematic practices (Figure 20.2).

Interestingly enough, when I sought to learn how to interview eyewitnesses in a manner that would be effective for creating composite sketches, I realized there was no specific course, training, or book that focused on interviewing cooperative eyewitnesses for sketch artists. While Karen Taylor's (2001), *Forensic Art and Illustration*, made clear the complexities of composite art it arrived too late for me as I had already completed my fifth year as a police artist and had completed well over 1,800 composite sketches. Even she allowed novice forensic artists to contemplate what interview style might work better for them. The route for many investigators to learn authentic eyewitness memory interview techniques is reserved for special workshops, manuals, instructional books, and conferences touting techniques that encourage strategies that discern how eyewitnesses may be withholding information from your investigation.

I believe there may be too much ambiguity in how best to train law enforcement personnel to interview cooperative eyewitnesses, and even fewer administrators seeking definitive standards for gathering the most reliable eyewitness evidence. If local law enforcement agencies just considered the information published by highly respected law enforcement entities since 1999 and implemented a majority of their recommendations, we might begin to appreciate the request for collaboration with researchers to better define next steps in preserving eyewitness evidence. Instead, we rely on practitioners like myself to inform researchers, law enforcement, prosecutors, loss prevention agents,

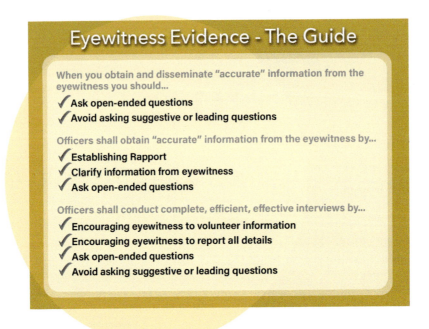

Figure 20.1 Highlights of the Guide. From *Eyewitness Evidence: A Guide for Law Enforcement*, DOJ, 1999.

human resource managers, and criminal justice students on how to gather more reliable eyewitness evidence.

We know there are more cooperative eyewitness interviews happening every year than there are violent crimes being investigated and yet we have no real data on how these interviews are being conducted and whether they result in reliable information. We might look to clearance rates to give us an idea of how these eyewitness statements might lead to arrests from interviews, but we have no idea whether the information actually led to the identification of the culprit or not. The FBI cautioned us not to rely on their UCR Program numbers for any significant meaning; even so, we have to believe the 25% clearance rate for robberies in 2020 had to be somewhat close (Lartey & Li, 2022). We've also discussed the misidentification and wrongful convictions that were often initiated by eyewitness testimony that was either unreliable or manipulated in some way by law enforcement officials – sometimes while following accepted interview norms.

My perspective on this issue of accountability for interviewing eyewitnesses is based somewhat on the lack of recognition the National Institute of Justice considered when they published the 2009 report on forensic disciplines that were featured as advancing forensic science. Forensic art was not mentioned, nor scrutinized, and I felt the report was missing a large number of practitioners who were interviewing eyewitnesses that often led to amazing apprehensions of heinous criminals. We know that a few of the over 300 exonerations began with forensic artists creating a composite sketch, and still their

EXPECTATIONS AND FUTURE RESEARCH

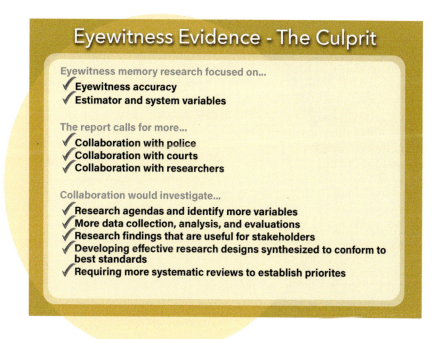

Figure 20.2 Highlights of Identifying the Culprit. From *Identifying the Culprit: Assessing Eyewitness Identification*, National Academy of Sciences, 2014.

interview process has not been scrutinized to garner enough calls for change. We know that photo line-ups were highly criticized for their process and agencies across the country adhered to systematic changes that considered years of evidence-based research on eyewitness accuracy. Nevertheless, if we consider the epistemology of eyewitness interviews that investigators must master in order to perform at the highest levels we have to agree on the standards for the outcomes of these interviews. In other words, if we are seeking the truth from these eyewitness interviews we must acknowledge that eyewitnesses are limited in their ability to recall specific details; justifying interview tactics that consider these limitations as confederate actions should not be accepted as the norm. If we don't begin to evaluate this issue, agency leaders will never understand the impact eyewitness memory deficits have on their investigative interviews until they are debriefing their interview process in a wrongful conviction case.

I look forward to collaborating with local police agencies, district attorney and public defender offices, and private investigative firms to assist them in evaluating their eyewitness interviews so they can identify issues that can be corrected with proper training. I look forward to building relationships with law enforcement academies to create new learning curricula that focus on more practical exercises and formative assessments that instill proficiency and confidence, post academy and field training programs. I look forward to working with health administrators, human resource managers, and loss prevention agencies from around the country in instituting annual eyewitness interview exercises that consider the latest in eyewitness memory research and incorporate formative and summative assessments to improve their important interview outcomes.

Finally, I look forward to working with researchers in eyewitness memory to begin to develop new studies that measure the effectiveness of the *interviewers* to gather reliable cognitive evidence and not just about the accuracy of the people (eyewitnesses) making choices. Many friends and colleagues in law enforcement over the years have asked me about critiquing the quality of a composite sketch they saw on the news because of the cartoon-like quality – they assumed the unrealistic quality meant it was not useful for the investigation. I always reminded them to be more concerned about how questions were asked and what the eyewitness said to confirm the features drawn, and not about how well the sketch resembled a portrait of a person. The retrieval of reliable cognitive evidence should always be the main objective, regardless of whether you are gathering cognitive evidence for a composite sketch of a murderer or suspect who committed a petty theft.

APPENDIX A
CATEGORY OF COMMENTS AND QUESTIONS

Every transcript is reviewed, and each line of the transcript is labeled with one of these types of questions. When there is a difference in coding about the question category, after two reviews, a third review is conducted; the eyewitness responses are considered, including the questions asked before and afterwards to determine the best label assignment.

Table A.1 Category of Questions and Comments

Question Type	Definition	Examples	Cognitive Evidence Reliability	Type 1–4
ACQ	Accusatory Comment or Question	Why did you lie about the race of the suspect? Have you been drinking?	Diminish Reliability of Cognitive Evidence (DRCE)	Type 2
AL	Active Listening	Any words, or non-verbal communications that signal you are paying attention to every word the eyewitness is saying.	Improve Reliability of Cognitive Evidence (IRCE)	Type 4
AQC	Administrative Question or Comment	How are you doing today? DYKWYAH? I'm going to ask you questions in three phases.	No effect on reliability of cognitive evidence	Type 1
EC	Empathetic Comment	I'm sorry that happened to you. I can imagine you were very scared.	Improve Reliability of Cognitive Evidence (IRCE)	Type 4

(*Continued*)

APPENDIX A

Table A.1 (Continued) Category of Questions and Comments

Question Type	Definition	Examples	Cognitive Evidence Reliability	Type 1–4
FC	Force-Choice	Does he have short hair or long hair? Is the jacket leather or canvas?	Diminish Reliability of Cognitive Evidence (DRCE)	Type 2
LQ	Leading Question	You called the police after 1PM didn't you? You hadn't seen the suspect before the incident, had you?	Diminish Reliability of Cognitive Evidence (DRCE)	Type 2
MCQ	Multiple-Choice Question	Was he wearing a blue, black, or brown jacket? Was the vehicle a Ford, Chevy, or Dodge?	Diminish Reliability of Cognitive Evidence (DRCE)	Type 2
MP	Mirror Probe	Used after a word or phrase that you would like the eyewitness to elaborate on. For instance, if the eyewitness says he saw a black car, you might ask, "A black car?"	Improve Reliability of Cognitive Evidence (IRCE)	Type 3
MQ	Multiple Questions	What was his race, how about his age, and was he a big guy?	Diminish Reliability of Cognitive Evidence (DRCE)	Type 2
MLQ	Multiple Leading Questions	So, you must have been on this side of the street, did you hear him yell at the women in the car? Did he use profanity or was it too loud to hear anything else?	Diminish Reliability of Cognitive Evidence (DRCE)	Type 2

(Continued)

APPENDIX A

Table A.1 (Continued) Category of Questions and Comments

Question Type	Definition	Examples	Cognitive Evidence Reliability	Type 1–4
MRP	Mindful Rapport	In MIM, rapport is established through the entire interview process. Every exchange with the eyewitness is an opportunity to build and establish trust so they are compelled to offer you as much information as possible.	Improve Reliability of Cognitive Evidence (IRCE)	Type 3
NR	Narrative Review	This question was added after reviewing interview transcripts from other investigators. These types of comments or questions focus on reviewing certain details that were covered initially.	No effect on reliability of cognitive evidence	Type 1
OEQ	Open-Ended Question	What was his age? How did she comb her hair? What color was the car?	Improve Reliability of Cognitive Evidence (IRCE)	Type 3
PQ	Probing Question	Usually, a follow-up to an OEQ. What did he say? You said it was dark outside?	Improve Reliability of Cognitive Evidence (IRCE)	Type 3
PLQ	Probing Question Leading	Usually, a follow-up to an OEQ. So, he must have been older than you? You must have turned on the lights when you came outside?	Diminish Reliability of Cognitive Evidence (DRCE)	Type 2

(*Continued*)

APPENDIX A

Table A.1 (Continued)   Category of Questions and Comments

Question Type	Definition	Examples	Cognitive Evidence Reliability	Type 1–4
SRP	Standard Rapport	Standard rapport is practiced by most interviewers and involves checking in on the eyewitness for their satisfaction for environmental conditions, personal needs, questions about the investigation, and any comment made to improve communications.	No effect on reliability of cognitive evidence	Type 1
COR	Confidence of Recollection	A question(s) asked before starting the interview to evaluate the confidence of the eyewitness regarding the suspect's face and/or elements of the crime.	May affect the reliability of cognitive evidence if the eyewitness is reluctant to offer information about the event.	COR rating is deducted from the RCE
DYKWYAH	Acronym for Do You Know Why You Are Here?	Acronym for Do You Know Why You Are Here? This question may be asked before starting the interview or during Topic 1.	May affect the reliability of cognitive evidence if the eyewitness is unsure whether they can offer information about the crime event.	May contribute to the COR rating.
TIATI	That Is All There Is	A MIM principle that adheres to the philosophy that sometimes the eyewitness does not remember details of the crime.	Posing questions to the eyewitness after signaling that they do not recall may negatively affect the reliability of cognitive evidence.	Type 2

APPENDIX B
SAMPLE MINDFUL INTERVIEW METHOD SCRIPT

SAMPLE MINDFUL INTERVIEW METHOD SCRIPT

INV: Good afternoon, my name is Gil and I'll be interviewing you today. I want to thank you for coming in today and for helping us with this investigation. First of all, do you know why you are here?

EW: Response.

INV: Okay, so if you saw the suspect again would you recognize him?

EW: Response.

INV: Very good. Do you need anything or have any questions before we get started?

EW: Response.

INV: The way this works is I'm going to ask you some general questions about the suspect's face and then I'd like you to answer to the best of your knowledge. Most people don't remember everything in great detail, but most people, when they're here and focused on the questions tend to remember a lot of information. Now, I'm going to ask you to close your eyes so you can focus on the questions, and I'm going to ask you to give me a couple of deep breaths to help you get calm before we get started.

After about five to ten minutes I'm going to ask you to open your eyes and I'm going to ask you tell me what happened. I want you to tell me what happened starting from before you saw the suspect until police were called. I want you to understand that our memory is not perfect and so if I ask you a question about something and you don't remember, just say you don't recall. If I need to, I may ask you a different question. I just want you to do the best that you can. Do you understand?

EW: Response.

INV: Okay, now close your eyes and give me a couple of deep breaths (take the same deep breaths with the EW) and relax.

EW: (Closes eyes and takes deep breath.)

INV: Very good, we'll begin …

INV: Tell me about the race (ethnicity) of this person?

INV: His/her age? (After learning the gender continue with proper pronoun.)

INV: What about the body build?

INV: Tell me about the face shape?

INV: What about the hair?

INV: How would you say they comb their hair?

INV: How about the texture of the hair?

APPENDIX B

INV: (Ask about color, length, or style, if not already revealed.)
INV: Tell me about the forehead?
INV: What about the ears?
INV: Tell me about the nose?
INV: How about the mouth and lips?
INV: Tell me about the chin?
INV: What about the cheeks?
INV: Tell me about the texture of the skin?
INV: What about the color of the skin?
INV: Tell me about the neck?
INV: What type of clothing they were wearing?
INV: Tell me about the eyes?
INV: What about the eyebrows?
INV: What about the attitude?
INV: Can you think of anything else about the face?
INV: What would say is his most distinctive feature? (Ask whether they have forgotten to mention something else about the person)
INV: Okay, you can open your eyes now. Do you need anything before we move to the next phase?
EW: Response.
INV: Okay, now what I want you to do is to tell me what happened. I want you to tell me what you were doing just before you saw this suspect. Focus on everything before you saw them and then take me all the way through until police were called. Do you understand?
EW: Response.
INV: Okay.
EW: Response.
INV: (Engage in active listening with occasional mm, uh-huh, and head nods, along with MP questions, PQ questions, and no interruptions. Be mindful of keeping eyewitness on topic and guide them to return to the topic (if needed). Do not ask leading questions and make any accusatory statements.)
INV: Very good. I just have a couple of questions about some items you covered. Can you tell me about …? (Focus on specific items and only ask OEQ questions with follow-up probing and some force-choice and multiple-choice questions when appropriate.)
INV: Is there anything else you want to add?
EW: Response.
INV: Very well, that's all I have for you today. Keep in mind that you may remember more details of the event after you leave today, so if you do remember something, please don't hesitate to call me and let me know. We may also contact you again and ask you more questions if we need some clarification about something. Will that be okay? If this case goes to court you may be asked to testify in person, but we'll let you know in advance.
Here's my card, feel free to contact me if you have any questions about the investigation. Do you have any other questions?
EW: Response.
INV: Very good, I'll walk you out. Thanks again for coming in. Have a good day!

APPENDIX C
FORENSIC ART INDEXING

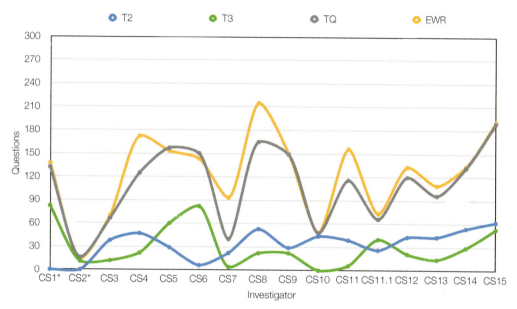

*Topic 2 was not accessed for CS 1 and 2 because the suspect was known.

Figure 23.1 Line graph of interview interactions throughout all case studies.

APPENDIX C

Table C.1 Operationalizing Questions for Cognitive Evidence Reliability - Forensic art interview sessions; Percentages used to quantify each interview domain, confirmed March 25, 2023

	DRCE			IRCE			MR			EWR			T2			T3			TSQ		
		SD	M		SD	M		SD	M		SD	M		SD	M		SD	M		SD	M
CS3	4		10	68		10	61		10	20		50	51		84	91		88	60	0	2
CS4	4		10	55		34	62		24	49		50	88		81	98		70		0	2
CS6	8		2	76		9	83		-1	50		89	96		88	116		5			7
CS8	3		9	60		25	67		15	50		92	85		98	70				0	2
CS9	1		7	63		16	56		6	48		95	88		96	68				0	2
CS10	18		12	71		2	64		12	50		80	87		0	28		3			5
CS11	6		12	63		10	56		20	50		91	84		90	62				0	2
CS12	11		17	57		11	64		21	50		78	85		80	52		2			0
CS13	14		8	66		9	59		19	50		83	90		85	57				0	2
CS14	11		17	66		10	59		20	50		85	78		83	55				0	2
CS15	16		10	76		1	69		11	51		73	80		89	61		2			0
AVG.	9	6	10	66	7	64	12	10	15	50	1	50	85	7	86	81	28	64	1	2	

DRCE: Diminish Reliability of Cognitive Evidence, IRCE: Improve Reliability of Cognitive Evidence, MR: Mindful Rapport, EWR: Eyewitness Responses, T2: Topic 2, T3: Topic 3, TSQ: Topic Sequence, SD: Standard Deviation, M: Mean.

APPENDIX C

Table C.2 Standard deviation for T2 and T3, all case studies, n=16; confirmed March 25, 2023

	Felony or Misdemeanor	TYPE	T2	SD	MEAN	T3	SD	MEAN	TQ	REW	TOTAL EXCH
CS1	Felony	CRIMINAL	0		27	83		107	130	137	285
CS2	Felony	CRIMINAL	0		27	11		35	16	13	31
CS3	Misdemeanor	FORENSIC ART	36		9	12		-12	64	70	141
CS4	Felony	FORENSIC ART	47		20	22		-2	125	173	350
CS5	Felony	CRIMINAL	29		56	36		60	149	162	332
CS6	Felony	FORENSIC ART	120		93	76		100	248	274	548
CS7	Civil	CRIMINAL	22		-5	4		28	40	72	158
CS8	Felony	FORENSIC ART	53		26	22		-2	165	220	438
CS9	Felony	FORENSIC ART	29		2	21		-3	148	158	327
CS10	Felony	FORENSIC ART	44		17	0		24	48	49	98
CS11	Felony	FORENSIC ART	39		12	6		-18	114	127	253
CS11.1	Felony	CRIMINAL	26		53	35		59	61	60	127
CS12	Misdemeanor	FORENSIC ART	43		16	21		-3	119	133	264
CS13	Misdemeanor	FORENSIC ART	44		17	14		-10	97	109	216
CS14	Misdemeanor	FORENSIC ART	53		26	29		5	128	144	286
CS15	Felony	FORENSIC ART	55		28	52		28	178	187	367
		Total Averages	40	27	26	28	24	25	114	131	264

271

APPENDIX C

Table C.3 Standard Deviation for non-forensic art case studies, n= 5; confirmed March 25, 2023

	Felony or Misdemeanor	TYPE	T2	SD	MEAN	T3	SD	MEAN	TQ	REW	TOTAL EXCH
CS1	Felony	CRIMINAL	0		27	83		107	130	137	285
CS2	Felony	CRIMINAL	0		27	11		35	16	13	31
CS5	Felony	CRIMINAL	29		56	36		60	149	162	332
CS7	Civil	CRIMINAL	22		-5	4		28	40	72	158
CS11.1	Felony	CRIMINAL	26		53	35		59	61	60	127
		Total Averages	15	14	32	34	31	58	79	89	233

272

Table C.4 Standard Deviation for all forensic art case studies, n=11; confirmed March 25, 2023

	Felony or Misdemeanor	TYPE	T2	SD	MEAN	T3	SD	MEAN	TQ	REW	TOTAL EXCH
CS3	Misdemeanor	FORENSIC ART	36		9	12		-12	64	70	141
CS4	Felony	FORENSIC ART	47		20	22		-2	125	173	350
CS6	Felony	FORENSIC ART	120		93	76		100	248	274	548
CS8	Felony	FORENSIC ART	53		26	22		-2	165	220	438
CS9	Felony	FORENSIC ART	29		2	21		-3	148	158	327
CS10	Felony	FORENSIC ART	44		17	0		24	48	49	98
CS11	Felony	FORENSIC ART	39		12	6		-18	114	127	253
CS12	Misdemeanor	FORENSIC ART	43		16	21		-3	119	133	264
CS13	Misdemeanor	FORENSIC ART	44		17	14		-10	97	109	216
CS14	Misdemeanor	FORENSIC ART	53		26	29		5	128	144	286
CS15	Felony	FORENSIC ART	55		28	52		28	178	187	367
		Total Averages	51	24	24	25	22	10	130	149	299

273

APPENDIX C

Table C.5 Proficiency Range for each interview domain - confirmed March 25, 2023

Cognitive Evidence Effect	More than Acceptable = 3	Acceptable = 2	Less than Acceptable = 1
Diminish Reliability (DRCE)	< 7%	7% - 10%	> 10%
Improve Reliability (IRCE)	> 61%	61% - 57%	< 57%
Mindful Rapport (MR)	> 9%	9% - 4%	< 4%
Eyewitness Response (EWR)	> 49%	49% - 48%	< 48%
Topic 2 (T2)	> 82%	82% - 78%	< 78%
Topic 3 (T3)	> 59%	59% - 45%	< 45%
Topic Sequence (TSQ)	< 1	1 - 2	> 2
Reliability of Cognitive Evidence scores	**Highly Reliable** 21 - 18	**Reliable** 17 - 14	**Less Than Reliable** 13 - 7

Mean scores derived from forensic art sketch interviews (n=11)

Table C.6 Acceptable Proficiency Scores for each domain – Confirmed March 25, 2023

DRCE	IRCE	MR	EWR	T2	T3	TSQ
10	65	14	50	86	73	2

Figures derived from eleven forensic art sketch interviews randomly selected. Proficiency ranges: The acceptable proficiency scores (APS) were derived by taking 50% of the average mean scores for each cognitive evidence domain. The proficiency range was based on the APS minus 50% of the (SD) for each level: APS - SD/2 = Acceptable Proficiency Score

Table C.7 Total number of questions for case studies: Topics 2 & 3

TYPE	T2	T3	TQ	EWR	TOTAL EXCH
CS1*	0	83	130	137	285
CS2*	0	11	16	13	31
CS3	36	12	64	70	141
CS4	47	22	125	173	350
CS5	29	36	149	162	332
CS6	120	76	248	274	548
CS7	22	4	40	72	158
CS8	53	22	165	220	438
CS9	29	21	148	158	327
CS10	44	0	48	49	98
CS11	39	6	114	127	253
CS11.1	26	35	61	60	127
CS12	43	21	119	133	264
CS13	44	14	97	109	216
CS14	53	29	128	144	286
CS15	55	52	178	187	367
Averages	**40**	**28**	**114**	**131**	**264**

* Topic 2 was not accessed because the suspect was known. Case 11.1 was an interview that morphed into the investigator asking extensive questions about the crime; i am including it as another example of interviewing by law enforcement investigators.

APPENDIX D
LIST OF ALL CASE STUDIES

Table D.1 List of All Case Studies and Their Reliability of Cognitive Evidence Scores

Case Study	Year	Agency	Class of Crime	Gender of Victim	Type of Crime	Type of Investigator	RCE Score
CS1	2016	California Highway Patrol	Felony	Male	Officer misconduct	Criminal	12
CS2	2016	California Highway Patrol	Felony	Female	Officer misconduct	Criminal	10
CS3	2010	Mountain View Police	Misdemeanor	Female	Annoying children	Forensic Artist	21
CS4	2012	San Jose Police	Felony	Female	Assault with a deadly weapon	Forensic Artist	18
CS5	2021	San Jose State University	Mock felony	Male	Mock robbery	Mock Criminal	10
CS6	2019	San Ramon Police	Felony	Female	Attempted kidnapping	Forensic Artist	18
CS7	2017	Private party	Civil	Male	Alleged fraud – report analysis	Forensic Artist	12
CS8	2013	Mountain View Police	Felony	Male	Home invasion	Forensic Artist	20
CS9	2019	Mountain View Police	Felony	Female	Robbery	Forensic Artist	20
CS10	2005	San Jose Police	Misdemeanor	Male	Suspicious person trespassing	Forensic Artist	13
CS11	2013	Los Gatos Police	Felony	Female	Robbery	Forensic Artist	21

(*Continued*)

APPENDIX D

Table D.1 (Continued)   List of All Case Studies and Their Reliability of Cognitive Evidence Scores

Case Study	Year	Agency	Class of Crime	Gender of Victim	Type of Crime	Type of Investigator	RCE Score
CS11.1	2013	Los Gatos Police	Felony	Female	Robbery	Criminal	**8**
CS12	2006	San Jose Police	Misdemeanor	Female	Indecent exposure	Forensic Artist	**16**
CS13	2006	San Jose Police	Misdemeanor	Female	Indecent exposure	Forensic Artist	**18**
CS14	2017	San Jose Police	Misdemeanor	Female	Indecent exposure	Forensic Artist	**19**
CS15	2018	Morgan Hill Police	Felony	Male	Attempted kidnapping	Forensic Artist	**14**

For more information go to: www.mindfulinterviews.com/CStranscripts
Transcripts C3 through C15 have been de-identified and edited to maintain confidentiality.

APPENDIX E
CASE STUDY TRANSCRIPTS AND EFFICACY OF EYEWITNESS INTERVIEW ASSESSMENT REPORTS

Case studies 1 through 5 include the coded transcripts as well as the complete EEIA narrative and summary reports. Case studies 6 through 15 include the coded transcripts and the EEIA Summary Report for each evaluation. For complete EEIA reports for case studies 6 through 15 go to www.mindfulinterviews.com/CaseStudies.

Each case study was evaluated and prepared for EEIA processing. Every attempt was made to standardize the evaluation and coding process for every case study. Any errors in coding, calculations, or assignment of RCE score, should be directed to the author. All of the transcripts were anonymized for instructional purposes, any resemblance to specific investigations is purely coincidental. The crime types and agencies are listed for informational purposes and to give the reader an idea of the variety of cases used in applying *The Mindful Interview Method*.

APPENDIX E

CASE STUDY #1

For more information about Case Study #1 see Chapter 15 for instructional content. This section includes: a. Complete EEIA report, b. Coded transcript, and c. EEIA summary report.

Eyewitness Interview Data Collection
This diagnostic report is part of the Efficacy of Eyewitness Interview Assessment℠

Date	5/20/22
Type of event	CASE STUDY #1
Type of investigator	Criminal

Table 1 - Topic Descriptions

Topics	Topic Description
1	Welcome, Introduction, Assess
2	Suspect Description
3	Crime Elements
4	Confirmation, Clarification, Review
5	Conclusion, Follow-up, Q&A

Table 2 - Topic Access per Interview

Topic	Questions per topic	Questions per interview	Eyewitness Responses	Responses per interview
1	46	35%	57	42%
2	0	0%	0	0%
3	83	64%	79	58%
4	0	0%	0	0%
5	1	1%	1	1%
Total	130	Total	137	
Average Questions	26	Average Responses	27	

Table 3 - Question Category from Transcript Review

Topic	AQC	ACQ	EC	FC	LQ	MCQ	MP	MQ	MLQ	NR	OEQ	PQ	PLQ	AL	Questions Only	Topic Totals	EWR
1	7			1	1	1		3			15	8	10	15	46	61	57
2															0	0	0
3	3	5		7	12		3	3	3		19	16	12	3	83	86	79
4															0	0	0
5	1														1	1	1
Totals	11	5	0	8	13	1	3	6	3	0	34	24	22	18	130	148	137

Table 4 - Reliability of Cognitive Evidence (RCE) Rating

Highly Reliable	Reliable	Less Than Reliable	Reliability of Cognitive Evidence
21 - 18	17 - 14	13 - 7	12

Table 5 - Confidence of Recollection (COR) Rating

Confidence is confirmed	Confidence is questionable	Confidence is unreliable	COR Rating
0	-1	-2	-1

Reliability of Cognitive Evidence

Table 4 - Reliability of Cognitive Evidence Scale

Cognitive Evidence Effects	More than Acceptable (3)	Acceptable (2)	Less than Acceptable (1)
Diminish Reliability	< 7%	7% - 10%	> 10%
Improve Reliability	> 61%	61% - 57%	< 57%
Mindful Rapport	> 9%	9% - 4%	< 4%
Eyewitness Response	> 49%	49% - 48%	< 48%
Topic 2	> 82%	82% - 78%	< 78%
Topic 3	> 59%	59% - 45%	< 45%
Topic Sequence Deviation	< 1	1 - 2	> 2

Mean scores derived from Mindful Interview Method in forensic art sketch interviews.

Table 5 - Reliability of Cognitive Evidence for Interview

Cognitive Evidence Questions	Results	RCE
Diminish Reliability (DRCE)	39%	1
Improve Reliability (IRCE)	41%	1
Mindful Rapport (MR)	12%	3
Eyewitness Response (EWR)	48%	2
Topic 2 (T2)		2
Topic 3 (T3)	48%	2
Topic Sequence Deviations (1 - 5), (TSQ)	1	2
Confidence of Recollection		-1
Reliability of Cognitive Evidence (RCE)		**12**

APPENDIX E

Topic Sequence Overview and Topic 2 & 3 Focus

This diagnostic report is part of the Efficacy of Eyewitness Interview Assessment℠

Table 1 - Sequence of Topics

Total Deviations	Sequence	1	2	3	4	5						
1	Topics	46	0	83	0	1						

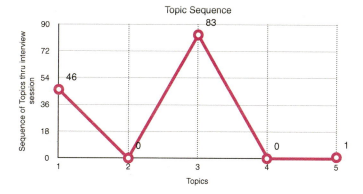

Table 2 - Topic 2 & 3 Questions

	Total Interview Questions (Type III & IV)	Proportion of questions
Topic 2	0	
Topic 3	41	48%

Topics 2 & 3 cover suspect description and crime elements.

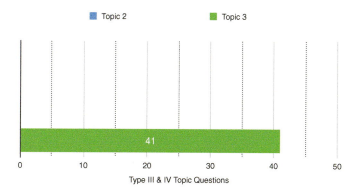

APPENDIX E

Question Examination and Eyewitness Responses

This diagnostic report is part of the Efficacy of Eyewitness Interview Assessment[SM]

Table 1 - Examination of Questions from eyewitness interview			
Type	Questions	Total	Proportion
I	AQC, NR	11	7%
II	ACQ, FC, LQ, MCQ, MQ, MLQ, PLQ	58	39%
III	MP, OEQ, PQ	61	41%
IV	EC, AL	18	12%
EWR	EW Responses	137	48%
	Total	**285**	

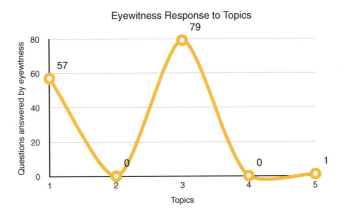

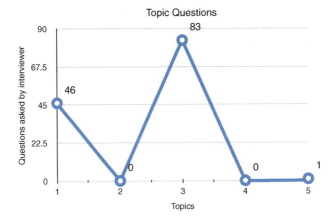

282

APPENDIX E

EYEWITNESS INTERVIEW ANALYSIS (EIA)
CONFIDENTIAL TRANSCRIPT REVIEW

The transcripts have been anonymized to protect the innocent. Any reference to persons or places in this transcript is maintained purely for dialogue consistency and the evaluation of interview strategies. The crime type and number of eyewitnesses remain to offer the reader some perspective on the type of case featured. For this book, all case studies that included a composite sketch from forensic artist Gil Zamora included some evaluation of COR. Some of these transcripts will include the COR evaluation, while others may have been evaluated outside of the interview transcript. Other case study transcripts evaluated for COR may include notes that address this outcome. Each case study will include the EEIA (Data Collection page and Summary Report). The Data Collection page includes all the question types attributed to the transcript review. Each transcript review was conducted a minimum of three times before generating the complete EEIA.

Date of transcript review: May 20, 2022

Crime type: Officer misconduct

Notes:

Topic 1

ARC 1. INV: Okay Officer McGrew, have you spoken to anyone besides your representative regarding the nature of this investigation?

2. SUSP: No.

ARC 3. INV: How long have you been employed as a peace officer with the California Highway Patrol?

4. SUSP: Over thirteen years

ARC 5. INV: Okay And when did you first begin your training at the California Highway Patrol Academy?

6. SUSP: December of 2002

ACC 7. INV: Okay When did you graduate from the academy?

8. SUSP: June of 2003

DEQ 9. INV: Can you give us an explanation as to why you wanted a career in law enforcement?

10. SUSP: It was a good career. I wanted to help the public and have a good retirement, make a difference.

PQ 11. INV: Okay Where have you been assigned since you've graduated from the CHP Academy?

12. SUSP: West Valley CHP

APPENDIX E

 13. INV: Okay So for the duration of the 13 and a half years that you've indicated, you've been at West Valley the whole time?

14. SUSP: Yes

 15. INV: Okay And what is your current assignment

16. SUSP: at the West Valley Area? I was the VIN -- VIN inspection officer.

 17. INV: Okay And is this considered a special duty position?

18. SUSP: Yes

 19. INV: How long have you been assigned to this position?

More basic inquiries about topic 1

 20. INV: Okay Please describe your duties and responsibilities as the West Valley Area VIN Officer?

21. SUSP: Primary duty is locating stolen vehicle components and verifying safety standards are met with the vehicles.

 22. INV: Such as air bags and seat belts?

23. SUSP: Yes

 24. INV: Okay And is there any part of the process that you do that has to do with verifying information through the Department of Motor Vehicles?

25. SUSP: Yes

 26. INV: Or CLETS?

27. SUSP: Yes

 28. SUSP: And what is that?

29. SUSP: Making sure the vehicle's not stolen, running vehicle components, mainly the VIN to make sure the vehicle's not stolen.

 30. INV: Okay As part of your duties, do you have any requirement to do any monthly or quarterly paperwork?

31. SUSP: Yes

 32. INV: And what does that entail?

33. SUSP: I do two forms for any blue tags that were issued, unnumbered blue tags as well as numbered blue tags.

 34. INV: Do you know -- I'm sorry...

35. SUSP: I also complete a 136 form which is a vehicle -- vehicles that were stolen or recovered in our area reported by our office officers

 36. INV: Okay And the two forms that you reference with regard to the blue tag, do you know what those form numbers are and what they"re called?

37. SUSP: 36 and number 97A

38. INV: Okay

More topic 1 questions...

39. INV: Okay.

Topic 1

284

APPENDIX E

40. SUSP: Then I make sure that they've already been to the DMV. And if they haven't been to the DMV, then I'll refer them to the DMV, and then I go about getting their name, phone number, year and make of the vehicle, and make sure they have the appropriate documentation.

AR 41. INV: Okay So then the information that you take from them, the information you just described, what do you then do with that information to keep take of who"s coming and going for your appointments?

42. SUSP: I put it into a computer, name and phone number.

AL 43. INV: Okay.

44. SUSP: And the year of the vehicle and the make

AL 45. INV: Okay And…

46. SUSP: In an appointment block to document what time their appointment is, day and time.

PLR 47. INV: And you indicate you put it into a computer. You're referring to Microsoft Outlook calendar where you keep track of your appointments there?

48. SUSP: Yes

PLR 49. INV: Okay And nobody besides you makes those entries? You're the only one that has access to that and keeps track of your own appointments and enters that information?

50. SUSP: Yes

PLR 51. INV: Okay So let's say a clerical person couldn't accept a phone call for you and has access to your calendar and schedule an appointment for you, you're responsible for scheduling your own appointments?

52. SUSP: Correct.

MQ 53. INV: Okay With regard to the Microsoft Outlook program and your familiarity with it, when you enter an appointment in an -- let's say an hour block of time just to allow for an appointment. There's the ability to classify each appointment, and by classify, I mean, it allows you to make it urgent, a low priority, follow-up, or personal. Can you explain how these appointments get classified by you?

54. SUSP: You're talking about changing the color in the block?

AL 55. INV: Yes.

56. SUSP: Okay I just, for me, I just selected green for a VIN appointment that was completed and there's no further follow-up to be done.

AL 57. INV: Okay

58. SUSP: I would use red for VIN appointments that did not show up and blue for blue tag

AL 59. INV: Okay

60. SUSP: And I think it was a salmon color, light orange, that was a VIN appointment that needed to be followed through. So if their air bag system wasn't working right or usually it's air bags. So if

APPENDIX E

the air bag system wasn't working right, then they would have to come back after they fixed the air bag system

61. INV: Uh-huh.

62. SUSP: ...come back for a follow-up appointment, no appointment needed. I would write information on their copy of what they got from DMV and give it back to them, tell them that they needed to fix the air bag system at any -- any place, bring back that documentation as well as calling first to make sure that I was there that day, that I didn't have court, that I wasn't at training, to make sure, talk to me and ask to make sure that I was there that day that they could come in and finish their appointment.

63. INV: Okay.

64. INV2: Can I ask a question real quick?

65. INV: Yes

66. INV2: Green was just for a VIN inspection that went A-O-kay?

67. SUSP: Right

68. INV2: Okay.

69. INV: So when I asked you that question, I listed four items that are attached to each one of the appointments. Do you use or were you the one who entered or classified those appointments under those headings or were those already a preset on the Microsoft program–you're using colors?

70. SUSP: They were preset in the Microsoft program

71. INV: Okay

72. SUSP: I just used the colors

73. INV: Okay So when somebody comes in for a VIN appointment, can you just explain the normal process for how you proceed with that appointment with the...

74. SUSP: To make a VIN appointment? Or...

75. INV: No– No When somebody comes in for a VIN appointment. What's the normal process for you?

76. SUSP: I'll meet them at the front desk, make sure that they have the paperwork for the vehicle. If they don't have -- I've had in the past they came in with no paperwork for the vehicle. So then I would tell them they had to return, bring in the paperwork, because when I made the appointment on the phone, I told them to bring driver's license, current valid California driver's license, DMV papers, the title, and anything else that they had paperwork for the vehicle as well as the vehicle itself.

77. INV: And with regard to other paperwork, are you talking receipts? Or...

APPENDIX E

78. SUSP: Right If they don't have the title, then a Bill of Sale or receipts for components that were replaced, yes

OEQ 79. INV: Okay And if they don't have the paperwork you've requested, what happens next?

80. SUSP: Then they would have to come back and reschedule, because it's not just a quick air bag system check. They would have to reschedule whenever my next free block was or if I had a cancellation the next day, then I could fit them in the next day.

PLQ 81. INV: So if they didn't bring their required documents, you wouldn't be able to conduct the inspection properly?

82. SUSP: Correct Because I need the DMV documents showing, you know, telling me the reason for the VIN inspection as well as the title to make sure that they have the title for the vehicle or a Bill of Sale or some type of ownership documentation for the vehicle.

PLQ 83. INV: Okay Are there times when your inspection takes place in the front parking lot versus in the auto bay in the back of the West Valley Area?

84. SUSP: Yes

OEQ 85. INV: Okay Can you describe what the difference is or what the circumstances are?

86. SUSP: Usually, if it's just an air bag re inspection, I can complete that in the front parking lot. Motorcycles, I would usually do in the front parking lot, and pretty much I can't think of any exception. All of the other inspections would be completed in the back parking lot because I'm looking at confidential VIN locations and crawling underneath the vehicle so…

PLQ 87. INV: Okay So…when you're taking these people's documents, you don't make copies of everything that they bring necessarily? You said you make a copy of the title or the salvage certificate and their driver's license.

88. SUSP: Yes

OEQ 89. INV: The purpose of copying their driver's license on to the piece of paper is for what?

90. SUSP: Just if there's a later date when the vehicle does come back stolen or I have just the documentation of the actual individual that brought the vehicle in.

OEQ 91. INV: Okay And as far as your records go with regard to your completed VIN appointments, how do you maintain your records and where do you keep those?

92. SUSP: The completed records were in a file cabinet above my desk

MLQ 93. INV: Okay And how do you…how do you maintain those? Do you keep them in monthly folders together?

94. SUSP: Yes monthly folders

PLQ 95. INV: In a chronological order? How you completed the inspection? Is that how you had them organized?

96. SUSP: Yes

287

APPENDIX E

 97. INV: Okay Can you explain the reasons why a vehicle, outside of not having the paperwork, why a vehicle might be passed on an inspection as opposed to, I think refused is the terminology that's used if it's -- if it doesn't pass that day or you can't sign off?

98. SUSP: Say that again?

 99. INV: When you're conducting a VIN inspection, a vehicle either passes or fails? Essentially...

100. SUSP: Right

 101. INV: So, under the circumstances when a vehicle would fail, what are some of the reasons?

102. SUSP: Usually air bags. If they have multiple components that do not have VIN numbers, then I can refuse them and have them bring in receipts where they got those components from.

 103. INV: Okay

104. SUSP: Those are the two main reasons that I can think of

 105. INV: And in your Microsoft Outlook calendar, do you make notes to yourself when somebody fails?

106. SUSP" Yes

 107. INV: What do you put there?

108. SUSP: Usually I'll block it red that they failed, indicating on a if I look at a weekly calendar, I can see fail, fail really quickly

 109. INV: Okay.

110. SUSP: And then I'll put usually the reason for it, air bag, you know, if it's a -- if I turn them away, no paperwork.

 111. INV: And...

112. SUSP: Or if they're late to the appointment.

113. INV: Okay Do you also make notes on the copied notes sheet that you referred to earlier with the title and their driver's license? Do you make notes on there as well as to what their -- the status of their appointment was?

114. SUSP: Yes

More questions about operations...

115. INV: Okay So once a vehicle does not pass, you give these individuals direction on what they need to do to satisfy the requirements for you to sign off your paperwork, their paperwork?

116. SUSP: Yes

117. INV: Okay During a VIN inspection, is it necessary or do you find yourself needing to question the person who brought the vehicle in about the vehicle or the components or the paperwork?

118. SUSP: Sometimes yes

APPENDIX E

119. INV: Okay During a VIN inspection -- I'm sorry. Why would you why would you question them about what's the purpose of it if you have any question about it?

120. SUSP: If they're missing NHTSA labels I would just ask them if that component was purchased from a salvage yard or if the NHTSA label is missing, if there was -- they purchased it that way, just clarification.

121. INV: Okay.

Topic 3

122. INV: During a VIN inspection, does your conversation with members of the public ever deviate from the questions which are necessary to conduct the inspection?

123. SUSP: Questions? Not at the beginning–no

124. INV: Okay I'll repeat the question. During a VIN inspection, does your conversation with members of the public ever deviate from the questions which are necessary to complete the inspection?

125. SUSP: Ever? Yes

126. INV: And can you elaborate on that?

127. SUSP: The reason for this investigation, inappropriate comments

128. INV: And what do you mean by that?

129. SUSP: Making comments to the public that don't have anything to do with the inspection.

130. INV: Are you referring to a specific comment that you make? Or are you referring to a conversation that takes place? Or what specifically are you referring to when you say making inappropriate comments?

131. SUSP: Conversations that have taken place in the past.

132. INV: Okay

133. SUSP: Some of the people that came in for VIN inspections

134. INV: Is there anything that you specifically remember?

135. SUSP: Specifically, the last -- the appointment that she complained, I was trying to explain to her that she had to get the air bag system was fixed she could either bring the vehicle back to the office or get a hotel room.

136. INV: Okay So you had a VIN appointment with somebody. Do you remember when this was? The specific person you're just referring to?

137. SUSP: It was the beginning of (redacted)

138. INV: Do you remember this person's name?

139. SUSP: No.

289

APPENDIX E

 140. INV: Was it a man or a woman?

141. SUSP: A woman

 142. INV: Okay You explained that she needed to get her air bag system fixed, and you gave her two options it sounds like.

143. SUSP: No–I gave her one option, to fix the air bag system

 144. INV: Okay But after the air bag system was fixed, you gave her two options as to what to do next. You said you can either come back for an inspection at the office? Yes?

145. SUSP: That I would complete the VIN inspection–that I would complete the air bag inspection either way, yes.

 146. INV: Okay So she needed to have an air bag system fixed, you meaning you weren't going to pass her like you had just previously described? You suggested to her that she come back for a re-inspection at the West Valley office?

147. SUSP: Yes

 148. INV: Okay Which is normal for you, right? And then the other option you just said was to get a motel room?

149. SUSP: To get the air bag system fixed, yes.

 150. INV: What do you --

151. SUSP: I mean, I could

 152. INV: I–what did you mean when you asked her -- when you told -- suggested to her to get a motel room? What does that mean?

153. SUSP: To be intimate

 154. INV: Did you tell her that?

155. SUSP: No.

 156. INV: What did you tell her?

157. SUSP: What I said, to fix the air bag system and then either come back to the West Valley office or to get a motel room.

 158. INV: Okay So you were proposing to her a motel room for the purpose of having sexual relations with her?

159. SUSP: Yes

 160. INV: How long into this appointment did this conversation take?

161. SUSP: It was at the end of the appointment after I had completed the inspection

 162. INV: Okay So when I asked you earlier does your conversation with members of the public ever deviate from questions which are necessary to complete the inspection, and you said yes, is this normal for you?

APPENDIX E

163. SUSP: No.

 164. INV: Why did it happen that day?

165. SUSP: I don't know

 166. INV: Was is it something that she said to you that prompted you to ask her this?

167. SUSP: I had to -- I think she didn't speak very good English, and I didn't -- I was trying to explain to her what to do, and I kept explaining it to her, explaining it to her, and she didn't understand

 168. INV: Okay Did she, in any way, infer that that's what she wanted--was to go to a motel room?

169. SUSP: Not to a motel room, no.

 170. INV: Did she do anything to make it appear that she was attracted to you?

171. SUSP: I don't remember

 172. INV: Was this your idea? The motel room?

173. SUSP: Yes

 174. INV: Yes? That was a yes?

175. SUSP: Yes

 176. INV: When you suggested the motel room, did you suggest a time?

177. SUSP: No.

 178. INV: Did you suggest a location?

179. SUSP: No

 180. INV: How, in your mind, did you anticipate that playing out?

181. SUSP: I didn't think she would understand me because she -- I couldn't explain to her that she needed to get the air bag system fixed.

 182. INV: You didn't think that she would understand the fact that you had asked her to a motel room?

183. SUSP: I didn't think she would understand

 184. INV: So if you didn't think she would understand what you were saying, why did you say it to begin with?

185. SUSP: I don't know.

 186. INV: So if you asked this woman, who you'd only met that day for her VIN appointment, is that a yes?

187. SUSP: Yes

291

APPENDIX E

MLQ 188. INV: So you asked this woman that you only met that day if she wanted to go to a motel room with you to have sexual relations, how did you anticipate or expect that to work out? When was this going to happen?

189. SUSP: I didn't expect it to happen.

PLQ 190. INV: Okay Was it–you just expressed the intent of having being intimate with her. So was there– did you have a plan in place?

191. SUSP: No

MP 192. INV: No?

OEQ 193. INV: How many times has this happened?

194. SUSP: I don't know

FC 195. INV: More than once?

196. SUSP: Yes

PLQ 197. INV: Twice?

198. SUSP: More than twice

FC 199. INV: So since you've been a VIN officer, since (redacted) has this happened on numerous occasions during that period of time?

200. SUSP: More than twice–I don't know how many times

PLQ 201. INV: Ten?

202. SUSP: I don't know.

PLQ 203. INV: Twenty?

204. SUSP: I don't know

PLQ 205. INV: Is it possible that you've done this twenty times?

206. SUSP: In two years, I don't -- that -- not twenty

OEQ 207. INV: How many?

208. SUSP: I don't know–I'd have to–I don't–I don't know

OEQ 209. INV: Has anybody, with regard to CHP employees ever been present when you've done this?

210. SUSP: No

PQ 211. INV: Does anybody know that you do this?

212. SUSP: No

PQ 213. INV: So you're the only one who's been there when this has occurred, along with the individual who's having the VIN inspection?

APPENDIX E

214. SUSP: Yes

PQ 215. INV: So nobody else would know how many times this has occurred other than you?

216. SUSP: Yes

ACQ 217. INV: You've indicated you don't know how many times, but I'm going to -- I'm going to ask you, how many times -- and I'll give you time to think about it. How many times do you think that you have asked somebody to go to a motel during a VIN appointment?

218. SUSPREP: Okay You're asking him for an estimation now or a guess? Because he stated that he can't remember. He said that it's more than two, but not more than twenty.

AQC 219. INV: Okay Yes–So I'm asking for a clarifying number

220. SUSPREP: Okay If he can't remember an exact number, as we stated at the beginning of this, he's not supposed to speculate or guess, and he's narrowed it down from two to twenty. So I don't know–if you don't want–if he's not to guess, how's he supposed to narrow it down more than that?

ACQ 221. INV: Given the fact that he's the only one who's been present at these appointments, I'm going to give him an opportunity to think about it and to think back as to how many times he thinks this has occurred. So it's somewhere between two and twenty. Can you think back to any other specific occasions when this has occurred?

222. SUSP: Not specific occasions–no

PQ 223. INV: Okay Is there -- you said it's happened twice?

224. SUSP: More than twice

PQ 225. INV: Okay Can you think of one other occasion when it's occurred?

226. SUSP: Not specifically, no

OEQ 227. INV: Okay The woman you were just talking about that you said you gave her the option of coming back to the office for the inspection or going to a motel room, who was with her that day?

228. SUSP: I think her son was with her.

MP 229. INV: Her son? How old was her son?

230. SUSP: I don't remember

PLQ 231. INV: Was it an infant?

232. SUSP: I don't remember

PLQ 233. INV: Was this son a baby?

234. SUSP: No

LQ 235. INV: Okay So this was a child that was walking around with her, right?

236. SUSP: Yes

APPENDIX E

LQ 237. INV: A child that presumably can carry on a conversation and understand what's being said?

238. SUSP: Yes

FC 239. INV: So did you make that comment to this woman in front of her son?

240. SUSP: No

OEQ 241. INV: Where was her son when you asked?

242. SUSP: He was outside of the car.

OEQ 243. INV: And where were you when this happened?

244. SUSP: I was–I think I was sitting in the driver's seat showing her the air bag light.

PQ 245. INV: And she was in the car as well?

246. SUSP: She was standing beside the car.

FC 247. INV: In the front parking lot?

248. SUSP: Yes

PQ 249. INV: You don't remember her name?

250. SUSP: No, sir

OEQ 251. INV: Would you recognize her if you saw her again?

252. SUSP: No

ACQ 253. INV: Why does that particular appointment or that particular woman stick out in your mind and you're unable to remember the others?

254. SUSP: Because she went into the office to complain.

ACQ 255. INV: Has this happened so many times that you can't keep track of it?

256. SUSP: No I just don't remember because some of them were possibly a year ago. I don't…

LQ 257. INV: Okay So going back during your assignment as the VIN officer, (redacted) of (redacted) to (redacted) of (redacted) you think that it's possible that this happened as long ago as a year ago?

258. SUSP: Possibly

PLQ 259. INV: Okay Is it ever necessary for you, when you're doing a VIN appointment, to contact the individual after they've left?

260. SUSP: No.

PLQ 261. INV: Okay And I'll clarify that, after you've passed somebody for their VIN appointment, is it necessary for you to ever contact them?

262. SUSP: Sometimes, yes, to follow up on the appointment if I refuse them. In the past I've contacted people to do follow-up to make sure that they're going to come back to complete their inspection, yes.

APPENDIX E

PLQ 263. INV: Okay So the question was—for VIN inspections where you've passed them, when they've passed, is it necessary for you to contact them after they've left?

264. SUSP: Passed—no

AL 265. INV: Okay

AQC 266. INV2: Yeah.

AQC 267. INV: Go ahead

PR 268. INV2: Morgan, you mentioned that—you mentioned a motel room to her?

269. SUSP: Yes

MQ 270. INV2: What motel were you going to? What one did you have in mind specifically?

271. SUSP: I didn't have any hotel room in mind

PLQ 272. INV: And did she seem happy about the comment?

273. SUSP: She was confused and then unhappy

LQ 274. INV: Did she repeat the question to you for verification once you mentioned motel? Did she ask you what or ask you to specify what you meant?

275. SUSP: I don't remember

AL 276. INV: Okay Okay

PR 277. INV: When you said somebody fails an appointment that you needed to re-contact them for—or if there was a need to re-contact them, how do you normally do that?

278. SUSP: By phone

LQ 279. INV: Okay the office phone?

280. SUSP: Yes

FC 281. INV: Have you ever had occasion to contact them on your cell phone?

282. SUSP: I don't think so

OEQ 283. INV: Okay And how long does a typical VIN appointment take to complete?

284. SUSP: About an hour

MLQ 285. INV: Is that the average or is that kind of–is it maximum of an hour and some take less than that?

286. SUSP: For a newer vehicle, up to an hour. For an older vehicle, it could take more than–more than two hours

OEQ 287. INV: And about how long does a re-inspection take if you've already seen this vehicle?

288. SUSP: That takes less than 30 minutes

295

APPENDIX E

Topic 5

AQC 289. INV: Okay, Okay We're going to move on from the topics we just talked about. We need to move into some policy stuff and discuss that with you right now. Okay So we're just going to go through some documents, and I think before we'll do that, we're going to take a ten-minute break. Okay? So it's, by my clock it's 8:45 right now, and we'll come back…

290. SUSP: Okay

16 responses within T3 were less confident and investigator resorted to asking questions that diminished RCE.

16/79 (T3) = 20%; COR −1

END OF INTERVIEW

APPENDIX E

EEIA Summary Report

This report is part of the Efficacy of Eyewitness Interview Assessment℠

Date	5/20/22	Type of event	CASE STUDY #1	Type of investigator	Criminal

Topic Descriptions

Topics	Topic Description
1	Welcome, Introduction, Assess
2	Suspect Description
3	Crime Elements
4	Confirmation, Clarification, Review
5	Conclusion, Follow-up, Q&A

Topic Sequence (chart): Topic 1 = 46, Topic 2 = 0, Topic 3 = 83, Topic 4 = 0, Topic 5 = 1

Total Questions	130	Total Responses	137	Average Questions	26	Average Responses	27

Topic Access per Interview

Topic	Questions per topic	Eyewitness Responses
1	46	57
2	0	0
3	83	79
4	0	0
5	1	1

Examination of Questions Types

Type	CE Effect	Questions	Total	Proportion
I	SRP	AQC, NR	11	7%
II	DRCE	ACQ, FC, LQ, MCQ, MQ, MLQ, PLQ	58	39%
III	IRCE	MP, OEQ, PQ	61	41%
IV	MR	EC, AL	18	12%
		EW Responses	137	48%
		Total	285	

Topic 2 & 3 Questions (Type III & IV) (bar chart): Topic 2 = 0, Topic 3 = 41

Reliability of Cognitive Evidence Scale

Cognitive Evidence Effects	More than Acceptable (3)	Acceptable (2)	Less than Acceptable (1)
Diminish Reliability	< 7%	7% - 12%	> 12%
Improve Reliability	> 56%	56% - 50%	< 50%
Mindful Rapport	> 9%	9% - 4%	< 4%
Eyewitness Response	> 48%	48% - 47%	< 47%
Topic 2	> 82%	82% - 79%	< 79%
Topic 3	> 55%	55% - 41%	< 41%
Topic Sequence Deviation	< 3	3 - 4	> 4

RELIABLE COGNITIVE EVIDENCE COLLECTED	HIGHLY RELIABLE: 21 – 18. RELIABLE: 17 – 14 LESS THAN RELIABLE: 13 – 7

COR:	DRCE:	39%	IRCE:	41%	MR:	12%	EWR:	48%	T2:		T3:	48%	TSQ:	1	RCE
-1		1		1		3		2		2		2		2	12

Confidence of Recollection (COR): 0 = Confidence is affirmed; -1 = Confidence is questionable; -2 = Confidence is unreliable

APPENDIX E

CASE STUDY #2

For more information about Case Study #2 see Chapter 16 for instructional content. This section includes: a. Complete EEIA report, b. Coded transcript, and c. EEIA summary report.

Eyewitness Interview Data Collection
This diagnostic report is part of the Efficacy of Eyewitness Interview Assessment℠

Date	3/1/22
Type of event	CASE STUDY #2
Type of investigator	Criminal

Table 1 - Topic Descriptions

Topics	Topic Description
1	Welcome, Introduction, Assess
2	Suspect Description
3	Crime Elements
4	Confirmation, Clarification, Review
5	Conclusion, Follow-up, Q&A

Table 2 - Topic Access per Interview

Topic	Questions per topic	Questions per interview	Eyewitness Responses	Responses per interview
1	2	13%	4	31%
2	0	0%	0	0%
3	11	69%	8	62%
4	0	0%	0	0%
5	3	19%	1	8%
Total	16	Total	13	
Average Questions	3	Average Responses	3	

Table 3 - Question Category from Transcript Review

Topic	AQC	ACQ	EC	FC	LQ	MCQ	MP	MQ	MLQ	NR	OEQ	PQ	PLQ	AL	Questions Only	Topic Totals	EWR
1					1							1			2	2	4
2															0	0	
3	7							1		1	2		2		11	13	8
4															0	0	
5	2										1				3	3	1
Totals	9	0	0	0	1	0	0	1	0	2	2	1	2		16	18	13

Table 4 - Reliability of Cognitive Evidence (RCE) Rating

Highly Reliable	Reliable	Less Than Reliable	Reliability of Cognitive Evidence
21 - 18	17 - 14	13 - 7	10

Table 5 - Confidence of Recollection (COR) Rating

Confidence is confirmed	Confidence is questionable	Confidence is unreliable	COR Rating
0	-1	-2	-1

Reliability of Cognitive Evidence

Table 4 - Reliability of Cognitive Evidence Scale

Cognitive Evidence Effects	More than Acceptable (3)	Acceptable (2)	Less than Acceptable (1)
Diminish Reliability	< 7%	7% - 10%	> 10%
Improve Reliability	> 61%	61% - 57%	< 57%
Mindful Rapport	> 9%	9% - 4%	< 4%
Eyewitness Response	> 49%	49% - 48%	< 48%
Topic 2	> 82%	82% - 78%	< 78%
Topic 3	> 59%	59% - 45%	< 45%
Topic Sequence Deviation	< 1	1 - 2	> 2

Mean scores derived from Mindful Interview Method in forensic art sketch interviews.

Table 5 - Reliability of Cognitive Evidence for Interview

Cognitive Evidence Questions	Results	RCE
Diminish Reliability (DRCE)	17%	1
Improve Reliability (IRCE)	22%	1
Mindful Rapport (MR)	11%	3
Eyewitness Response (EWR)	42%	1
Topic 2 (T2)		2
Topic 3 (T3)	38%	1
Topic Sequence Deviations (1 - 5), (TSQ)	2	2
Confidence of Recollection		-1
Reliability of Cognitive Evidence (RCE)		**10**

APPENDIX E

Topic Sequence Overview and Topic 2 & 3 Focus

This diagnostic report is part of the Efficacy of Eyewitness Interview Assessment℠

Table 1 - Sequence of Topics

Total Deviations	Sequence	1	2	3	4	5							
1	Topics	2	0	11	0	3							

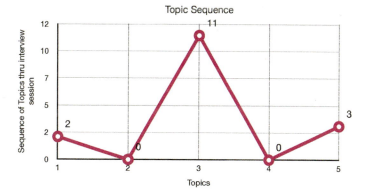

Table 2 - Topic 2 & 3 Questions		
	Total Interview Questions (Type III & IV)	Proportion of questions
Topic 2	0	
Topic 3	5	38%

Topics 2 & 3 cover suspect description and crime elements.

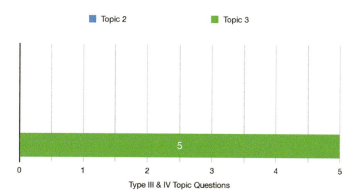

299

APPENDIX E

Question Examination and Eyewitness Responses

This diagnostic report is part of the Efficacy of Eyewitness Interview Assessment℠

Table 1 - Examination of Questions from eyewitness interview			
Type	Questions	Total	Proportion
I	AQC, NR	9	50%
II	ACQ, FC, LQ, MCQ, MQ, MLQ, PLQ	3	17%
III	MP, OEQ, PQ	4	22%
IV	EC, AL	2	11%
EWR	EW Responses	13	42%
	Total	31	

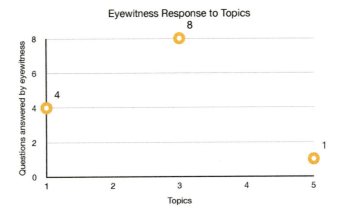

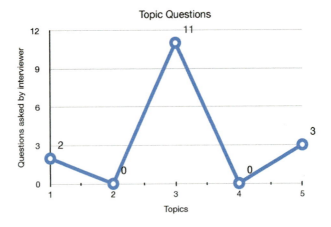

APPENDIX E

EYEWITNESS INTERVIEW ANALYSIS (EIA)
CONFIDENTIAL TRANSCRIPT REVIEW

The transcripts have been anonymized to protect the innocent. Any reference to persons or places in this transcript is maintained purely for dialogue consistency and the evaluation of interview strategies. The crime type and number of eyewitnesses remain to offer the reader some perspective on the type of case featured. For this book, all case studies that included a composite sketch from forensic artist Gil Zamora included some evaluation of COR. Some of these transcripts will include the COR evaluation, while others may have been evaluated outside of the interview transcript. Other case study transcripts evaluated for COR may include notes that address this outcome. Each case study will include the EEIA (Data Collection page and Summary Report). The Data Collection page includes all the question types attributed to the transcript review. Each transcript review was conducted a minimum of three times before generating the complete EEIA.

Date of transcript review: March 1, 2022

Crime type: Officer misconduct

Notes:

APPENDIX E

Topic 1

1. EW: Then he started saying to me, well, you know what? You want me get one motel room for me and you? I said, what?
2. EW: A motel room for me and you?
3. **LQ** INV #1: Is there any way that she could — is there any way she misunderstood? Is there any way that you misunderstood what [the officer] was saying?
4. EW: No, I understand everything.
5. **PUQ** INV #2: You don't need anybody to speak in Spanish. You understand English?
6. EW: I understand English, but...

Topic 3

7. **ACQ** INV #3: Just to tell you, this is highly unusual for a citizen to tell me this with this officer. I just - I'm not saying I don't believe you. I was just thinking it's very out there, you know? It's very out in left field for this exchange to happen, so...
8. EW: No, but I don't lie. I tell you exactly what he's saying.
9. **ACQ** INV #3: I don't believe you're lying to me, but understand that this is very unusual.
10. **ACQ** INV #1: Ma'am, did you have any alcohol to drink last night? Nothing that would...
11. EW: No, sir. I don't drink alcohol. I don't do drugs. I don't smoke.
12. **AL** INV #1: OK.
13. EW: I have four kids. I'm mother to four kids.
14. **AL** INV #1: OK.
15. **ACQ** INV #1: I just - I feel like I smell some alcohol in here, and I mean no disrespect or anything, but I just - that's why I asked.
16. EW: No, no.
17. **PQ** INV #3: You haven't had something to drink in the last 12 hours?
18. EW: Nothing.
19. **AQC** INV #1: Can I - I'm just going to walk over there. I'm going to have you follow my finger.

APPENDIX E

20. EW: Yeah, yes, sure. We can leave my son here?

ACQ 21. INV #1: Oh, no, this will just be right here. I was just going to have you follow my finger with your eyes. Try not to move your head, OK? OK, thank you, ma'am. I just sometimes - I don't know if it's this room, but I felt like I was smelling alcohol. Maybe it's from that breath machine right there, so I apologize.

MLQ 22. INV #3: Is there any reason why you think he would say this to you? Is it maybe to help you get a certificate or help you pass to get registration for your vehicle?

PQ 23. INV #3: Why do you think he was asking for a motel room for you and him?

24. EW: Because he no respect the ladies.

OGR 25. INV #3: What does that mean?

26. EW: He no respect the ladies because...

27. INV and EW speak Spanish...

AQC 28. INV #3: OK. She said, well, it's disrespect to her. And I go, what does that mean to you? And she says, sex between him and - her and the officer.

29. INV #1: OK.

30. INV #3: In Spanish.

Topic 5

OGR 31. INV #3: Do you have any questions for us?

32. EW: No. (Speaking Spanish).

AQC 33. INV #3: She's describing that she's scared, confused, and she doesn't understand this department, that she's worried that we're going to protect him. And she - there wasn't a reason for this to happen.

AQC 34. INV #1: Well, ma'am, we take complaints seriously, and we will fully investigate this incident. So just know that we're not going to dismiss this and think that it's no big deal. It's a big deal to us.

END OF INTERVIEW

APPENDIX E

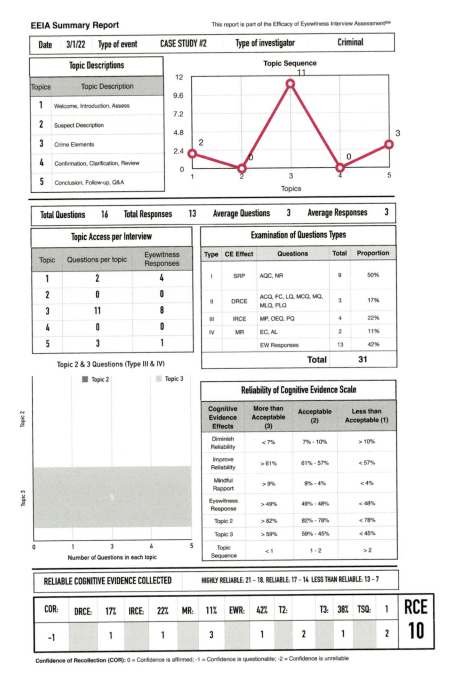

APPENDIX E

CASE STUDY #3

For more information about Case Study #3 see Chapter 17 for instructional content. This section includes: a. Complete EEIA report, b. Coded transcript, and c. EEIA summary report.

Eyewitness Interview Data Collection
This diagnostic report is part of the Efficacy of Eyewitness Interview Assessment℠

Date	3/15/22
Type of event	CASE STUDY #3
Type of investigator	Forensic Artist

Table 1 - Topic Descriptions

Topics	Topic Description
1	Welcome, Introduction, Assess
2	Suspect Description
3	Crime Elements
4	Confirmation, Clarification, Review
5	Conclusion, Follow-up, Q&A

Table 2 - Topic Access per Interview

Topic	Questions per topic	Questions per interview	Eyewitness Responses	Responses per interview
1	7	11%	9	13%
2	36	56%	38	54%
3	12	19%	15	21%
4	6	9%	6	9%
5	3	5%	2	3%
Total	64	Total	70	
Average Questions	13	Average Responses	14	

Table 3 - Question Category from Transcript Review

Topic	AQC	ACQ	EC	FC	LQ	MCQ	MP	MQ	MLQ	NR	OEQ	PQ	PLQ	AL	Questions Only	Topic Totals	EWR
1	5										2			2	7	9	9
2	3			3			2				20	8		1	36	37	38
3	2						2				2	6		4	12	16	15
4											3	3			6	6	6
5	3													3	3	3	2
Totals	13	0	0	3	0	0	4	0	0	0	27	17	0	7	64	71	70

Table 4 - Reliability of Cognitive Evidence (RCE) Rating

Highly Reliable	Reliable	Less Than Reliable	Reliability of Cognitive Evidence
21 - 18	17 - 14	13 - 7	21

Table 5 - Confidence of Recollection (COR) Rating

Confidence is confirmed	Confidence is questionable	Confidence is unreliable	COR Rating
0	-1	-2	0

Reliability of Cognitive Evidence

Table 4 - Reliability of Cognitive Evidence Scale

Cognitive Evidence Effects	More than Acceptable (3)	Acceptable (2)	Less than Acceptable (1)
Diminish Reliability	< 7%	7% - 10%	> 10%
Improve Reliability	> 61%	61% - 57%	< 57%
Mindful Rapport	> 9%	9% - 4%	< 4%
Eyewitness Response	> 49%	49% - 48%	< 48%
Topic 2	> 82%	82% - 78%	< 78%
Topic 3	> 59%	59% - 45%	< 45%
Topic Sequence Deviation	< 1	1 - 2	> 2

Mean scores derived from Mindful Interview Method in forensic art sketch interviews.

Table 5 - Reliability of Cognitive Evidence for Interview

Cognitive Evidence Questions	Results	RCE
Diminish Reliability (DRCE)	4%	3
Improve Reliability (IRCE)	68%	3
Mindful Rapport (MR)	10%	3
Eyewitness Response (EWR)	50%	3
Topic 2 (T2)	84%	3
Topic 3 (T3)	88%	3
Topic Sequence Deviations (1 - 5), (TSQ)	0	3
Confidence of Recollection		0
Reliability of Cognitive Evidence (RCE)		**21**

APPENDIX E

Topic Sequence Overview and Topic 2 & 3 Focus

This diagnostic report is part of the Efficacy of Eyewitness Interview Assessment℠

Table 1 - Sequence of Topics

Total Deviations	Sequence	1	2	3	4	5						
0	Topics	7	36	12	6	3						

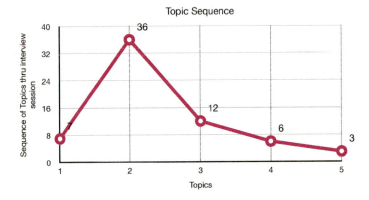

Table 2 - Topic 2 & 3 Questions

	Total Interview Questions (Type III & IV)	Proportion of questions
Topic 2	31	84%
Topic 3	14	88%

Topics 2 & 3 cover suspect description and crime elements.

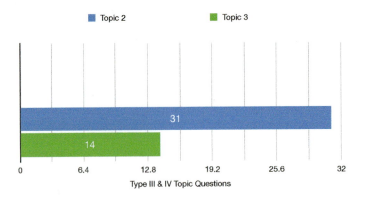

306

APPENDIX E

Question Examination and Eyewitness Responses

This diagnostic report is part of the Efficacy of Eyewitness Interview Assessment[SM]

Table 1 - Examination of Questions from eyewitness interview

Type	Questions	Total	Proportion
I	AQC, NR	13	18%
II	ACQ, FC, LQ, MCQ, MQ, MLQ, PLQ	3	4%
III	MP, OEQ, PQ	48	68%
IV	EC, AL	7	10%
EWR	EW Responses	70	50%
	Total	**141**	

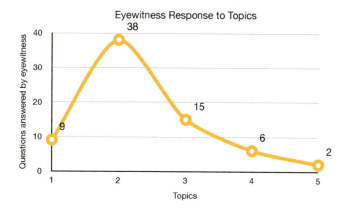

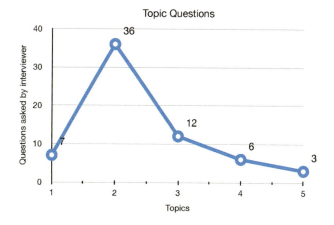

307

APPENDIX E

EYEWITNESS INTERVIEW ANALYSIS (EIA)
CONFIDENTIAL TRANSCRIPT REVIEW

The transcripts have been anonymized to protect the innocent. Any reference to persons or places in this transcript is maintained purely for dialogue consistency and the evaluation of interview strategies. The crime type and number of eyewitnesses remain to offer the reader some perspective on the type of case featured. For this book, all case studies that included a composite sketch from forensic artist Gil Zamora included some evaluation of COR. Some of these transcripts will include the COR evaluation, while others may have been evaluated outside of the interview transcript. Other case study transcripts evaluated for COR may include notes that address this outcome. Each case study will include the EEIA (Data Collection page and Summary Report). The Data Collection page includes all the question types attributed to the transcript review. Each transcript review was conducted a minimum of three times before generating the complete EEIA.

Date of transcript review: March 15, 2022

Crime type: Suspicious person, annoying children

Notes:

Topic 1

[ARC] 1. INV : ...Ok the way this works is that I'm going to ask you about the person's face.
2. EW : ok
[ARC] 3. INV : and was it one suspect?
4. EW: yeah
[ARC] 5. INV : I'd like you to go ahead and answer to the best of your knowledge.
6. EW : ok
[ARC] 7. INV : Most people don't remember everything in great detail; however, a lot of folks tend to remember a lot of information especially when they're here and focus on the questions.
8. EW : ok
[ARC] 9. INV : You're going to have your eyes closed for about 5 minutes : that's going to help you relax and focus on the questions. It's makes it a little easier to describe. Then after that I'm going to ask you to open your eyes and I'm going to ask you to tell me what happened and then I'll show you the sketch and if we need to, we'll make some changes. Do you understand?
10. EW : mhmm
[OEQ] 11. INV : Now, so there's two of you so um. Can you give me an idea of the location where you were? You were together when this happened?
12. EW : Ah no she was playing in the playground like maybe a block away from our apartment
[AL] 13. INV : ok
14. EW : It's inside our apartment
[AL] 15. INV : ok

APPENDIX E

16. EW : There were a group of kids : like maybe 10 or 12 kids playing together and in that, 4 were girls ranging from 6 years to 12 years of age and my daughter she was playing and I think a couple of more kids were doing the same thing and she tells me that this guy… like a little bit away from them was taking pictures and he had a cellphone and then she could notice that he was videotaping when he came closer to them. And I asked her like how you suspect that he's videotaping you and she says : she's had a cellphone since 7 years of age so knows how to take a picture and how to take a video recording and he was holding the camera horizontally pointing it towards them and especially toward the body part.

17. INV : ok so when did you see him?

18. EW : Umm then what happened she suspected that and said to her friend hurry up, let's go home so all of them came home and she described the situation. My husband was at home, so I told him around 7:15 in the evening and I was explaining to him suddenly that person appeared in front of my apartment looking for them. And I had the idea that something was wrong, and I was about to go out and you know this guy just … and I ask him why are you following them and he said no I'm not following. I said you are taking picture and he said no I'm not taking picture : I was talking on my cell phone, and he started walking very fast. And I think he suspected something so his car was parked right in front of my apartment : a little bit on the left side, but it was… so he just went and sat in his car. That's how my husband went inside to get the camera to take a picture but by the time I go there he was sitting in his car…

Topic 2

19. INV : Ok that gives me a better idea because I'm going to ask you the same questions–I'm going to ask all of my questions to your mom, ok? So, you both have cell phones. You want to make sure they're on silent, so we don't get interrupted. So, all of my questions are going to be to you.

20. EW : ok

21. INV : So you go ahead and answer to the best of your knowledge. Just tell me everything, ok. And then umm after when I show you the sketch, then you'll have an opportunity to make comments if you need to ok? So, all of my questions will be to her. You just sit back and relax. You'll also need to close your eyes and relax as well. Ok? Do you have any questions for me?

22. EW : No

23. INV : Ok go ahead and close your eyes and give me a nice deep breath and we'll begin. First of all, what would you say is the race of this person?

24. EW : White.

25. INV : Age range?

26. EW : 40:45

27. INV : Body build?

28. EW : skinny

29. INV : When you think about the shape of this guy's face, what shape are we talking about?

30. EW : umm a little bit on the longer side.

31. INV : tell me about his hair

32. EW : no hair. Totally bald.

33. INV : he was bald?

34. EW : mm

35. INV : some men when they have a bald head their shape is a little distinctive. Anything unusual about the shape?

36. EW : It was totally round and nicely shaped.

37. INV : ok perfect. Tell me about his ears.

38. EW : um the ears I couldn't notice. Since he was white it was obvious, I could see his ears nicely.

39. INV : Ok any earrings on this guy?

40. EW : No.

41. INV : Tell me about his nose.

APPENDIX E

OEQ 42. EW : Straight nose.
OEQ 43. INV : His mouth and his lips?
44. EW : Lips were kind of thin?
MP 45. INV : Thin?
46. EW : Yeah
OEQ 47. INV : Uhuh. What was his attitude?
48. EW : Ah he was pretty arrogant.
PQ 49. INV : Ok. Any facial hair?
50. EW : Ah no
OEQ 51. INV : Tell me about his chin.
52. EW : His chin was kind of pointy.
PQ 53. INV : Any hair on the chin?
54. EW : No.
OEQ 55. INV : And his cheeks? What were they like?
56. EW : They were kind of flat.
OEQ 57. INV : Skin color?
58. EW : White
OEQ 59. INV : The texture of his skin?
60. EW : Kind of shiny
PQ 61. INV : Any scars or marks on his face and neck?
62. EW : No
OEQ 63. INV : And tell me about his neck.
64. EW : Um his heck was like kind of normal. He was wearing a white t:shirt.
MP 65. INV : A white t:shirt?
66. EW : Mm.
OEQ 67. INV : Have you ever seen this guy before?
68. EW : No
OEQ 69. INV : Tell me about his eyes?
70. EW : His eyes were like cat eyes um maybe a little bit of greenish blue.
PQ 71. INV : Ok. And what do you mean by cat eyes?
72. EW – Um, it's like : it's not totally black it's a mixture of green and blue.
AC 73. INV : Ok I see what you mean : the color.
74. EW : Yeah
OEQ 75. INV : Tell me about the overall look in his eyes : the size of his eyes : things like that
76. EW : Could you explain?
PQ 77. INV : Um the size of his eyes?

310

APPENDIX E

78. EW : They were kind of normal. Not too big not too small.
PQ 79. INV : Ok and then the look in his eyes.
80. EW : Scared
OEQ 81. INV : Ok. And eyebrows?
82. EW : Eyebrows are normal
FC 83. INV : When you saw this guy, was it daytime or nighttime?
84. EW : It was evening and light.
FC 85. INV : And this happened indoors or outdoors?
86. EW : It was outdoors.
OEQ 87. INV : And what do you remember the most about this guy's face?
88. EW : His nose
PQ 89. INV : And why do you remember the nose most?
90. EW : Sharp nose like straight
FC 91. INV : Does this guy have a mannish face or a boyish face?
92. EW : A mannish face
OEQ 93. INV : How close did you get to him?
94. EW : Mm, like a couple of feet.

Topic 3

AQC 95. INV : Alright you can open your eyes. Now what I want you to do is I want you to tell me what happened. I want you to tell me what you were doing just prior to running into this guy and then take me through the incident up until the police get involved.

96. EW : Ok, so um I explained to you that I confronted him then I followed him, and I saw he was sitting in his car. By the time I go there he was taking a …

MP 97. INV : He was taking what?

98. EW : He was about to leave.

AL 99. INV : Mm.

100. EW : So I could read his number plate and I was repeating it loudly and starting with the 2FP. And there were some numbers, and I was repeating that loudly so by the time he just went away, and I get inside and I told that number to my husband and he immediately called 911. And they transferred us to another dispatch–police officer–so he showed up between 3:4 minutes and he came there and he asked what happened and I told him and he talked to my daughter and the kids and asked them if what he was wearing, how tall he was, if he touched them or did he talk to them : all those kinds of questions and he asked us if we saw this man before and then somebody told us : the neighbors told us : that we have a video camera near our apartment and I told him and he went to the manager's apartment.

PQ 101. INV : Who went to the manager's apartment?

102. EW : The police officer

APPENDIX E

AL 103.INV : Oh ok.

104.EW : But she said the cameras were off. It was not on.

AL 105.INV : Ok

106.EW : So he came back, and he said do you remember the make of the car and I couldn't. I just gave him the 2FP and the numbers and he took down my driver's license and my phone number and said he would call if he would call if he needed you there and how good is your memory– would you recognize him, and we said yeah, we could recognize him and after that he left. And around 10:30 he called again, and he said do you know the make of the car : do you suspect it can be some car and I said umm I don't really remember because I was totally concentrating on the number plate. And the detective called, and he gave me the number to call you.

PQ 107.INV : Did they stop anybody for you to look at that night?

108.EW : Repeat that.

PR 109.INV : Did they stop anybody for you to look at that night?

110.EW : No. The police officer said he will roll through the database um you know to look for the car, just to see whether there is anybody who lives nearby and need to make sure that's not and I couldn't find anybody. No. Not like that person.

PQ 111.INV : Right. Did your husband see the car?

112.EW : No he just went inside. Actually, he was inside when this guy came and we were near our door about to leave, but since he showed up and he started running, my husband went in to just get a camera to take a picture, but this guy was next to our apartment, and he just ran by the. But he saw that person.

MP 113.INV : He did see him?

114.EW : Yes.

OEQ 115.INV : How did he see him?

116.EW : Because we were standing near our door about to go out just to see what happening…

AL 117.INV : Oh..

118.EW : At the park and immediately this guy showed up just to see where the kids are basically following them all over to our apartment.

OEQ 119.INV : How many other kids were there?

120.EW : Because there were kids, the younger one was 6, and one was 6 1/2 and the other was 12 years old.

PQ 121.INV : And do you know them all?

122.EW : Yes.

PQ 123.INV : And what area was this?

124.EW : Umm it's in …off … near the ...

AQC 125.INV : Oh ok. Alright I'm going to show you the sketch.

(The sketch is shown to EW#1 and then EW#2: this portion has been edited to focus on the retrieval of cognitive evidence and not on the forensic art process)

Topic 4

OER 126.INV : And what kind of camera did he have?
127.EW2 : Um it was a cell phone that had a camera in it.
PR 128.INV : So what kind of cell phone?
129.EW2 : It looked very much like mine.
PR 130.INV : And what kind do you have?
131.EW2 : Mine is a …
OER 132.INV : Have you ever seen this guy before, …?
133.EW2 : No.
PR 134.INV : No? How about your friends?
135.EW2 : No, none of us had ever seen him.
OER 136.INV : Have you guys been talking about it?
137.EW2 : Sometimes.

Topic 5

AQC 138.INV : Mm. And … the initials to your name?
AQC 139.INV : … Got it. Ok. Here's my card. If you have any questions, you can give me a call.
140.EW : Sure.
ARC 141.INV : And I will give this to the detective.
142.EW : Ok sounds good. Thank you.

End of Interview

APPENDIX E

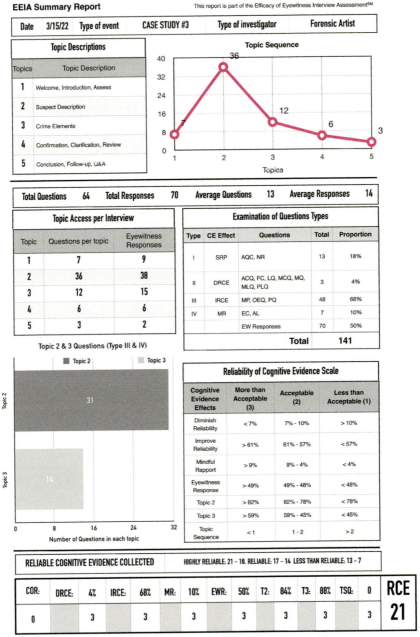

APPENDIX E

CASE STUDY #4

For more information about Case Study #4 see Chapter 18 for instructional content. This section includes: a. Complete EEIA report, b. Coded transcript, and c. EEIA summary report.

Eyewitness Interview Data Collection
This diagnostic report is part of the Efficacy of Eyewitness Interview Assessment℠

Date	3/28/22
Type of event	CASE STUDY #4
Type of investigator	Forensic Artist

Table 1 - Topic Descriptions

Topics	Topic Description
1	Welcome, Introduction, Assess
2	Suspect Description
3	Crime Elements
4	Confirmation, Clarification, Review
5	Conclusion, Follow-up, Q&A

Table 2 - Topic Access per Interview

Topic	Questions per topic	Questions per interview	Eyewitness Responses	Responses per interview
1	9	7%	11	6%
2	47	38%	63	36%
3	22	18%	53	31%
4	45	36%	45	26%
5	2	2%	1	1%
Total	125		Total	173	
Average Questions	25		Average Responses	35	

Table 3 - Question Category from Transcript Review

Topic	AQC	ACQ	EC	FC	LQ	MCQ	MP	MQ	MLQ	NR	OEQ	PQ	PLQ	AL	Questions Only	Topic Totals	EWR
1	1		3					4	1		3				9	12	11
2	1			6			1	21	18		17				47	64	63
3	1					11			10		31				22	53	53
4	9		4					10	22		1				45	46	45
5	1		1												2	2	1
Totals	13	0	8	6	0	0	11	1	0	0	35	51	0	52	125	177	173

Table 4 - Reliability of Cognitive Evidence (RCE) Rating

Highly Reliable	Reliable	Less Than Reliable	Reliability of Cognitive Evidence
21 - 18	17 - 14	13 - 7	18

Table 5 - Confidence of Recollection (COR) Rating

Confidence is confirmed	Confidence is questionable	Confidence is unreliable	COR Rating
0	-1	-2	0

Reliability of Cognitive Evidence

Table 4 - Reliability of Cognitive Evidence Scale

Cognitive Evidence Effects	More than Acceptable (3)	Acceptable (2)	Less than Acceptable (1)
Diminish Reliability	< 7%	7% - 10%	> 10%
Improve Reliability	> 61%	61% - 57%	< 57%
Mindful Rapport	> 9%	9% - 4%	< 4%
Eyewitness Response	> 49%	49% - 48%	< 48%
Topic 2	> 82%	82% - 78%	< 78%
Topic 3	> 59%	59% - 45%	< 45%
Topic Sequence Deviation	< 1	1 - 2	> 2

Mean scores derived from Mindful Interview Method in forensic art sketch interviews.

Table 5 - Reliability of Cognitive Evidence for Interview

Cognitive Evidence Questions	Results	RCE
Diminish Reliability (DRCE)	4%	3
Improve Reliability (IRCE)	55%	1
Mindful Rapport (MR)	34%	3
Eyewitness Response (EWR)	49%	2
Topic 2 (T2)	88%	3
Topic 3 (T3)	98%	3
Topic Sequence Deviations (1 - 5), (TSQ)	0	3
Confidence of Recollection		0
Reliability of Cognitive Evidence (RCE)		**18**

APPENDIX E

Topic Sequence Overview and Topic 2 & 3 Focus

This diagnostic report is part of the Efficacy of Eyewitness Interview Assessment℠

Table 1 - Sequence of Topics

Total Deviations	Sequence	1	2	3	4	5						
0	Topics	9	47	22	45	2						

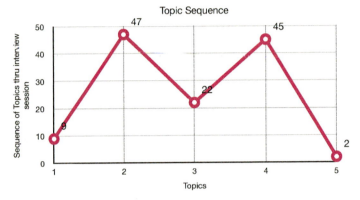

Table 2 - Topic 2 & 3 Questions

	Total Interview Questions (Type III & IV)	Proportion of questions
Topic 2	56	88%
Topic 3	52	98%

Topics 2 & 3 cover suspect description and crime elements.

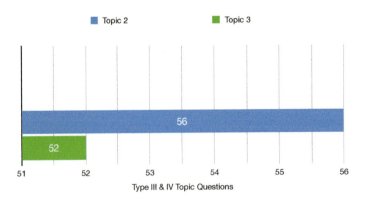

316

APPENDIX E

Question Examination and Eyewitness Responses

This diagnostic report is part of the Efficacy of Eyewitness Interview Assessment℠

Table 1 - Examination of Questions from eyewitness interview			
Type	Questions	Total	Proportion
I	AQC, NR	13	7%
II	ACQ, FC, LQ, MCQ, MQ, MLQ, PLQ	7	4%
III	MP, OEQ, PQ	97	55%
IV	EC, AL	60	34%
EWR	EW Responses	173	49%
	Total	**350**	

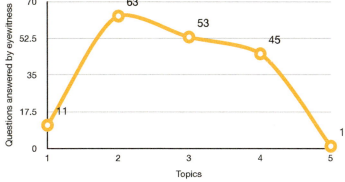

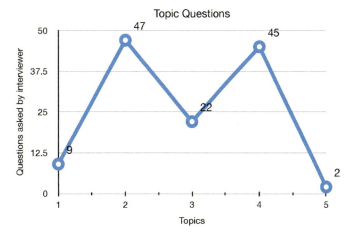

317

APPENDIX E

EYEWITNESS INTERVIEW ANALYSIS (EIA)
CONFIDENTIAL TRANSCRIPT REVIEW

The transcripts have been anonymized to protect the innocent. Any reference to persons or places in this transcript is maintained purely for dialogue consistency and the evaluation of interview strategies. The crime type and number of eyewitnesses remain to offer the reader some perspective on the type of case featured. For this book, all case studies that included a composite sketch from forensic artist Gil Zamora included some evaluation of COR. Some of these transcripts will include the COR evaluation, while others may have been evaluated outside of the interview transcript. Other case study transcripts evaluated for COR may include notes that address this outcome. Each case study will include the EEIA (Data Collection page and Summary Report). The Data Collection page includes all the question types attributed to the transcript review. Each transcript review was conducted a minimum of three times before generating the complete EEIA.

Date of transcript review: March 28, 2022

Crime type: Assault with deadly weapon

Notes: Eyewitness arrives to interview with bandage on head.

Topic 1

[ARC] 1. INV - Hi..., I'm...Nice to meet you.
[PR] 2. INV - Alright. Do you know why you're here today?
3. EW - Yeah ...
[OER] 4. INV - Ok, what happened to you? I just want to know what was the crime. I don't need to know the story right now.
5. EW - Ok. Well he hit my truck.
[AL] 6. INV - Uh huh.
7. EW - Like bumped it a little bit. So I pulled over obviously.
[AL] 8. INV - Mhm.
9. EW - I got out of the truck and he said that he didn't have .....(inaudible)   So I told him to give me money. And he said he didn't have it so he went to the truck to supposedly to get it and he came back .... (inaudible).
[EC] 10. INV - Oh I'm sorry. It was like a robbery?
11. EW - Yeah he took all the stuff from my truck.
[EC] 12. INV - Ok. And you're ok right now?
13. EW - Yeah I had a CT scan because I was swollen and I was bleeding like crazy.
[EC] 14. INV - Oh I'm sorry. Ok. And you're feeling better?
15. EW - Mhm. I still feel like paranoid.

318

APPENDIX E

AL 16. INV - Oh yeah.
17. EW - Like whenever I drive.
OEQ 18. INV - Oh I can imagine. When did this happen?
19. EW - The day before yesterday.
OEQ 20. INV - Ok. And how's your memory about this guy?
21. EW - Pretty good.
OEQ 22. INV - Ok. And if you saw him again would you recognize him?
23. EW - Yeah.

Topic 2

AQC 24. INV - Ok. Very good. I'm going to move a little closer so you can hear me. The way this works is I'm going to ask you some general questions about the person's face. I'd like you to go ahead and answer to the best of your knowledge. Most people don't remember everything in great detail however a lot of folks tend to remember a lot of information especially when they're here and they focus on the questions. You're going to have your eyes closed for about 5 minutes to help you relax. It helps you to focus on the questions and it makes it a little easier to describe. Then after that I'm going to ask you to open your eyes and ask you to tell me what happened and then I'll show you the sketch and if we need to we'll make some changes. Do you understand that? Do you have any questions for me?
25. EW - No.
OEO 26. INV - All right go ahead and close your eyes. Give me a nice deep breath. I want you nice and relaxed. Very good. Ok? First of all, what would you say is the race of this person?
27. EW - I would say Chicano.
OEQ 28. INV - Ok. Age range?
29. EW - Around 28-35.
OEQ 30. INV - Very good. Body build. What would you say his body is like?
31. EW - He was slim but not super slim.
OEQ 32. INV - Ok. Tell me about his face shape. What was that like?
33. EW - It was round.
OEQ 34. INV - Ok. Tell me about his hair. What was that like?
35. EW - His hair - um it was like a guys haircut. The ones that go like - I don't know how to explain it.
AL 36. INV - It's ok. Go ahead.
37. EW - It was like - oh what's it called - they told me - those haircuts that were all one size but they go like…do you know what I'm talking about?
PQ 38. INV - Was it short?
39. EW - No it wasn't. It was like grown out.
OEQ 40. INV - Ok and the color of his hair?
41. EW - It was black.
PQ 42. INV - Ok and is it long enough to comb?
43. EW - No, it was probably like an inch or a little shorter.

319

APPENDIX E

FC 44. INV - All right and um does he have any parts in his hair?
    45. EW - No.
PQ 46. INV - Ok and - what were you going to say?
    47. EW - Um it wasn't like a - I don't know what it's called.
PR 48. INV - You said somebody told you something?
    49. EW - Yeah, my boyfriend told me the haircut...
PQ 50. INV - Was he there?
    51. EW - No but I told him how and he told me what it was.
AL 52. INV - Hmm
    53. EW - I'm trying to remember what it's called...
PQ 54. INV - Is it a unique look?
    55. EW - No. A lot of guys get it.
AL 56. INV - Mhm.
    57. EW - Those when they get faded.
AL 58. INV - Mhm.
    59. EW - It goes like this and it goes like that. You know it was all one size.
PQ 60. INV - All one length?
    61. EW - Yeah.
AL 62. INV - Ok.
    63. EW - And some get it long at the top and short at the bottom.
PQ 64. INV - Not him?
    65. EW - Not like that, no. It was all one size.
PR 66. INV - Ok and the color of the hair again?
    67. EW - It was black.
OEQ 68. INV - Ok. Tell me about his ears. What were they like?
    69. EW - They were not big or....they were just normal size.
FC 70. INV - Ok and was he wearing any earrings?
    71. EW - No.
OEQ 72. INV - Ok and what about his forehead? What was that like?
    73. EW - Um it wasn't too big because he had bushy eyebrows.
AL 74. INV - Ok.

APPENDIX E

OEQ 75. EW - It was just like perfect.

OEQ 76. INV - Ok. Tell me about his nose.

77. EW - His nose was like…it wasn't wide but it wasn't closes, you know what I mean? It wasn't narrow. It was like a medium size.

OEQ 78. INV - Ok very good. His mouth and his lips?

79. EW - Um, his lips, they were pretty small I think. (inaudible) His mouth - cuz he was covering it a lot of the time.

PQ 80. INV - With what?

81. EW - His hand.

AL 82. INV - Ok.

83. EW - He was also smoking, so…

OEQ 84. INV - What's his attitude like?

85. EW - It was like really relaxed but nervous. Like he would hardly speak but he didn't seem like panicked. He was just nervous, I'm guessing, that's why he didn't speak much but I didn't think (inaudible).

PQ 86. INV - Any facial hair on this guy?

87. EW - Um not that I remember because I told them he did but I believe that he didn't because at first I thought he had like something here…

AL 88. INV - Mhm.

89. EW - but then I don't think he did.

OEQ 90. INV - And when you say you told them he did, who were you talking about?

91. EW - I told the sheriff.

AL 92. INV - Oh ok.

93. EW - I thought I saw a goat tee but then I thought about it and remembered.

PQ 94. INV - So now you're saying probably not?

95. EW - No.

OEQ 96. INV - Ok. And um what's the chin like?

97. EW - It was round. Everything came along with his face you know how some chins stick out? His fit.

FC 98. INV - Does he have a mannish face or a boyish face?

99. EW - I think he had a boy face. Like a little kids face.

OEQ 100. INV - Mhm. Tell me about his skin.

APPENDIX E

101. EW - His skin was very light. Maybe a little lighter than me but the reason I said he was Chicano was that I was speaking to him in English but some of the words came out in Spanish...

PQ 102. INV - For you?

103. EW - Yeah for me. And I was like, "Do you speak Spanish?" And he was like, "Kind of. I understand it." (inaudible)

FC 104. INV - And he told you in English?

105. EW - Yeah.

AL 106. INV - Ok.

107. EW - (inaudible)

OEQ 108. INV - Mhm. Tell me about his neck. What was that like?

109. EW - I didn't see his neck because he was wearing a hoodie - a dark hoodie - and it went pretty high.

AL 110. INV - Mhm.

111. EW - But I think it was short because he covered it.

OEQ 112. INV - And go ahead and tell me how he was dressed.

113. EW - He was wearing a dark hoodie, just like this, With no zipper and I believe he had a white tee on the bottom and long jean shorts down to his knee, maybe a little bit longer. I didn't see his (inaudible). And they were light - they weren't dark.

PQ 114. INV - What was light?

115. EW - The pants.

AL 116. INV - Ok.

117. EW - They were light blue.

AL 118. INV - Mhm.

119. EW - His shoes I didn't see. I didn't pay attention.

MQ 120. INV - Any scars, marks or tattoos?

121. EW - No, not that I saw.

AL 122. INV - Mhm.

OEQ 123. INV - Tell me about his eyes.

124. EW - His eyes were kind of round but stretched out. Kind of like Asian but not too Asian. They were like oval but stretched out a little. (inaudible)

PQ 125. INV - And the color of his eyes?

126. EW - Black/brown. Dark.

APPENDIX E

OEQ 127. INV - And tell me about his eyebrows.

128. EW - They looked kind of bushy.

AL 129. INV - Mmm

130. EW - Not super bushy, but a little bit.

OEQ 131. INV - Did you ever see this guy before?

132. EW - That guy looked like a guy I went to high school with but the guy I went to high school with was like more taller....more (inaudible) basically the same thing but the guy I met in high school had facial hair.

PQ 133. INV - When did you see that guy?

134. EW - Back in high school.

PQ 135. INV - So you haven't seen him since?

136. EW - No.

PQ 137. INV - Oh ok. But you're saying he kind of reminded you of him?

138. EW - Yeah that was my first impression when I saw him. That he looked like him.

AL 139. INV - Mhm.

140. EW - His color. Just his face.

FC 141. INV - Mmm. Did this happen during the day or at night?

142. EW - At night. It was like 10 or 9:50.

OEQ 143. INV - Oh really. What was the lighting like?

144. EW - I think there was just one light there on the street. The ones on the big pole. And my truck lights. But I could see his face.

FC 145. INV - And he was in front of you or behind you?

146. EW - He wasn't...we were standing side to side.

AL 147. INV - Mhm.

148. EW - And I would sometimes face him but he was always to the side.

OEQ 149. 8. INV - Mmm. Anything else you can tell me about his face?

150. EW - ... (inaudible) looked like - not a baby you know - a young person, you know? Like he didn't have no acne. Nothing like that.

Topic 3

AQC 151. INV - Nothing like that. All right you can open your eyes. Now what I want you to do is tell me what happened. I want you to tell me what you were doing just prior to running into this guy and then take me through the incident up until the police got involved.

323

APPENDIX E

152. EW - Ok. So I was actually going to Savemart right here to go get milk and I pulled out and...

MP 153. INV - You pulled out?

154. EW - Yeah I pulled out of Savemart And I went to the strip mall by...

MP 155. INV - Savemart?

156. EW - Yeah. And think I went past the light and I saw him.

MP 157. INV - You saw him?

158. EW - Yeah. Not him. I saw the truck. The way I recognized the truck is the lights were dim cuz one of the lights didn't work. (inaudible)

MP 159. INV - One of the lights?

160. EW - Huh?

PQ 161. INV - One of the lights, you said?

162. EW - Yeah and um ok whatever and he was still (inaudible). And I went to Mobil I think it's called - the gas station on Oak

AL 163. INV - Mhm.

164. EW - And I put gas in but there wasn't too many people. There was just like a little bit so I could see everyone around cuz it was small and I could see everything so I put gas in and I pulled out and I was already coming back towards Oak.

AL 165. INV - Ok.

166. EW - Because I didn't...

MP 167. INV - Towards Oak?

168. EW -Yeah and (inaudible) once I hit the light on Oak towards (inaudible) he was coming. The truck.

PQ 169. INV - He was coming so you knew it was him?

170. EW - Yeah I knew it was him cuz of the light.

AL 171. INV - Got it.

172. EW - So like, that's weird, you know. So I saw the light (inaudible) so um how do I explain it to you... the light..was red.

PQ 173. INV - Oh the signal light?

174. EW - Yeah. I stopped there and he was coming in the same lane I was going to turn. I was going to turn left and he came right behind me and he just like hit my truck. Like bumped it not even hard.

MP 175. INV - He bumped your truck?

324

APPENDIX E

176. EW- Yeah. I was like great. What are you doing? So I looked out my window (inaudible) the mirror

MP 177. INV - Oh ok you looked at the mirror?

178. EW - Yeah and he was looking at me cuz he told me to pull over. He told me to pull over. I was like ok but I wasn't going to pull over to there because there was no space. So I turned to watch the road but the bridge was really narrow so I couldn't pull over there so I went to the first block and I wasn't even to the edge so he pulled over to the edge...

MP 179. INV - He pulled over to the edge?

180. EW - Yeah and I was like inside the lane like whatever and I tried to look in my mirror to see if I could see the truck - my truck or his truck but I couldn't so I pulled down my window but I couldn't so I just go out to see the truck - the back of my truck. So one of his lights - remember his light?

AL 181. INV - Yes.

182. EW - So one of his lights was all the way in so I thought that happened when he crashed my truck because I saw obviously the dim light but I wasn't that close so I could see it was pushed in so I was like ohhh. So I got out and my truck was just scratched and he got out too and I was like, "What were you thinking? You're not going to tell me you didn't see me because I was right there stopped at the light. Obviously you could see me."

AL 183. INV - Mhm.

184. EW - And he was like oh I'm sorry. And he was like, "I was trying to light up my cigarette." So when he told me that he actually started to light up his cigarette and I was just like oh my god. And he said, "So what are you trying to do about it. And I was like, "I have full insurance. I have everything. Do you have insurance?" And he was like, "No I don't have nothing." And I was like oh my god I don't know what to do. And I was like, "I want to call the cops." And he was like, "No, no. Let's try to fix something."

MP 185. 9. INV - He said, "Let's try to fix something?"

186. EW - Yeah and I was like ok cuz you know I've never been in an accident you know and I just got the truck so...

AL 187. INV - Ok.

188. EW - So I called my boyfriend and I told him what happened and I was like I don't know what to do..

MP 189. INV - You called your boyfriend?

190. EW - Yeah.

PQ 191. INV - While you were there?

APPENDIX E

192. EW - Yeah. I was like, "I don't know what to do. What should I do?" And he was like, "Well ask him for money or something." And I was like ok (inaudible) for money and so he said, "Let me talk to him." But the guy wouldn't say many words. He was like, "Yeah. No." Like he wasn't… (inaudible) I guess he told him his name and he told him some phone numbers.

193. INV - He told your boyfriend his name?

194. EW - Yeah.

195. INV - Ok.

196. EW - He told him phone numbers. Obviously it wasn't… (inaudible) And um so he just passed him to me and he was like, "Talk to him." And I was like - talk to my boyfriend. And I told him like what did you guys say? And he was like, "Well he's gonna give you $200. He said he has it in his truck." So I was like, "Ok. So what's going to happen with the incident?" And he was like, "Just report that somebody hit you or something else." And I was like ok. So I was like, I told the guy, but I was on the telephone with him, "So do you have the money with you?" And he was like, "Yeah." And I'm like, "Ok." But I was expecting him to pull it out or go get it or something.

197. INV - Right.

198. EW - And my boyfriend was like, "What is he doing?" And (inaudible) he was like, "Ask him for the money." And I was like, "So do you have the money with you or do you have it in the bank. Do we have to go somewhere?" And he was like, "No (inaudible)." And I was like, "Give it to me."

199. INV - Right.

200. EW - And he wouldn't do it it. He was just standing there thinking about what to do - I don't know. So umm he actually got - I guess he was just standing there and I wasn't saying anything and so he got impatient (boyfriend) and he was like, "Tell him. Tell him to give you the money." And I was like, "Ok, well take it out. Take out the money." And he was like, "Ok." He said ok again and I was like, "Ok I'll wait for you right here. Go get it." Cuz I was like, "Is it in your truck? He was like, "Yeah." So he went to his truck.

201. INV - Ok.

202. EW - And he went to his passenger seat and he bent down and he like got something. And he went to the side he was driving. I don't know why but he did. And he was walking towards me slowly (inaudible) but he was looking around and I was like ok this is weird and so was walking toward me and he pretended to put something under his sweater maybe to make me think he was putting the money in there cuz as he was coming up to me he had his sweater like this…

203. INV - Mhm.

204. EW - He was pretty close to me already and I still had the phone on my ear…

AL 205. INV - OK.

206. EW - and whenever - he was going to get the money..

AL 207. INV - Ok.

208. EW - I was writing down his plate number.

AL 209. INV - Ok.

210. EW - And um once he was right next to me - actually he pulled out his hand and I pulled out my hand so he would like give it to me and he hit me, like right there (inaudible) he hit me right here and my glasses fell off my ear and he kept hitting me and hitting me in the face and all over my head.

MP 211. INV - He just kept hitting you.

212. EW - Yeah my face, my head, my nose. And probably like three times and I fell to the ground.

AL 213. INV - Ok.

214. EW - And he hit me one more time and I was screaming (inaudible) so he could get the point and once I didn't say anything, he stopped. So he basically thought he had knocked me out. I wasn't right. And he reached down to the floor and grabbed my phone and went inside my truck and took my bag and I think he took the milk because it (inaudible) the milk was on top of the (inaudible) It was on top of my purse. It was a little carton. It wasn't big. He grabbed it and took it and my purse was wide open. It was really open

AL 215. INV - Mmm.

216. EW - and it's big so anything could have fallen out. So he got the purse and he went in the truck and he (inaudible). And I looked if he was fully gone, I just got in the truck and I just turned on the truck and pressed the gas and I pulled into this driveway

AL 217. INV - Mhm

218. EW - Because this truck was pulling out and I got out of the truck. I put it in park and I got out of the truck and I was bleeding like a lot and my nose and (inaudible) and I told these guys - there were two young guys - they were like 20 something almost 30 and I told them, "Can you guys help me? Can you call the police?" And they were like, "No!" They were like scared.

PQ 219. INV - Oh were they?

220. EW - Yeah and I was like, "Can you please at least call them." "What happened to you?" And then when I told them that the truck had been robbed they were like, "Well ok." Because they were scared - I don't know what they were afraid of.

PQ 221. INV - Mhm. And what did they do?

APPENDIX E

222. EW - They got out of the truck and they were standing right there and I was like, calm down and the other guy was like, "Calm down!" telling me to calm down because I was freaking out and - the dad I guess got out of the house and he was like, "What happened?" And I told him. And he was like, "You need to just breathe. You're ok." He was trying to calm me down. He was like, "You're in one piece. You don't have to fight still." And I was like ok. So he went to call (inaudible) back for me and (inaudible) my glasses and I kept seeing him (inaudible) so um I told the guy I was like, "Will you go see if my glasses are over there? I don't know if he ran them over or if he took them or..." And he was like, "Yeah, yeah." And he was looking for them on the floor and he got them but he didn't want to pick them up because (inaudible)

223. INV - Evidence. Right.

224. EW - He was like, "They're right here." But cars are coming and he had to pick them up.

225. INV - Oh. It was on the street.

226. EW - Yeah it was in the middle of the street. And so he picked them up and I put them on because I couldn't see, you know.

227. INV - Right.

228. EW - But I was bleeding so I just took them off. (inaudible)

229. INV - Mmm.

230. EW - And so first the paramedics came- no, no, the ambulance and then the paramedics came. So I'm guessing, I'm not sure cuz my boyfriend called the cops, too (inaudible). So two cops came. First one, and then another one. I don't know if they came together.

231. INV - Ok. Got it.

232. EW - The other guy. First the paramedics sat me down and took my blood pressure and (inaudible). I was sitting down and (inaudible) he took me to the ambulance. (inaudible) And then my boyfriend arrived and he go there and he was (inaudible) because he didn't know what happened and they were like hold on, hold on, and they were like, "We need to have the police." Oh and after that they were like, "Are you sure you don't want us to take you to the hospital." And I was like, "No because I don't have insurance."

233. INV - Mhm.

234. EW - And I went to the side to speak to the cop.

235. INV - Mhm.

236. EW - (inaudible) And after that they took me to my truck and so the cops went to my truck (inaudible) and after that ok, I gave them all the information and the other cop, he came back because I guess he found my wallet...

328

APPENDIX E

AL 237. INV - Oh, ok.

238. EW - So what the cop thought that since my bag was open that probably when he (inaudible) he got it, my wallet fell out cuz he found it I guess on the edge...

PQ 239. INV - Nearby?

240. EW - Yeah nearby I don't know if he threw it out or... So then they gave it to me and everything was in there. Everything not even my money was gone.

AL 241. INV - Oh.

242. EW - That's why I don't know.

AL 243. INV - Mhm.

244. EW - (inaudible) That's when he told me what he thought happened. So he gave me his card.

AL 245. INV - Mhm.

246. EW - And he's like,"I'm gonna be gone until Sunday." So maybe another cop will take the case. I was like, ok...take her home.So (inaudible) cuz I live in Watsonville.

AL 247. INV - Right.

248. EW - My cousin I live with...

AL 249. INV - Mhm, *EW* she and her husband always go to bed super early cuz they work really early so (inaudible) they're not going to be able to take care of me.

AL 250. INV - Right.

251. EW - And I'm like - so they took me to their house and I started calling my checking..

AL 252. INV - Right.

253. EW - and all those places.

PQ 254. INV - Right. So did the police show you any pictures of possible suspects?

255. EW - They said they didn't want to confuse me cuz the picture was fresh in my head of my head.

Topic 4

AQC 256. 1. INV - Right. All right, I'm going to show you the sketch. When you look at the sketch, I don't need you to tell me whether or not it looks like him just yet. What I want you to do is just look at the sketch, see what I'm doing. After you look at it for a few seconds, we're going to go over the same questions again, but this time you'll be looking at the sketch. As I ask you about each feature, I want you to tell me whether we're in the ball park or whether you want me to make changes.

257. EW - ok.

APPENDIX E

PQ   258. INV - Do you understand that?

259. EW - Yes.

AQC   260. INV - We're never gonna be exact because your memory isn't exact.

261. EW - Yeah.

AQC   262. INV - But we want to be very, very close. So when you look at it, it helps you to remember. Alright? This is what I have so far... First of all, just the shape of the face. How's the shape of the face?

263. EW - Pretty good.

OBQ   264. INV - Ok. The hair on his head?

265. EW - Yeah.

PQ   266. INV - Something like that? And dark? His hair?

267. EW - Yeah.

OER   268. INV - Ok. The ears I gave him?

269. EW - Yeah. Oh maybe a little bigger.

PQ   270. INV - In what way?

271. EW - Like...

OBQ   272. INV - Ok...Tell me about his nose.

273. EW - His nose looks about right.

OER   274. INV - His mouth and his lips?

275. EW - Yeah.

OEQ   276. INV - Yep. His chin and his cheeks?

277. EW - His cheeks maybe a little thinner.

PQ   278. INV - A little thinner. Mhm. (drawing...) So it looks like um... so did he end up taking anything after all? I mean, I don't remember now.

279. EW - (inaudible)

EC   280. INV - Oh, he did get the bag. Got it. (drawing) So did you end up going to the doctor or hospital?

281. EW - Yesterday.

EC   282. INV - What did they say?

283. EW - They took a CT scan and they said everything was ok.

EC   284. INV - Ok. Just headaches or something like that?

285. EW - Yeah it hurts. My face.

APPENDIX E

EC 286. INV - Yeah I can imagine.

287. EW - (inaudible)

OEQ 288. INV- Yeah I know. Ok. Umm the eyes?

289. EW - The eyes need to be a little more open.

PQ 290. INV - Ok. More open?

291. EW - Yeah they were like kinda stretched out but big.

PQ 292. INV - Alright I can do that.(drawing) I don't remember but did he take your truck?

293. EW - No. Thank God.

AL 294. INV - Ok.

295. EW - The cops said he stole the truck he was in.

PQ 296. INV - Oh really? Oh yeah, that's right because you wrote down the license plate. They have that?

297. EW - Yeah.

PQ 298. INV - Good. That was pretty smart of you. And he didn't see you doing that, huh?

299. EW - I guess not cuz then he would have (inaudible)…

PQ 300. INV - yeah. (drawing…) So what about the name he gave your boyfriend?

301. EW - It was Emilio (inaudible).

PQ 302. INV - And you guys already told the police that, right?

303. EW - Yeah. (inaudible)

OEQ 304. INV - Did your boyfriend recognize the name or anything?

305. EW - No.

PQ 306. INV - (drawing) How's that on the eyes?

307. EW - Yeah.

PQ 308. INV - Better?

309. EW - Yeah.

PQ 310. INV - The eyebrows?

311. EW - Um they weren't that long.

PQ 312. 25. INV - Mhm. How about the thickness?

313. EW - I think it's about (inaudible)

AQC 314. INV - So I made one thicker than the other. Which one is it more like? This one on the right or the one on the left?   On the right? When you say longer you mean take it away from here?

APPENDIX E

AQC 315. EW - Yeah…You're good.
316. INV - Oh, thank you. Well you have a good memory, too, so that's good.
317. EW - Not really. (inaudible)
PQ 318. INV - How's that?
319. EW - Yeah.
OEQ 320. 28. INV - How about his age? How are we doing on his age?
321. EW - He kinda looks younger but he did still look young.
PQ 322. INV - Yeah, how old does this guy look here?
323. EW - I don't know. Like 18?
PQ 324. INV - It's up to you. So you want him a little older or are we ok?
325. EW - Maybe a little bit older. I don't know.
OEQ 326. INV - Ok, what about the sweatshirt?
327. EW - Yeah that's fine.
PQ 328. INV - ok. And no scars or marks?
329. EW - (inaudible)
AQC 330. INV - Ok. I'm just going to finish him up a little bit. (drawing) So were you able to cancel everything?
331. EW - Yeah.
AQC 332. INV - Good. (drawing) The next time you see this sketch, you might see the sweatshirt. The hoodie. You might see it black, like really dark. So I'm not gonna have you sit here to fill it all in. So I'm just letting you know if you ever see it again, you'll notice that it's considerably darker than what it is today. I just worked on his age a little bit. What I want you to do is ask yourself, "Does it remind me of him." If there's something else that you want me to change or adjust, just let me know and I'll take care of it, ok?
OEQ 333. INV - Does that remind you of him?
334. EW - Yeah.
PQ 335. 36. INV - Do you want to make any changes?
336. EW - I don't get the hair.
PQ 337. INV - How do YOU want it? I just filled it in.
338. EW - Is it slicked back, or how is that?
PQ 339. INV - If you want it slicked back, I can make it slicked back. I don't have it slicked back.

APPENDIX E

340. EW - It was like normal.

AQC 341. INV - Yeah. Standing up. That's the way I had it. If you look at the edges here - watch - (drawing)

342. EW - It was just like normal. (inaudible) Yeah.

PQ 343. INV - Something like that? Good. Anything else?

344. EW - I don't think so.

APC 345. INV - Ok. About as close as we're gonna get?

346. EW - Yeah.

Topic 5

APC 347. INV - Good job! Ok. (drawing) The initials to your name are AU? And this happened to the 22nd at 22 hours. If you have any questions, you can always call. They wanted you to talk to somebody? Did you know who that was?

348. EW - (inaudible)

EC 349. INV - Ok. I'll walk you out. Take care of yourself, all right?

End of Interview

APPENDIX E

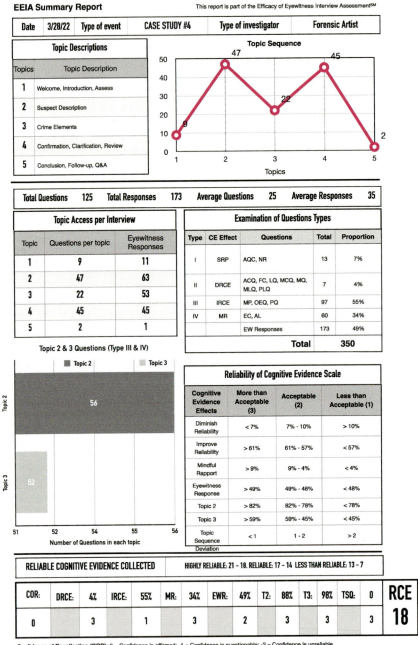

APPENDIX E

CASE STUDY #5

For more information about Case Study #5 see Chapter 19 for instructional content. This section includes: a. Complete EEIA report, b. Coded transcript, and c. EEIA summary report.

Eyewitness Interview Data Collection
This diagnostic report is part of the Efficacy of Eyewitness Interview Assessment℠

Date	4/10/22
Type of event	CASE STUDY #5
Type of investigator	Mock Criminal

Table 1 - Topic Descriptions

Topics	Topic Description
1	Welcome, Introduction, Assess
2	Suspect Description
3	Crime Elements
4	Confirmation, Clarification, Review
5	Conclusion, Follow-up, Q&A

Table 2 - Topic Access per Interview

Topic	Questions per topic	Questions per interview	Eyewitness Responses	Responses per interview
1	5	3%	5	3%
2	29	19%	28	17%
3	26	17%	33	20%
4	70	47%	75	46%
5	19	13%	21	13%
Total	149		Total	162
Average Questions	30		Average Responses	32

Table 3 - Question Category from Transcript Review

Topic	AQC	ACQ	EC	FC	LQ	MCQ	MP	MQ	MLQ	NR	OEQ	PQ	PLQ	AL	Questions Only	Topic Totals	EWR
1	1			1							1	2			5	5	5
2	1			1			3	1	7		5	6	5	2	29	31	28
3	2		3		1		1	2	2		2	5	8	8	26	34	33
4	8			3	2		6	2	6	9	1	20	13	9	70	79	75
5	9		9					1						2	19	21	21
Totals	21	0	12	5	3	0	10	6	15	9	9	33	26	21	149	170	162

Table 4 - Reliability of Cognitive Evidence (RCE) Rating

Highly Reliable	Reliable	Less Than Reliable	Reliability of Cognitive Evidence
21 - 18	17 - 14	13 - 7	10

Table 5 - Confidence of Recollection (COR) Rating

Confidence is confirmed	Confidence is questionable	Confidence is unreliable	COR Rating
0	-1	-2	-1

Reliability of Cognitive Evidence

Table 4 - Reliability of Cognitive Evidence Scale

Cognitive Evidence Effects	More than Acceptable (3)	Acceptable (2)	Less than Acceptable (1)
Diminish Reliability	< 7%	7% - 10%	> 10%
Improve Reliability	> 61%	61% - 57%	< 57%
Mindful Rapport	> 9%	9% - 4%	< 4%
Eyewitness Response	> 49%	49% - 48%	< 48%
Topic 2	> 82%	82% - 78%	< 78%
Topic 3	> 59%	59% - 45%	< 45%
Topic Sequence Deviation	< 1	1 - 2	> 2

Mean scores derived from Mindful Interview Method in forensic art sketch interviews.

Table 5 - Reliability of Cognitive Evidence for Interview

Cognitive Evidence Questions	Results	RCE
Diminish Reliability (DRCE)	32%	1
Improve Reliability (IRCE)	31%	1
Mindful Rapport (MR)	19%	3
Eyewitness Response (EWR)	49%	2
Topic 2 (T2)	52%	1
Topic 3 (T3)	56%	2
Topic Sequence Deviations (1 - 5), (TSQ)	7	1
Confidence of Recollection		-1
Reliability of Cognitive Evidence (RCE)		**10**

APPENDIX E

Topic Sequence Overview and Topic 2 & 3 Focus

This diagnostic report is part of the Efficacy of Eyewitness Interview Assessment℠

Table 1 - Sequence of Topics

Total Deviations	Sequence	1	2	3	2	3	4	3	4	3	2	4	5	
7	Topics	5	7	10	12	30	23	7	9	16	12	14	22	

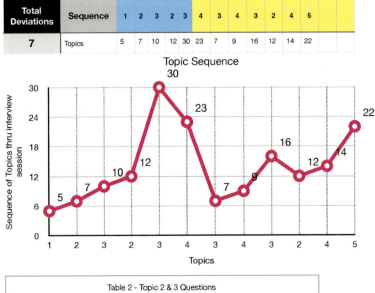

Table 2 - Topic 2 & 3 Questions

	Total Interview Questions (Type III & IV)	Proportion of questions
Topic 2	16	52%
Topic 3	19	56%

Topics 2 & 3 cover suspect description and crime elements.

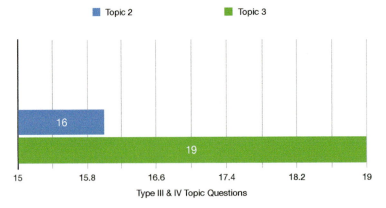

336

APPENDIX E

Question Examination and Eyewitness Responses

This diagnostic report is part of the Efficacy of Eyewitness Interview Assessment[SM]

Table 1 - Examination of Questions from eyewitness interview

Type	Questions	Total	Proportion
I	AQC, NR	30	18%
II	ACQ, FC, LQ, MCQ, MQ, MLQ, PLQ	55	32%
III	MP, OEQ, PQ	52	31%
IV	EC, AL	33	19%
EWR	EW Responses	162	49%
	Total	**332**	

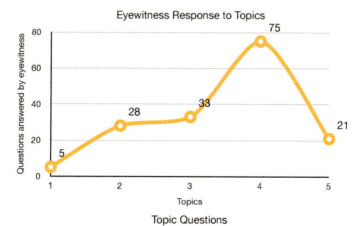

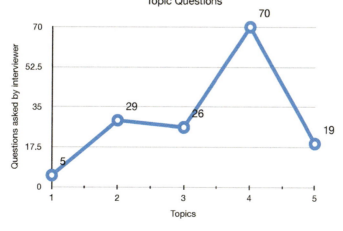

337

APPENDIX E

EYEWITNESS INTERVIEW ANALYSIS (EIA)
CONFIDENTIAL TRANSCRIPT REVIEW

The transcripts have been anonymized to protect the innocent. Any reference to persons or places in this transcript is maintained purely for dialogue consistency and the evaluation of interview strategies. The crime type and number of eyewitnesses remain to offer the reader some perspective on the type of case featured. For this book, all case studies that included a composite sketch from forensic artist Gil Zamora included some evaluation of COR. Some of these transcripts will include the COR evaluation, while others may have been evaluated outside of the interview transcript. Other case study transcripts evaluated for COR may include notes that address this outcome. Each case study will include the EEIA (Data Collection page and Summary Report). The Data Collection page includes all the question types attributed to the transcript review. Each transcript review was conducted a minimum of three times before generating the complete EEIA.

Date of transcript review: April 10 2022

Crime type: Mock robbery

Notes:

Topic 1

AQC 1. INV: All right so, I'm very sorry this happened to you Mr. Greg–I'm just trying to figure out what happened exactly, so where were you at?

2. EW: It happened right in front of the seventh street garage I was walking to MacQuarrie hall but I was on San Fernando

FC 3. INV: Okay were you on the campus side? Or were you on the other side of the seven eleven side in that area?

4. EW: I was on SJSU.

PQ 5. INV: Okay so did you know these two guys at all?

6. EW: No I was just walking to class

OEQ 7. INV: And how long ago did this happen?

8. EW: Well, Mm It happened around my lunch time so probably about twelve thirty.

PQ 9. INV: Twelve thirty so it's about one forty right now, so about an hour ago?

10. EW: Yeah

APPENDIX E

Topic 2

PQ 11. INV: Okay and you said it was two males?

12. EW: Yeah was definitely to two guys.

OEQ 13. INV: What color clothing did you notice on one or the other?

14. EW: Yeah some there is one guy who was wearing a blue sweater with the bear I think it was Cal Berkeley bears sweater. He was a white guy and then I think he was wearing some like basketball shorts or something and then…

PQ 15. INV: Do you, do you know what color the basketball shorts were?

16. EW: I dunno.

PQ 17. INV: Okay did you notice anything about the shoes by chance?

18. EW: I don't know sorry.

MLQ 19. INV: Okay was he, did he have black hair, red hair, blonde hair?

20. EW: I think he had blonde hair but it was more like it was if it was covered by the hoodie he was wearing and so I only got to look at his skin color which is why his face kinda had acne on it

OEQ 21. INV: Okay Do you think you'd recognize this guy again if you saw him?

22. EW: Yeah

AL 23. INV: Okay all right.

Topic 3

PLQ 24. INV: What direction did he head off in? Cause you said you were walking by the seventh street garage so you're walking (EW: yeah) you're walking westbound on the North side walk right?

25. EW: I was walking towards MacQuarrie Hall yeah

OEQ 26. INV: Okay so what direction did this guy head off after that?

27. EW: Honestly, I am a little disoriented because, I fell to the floor after being hit by something

PLQ 28. INV: Okay When did the white guy hit you, or did the other guy hit you?

29. EW: They both kinda hit me it's just (INV: okay) the one who hit me on the head was the white guy and he he's the one who stopped me in my tracks in the first place.

LQ 30. INV: What did he say to make you stop in your tracks?

31. EW: Well that's not what he said I mean he stood right in front of me as I was walking and then I told them I was listening to my headphones I took them I took out my AirPods and then I asked him what's up how can I help you he's that just like we're taking your backpack and it kinda happened from there.

PLQ 32. INV: Okay so did he brandish a weapon? Did he physically stop you like this? Or did he grab you? Or did he just stand there and block your way?

MLQ 33. EW: He, he stood in front of me I don't know what he pulled or what he hit me with–I don't know what he had, but it was hard as hell because it left a big hole cut right here in my forehead

PQ 34. INV: Okay Who put the bandage on you and where did you go to get that fixed outa curiosity?

35. EW: Actually there was a kid who help me afterwards his name's Alan

MP 36. INV: Alan. (EW: yeah)

339

APPENDIX E

AQC 37. INV: Okay, all right, so now I got a decent description of the first guy.

Topic 2

OEQ 38. INV: What did the second guy look like?

39. EW: He was kind of tanned I want to say maybe Hispanic. I'm Mexican. I want to say Mexican. He was–he had kind of long hair, I don't know.

OEQ 40. INV: Okay Um, what type of clothing was he wearing?

41. EW: What was he wearing? He was wearing a white hoodie with some pants I wanna say jeans.

PQ 42. INV: Okay Did you notice anything about shoes or tattoos or anything?

43. EW: No well he was covered. I didn't get a look at the shoes he came from behind–that one

MP 44. INV: So he came from behind?

45. EW: yeah

MCQ 46. INV: Um, these guys were they–the white guy, was he tall? Short? Fat? Skinny?

47. EW: He was kind of skinny

MP 48. INV: Skinny?

49. EW: Yeah The white guy was kinda skinny the other guy was kind of bulky

MP 50. INV: Bulky?

51. EW: Yeah

PQ 52. INV: Um, about how tall how tall are you outa curiosity?

53. EW: I'm six feet tall.

FC 54. INV: You're six feet tall. Okay was the white guy–was he taller or shorter than you?

55. EW: Yeah he was a little bit shorter.

PLQ 56. INV: Okay was he like five-five or was he a lot shorter? I'm five-nine so would you say hypothetically he was about my height?

57. EW: Yeah, I just I mean he wasn't too much shorter than me.

PQ 58. INV: Okay so what about the other guy?

59. EW: I, I honestly I couldn't tell you because he came from behind me and then the next thing I know I was on the floor.

MCQ 60. INV: Okay so did you see a hat? Was he wearing a hat or a backpack, or anything of that nature?

61. EW: Um, No they wanted my backpack. They kept on saying just take it off or just give it to us, and then they just kept on hitting me, so.

Topic 3

OEQ 62. INV: Okay so where did they hit you at?

63. EW: Well I have a bruised rib right here I can feel it. Um, the guy who hit me in the head and struck me made my forehead right here so it's bleeding all on the front of my forehead but it hurts like in the back of my head

AL 64. INV: Okay

APPENDIX E

PLQ 65. EW: Um, and then when they took my backpack I was also holding on because they pulled it over my head and my right arm got caught in it because I didn't want to let it go and so one of them kicked me in the shoulder and now I'm kind of, I'm I feel like I'm bruising around this area.

PLQ 66. INV: Okay, so is it your collar bone? Does it feel like it, so you got kicked basically in your collar bone area?

67. EW: Yeah, it's more it's more like the shoulder area

AQC 68. INV: Shoulder area? Okay so with that you wanna have somebody pick you up and have you do you want me to call an ambulance to get you checked out and that type of stuff? (EW: No) because your head injuries, those can be with head injuries especially. I'm not a doctor I mean I've had some little medical training (EW: yeah) probably you need to get your head checked out because you could have a concussion and it just to be safer on that side okay?

69. EW: That's okay I'll go on my own.

PQ 70. INV: You sure?

71. EW: Yeah that's fine.

Topic 4

OEQ 72. INV: Okay that's all right. So, then I'm going to ask you some more questions here (EW: OK), and so this is just to establish like what exactly was taken. So you had your backpack, what's your backpack look like?

73. EW: It's a black Michael Kors backpack and inside that I had my stuff for my project that I was gonna go work on which included my laptop a textbook, some pens, and pencils and my notebook.

PLQ 74. INV: Okay so with the Michael Kors backpack, and those are pretty expensive, about how much would you would you say that's worth roughly?

75. EW: It was a gift for Christmas but I think it was like six hundred dollars

PQ 76. INV: Okay it's six hundred bucks on that (EW: yeah) with the laptop what type of laptop is it?

77. EW: Macbook pro

MP 78. INV: Macbook pro?

79. EW: Yeah

PQ 80. INV: Okay about how much is that one worth?

81. EW: Well I enhanced it so about two grand.

MP 82. INV: So two thousand dollars?

83. EW: Yeah

PQ 84. INV: Okay Now Do you know the serial number for that?

85. EW: I couldn't tell you

PQ 86. INV: Okay well outa curiosity do you have the box back at home?

87. EW: I do, I do.

AQC 88. INV: Okay that'll be perfect because what we do is we can get that serial number and put it into our APS which is our stolen items stuff and if another officer runs across it we can find it that way.

89. EW: Okay Thank you

Topic 3

APPENDIX E

AQC 90. INV: So we definitely want to get some follow-up stuff you'll probably need to get checked out by the doctor first and we can get back to that later

91. EW: Okay

Topic 4

PLQ 92. INV: Anything else? You said a text book what type of text book?

93. EW: It was just a school textbook for my justice studies course

MQ 94. INV: Okay it's kind of a weird thing so if we stop somebody what kind of book was it exactly? Just because if we find somebody and then you have your name in it or anything…

95. EW: Well I checked it out from the library but financial aid paid for it so I couldn't tell you how much it costs

PQ 96. INV: Okay did you have any identifying markings on the laptop?

97. EW: Yeah there's a Nike logo on it–it's like a sticker.

PQ 98. INV: Okay Awesome where was it located on the laptop?

99. EW: It was in the front upper–well if you close the laptop it's in the front upper right

MP 100. INV: Okay upper right?

101. EW: Yeah

MLQ 102. INV: With the backpack, you said it was a Michael Kors, did it have anything on the outside? Did it have your name on it anywhere? Or like a luggage tag something of that nature?

103. EW: No I was going for the more minimal things so I did't customize it or anything like that

PQ 104. INV: Okay anything else in the backpack that got taken?

105. EW: I think I had my SJSU hoodie

MP 106. INV: SJSU hoodie?

107. EW: Yeah

PLQ 108. INV: Okay all right. Was it a blue one a yellow one?

109. EW: It was a gray

PLQ 110. INV: Gray one Okay, did they have your name in it or anything?

111. EW: No, it didn't, but it did kind of have a little tear in the in the stomach pot pouch

PLQ 112. INV: Um, did you have a notebook in the backpack like papers with your handwriting or anything?

113. EW: Yeah I was working on a project, that's why I was going to MacQuarrie hall

PQ 114. INV: What color was the notebook?

115. EW: It was purple

PLQ 116. INV: Purple, any other like distinguishing stuff with that?

117. EW: Um, in sharpie I wrote my class my class on it I think it's like JS one-eighty-five or something

PQ 118. INV: All right, right. Estimated cost for the hoodie and the notebook?

119. EW: I think the hoodie was somewhere around sixty dollars and then my notebook was like a dollar

MP 120. INV: A dollar, okay.

Topic 4

APPENDIX E

PLQ 121. INV: So now this is just to narrow down the area that you're at. You said you were at San Salvador right?

122. EW: Um..I think so.

PQ 123. INV: Okay, so you say you're in the seventh street garage area right?

PQ 124. INV: Well, the reason why I asked is we have some cameras in that area so I'm gonna try to see if we can really narrow down the area. So you know where the police department is?

125. EW: Um, like on campus?

AL 126. INV: Yeah, yeah

127. EW: Er, is that…

AQC 128. INV: It's at the seventh street garage area you could actually cut through the building when you pull into the garage.

129. EW: Okay

PLQ 130. INV: Okay, so we're on both sides of that area. So you said you're on San Salvador right there right on that street okay. Well, were you closer to where you got hit; you were going to MacQuarrie so you're going around the garage and then over to MacQuarrie hall?

131. EW: Well I had gone to an ATM right before that because I know campus has an ATM…

PLQ 132. INV: – Okay So are you over at like lot four? Where we have the four ATMs?

133. EW: Um, I think so.

PLQ 134. INV: – All right, is it by the student union?

135. EW: Yeah is that where the Wells Fargo is on?

AQC 136. INV: I think that's where the Wells Fargo is, yes…

137. EW: …probably over there

MLQ 138. INV: Okay so were you there before? Didn't you say that's where you started off before you went over to MacQuarrie hall?

139. EW: Yeah, so I was walking through the campus but it happened kind of around there

PLQ 140. INV: Oh, it happened over there over by the ATMs?

141. EW: No. so I I had gone to the ATM for a little bit, and I don't know if they were following me since then but (INV: okay) it happened around the seventh street garage area

FC 142. INV: So, okay you were you on the North side of the garage or were you on the street side?

143. EW: No I was I was on campus

PQ 144. INV: You're on campus. Okay, so you weren't on the road whatsoever there; by the sidewalk when I asked you if you were on the actual North side of the garage where there's not that street

145. EW: I think, I think my problem is that because I could see it; it's I'm just kind of identifying where it's at but I I was on campus for sure

PLQ 146. INV: Okay so do you know if you were by the building right next to MacQuarrie?

147. EW: Um…

PLQ 148. INV: Sweeney Hall. It's got like an open courtyard area

149. EW: I was in an open courtyard area but I I couldn't tell you. I'm a justice studies major so the only building I need to go to is MacQuarrie hall

PLQ 150. INV: Okay, okay so you just weren't at MacQuarrie

APPENDIX E

151. EW: Yeah
PQ 152. INV: But you're by the Seventh Street garage
153. EW: Yeah
FC 154. INV: And you come from the ATMs
155. EW: Yeah
MLQ 156. INV: Um, okay all right, when you think you're–so, what were you–if you were over by the ATM did you walk back towards MacQuarrie and if so like what route did you take? Did you go through the south of the student union or south of the event center? Do you know?
157. EW: Um, I think I went south of student union (INV: okay) I I took the most direct route because this route is from my time at SJSU, it's been the fastest
MLQ 158. INV: Okay so, so you kind of went if you were at–from the ATM went south of the student union and then over onto Seventh Street Plaza, right? Okay and then walking towards MacQuarrie did you then walk through like the San Carlos Plaza area?
159. EW: Um, I don't think so. I think I could have very briefly, yeah, I was listening to my headphones so… (INV: okay) I wasn't exactly paying attention to where…
PQ 160. INV: Gotcha, so could you see MacQuarrie from where these guys beat you up at?
161. EW: Yeah it was, it was within my sight but like it would take me about a minute to get there walking
PQ 162. INV: Okay, okay so you were kind of in that courtyard area between Sweeney and MacQuarrie and the seventh street garage. There's that kind of like courtyard area between those three (EW: yeah I was about…) and you got to San Carlos Plaza like just to the north of you there…
163. EW: Yeah, well the plaza, yeah, I mean I could see I know what area you're talking about I can't say where exactly it took place because it was kind of like they stop me in one area and then the actual area where I got hit happened in like a little bit more towards another area
ARC 164. INV: Okay, okay so just for your–if it happened in that area of that plaza between Sweeney and MacQuarrie we have–or we used to have at least have a camera up there so I can go and check that footage for you
165. EW: okay

Topic 3

OGQ 166. INV: Back to how they hit you. So you said you got hit in the head first right?
167. EW: Yeah so some guy stood in front of me–the white kid and then he told me we're taking your backpack and I kind of felt somebody behind me feeling my back pack up and then that's when I kind of lunged forward to get the person behind me to stop feeling my backpack and then that's when I got hit in the head I don't know by what
AL 168. INV: Okay gotcha
169. EW: …and then I kind of curled up and then as I was curling up because you know my forehead hurt the guy behind me who already had my backpack in his hand started pulling my backpack above me like up from me like that kinda, and then almost took it off and that's when my arm got hooked in to one of the straps on my backpack, um…and then after that I kept on getting kicked in the legs. I I think they wanted like to put me to the ground or something…

344

APPENDIX E

PQ 170. INV: So when you're curled up, were you like curled up in a ball but not on the ground like kinda hunched over?

171. EW: Yeah I'm like in fetal but standing (INV: Okay) Like it's kinda like that because I didn't know how I don't want to be blushing gut–gushing blood (INV: Okay) but I didn't know, you know, I've never been thru something like this. Its never happened to me before so I don't know how to react…

MCQ 172. INV: Okay, so you got hit in the head when you went down they tried pulling it off your arm and it got hooked. How many times did they kick you in the–was it your right leg or left leg?

173. EW: So I got kicked on my right leg for sure, um, in the back of the knee and that's kind of where my knee pain comes from (INV: okay) because that one kind of–that one fucked me up and dropped me to the ground. And then, sorry…

PQ 174. INV: No, no about how many times did you get kicked in the right leg?

175. EW: Probably maybe two really good kicks

PLQ 176. INV: Okay, now did you get kicked anywhere else?

177. EW: Yeah my shoulder (INV: okay) it was when I was trying I was holding on to my backpack because I didn't want them to take it and then the guy who hit me–the white kid who hit me in the head he ended up kicking the shit out of my shoulder and that's when I lost my grip on my back

PLQ 178. INV: Okay did the other guy–did he just pull the backpack off or did he kick you also?

179. EW: So the guy who was behind me, and I think I I'm pretty sure he's the one who kicked me in the back of my knee so that's why my knee is like throbbing right now, but I can't say if he hit me anymore because after that I was pretty much was like I wanted it to stop while I was in the fetal position

Topic 4

AQC 180. INV: Okay all right. So that's so I can–just for simplification–just so I can get an idea, you're somewhere in that courtyard area. I'm just gonna summarize real quick what I got so far.

NR 181. INV: You're in a courtyard area walking from class. You just come from the ATMs, you don't notice the guys beforehand (EW: okay), but the white guy stands in front of you, stops ya and then they're taking your backpack. You feel the other guy come up behind you–grab it right?

182. EW: Right

MQ 183. INV: Um, then you get hit on the head, but you don't know by who or with what, but you think it's the white guy, but you don't know for sure and you don't know if he had a weapon or anything. Or you just think it's just–do you think it was a fist or hand slap or…

184. EW: No, so this has never happened to me before, but I've kinda been and kind of like–because I have brothers so I know what a punch feels like and it didn't feel like a…

PQ 185. INV: – Not like a punch Okay. Gotcha, but you got hit with something though

186. EW: Yeah

NR 187. INV: …and you kind of go down to the ground. You're in kind of a standing fetal position

188. EW: Yeah

NR 189. INV: …and then they try to pull the backpack off you and you get kicked in the shoulder because it gets stuck there and then they keep kicking you in your right knee a couple times–one time really hard that drops you to the ground okay?

345

APPENDIX E

190.EW: So, I think I got hit and then I kind of bent over, and then as I was going to go to the ground, after I got hit in the head, I got kicked in the knee and that's what took me to the ground

AL 191.INV: Okay

PQ 192.EW: …As I was going to the ground they pulled my backpack off and then my arm got stuck (INV: okay) so this is as I'm going to the ground.

193. INV: Okay–so head, so you get hit in the head first, then the knee, then they're pulling the backpack, shoulder gets kicked, and then you go down to the ground. Did you get kicked or hit any time after that?

194. EW: Um, I think after that they must've been running by then because my backpack was gone. I guess that's all they wanted because I looked up and they were both running in different directions.

PLQ 195. INV: Okay, gotcha, so they were running in separate directions from you?

196. EW: Yeah I couldn't tell you which specific one was running where.

Topic 3

MQ 197. INV: Okay Gotcha Do you know, can you give me just a general idea of which–I don't know–a general idea of which way each of them went? It doesn't have to be exactly specific about whether the white guy went this way, or the other guy went that way I just need a general idea.

198. EW: One was running towards MacQuarrie Hall and then the other one was running towards in a diverted direction not towards MacQuarrie Hall. I don't know where he was running…

PLQ 199. INV: Gotcha Okay So you said the person that bandaged you up–did they see all this by chance?

200. EW: Yeah Alan

MP 201.INV: Alan?

202.EW: Yeah

MQ 203. INV: Do you have–do you know how I can get a hold of Alan by chance? Did you get a phone number? Do you know him from something else?

204. EW: Honestly Alan is just some Asian student at SJSU who kind of saw the whole thing and he told me, he's like, Tony, I saw–well, he didn't say "Tony" he told me, he was like, hey I saw the whole thing…

AL 205. INV: Okay

206. EW: …but there were people starting to crowd around and he's the one who helped me

PQ 207. INV: Okay was there anybody else in the area that might have seen these guys?

208. EW: Yeah, yeah for sure there were other people in the area, but I don't know if they were paying attention to it.

MLQ 209. INV: Okay, um, with that I just have to decide did you fear at all that you were gonna get hurt? Or that they–that they were going to hurt you during this whole process?

210. EW: Honestly, because okay, I've usually kind of been able to avoid situations like this because I'm six feet. Well, when it's two against one you kind of start, you know, I don't want to say that I was like a little bitch or anything, but it definitely humbled me in the sense that I I didn't want it to continue for sure.

PLQ 211. INV: Okay, gotcha, and then they obviously–they didn't have permission to take your stuff?

212.EW: Of course not

346

APPENDIX E

PLQ 213. INV: And you were fearful that they were going to beat you up a little more right?

214. EW: Right, I don't know what they wanted and okay I kind of was just hoping that I wasn't going to die.

EC 215. INV: Okay, um, Okay yeah You were hoping that you're not gonna die that's definitely (EW: yeah) that's definitely good, I mean glad you're glad–you're not in the best situation which you could obviously be in and you're a little beat up, but you're here and you're safe right now and you're okay, and um, the reality is, well the thing is that these are just items that were taken and they can be replaced–yes it's a pain in the butt, and no it's not–it's a violation of you–of them taking all your stuff, but for the most part it's we–they can be replaced you can't…

216. EW: Yeah, but I had so much data on that laptop–so much data.

Topic 4

PQ 217. INV: So, do you track your laptop at all with like *Find My* phone app? Sort of application or anything of that nature?

218. EW: Well I have an iPhone so I know my account. Ahh, my phone account is logged in my apple account

PQ 219. INV: Okay, well I believe we can use it if you have the *Find My iPhone* app. Does it connect up to the computer? We could possibly find out where it's at.

220. EW: Yeah, I can–my my main concern is what if they smash it. I have a whole lot of stuff on that computer.

PQ 221. INV: Okay well, well, well, we can–do you have your phone with you right now? We can just pull it up real quick to see if it's, if it's showing up anywhere.

222. EW: I don't. I don't have my phone on me (INV: okay) I don't want to say it's with my backpack but it could be in my sweater I don't know where it's at right now (INV: okay) I could have left it in my car.

PQ 223. INV: Okay Gotcha Do you have your keys to your car?

224. EW: Yeah, they're in my pocket.

PQ 225. INV: Okay was there anything that had like your address on it in your backpack?

226. EW: Um, like I I know that my–my wallet was in my backpack and my wallet's got my ID and then so yeah.

PLQ 227. INV: But there weren't keys to your house in there were there?

228. EW: Not to my house, no because I have all my keys on the same link as my car keys

Topic 2

OEQ 229. INV: Okay, um did you ever–have you never seen these guys before whatsoever or seen them around campus at all?

230. EW: No, I I could recognize them, but I couldn't tell you anything about them all.

PLQ 231. INV: Okay you would recognize both of them, or just the one guy?

232. EW: Well, definitely the white kid with acne who stood in front of me because he kind of had this grin on his face before he said, "We're taking your back" but the other guy, all I know is that he had longer hair and he was kind of like darker complexion.

347

APPENDIX E

PLQ   233. INV: Okay, um, they weren't wearing sun– and this is gonna sound odd, especially in COVID times, were they wearing a mask or not?

234. EW: Yeah, well yeah, they were wearing a mask for sure.

PQ   235. INV: What color masks were they wearing do you know?

236. EW: Well the one in the white sweater was wearing a white mask, probably to blend in more, and the other one was with the one in the blue sweater, he was wearing blue.

MLQ   237. INV: Was it a hoodie? Was it a zip-up, anything like that?

238. EW: It was, it was a hoodie as well. It was just white and I couldn't–I I didn't get a clear look at any logo's on it but it looked like a plain white sweater to me

MLQ   239. INV: Okay, gotcha–gotcha–gotcha–so nothing with his jeans? Um, did you notice any jewelry? Did they have any watches? Or rings? Or earrings?

240. EW: Nothing immediate, um, I couldn't see earrings they were covered by hoods.

MLQ   241. INV: Okay, um, no tattoos? You didn't see them on a bike? Or anything of that nature either?

PLQ   242. INV: Or did you see anybody else with them beforehand?

243. EW: No, honestly I didn't notice them until what was happening happened.

AC   244. INV: Okay.

MLQ   245. INV: Um, but it was just them for sure? There wasn't anybody else?

246. EW: No.

MLQ   247. INV: All right, so these two guys–the white guy and you think he's Hispanic or would you say Asian or…?

248. EW: Well, all I know is that is hair was kind of wavy (INV: okay) I don't know if that matters at all but

AQC   249. INV: It just helps sometimes just to–with that stuff.

Topic 4

MLQ   250. INV: Um, so, all right, so two males, the skinny, skinny white guy he's about five nine-ish around there with the blue sweater and basketball pants, blue Cal Bears sweater, basketball pants and he had blonde hair–he's the one that um stopped you originally and said we're taking your backpack, right? And then you have the possibly Hispanic male with longer hair with a white hoodie and jeans, he was shorter than you also. And he was a little heavier right?

251. EW: He was. He was definitely bulkier, but he was taller than me.

MP   252. INV: He was taller than you?

253. EW: In the white sweater, yeah I would say he's about easily six two.

PLQ   254. INV: Six two, okay, so six two long haired Hispanic, white hoodie, with jeans, no backpack or anything like that?

255. EW: No, well they have my back–they didn't have a backpack

PQ   256.INV: But, but no back pack?

PLQ   257. INV: So both of them showing up with no weapons or anything seen of that nature right?

258. EW: I didn't see a weapon no, but, okay like I said, I got hit over the head with something and then I can take a punch, but whatever that was they–yeah got me.

348

APPENDIX E

NR— 259. INV: Gotcha, okay, and they take your Michael Kors black backpack worth about six hundred bucks with your MacBook pro which was upgraded and worth about two thousand dollars, a SJSU gray hoodie with a tear in the stomach that was about sixty bucks, your notebook which is about a dollar and you think your phone might be in there but you're not sure.

260. EW: Well, it could be in my backpack, it could be in my car. I'd have right now but I'm in, I'm in the office at SJSU.

PQ 261. INV: Okay and your wallet was also in your backpack right?

262. EW: My wallet was in my backpack.

AQC 263. INV: Um Have you checked to see if there's, I know it's a little early but we need to check to make sure the cards aren't being used–that they've been canceled too on that end okay?

264. EW: Okay, um, I don't have my phone on me so I can't really–I don't have access to them right now and I'm in the nurse's office–they're just letting me use this to talk to you guys

PQ 265. INV: Okay, um, what type of debit or credit cards did you have there?

266. EW: I have, let's see I have about two credit cards and one debit card–my debit card is Wells Fargo

MP 267. INV: Debit is Wells Fargo?

268. EW: Yeah

PQ 269. INV: Okay what are the two credit cards?

270. EW: Um, one is Capital one for sure and then the other one might be American Express.

PLQ 271. INV: Okay, what was your last purchase–obviously I'm guessing your debit card was the last time you used–it was at the ATM?

272. EW: Yeah I took out forty bucks.

PQ 273. INV: Okay So you take out forty dollars. So that was the last time you used that card, do you know the last time you used the Capital One or the Amex card?

274. EW: I don't know specifically I couldn't tell you–probably something on Amazon I don't know

AQC 275. INV: Okay Amazon So another thing that we really want. A lot of times we can get really good surveillance footage of who uses these, so after the fact, so if you can give me those credit card numbers and if they've been used at another place a lot of times–they usually have only a couple weeks of window to where we can actually get footage. But if you can give me those, if they're used at all then we can go get surveillance footage and hopefully identify these guys that did this okay?

276. EW: Oh, okay I don't have that information right now.

Topic 5

AQC 277. INV: And I understand that. I'm just saying when you get home well, I'd love to say, hey go home and rest, but it's kind of helpful for solving this–if we can get the serial numbers from your computer and credit card and debit card numbers so that way we can get it all entered in and then if it's used we can go and find out who's using that and kind of track it back.

278. EW: Yeah Okay

PQ 279. INV: All right, um where, how did you get to campus? Do you have any more questions or anything right now?

280. EW: Um, well, not really, what should I do now?

349

APPENDIX E

281. INV: Okay so what I'm gonna give you is, I'm gonna give you a report receipt with your case number here okay. It's gonna have my name, my phone number and my badge number. Um, I'm probably going to follow up with you will later today to–

282. INV: Well one, are you sure you don't want to go the hospital for one? (EW: No, I'm OK) At least get checked out?

283. INV: I would suggest going to at least your primary care doctor or over to the wellness center here at least to get checked out by them okay?

284. EW: Okay

285. INV: I'm gonna give you this report receipt. It's got my name on it, case number, all the stuff. That's just to identify your case number and what not. Hold on to that. I got some victim assistance stuff that I can give you too and I'm gonna give you a card that tells you like what's what and things that are available to you on campus here you know. We do have our escort program–you're a big guy you might not want to at times, I get that, but at night time, it's dark, you can call the police department and either our cadets or officers will escort you back and forth to and from your car, or however you get on campus at night

286. EW: Ah, okay.

287. INV: Um and that's kind of where we're at here as of this point. Um, did you drive to campus?

288. EW: I did yeah.

289. INV: Okay Are you gonna be okay to drive with your head injury?

290. EW: Um, well I don't know, can a person drive? I mean I feel fine but…

291. INV: I'm just saying you might not want to drive. You may want to call somebody to come pick you up especially since you said you're feeling something in the back of your head, you got hit in the front. Sometimes it's kind of a sign of a concussion so the last thing I want you to do is pass out behind the wheel after this whole thing, so you might just want to get somebody to pick you up and then take you to your primary care doctor okay? Just to get checked out–if you're saying you got hit up front and then you're hurting on the back of your head that usually means it's kind of a sign of a concussion. So, you either need to go get you checked out by an adult–I mean you're–how old are you?

292. EW: I'm twenty five

293. INV: Yes, so you're an adult you got the rights to do whatever you want to do on that end, but I would suggest you to go on an ambulance, or at least have a buddy take you to the doctor to go get that checked out because I don't want you to drive. I personally, then this is me being a person, I want you getting medical care because that might be a concussion and the last thing you want to do is pass out behind the wheel okay?

294. EW: That makes sense

295. INV: So let's, let's go and see if you got a buddy that we can call to come pick you up and drive you to the doctor. That sounds like a good idea to me

296. EW: Okay

297. INV: Okay, so we'll get that taken care, I'll stand by with you here until he shows up and you can go off and get checked out by them.

298. EW: Yeah, I am I gonna get my stuff back?

APPENDIX E

AQC 299. INV: I'll be honest um, you might not. That is, the quicker you can give me some of that information the more likelihood it is that we will get–we can hopefully recover it, but I'm not gonna tell you everything's all great and gravy and that you were going to get this stuff back, okay?

300. EW: That's fair

AQC 301. INV: I will say that the more likelihood of getting things back is a lot better when we have serial numbers, and that type of stuff, and the credit card numbers, because we can track back and at that point it's easier for us also to find people and prosecute them. I'd love to say it's my job now–I can go find and do the stuff but I need your help by getting me this information so that we can find these people and arrest them for the robbery here okay?

302. EW: So I should just get home as soon as possible then?

EC 303. INV: Well I'd say go to the doctor first–get that checked out and then give me that information okay? Your health and well being is more important to us than finding these guys right now okay?

304. EW: Okay, okay all right so I can call somebody then I'll be good.

EC 305. INV: Yep…I'll stand by here with you 'till they get here–to make sure you get to the car and head off, okay?

306. EW: okay

AQC 307. INV: Um you got the report receipt, you got my phone number, if anything else comes up. I might call you in a day or two just to follow up, um this has kind of been a traumatic experience for you. We also have counseling services available here on campus if you feel like you need to talk to somebody and I'll probably call you in a day or two to see if you remember anything else about this–to see if, um, like you know maybe over time thinking about things if you remember something else and that type of stuff okay?

308. EW: Is it, is it possible that I could use your phone to call Gil Zamora right now?

AL 309. INV: That's no problem

310. EW: Okay

AL 311. INV: All right

312. EW: Okay yeah I'll call Gil right now.

AQC 313. INV: All right I'll stand by here and wait for him till he gets here and then we can head off from there. So any other questions or concerns?

314. EW: No, I just kinda want my stuff back. I wish this never happened to me. I'm kind of mad. I'm kind sad and I don't know how to handle this but…

EC 315. INV: Those are all kinda normal responses to this–um, they violated and you feel like you should be able to walk across the street here and on campus and feel safe. Yeah and this unfortunately happened to you, and there are pain in the butt people everywhere around and unfortunately you got kind of picked on today to meet one–two of them in this situation

316. EW: My luck

AL 317. INV: Yeah

318. EW: Okay so, well thank you.

End of Interview

APPENDIX E

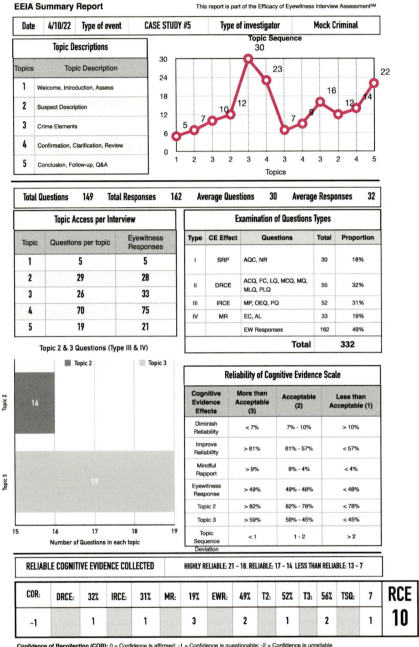

APPENDIX E

CASE STUDY #6

This section includes: a. Coded transcript, and b. EEIA summary report. For complete EEIA reports for case studies 6 through 15 go to www.mindfulinterviews.com/CaseStudies.

Each case study was evaluated and prepared for EEIA processing. Every attempt was made to standardize the evaluation and coding process for every case study. Any errors in coding, calculations, or assignment of RCE score, should be directed to the author. All of the transcripts were anonymized for instructional purposes, any resemblance to specific investigations is purely coincidental. The crime types and agencies are listed for informational purposes and to give the reader an idea of the variety of cases used in applying *The Mindful Interview Method*.

EYEWITNESS INTERVIEW ANALYSIS (EIA)
CONFIDENTIAL TRANSCRIPT REVIEW

Date of transcript review: April 17, 2022

Crime type: ATTEMPTED KIDNAPPING

Notes:

Topic 1

OEQ   1. INV: Ok, so do you know why you're here?
2. EW: Yes.
PQ   3. INV: Why?
4. EW: Because there was someone in a car asking me to come with them and I didn't know who it was and they grabbed me by the hand and tried to pull me into the car.
OEQ   5. INV: Ok and if you saw him again, would you recognize him?
6. EW: Yes I would.
AQC   7. INV: Fantastic. Ok, how this works is (Oh there's water there for you - that's for you, this is for me.) um the way this works is I'm going to ask you some general questions about this person's face. I'd like you to go ahead and ask to the best of your knowledge. Most people don't remember everything in great detail, however a lot of folks tend to remember a lot of information, especially if they're here and focus on the questions. Um I'm going to ask you to close your eyes. It helps you to relax and focus on the person's face. It makes it a little bit easier to describe and then after that I'm going to ask you to open your eyes. I'm going to ask you to tell me what happened. I don't know anything that happened, ok, so I'm going to be hearing it from you for the first time. And then after that, I'll show you the sketch and if we need to, we'll make some changes. Alright? Do you understand that?
8. EW: Yes.
OEQ   9. INV: Fantastic. Do you have any questions?
10. EW: Not right now.

353

APPENDIX E

ARC 11. INV: Alright. Go ahead and close your eyes. You're going to hear me drawing right from here, ok?

12. EW: Mhm.

Topic 2

OEQ 13. INV: Take a nice deep breath to let me know you're ready to begin. Ok. First of all, tell me about the race of this person.

14. EW: Uh he was Indian. He had very dark skin.

OEQ 15. INV: Mhm. Age range?

16. EW: Uh about 30-50.

PQ 17. INV: Body build?

18. EW: Ah from what I could tell, not muscle, it wasn't muscle, it was kinda normal. Averaged out.

OEQ 19. INV: Average. Ok. Have you ever seen him before?

20. EW: Ah no I have not.

OEQ 21. INV: Ok. Tell me about the shape of his face. What was that like?

22. EW: It was round.

OEQ 23. INV: Round. Alright, tell me about his hair. What is that like?

24. EW: Shaggy. Not covering his ears though.

OEQ 25. INV: What about the length of his hair?

26. EW: It was up to his ears on the side but down to his lower neck.

PQ 27. INV: Mhm. And when you say shaggy, what do you mean by that?

28. EW: It was kind of messy and it was long enough to go down to the middle of his neck. Not too long.

OEQ 29. INV: Mhm, what was the style of his hair?

30. EW: Ah it was to the side - it was parted to the side.

FC 31. INV: Which side?

32. EW: Left.

MP 33. INV: His left side?

34. EW: Yeah, his side.

PQ 35. INV: From the part, what happens?

36. EW: Ah, wait I'm confused.

FC 37. INV: So you're telling me he parts his hair on the left, right?

38. EW: Mhm.

FC 39. INV: So his part that's closest to the ear, is that part, from the part, is it going back or is it going down or to the side?

40. EW: Oh, it's back. Like this.

PQ 41. INV: And you just motioned around your ear. Is it around his ears?

42. EW: Yes, on one side his hair was like here - it was not to his ear. But I couldn't see the other side. I could see there was hair behind his ears.

MQ 43. INV: OK and then the other side of the part. We have the part now, we talk about the part that goes behind his ear. The other side on top of his head. What is that? What's the direction of that hair? What does that do?

44. EW: The direction of?

ARC 45. INV: The hair. So we talked about the part near the ear…

46. EW: Going this way?

PQ 47. INV: Yes now I want to talk about the other side. So how does the hair go on that part?

48. EW: Uh it was going back but his hair was shorter near his ears.

PQ 49. INV: And what about the top of his hair?

50. EW: Uh it was facing - it wasn't straight down. It was back.

APPENDIX E

PQ 51. INV: It was going back as well?

52. EW: Mhm.

OEQ 53. INV: And the color of his hair?

54. EW: It was black and messy

MP 55. INV: Mhm. And you say - you used the word messy..

56. EW: Yeah.

OEQ 57. INV: Mhm. And overall length of the hair. What is that like?

58. EW: To the middle of his neck. Not too long.

MP 59. INV: Not too long. Is he wearing any sideburns?

60. EW: No.

OEQ 61. INV: No. Tell me about his forehead.

62. EW: His forehead is right in the middle. Not too deep down his face. Not too high.

OEQ 63. INV: Tell me about his ears.

64. EW: His ears are kinda curved a little. Where his earlobe is kinda goes in and out.

AL 65. INV: Mm.

66. EW: But I only saw his right ear.

PQ 67. INV. Why is that?

68. EW: Because he was in the car and I could only see one of his ears.

OEQ 69. INV: Mhm. Was he wearing any earrings?

70. EW: No.

OEQ 71. INV: Overall what would you say his ears were like?

72. EW: Um average size maybe a little bigger.

PQ 73. INV: Mm and did I ask you if he was wearing any earrings?

74. EW: Yes, he was not.

PQ 75. INV: Do you know what sideburns are?

76. EW: Yes.

PQ 77. INV: Did he have any sideburns?

78. EW: No he did not.

OEQ 79. INV: Tell me about his nose. What was that like?

80. EW: His nose was big. It was kind of big. It was going down here and then it kinda went out down his face.

PQ 81. INV: What about the overall length of his nose?

82. EW: Uh it was an average height but it was big on the sides.

83. INV: Mm. And the nostrils. What are they like?

OEQ 84. EW: I would say average.

PQ 85. INV: So when you say big, what do you mean?

APPENDIX E

86. EW: Uh I'm saying that it came down but instead of going straight down like and average or small nose, his nose kinda went out.
OEQ 87. INV: Mhm. Tell me about his mouth and his lips.
88. EW: Uh I feel like they were normal size just yeah.
PQ 89. INV: So his mouth was more normal size?
90. EW: Yes. His bottom lip was a little bigger than his top lip.
PQ 91. INV: Did he have any facial hair?
92. EW: Yes he had a mustache.
OEQ 93. INV: Tell me about it.
94. EW: It was kinda like down. It wasn't like a lot it was just a little bit but enough that you could see it.
PQ 95. INV: So when you say it wasn't a lot what do you mean by that?
96. EW: It wasn't long.
PQ 97. INV: Mhm. Do you know what stubble is?
98. EW: Yes.
FC 99. INV: Was it more than stubble?
100. EW: Yes.
OEQ 101. INV: And the color of his mustache?
102. EW: It was black.
OEQ 103. INV: What was his attitude like?
104. EW: Kinda like harsh.
OEQ 105. INV: Tell me about his chin?
106. EW: When his whole face was kinda round, his chin was like - how like if he had an oval face it would be kinda lower and that's how his chin looked. It didn't quite match his face or how it would normally be lower.
OEQ 107. INV: So overall what is the chin like?
108. EW: It doesn't really blend in with the face.
PQ 109. INV: What does it do?
110. EW: Um it's kinda farther from the mouth.
OEQ 111. INV: Mhm and what about the cheeks. What are they like?
112. EW: Normal.
MP 113. INV: Normal?
114. EW: Mhm
FC 115. INV: And any scars or marks on his face?
116. EW: No.
OEQ 117. INV: What about the color of the skin?
118. EW: It was dark.

356

PQ 119.INV: How dark?

120.EW: Um it was dark brown.

FC 121.INV: Lighter than you? Darker than you?

122.EW: Darker than me.

FC 123.INV: Mhm. Did this happen in the day or at night?

124.EW: It happened at around 5:30.

OEQ 125.INV: How close did you get to him?

126.EW: I was like two feet/three feet from the car.

OEQ 127.INV: What was the car like?

128.EW: It was a white Nissan.

MP 129.INV: Nissan?

130.EW: I'm not sure but the car was a little curvy. It stood out from the others.

OEQ 131.INV: Tell me about his neck. What's that like?

132.EW: I didn't get a chance to see it because he was wearing a hood.

MP 133.INV: A hood?

134.EW: He was wearing a hood and when he reached to grab me his hood fell off and then his ear wasn't normal - it was kind of bent . When I said it went in and out. And I noticed his hair was shaggy.

PQ 135.INV: So he was wearing a hood the whole time?

136.EW: No I saw the same guy walk past me before he got into the car.

OEQ 137.INV: Oh, this guy. And how did you know he was the same guy?

138.EW: Because he was wearing the same clothes.

OEQ 139.INV: Mhm, and what are they like?

140.EW: He was wearing a Nike t-shirt - it was bluish grey

AL 141.INV: Mhm

142.EW: Lighter, not dark. And he was wearing a black jacket over it.

MP 143.INV: A black jacket?

144.EW: Mhm

PQ 145.INV: And what was the jacket like?

146.EW: Uh I - it looked shiny so I assumed it was leather but it didn't have the texture to be leather.

AL 147.INV: Mhm.

148.EW: So I assumed some sort of athletic wear.

PQ 149.INV: You mentioned a hoodie earlier, so what was the jacket like?

150.EW: It..

FC 151.INV: Is the jacket the hoodie? Is that what you're saying?

152.EW: No I'm saying the jacket - it was kinda like when I was walking in the daylight, it shined off it and he wasn't wearing a hood when he walked past me.

APPENDIX E

PQ   153.INV: Oh but you're saying in the car he had a hoodie on?

154.EW: Yes.

—   155.INV: So…

156.EW: The only time it came off is when he reached out to grab me.

PQ   157.INV: Mmm, but you're confident it was the same guy?

158.EW: It was the same guy.

ARC   159.INV: So you know what? We're going to draw him without the hoodie. Is that ok?

160.EW: Yes.

PQ   161.INV: Alright good. So getting back to what he was wearing before he got in the car. You said it was a t-shirt?

162.EW: Mhm.

PQ   163.INV: And what's the color like?

164.EW: The color - It was just a circle around his neck. Like the one I have on right now.

FC   165.INV: Mhm. And so was it a dark blue? Light blue?

166.EW: It was light.

PQ   167.INV: And you said he was wearing a jacket.

168.EW: Yes.

PQ   169.INV: And you mentioned "shiny"

170.EW: Mhm.

PQ   171.INV: Why do you think it was shiny?

172.EW: Because I could see like the spot–the light hit the jacket, it kinda shined.

AL   173.INV: Mhm.

174.EW: The sunlight reflected off it?

OEQ   175.INV: What did you think about that?

176.EW: I don't know. I don't think it was a jacket like I have now because this is like a fabric.

PQ   177.INV: Mhm. But I thought you said it was black.

178.EW: It was.

FC   179.INV: Huh, and it was shiny as well?

180.EW: Yes.

PQ   181.INV: Um did he have any scars or marks on his face?

182.EW: No.

OEQ   183.INV: Let's talk about his eyes. What are they like?

184.EW: Uh they were big. On his right eye he had a faint blue line around one of his eyes.

OEQ   185.INV: A faint blue line? What does that mean?

186.EW: Um his eyes were really round to the point where they were almost black and the point where the iris and the whole white place like where they meet it was almost brown. Not brown - blue. Sorry. Just a faint line. It wasn't all over, just one corner of it.

APPENDIX E

PQ 187.INV: Mm. And his eye color was what?

188.EW: A really dark brown.

PQ 189.INV: And what was the look in his eyes?

190.EW: Um you could tell he was really harsh but he tried to be gentle but he was being really rough when he was talking.

OEQ 191.INV: Mmm (drawing). So let me ask you about this blue line. Where was the blue line?

192.EW: When he looked at me it was right underneath. On his right eye the bottom left near the white and where the brown touch.

PQ 193.INV: Mm have you ever seen that on a guy?

194.EW: Uh no but my mom has one like it and it's brown.

PQ 195.INV: Has what?

196.EW: A line. But her's isn't blue, it's brown. I've seen a lot of people with blue, actually like my grandpa's. They used to have that.

PQ 197.INV: Oh really? What does it signify?

198.EW: I don't know.

PQ 199.INV: Did you tell your mom and dad about this guy?

200.EW: They were the first people I told after I ran.

PQ 201.INV: You told them?

202.EW: Mhm.

OEQ 203.INV: Did you tell them about the description of the guy?

204.EW: No, I just said there was a guy who tried to grab me and put me inside his car.

OEQ 205.INV: Mhm. What about his eyebrows? What are they like?

206.EW: Bushy but they weren't big. They were small. They were average size but they were busy.

OEQ 207.INV: Mm. Were you afraid of this guy?

208.EW: Well when I saw him walking down the street when he passed by me.

AL 209.INV: Mhm.

210.EW: He looked at me in a way that made me uncomfortable. I wasn't scared of him, he just made me uncomfortable.

AL 211.INV: Mhm

212.EW: But when I saw the same guy trying to grab me, that's when I felt scared.

OEQ 213.INV: Mm. So when you saw him the first time you were where?

214.EW: I was just walking down the sidewalk and he walked.

PQ 215.INV: What street were you on?

216.EW: I was walking on the sidewalk on Fallen Leaf.

MP 217.INV: Fallen Leaf?

218.EW: Mhm.

PQ 219. INV: Do you know which direction?

APPENDIX E

220.EW: Like north? I don't know which direction the road was facing.

PQ 221.INV: Alright, so you were walking on Fallen Leaf and where was this guy?

222.EW: He was walking on the same street but in the opposite direction on the left side.

PQ 223.INV: Mm. So you would literally pass right in front of you?

224.EW: Yeah, he didn't say or do anything. He looked at me in a way that made me uncomfortable so I just walked faster.

PQ 225.INV: Mhm. Where were you coming from?

226.EW: I was coming from my house on the Iron Horse Trail going to my class.

PQ 227.INV: Which class?

228.EW: My singing class.

PQ 229.INV: Oh is this a class you attend regularly?

230.EW: Uh no depending on the teacher's schedule. It is mostly a regular class, yes.

PQ 231.INV: So what time does class start?

232.EW: Class, still depends on the teacher's schedule, but between 5-6.

PQ 233.INV: How do you know from day to day when it's going to start?

234.EW: My mom has a group and they will put the times on there and what I need to bring to the class.

PQ 235.INV: Mm Do you normally walk alone?

236.EW: Uh sometimes I walk alone or sometimes with my Dad, most of the time my Dad drops me off. He usually never lets me walk alone. And before I left my mom told me not to. She said it wasn't safe. I said it was fine and I just walked.

PQ 237.INV: So was that the first time?

238.EW: That I walked alone?

AL 239.INV: Yes.

240.EW: Uh probably yes

PQ 241.INV: Well do you remember a another time?

242.EW: I did walk alone with a friend once but I wasn't alone, I was with a friend.

PQ 243.INV: Oh ok. But I meant to this singing class at this time.

244.EW: No.

PQ 245.INV: That was the first time?

OER 246.INV: So you said his eyebrows were kind of bushy but thin? And what was the look in his eyes?

247.EW: Well when he tried to grab me it was kind of rage.

PQ 248.INV: But how about before? Since we're drawing him when he was walking past you. How about that?

249.EW: Oh, um he was kind of staring me down like I did something wrong.

PQ 250.INV: Any scars or marks on his face?

251.EW: No

APPENDIX E

OEQ 252.INV: So how many times did you see this guy?

253.EW: Once when I was walking on the sidewalk and once in the car.

OEQ 254.INV: Mhm. So have you ever seen this guy before?

255.EW: No.

OEQ 256.INV: Any other things you can remember about this guy's face that you want to tell me?

257.EW: There's nothing I remember on his face.

Topic 3

AQC 258.INV: Ok. You can open your eyes. Now what I want you to do is I want you to tell me what you were doing just prior to running into this guy and then take me through the incident up until the point where he tries to grab you. So go through them and tell me everything that happened.

259.EW: I was at home. It was 5:15...

AL 260.INV: Mhm.

261.EW: And usually the class is at 5:15 but sometimes it's between 5:00-6:00 so I thought I was late and I told my mom I was going to leave and she was like, "It's not safe."

PQ 262.INV: So you said you told your mom - she was home?

263.EW: Yes. She actually has a music class that she teaches so she wasn't able to drop me off that time so I said, "That's ok." And she said, "Be safe."

AL 264.INV: Mhm

265.EW: And I just ran to my class.

PR 266.INV: Mhm - how far do you have to go?

267.EW: Not that far. Maybe 5 minutes.

AL 268.INV: Ok.

269.EW: And I saw this guy when I was walking there to the house...

AL 270.INV: Mhm.

271.EW: And he looked at me in a way that made me uncomfortable so I started walking faster...

AL 272.INV: Mhm

273.EW: And I rang the doorbell and then they opened the door and they said class was at 6.

PQ 274.INV: Rang what doorbell?

275.EW: Uh their house doorbell.

PR 276.INV: Of the place you're going to get lessons?

277.EW: Mhm.

AL 278.INV: Ok, got it.

279.EW: And I went - I started walking further cuz my friend's house was like a minute or two away and before I got there I called my mom to make sure it was ok, if I could go there.

AL 280.INV: Oh.

281.EW: And she said it's ok. Just come back...

Mindful Interview Method ©2022

APPENDIX E

MP 282.INV: Come back?

283.EW: Home.

AL 284.INV: Home. Ok.

285.EW: And then I started walking back and once I got to the house - there was a big white box outside of the house - I got there and I heard a car and I turned around and I saw the same car that was parked there when the guy was passing me.

PQ 286.INV: Ok, did you already tell me when you saw him the first time?

287.EW: Yes.

PQ 288.INV: You did?

289.EW: Yes, I told you about when I saw him the first time. I don't think I told you about the car.

MQ 290.INV: Well let's go there first. When did you see him the first time? When you went to the house for class and you were early?

291.EW: Mhm.

AL 292.INV: Ok, and that was on the following (inaudible).

293.EW: Mhm.

PQ 294.INV: And when did you see… where's this house that you're going to?

295.EW: Fallen Leaf as well.

OEQ 296.INV: Oh, it's on Fallen Leaf. Ok. Got it. So then what happened?

297.EW: And then my mom said no come home and I was walking back the way I came from and then I saw this guy pull up in a car. The same guy that had walked past me and then he told me, "Oh, hi, I'm your dad's friend. We work together and he asked me to pick you up and drop you home and then I said, "No" and he said, "Come on, I'll open the door for you." And I started backing away and he reached out and grabbed my hand. He didn't grab it; he tried to. He touched my jacket but I pulled it away before he could grab it and I took off running and he followed me in the car and there was a curb and I ran to the right and I ran into one of the bushes because there were people around there. I don't think they noticed me because they were busy taking…

AL 298.INV: Mhm.

299.EW: And then I called my mom right after and I heard the man screaming and I heard him speeding away.

MP 300.INV: You heard the guy screaming?

301.EW: Mhm.

PQ 302.INV: Screaming what?

303.EW: I don't know. It was in a different language.

OEQ 304.INV: Mhm. And what did you tell your mom?

305.EW: I told my mom that a guy tried to grab me from the car and she asked me where I am and um what happened and everything. I was running home at that point on the trail.

OEQ 306.INV: Mhm. And what happened after that?

307.EW: I just went home. My dad called the police.

OEQ 308.INV: And what happened after that?

APPENDIX E

MP 309.EW: They said they were going to send an officer and that's the lady I talked to yesterday.
310.INV: So they sent an officer?
311.EW: Mhm.
PQ 312.INV: They talked to you?
313.EW: Mhm.
OEQ 314.INV: And what happened when you talked to her?
315.EW: She just asked me all the details what happened, like what I remembered about him and what he was wearing and like what car he was in and things like that.
PC 316.INV: And you told her about seeing him twice?
317.EW: Mhm.
OEQ 318.INV: So you said he pulled up to you. So how was he doing that?
319.EW: Well he was just in the car and the car just came up behind me and stopped next to me.
PQ 320.INV: So you're on the sidewalk, right?
321.EW: Mhm.
PQ 322.INV: And he pulls up behind you?
323.EW: No. I'm right here and he pulls up right here and he turns...
PQ 324.INV: So he parks beside you?
325.EW: He doesn't park. He's just standing there.
PQ 326.INV: You mean in the car?
327.EW: Yeah, in the car.
PC 328.INV: You mean your left or your right?
329.EW: Uh, left.
PQ 330.INV: You're looking left at him so is he looking at you from what side of the car?
331.EW: The driver.
MP 332.INV: He's on the driver's side?
333.EW: Yeah.
PC 334.INV: And is he with traffic or against it?
335.EW: Ahh. I don't know.
PQ 336.INV: Hm. So you said you turned left and you see him. Which way is his car facing?
337.EW: His car - when I was looking this way...
R 338.INV: Right, you looked at him.
339.EW: His car was facing this way.
AQC 340.INV: You're looking that way - left. So go ahead - turn that way. So which way is his car facing?
341.EW: It's facing that way.
PQ 342.INV: So he's looking that way, right?
343.EW: Yeah.

APPENDIX E

PQ 344.INV: So if he's going that way then the driver - where's he at?

345.EW: He's in the car and he's looking at me. There's no one in the passenger seat.

PQ 346.INV: Oh, so he's doing it from across? Got it.

347.EW: Mhm.

AQC 348.INV: He tells you - well you notice him first...

349.EW: Mhm.

OEQ 350.INV: And then what happens after you notice him. Let's kind of slow down about what happened. So you notice him and then what?

351.EW: Uh he - I hear him pulling down the windows and I hear him saying something in another language. I can't understand what he's saying and he starts talking to me and he's saying, "Oh hi, I'm here to pick you up. I'm here to drop you off at home."

PQ 352.INV: In English?

353.EW: Yeah, but he had an Indian accent and he was like um me and you dad work together, we're friends and he asked me to drop you off at home and I said, "No." And he was like, "Come on, I'll open the door for you." And I said, "No." And I backed off and he reached out to grab my hand.

PQ 354.INV: How did he do that?

355.EW: He was - his height was like the roof of the car.

AL 356.INV: Mhm.

357.EW: And when he tried to reach out to me - he wasn't wearing a seatbelt so he had to kind of bend his head a little bit and he just reached out of the window completely and he tried to grab me but he touched my jacket like right here, but I pulled back...

PQ 358.INV: So how close were you to the car?

359.EW: Like 2-3 feet.

MP 360.INV: 2-3 feet from the car?

361.EW: Yeah, not far, actually.

PQ 362.INV: How did you get so close to the car?

363.EW: I was walking on the left of the sidewalk when I came back and I was walking on the right of the sidewalk when I was going so I always walk on the same side...

PQ 364.INV: Right. And he was on the street, right?

365.EW: Mhm

PQ 366.INV: Did he get really close or did he stay on the street? What happened?

367.EW: Yeah, uh when, like the place that it happened, it was like, the sidewalk kind of goes straight and then it dips down a little bit and then it goes back up so it was at the part where it dipped down so it was really close to actually getting on the sidewalk.

AL 368.INV: Oh.

369.EW: So the car was really close even if I was at that part of the sidewalk.

PQ 370.INV: Ok. But then he reaches across from the car?

364

APPENDIX E

PQ 371.EW: Yeah, there's no-one in the passenger side.
PQ 372.INV: And what do you do when he's starting to reach out from the car?
373.EW: I like kinda - I don't do anything. I was just standing there and it happened really quick and I didn't know what to do but then once he touched my jacket, I pulled away from him
AL 374.INV: Mhm
375.EW: He screams and then I run.
PQ 376.INV: He screamed at you? What did he say?
377.EW: I don't know what he said.
PQ 378.INV: And then so you said he screams and then you run?
379.EW: Yeah.
PQ 380.INV: And which way do you run?
381.EW: I run the same way I was walking back home, so the car was facing this way.
OEQ 382.INV: So how far away was your home from that location?
383.EW: Uh the same. So if I was running, probably two minutes.
MQ 384.INV: Two minutes? You didn't go home - you said you went in the bushes?
385.EW: I went in the bushes.
OEQ 386.INV: And do you know whose bushes they were?
387.EW: Uh, actually it wasn't at somebody's house. They were just there where the trail was so it wasn't like - it didn't belong to anyone.

Topic 4

AQC 388.INV: Oh. I see. Alright, I'm going to show you the sketch. When you look at the sketch, I don't need you to tell me if it looks like him or not. What I want you to do is just look at the sketch and kinda see what I've been doing. After that, I'm going to ask you the same questions I did before, but this time you'll be looking at the sketch.
389.EW: Mhm.
AQC 390.INV: As I ask you about each feature, I want you to tell me whether we're in the ballpark or whether you want me to make some changes. Do you understand that?
391.EW: Yeah.
AQC 392.INV: We're never going to be exact. Never, because no-one's memory is exact, however, we can get pretty close to what the person looks like if all the information is here, ok?
393.EW: Mhm.
OEQ 394.INV: Alright so this is what I have so far. First of all, the shape of the face. How are we doing with the shape of the face?
395.EW: Ok.
PQ 396.INV: It's ok?
397.EW: Yeah.
OEQ 398.INV: Alright the hair on his head - is that ok?

365

APPENDIX E

399. EW: Yes.

AQC 400. INV: As I tell you about each feature I need you to tell me if it's fine or if I have to make a change, ok?

401. EW: Mhm

OEQ 402. INV: And forehead?

403. EW: Yes.

OEQ 404. INV: And ears?

405. EW: Yes.

OEQ 406. INV: And the nose?

407. EW: Yes.

OEQ 408. INV: And then the mustache?

409. EW: Yes.

PQ 410. INV: So um you see I gave him a little (mustache) because you said it wasn't - I don't think you used the word thick. It wasn't thick?

411. EW: No.

PQ 412. INV: So is that enough there?

413. EW: Yes.

OEQ 414. INV: Ok and the lips and the mouth?

415. EW: Mhm

OEQ 416. INV: The chin and the cheeks?

417. EW: Yes.

OEQ 418. INV: The tee shirt and the jacket?

419. EW: Yes.

PQ 420. INV: So the jacket is black but it's shiny, right?

421. EW: His jacket goes more in. I could only see a little bit of his shirt so like this...

PQ 422. INV: Oh, so not as open, you're saying?

423. EW: Yeah, it is open but when he reaches out I see the Nike on...

PQ 424. INV: On the tee shirt?

425. EW: Yeah it's about this size but it's like a little bigger.

AQC 426. INV: Oh the swish you mean. Oh. Ok, well I'm just going to...draw it later. I'm going to say there's a Nike swish there. That will remind me. Um but the tee shirt, neck area, how does that feel?

427. EW: Yes.

OEQ 428. INV: Ok, the eyes?

429. EW: Correct.

OEQ 430. INV: Does he look about the right age?

431. EW: Yes.

APPENDIX E

OEQ 432.INV: So you said 30-50. How old is your dad?
433.EW: My dad is 45.
FC 434.INV: Do you think this guy is older or younger?
435.EW: My dad?
PQ 436.INV: No, this guy. Does he look older than your dad?
437.EW: Umm...
PQ 438.INV: What do you think? Since you know your dad is 45.
439.EW: Yeah, my dad doesn't really look 45.
PQ 440.INV: How old does he look?
441.EW: He probably looks 40.
AL 442.INV: Ok.
443.EW: But this guy, he looks about 35-40.
AL 444.INV: Mhm. ok.
445.EW: Not that old.

Topic 3

OEQ 446.INV: Did anything like this ever happen to you before?
447.EW: No.
PQ 448.INV: Your friends?
449.EW: No.
OEQ 450.INV: (drawing) What do you think this guy wanted?
451.EW: Um I don't really know. I don't know if it has to do with school or anything.
OEQ 452.INV: So why did your mom mention that, I think you used the word - it would be dangerous to go, for you to go out?
453.EW: Because she's overprotective. All the time. Like even if I'm going to school, like after school I'm like, "Can I go with my friends to marketplace. She usually says no, like, she doesn't want me to go alone. She says that there should always be an adult with you.
AL 454.INV: Mm.
455.EW: So at the same time, my dad's not as overprotective as my mom but, but he still like thinks I shouldn't go alone but I thought it would be fine so I just went.
PQ 456.INV: Do you have any siblings?
457.EW: Yes, I have one brother.
PQ 458.INV: How old is he?
459.EW: He's 10.
OEQ 460.INV: Did you tell him about this?
461.EW: Yes.
462.INV: What does he think?

367

APPENDIX E

463.EW: I didn't tell him - he kinda just figured it out.
PQ 464.INV: Oh really?
465.EW: Mhm.
PQ 466.INV: What about your friends?
467.EW: No-one knows.
MP 468.INV: No?
469.EW: No.
PQ 470.INV: So you were with the officers today?
471.EW: Yes.
PQ 472.INV: Where were you?
473.EW: Fallen Leaf.
PQ 474.INV: So you showed them where everything happened? You showed them where the car was?
475.EW: Yes.
PQ 476.INV: And you said, what kind of car was it again?
477.EW: Nissan.
MP 478.INV: Nissan?
479.EW: White.
PQ 480.INV: Did they show you pictures of any white Nissan?
481.EW: I actually searched it up.
RQ 482.INV: On your own?
483.EW: I searched it up on my dad's phone. The officer, the lady that came to my house Friday, she asked me if I have time I can see, I could look at pictures of white Nissans and if I figure out which one is close to the one I saw, and I found one. I didn't know what it was but it looked like the one I saw the other day.
AL 484.INV: Hm
485.EW: So, I sent that to them.
PQ 486.INV: Oh, you did already?
487.EW: Mhm

Topic 2

OEQ 488.INV: So how tall was this guy?
489.EW: He looked about average height I would say because the car wasn't too big…
PQ 490.INV: Well you saw him walking…
491.EW: Mhm.
PQ 492.INV: That's what I mean. You saw him walking so..
493.EW: He wasn't that tall. He was average height. A little taller than average actually.
MQ 494.INV: So have you been to your singing class yet? Was it a voice class?

APPENDIX E

PQ 495.EW: It's a singing class, yes.
    496.INV: So have you been to that class since?
    497.EW: No I have not.

Topic 4

AQC 498.INV: (Drawing). Alright, I'm going to show you the sketch one more time. When you look at it, I want you to ask yourself, "Does it remind me of him?" If it does, what I want you to do is I want you to tell me it does. If it doesn't and you want me to make a change on something, just let me know and I'll make the change, alright?
    499.EW: Mhm.
PQ 500.INV: It's like before, we want to be very close. It's never going to be exact but we want to be close. (drawing) So somebody seeing him, just walking right, would they notice that color on the eye underneath there?
    501.EW: Um I mean if the eye didn't look like, sometimes you know how the eyes are red…
AL 502.INV: Mhm.
    503.EW: And like a little yellow, not perfectly white. I think they would if it was.
FC 504.INV: Because it's on the eye or on the skin?
    505.EW: It's on the eye. It's in the eye.
MP 506.INV: It's In the eye?
    507.EW: It's there, yeah. It's inside. It's not on the skin
PQ 508.INV: Ok. So they put something on the eye? I think you said someone in your family wears something like that.
    509.EW: No, it's not…It's just there.
PQL 510.INV: Oh you mean it's a condition they have.
    511.EW: I don't think it's a condition. I think it's just there.
PQ 512.INV: Really?
    513.EW: Yeah.
AQC 514.INV: Ok, so it's in the eye in the white area of the eye near the brown part.
    515.EW: Yes.
PQ 516.INV: On the lower side?
    517.EW: Mhm
PQ 518.INV: So when you saw him walking, did you see it then?
    519.EW: No.
PQ 520.INV: But you saw it when.
    521.EW: He was close to my face trying to grab me.
FC 522.INV: Got it. And he's reaching out with the left or the right arm?
    523.EW: Right.

APPENDIX E

PQ 524. INV: Right arm. And you're seeing it in his right eye?
525. EW: Mhm.
PQ 526. INV: Got it. Ok. How's that? Does it remind you of him?
527. EW: Mhm
OEQ 528. INV: Do you want to make any changes?
529. EW: No, it's right.

Topic 5

AQC 530. INV: Good. Very good. (drawing). The next time you see this, if you ever see it, I'm going to indicate it in this area ok. So you'll see that there.
531. EW: Mhm

Topic 3

FC 532. INV: (drawing) So was the car on or off?
533. EW: It was on.
PQL 534. INV: Did he have anything going on in the car, the radio?
535. EW: No, I could just hear the engine running.
PQ 536. INV: Mhm Were there a lot of cars around?
537. EW: No there was actually no-one around except for on the trail.
MP 538. INV: On the trail?
539. EW: Yeah.
PQ 540. INV: Got it. But this is like a residential area, right?
541. EW: Mhm.
AQC 542. INV: And you're walking - it sounded like he might have gone in somebody's driveway, huh? Because I think you described the sidewalk going down and then.
543. EW: Mhm, he was really close to getting on the sidewalk but then he was not
PQ 544. INV: Ah, ok. So he was still on the street?
545. EW: Mhm.

Topic 5

AQC 546. INV: Got it. (drawing) Ok. So I need your initials to your name.
547. EW: (initials)___
PQ 548. INV: And this happened what date? Yesterday?
549. EW: Friday, that was yesterday right?
PQ 550. INV: _____ Around what time?
551. EW: 5:30.

END OF INTERVIEW

APPENDIX E

EEIA Summary Report

This report is part of the Efficacy of Eyewitness Interview Assessment℠

Date	4/17/22	Type of event	CASE STUDY #6	Type of investigator	Forensic Artist

Topic Descriptions

Topics	Topic Description
1	Welcome, Introduction, Assess
2	Suspect Description
3	Crime Elements
4	Confirmation, Clarification, Review
5	Conclusion, Follow-up, Q&A

Topic Sequence

Values across topics: 5, 122, 65, 29, 20, 5, 16, 1, 7, 3

Total Questions	248	Total Responses	274	Average Questions	50	Average Responses	55

Topic Access per Interview

Topic	Questions per topic	Eyewitness Responses
1	6	6
2	120	127
3	76	93
4	42	45
5	4	3

Examination of Questions Types

Type	CE Effect	Questions	Total	Proportion
I	SRP	AQC, NR	17	6%
II	DRCE	ACQ, FC, LQ, MCQ, MQ, MLQ, PLQ	23	8%
III	IRCE	MF, OEQ, FQ	208	76%
IV	MR	EC, AL	26	9%
		EW Responses	274	50%
		Total	**548**	

Topic 2 & 3 Questions (Type III & IV)
Topic 2: 113
Topic 3: 81

Reliability of Cognitive Evidence Scale

Cognitive Evidence Effects	More than Acceptable (3)	Acceptable (2)	Less than Acceptable (1)
Diminish Reliability	< 7%	7% - 10%	> 10%
Improve Reliability	> 61%	61% - 57%	< 57%
Mindful Rapport	> 9%	9% - 4%	< 4%
Eyewitness Response	> 49%	49% - 48%	< 48%
Topic 2	> 82%	82% - 78%	< 78%
Topic 3	> 59%	59% - 45%	< 45%
Topic Sequence Deviation	< 1	1 - 2	> 2

RELIABLE COGNITIVE EVIDENCE COLLECTED

HIGHLY RELIABLE: 21 - 18, RELIABLE: 17 - 14, LESS THAN RELIABLE: 13 - 7

COR:		DRCE:	8%	IRCE:	76%	MR:	9%	EWR:	50%	T2:	89%	T3:	88%	TSQ:	5	RCE
0			3		3		2		3		3		3		1	**18**

Confidence of Recollection (COR): 0 = Confidence is affirmed; -1 = Confidence is questionable; -2 = Confidence is unreliable

APPENDIX E

CASE STUDY #7

This section includes: a. Coded transcript, and b. EEIA summary report. For complete EEIA reports for case studies 6 through 15 go to www.mindfulinterviews.com/CaseStudies.

Each case study was evaluated and prepared for EEIA processing. Every attempt was made to standardize the evaluation and coding process for every case study. Any errors in coding, calculations, or assignment of RCE score, should be directed to the author. All of the transcripts were anonymized for instructional purposes, any resemblance to specific investigations is purely coincidental. The crime types and agencies are listed for informational purposes and to give the reader an idea of the variety of cases used in applying *The Mindful Interview Method*.

EYEWITNESS INTERVIEW ANALYSIS (EIA)
CONFIDENTIAL TRANSCRIPT REVIEW

Date of transcript review: May17, 2022

Crime type: Civil Case consultation

Notes: I consulted on a case where the litigant wanted the crime report analyzed for gathering reliable information and whether a composite sketch could be created from the initial witnesses from this interview. One of the witnesses in this interview agreed to be interviewed for a sketch.

Topic 3

1. [PLQ] INV: When you were treating the victim the other night, do you recall if he was wearing glasses when you first contacted him?
2. EW1: I don't believe so. Not that I remember–I don't remember taking them off of him–I guess.
3. [PLQ] INV: OK Do you remember seeing any glasses anywhere at the scene?
4. EW1: Not that I recall - no.
5. [PLQ] INV: OK, and....Let's see what was the other thing I was going to ask you? (pause). Do you remember, um, if you discarded any wrapping from the gauze into a trash can - that was in that room?
6. EW1:(pause) The only the–only thing that we left in that room when I tore–when I tore open the gauze…
7. [AL] INV: Hmmm
8. EW1:–the outer wrapper - I left on, I left a few of those floor
9. [AL] INV: OK
10. EW1: but the actual gauze itself, um, stayed on him.

372

APPENDIX E

11. INV: OK
12. EW1: Cause we put it on and wrapped it and then, uh we applied more when we got into the ambulance.
13. INV: OK, inaudible Go ahead
14. EW1: …thinking one more thing, I don't know if it's even relevant or not.
15. INV: What's that?
16. EW1: Um, I was trying to think if we saw anybody at all like the entire time we were sitting there.
17. INV: Mmm

Topic 2

18. EW1: And there was one man we saw and you know people walk to the parking lot all the time so I guess I didn't even really think about it. (clear throat) There was a man that walked to - he was over 6 feet tall - really big guys and the sense just like big-boned, big broad shoulders and he had long black curly hair and I just remember him slowly walking up like he was going to come talk to us. And then he kind of just walked by…and I don't know if that's relevant.
19. INV:–At what point, and it was–was that when you were parked? Before you got called?
20. EW1: Yeah, yeah, when we were parked and I was trying to think in relation to the call like what time that was…
21. INV: Mmm
22. EW1: and I just - I don't exactly remember. I just know it was–it wasn't like earlier in the day, like when we first got there it was later.
23. INV: You mean this is while you were Sta–Sitting there staged or not staged. Ah, but posted.
24. EW1: Posted yeah, yeah
25. INV: OK
26. EW1: Cause I remember we're just sitting there talking and I remember he was walking and I kinda looked at Robert and I was like, oh he's kinda goofy looking or something. I made a joke about it or something and I mean he didn't, he didn't make any gestures or (inaudible) he slowly walked away and maybe he was going to work. I don't know, but I remember nodding my head at him, kinda like, you know, you nod your head like you're saying, "Hi" type-thing. I remember doing that and he just kinda glared at me and kept walking by.
27. INV: Do you remember anything about what he might be wearing?
28. EW1: Uh, he was wearing white t-shirt and (inaudible) navy pants or jeans, I mean.
29. INV: OK
30. EW1: That's about all I remember of him. He was, he was pretty tall and pretty big. He was whatever 6' tall for sure.
31. INV: Mhmm, OK
32. EW1: I guess I really didn't think about it until this morning, cause I guess people walk through that parking lot all the time so that's not overly suspicious to have somebody walking through the fairgrounds, but…
33. INV: Any idea um race he was?
34. EW1: He was white.
35. INV: He was a white guy?
36. EW1: Yeah.
37. INV: And age?
38. EW1: Oh, if I had to guess, he would be in his 30s - somewhere in his 30s.
39. INV: With long dark curly hair?

373

APPENDIX E

40. EW1: And it was black.
41. INV: Black hair, yeah?
42. EW1: Yeah.
43. INV: OK Glasses or anything? Tattoos?
44. EW1: No glasses, I didn't, I didn't see, I don't remember if he had tattoos or not.
45. INV: OK Nothing…
46. EW1: No, I was - Robert and I were in pretty in depth conversation about nursing and things like that, so I didn't overly pay attention to him. I just remember kinda looking at him cause I thought OK, he's gonna - like he, he approached the ambulance almost like he was gonna come talk to us…
47. INV: Mhmm
48. EW1: but I went to roll down the window but then he just–nodded at him and just kept walking by, so…
49. INV: OK And where did you last see him walking?
50. EW1: Um, I liked, I tried looking in the mirror to see where he was going and I didn't see him. I mean he was just walking away from the ambulance at that time, then I didn't look again.
51. INV: He approached you?
52. EW1: So he was walking. Yeah
53. INV: OK So he was coming from the north/south
54. EW1: To south.
55. INV: OK
56. EW1: He was walking north - he was coming from the South.
57. INV: OK You guys were facing south at the time, or?
58. EW1: We were facing south, Yes.
59. INV: OK
60. EW1: So, he came from the um, the first time I saw him, he was walking down kinda that gravel drive there…
61. INV: Mhmm.
62. EW1: in between um, in between the driveway of those three buildings and the other two buildings that are kinda off to the West there.
63. INV: OK. OK.
64. EW1: Like I said, I really didn't think about it before, just cause people walk through there all the time and it didn't seem overly suspicious. I mean, he was just walking. He wasn't doing anything wrong, um, so…
65. INV: You think it would…(inaudible) close to the time that you had this call?
66. EW1: I do feel like it was within that (pause) frame, it–maybe within an hour or two.
67. INV: OK.
68. EW1: It definitely wasn't like when we first–cause we were there for a couple hours at least. I just remember we were pretty in depth conversation by then it was, you know, we had been sitting there over an hour, so I would say it was probably within the hour of the call happening.
69. INV: OK. Alright, well if you think of anything else just give me a call.
70. EW1: OK. Sounds good. I'm happy to help.

Follow-up interview with same eyewitnesses

Topic 1

APPENDIX E

71. INV: OK, ummm, investigator Brunswick, I'm–no idea what day it is, it's May 8th and it's about 2:45pm and I'm with Red paramedics Robert and Ben at the Red station Civic Plaza Drive. OK. So you guys wanna tell me what happened?

72. INV: I mean Ben you already said that you were posted at the fairgrounds, right?

73. EW1: Yup,, do you want me to explain?

74. EW2: Either way.

Topic 2

75. EW1: So we, so we were posted at the fairgrounds, um kind of that new mail parking lot. The paved area there if that makes sense.

 76. INV: So there's (inaud)

77. EW2: (inaud) (cross talk) Three (inaud) east of the grandstand

78. EW1: Yeah

 79. INV: OK

80. EW1: Yeah

81. EW1: And so we were posted there we had heard the radio traffic over LAC, um, but we were unsure where, where the location was, um, we heard another crew member say they were, they were in route to the EOC and my partner and I were trying to decipher is that (inaud) we used to LAC but I never heard the term EOC.

82. INV: oh

83. EW1: So, so we weren't, weren't quite sure exactly where that was.

84. INV: Mmm

85. EW1: Um, so at that time we drove right past the EOC and took a left down, um, would that be third (EW2 - Third) third avenue, um, and started heading, um (EW2 - toward LAC) North

 86. INV: So that would be North?

87. EW1: Yeah, we started heading North towards the LAC because we thought thats, that was the area, um, when we saw multiple police officers coming towards us we quickly–it kinda clicked in our brain, that no it's the building we just passed. I don't recall seeing anything when we passed the building, um cuz we're kinda focused on where, where's this (INV: Mmm) coming from. Um, so we turn around we follow the police cars in–we arrived at the same time the police cars did. I remember when I got out I heard squealing tires and I turned and looked and I saw a man and it looked like, like a Jeep Cherokee, or like a four door suburban type thing. I just remember hearing the tires and I looked and I saw him speeding out…turning left like he was pulling out (inaud–this is Robert…) and at the time I didn't I didn't really think of it because, I, I didn't know if you know if he was just trying to get out of the way or like it didn't really register at the time that you know maybe that's the suspect. But he was definitely burning his–I mean he was really booking. Um.

88. INV: When you say he turned left, what…

89. EW1: So he was, so he went. I'm sorry let me elaborate more. So it looked as though he was turning, ahh, North on Third Avenue there, that's Third Avenue correct?

APPENDIX E

90. INV: Yes

91. EW1: OK, so he was turning North on Third Avenue, and it was either a red or green Jeep I don't remember what it was (inaudible) to, I just can't recall off the top of my head. Um, it looked, it looked as though he had something black on his head maybe a scarf or something like that.

92. INV: And you thought he was a male?

93. EW1: It did look like a male, yeah. He was kinda hunched down in his seat so I didn't get I didn't get a very good look at him at all.

94. INV: OK

Topic 4

95. EW1: So at that time the officers had gone in, um, found the patient and that's when they directed us to come in right away, and they said this hall way is clear we haven't cleared anything else yet, but you're safe to come into this room. Ah, so Robert and I went into the room and I asked the officer to shut the door so there was an officer–I don't know if they did or not, but there was officers around the door.

96. EW2: Officers, yeah securing the hallway

97. EW1: Secured, they secured the–the area there…

98. INV: OK

99. EW1: Um, and then at that time ah Robert started talking to the patient I had noticed, um, he had a laceration to his neck ah he was laying in the prone position over what looked like a box, or over computers or something, and then his left arm had a very deep laceration, um, I could see bone ah to his left arm and then his hand, um so at that time Robert was talking–we're were both talking to him to kind of assess where his injuries are and where to start from and–and I started to put gauze on the arm and then we rolled him over to assess his airway and that cause he didn't seem to be having trouble breathing but we were concerned with the laceration to the neck, um, and then you know we got him out and transported from there.

100. INV: OK

101. EW1: I don't know what more detail you need.

102. INV: That's good

103. EW1: OK (I'm gonna go with Robert) I did–I did cut his pants off.

104. INV: OK

105. EW1: That was the only–I don't think we cut his shirt, did we? I–I…did cut his pants.

106. INV: And where are those? Are those with him at St.

107. EW1: They were–they were never…

108. INV: OK, there's somebody on the way…

109. EW1: But I–I did cut his pants

110. INV: OK

111. EW1: At that–when I–when I did my assessment of his legs I did not see any stabs or injuries. Um, or any–I didn't see any thing on his pants at that time.

APPENDIX E

112. INV: OK
113. EW1: When I cut'em–through his pants.
114. INV: OK, So what about you Robert? So you hear the–you hear the call and you're thinking it maybe LAC cause it doesn't seem to be clear?
115. EW2: Well I wasn't–I wasn't totally sure where EOC was
116. INV: OK
117. EW2: Then Joe said that and we were discussing that when we got on Third Street (inaud) what we (inaud) then we saw the cop cars coming and we knew (INV: OK) we should be back there and we turned–we were–I mean we watched them go through the door. We were that close.
118. INV: OK
119. EW2: So, and like I said they…
120. INV: you mean the officers go through the door?
121. EW2: Yeah goin' in
122. INV: OK
123. EW2: I didn't see the car, but I got the other side of the truck and–cause one of us grabbed–I grabbed the bag and he grabbed the monitor.
124. EW1: I just happened to look just 'cause I heard–I heard the tires squealing'.
125. EW2: And you were at the back door looking that way where I was looking at the truck
126. EW1: No I–I was the driver and I–I stopped and looked around cause I just heard the tires.
127. EW2: OK, when we first got there.
128. EW1: Yeah and then I–at the time I didn't think anything of it.
129. INV: OK
130. EW1: Just coming on.

Detective uses smartphone to pull up the location on a map and asks EW1 and EW2 to help locate the area they were posted prior to the call. Detective tells them where EOC and Third Street are on the map and asks them to identify the place where they were posted. Detective tells them that they had parked at the same location many times before on patrol. Eventually detective asks where they were when they heard the squealing tires.

131. EW1: So I'll just zoom this in. (INV:Yup) So we had parked–I'll just point with my pen there–we parked facing this way here.
132. INV: OK, and that's the front door right there
133. EW1: Yup, and I was driving, so when I got out I heard it and I turned and looked I saw him right about here going this way weaving between a car.
134. INV: OK
135. EW1: So, It was–it was about here but the angle of the car–it wasn't straight like he was clearly turning
136. INV: Mmm
137. EW1: North. Um, but that's when I saw him.

APPENDIX E

138. INV: And so prior to when you turned around and you drove back in here did you see where that vehicle was at all?

139. EW1: No cause when we initially pulled in my focus was on the officer at the door directing

140. INV: OK

141. EW1: Directing us so at that time, no I didn't see any

142. INV: OK

143. EW1: I don't recall that.

144. INV: So when the–when the call came out I'm assuming there's probably a little bit of panic going on even at the LEC with the dispatchers–ah because…this is a county employee–county deputy.

145. EW1: Something you never want to hear.

146. INV: Yeah, and so they didn't give out the address right away, probably.

147. EW1: Um, there was never–our dispatcher. EW2: I don't think they ever gave us–us the address. EW1: All we heard was EOC and that's what the problem was

148. INV: Yeah

149. EW1: And I asked our dispatcher, I said where is–what is EOC and where is it?

150. INV: OK

151. INV: And there was no reply but at that time.

152. EW2: Cause she had said, I think she was trying–at one point she said the call is coming in right now (EW1 - Yeah) But we just followed them (Inaudible)

153. EW1: Cause we just scan LAC

154. INV: Mmm

155. EW1: We hear obviously (INV: yup) before dispatchers so that–that was part of the communication error there.

156. EW2: And we only get part of what they do because if our dispatcher talks (inaud) then it kicks it out, yeah, yeah.

157. INV: OK

158. EW2: And that was the other (inaud) I was discussing (laughs)

159. INV: OK

160. INV: Who was putting chatter on the radio that we didn't need.

Topic 2

161. INV: OK and so you think it was Jeep Cherokee or a like four-door suburban?

162. EW1: It was definitely a four-door

163. INV: OK

164. EW1: Vehicle I–I thought it was a Jeep Cherokee it appeared to be that. He was going so fast, I mean things were going quick but…

165. INV: OK

378

APPENDIX E

PLQ 166. EW1: I definitely remember four doors for sure.

167. INV: Anything else about the vehicle you can remember, any stickers, or paint, or rust or…

168. EW1: No But I remember is a ol–it wasn't newer it was an older…Jeep.

AL 169. INV: OK. Yeah.

170. Being a car guy I would say it's probably in the early nineties… late nineties.

AL 171. INV: OK

PQ 172. INV: And, how about the guy? I mean you could tell–you could see enough that you thought it was a guy.

173. EW1: I saw something black on the head whether…

MP 174. INV: Black on the head?

175. EW1: Whether, whether that was hair or a mat, I mean I don't know. I just–he was kinda crunched down like this

AL 176. INV: OK

177. EW1: When–when I saw him and I just saw him briefly. I–I mean I didn't see skin color or anything like that, it was so quick.

AL 178. INV: OK

Topic 5

OEQ 179. INV: Anything else you guys can think of?

180. EW1: I'm sorry no.

XL 181. INV: Oh, no that's OK. OK.

QC 182. INV: I'm gonna go ahead and stop this.

4/28 = 14% negligible effect on COR
COR rating = 0. Transcripts did
not indicate QQ asked during
interview.

END OF INTERVIEW

APPENDIX E

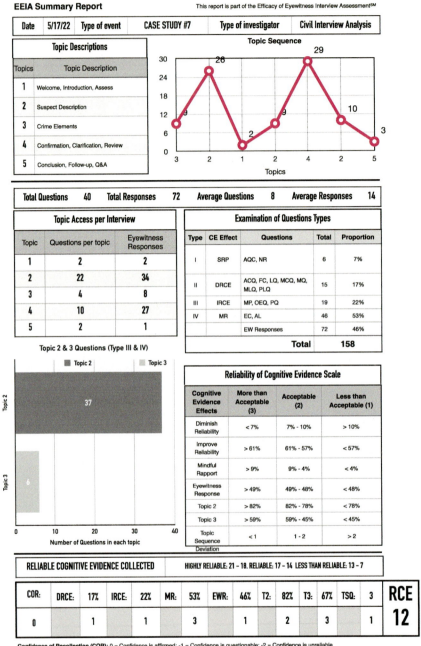

APPENDIX E

CASE STUDY #8

This section includes: a. Coded transcript, and b. EEIA summary report. For complete EEIA reports for case studies 6 through 15 go to www.mindfulinterviews.com/CaseStudies.

Each case study was evaluated and prepared for EEIA processing. Every attempt was made to standardize the evaluation and coding process for every case study. Any errors in coding, calculations, or assignment of RCE score, should be directed to the author. All of the transcripts were anonymized for instructional purposes, any resemblance to specific investigations is purely coincidental. The crime types and agencies are listed for informational purposes and to give the reader an idea of the variety of cases used in applying *The Mindful Interview Method*.

EYEWITNESS INTERVIEW ANALYSIS (EIA)
CONFIDENTIAL TRANSCRIPT REVIEW

Date of transcript review: May17, 2022

Crime type: Home invasion

Notes:

Topic 1

1. INV: Hi, I'm Gil. Go ahead and take a seat. Do you mind - we're gong to put our stuff away right now. Um so I guess something happened to you guys, right?

2. EWS - Yeah.

3. INV: Wait, what did you say?

4. EW: I said yes.

5. INV: Ok. I got it. Sorry. And this happened when?

6. EWS: A month ago.

7. INV: Ok, something like that. Ok, I'm the same way, trust me. Like when something happens, I won't know the exact day unless I look at the calendar or my phone, and right now I'm out of sorts because I just realized I don't have my IPhone with me - it's at home - so I'm lost right now. So anyway...

8. EW: (inaudible)

9. INV: So I'm Gil. Gil Zamora. I'm going to be helping out with a sketch of apparently some guys that you saw - this was a home invasion/robbery, something like that. Can you give me an idea of your confidence of what you remember. So, just answer this one question: if you saw this person again would you recognize him?

10. EW1: Yes.

11. EW2: If a saw a picture...

12. INV: If you saw this person again would you recognize him?

13. EW2: Yeah.

APPENDIX E

PQ   14. INV: Ok, that's great. Did you see the same person?

15. EW1: There was two guys.

16. EW2: I saw one guy more than the other guy but I would still recognize both.

OEQ   17. INV: So let's do this. We have Guy 1 and Guy 2. I'm going to say Suspect 1 and Suspect 2. That's usually the way the cops put it down so, we know there are two. So Suspect 1 - he's the guy that comes first. So who saw Suspect 1?

18. EW2: I did.

PQ   19. INV: Ok. Did you see Suspect 2?

20. EW1: Yes.

PQ   21. INV: Ok. Did you see Suspect 1?

22. EW1: Um vaguely but I really remember his face.

PQ   23. INV: Alright, did you see Suspect 2?

24. EW2: Yeah but again it was just passing so I probably wouldn't remember his face.

ARC   25. INV: OK, good. Well that's what we're going to do. We're going to - I'll interview you for Suspect 1, and I'll interview you for Suspect 2. Um the interview itself should take between 1/2 hour and 45 minutes. You're going to be out, you're going to be in. Once we're done, then I'll meet with him and you'll be out so you can relax. After we're done with both sketches, what I'd like to do is show you #1 and show you #2 and get your thumbs up.

26. EW2: Um I had a question about this because we already know the guy that set us up...

ARC   27. INV: That's fine. That's additional information.

28. EW2: We were asking the cops to hack his Facebook so we could see his face with friends because what if this gives us an idea of what the guys look like.

PQ   29. INV: You mean the sketch?

30. EW2: Yeah.

ARC   31. INV: Well here's the good thing: I am only interviewing you from your memory. I'm not going to show you pictures, nothing. So whatever you say, that's what it is.

32. EW2: Mhm.

ARC   33. INV: No issues. That's my business card. You can take one and I'll give one to Brian. And then you'll go out with the detective and he's going to sit you somewhere else and we'll see you back in a little bit, ok? Detective Goodman? Is he still here? Oh there he is. So he's going to wait while we conduct the interview with him. Ok, sounds good. (Door shuts). Right here if you don't mind.

ARC   34. So I'm going to sit like this and you'll be here. I don't want you distracted by anything else. So this is the way this goes. I'm going to ask you some general questions about the person's face. I'd like you to go ahead and answer to the best of your knowledge. Most people don't remember everything in great detail however a lot of folks tend to remember a lot of information especially when they're here and focused. You're going to have your eyes closed for about five minutes. That's going to help you to relax, to focus on the questions. It makes it a little easier to describe. After that I'm going to ask you to open your eyes. I'm going to ask you to tell me what happened and I'll show you the sketch. If we need to, we'll make some changes.

35. EW: Alright.

ARC   36. INV: I don't know anything about the case. I work with a lot of agencies around the world. I was contacted by this agency and I told them to give me the case number and that's it. So you might remember some things today that you didn't remember before. That's normal. You might not remember things today that you remembered before and that's ok. All I'm dealing with today is the person's face and in this case, we talked about Suspect 1. If you think about Suspect 2, you need to tell me otherwise I'll assume it's Suspect 1.

37. EW: Yeah.

ARC   38. INV: We're just dealing with your memory, so if you don't remember, just say, "Hey, Gil. I really don't remember that." I may prod you more. Don't take that as you don't know that - I

39. EW: No.

 40. INV: Alright. Close your eyes, give me a nice deep breath and let me know when you're nice and relaxed and we can begin.

Topic 2

41. EW: I'm ready.

 42. INV: Ok. First of all, what would you say is the race of this person?

43. EW: He was black.

 44. INV: Age range?

45. EW: I would say like 24-26.

 46. INV: Body build?

47. EW: Husky.

 48. INV: When you think about the shape of this guy's face, what shape does it look like?

49. EW: I would say like a pear. Like the top of his head does what a pear does.

 50. INV: Hm

51. EW: (inaudible)

 52. INV: Ok. That's good. Tell me about this hair. What is that like.

53. EW: Short and nappy.

 54. INV: Color?

55. EW: Black.

 56. INV: So what would you say about the length of the hair?

57. EW: Very short. One or maybe a two on the razors.

 58. INV: Mhm. What's the hairline like?
EW: Um I don't really remember that real well, but it goes right across. I don't know if it was that clean cut though.

 59. INV: Mhm. Tell me about his ears. What are they like?

60. EW: Um they really didn't stick out that much.

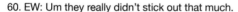 61. INV: Was he wearing any earrings?

62. EW: No, he was trying to keep a hood up and the hood was up like this almost at all times but his face was clear but you couldn't see his ears that well.

 63. INV: Ok. Any earrings?

64. EW: Not that I noticed.

APPENDIX E

OER 65. INV: Mhm. Tell me about his forehead. What was that like?

66. EW: Um it was kinda big, a little bit bigger than the average but it wasn't wrinkled. It was flat.

OEQ 67. INV: Mhm. Tell me about his nose. What was that like?

68. EW: He had a wide nose and it didn't stick out very far.

PQ 69. INV: It did not?

70. EW: It didn't. It was wide and flat.

OEQ 71. INV: (drawing) What about the nostrils. What are they like?

72. EW: Um they were flared but I don't know if that was him in the heat of the moment or if it was just normal.

AC 73. INV: Mhm

74. EW: but they were all super flared out in the struggle at least.

OEQ 75. INV: Mhm. Tell me about his ~~nose~~ mouth and his lips.

76. EW: Um let's see. He - they were kinda big but I don't really know.

PQ 77. INV: Mhm. And what do you mean by big?

78. EW: Um they came out kinda far like mine come out to here and I felt like his were here and …(inaudible).

PQ 79. INV: Ok. Anything distinctive about his mouth?

80. EW: Not particularly. I feel like it was too big for his chin. Like his chin - cuz his cheeks were kinda chubby so they kinda wrapped up and then his chin poked out like just this much.

OER 81. INV: Mhm. What was his attitude like?

82. EW: Um he was nervous, he was scared but he was aggressive but he definitely wasn't (inaudible) by any means. He was just on, it felt like.

PQ 83. INV: Hm. And this guy we're calling him Suspect 1, correct?

84. EW: Yup.

PQ 85. INV: And you felt he wasn't the leader?

86. EW: No, he wasn't the leader at all. He was the guy that knocked on the door and (inaudible) me.

OEQ 87. INV: Got it. Any facial hair on this guy?

88. EW: Ah scrappy like he hadn't shaved in two or three days ish but it wasn't think by any means, it was more patchy than anything.

PQ 89. INV: Hm and where was the patch?

90. EW: It was just kinda like, he had facial hair all the way up here but it wasn't - it was probably kinda like mine like it wasn't thick all the way through it was like kinda heavier

APPENDIX E

here and up here not so heavy and then it wasn't coming out all the way, you know what I mean?

91. INV: Mhm ok. And then tell me about the cheeks. I mean, excuse me, the chin.

92. EW: Chin was kind of small, um but I think it was just because his lips were a little bit big and his cheeks were husky or so his chin kind of just sank into his face a little bit but still stuck out. I feel like my chin sticks out but his didn't at all.

93. INV: His did not?

94. EW: His did not just like you could only see this much of his chin.

95. INV: Ok. And you said earlier that there might be some hair on it?

96. EW: yeah it was just kinda scruffy. Just like one or two days…

97. INV: Mhm. And then tell me about the cheeks.

98. EW: Um they were kinda like the fattest part of his face um.

99. INV: And what was that like?

100. EW: I don't want to say Fat Albert but just like wider, puffy almost like he was holding air but he wasn't.

101. INV: This guy, um, tall guy, short guy, medium guy?

102. EW: He was about my height.

103. INV: Mhm. Any scars or marks on his face?

104. EW: Not that I noticed really.

105. INV: What about the color of his skin?

106. EW: Um, if you noticed, Andre's a little bit darker than Andre, but not that much.
INV: Mhm. (drawing) Tell me about his neck.

107. EW: Um he had kinda a wide neck. It wasn't very long, it was kinda short um like his head almost sat on his shoulders a little bit.

108. INV: Mhm

109. EW: and uh it was wide - he was broader shouldered than me.

110. INV: And what is he wearing for clothing.

111. EW: Um he had like his hoodie jacket on and it like zipped up and he was trying to keep it up off his face but he wasn't focused on it.

112. INV: Color of this jacket?

113. EW: I want to say gray but it's not that clear. I wasn't really focused on his jacket.

114. INV: Mhm. (drawing) Tell me about his eyes.

115. EW: Um they were kinda squinty I guess. Not as wide-eyed but um. I want to say they were kinda narrow, just kinda smallish but I'm not entirely sure on that.

APPENDIX E

PQ 116.INV: Mhm. Eye color?

117.EW: I want to say brown but I'm not sure but brown sticks out for whatever reason.

AL 118.INV: Ok.

119.EW: I'm like a 4 out of 10.

PQ 120.INV: We could say dark though, right?

121.EW: Yeah.

PQ 122.INV: Is that good enough?

123.EW: Yeah, dark is fine.

OEQ 124.INV: Ok, tell me about eyebrows.

125.EW: They were kinda bushy.

AL 126.INV: mhm.

127.EW: They kinda, like his forehead was larger so his eyebrows match that but they were too big for his eyes.

FC 128.INV: Mhm did you see him during the day or at night?

129.EW: It was right after sunset so it was nighttime.

OEQ 130.INV: What was the lighting like?

131.EW: It was like 6:00 so it was dark around here and there was lighting in my house but other than that the lighting wasn't great.

FC 132.INV: Mhm so you saw him, would you say inside or outside?

133.EW: I opened the door and he was standing on the front porch so there was - my porch light was on but there wasn't any kind of directional light.

AL 134.INV: Mhm.

135.EW: There was a flood light right over his head and then I saw him in the living room but his back was to the light most of the time.

AL 136.INV: Mhm

137.EW: Not a coincidence.

PQ 138.INV: You don't think it was part of concealment?

139.EW: Yeah I don't think he was trying to do that but..

PQ 140.INV: It just happened that way.

141.EW: Yeah I was either up against the wall or on the floor so the light was behind him most of the time.

OEQ 142.INV: Did you ever see this guy before?

143.EW: No.

APPENDIX E

OEQ 144.INV: So what was his name?

145.EW: I don't know his name.

PQ 146.INV: Was there a name that they called him?

147.EW: No.

AL 148.INV: Ok.

149.EW: (inaudible)

OEQ 150.INV: How long would you say you saw this guy there?

151.EW: Um he was in the house for probably 20 minutes, give or take.

152.INV: (drawing)

153.EW: But I was face to face with him for the first 5-10 minutes. After that I was I was kinda rolled over on the carpet.

PQ 154.INV: Mhm did you see a weapon?

155.EW: Yeah they had a gun.

PQ 156.INV: Did this guy? Suspect 1?

157.EW: He didn't come in with any weapon that I saw. He was trying to act like he had a gun in his pocked but I thought if he had a gun in his pocket he would have had it out already so I don't think he actually had a gun...

AL 158.INV: Mhm

159.EW: But he had picked up my hammer.

MP 160.INV: You had a hammer out?

161.EW: Yeah. We were trying to install our screen door actually like earlier that week so we were - I was using it to try to get the door in. I left it on the TV stand.

AL 162.INV: Hmm

163.EW: (inaudible)

OEQ 164.INV: (drawing) So what would you say this guy's attitude was like?

165.EW: He was, I'm just going to say he was a goon but he was following orders more than anything as far as I could tell.

AL 166.INV: Mhm.

167.EW: He was expecting a pay day but he was not the leader by any means. Suspect 2 was the (inaudible) but they were both reporting back to someone else.

AL 168.INV: Hm.

169.EW: They were by no means the master minds.

FC 170.INV: Any scars or marks on this guy's face?
EW: No.

387

APPENDIX E

Topic 3

AQC 171.INV: Alright, you can open your eyes. Now what I want you to do is I want you to tell me what happened. I want you to tell me what you were doing just prior to running into this guy and I want you to take me through the incident up until police get involved.

172.EW: Um we were playing - me and Andre were both playing Starcraft II on our computers. We were together and then we got a knock on the door and that's not terribly unnatural because we just have people from school or whatever coming through a lot.

MP 173.INV: Mhm coming from school?

174.EW: Coming from school or just friends from class coming through. I opened the door and I didn't recognize them at first but I thought he could have been one of Andre's friends from Fairfield or something like that

AL 175.INV: Mhm

176.EW: So I was like "Who are you?" and that's when he stepped both feet inside the door and I said, "Hey how's it going, man? Like what's up?" and then I was kinda like, who are you? What's going on here? and I saw Suspect 2 running up the stairs trying to zip up his hoodie like over his face..

AL 177.INV: Mhm.

178.EW: (inaudible) large red flag and that's when I tried to push Suspect 1 out the door.

AL 179.INV: Mhm.

180.EW: But he was obviously pushing back and Suspect 2 pushed his way in through the door and at that point that's when I started to push him out and I yelled for Andre - like shit's about to happen.

PQ 181.INV: Where was Andre?

182.EW: Andre was in his room which is the first door on the left from the front room so he was pretty close.

AL 183.INV: Mhm.

184.EW: But he couldn't see what was going on so I called for him in a way that he would know that I needed some help.

AL 185.INV: Mhm.

186.EW: And so he kinda came running but the dude was already inside the house and tackled him as he was headed toward the doorway.

PQ 187.INV: Which suspect?

188.EW: Suspect 2 tackled him, so they were struggling on the bed fighting the whole time I was fighting the first guy.

AL 189.INV: Mhm.

190.EW: So pretty much right after the first guy ran in the other guy kinda grabbed me at hit me up against the wall.

APPENDIX E

191.INV: Mhm.

192.EW: And he was like, "Don't yell, don't say nothing. I don't want to hurt you."

193.INV: Mhm.

194.EW: That's when I started fighting back cuz I'm like, fuck this dude. (inaudible)

195.INV: Right.

196.EW: So I started fighting back and then in the struggle he picked up the hammer and hit me on the head a couple of times with it and we were continuing to struggle, grappling and like I was trying to get some hits in but I don't think I got anything good other than preventing him from doing more damage to me.

197.INV: Mhm.

198.EW: Um eventually I ended up on the floor, he was still hitting/kicking me a couple of times but I was able to grab the hammer and stop him but then he was using his fists, trying to get the hammer away from me.

199.INV: Mhm

200.EW: Um the whole time that was going on, the other dude pretty much beat Andre just where he wasn't fighting anymore and he stopped hitting Andre when he stopped fighting. They made Andre come out and take down the video cameras we had plugged in over my desk and stuff but they weren't actually working or anything, they were just decoys - scare tactics I guess.

201.INV: Mhm.

202.EW: Only because we had been robbed before but um so he made Andre take those down. Once Suspect 2 made Andre take them down he then zip tied Andrea and Suspect 1 at this point was emptying out Alex's bag and just looking for a stash.

203.INV: Who's Alex?

204.EW: Alex is the guy on the couch. He was kinda staying with us.

205.INV: Oh, there was a third guy.

206.EW: He wasn't there.

207.INV: Oh, got it.

208.EW: He wasn't there but he's the guy on the couch - he stays there. Um he was at work, though. Then these guys, um they were asking me where stuff was, where the money was. And we were like, "We don't have money."

209.INV: Mhm

210.EW: Like we have weed- it's on the desk.

211.INV: Mhm.

212.EW: If you're here for that, take it and go. And then they dragged me and Andre into Andre's room. Andre was still zip tied but they didn't bother to zip tie me only because I wasn't responding to them so I think they thought I was more hurt than I was and if they thought I wasn't going to argue so I just kinda like laid there and didn't respond to them

389

APPENDIX E

and tried to stay conscious. Andre and I were (inaudible) lost consciousness but I don't think I ever did.

213.INV: Mhm

214.EW: I just didn't respond for a few minutes because I didn't want them to know I was responsive.

215.INV: Right.

216.EW: Um then they continued to ransack the place for a little while looking for a stash of money. They called a third person on the phone who was then walking them through our house. Telling them where the valuable stuff should be.

217.INV: Oh really?

218.EW: Yeah. That's why we kinda know they weren't the master minds by any means. They were just goons so they were on speaker phone with this guy who's like, "Go check by the desk, go check the rooms, check under the beds." And it's like, "Look man, like, clearly you would have found it by now."

219.INV: And you could hear him?

220.EW: Yeah, I could't hear him that well but I knew he was on the phone and I kinda heard a voice but it wasn't - I could just hear he was on the phone.

221.INV: Mhm

222.EW: Um, Andre (inaudible) I and believed him.

223.INV: So what happened after that?

224.EW: After they kinda checked the whole place they were still talking on the phone with the dude and they said, "Pull around, we're all done. We're leaving." And so then the guy pulled around and they ran out the front door and they took off and they took off before Andre could get up and look out the window but he got up and locked the door.

225.INV: Who got up?

226.EW: Andre got up. I was still lying on the floor.

227.INV: Mhm

228.EW: Um I was still on the floor trying to catch my breath and make sure it was all actually over.

229.INV: Mhm.

230.EW: Um once Andre went to go get the knife, I kinda rolled over and I had blood all over my eyes so I couldn't really see anything at that time either but he handed me the knife so I could cut his zip ties off and then Andre kinda cleaned up and like himself a little. He got himself ready to do whatever was next and I got up and headed to the bathroom to see what I was looking like and my face wasn't looking too good and he was asking me if we needed to call an ambulance and I was like, um I really don't want to pay for an ambulance but I think I need to get to a hospital because I'm getting kinda dizzy here.

231.INV: Mhm

APPENDIX E

232.EW: And so he said he would just call our friend who lives like two houses down and he came (inaudible) and I got my stitches, I got my CT scan and it checked out fine.

233.INV: MHm

234.EW: But um they called the Oakland police there to respond to the incident and Oakland (inaudible) wasn't their jurisdiction and they never showed up. They didn't say that, they just didn't show up so the next morning after getting back from the ER and everything we're like, "Aren't the cops supposed to be showing up?" So we called PPT and was like, "Hey so, (inaudible)." And so the Emeryville came out and they checked us out and all that kinda stuff.

235.INV: Did they show you any pictures of possible suspects?

236.EW: No, at the time we were um still really unsure who it was.

237.INV: Mhm

238.EW: We were going over suspects in our head and we gave them who we thought it might be at the time.

239.INV: Names?

240.EW: We gave him the name of one person who we thought it could have been, like the mastermind of it because like he was kinda ghetto when he talked around me before so we said it could have been this guy because had talked about doing this kind of thing before and we kinda know him as a (inaudible) guy but he - we still thought he was cool um. Later like I didn't realize it but I had like a friend in my class who asked for phone numbers for anyone we thought could be involved so we gave him like this guy's phone number and this other guy, Hector, called the next day also to see if we were ok but we hadn't told anybody about it so it was kinda, it was weird. So we gave him Hector's number and one other guy's phone number.

241.INV: It was weird that he knew something had happened?

242.EW: He never said something had happened but he called to check up on us and like, "Hey, how's it going? Are you, you know, how's things? Is B around? Is B ok?" And it was like, we never said anything about like yeah. So that was kinda a big red flag in our head cuz we were still just trying to recover before we told anyone what happened and then you know he called to see what was up but he never calls Andre so that was just a big red flag in our head.

243.INV: And you gave that information?

244.EW: I gave that information to a friend of mine in class who was like, "Do you know any of their phone numbers?" And so then he came back with me the next day and he said he did some like random searches on their phone numbers and stuff like that and he said our names came up on Hector's phone, both of our names came up in Hector's phone at least seven times or something like that, each.

245.INV: Hm

246.EW: Along with like "gun" and "rob" and a bunch of other key words that he ran.

247.INV: Oh, really?

248.EW: Yeah, the other guys didn't pop up with us at all, like weed popped up but that wasn't anything conclusive.

APPENDIX E

249.INV: Mhm

250.EW: ….didn't show up at all or anything like that though.

251.INV: And what did you do with that information?

252.EW: We took what we could and we gave it to the cops and we just said, "We don't think it's this guy anymore. Hector's now the guy we think set us up because not only is he acting weird but um we didn't ask him to do it but he looked at all the text records and stuff like that and random key work searches and found that stuff. But when we told him we wanted (inaudible) he kinda got scared. The guy from my class, the hacker guy or whatever,

253.INV: What's his name?

254.EW: Um I really don't want to give his name.

255.INV: Oh ok.

256.EW: Out of respect for him or whatever but…

257.INV: But he helped you out.

258.EW: He helped me out kind of whenever (inaudible) he kinda backed down a little bit and what I'm doing is illegal…

259.INV: Oh.

260.EW: So I really don't want him to come up on any kind of radar and so he kinda said, "Well if you could give us like a (inaudible) version that still says what's what without any kind of information that leads to you, we'd appreciate it." So we got that and sent that over to the cops.

261.INV: Via email or on paper?

262.EW: Um I think we just emailed him what we got via email.

263.INV: So one of the detectives?

264.EW: Yeah, we forwarded the email.

265.INV: And how long ago was that?

266.EW: Um the text message stuff was probably a month ago.

267.INV: Mhm.

268.EW: Could be a little bit less.

269.INV: Alright and um it seem like you guys were doing a little bit of sleuthing, right? Kinda looking around? So Andre said something about Facebook or something. Did you guys start looking for somebody?

270.EW: We were, we kinda like once Hector kinda came up with a suspect in our heads like it kinda, Andre says that the phone call clicked it in his mind that the voice was the voice of the phone. When Hector called the next day, he said that's when he recognized it and so from that point we kind of like starting looking into Hector a little bit just like as much as we could, just looked him up on Facebook to see if he had any new friends that would jog our memory, you know just spark a recognition in our head.

APPENDIX E

AL 271.INV: And?

272.EW: All of his friends are hidden unless you're a mutual friend.

AL 273.INV: Got it.

274.EW: So we couldn't see anything.

AL 275.INV: Ok.

276.EW: That's why he's hot on the police to hack his Facebook for us real quick. I don't know, I'm not as optimistic about his Facebook as he he is.

PQ 277.INV: Andre, you mean?

278.EW: Yeah Andre thinks that Facebook could crack the case and I'm kinda like, I don't know.

Topic 4

AQC 279.INV: OK. Alright, I'm going to show you the sketch. When you look at the sketch, I don't want you to tell me whether or not it like him just him. Ok, not just yet. What I want you to do is look at the sketch, see what I've been doing. After you look at it for a few seconds, we're going to go over the same questions again, but this time you're going to be looking at the sketch. As I ask you about each feature I want you to tell me whether we're in the ballpark or whether you want me to make some changes.

280.EW: Ok.

AQC 281.INV: We're never going to be exact, but we want to be very, very close so when you look at it, it helps you to remember. Alright?

282.EW: Mhm.

AQC 283.INV: (shows sketch) This is what I have so far.

OEQ 284.First of all, just the shape of the face. How's the shape of the face?

285.EW: It's pretty good.

AL 286.INV: Ok.

287.EW: I would just kind of, not thin it out, but narrower I guess.

PQ 288.INV: In the cheek area?
EW: Just kinda, his cheeks are good as far as his head goes but I think the head in general is just a little bit tighter.

PQ 289.INV: Thinner?

290.EW: Yeah.

PQ 291.INV: Ok. So bring it in a little more?
EW: Just a little more.

PQ 292.INV: Ok. I'm going to do a little something here and see if that helps. Anything like this ever happen before?

293.EW: Um my apartment had been robbed but I wasn't home. My roommate was home.

APPENDIX E

PQ 294.INV: How long ago was that?

295.EW: That was a year ago or something.

PQ 296.INV: Out here?

297.EW: Yeah.

PQ 298.INV: How's that feel?

299.EW: Yeah, that's better.

OEQ 300.INV: Ok. The hair on his head?

301.EW: Hair is good. I feel like it came out a little more.

PQ 302.INV: Bring it in? Ok, very good.

303.EW: And then the top, I feel like it arched down. Like it wasn't really receding but just a little bit. Not as receded in the middle.

AL 304.INV: Ok.

305.EW: Just like it hadn't been edged up lately at all.

OEQ 306.INV: (drawing) How's that feel?

307.EW: Yeah.

OEQ 308.INV: Ok, the ears on his head?
EW: Ears are good. I don't remember much about his ears but those look good.

309.INV: Mhm. The nose?

310.EW: Yeah, nose I feel like could be a little less wide but not by much.

PQ 311.INV: The nostrils you're talking about? Ok, less?

312.EW: Yeah, just a little less.

OEQ 313.INV: (drawing) How's that?

314.EW: It's ok.

OEQ 315.INV: Ok, the mouth and lips?

316.EW: Um that's all good.

PQ 317.INV: Mhm, see the little mustache I gave him? Is that ok.

318.EW: Yeah it kinda goes all the way over, I feel like.

AL 319.INV: I can add it.

320.EW: But it was just about that thickness, just not very much.

AL 321.INV: Ok.

322.EW: I wouldn't even call it a mustache, it's if you would call what I have a mustache, (laughs).

APPENDIX E

AQC 323.INV: Ok. He's been growing that for years. Kinda like that.

324.EW: Yeah kinda like the same thing - it kinda came back on his cheeks.

AQC 325.INV: OK, I'm going to kinda of give a hint of stuff.

326.EW: Like he was trying to grow one but weak.

AQC 327.INV: Ok. It may look a little more here only because the police are going to make copies and I want the guys on the streets and in the cars to remember hey there's something there so don't give up. Is that alright?

328.EW: Yeah.

OEQ 329.INV: The lips, the mouth?

330.EW: Um the lips and mouth look good to me.

OEQ 331.INV: Mhm. Chin and cheeks?

332.EW: Those are good.

OEQ 333.INV: Mhm, and then the eyes?

334.EW: Eyes could be a little bit less just like the bottom of the eyes can come down a little more I feel like.

PQ 335.INV: So you want the eyes more open?

336.EW: Yeah, just a little bit.

OEQ 337.INV: Ok. How's the look? How does that look for you?

338.EW: It's ok.

339.INV: (drawing)

340.EW: Not quite that squinty.

OEQ 341.INV: Ok. So what were these guys looking for?

342.EW: A stash of money.

AC 343.INV: Mhm.

344.EW: Um

PQ 345.INV: You guys have a lot of money or something?

346.EW: No, um we used to grow semi-moderate scale, I would say.

PQ 347.INV: For family and friends or what, just you guys?

348.EW: Mostly just us and students with their cards but we couldn't let them know we had enough if they needed some, that type thing. And Hector being in Andre's class would be one of them, and so um I didn't think he knew we were still doing it but he knew we were at least one point in time and so for whatever reason he felt like we had a bunch of money stashed in our house somewhere and it was like we don't keep money like that in the house.

APPENDIX E

OEQ 349.INV: How does that feel?

350.EW: Yeah, much better.

OEQ 351.INV: How about his age? How are we doing on his age?

352.EW: Um he looks just a little bit older.

PQ 353.INV: Mhm, how old does this guy look?

354.EW: He looks 26-28 and it's still about right. I feel maybe he looked a little more immature.

OEQ 355.INV: Mhm, and what about the eyebrows?

356.EW: They could be a little more bushy. They could bush up a little more.

PQ 357.INV: Hm really?

358.EW: They were like pretty bushy.

PQ 359.INV: Ok. So did the police get the hammer?

360.EW: No. (inaudible)

PQ 361.INV: Who?

362.EW: The guys.

FC 363.INV: As in these guys or the police?

364.EW: No, the suspects.

AQC 365.INV: Oh, they took the hammer. Oh, ok. I'm sorry I thought the hammer was there.

366.EW: No, we were looking for the hammer but it never turned up.

PQ 367.INV: So when you said you guys were playing the game early on, are you playing the game together in the same room?

368.EW: Not in the same room, but in the same game so we were each on our own computers. Andre was in him room, my desk was in the living room at the time.

PQ 369.INV: And what was that game?

370.EW: Starcraft II. We were actually playing an arcade game using Starcraft II platform. They just have a build-your-own-game type thing in there so you can use all their units with image and all that kinda stuff but you can set your own rules so we were playing a tug-of-war game, I think.

PQ 371.INV: So, when Suspect 1 knocks at the door, do you have to pause or something?

372.EW: Yeah. Andre was paying attention to the game while I was getting the door. We didn't pause but I stopped.

PQ 373.INV: And so you say they eventually put you in the same room. And what room was that?

374.EW: Andre's room.

NR 375.INV: And you said when you saw him, he was tied?

APPENDIX E

376.EW: Yeah. I was still in the living room. I heard them zip-tying Andrea and I heard them talk about zip-tying me but then they just dragged me into the room then put him on the floor next to me. I knew I was bleeding pretty bad and I was letting them get scared by that cuz I mean blood is scary.

PQ 377.INV: Mhm, did you know they were concerned about it?

378.EW: They didn't say anything but I could just tell by the way the guy didn't want to touch me, he didn't drag me by my arms or legs or anything. He grabbed me by the shirt and the way they were addressing me from that point on, they didn't want to look at me or touch me or think about me because I think they thought I was dead or dying so they just didn't want to worry about that right now.

PQ 379.INV: How big was this hammer?

380.EW: Probably not a standard weight, like a, it was still supposed to be like a regular hammer but it was in like a cheap tool set so it was lighter like aluminum not heavy like iron ones.

OEQ 381.INV: So what did they end up getting?

382.EW: They grabbed some weed mostly. They grabbed a couple hundred dollars in cash that I had in my room but that's about it.

PQ 383.INV: Where'd they find that?

384.EW: The cash?

AL 385.INV: Mhm.

386.EW: They just went through my dresser and I had it in my (inaudible).

OEQ 387.INV: And how did they leave?

388.EW: They were still on speaker phone with the guy, still kinda looking for stuff. And they said they were all done looking, pull around, and as soon as the guy pulled around they ran out the door.

PQ 389.INV: Did they leave anything behind?

390.EW: They left a loaded clip but we didn't even see it until the next day when the cops showed up. They spotted it.

PR 391.INV: In your place? And they took it?

392.EW: yeah the cops took it. But our house was ransacked and dirty. We honestly didn't try to clean it so we didn't even notice the loaded clip amongst the clutter.

FC 393.INV: But it's usually clean, or pretty much?

394.EW: I try to keep it clean but with three people living in there, it doesn't stay as clean as I like it.

PR 395.INV: So how about the other guy on the couch?

396.EW: He was just a work. They were asking about him, actually. The robbers were asking where he was.

PQ 397.INV: Asking by name?

397

APPENDIX E

398.EW: They didn't, I don't think they knew his name, they were asking where the other guy was. Where's the other guy?

AL 399.INV: Hm.

400.EW: There's a third guy - where is he?

PQ 401.INV: How long has he been there?

402.EW: Two months maybe. Three months.

AL 403.INV: Mhm.

404.EW: He actually lived down here like a year or two ago and then his parents moved to Washington and he wanted to stay and he was 18 but they kinda said you have to come with us, so he went with them but then right before he moved down here, he was like getting kicked out of his house up there and it was, (inaudible) and he actually wants to do what Andre's doing for school and stuff like that so we said if you want to sleep on the couch, we don't mind if you want to come down here and so he was on the train the next week.

Topic 5

AQC 405.INV: Alright I'm going to show you the sketch one more time, when you look at it I want you to ask yourself does it remind me of him. If there's anything else that you want me to change or adjust, just let me know and I will take care of it. Alright?

406.EW: It looks good.

PQ 407.INV: In the ballpark?

408.EW: Yeah.

PQ 409.INV: See the hoodie, the way I put it. You said it was grey, so I kind of left it lighter. Does that remind you of him?

410.EW: Yeah. The only thing I could say is that the hoodie kinda went up - it was kinda like this.

AQC 411.INV: Yeah, I'll leave it down there so everybody won't get mistaken about the hair.

EC 412.Alright very good. So what did the doctor say?

413.EW: No brain damage. I had 10 stitches on my face.

MO 414.INV: On your face?

415.EW: Yeah, it's all up here, right there. You see the scar I have here and this one over here.

AL 416.INV: Wow.

417.EW: Yeah, I wasn't looking too great.

PQ 418.INV: So you didn't miss any class?

419.EW: I did. I missed the following day - I missed one class and then I went the day after that but I told my teacher I was like, I'm on painkillers, I'm not going to turn in any work today. I'm here to take notes. So I felt (inaudible) but honestly I missed more days trying to keep my mother from freaking out too much. I missed like one or two days of myself just resting and then I missed two or three days just helping my mom out.

420.INV: So, how's the screen door?

421.EW: We put it up.

422.INV: What kind of screen door was it?

423.EW: Just a metal screen door.

424.INV: Do other people have them around there?

425.EW: Yeah.

426.INV: Why didn't the landlord put it up?

427.EW: He paid for it, we just had to put it up.

428.INV: So what are the initials to your name?

429.EW: E S

430.INV: Ok, do you happen to know the case number on this?

431.EW: No.

432.INV: That's fine. And this happened when? The date?

433.EW: The 5th of December.

434.INV: OK. I'll walk you out. It was nice meeting you.

435.EW: It was nice meeting you too.

END OF INTERVIEW

APPENDIX E

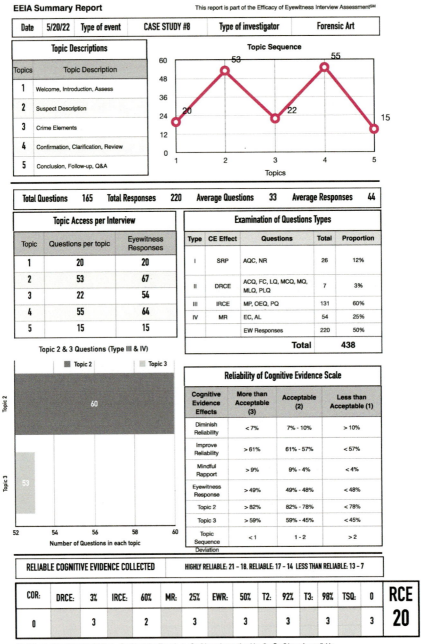

400

APPENDIX E

CASE STUDY #9

This section includes: a. Coded transcript, and b. EEIA summary report. For complete EEIA reports for case studies 6 through 15 go to www.mindfulinterviews.com/CaseStudies.

Each case study was evaluated and prepared for EEIA processing. Every attempt was made to standardize the evaluation and coding process for every case study. Any errors in coding, calculations, or assignment of RCE score, should be directed to the author. All of the transcripts were anonymized for instructional purposes, any resemblance to specific investigations is purely coincidental. The crime types and agencies are listed for informational purposes and to give the reader an idea of the variety of cases used in applying *The Mindful Interview Method*.

EYEWITNESS INTERVIEW ANALYSIS (EIA)
CONFIDENTIAL TRANSCRIPT REVIEW

Date of transcript review: May17, 2022

Crime type: Robbery

Notes:

Topic 1

1. INV: The way this goes is I'm gonna ask you some general questions about a person's face. I'd like you to go ahead and answer to the best of your knowledge. Most people don't remember everything in great detail however a lot of folks (EW: Especially days after)_yeah, so most people tend to remember a lot of information especially when they're here and their focused on the questions.

2. INV: First of all do you know why you're here?

3. EW: Yes I want to try to describe the guy who came in and tried to rob the place?

4. INV: Good, and how's your memory about that?

5. EW: I remember him I can't remember exact details. He's probably around like forties forty five?

6. INV: If you some again would you recognize him?

7. EW: Oh yeah .

8. INV: Good. That's all I need. So the way this works is I'm gonna ask you some questions. The way that I ask you the questions–you're gonna have your eyes closed for about five minutes that's a help you to kind of relax kinda get into it here stay here and then–so you're are nice and present and then after I ask you the questions I'm asking open your eyes and I'm going to show you the sketch and if we need to make some changes. All right?

9. EW: OK.

APPENDIX E

OEQ 10. INV: Do you have any questions?

11. EW: Uhm, not that I know of. So if there's something that I'm kind of fuzzy on like should I still like if you say if you have facial hair or not, uhm, I kind of remember him with facial hair, like shruggy at the same time like I can also picture him like yeah I can't picture him without facial hair so I guess he did see.

AQC 12. INV: You see already answered you question.

13. EW: Yeah.

AQC 14. INV: So, so here's basically your role, when I ask you a question whatever comes your mind just tell me what it is.

15. EW: Okay

AQC 16. INV: If one of the things is "I don't remember" then you tell me you don't remember. That's it.

17. EW: Okay

AQC 18. INV: If I need more information I may ask you another question to try to get something out of you, but if we have nothing–we have nothing don't worry about it okay?

19. EW: OK, yeah I'm not gonna worry.

AQC 20. INV: You're fine all right? So take a deep breath and close your eyes and we'll begin

Topic 2

OER 21. INV: First of all what is the race of this person?

22. EW: He was African American

AL 23. INV: Mhm

OEQ 24. INV: Age range?

25. EW: Forty to forty five?

OEQ 26. INV: Body build

27. EW: He was tall maybe six feet, maybe six-two would be kind of reaching it. He wasn't big he was kind of scrawny, um, his face wasn't slim though it wasn't like he was super skinny

OER 28. INV: Okay, tell me about the shape of the face, what is that like?

29. EW: It wasn't round, but it didn't have a sharp point and his chin he kind of had like above was round and then it kind of just came together towards the bottom

PQ 30. INV: So it was king of round and what?

31. EW: Like cheekbones down it kind of narrowed down to like his chin so it kind of…

AL 32. INV: Mmhm

OER 33. INV: Tell me about his hair, what was that like?

34. EW: He had short hair uhm like maybe an inch or even less than an inch on top of his head

AL 35. INV: Mhm

PQ 36. INV: What was the color of his hair?

37. EW: It was dark maybe black

402

APPENDIX E

AL 38. INV: Mhm

39. EW: I think he had a little bit of a gray in it maybe, but not too noticeable

PR 40. INV: What was the textured of the hair like?

41. EW: Uhm, it was all one level it seemed kind of like African American hair length like curly, but short

AL 42. INV: Mhm

PR 43. INV: Tell me about his hairline, what is that like?

44. EW: Uhm, maybe three your four fingers above his eyebrows, uhm, I wasn't too far back

45. EW: He had brown eyes

OEQ 46. INV: Tell me about his ears, what were they like?

47. EW: They were medium like they weren't too big t

PR 48. INV: Was he wearing any earrings?

49. EW; No

OEQ 50. INV: Tell me about his nose, what was that like?

51. EW: Uhm, he kind of had like a medium size knows his nostrils were from out kind of big–just like a regular person's nose it didn't have any piercings on it, sorry that's all

AL 52. INV: No that's fine

OER 53. INV: Tell me about his mouth and his lips?

54. EW: I have a feeling it was kind of hard to see his upper lip just maybe because he had hair

AL 55. INV: Mhm

56. EW: Uhm, they weren't pink pink but they had a little bit of pink in them–he kind of had a big mouth

OEQ 57. INV: What was his attitude like?

58. EW: He first came on friendly and like we had a conversation with me he didn't seem like he was someone that I needed to look out for

AL 59. INV: Mhm

60. EW: He acted like he was gonna buy some shoes and said that he had a wife. I do remember a ring, I think it was on his pinky finger

OEQ 61. INV: Tell me about his chin

62. EW: it wasn't a point but it was kind of like round, kind of like my face kind of round out the bottom I believe he had a little bit of a like scruff on his face

AL 63. INV: Mhm

APPENDIX E

64. EW: Uhm, and I believe that was dark and maybe had a little bit of gray in it

65. EW: I don't remember seeing like his cheek bones–not that much maybe only a little bit of hair

83. EW: I think the jacket was like gray, like not too dark of a gray but uhm and the shirt was just a regular you black t-shirt you can buy at Target or Walmart it wasn't expensive or anything, but just like something you can sleep in

FC

84. INV: So any scars or marks on his face?

85. EW: No, he didn't have any like that

OEQ

86. INV: Tell me about his eyes, what are they like?

87. EW: Kind of hard to say they weren't round but they weren't like–not to be racist or anything, like they weren't like Asian eyes they didn't have a long there were kind of normal you know. I didn't really pay much attention to him because there are a lot of people in the store but he waited outside after he looked at some shoes and I thought that was kind of weird. Uhm and when he went outside he said that he was gonna wait for wife outside, but then he came back in kind–kind of antsy. He said that his wife needed to hurry up and that she was taking too long and that's when he went around and told me to come with him. At that point I was kind of confused and I looked at him and he told me to go to the back because he thought that we had a safe back there.

88. EW: He had big hands–I remember he had big hands.

OEQ

89. INV: What about his eyebrows?

90. EW: They were medium they weren't too thick, uhm but they also weren't like cleanly done

OEQ

91. INV: How would you describe the look in his eyes

92. EW: When he first came in he seemed calm and settled. Once he left outside and waited for a while but when he came back in he was more alert, uhm he was looking around to see if–I think if there was anything anyone in the lanes…

MP

93. INV: In the lanes?

94. EW: Yeah, shoe lanes, but he tried–he tried not to look at me and he kept wanting so follow me and he didn't want to be next to me.

OEQ

95. INV: And the color of his eyes?

96. EW: I believe they were brown, yeah

PQ

97. INV: Any other distinguishing marks or characteristics about his face?

98. EW: Not that I can remember it was just so off guard you know, uhm, I see a lot of African American people…uhm like if they kind of look like him like I have to stare at them to make sure it's not him and notice this…

PR

99. INV: Oh, since the incident?

100. EW: Yeah and I notice that he whenever I look at tan African man and they're clean shaven I don't feel as scared, but when I see someone with a little bit of scrug I start freaking out and...

101. EW He sounded prepared he sounded like he knew–he knew what he was doing–he knew, he was shocked when I turned around and I reached for him

Topic 3

102. INV: Alright, you can open your eyes. Now what I want you to do, Is I want you to tell me what happened–I know you started to tell me a little bit but really focus on what you were doing before you saw this guy, and then take me through the incident up until police get involved.

103. EW: Okay, so I–me and my coworker we were both running late to work and I have a three year old so I had to drop him off at school before I had to work and so she was also running late and she got there before me to open up the store, and by the time that I walked in we already had a couple customers. Uhm, I don't know if you've ever been into that store but ...

PQ 104. INV: What's the store?

105. EW: It's Payless...

PQ 106. INV: Okay, Shoe Source?

107. EW: Yeah right here in Mountain View near Walmart. I was cleaning shoes which means I'm unpacking them from the shoe box and taking out the stuffing and putting security tags on them. And that was in the corner of the store and that's what I usually do since I'm kind of quick at it. And people keep walking in and I greet them–hi welcome in, hi hello, and he walks in and I say hi welcome in and he says oh hey my wife told me to come over she's over at Walmart shopping and she saw that you guys were having a sale and told me to come over and pick out some shoes. I say okay what size are you? Oh nine and a half and OK well, if you can come over here and these are the shoes we have. He asked do you have any steel point toe shoes. I said the only steel point toe shoes we have are this one and then we have this one, but it looks like these are the only two we have.

108. EW: Oh I'm kinda liking–he responded okay I'm kinda liking these ones right here and then he pushed on top of like the toe to make sure that they were steel and he said that feels like it's steel all right. Yeah well if you have anymore questions let me know. So walk over to my corner again it's in the same lane like right next to like in the same isle I guess... (INV: OK)

 109. INV: So same lane

110. EW: Yeah but it's like the corner in the store I was right here and like this was the open like this was all open to the front lines anyone can see and he was here like in the shoe lane and then there were shoe lanes here, and so I had my back to him almost the whole time so I just didn't think much of it (INV: Right) when he left... he said he was going wait outside

APPENDIX E

MP 111. INV: He told you?

112. EW: Yeah he's like oh I think I'm gonna wait outside for my wife until she gets here he and I thought that that was kind of weird because I mean who would wait outside when we have chairs you can sit on you can look at other shoes, uhm you know there was a lot of things there that he could have done except waiting outside so I thought that that was kind of weird and I went back to see if he stole the shoes because I thought that he had.

PQ 113. INV: Oh, you thought that?

114. EW: Yeah and I looked at the box I saw that it was empty and then I realized that he just didn't put them back in the box and he just put them in the wrong place

PQ 115. INV: Oh, you saw them

116. EW: Yeah and uhm and so I just I think I left them there wherever he put them as long as I just saw them there that was fine uhm and then I went back to continue in that corner and my coworker came over to me because she was putting the shoes away and where they belong on the shelf

PQ 117. INV: It's just you two?

118. EW: Yes and she came over to me and we were just talking and there's a window that I'm facing but on the window there's signs because they're going out of business and she noticed him and she like she made a face like what and she's like oh I don't know just someone just standing out there and I tried to look but uhm if I looked even more I would have knocked things over I don't look around the signs, uhm but I couldn't see him I was like oh yeah he said he was gonna wait for his wife or something

PQ 119. INV: So you assumed it was the same guy?

120. EW: Yes

AL 121. INV: Okay

122. EW: And uhm she was like oh that's weird and I was like yeah I don't know and we continued I continued working and we continued talking because she wanted to order some breakfast because she was hungry and so…customers left and customers came and he was still outside and a guy came to deliver the food she did Door Dash and so I had she got me a Saibo so I had that by my shoes and I have yet eaten it and she hasn't yet eaten hers because she wouldn't she wanted to finish putting away a cart of shoes before she does that and so she was in the eight and half nine women's section and it was just me and her in the store and he came in he said this woman is taking for ever and she needs to hurry up and I kind of didn't much pay attention to him…since I have a three year old I know what they do to try to get attention so I know it's best to not really ignore them but just like I kind of chuckled to myself

most yeah I don't really know what to say to you about that uhm...and he went as if he was going to the men's section again but since I'm right in that lane he went around where we have our socks and basically I was cornered because there was a wall there was the shoes that I was cleaning and here was where we kept our socks, so I was in the middle of that and he... uhm he was like where we have our sandals and socks and he says come with me come to the back and let's go open the safe

123. INV: He said it like that?

124. EW: Yeah like come with me and I was confused at first and I turned and I vaguely looked at him but I saw his hand out he had the gun and I kinda stammered I didn't really know what to say you know I kind of freaked out and so I was just so uhm okay and I started kind of walking towards the back. Uhm and once we kind of got to where I showed him his shoes I turned around he was holding the gun in his right hand so that makes me think that he was a righty

125. INV: Mmhm

126. EW: And he was holding the gun in his right hand and since I had brace on I'm not very mobile with it and so I tried to grab him with my left hand but I kind of got his jacket and he pulled away and that's when he hit me in the head once really hard and I like put my hands up in the air like trying to like protect myself, and then he hit me again and that's the second time that's when I yelled for my co-worker and uhm he left he just walked away they did't run he didn't do anything he didn't touch her he walked by her and walks towards Walmart.

127. EW: And I didn't realize that I was bleeding until like I was shaking she said call the cops and so I pulled out my phone I dialed 9-1-1 and I was on the phone with them as hi someone tried to rob this place he had a gun and he hit me on the head and dispatch said okay like we someone on the way stay on the phone with me...so I stayed on the phone but when I brought my phone down from my ear to look at it to put it on speaker there was just blood everywhere on my phone that's how I found out that I was bleeding, and by then I was freaking out I was shaking I felt instantly like cold and then....uh my husband he called the store cause I had texted him that's why I put him on speaker so I could tell him like Hey this happened

128. INV: Oh, you were telling them what was happening

129. EW: No I just texted him like Hey someone tried to rob the place like he had a gun and he hit me in my head and that's all that I told him I was just trying to figure everything out and the cops were there pretty soon...one of the officers says that he was driving by like a minute ago and that if he had driven slower or the timing like he would have been there so to me it kind of made it seem like he kind of felt guilty or it was his fault

130. INV: The police officer?

APPENDIX E

131. EW: Yeah that like he just had missed him, uhm, we didn't have any security cameras the officers are asking up cameras and what had happened and I explained to them the story and I show them the shoes that he had and they took the shoes the EMT came they treated my wounds and check my vitals uhm…there is just like a lot of officers in the parking lot there was at Walmart there were offices all outside they did bring someone in handcuffs an African American guy he and they told me that they picked him up time but it could not be the guy don't think that just because they have him it means it's him and yeah I definitely don't want to put the wrong person in and my coworker was watching like looking at him off the window and I believe the EMT someone told me that I should go also check and

MP 132. INV: Check what?

133. EW: To see if it was the guy

AZ 134. INV: Oh I see

135. EW: Yeah and so as I walked over the officer that was with my coworker told me that it was only one at a time and I was like okay, okay, sorry and I kind of stepped away, uhm…and then she gave them like whatever she thought and then I went up and instantly I said no that's not him and I noticed once they turned around I saw that he was in handcuffs I saw that there was a ring on his finger and that's what made me remember that the guy had a ring on his finger on his left hand…yes…

PQ 136. INV: And this guy had a ring…also…which hand?

137. EW: Yes, I couldn't really tell if his hands were crossed or…

PQ 138. INV: But the ring triggered your memory about him

139. EW: Yeah

140. INV: And then what happened?

141. EW: The EMT told me to sit down…different officers came in to ask me the same question that another officer asked me. I did give them the details immediately about the ring right when I saw it, then I got sat on the stretcher…and they rolled me into the parking lot that that's when I saw that a cop car was down at Walmart, and then they took me away to El Camino Hospital.

OEQ 142. INV: Has anything like this ever happened to you before?

143. EW: No nothing like this

OEQ 144. INV: And have you seen any pictures of possible suspects since then?

145. EW: No. And I I would like to just because I feel like it would help like I think that I would be able to identify him by a picture cause like I hear his voice and I feel him next to me and…it was just like like what he was hitting me I just felt like he was just towering over me

APPENDIX E

AL 146. INV: Oh really?

147. EW: Yeah and that's what made me saved me I'm guessing he's like six feet…not just because the towering as he held himself when he walked in he was pretty tall

EC 148. INV: Well, I'm glad you're here able to tell me what happened

149. EW: Me too…

EC 150. INV: How's your baby?

151. EW: He's good

EC 152. INV: And your husband? How is he dealing with all this?

153. EW: He doesn't want me to work there anymore and so is the co-worker that was there during the incident she also doesn't want to work there anymore. This is the second time within a month that we have been robbed

PQ 154. INV: But you weren't there for that other time?

155. EW: Yeah I wasn't there for the first but I don't think that they had a weapon that time and they actually took stuff that this guy didn't even take anything

Topic 4

AQC 156. INV: All right I'm gonna show you the sketch when you look at the sketch I don't need you to tell me whether it looks like him or not not just yet. What I want you to do is just look at the sketch to see what I've been doing. After you look at it for a few seconds I'm gonna ask you the same questions I asked you before, but this time you'll be looking at the sketch. As I ask you about each feature I want you to tell me whether we're in the ballpark or whether you want me to make some changes. We're never going to be exact because your memory isn't exact

157. EW: Yeah I know…

AQC 158. INV: But we want to be close enough so that when you look at it it helps you to remember what this guy looks like all right?

159. INV: This is what I have so far…(showing the sketch for the first time)

OER 160. INV: First of all just the shape of the face how's the shape of the face?

161. EW: Uhm, the shape is okay

OER 162. INV: The hair on his head, how does the feel?

163. EW: It's too tall, it wasn't that long

AQC 164. INV: So do you see the different lengths I have do you want me bring it down to something like this?

APPENDIX E

PQ 165. EW: Yeah and he didn't have that big of a forehead.

PQ 166. INV: okay so I can bring it down?

167. EW: Yes

FC 168. INV: Mmhm a little? A lot, or?

169. EW: Uhm a little yeah…

AQC 170. INV: Let me bring that down first before I cut off the hair at the top okay?

PQ 171. INV: So that's what I'm gonna do. You see that?

172. EW: Yeah…

PQ 173. INV: Is that better? It made my heart kind of… *EW*

AQC 174. EW: Good, I mean he's not here but this is good…

OEQ 175. INV: So what did he hit you with?

176. EW: The bottom of his gun

AL 177. INV: Oh

PQ 178. INV: Did you lose consciousness and all?

179. EW: No, but I felt like if he had hit me a couple more times like two or three more times that would…I probably would of either blacked out or fell to the ground

OEQ 180. INV: How does that feel–the hair?

181. EW: Yeah

OEQ 182. INV: All right the ears I gave him?

183. EW: Yes the ears are okay

OEQ 184. INV: The nose?

185. EW: Yes the nose is good too

OEQ 186. INV: What about the scruffiness on his beard?

187. EW: Yeah that's good

OEQ 188. INV: Okay and the lips and the mouth?

189. EW: Yeah

OEQ 190. INV: His eyes?

191. EW: I feel like his eyes might have been a little bit bigger

PQ 192. INV: As in what way?

410

APPENDIX E

OEQ 194. INV: How about his age?

193. EW: Like the corners of his eyes were like this I guess like more larger?

195. EW: He looks pretty young in this picture

PQ 196. INV: How old does he look here?

197. EW: Like five-twenty, thirty?

AQC 198. INV: So we want to go forty, forty-five so about ten years all right, let me see what I can do...

199. EW: I wish I just had kept the conversation with him though...

PQ 200. INV: Why?

201. EW: Cause usually when customers in and I try to have a conversation with them not about personal things but if it does get to that I should have asked him like oh how long have you guys been married or like do you guys have any kids or anything like that just so I could of... more seconds would have been seeing what he's like

AL 202. INV: Oh, I see

203. EW: And just seeing his face you know

OEQ 204. INV: So at the other robbery who was there?

205. EW: My manager Martina and a co-worker named Jessica

PQ 206. INV: Did they call the call police?

207. EW: I believe so I believe they took I think eleven pairs of shoes and a couple purses

EC 208. INV: Oh wow...

209. EW: Yeah

PQ 210. INV: So it was a lot

211. EW: And I think they pushed my manager...

PQ 212. INV: Did they call police?

213. EW: Yes

PQ 214. INV: And do they have video or something?

215. EW: No, we don't have any security cameras

PQ 216. INV: And she didn't want to do a sketch?

217. EW: Yeah, I don't know

PQ 218. INV: You don't know?

APPENDIX E

OEQ   219. INV: You have a feeling, what's your feeling?

220. EW: Yeah that they don't really care anymore just because it's going out of business…

PQ   221. INV: Are all of them going out of business or just that one?

222. EW: Yes every Payless across the US

PQ   223. INV: Oh wow…When's the last day?

224. EW: I wanna say like towards the end of April uhm, but just the other day my manager told me that they were still weren't gonna put security cameras in there and that didn't make me feel comfortable at all

PQ   225. INV: How long have you been there?

226. EW: A month

PQ   227. INV: What? Oh wow…

228. EW: I started maybe like in February…yeah like February seventh or something

PQ   229. INV: And where is this Payless Shoe Source?

230. EW: it's on Showers Drive

MP   231. INV: Shower…In Mountain View?

232. EW: And I feel like that's starting to become a hot spot

OEQ   233. INV: Oh really, why is that?

234. EW: Because I feel like people have gotten away with it and they're just gonna go and…

AL   235. INV: Oh I see

236. EW: …you know hey I think they got away with this next time come with me type of thing. Like I have a feeling that he's gonna come back I even told my husband that like I feel like he's gonna come back and get revenge and he's like revenge on what? Revenge on me interfering with what he wanted to do.

OEQ   237. INV: Let me ask you about that. Why..

238. EW: Fight back?

OER   239. INV: Why did you grab him?

AQC   240. INV: It's sounds like when you said as he was asking you to go back…

241. EW: We were walking yeah and then I turned around I tried to grab his forearm…

OEQ   242. INV: Why?

412

APPENDIX E

243. EW: It was just an instant you know I don't even think about turning around I just did it…you know and after that like I after the incident happened like these past couple days I've been constantly thinking about that–me turning around and like I wish I had done something other than just try to grab his forearm, you know, like as he was hitting me his hands were like up in the air like I wish I would have just punched him in the stomach or kicked out his knees like if I had grabbed his arm like I probably break his arm where his elbow is at, like…I don't know

PQ 244. INV: Do you think yo could have done that?

245. EW: Yeah

PQ 246. INV: You do?

247. EW: Yeah

PQ 248. INV: How do you know?

249. EW: I don't know that I could've done it but I have a pretty strong punch and kick just because I have experience with fighting…

PQ 250. INV: From where?

251. EW: I used to do Moi Tai at a gym–kickboxing

AC 252. INV: Oh okay

253. EW: But I stopped that in high school once I got pregnant, uhm but I've always I still have a kick boxing bag at home and I was just doing that a couple days before this happened and I know my strength and I know I'm strong for my height and my size…and I just feel like lately I've been kind of working out so I feel like I those punches and stuff would have been so much more harder than they who would have been if I'd hadn't worked out

PQ 254. INV: So he ended up not taking anything

255. EW: Yeah

PQ 256. INV: What about your friend why isn't she here helping describe this guy?

257. EW: Uhm I don't know I don't think anyone contacted her about it

PQ 258. INV: You don't think so

259. EW: Yeah

PQ 260. INV: Did you tell her you were coming here today

261. EW: Yes she knows. She actually should be there at the store right now…

PQ 262. INV: She's the one that's covering your spot?

413

APPENDIX E

263. EW: Ah yes. She actually was late so my manager had to come in, uhm, but then once Corina comes then my manager will most likely leave

AQC 264. INV: All right so I made some adjustments so what I want you to do is I want you to ask yourself, does the sketch remind me of the guy. That's all I want you to ask yourself. If it does we're good. If there's something that you want me to change or make an adjustment to just let me know and I will focus in on that all right? (Showing sketch)

OEQ 265. INV: What do you think?

266. EW: He looks different but like maybe a bigger nose, like nostrils

OEQ 267. INV: Well I did it originally like you said so I just left it alone (EW: yeah, yeah, yeah) I really didn't do anything more. How's the age?

OEQ 268. INV: I made him little bit older. How does that feel?

269. EW: I feel even older

PQ 270. INV: He's looking now–what age?

271. EW: Like thirty to thirty five I wanna say…

AL 272. INV: Oh still the same?

273. EW: Before it was like twenty-five thirty and now he's maybe…

PQ 274. INV: So just a little bit older?

275. EW: Yeah maybe he wasn't like…maybe he wasn't…he wasn't old enough to not like have any …I don't know like when you're age fifty like I don't know like how you're health is

AQC 276. INV: Well I mean you know we're talking about appearance here so (EW: yeah) it's not about health

277. EW: So maybe…but the bottom face does that does look like him

AQC 278. INV: Good like we said it's never gonna be exact

279. EW: Yeah

AQC 280. INV: As long as it's close enough.

Topic 5

281. EW: Do you know if I'm going to see any photos…

AQC 282. INV: Yeah they want to do this first because…this is better so that if they have an idea who it is then they can kind of concentrate on that if they have any suspects for you to for you to look at so…

283. EW: Okay

APPENDIX E

AQC 284. INV: So once they get this information they'll follow up and then if they do identify somebody that they think that you can look at they will do that...

285. EW: How long have you been doing this for?

AQC 286. INV: Since nineteen ninety-three

287. EW: That's cool. I'm guessing you like...

AQC 288. INV: Yes, I get to help somebody like you

289. EW: And you enjoy doing it

DEQ 290. INV: So would you want to do after working at Payless Shoe Source?

291. I'm currently going to school right now and...

PQ 292. INV: What are you studying?

293. EW: I'm trying to get my general ed out of the way, eventually I think I want to be a child therapist or a teacher something has to do with children. I've have been in many, many therapies and all my life and...I've been through a lot so I think that from my experiences and knowledge will help other people that are going through the same in the same situation or thinking about things you know

EC 294. INV: That's very admirable

295. EW: Yeah I think I'd be really good at that and I for some reason I give good advice don't follow it but

AQC 296. INV: Okay do what I say and not what I do?

297. EW: Yeah I always look out for others more that I look out for myself so...I feel like..

PQ 298. INV: Yeah what would you tell your friend who ran into this situation and who fought this guy what would you tell her now?

299. EW: I told both my co workers what that wasn't there but like we became friends there at work and her name is Rosa and Corina was there with me I told them that I don't feel comfortable with them going there anymore to work so I don't want for them not to come to work, but...I don't feel like they're safe there and I know that I don't want them to deal with something like that. I even told...yesterday was my first day back and I had a therapy session right after and I told her that I was kind of happy that it was me and not them...

PQ 300. INV: Why is that?

301. EW: Because I felt like I not handled it better than them, but like I feel like I'm more tougher than them I have thicker skin and it's kinda hard to get to me, you know...and just the many things that I have been through in life I think that this is just not another obstacle but something

415

APPENDIX E

that you know happened and I feel like if it if had been them–I just wouldn't have felt the same about the situation...you know...but the one that was with me she is no longer going to work there at Mountain View

PQ 302. INV: Oh she's not?

303. EW: Yeah she already talked, well...and you see that's the thing at work someone–there's a security guard there

PQ 304. INV: Oh there is?

305. EW: Yeah that not specifically for Payless but for the whole lot, so he walks around here she walks around with from Walmart all the way down to like Kohls and then on the way the Trader Joe's like the whole lap. And he came into the store yesterday and he says that someone said that I jumped on the guy in that I had seventeen stitches and that I got the crap beat out of me and I was just where is this coming from? And I'm pretty sure it just all comes back to this one coworker that I already had an issue with and like she's right now telling my manager that I told the girls not to go to work so I like had to clear that up with my manager. I was like hey it's not that I'm telling them not to come to work it's just me telling them that if they're here they need to be careful (INV: right) and to be aware who comes in...

AQC 306. INV: That's good advice

307. EW: Yeah and I just don't feel comfortable with them being here just because Rose is a minor she gets hurt that's even more of a problem because they're making it seem like it was my fault that that happened and they also tried to even fire me over it

PQ 308. INV: Over this issue?

309. EW: Yes

EC 310. INV: Oh my God I'm sorry

311. EW: So I got a write-up because of it and my manager got a write-up because of it and it's just like I feel like they don't want me to like pursue more than what I already have. (INV: right, I se) It was a big problem for them about me getting injured right now yeah

AQC 312. INV: That makes sense

313. EW: And that's frustrating to me because I mean that would have happened or they would have caught the person that they had just freaking security cameras, you know and was just like this could happen so many more times and still like you you're not gonna do anything about it (INV: right) you know the second time this month you still should not have put security cameras and happened again don't blame the person...you know

OEQ 314. INV: All right, how does that feel?

416

APPENDIX E

315. EW: Yeah much better yeah

AQC 316. INV: Because I worked on the age and everything else

317. EW: Yeah

PQ 318. INV: Good, all right so what do you think–are they gonna–they're not going to put security cameras till now when or are you back at work now

319. EW: Yesterday was my first day back and then after this unless I go back but this does it's scary for me

AQC 320. INV: The initials to name

321. EW: AM

AQC 322. INV: And this occurred what date what day?

323. EW: The sixteenth three sixteen twenty nineteen

AQL 324. INV: And around what time?

325. EW: Ten forty-five, that's when we were in the physical alteration. Ten fifty-one that's when I called the police

AQC 326. INV: Okay perfect

AQC 327. INV: All right well you have my business card there I'm going to follow up with the detectives and if they have any more questions for you they'll get a hold of you.

328. EW: Yes I'm constantly wondering like what's happening and I wonder what I could do…

AQC 329. INV: Yeah they were just waiting for this sketch

END OF INTERVIEW

APPENDIX E

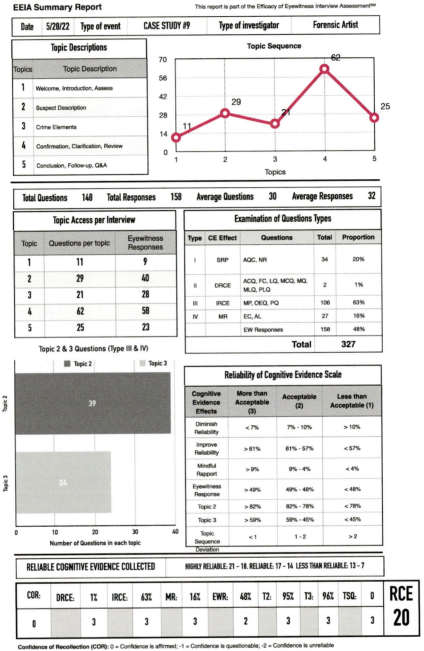

APPENDIX E

CASE STUDY #10

This section includes: a. Coded transcript, and b. EEIA summary report. For complete EEIA reports for case studies 6 through 15 go to www.mindfulinterviews.com/CaseStudies.

Each case study was evaluated and prepared for EEIA processing. Every attempt was made to standardize the evaluation and coding process for every case study. Any errors in coding, calculations, or assignment of RCE score, should be directed to the author. All of the transcripts were anonymized for instructional purposes, any resemblance to specific investigations is purely coincidental. The crime types and agencies are listed for informational purposes and to give the reader an idea of the variety of cases used in applying *The Mindful Interview Method*.

EYEWITNESS INTERVIEW ANALYSIS (EIA)
CONFIDENTIAL TRANSCRIPT REVIEW

Date of transcript review: May17, 2022

Crime type: Suspicious person, possible kidnapping

Notes: The transcript starts after an initial greeting and QQ. The transcript only captures topics 1 and 2. Topics 3 - 5 were not captured in this transcript. Nevertheless, the topics were eventually covered as a sketch was completed for this investigation. This transcript was included because of the unique characteristics of the interview.

Topic 1

 1. INV: Ok, the way this works is I'm going to ask you some general questions about the person's face and what I'd like you to do is go ahead and answer to the best of your knowledge.

2. EW: Ok.

 3. INV: Most people don't remember everything in great detail…

4. EW: Yeah.

 5. INV: but a lot of people do remember a lot of information when they're here and they're concentrating on the sketch. You're going to have your eyes closed for about 5 minutes and then I'm going to ask some questions about her face and then after I'll have you open your eyes, I'll have you tell me what happened, what you saw, and I'll show you the sketch and if we need to we'll some changes.

6. EW: Ok.

 7. INV: Alright? Do you have any questions for me?

8. EW: No questions.

9. INV: Ok, good. We're just going to do the gal that you saw with short hair. So all of my questions are going to be about her. OK?

10. EW: Ok.

APPENDIX E

PQ   38. INV: Small earrings?

       39. EW: Yes.

FC   40. INV: Are they studs or are they hoops?

       41. EW: They're studs.

MP   42. INV: Studs?

       43. EW: Yeah.

OEQ   44. INV: Ok. Tell me about her nose. What was that like?

       45. EW: A little bit bigger.

PQ   46. INV: What do you mean by that?

       47. EW: Like a little bit like mine but a little more. More down.

OEQ   48. INV: More down, ok. What about her lips? What are her lips like?

       49. EW: Ah very, not too big but normal. Normal lips.

FC   50. INV: Did she wear any lipstick?

       51. EW: Yeah and…

PQ   52. INV: Did she wear any lipstick?

       53. EW: Yeah.

PQ   54. INV: What color?

       55. EW: Brown.

OEQ   56. INV: (drawing) What was her attitude like?

       EW: Um she was very like, you know, yelling at me.

MP   57. INV: Yelling?

       EW: Yeah. Because she said, "I'm going pick up my kids." And I said, "I never see you at this school. Why don't you go to the office?" And that the time the (inaudible) started and I see her take a phone and I think maybe she call the other lady and the other lady call (Inaudible) and say, "Oh security, security, security, excuse me, I need to go to the office and when they go inside the car, they just go straight to the street.

OEQ   58. INV: Mhm. Tell me about her chin. What was that like?

       EW: You're talking about…

PQ   59. INV: Her chin and her cheeks on her face.

       60. EW: She's got some dark…

PQ   61. INV: What?

       62. EW: She's got some dark things like maybe she put something on her face.

MP   63. INV: Some dark things?

       EW: No like to make her like, you know, more clearly.

PQ   36. INV: Very little. Are there any earrings? Does she wear earrings?

       EW: Yes.

OEQ   37. INV: And what are they like?

       EW: Little.

APPENDIX E

PQ 64. INV: So she was like wearing makeup?

65. EW: Yeah.

MCQ 66. INV: What about her cheeks. What are they like? Her cheeks. Chubby cheeks, skinny cheeks, medium cheeks.

67. EW: Skinny.

OEQ 68. INV: What about her neck?

69. EW: Not too big.

OEQ 70. INV: What kind of clothes was she wearing?
EW: She wore like a small things right here but all of this out. (Inaudible) you know, very tight.

PQ 71. INV: Mhm. What color was the shirt?
EW: Um like a little bit brown.

FC 72. INV: Mhm. Did it have sleeves and a collar?
EW: No sleeve.

MP 73. INV: No sleeves?

74. EW: Yeah, no sleeves. She dressed like she was going to go to fitness and just (inaudible) and she got the white sneaker.

MCQ 75. INV: Mhm. (drawing) Does she have any tattoos, scars or marks on her face?

76. EW: No, I don't see any.

OEQ 77. INV: And what about the color of her skin.

78. EW: Light skin almost like me, you know my hand.

OEQ 79. INV: Mhm. Tell me about her eyes.

80. EW: Eyes a little bit round.

OEQ 81. INV: What about the look in her eyes?
EW: Look in eyes?

PQ 82. INV: Mhm, what is that like?

83. EW: A little bit brown, like dark inside.

MP 84. INV: Dark inside?

85. EW: Yeah.

AL 86. INV: OK

TRANSCRIPT OF INTERVIEW ENDS

APPENDIX E

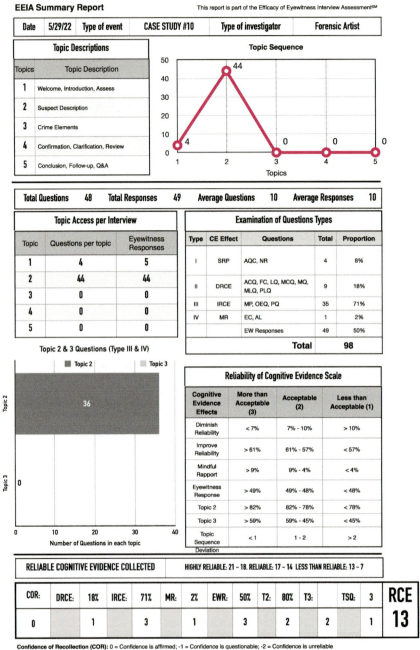

APPENDIX E

CASE STUDY #11

This section includes: a. Coded transcript, and b. EEIA summary report. For complete EEIA reports for case studies 6 through 15 go to www.mindfulinterviews.com/CaseStudies.

Each case study was evaluated and prepared for EEIA processing. Every attempt was made to standardize the evaluation and coding process for every case study. Any errors in coding, calculations, or assignment of RCE score, should be directed to the author. All of the transcripts were anonymized for instructional purposes, any resemblance to specific investigations is purely coincidental. The crime types and agencies are listed for informational purposes and to give the reader an idea of the variety of cases used in applying *The Mindful Interview Method*.

EYEWITNESS INTERVIEW ANALYSIS (EIA)
CONFIDENTIAL TRANSCRIPT REVIEW

Date of transcript review: May17, 2022

Crime type: Robbery

Notes: The interview takes place with the case investigator present. The case investigator is allowed to ask questions between sections of the sketch interview where there is a natural break in between asking questions related to the suspect. The interview portion between the investigator and this eyewitness is included in a separate case study (11.1) for reference purposes, and to show the contrast in interview styles (with the same eyewitness).

 Topic 1

AQC 1. INV: Thanks for coming in. I appreciate that.

2. EW: You're welcome.

AQC 3. INV: So, I already talked to you yesterday.

4. EW: Ahah.

AQC 5. INV: A little bit about what's going to happen today. I'm going to ask you some general questions about this person's face.

6. EW: Ok.

AQC 7. INV: And then I'd like you to answer to the best of your knowledge.

8. EW: Ok.

AQC 9. INV: Most people don't remember everything in great detail however they tend to remember a lot of information when they're focused on the questions.

10. EW: Ok.

APPENDIX E

AQC   11. INV: So that's kinda what we're going to do here and another thing that I do is you want to relax. You want to sit back a little bit. It's probably going to be about 40 minutes, right in there, 45 at the max.

12. EW: Ok.

AQC   13. INV: So the way I know that you're relaxed is you're going to have your eyes closed. You're going to give me some nice deep breaths and then I'm going to ask you questions about the person's face - that'll last 5-8 minutes then after I'm going to ask you to open your eyes. I'm going to ask you to tell me what happened and then I show you the sketch and if we need to we'll make some changes.

14. EW: Ok.

PR   15. INV: Do you understand?

16. EW: Yes.

OEQ   17. INV: Alright, do you have any questions for me?

18. EW: No.

AQC   19. INV: Obviously, Det. Connington's going to be in the room. He's not going to say anything or ask anything until I'm pretty much done and then if he has some questions, he'll ask you. If he doesn't, then we move on. Alright?
EW: Ok.

— 20. DET: And if I bug you, I can leave too.

— 21. EW: You don't bug me.

———— Topic 2

OEQ   22. INV: Alright go ahead and close your eyes and give me a nice deep breath and we'll begin. First of all what would you say is the race of this person.

23. EW: African American.

OEQ   24. INV: Mhm. Age range?
EW: Ah 20 - late 20s.

OEQ   25. INV: Mhm. Body build?

26. EW: Um average to slender.

 27. INV: When you think about the shape of his face, what kind of shape does it make?
EW: Um well it's not long and it's not chubby. Um it's ah I'm not sure what other shapes are. I mean I think of a circle and it wasn't a round face and he didn't have a long face.

PQ   28. INV: Was it an unusual shape.

29. EW: No.

FC   30. INV: Ok, was it pretty average?
EW: yes.

OEQ   31. INV: OK that's fine with me. Tell me about his hair. What is that like?

32. EW: Um short black or dark brown. Cut very close to his hair but not shave.

APPENDIX E

MP 33. INV: Not shaved.

34. EW: Mhm.

OEQ 35. INV: And what was the hairline like.

36. EW: Um he had a hat on. It was either turned around backwards a baseball cap or smaller kinda of a beanie. So you saw like two inches over his hears of hair.

PQ 37. INV: And what did you tell police about the cap.

38. EW: It was light color, mostly white.

FC 39. INV: Mhm. Did you say it was a cap or beanie?
EW: I said a cap. I believed it was probably a baseball cap turned around backwards.

PQ 40. INV: Ok, any markings on the cap?
EW: No.

PQ 41. INV: And it was light colored?

42. EW: Yes.

PR 43. INV: And you're able to see some hair on the sides?

44. EW: Mhm not like cut with scissors, um so it didn't touch his ears.

PQ 45. INV: Ok. And the color of the hair?

46. EW: Ah dark brown to black.

OEQ 47. INV: Mhm. Tell me about his ears. Yes his ears, what are they like?
EW: Um they didn't stick out.

MP 48. INV: They did not stick out.

49. EW: No I think they just laid nicely.

PR 50. INV: Mhm. Any earrings on this guy?
EW: I don't recall any earrings.

OER 51. INV: Mhm. Tell me about his forehead.

52. EW: Um average. It wasn't large. He didn't have any large features.

OEQ 53. INV: Very good. Tell me about his nose.

54. EW: Average, not flat like a lot of times, other ethnicities are.

PQ 55. INV: What about the overall length of the nose?

56. EW: Um it was not long. I don't remember it looking big or long or anything.

PR 57. INV: Ok. And are you able to see his nostrils?

58. EW: I don't recall seeing them.

OEQ 59. INV: Ok. Tell me about his mouth and his lips.

60. EW: Um his mouth was closed. He didn't talk or say anything.

AL 61. INV: Mhm.

62. EW: I don't, I think that it was more average. It wasn't um, he didn't have large lips or I don't recall them being large.

APPENDIX E

OEQ 63. INV: Mhm. What was his attitude like?

EW: Um when he walked up, he was very calm and then he sort of scattered as he ran.

AL 64. INV: Hm.

65. EW: He walked up to the group, hit her and then scattered really fast.

OEQ 66. INV: Tell me about his chin.

67. EW: Um I don't recall having any distinctive features, like bumps or anything. It was more rounded.

OEQ 68. INV: Mhm. Tell me about his neck.

69. EW: Um you could see his skin because he had a tee shirt on so it wasn't like he was a squished neck or that you saw a lot of length.

AL 70. INV: Mhm.

71. EW: But you know he was younger not toned or anything but it wasn't like he had any, you know any skin or extra things in between.

OEQ 72. INV: Mm. What kind of shirt is he wearing?

73. EW: Tee shirt, like an undershirt.

FC 74. INV: Crew neck or v neck?

75. EW: Crew neck.

PQ 76. INV: Any markings on his shirt?

EW: No. All white.

OEQ 77. INV: Mhm. Tell me about the skin tone. What is that like?

78. EW: Um, lighter black skin, so almost like Hispanic. It wasn't super dark.

OEQ 79. INV: Did he say anything to you?

80. EW: No.

OEQ 81. INV: Have you ever seen him before?

EW: No.

PQ 82. INV: Any scars or marks on his face or neck?

EW: Ah no, his skin, if I recall was more just gentle. Smooth.

OEQ 83. INV: Ok. Tell me about his cheeks.

84. EW: Um, they were regular. They weren't full or rounded but it wasn't like he had a super skinny face.

OEQ 85. INV: Tell me about his eyes.

426

APPENDIX E

86. EW: I remember that he was looking down which is why the woman in front of me stepped aside because she thought they were going to collide, you know when you're walking toward each other and the person's not paying attention…

OEQ 87. INV: Mhm. So what about eye color, eye shape, things like that?

EW: Um I don't recall. They were not.. I'm assuming they're brown because I don't remember them being light colored.

AL 88. INV: Mhm.

89. EW: But his focus was more down.

MCQ 90. INV: Big eyes, medium eyes, small eyes?

91. EW: I think medium.

FQ 92. INV: Eyebrows?

93. EW: I don't remember his eyebrows. They must not have been that big.

OEQ 94. INV: Anything else you can tell me about his face?

95. EW: No.

Topic 3

ARC 96. INV: You did a really good job. Alright go ahead and open your eyes. Now what I want you to do is I want you to tell me what happened. I want you to tell me what you were doing just prior to running into this guy and then take me through the incident up until police got involved.

97. EW: Mhm. Um so I pulled up into the parking spot in front of our dance school and Jennifer, the other woman, pulled up next to me.

MP 98. INV: Jennifer?

99. EW: And - yes, that's her name as well. And then she got out first and then I got out and as she was crossing over to the entrance to the dance school, her daughter was taking class, coming in to go into class, she noticed some other parents so she went to the left to say hi to them and as she was moving out of the way of a gentleman who was coming down the walkway and I had already, I wasn't really paying that much attention cuz she was going to go off to talk to the other ladies and I was going to go in to the dance school.

AL 100. INV: Mhm

101. EW: And then the gentleman just punched her in the face. I didn't see him punch her cuz I was behind her…

AL 102. INV: Mhm

427

APPENDIX E

[PQ] 103.EW: But she fell down to the ground so and hit her head on the cement and then someone said to call 911 and my phone was in the car, so I went back in the car to get my phone and when I came back out from my car, someone had said that he punched her cuz I was on the phone and I said that she had been assaulted and maybe pushed down in some way and then the other person said, no I saw - he punched her in the face.

[PQ] 104.INV: And who is this person who told you that?

105.EW: Um, Lisa.

[AL] 106.INV: Oh, ok.

107.EW: So she was on the other side.

[O EQ] 108.INV: And do you know Jennifer?

EW: I don't know her.

[AL] 109.INV: Alright.

110.EW: The kids all take dance together but she's not a friend.

[PQ] 111.INV: Alright. And what did the suspect do? What did he do?

112.EW: He just punched her and then pivoted and ran so I actually thought that maybe he had stolen something. And then as he started to run down the walkway, a couple of the other moms then ran down the end to see which way he was running down the street so we could tell police.

[PQ] 113.INV: And where did he go?

114.EW: Um he went up Harwood.

Topic 4

[ARC] 115.INV: (drawing) Alright I'm going to show you the sketch. When you look at the sketch, I don't need you to tell me whether it looks like him or not, not just yet.

116.EW: OK.

[ARC] 117.INV: What I want you to do is just look at the sketch and kinda see what I've been doing. After you look at it for a few seconds, we're going to go over the same questions again but this time you'll be looking at the sketch but this time as I ask you about each feature, I want you to tell me if we're in the ballpark or whether we need to make some changes, understand?

118.EW: Ok.

[PQC] 119.INV: We're never going to be exact, that's a given. However, we definitely want to be somewhere where we eliminate a lot of other people just to make sure we're in the right spot, ok?

APPENDIX E

120.EW: Ok.

OEQ 121.INV: Alright. Now you say he was African American. Why do you say that?

122.EW: Because of his coloring and the way his hair laid on his head.

PQ 123.INV: So texture?
EW: Yeah.

PQ 124.INV: Ok. Had you not seen his hair?

125.EW: Then I may have said Hispanic.

OEQ 126.INV: Ok. Good. That's very good. Did you discuss they way he looked like with other people?
EW: Um, not just as we were talking to the officer.

AL 127.INV: Mhm.

128.EW: And the people on the other side said the he was definitely African American.

PQ 129.INV: Oh, you had heard that?

130.EW: Yes.

OEQ 131.INV: Ok, so what about sideburns? Was he wearing any sideburns?

132.EW: Um I don't recall hair passing his ears.

OEQ 133.INV: Ok. Alright this is what I have so far. First of all, just the shape of his face. How's the shape of his face?
EW: I think that's...

PQ 134.INV: Ballpark?

135.EW: Yeah.

136.INV: OK, now the cap that he was wearing, how it lays on his head and so forth and how much you see. How does that feel for you?

137.EW: I think I saw more like up to here.

MQ 138.INV: As in hair? On the side?
EW: Yeah, I think I could see more hair.

PQ 139.INV: How about in the front?

140.EW: No I don't remember seeing hair in the front...

PQ 141.INV: No, I mean the cap. Do you need it lower on the head or is that ok?

142.EW: It may have been a little bit lower because I - that to me looks like for sure it's a baseball cap turned around.

APPENDIX E

ARC 143.INV: That's what I did because you said eventually you'd rather say it's a baseball cap…

144.EW: Than a beanie, yeah.

ARC 145.INV: So because there's the back of it in the back.

146.EW: Mhm

ARC 147.INV: So we'll just go with that.

148.EW: Yeah I don't remember actually seeing the bill but…

ARC 149.INV: It makes sense because it's behind.

150.EW: But I do remember seeing a little bit more hair on the sides.

ARC 151.INV: Mhm. You saw him at different vantage points, different angles, so obviously we're focused just on the front so it may not look like a lot and I'm trying to make sure I have the right perspective so um, you'll have to bare with me on that.

152.EW: Ok.

PR 153.INV: So I'll show just a little bit but I'm more concerned with that face-forward look. How's that feel?

154.EW: I still think I saw even more of his hair.

ARC 155.INV: Mhm. We'll let that go because I'm saying if I turn him around I can show it but we're looking at him forward and as long as we see some hair.

156.EW: Oh, ok.

OER 157.INV: The ears? How are we doing?
EW: Mhm.

OER 158.INV: You can see I didn't finish that one, I just wanted to get a sense for size. And then the nose? How are we doing there?

159.EW: I think that's fine.

OER 160.INV: Mhm. The mouth and the lips?

161.EW: Yes.

OER 162.INV: The chin and the cheeks.

163.EW: Mhm

OER 164.INV: The neck area?

165.EW: Um his shirt was open more so I saw more.

PR 166.INV: Ok, very loose?

APPENDIX E

167. EW: yes.

PQ 168. INV: (Drawing) How's that?

169. EW: Yeah.

OER 170. INV: And then the color of his skin?

171. EW: I think it was a little darker than that.

PQ 172. INV: A little darker? Ok, so if I kinda stayed in this range would we be ok? So I made this lighter up here. Something like that overall?

173. EW: Yeah but it was darker than that. That looks lighter to me.

PQ 174. INV: Mhm, so darker?

175. EW: Yeah.

FC 176. INV: (drawing) And we said no scars or marks that you remember. Like that. (drawing) Have a boyish face or a mannish face?

177. EW: Um, in between. He didn't look like a teenager to me but he didn't look like a dad.

FC 178. INV: Got it. Concentrating on the color more, the shading on this side. So is that ok? Something like that or darker?

179. EW: Not darker.

PQ 180. INV: Are we ok right here?

181. EW: I think so.

OER 182. INV: Ok, good. And the eyes again. How are we doing on the eyes?

183. EW: They may have been darker.

MQ 184. INV: The shape and things like that? Size?

185. EW: Um they may have been bigger.

PQ 186. INV: Mhm a little bit?

187. EW: Yeah.

ARC 188. INV: Ok, I'm going to darken them. Maybe that will help you.

189. EW: Cuz his eyes were not something that I was drawn to. You know usually when you look at someone you remember the eye color but I think that might have been because his focus was more down.

OER 190. INV: Right. (drawing) What was he wearing for clothing?

191. EW: Just a loose, white undershirt and very baggy jeans.

APPENDIX E

PQ   192.INV: Color?
      EW: Blue and you could see his underwear, or they were hanging lower.

PQ   193.INV: And his shoes?
      EW: I don't remember.

OER 194.INV: Do you think you've seen him before?
      EW: No.

PR   195.INV: (drawing) I just worked on the eyes. Made them a little darker. How's that feel?

196.EW: It feels better.

DTR 197.INV: Mhm. Overall age? How we doing there?
      EW: It looks maybe a little bit younger.

PQ   198.INV: What does he look like for you?

199.EW: For me, this looks like late teenager early 20s so I think maybe he looked a little bit older.

MP   200.INV: Ok, so you want him a little older.

201.EW: Yeah.

PQ   202.INV: See how I left his eyebrows not as descriptive? Are we ok with that or do you want me to show something?
      EW: No, I don't really remember his eyebrows very much.

AQC 203.INV: Alright. I'll work on this a little bit. (drawing) (To detective) If you have questions, you can go ahead and ask them if you'd like.

Detective assumes interview...

Back to forensic artist interview

PR   204.INV: (drawing) So if he did have eyebrows, it would probably be unusual. You would have noticed that maybe?

205.EW: Yeah, like if he had no eyebrows?
AL   INV: Yeah.

206.EW: Yeah.

ARC 207.INV: Because when you see this, I'm going to show some because that's what I want to do because unless you tell me he doesn't have any, he probably does. They're just unremarkable.

208.EW: Yeah.

ARC 209.INV: Which is normal, so um just keep that in mind when I show it to you.

210.EW: Ok.

432

APPENDIX E

PQ 211.INV: And did we say his hair was black, correct?
    EW: Either dark brown or black, but it was dark.

OER 212.INV: Ok. (drawing) Have you ever witnessed anything like this before?
     EW: No.

OER 213.INV: How long have you been going there?

     214.EW: Um just since the Fall.

PQ   215.INV: And that area, is it ok area? What's it like.

     216.EW: Mhm. Just a little strip mall amongst a residential area.

EC   217.INV: (drawing) Mhm. So pretty shocking, maybe?

     218.EW: Mhm well on that side of the mall is very quiet because it's really, the dance school is the only place you usually see people coming in and out of.

AC   219.INV: Oh.

     220.EW: There's a couple of other businesses there but two of them are restaurants and the other is a photographer so it's always closed by the time we get there.

AC   221.INV: Mhm

Detective returns and assumes interview…

Forensic artist assumes interview

——— **Topic 5**

AQC 222.INV: So when I show this one more time, what I want you to do is ask yourself, "Does that remind me of him?"

     223.EW: Ok.

AQC 224.INV: If there's something that you're looking at and you're thinking, "Well maybe we can adjust this or change that, um just kind of focus in on that and let me know, otherwise, I think we should be ok.

     225.EW: Ok.

     226.INV: (shows sketch)
     EW: Yeah.

PQ   227.INV: In the ballpark?

433

APPENDIX E

228.EW: Yeah. The only thing that I question maybe is that it's too dark, but other than that, I mean now there's a little more texture in the hair and that's what I sort of remember the short but it didn't touch his ears or anything.

AQC 229.INV: No, it's not touching the ears. Ok, good. Alright, and how about the age? Did we fix up the age a little bit for you?

230.EW: Yeah.

Detective assumes interview...

I recall speaking to EW on a call prior to this interview. In this call I asked her the QQ and she responded positively (see question 3). Since the case detective was in this interview I allowed them to ask questions in between refining the sketch (usually about 5-10 minutes). For more information on their interview see CS 11.1.

INTERVIEW ENDS

APPENDIX E

EEIA Summary Report
This report is part of the Efficacy of Eyewitness Interview Assessment℠

Date	5/29/22	Type of event	CASE STUDY #11	Type of investigator	Forensic Artist

Topic Descriptions

Topics	Topic Description
1	Welcome, Introduction, Assess
2	Suspect Description
3	Crime Elements
4	Confirmation, Clarification, Review
5	Conclusion, Follow-up, Q&A

Topic Sequence (values by topic): 1→10, 2→39, 3→6, 4→55, 5→4

Total Questions	114	Total Responses	127	Average Questions	23	Average Responses	25

Topic Access per Interview

Topic	Questions per topic	Eyewitness Responses
1	10	10
2	39	43
3	6	10
4	55	59
5	4	5

Examination of Questions Types

Type	CE Effect	Questions	Total	Proportion
I	SRP	AQC, NR	25	20%
II	DRCE	ACQ, FC, LQ, MCQ, MQ, MLQ, PLQ	8	6%
III	IRCE	MP, OEQ, PQ	80	63%
IV	MR	CO, AL	13	10%
		EW Responses	127	50%
		Total	**253**	

Topic 2 & 3 Questions (Type III & IV)
- Topic 2: 39
- Topic 3: 9

Reliability of Cognitive Evidence Scale

Cognitive Evidence Effects	More than Acceptable (3)	Acceptable (2)	Less than Acceptable (1)
Diminish Reliability	< 7%	7% - 10%	> 10%
Improve Reliability	> 61%	61% - 57%	< 57%
Mindful Rapport	> 9%	9% - 4%	< 4%
Eyewitness Response	> 49%	49% - 48%	< 48%
Topic 2	> 82%	82% - 78%	< 78%
Topic 3	> 59%	59% - 45%	< 45%
Topic Sequence Deviation	< 1	1 - 2	> 2

RELIABLE COGNITIVE EVIDENCE COLLECTED
HIGHLY RELIABLE: 21 - 18. RELIABLE: 17 - 14 LESS THAN RELIABLE: 13 - 7

COR:	DRCE: 6%	IRCE: 63%	MR: 10%	EWR: 50%	T2: 91%	T3: 90%	TSQ: 0	RCE
0	3	3	3	3	3	3	3	**21**

Confidence of Recollection (COR): 0 = Confidence is affirmed; -1 = Confidence is questionable; -2 = Confidence is unreliable

APPENDIX E

CASE STUDY #11.1

This section includes: a. Coded transcript, and b. EEIA summary report. For complete EEIA reports for case studies 6 through 15 go to www.mindfulinterviews.com/CaseStudies.

Each case study was evaluated and prepared for EEIA processing. Every attempt was made to standardize the evaluation and coding process for every case study. Any errors in coding, calculations, or assignment of RCE score, should be directed to the author. All of the transcripts were anonymized for instructional purposes, any resemblance to specific investigations is purely coincidental. The crime types and agencies are listed for informational purposes and to give the reader an idea of the variety of cases used in applying *The Mindful Interview Method*.

EYEWITNESS INTERVIEW ANALYSIS (EIA)
CONFIDENTIAL TRANSCRIPT REVIEW

Date of transcript review: May17, 2022

Crime type: Robbery

Notes: This excerpt highlights the investigator questions with the same eyewitness from cases study #11. The investigator was present during the sketch interview and was allowed to ask questions near the end of the interview. This analysis focuses on topics 2 and 3. Since the eyewitness experienced topics 1, 4 & 5, in this same session, we are not subjecting this interview to the same scrutiny in these topics (see Topic Sequence deviations). The excerpt is presented to show the contrast in interview styles with the same eyewitness.

1. INV: Alright. I'll work on this a little bit. (drawing) (To detective) If you have questions, you can go ahead and ask them if you'd like.

   Topic 2

   Detective assumes interview

   PLQ
2. DET: You know um when you were talking about his height, um we've got a little bit of a range from the other folks, so how certain are you of his height and I believe, and I don't want to put words in your mouth, but…
3. EW: I thought like 5'10 um only based on my own height because I saw him this way and he was definitely taller than me but it wasn't…

   PR
4. DET: How tall are you?
   EW: I'm 5'6, so that's why I was thinking maybe 5'10.

   PLQ
5. DET: Is it possible that he's taller?
6. EW: Yeah, but I wouldn't say like 6 foot. Unless he was carrying himself sort of you know low, but the way he was standing, I wouldn't say he was over 6 feet.

APPENDIX E

7. DET: He quickly ran back the direction he came from. You know sometimes when people run, they crouch, particularly if they're running fast. Is your memory from that moment or from when he's approaching you, cuz if he's running crouched, he might appear shorter than he really is.

8. EW: I was thinking more the memory when he was walking towards, as he ran off he was definitely crouched down and more my height.

9. DET: So is it fair to say you're pretty confident he was between 5'10-6 ft? Or is it possible he can be even taller than 6 ft?
EW: Well he could be taller if, I mean I know a lot of the, not to be stereotypical, but the men who wear the baggy jeans and things, they kinda walk, they don't stand up tall, so..

10. DET: So possible taller if he had bad posture.

11. EW: Yes.

12. DET: I'm going to grab, I just have a little sketch of the area and we can make sure we're on the right page where you were at and where she was at.

13. EW: That's fine.

14. DET: I'll be right back. Does anyone want water?
INV: I'll have a water.

15. EW: I'll have water. Thank you.

Detective returns and assumes interview

16. DET: This might be off a little bit, but you know obviously here is our strip mall and the Walgreens jut out, here's the end, you go back around and obvious Harwood is right here, um based on what I've heard from our victim is that she parked maybe three stalls from the jut out…

17. EW: Yeah we were both parked here.

18. DET: So you were…

19. EW: Right next to her.

20. DET: You were right next to her here?
EW: Yeah.

21. DET: Ok, this sounds kinda weird but um the make and color of your car so if I have video I can see…

22. EW: Oh, it's a Honda Odyssey dark green. It almost looks dark grey, it's like a dark green.

23. DET: Ok, you don't happen to have the license plate, do you?
EW: I don't but I drove it here.

24. DET We can check afterwards. So you were parked immediately to the East one stall.

25. EW: Correct.

26. DET: Ok. And she kinda recalled her daughter coming out first and running into, then she followed the daughter out…

27. EW: Mhm

APPENDIX E

28. DET: it was two-weeks break and everyone was excited to come back to class.
29. EW: Mhm.
30. DET: Most people were looking forward to the mini reunion here. Ah so she was here, you were here in the vehicles, um and then you both were walking along the sidewalk, is that correct?
31. EW: Correct, my daughter was coming out of class so they had one little girl that was still in the car but the daughter, you know, she got out and ran in and her mom got out and as soon as they crossed in front of me, then I stepped out.
32. DET: Ok, and, this is approximately where the studio is, is that correct? So you were like 2,3,4 stalls away from the studio?
    EW: Yeah probably three because she fell right in front of one car and then there was another car and mine.
33. DET: Oh so actually I have the car that she fell…
34. EW: It was directly in front of the studio, like wherever the front door is, she was literally right in front of the studio.
35. DET: So, I have some photos, though, of the scene. I'll show those real quick.
36. EW: Ok.
37. DET: (inaudible))
38. EW: That's fine.

Forensic artist assumes interview and completes refinement of sketch

Detective assumes interview

39. DET: Any potential that the face was longer, or the nose was bigger?
40. EW: You know, he didn't to me didn't have, at least what I recall, more like a stereotypical African American features because…
41. DET: (interrupts) I mean, I'm a mutt, most people have mixes of all different types of race or backgrounds or ethnicities…
42. EW: Yeah.
43. DET: So any potential there that he was of mixed race, of multiple races?
44. EW: Um it didn't look like a mix of like black/white, so to speak, where it's very light skinned.
45. DET: Ok.
46. EW: Um but he definitely didn't have a jet black complexion.
47. DET: Ok.
48. EW: It did definitely did to me look like it could have been Hispanic in coloring but the way that I remember his hair, I would say more African American, more than Hispanic.
49. DET: Ok. So, here's the photo of the…
50. EW: Yeah this is where she fell.
51. DET: Yeah, right here. And so this is the car parked just East to the doors.
52. EW: OK, so …

438

APPENDIX E

53. DET: There was a sedan that was there at the time, this is this car afterwards, parking spots always hard to find.

54. EW: Yeah, it was a different woman.

55. DET: So this is probably what would be the front door of the studio is what I imagine, and I could be a couple of spaces off but.

56. EW: Yeah, see how the front door is literally where the line is.

57. DET: Yeah.

58. EW: And that right where she…

59. DET: (Interrupts) that's kinda what I have right here.

60. EW: Ok.

61. DET: But you think it's maybe three spaces or.

62. EW: So if this is the…

63. DET: This is this vehicle right here - there's the front door.

64. EW: Ok. then I was, gosh I don't remember there being this many parking spots there. Um, I thought there were only….I thought we were more like here though

65. DET: (Interrupts)…perhaps this, what I can do is count back because I counted this way.

66. EW: Did we count where her car was?
    DET: Um this is from her memory

67. EW: Ok.

68. DET: So this, I'll have to move this, possible to move these two things over.

69. EW: Yeah I'm thinking all of this in general might be over just a little bit..

70. DET: Ok.

71. EW: Because I don't think there are this many parking spots in between Walgreens and the dance studio…

72. DET: (Interrupts) So here's kind of that view, um and you see here is a car and you can see here the edge and if you count, there's actually about 10 spots from here - one, two, three, four, five, six, seven, eight, I'm sorry nine spots.

73. EW: It's ok.

74. DET: So um counting this way, that puts you closer this way.

75. EW: Ok. Well, then I guess..

439

APPENDIX E

AQC 76. DET: That's fine. It's more of a concept sketch for me.

77. EW: I thought we were a little bit closer, like maybe…

PLQ 78. DET: (Interrupts) but you were walking behind her so she would have been approximately right here…

79. EW: Yes.

AQC 80. DET: when she was hit.

81. EW: Your other picture was showing right in front. She was right here.

AQC 82. DET: Right here at the corner. She hit part of the vehicle when she fell.

83. EW: Well, she fell into this car.

AQC 84. DET: This car wasn't here.

85. EW: But you know what I mean, yeah.

PQ 86. DET: And you were how far behind her, you believe, when she was hit?

87. EW: Maybe four steps.

AL 88. DET: ok.

89. EW: Because I was not in front of the car she fell on and I think my car was only two away and I had enough time to notice, because there aren't usually other people, especially men, in that area - it's mostly all moms picking up their kids or dropping them off- So I noticed that he was there.

AQC 90. DET: Um, in this group here, we have Stephanie and Lisa and Alicia

91. EW: Mhm.

LQ 92. DET: They were - um, someone remembers him being closer to the car here but somebody remembers him being on the sidewalk.

93. EW: No, they weren't on the sidewalk, they were like in between the cars.

PQ 94. DET: Ok, in between the cars, like in here?

95. EW: Yeah, cuz I came in, I think I came in either this way or this way. I went to the grocery store in between when they were in class and I saw, I could see them all before I parked.

AL 96. DET: Ok.

97. EW: I go to school with both Stephanie and Lisa and I remembered seeing them both.

PQ 98. DET: Ok. So but you believe they were probably out in between the parking spots?

APPENDIX E

99. EW: Oh, yeah, all the cars, all of those spots were full so they were , I mean I could see them and…

ACR 100. DET: (interrupts) but they weren't

101. EW: they were down enough

AR 102. DET: (Interrupt) they were..

103. EW: like standing in the middle of the road

PQ 104. DET: Ok and do you know Sandy C_____?

105. EW: yes.

FC 106. DET: So she was parking illegally?

107. EW: Yes.

PQ 108. DET: I told her I wouldn't give her a ticket. But is this an approximate location to where she was at relatively, as you remember?

109. EW: I mean it would make sense. I mean she wasn't as far here. She would have been, if Stephanie and those guys were there it would make sense she was there or a little more this way.

PQ 110. DET: Ok, so in the concept sketch is it generally close to what you remember?

TOPIC 2 111. EW: Yes.

AQC 112. DET: Ok, this help me visualize this and also when I'm trying to collect additional evidence for video and things like that, just seeing, you know, where he might have ran.

113. EW: Yeah and the only thing that we all remembered after, because there was only one car they had asked, did you see anybody leave, was like a white pick up truck that left.

PQ 114. DET: No, I recall I spoke to one about that. Did you see the white pick up truck?

115. EW: I did.

ACR 116. DET: You didn't mention that, though, to the initial officer.

117. EW: No, because it wasn't, we weren't really talking about…

PQ 118. DET: (Interrupts) Kimberley saw the - you saw the….?

119. EW: We all saw it because on the of the other moms said, do we think he could be in that car because it was sort of…

PQ 120. DET: (Interrupts) How much time passed until you saw the truck?
EW: Um I would say within a minute.

PQ 121. DET: Ok. And you recall the truck color?

441

APPENDIX E

[PQ] 122. EW: It was a white pickup truck and there was only one man inside?
DET: And what type of truck?
EW: Not a big one, so it reminded me more of like an older, like Toyota. Like a traditional pick up truck, not a fancy Ram truck, you know what I mean.

[MQL] 123. DET: So, but you have your Toyotas, you have Nissans, you have the S10, you have the Ford Ranger.

124. EW: My recollection it was sort of box - it looked very traditional with a traditional flat bed...

[PQ] 125. DET: (Interrupts) Do you recall....?

126. EW: Didn't have any other color.

[PQ] 127. DET: You don't recall any other (inaudible) or anything

(128.) EW: I don't remember anything on it except...

[PQL] 129. DET: (Interrupts) damage or any bumper stickers or anything

130. EW: I don't think it had bumper stickers but it was definitely white but it wasn't fancy...

[MQC] 131. DET: (Interrupts).....some people saw, some people didn't but so that's good. I'm glad (inaudible) if you were to put a time frame on it in terms of its age, what would you think? Would you say 60s, 70s, 80s, 90s

132. EW: So I was in high school in the 80s, and I recall that style of truck that teenagers drive.

[PQL] 133. DET: So if teenagers were driving in high school it may have been older.

134. EW: Yeah, but it didn't look like a clunky old car but it definitely didn't look...

[PQL] 135. DET: (Interrupts) 80s is fair?

136. EW: Yeah.

[LQ] 137. DET: Similar to a Toyota?

138. EW: Yeah, it reminded me of the traditional Toyota trucks with the kids used to drive.

COR: 7/61 questions (T2-T3) - Negligble effect. (11%) See COR Table.

SEGMENT OF INTERVIEW ENDS

APPENDIX E

EEIA Summary Report

This report is part of the Efficacy of Eyewitness Interview Assessment℠

Date	5/29/22	Type of event	CASE STUDY #11.1	Type of investigator	Criminal

Topic Descriptions

Topics	Topic Description
1	Welcome, Introduction, Assess
2	Suspect Description
3	Crime Elements
4	Confirmation, Clarification, Review
5	Conclusion, Follow-up, Q&A

Topic Sequence

Values plotted: 0, 8, 12, 5, 31

Total Questions	61	Total Responses	60	Average Questions	12	Average Responses	12

Topic Access per Interview

Topic	Questions per topic	Eyewitness Responses
1	0	0
2	26	22
3	35	38
4	0	0
5	0	0

Examination of Questions Types

Type	CE Effect	Questions	Total	Proportion
I	SRP	AQC, NR	18	27%
II	DRCE	ACQ, FC, LQ, MCQ, MQ, MLQ, PLQ	23	34%
III	IRCE	MP, OEQ, PQ	20	30%
IV	MH	EC, AL	6	9%
		EW Responses	60	47%
		Total	**127**	

Topic 2 & 3 Questions (Type III & IV)

Topic 2: 10
Topic 3: 16

Reliability of Cognitive Evidence Scale

Cognitive Evidence Effects	More than Acceptable (3)	Acceptable (2)	Less than Acceptable (1)
Diminish Reliability	< 7%	7% - 10%	> 10%
Improve Reliability	> 61%	61% - 57%	< 57%
Mindful Rapport	> 9%	9% - 4%	< 4%
Eyewitness Response	> 49%	49% - 48%	< 48%
Topic 2	> 82%	82% - 78%	< 78%
Topic 3	> 59%	59% - 45%	< 45%
Topic Sequence Deviation	< 1	1 - 2	> 2

RELIABLE COGNITIVE EVIDENCE COLLECTED

HIGHLY RELIABLE: 21 – 18. RELIABLE: 17 – 14 LESS THAN RELIABLE: 13 – 7

COR:	DRCE:	34%	IRCE:	30%	MR:	9%	EWR:	47%	T2:	36%	T3:	41%	TSQ:	3	RCE
0		1		1		2		1		1		1		1	8

Confidence of Recollection (COR): 0 = Confidence is affirmed; -1 = Confidence is questionable; -2 = Confidence is unreliable

APPENDIX E

CASE STUDY #12

This section includes: a. Coded transcript, and b. EEIA summary report. For complete EEIA reports for case studies 6 through 15 go to www.mindfulinterviews.com/CaseStudies.

Each case study was evaluated and prepared for EEIA processing. Every attempt was made to standardize the evaluation and coding process for every case study. Any errors in coding, calculations, or assignment of RCE score, should be directed to the author. All of the transcripts were anonymized for instructional purposes, any resemblance to specific investigations is purely coincidental. The crime types and agencies are listed for informational purposes and to give the reader an idea of the variety of cases used in applying *The Mindful Interview Method*.

EYEWITNESS INTERVIEW ANALYSIS (EIA)
CONFIDENTIAL TRANSCRIPT REVIEW

Date of transcript review: May17, 2022

Crime type: Indecent exposure

Notes: The transcript starts after an initial greeting and QQ. The transcript only captures topics 1 and 2. Topics 3 - 5 were not captured in this transcript. Nevertheless, the topics were eventually covered as a sketch was completed for this investigation. This transcript was included because of the unique characteristics of the interview.

Topic 1

1. EW: So I'm just curious, if you don't mind me asking cuz I thought, that's kinda weird - a month later - I mean, has this guy been around?

AQL 2. INV: I have no idea.

3. EW: That is just weird.

AQC 4. INV: I do about 200 of these, I just get a call from the detective saying this person is going to contact you...

5. EW: Ok.

AQC 6. INV: So it depends - sometimes the detectives, they're working on something and then they realize, oh wow, maybe we can get a sketch, so I never know. Sometimes I get called right away, other times I don't, so we'll see how it works. The way this works is I'm going to ask you some general questions about the person's face. We're never going to be exact but we want to be very very close so when you look at it, it helps you to remember.

7. EW: Ok.

AQC 8. INV: You're going to have your eyes closed for about 5 minutes as I ask you the questions. This will help you to relax and focus on the questions and then maybe get a mental picture of this guy. It makes it a little easier to describe. After that, I'm going to ask you to open your eyes, tell me what happened and then I'll show you the sketch and if we need to we'll make some changes. Alright? Do you have any questions for me?

9. EW: (nods head)

APPENDIX E

ARC 10. INV: Alright, go ahead and close your eyes. Do you have a cell phone? Yeah, you need to turn that off.

11. EW: Sorry, he calls me all day long.

Topic 2

OEQ 12. INV: Yeah, yeah. Here we go. Take a nice deep breath, let me know you're relaxed. First of all, what would you say is the race of this person?

13. EW: He could have been not white but Greek with dark hair. Not blonde/blue eyed. He's a white guy with dark hair.

OEQ 14. INV: OK. Age range?

15. EW: Probably about no more than 40. About 38.

OEQ 16. INV: Body build?

17. EW: Um about 170-180 pounds.

MCQ 18. INV: How about fat, skinny, medium, that range?

19. EW: He was thin.

OEQ 20. INV: Ok. when you think of the shape of this guy's face, what kind of shape are we talking about?

21. EW: Um he was thin, so he had a narrow chin and his cheeks are a little high, though.

OEQ 22. INV: Tell me about his hair. What was that like?

23. EW: It was dark and a little thick, a little wave in it and it kinda went to his jaw line. Not like a mullet.

AL 24. INV: OK.

25. EW: It was thick.

OEQ 26. INV: How does he comb his hair?

27. EW: It went back.

PLQ 28. INV: Straight back.

29. EW: Mhm. Straight back with the wave.

OEQ 30. INV: And what about the sides of the hair?

31. EW: They were a little shorter around the side, around his ears a little.

PLQ 32. INV: And the color is black?

33. EW: Black.

PQ 34. INV: Any sideburns on this guy?

35. EW: No, clean face.

OEQ 36. INV: What is the hairline like?

37. EW: Like?

PQ 38. INV: Like where the hair meets the forehead.

445

APPENDIX E

MCQ   39. EW: Um, it was pretty normal. It wasn't high, it wasn't low. It was just normal.

40. INV: Mhm. And the forehead itself? Big forehead, small forehead, medium forehead?

41. EW: Just a normal average guy.

FC   42. INV: And then thick hair medium hair?

43. EW: It was medium. It was wavy, dark.

PR   44. INV: And does the hair cover the ears?

45. EW: Just like the tips of them - that's it.

PQ   46. INV: And speaking about the ears, any earrings or anything like that on this guy?

47. EW: No, I didn't see any.

OEQ   48. INV: Tell me about his nose. What's that like?

49. EW: He had a thin nose, a little longer, narrow. It wasn't a Greek nose at all.

PQ   50. INV: The nostril area?

51. EW: It looked normal to me. He didn't have big, protruding nostrils or anything.

OEQ   52. INV: And tell me about his mouth and his ears.

53. EW: Well, he had no facial hair so his lips were pretty normal. They weren't real small. Normal lips. He had no facial hair.

OEQ   54. INV: What was this guy's attitude like?

55. EW: Nonchalant, like he does this all the time. No big deal. Didn't seem nervous, nothing– absolutely nothing.

PQ   56. INV: Did he talk to you?

57. EW: No, no. I just realized when my daughter told me what he was doing or what hadn't any pants on, then he took off. He put the towel on his lap. He took off. But I saw him right before. This distance was right there and he had dark glasses on, like aviator glasses.

OEQ   58. INV: Tell me about his chin?

59. EW: HIs chin was a little long, he was thin right here in his cheeks so he wasn't a heavy guy.

AL   60. INV: Mhm.

61. EW: It was more round.

PQ   62. INV: The chin?

63. EW: Mhm.

PQ   64. INV: And any hair on the chin?

APPENDIX E

65. EW: No, he had no facial hair.

PQ 66. INV: Ok. Any scars or marks on his face?

67. EW: Mm no, not that I can remember.

OEQ 68. INV: And then his cheeks. What are they like?

69. EW: He hadn't - you could tell he had a little bit of high cheekbones. He was all thinner in here.

AC 70. INV: Mhm.

71. EW: It's like, you don't forget a face with something like that.

MQ 72. INV: And then tell me about his clothing, the neck area, things like that.

73. EW: He had just a white t-shirt on. Just a solid white t-shirt. Obviously, my daughter said he had no pants on. Who knows, they could have been down to his ankles and driving but when I saw him, he put the towel over his lap and just took off.

FC 74. INV: This guy overall, clean looking? Dirty looking?

75. EW: He seemed clean. He seemed like a normal guy.

OEQ 76. INV: Alright and then tell me about his eyes.

77. EW: I couldn't see his eyes because he had dark glasses on.

PQ 78. INV: So he had them on the whole time?

79. EW: He had them on the whole time.

PQ 80. INV: And you were saying they were aviator-type glasses?

81. EW: Yeah, aviator, dark glasses.

PQ 82. INV: Any frames on them?

83. EW: Silver frames. Cheap ones.

PQ 84. INV: Really?

85. EW: Yeah, you could tell they were cheap ones.

PQ 86. INV: And you're saying they're big?

87. EW: They were big. Mhm.

PQ 88. INV: And then the lens color?

89. EW: Dark. Dark black.

OEQ 90. INV: Skin color?

91. EW: He was fair. Pretty fair.

447

APPENDIX E

 92. INV: Anything else about his face distinctive that you remember?

93. EW: Uhuh.

 94. INV: Do you think you've seen him before?

95. EW: It's funny you ask but he looks like somebody and I cannot picture who.

 96. INV: Were you in an area that was familiar to you?

97. EW: Mhm.

 98. INV: Was it near a home or shopping or what?

99. EW: It was at Macy's shopping, Valley Fair.

 100.INV: And how long did you see him? About how long was it?

101.EW: Maybe at the most 10 seconds. Right in front of me.

 102.INV: And are you in a car or are you walking?

103.EW: I was walking.

 Topic 3

 104.INV: Alright you can open your eyes. Now what I want you to do is I want you to tell me what you were doing just prior to running into this guy and then take me through the incident up until police get involved.

105.EW: We were just walking out of Macy's, my daughter and I. I was on the right side, she was on the left side. So we were walking and he's driving slow, like waiting for us to get to our car.

 106.INV: Behind you?

107.EW: Yeah, like he was going to wait to see if he was going to get our spot.

 108.INV: Mhm.

109.EW: So we're walking and he speeds up a little and he's right next to us and that's when my daughter looked in the car and then as soon as she looked in the car she just looked at me and said, "Oh my God, did you see that? It was gross." And I said, "What Angelique?" She said, "Mommy, he was naked." And I said, "What?!"

 110.INV: Does he back up as she's telling you this?

111.EW: Well I think there was another gal on the other side.

 112.INV: Mhm

113.EW: Walking. There was a lady.

 114.INV: He couldn't go around yet?

448

APPENDIX E

115.EW: He couldn't go around yet and we were, we were right next to him. She could see like from here to your chair almost.

 116.INV: And then?

117.EW: So when I got to the end of my car and he realized my daughter told me, I turned around and as soon as I turned around then he was right here to me and I saw his face and that's when I saw him put the towel, he had the towel over his lap cuz I looked in the car. He had a towel over his lap.

 118.INV: Mhm

119.EW: And just drove off and I called the cops right away.

 120.INV: And did you wait there for police?

121.EW: Mhm.

 122.INV: And what happened when they got there?

123.EW: Um, I gave them the full description and they pulled some young kid over and asked us if we'd go see if it was him and it wasn't.

 124.INV: So you did go see?

125.EW: Yeah.

126.INV: And he was too young?

127.EW: Too young and no hair.

128.INV: He was bald?

129.EW: He had no hair, and we were like, "No, the guy that just left has a head of hair." Yeah.

 130.INV: Ok, way to go guys.

131.EW: And he was alone. The one they pulled over had a girl with him and it was a different car.

132.INV: Wow.

133.EW: Yeah,

 134.INV: And then after that, what happened?

135.EW: Um, nothing. He just talked to us and got all my information.

 136.INV: And have you seen any pictures of possible suspects?

137.EW: No. You never think you're going to go through that, you know. You know what, honestly, if I saw him, if I saw that same guy in that same car, I would (inaudible).

APPENDIX E

138.INV: Mhm. So you told me that for some reason he was familiar. Was this at the time of the event or was this after thinking about it?

139.EW: After thinking about it.

140.INV: Days later?

141.EW: Mhm. And even on the way here, I'm trying to think who does he look like and for the life of me I just cannot get the name out.

142.(inaudible)

143.INV: A little bit. And was this daytime or nighttime?

144.EW: It was probably like 5:15-5:30. So it was broad daylight.

145.INV: Mhm, and you weren't in a covered garage?

146.EW: Yeah.

147.INV: Oh, you were?

148.EW: Yeah we were in a covered garage.

149.INV: Did anyone else see this guy?

150.EW: I don't think the other person saw him cuz, you know, you're not paying attention and it just so happens - I wouldn't have seen anything if my daughter hadn't said something.

151.INV: What kind of car was it?

152.EW: It was either and Nissan Maxima 4 door car or a - something like that (inaudible)

153.INV: What was the car like?

154.EW: It was clean. It didn't, I mean maybe he was a (inaudible) - driving a car like that? (inaudible) Sad.

Topic 4

155.INV: I'm going to show you the sketch. When you look at the sketch, I don't need you to tell me whether or not it looks like him or not. Not just yet. What I want you to do is just look at the sketch, see what I've been doing. After you look at it for a few seconds, we're going to go over the same questions again. But this time, you'll be looking at the sketch. As I ask you about each feature, I want you to tell me whether we're in the ballpark or whether you're going to make some changes.

156.EW: Ok.

450

APPENDIX E

157. INV: Remember, we're never going to be exact. We just want to be very, very close. Alright, here's what we have so far. (shows sketch). First of all, just the shape of the face. How's the shape of the face?

158. EW: That's pretty close.

159. INV: In the ballpark?

160. EW: Mhm

161. INV: The hair?

162. EW: His hair was a little more wavier, so it was a little thicker here. A bit more wave in his hair.

163. INV: Ok, besides the wave, what about the volume that I have? Is that enough?

164. EW: It's fine.

165. INV: Ok. And then the sides are ok? I'm just talking volume.

166. EW: Yeah

167. INV: So we want to add more weight.

168. EW: Yeah, a little bit more right here.

169. INV: Any falling forward on the forehead?

170. EW: No, just that it was wavier so the way his hair went it was wavier so it wasn't perfect.

171. INV: Ok.

172. EW: And it wasn't real long, you could just see the wave. I saw the waviness.

173. INV: It was more than a perm? It wasn't tight?

174. EW: It was a natural wave. It wasn't perfect hair.

175. INV: Ok. (drawing) Ok, this is what's gonna happen. I'm just doing that side, something like that?

176. EW: Yeah.

177. INV: And I'll extend it over. Alright, the forehead that I gave him?

178. EW: I think it went down a little more. He didn't have such a high forehead.

179. INV: Mhm (drawing)

180. EW: He wasn't a bad looking guy. He just looked normal.

181. INV: Right. Had you been walking a while to get in your car?

182. EW: No. I just got out of the store. I mean obviously, he wasn't there to park. There was plenty of parking. He just took off.

451

APPENDIX E

OEQ 183.INV: (drawing) Alright, what about the ears?

184.EW: I don't remember the ears. They weren't big or protruding, I would know that.

PQ 185.INV: Ok, so I don't need to bring them out any more?

186.EW: No, and his face right here is almost perfect.

OEQ 187.INV: Ok, the nose?

188.EW: The nose, yeah, he had a nice nose.

AL 189.INV: Mhm

190.EW: He didn't have a big nose and his lips were normal.

PQ 191.INV: We're ok there?

192.EW: Mhm

PLQ 193.INV: So the chin and the cheeks are ok?

194.EW: Mhm.

OEQ 195.INV: The neck and the t shirt area?

196.EW: Mhm. I mean, it looks like him.

MQ 197.INV: The glasses, shape? So these are black?

198.EW: Yeah he had black dark, dark glasses.

OEQ 199.INV: Ok, how about his age? How are we doing on that?

200.EW: His age was not more than 40.

PQ 201.INV: I know, so how are we doing on the sketch?

202.EW: Perfect.

OEQ 203.INV: We're in the ballpark?

204.EW: Yeah. And he wasn't a bad looking guy either. He looked just like a normal guy.

AQC 205.INV: Right. Well, unfortunately, he's not a normal guy.

206.EW: No, exactly.

Topic 5

PQ 207.INV: (drawing) So where are you working?

208.EW: I'm an escrow officer at (inaudible) Title. I'm the branch manager so..

PQ 209.INV: Over there on Bascom?

452

APPENDIX E

210. EW: No, East San Jose. Over on White Road

211. INV: Is that the same company?

212. EW: Did you just do a transaction on Bascom?

213. INV: Years ago. I knew a guy name Brandon (inaudible). No, not Brandon - something else. John?

214. EW: Was he a rep or an escrow officer?

215. INV: I think he was like the loan guy.

216. EW: Oh, ok, well we don't do the loan part. We do the part when you do the loan and purchase your home that we sign you off and close your deal and do all that.

217. INV: Oh, that's right.

218. EW: We don't do the actual loans. Trust me my job is enough.

219. INV: You're the people who check everything.

220. EW: Mhm, I explain everything. Yeah. The realtors are nowhere to be found unless there's a problem. That's me. And I'm cutting these fat checks to the realtors.

221. INV: Realtors?

222. EW: Realtors and brokers that trust me.

223. INV: They didn't do anything? You did it all?

224. EW: They did absolutely nothing and they're ripping these people off but who am I?

225. INV: You can't tell them?

226. EW: No I can't say a word. Oh, trust me there's....

227. INV: Is this a great deal and you're like...

228. EW: Yeah, if you don't feel comfortable with this, talk to the other person. I can't advise you. And... (EW continues to chat about work)

Topic 4

229. INV: Ok, I'm going to show you this one more time. When you look at it, ask yourself does it remind me of him. If there's anything else we want to change, just let me know.

230. EW: His hair was a little longer right here.

231. INV: Ok.

232. EW: He had a little bit longer hair. It wasn't so short.

233. INV: So, I'm gonna do that. See that?

APPENDIX E

234.EW: Yeah it was fuller. You can see more of his hair here. Yeah.

235.INV: Ok.

Topic 5

236.EW: So how long have you been doing this?

237.INV: Well, I'm going on 14 years. I've been here 22 but I've been doing this for 14.

238.EW: Oh, wow. It's a talent to do that.

239.INV: Yeah, I enjoy it. When I found out that they actually paid somebody to draw all day, I thought how do I get that job? It took me about 8 years, but I got here.

240.EW: And you probably get all kinds of nice stories in here.

241.INV: Oh, yeah. Some are pretty bad, some are crazy. Alright, how's that?

242.EW: Much better. You know it's sad because when I went to the security guys there at the mall, they're all dumb shits, excuse my French, but they don't care. They were laughing and I look at them and went, "I don't think this is funny."

243.INV: They were laughing?

244.EW: They were kinda laughing, like, "What happened?" And I said, look someday you kids will grow up and have a daughter and that's one thing you're not going to wish your daughter to see.

245.INV: Was your daughter there when they were laughing?
EW: Yeah, and she was like, "Mom!"

246.INV: Well I hope you got a better response from the police.

247.EW: Oh, yeah, definitely. I was really surprised with how fast they got there.

248.INV: We usually respond on these pretty fast because these guys, that's how they start. They start doing this kind of gratification and then they, once this loses its excitement for them, they move on. So we need to find them before so now we know who they are. That's one of the reasons why we really get on his really hard.

249.EW: You know what and I remember when I was living in the Berryessa area and they had that Montgomery Wards there and that happened to me, getting out of the car and there he was. And back then they didn't have cell phones.

250.INV: Yeah, you're right.

251.EW: So I had to get a land line and by then, he was gone too.

252.INV: Did you call the police?

APPENDIX E

253.EW: Yeah, but I left.

PQ 254.INV: You did?

255.EW: Yeah, and I don't know why.

PQ 256.INV: So you didn't have to do a sketch then?

257.EW: No.

PQ 258.INV: You left, you never talked to police?

259.EW: No I called the police and said there's some perv here in this car, cruising the parking lot and he was disgusting. He was just gross. And this guy seemed like normal.

AQC 260.INV: Those are the worse ones.

261.EW: Clean, normal guy driving his family car and it was clean. And he wasn't a bad looking guy. Go somewhere. Pay for it. Find a girlfriend.

AQC 262.INV: OK, so how's this? (Shows sketch)

263.EW: Good

AQC 264.INV: Okay, your initials to your name?

AQC 265.INV: OK, I'll let you get back to your documents.

266.EW: OK, Thank you!

While there is no specific QQ in the transcript, the normal procedure for these interviews was to ask it as we walked to my office (or in the elevator). The question numbers that are circled signal a confidence in recollection that was maintained even though she was exposed to post event information. COR rating was negligible.

INTERVIEW ENDS

APPENDIX E

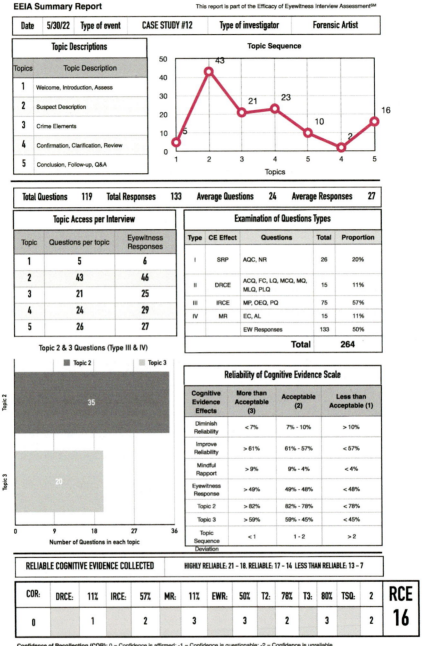

APPENDIX E

CASE STUDY #13

This section includes: a. Coded transcript, and b. EEIA summary report. For complete EEIA reports for case studies 6 through 15 go to www.mindfulinterviews.com/CaseStudies.

Each case study was evaluated and prepared for EEIA processing. Every attempt was made to standardize the evaluation and coding process for every case study. Any errors in coding, calculations, or assignment of RCE score, should be directed to the author. All of the transcripts were anonymized for instructional purposes, any resemblance to specific investigations is purely coincidental. The crime types and agencies are listed for informational purposes and to give the reader an idea of the variety of cases used in applying *The Mindful Interview Method*.

EYEWITNESS INTERVIEW ANALYSIS (EIA)
CONFIDENTIAL TRANSCRIPT REVIEW

Date of transcript review: May17, 2022

Crime type: Indecent exposure

Notes:

Topic 1

1. INV: The way this works is that most people, even though they have different views, they still have an idea of what the person looks like so I guess the question should be, if you saw him again, would you recognize him?

2. EW: Yes.

3. INV: Good, and that's all I need. The way we're going to do this is I'm gonna ask you some general questions about this person's face. What I'd like you to do is go ahead and answer to the best of your knowledge. Most people don't remember everything in great detail, however a lot of folks do tend to remember a lot more information when they're here and they're focused on the questions. You're going to have your eyes closed for about 5 minutes - that's going to help you to relax. People tend to remember more when they're nice and relaxed and they're focused. Some people also get an image of the person and it makes it easier to describe as well.

4. EW: Ok.

5. INV: After that, I'm gonna ask you to open your eyes. I'm gonna ask you to tell me what happened and then if we need to we'll make some changes to the sketch. Alright? Do you have any questions?

6. EW: No.

457

APPENDIX E

← Topic 2

 7. INV: First of all, give me a nice deep breath, let me know you're nice and relaxed and we'll begin. First of all, what would you say is the race of this person?

8. EW: Hispanic

 9. INV: Age range?

10. EW: Between late 20s - about 26 to early 30s, 32, 33 would probably be cutting it.

 11. INV: Ok. Body build?

12. EW: He wasn't heavy set. He didn't look like he did a lot of weight lifting, he just seemed kind of a regular non-weight lifter guy.

 13. INV: Mhm. When you think of the shape of his face, what kind of shape are we talking about?

14. EW: Kind of a larger head I guess you could say. He has not a small head, he has, it's more medium size, oval is what I can describe it.

 15. INV: Ok, anything unusual about it?

16. EW: No, he was just very clean cut is what I remember, hair wise.

 17. INV: How tall is this guy?

EW: He was sitting about, I'd say 5'7, 5'8, not much taller than that. He seemed shorter male.

 18. INV: Mhm. Tell me about his hair.

19. EW: Hair. Clean. I remember he looked like he'd just gotten a buzz on the side, or fade I guess you could call it. Top seemed cut to minimal. Not shaved. I remember seeing reflection of hair, so there was some hair at the top, mustache though, it was clean.

 20. INV: Tell me about the hair. How was it combed?

21. EW: It was, it long enough, it was combed, it looked like it was going in a back direction.

 22. INV: So it was too short to comb?

EW: Yeah it was too short to comb. It was shaved or cut at the top. Short.

 23. INV: And then are the sides shorter than the top.

24. EW: The side, yeah, it was like buzzed.

 25. INV: Is it like, there's a line?

26. EW: A fade? Yeah the line differentiates between the top to the side buzz.

 27. INV: Ok, and the color of his hair.

28. EW: Darker brown, like a chocolate color, but not black.

 29. INV: Any sideburns on this guy?

30. EW: It seemed short. Everything seemed clean here. Nothing outrageous.

 31. INV: Tell me about his ears. What are they like?

32. EW: Ears were smaller, not large at all. They seemed proportional to his head so that um they were just smaller in size, I guess.

 33. INV: Mhm. Any earrings on this guy?

34. EW: No, that I remember, no.

APPENDIX E

35. INV: (drawing) Tell me about his forehead. What does that look like?
36. EW: Um it didn't see very large at all because of the way his hair was cut, it seem like there was a fade in the front so it was a smaller forehead.
37. INV: Mhm and tell me about his nose. What was that like?
38. EW: His nose, there was nothing defining about it. It was, I couldn't see any bumps or anything. It seemed not to be very thick at the bottom, um more slender I guess.
39. INV: Mhm. So the nostrils. What were they like?
40. EW: Nothing interesting about the nose. Not very fat here, I just remember kind of slender. He looked slender.
41. INV: And tell me about his mouth and his lips.
42. EW: Lips were medium, not too thick, not too thin. They had slight shape, but I could tell there was a shape because of the way his mustache was cut that it was not covering his mouth.
43. INV: What was his attitude like?
44. EW: HIs attitude, I think he was frustrated with me because when I saw him from the side he knew I had been following him. He seemed, when I first first saw him, he was trying to get me to come towards the car and I wasn't. I refused to and he just um, the frustration was building, whatever it was. Kind of, I remember a (inaudible) feeling coming over him as well because I could tell he was getting nervous. He saw me on my phone. He saw that I wasn't stopping tailing him,
45. INV: Tell me about the mustache. What was that like?
46. EW: Mustache is very clean. It was, if I can remember, not thick. It didn't cover the mouth at all. There was a clean definition between the nose and the mustache so there was no hair here, it was trimmed, I guess.
47. INV: Does it go all the way across?
48. EW: No there's a little spot, bare area here and it stopped, I remember it stopping.
49. INV: At the corners?
50. EW: Yeah, or a guess where the lips would be.
51. INV: And what color is the mustache?
    EW: The mustache matched his hair. It was darker chocolate color but not black. I just remember his hair not being dark completely black.
52. INV: And so, this mustache looks pretty trimmed, like he's taking care of it?
53. EW: Like he had just gotten a hair cut or…
54. INV: What was his attitude like again?

459

APPENDIX E

55. EW: When I first saw him, it seemed that he was frustrated I wasn't coming towards the car, I could tell the frustration was building. From the side profile, he had this scared, kind of intense look, like he wouldn't come after me but he was trying to get away.

56. INV: Mhm

57. EW: So he wasn't going to be aggressive towards me, he just was trying to get away from my vehicle.

58. INV: Got it. Tell me about his chin. What does that look like?

59. EW: I remember from the profile that you could tell there was definition, um not square but more round but you could tell the jawline was defined.

60. INV: Mhm

61. EW: The end, there wasn't any, some people have that extra skin, you know there was just defined area between his jaw and his neck.

62. INV: And his neck, what was that like?

63. EW: His neck was slender, but I remember his shoulder, he had not big body builder shoulders but you know, they were longer here.

64. INV: Mhm. And tattoos, marks or scars on his face?

65. EW: No. Nothing on his face.

66. INV: Or neck?

67. EW: No.

68. INV: And white kind of shirt is he wearing?

69. EW: White, underneath, like the white undershirts. Just plain white.

70. INV: You mean like a t-shirt?

71. EW: Like a t-shirt. Guys I guess wear them underneath. My husband's in the military. He wears these white t-shirts under his uniform.

72. INV: Is it a v-neck, a crew neck?

73. EW: It was round.

74. INV: (drawing) What about his skin? What is that like?

75. EW: Clean, fair skinned. He was between a white shade, darker than I am but not dark. He's not out in the sun, he doesn't work in the sun. A lighter Hispanic shade, you could call it.

76. INV: And his cheeks. What are they like?

460

APPENDIX E

77. EW: His cheeks, I remember his face. His cheeks were not protruding extremely but you could tell there was that definition here when you - you can tell it wasn't a chubby face, it was, there was bone structure, I guess.

78. INV: Mhm. Cheek bones?

79. EW: Yeah.

80. INV: And the texture of his skin?

81. EW: It seemed smooth. It seemed taken care of.

82. INV: And this guy, does he have a mannish face or a boyish face?

83. EW: Mannish face, not young teenage, not even young 20 year old. It wasn't, he was getting older in his 30s.

84. INV: Any hair on the chin?

85. EW: Not that I remember, no, it all seemed fresh.

86. INV: (drawing) And tell me about his eyes.

87. EW: His eyes were almond shaped and they were medium to dark brown but they were like not circle more round. Not droopy either, they seemed fresh, kind of young looking. There was not heavy skin hanging over, droopy lids or what not and eyebrows seemed thicker but not too thick. They weren't groomed. They weren't plucked or anything. But they're also dark coffee looking color.

88. INV: Mhm. How close did you get to this guy?

89. EW: When I got out of my car after, he had, you know, been behind my vehicle. I got out to approach the vehicle. I was within about right here from the door so I'm leaning in towards him and that's when he reverses.

90. INV: And how long did you see him?

91. EW: At that front, direct front, less than 5 seconds. He had backed out as I approached him. I guess he got scared and then when the incident began, he was behind my car, I'm getting to my keys, and he starts to sign towards me. He's really close to the rear end of my car and I have to take a step so I can open my door, so within maybe 4-5 feet, if that. Then when I…

92. INV: How long was it total time maybe? The whole thing.

93. EW: Oh, the whole thing from start to the very last part that I saw him was 10 minutes.

94. INV: Ok. Did you think you knew him?

95. EW: No. I did not.

461

APPENDIX E

- Topic 3

 96. INV: Alright, you can open your eyes. Now what I want you to do is I want you to tell me what happened. I want you to tell me what you were doing just prior to running into this guy and I want you to tell me everything up until police get involved.

97. EW: Ok. I had just gotten out of the Walmart - I had gone there to get Capris. It was getting hot and it was that week where it started warming up here a lot in San Jose. So I'm exiting the Walmart...

 98. INV: In your car?

99. EW: No, I'm exiting the Walmart building heading towards my vehicle...

 100. INV: In the parking lot?

101. EW: In the parking lot of the Walmart, and as I'm approaching my car, I see that there are vehicles behind my car. I guess they were waiting there, probably a stopped car or what not a couple of cars away from where I'm parked. And I start reaching into my purse, and I have a lot of things in there and I'm looking for my keys and I'm struggling because I have a bag in my hand and I see the car still there and as I'm going through my bag I'm shuffling, I see that this car had stayed behind my vehicle and cars had all driven off so there was nothing blocking him, so I'm assuming he's waiting for my parking space and I'm still struggling to look through my stuff and my keys and he's still parked behind me and he starts to wave at me with his right hand to come towards his vehicle and I'm thinking he's telling me he's going to reverse and so I'm like ok...

 102. INV: So because is he blocking you?

103. EW: He's blocking me. He's completely behind the rear end of my car.

 104. INV: I know but like this? Like a T?

105. EW: Yes, exactly like that, yeah.

106. INV: Ok, got it.

107. EW: So he's waving and he continues to wave and I get a little apprehensive, like what's he doing now that it's obvious and it's clear that he wants me to come toward his car.

108. INV: Is he saying something to you.

109. EW: No, the window was up. I remember the window going down, he's still waving and I see his left hand is not visible on the steering wheel. It's down in his lap and I kind of turn and I look a little bit more...

110. INV: As you're walking?

111.EW: No, I'm stopped. I'm right here. Here's my car door, he's right here, and I'm looking through my purse and I look again as he's waving me and I see his hand motion going up and down. He's head is looking to me like it wants to go back in the seat. And I get my key opened and I can tell his pants are on but his zipper is down.

 112.INV: So you can see in his car?

113.EW: Yeah, I'm standing here. His car is not far from mine at all, from the back. So I'm looking and he's, I don't see anything, but you can tell his zipper is down. The vehicle is lower, it's not high SUV or what not. And I start to freak out and I get in my car and turn my car on. He's still behind my car. I see from the rear view mirror, I see his head go back out of either frustration or whatever you want to call it. I revved my car, saying you know get out of my way. I'm angry by this point, and as I rev my car, he moves forward and he stops as he moves forward and I guess expects me to get out of his way and keep going on my own, instead I stay up behind his vehicle and I honk. I'm honking, like what are you doing? He cuts across the divider between the two sides of the parking area and I follow him. I cut him off cuz there's no cars, I'm able to cut him off and park in front at an angle in front of him and he stops again. That's the point where I get out of my car and I run towards his vehicle and as he sees me coming, I can tell he's figgiting in his vehicle. I don't know if it was to put his pants up, I don't know what that is but...

 114.INV: Mhm

115.EW: I run up and I'm like, "What are you doing?" I'm cursing, I'm yelling.

 116.INV: Is his window still up?

117.EW: His window is up

 118.INV: Got it.

119.INV: And he has his face like he wants to get out of there. People are watching me get angry and no-one is coming and I forget what's around me. I run back to my car as he reversed and gone out toward the exit on Story, there's three lanes. One to go straight, one to turn right and to turn left. He's in the one turning toward the left hand sign. I am able to reverse and I get out and I follow and I'm behind his car. He sees me and he manages to cut across three lanes and go right trying to get out of my way or, and then there's a bus and he has to get out of the way of the bus that was in his way and I just follow him. I follow him to where Story turns into, I don't even know what it turns into but he makes a left onto Senter. He's in the turning lane and I'm following him and this is at the point where I had called 911. I make a left following his vehicle and he's swerving in and out and I'm tailing him. I'm able to get the license plate of the vehicle and describe it before he's able to pull off again into the traffic. He tries to make a U turn at one of the lights, I don't know what street it is, and I get up in front of his car and this is where we meet side by side. He gets out of my way, he's on this side of me and I turn and I look at him and that's how I get the profile of him sitting back in his car and he speeds off and so I have to wait for traffic to clear before I'm able to get back in there. We pass the Costco on our way and turn - It's Parrot or something.

120. INV: Mhm

121. EW: Make a right and he's going really quickly by this point. And then he makes a right and that's why I lose him because of the traffic coming at to make a right hand turn and I wait.

122. INV: And all this time you're on the phone?

123. EW: I'm on the phone so it's all recorded and I'm telling her what streets I'm going and it's what's making me go slower because I'm trying to drive stick and hold it.

124. INV: And what is she telling you?

125. EW: She's telling me police are coming, police are circling. What street are you on? Is he still on sight, what's he doing?

126. INV: Mhm

127. EW: And I guess the streets get confusing at one point because it turned into a one-way. I'm sure he's make a right hand turn or something around - there's an SJSU field for track or something. And some I'm sure he's gone done one of those ways and she tells me to wait in a specific area and I stop at the 7-11. I figured it's the most obvious point, and that's when Officer Best comes to the driveway and we meet. I know my make and models of my car but I couldn't figure out what his was. It had lights all across the back, like a Buick.

128. INV: So it's an older car?

129. EW: I would say like 90-91, white, colored, like a Mustang, like a coupe 2-door imagine. Yeah, because the door took over more than half the side angle and that's why the door is the main centerpiece.

130. INV: Right.

131. EW: I remember the interior being yellow colored, faded kind of. It was an older car, I'm thinking the Ford.

132. EW: I'm just angry because the reason I followed him was because I see people, I see kids and little girls and I know that there are kids getting out of school, and whether he thinks I'm younger or not, around 2:30-3:00 is when all the junior high and high school girls and kids get out of school and I can only imagine if this guy's still there. You know, kids go there for candy, gas station to get sodas or whatever and I didn't want him to stop and to harass another little kid.

133. INV: Did they stop anybody for you to look at that day?

134. EW: No, I had given them the license plate number, an officer guessed they got in contact with his brother or sister where he lived and that he was still driving around - he wasn't coming home.

135. INV: It was the right car, huh?

136. EW: I guess so. I guess the license plate I had given them. I was really close, I was tailing this guy, um and I had to make sure as best as possible to get at least that, you know. I made a scene in the parking lot because I wanted other people to come and help me and guys were just looking at me and I guess they thought maybe crazy girlfriend or you know something but no-one really made an effort.

Topic 4

AQC 137.INV: Alright, I'm going to show you the sketch. When you look at the sketch, I don't need you to tell me whether it looks like him or not. What I want you to do is just look at the sketch and kind of see what I've been doing. After you look at it for a few seconds, we're going to go over the same questions again but this time you'll be looking at the sketch. As I ask you about each feature I want you to tell me whether we're in the ballpark or whether we need to make some changes.

138.EW: Ok.

AQC 139.INV: Just remember, we're never gonna be exact, but we want to be very, very close so that when you look at it, it helps you to remember.

140.EW: Alright. Do you want me to stand up?

PR 141.INV: No, no, you're fine. And this happened how long ago?

142.EW: It's entering the second week.

AQC 143.INV: This is what I have so far (shows sketch)

144.EW: Yeah.

OEQ 145.INV: First of all, just the shape of his face. How's the shape of his face?

146.EW: You could make his jaw not so thin. It was a little more round just not full, not fat. I can't describe it.

MP 147.INV: A little more round?

148.EW: Yeah a little more round. Not so pointy.

PQ 149.INV: Ok. (drawing) Do you think this guy knew you?

150.EW: No. I was just a random - had to have been random.

OEQ 151.INV: The hair on his head?

152.EW: Yeah, it was, I would say less.

PC 153.INV: Less on the side or on the top?

154.EW: Yeah, less on the sides. It seemed more like a new fade.

AQC 155.INV: So what I'm doing…

156.EW: It's good, the definition between the top and the sides. But just the sides were a little bit..His were thinner.

MQ 157.INV: (drawing) Did you get your, what were you going to buy? Your shorts? Did you get them?

158.EW: Oh yeah, they were camouflage. I work with kids, the special ed kids like to be on the grass so I can't wear short. But this I can get dirty and not worry about it.

PQ 159.INV: How's that?

160.EW: Yeah, something like that.

APPENDIX E

OEQ   161.INV: Ok, the ears?

162.EW: Yeah, they're proportioned and small

OEQ   163.INV: And forehead?

164.EW: Yes, not too big.

OEQ   165.INV: The nose?

166.EW: I think just a little..

FC   167.INV: Rounder? Thicker?

168.EW: Yeah just a little bit. Not too much. But the slenderness from here to here is great.

PQ   169.INV: Ok. (drawing) How's that?

170.EW: Yes.

OEQ   171.INV: The lips?

172.EW: Perfect.

OEQ   173.INV: Mustache?

174.EW: Just clean. It was very clean um a little more space between the lip and the lower part of the mustache. It was very clean.

175.INV: (drawing)

176.EW: Yes.

OEQ   177.INV: Ok. The cheeks?

178.EW: Perfect.

OEQ   179.INV: The neck area, t-shirt?

180.EW: Yeah, he wasn't thick at all. Perfect. The white.

OEQ   181.INV: The eyes?

182.EW: Almond - very good.

OEQ   183.INV: What about his age. How are we doing on his age?

184.EW: A little older looking right here. He looks too fresh from here.

AQC   185.INV: I know that was a word you used a lot.

186.EW: Yeah, my mom uses it. It's young. He looks young.

PLQ   187.INV: Is he looking too young?

188.EW: He looks like he's about 22…

PQ   189.INV: So you want him a little bit older?

190.EW: Just a tad bit.

AQC   191.INV: Ok, I can do that. (drawing)

192.EW: The eyes, yeah. We looked directly at each other, twice, that I can remember.

APPENDIX E

Topic 5

RQ 193.INV: What time of day or night was it?

194.EW: Oh, um I had just gotten off of work - I'd say about 3:30 ish so it wasn't dark at all. I just remember it being a hot day. Yeah probably about 3:30.

PQ 195.INV: (drawing) So where are you teaching at?

196.EW: I'm a teacher's aid at the (inaudible) Center. It's a school for autistic children. Great job to have when you're a student at San Jose State.

AL 197.INV: Mhm.

198.EW: So it works with my hours.

PQ 199.INV: Are you getting your teaching credential?

200.EW: No, actually I want to be a lawyer so I'm a Justice Studies Major there.

AL 201.INV: Good for you.

202.EW: Kids just keep it entertaining. I need that right now.

AQC 203.INV: (drawing) Alright, I worked on his age a little bit.

204.EW: Ok. Yup.

PQ 205.INV: Is that alright?

206.EW: Yeah.

OEQ 207.INV: Anything else you want to change?

208.EW: No, that's it.

PQ 209.INV: We're in the ballpark?

210.EW: That's it.

PQ 211.INV: Alright, your initials?

212.EW: CK

AQC 213.INV: Alright, there's the sketch.

214.EW: Thank you so much!

INTERVIEW ENDS

APPENDIX E

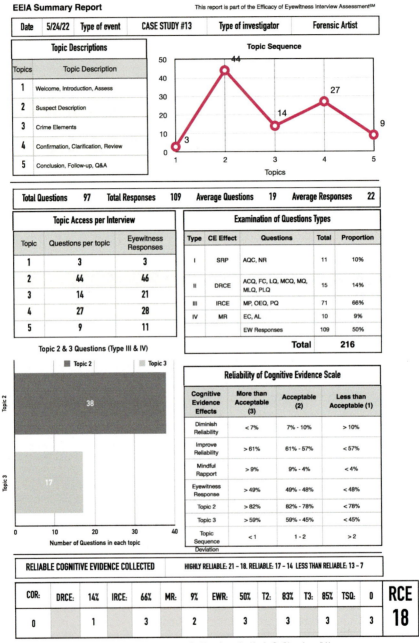

APPENDIX E

CASE STUDY #14

This section includes: a. Coded transcript, and b. EEIA summary report. For complete EEIA reports for case studies 6 through 15 go to www.mindfulinterviews.com/CaseStudies.

Each case study was evaluated and prepared for EEIA processing. Every attempt was made to standardize the evaluation and coding process for every case study. Any errors in coding, calculations, or assignment of RCE score, should be directed to the author. All of the transcripts were anonymized for instructional purposes, any resemblance to specific investigations is purely coincidental. The crime types and agencies are listed for informational purposes and to give the reader an idea of the variety of cases used in applying *The Mindful Interview Method*.

EYEWITNESS INTERVIEW ANALYSIS (EIA)
CONFIDENTIAL TRANSCRIPT REVIEW

Date of transcript review: May 17, 2022

Crime type: Indecent exposure

Notes:

Topic 1

 1. INV: Take a seat on the right.

2. EW: Ok.

 3. INV: Alright, here's my card for you for later if you have any questions. Let's see, so this happened to you when? How long ago?

4. EW: Ah, sorry I should remember the exact date, shouldn't I?

 5. INV: I have it, I was just asking in general.

6. EW: A few weeks ago.

 7. INV: A few weeks ago? Alright. So the way this works is I'm gonna ask you some general questions about the person's face…

8. EW: Ok.

 9. INV: I'd like you to answer to the best of your knowledge. Most people don't remember everything in great detail, however a lot of people tend to remember a lot of information, especially when they're here and they're focused on the questions.

10. EW: Ok

APPENDIX E

11. INV: You're gonna have your eyes closed for about 5 minutes. That helps you to kinda of relax and focus on the questions. It makes it a little bit easier for you to maybe visualize this subject, and then after, I'll ask you to open your eyes, I'll ask you to tell me what happened and then I'll show you the sketch and if we need to, we'll make some changes.

12. EW: Ok.

13. INV: Ok, alright. First of all, if you saw him again, would you recognize him?

14. EW: Um I honestly don't know, especially since he's wearing sunglasses at the time. So it's not like I saw his exact face.

Topic 2

19. INV: Ok, alright then, we'll give it a shot. We'll see what happens. Go ahead and sit back, relax, give me a nice deep breath and we'll begin. Ok. First of all, what would you say is the race of this person?

20. EW: He was caucasian.

21. INV: Mhm. Age range?

22. EW: Age range I'd say probably 30s but plus or minus 10 at the most. So like probably mid-30s.

23. INV: Ok. Body build?

24. EW: Sort of footballer-ish. So um so big with muscle and fat.

25. INV: I like that - "footballer-ish". I think you just made up a word.

26. EW: Possibly. I should coin it.

27. INV: One of is going to do that. (laughs) So think about the shape of his face. What's the shape of his face?

28. EW: I'd say round and but with like slightly squared jaw. Not completely boxy but roundish cheeks and a square jaw.

29. INV: Mhm. Tell me about his hair. What is that like?

30. EW: Um it was, I'd say reddish-brown. And it wasn't particularly short or long. If you need a length, I think it's stood up slightly.

31. INV: Stood up where?

32. EW: Sort of like, it was some volume around here and then I would probably guess that he has some sideburns but I'm not so sure. He did have a beard, though.

33. INV: Ok. So how would he comb his hair?

34. EW: Sorry, maybe make the front part stick up a little.

35. INV: Ok, go ahead and keep your eyes closed. That will help you when you're thinking about the questions.

36. EW: Ok.

APPENDIX E

PQ 37. INV: So um were there any parts in his hair?

38. EW: Not that I remember.

PQ 39. INV: Ok. And you said the color of his hair was what?

40. EW: Reddish-brown.

PQ 41. INV: Mhm. And you said that the thickness was what?

42. EW: The thickness was, I think, fairly thick.

AC 43. INV: Mhm

44. EW: I didn't see any balding spots or anything.

OEQ 45. INV: Mhm. And then the sides of the hair as far as length goes in relation to the top of the hair? What is that like?

46. EW: Um, I think it was, like, well pretty much a normal length so it wasn't long or shaggy or anything, so um I'd say, as far as hairstyles go around here…

OEQ 47. INV: Tell me about his ears.

48. EW: His ears, well I didn't notice anything about them so I'd say they were truly (inaudible)

AC 49. INV: Mhm.

50. EW: I do remember at the very least, the ear facing me was out of his hair.

PQ 51. INV: So the hair was around it?

52. EW: Mhm yeah.

PQ 53. INV: Ok. And you did talk about sideburns, right?

54. EW: Yeah.

PQ 55. INV: What were they like?

56. EW: Um, I sort of, well I think that his hair was, his beard went all the way up here, so I'm assuming his sideburns were there.

PQ 57. INV: Ok, got it. So that's part of the beard, you're saying?

58. EW: Yeah.

PLQ 59. INV: Any earrings?

60. EW: Um I don't think so

OEQ 61. INV: Mhm. Tell me about his forehead.

62. EW: Um it wasn't, well I would say slightly narrow, so his hair (inaudible) down his face.

PQ 63. INV: His hair was what, did you say?

64. EW: Forehead was slightly small I think.

PQ 65. INV: Oh, ok that's what you mean. Got it. What was the hairline like?

471

APPENDIX E

66. EW: I think it was sort of squarish so the hair just goes up, across and down.

 67. INV: Ok, very good. Tell me about his nose. What is that like?

68. EW: I think it was slightly, well I think it slightly hooked...

 69. INV: What do you mean by that?

70. EW: Um, so, actually no, sorry. That's not the way I would describe it. Um I think it was sort of, I mean it was fairly large and a bit bulbous around her,

 71. INV: Mhm

72. EW: And um but it wasn't particularly long or anything.

 73. INV: Ok. Are you able to see his nostrils?

74. EW: No.

 75. INV: Ok. Tell me about his mouth and his lips.

76. EW: I think they were a slightly darkish color. Um but then again his face was in shadows. He was inside the car and (inaudible) so I wouldn't be able to say if that's 100 percent correct and um his mouth was I'd say medium to large.

 77. INV: Were you able to see his teeth?

78. EW: No.

 79. INV: And you said he had a beard.

80. EW: Yeah.

 81. INV: And does this beard include a mustache (inaudible).

82. EW: Um I don't think he had a mustache.

 83. INV: So the beard, where does it cover on his face?

84. EW: So it just goes all the way down and up across his jawline.

 85. INV: So nothing above his upper lip.

86. EW: So, yeah.

 87. INV: Oh, ok. Is that unique to you or is that something you see a lot?

88. EW: I see it sometimes.

 89. INV: Mhm. Alright. Let's talk about his chin. What is that like?

90. EW: Well, since it was kinda covered by his beard, I would imagine it was sort of squarish. It didn't seem like it would be pointed or anything. I'm just assuming the square jaw continues to his chin as well.

APPENDIX E

OEQ   91. INV: And let's talk about the beard. What was that like?

92. EW: Um it was, I'd say, medium length and um it was slightly shaggy.

AL   93. INV: Mhm

94. EW: I don't think, it didn't seem to me as if he like kept it nice and clipped or anything.

OEQ   95. INV: Mhm. Talk about the thickness of his lips. What are they like?

96. EW: Say they were slightly thin, on the thin side.

AL   97. INV: Mhm.

98. EW: Yeah and they didn't exactly stick out or anything.

OEQ   99. INV: And what was the color of his beard?

100. EW: Same color as his hair, sort of reddish-brown/auburn color.

FC   101. INV: This guy, does he have a mannish face or a boyish face.

102. EW: I'd say mannish face.

OEQ   103. INV: Talk about his neck.

104. EW: Um, like it was on the thick side.

MP   105. INV: On the thick side?

106. EW: Yeah, like thick well it looked pretty strong so.

OEQ   107. INV: What was he wearing for a shirt?

108. EW: He was wearing a red t-shirt. I don't remember if it had a design or not though.

FC   109. INV: (drawing) Any scars or marks on his face?

110. EW: No, not that I know of.

PLQ   111. INV: Any tattoos?

112. EW: I didn't notice any.

AL   113. INV: Mhm.

114. EW: So I don't think there were any tattoos on the side that was facing me, so his right side.

AQC   115. INV: And you're touching your arm there.

116. EW: Mhm.

OEQ   117. INV: Tell me about his skin texture and skin tone, things like that.

APPENDIX E

118.EW: Um it sort of seemed to me like it had sort of reddish tinge, so and it didn't look completely smooth, like a bit bumpy and his face, I think he had some stubble around his mustache, um where his mustache would be, so his upper lip.

OEQ 119.INV: Mhm. And then let's talk about his eyes. What are they like?

120.EW: Um, it's hard. He was wearing really dark sunglasses so I really couldn't see.

OEQ 121.INV: Ok, that's good. So let's talk about that then. What were the glasses like?

122.EW: Um, I think they were completely black or at the very least I couldn't see through them and they were sort of like what my glasses look like except more like roundish on the bottom.

MCQ 123.INV: Mhm. Would you say they're large, small, medium?

124.EW: I would say they were medium.

PQ 125.INV: Mhm. What kind of frame are we talking about?

126.EW: So I mean I mean (inaudible) but they were like the Wellington-type glasses, if you know what I mean.

PQ 127.INV: No, help me with that.

128.EW: So they weren't like the sun visor type but they were sort of like what my glasses look like. Um so the bridge, they were, (inaudible) and then they were just like two semi circles and the entire, and the entire thing was just black including the lens and the fram.

PR 129.INV: Mhm. So there were no, there wasn't other material.

130.EW: I don't think so.

OEQ 131.INV: Have you ever seen this guy before?

132.EW: I don't think so.

PQ 133.INV: Mhm. And you said he was in a vehicle?

134.EW: Yeah.

OEQ 135.INV: What kind of vehicle?

136.EW: It was silver and I don't remember the car type. It was boxy and since his eye level was about where mine was, I'd say it was a very tall car.

PQ 137.INV: Any why do you say that?

138.EW: Because, like when for instance when my friend, she drives a sporty car but her car level is way below mine, when I get out on the sidewalk.

Topic 3

APPENDIX E

AQC 139.INV: Oh, I see. Alright, you can open your eyes. Now what I want you to do is I want you to tell me what happened. I want you to tell me what you were doing prior to running into this guy, and then take me through the incident up until police get involved.

140.EW: Ok. So I was walking home from Walgreens and I had a little bag on me and I was almost at my house and I was walking on the sidewalk down and, it's a fairly large street but and there were a number of cars parked not the side and when I passed one of them, the silver car...

MP 141.INV: Was he in the silver car?

142.EW: Yeah he was. And he said, the first thing he said was, "Excuse me." and that was when I turned around just looked to the side and

MP 143.INV: You looked to the side?

144.EW: Ahuh, and so I was right in front of the passenger seat. And so he was in the driver's seat but the passenger seat's window was open and that was when I looked straight at him and um his penis was out and I remember not really noticing it at first, so and then he just said, "Do you need a ride?" and that was when I realized - so my mind went slightly blank at first...

AL 145.INV: Mhm.

146.EW: but that was when I realized that his penis was out and fully erect so I just said, "No, no thanks." and then I walked home. My house is just around the corner so it was only a one to two minute walk.

AL 147.INV: Mhm.

148.EW: And so after arriving at my house, I realized that I should have taken his license, oh sorry, license plate number.

AL 149.INV: Mhm

150.EW: So I put on a hat, jacket and sunglasses and I tried to see if I could take a picture of his license plate.

PQ 151.INV: Oh, you went back outside?

152.EW: Yeah. So I went back outside. I creeped around the corner and but he had already gone by then.

PQ 153.INV: So what did you do after that?

154.EW: I just went home after that and I was debating whether or not I should call the police but in the end I decided to.

MP 155.INV: You decided to?

156.EW: Yeah. So the incident happened around just past 6.

APPENDIX E

MS 157.INV: 6?

158.EW: 6PM. And I think I called the police at 8pm after that and about an hour after that, so 9pm a police officer came to my house and he asked me re-live the scene and also showed him the place where it happened.

NV 159.INV: Mhm

160.EW: I guess that's how they (inaudible).

PQ 161.INV: Pardon me?

162.EW: So I guess…

PQ 163.INV: Oh, the whole thing. And have they shown you any pictures of possible suspects since then?

164.EW: No.

MQ 165.INV: And what did you say about the car? What was the car like?

166.EW: So it was silver. It was slightly like boxy on top and then with a hood that sort of, it like wasn't slanted, but flat and then rounded down.

OER 167.INV: Mhm. Has anything like this ever happened to you?

168.EW: No.

OER 169.INV: So when you're walking, you said, you'd just come back from where again?

170.EW: Walgreens.

PQ 171.INV: Walgreens. And what were you doing?

172.EW: I just went, I think I went to buy soap.

MQ 173.INV: Mhm. So when you're walking are you, is there anything going on besides that? Talking to anybody? Doing anything?

174.EW: Um no. I just generally listen to music but I don't think at that time I was.

PQ 175.INV: Ok. And when you said he said something to you - what did he say again?

176.EW: He said, "Excuse me."

PQ 177.INV: And when he said that, he was in his car?

178.EW: Mhm.

PLQ 179.INV: So he was in the driver's seat?

180.EW: Yeah.

476

APPENDIX E

PLQ 181.INV: And you said when you looked over, you mentioned that it was at the same eye level and you walking, so you think it was a big car?

182.EW: Yeah.

PQ 183.INV: Ok, and so you're able to see inside?

184.EW: Mhm.

PQ 185.INV: Now, his window was open, but was the car door open?

186.EW: No. And he didn't make any sort of move to get out.

AL 187.INV: Mhm. No, go ahead.

188.EW: All he did was sort of lean slightly over towards the passenger seat and look at me and, but yeah, he didn't try to get out or grab me or anything.

PLQ 189.INV: Did he make you feel that he wanted you to see him? Did he acknowledge that you were seeing him?

190.EW: Yeah.

PQ 191.INV: How did he do that?

192.EW: Um. Sorry, oh, are you saying did he try to make me look at his private parts?

PQ INV: His penis, yeah, or anything. Whatever. I mean did you get that sense?

193.EW: Well I guess because for one thing he, if he (inaudible) I would have walked past and not seen anything at all. I was just looking straight forward and there was no chance of me just looking at it from my free will.

OEQ 194.INV: So what was going on around you at the time?

195.EW: It was, I don't think there was anybody outside. There were a couple of cars just speeding past, but so I guess I could have called for help if I wanted to but…

PQ 196.INV: Oh, there were people around?

197.EW: Well, it was like right next to, well there were a lot of houses on the side and since there was nobody outside on the sidewalk, but there were cars just driving past so I think I could have made a scene if I wanted to.

PQ 198.INV: Oh, I see. And did he ever take off his glasses?

199.EW: No.

PQ 200.INV: Mhm. And you mentioned, I think you touched your arm when I asked you about tattoos. You don't think you saw any?

201.EW: I don't think I saw any at least on the side that was facing me, so his right side.

APPENDIX E

OEQ 202.INV: (drawing) And did he say anything to you after you looked at him?

203.EW: Um, all he said was, "Do you need a ride?"

AL 204.INV: Mhm

205.EW: To which I said, "No, thanks."

OEQ 206.INV: Have you talked to neighbors about this?

207.EW: No.

Topic 4

AQC 208.INV: Alright, I'm gonna show you the sketch. When you look at the sketch, I don't need you to tell me whether it looks like him or not, not just yet. What I want you to do is look at the sketch and kinda get a sense of what I was doing, sketching. And then I'm gonna ask you the same questions again, but this time you'll be looking at the sketch. As I ask about each feature, I want you to tell me whether we're in the ballpark or whether you might make some changes.

209.EW: Ok.

AQC 210.INV: We're never gonna be exact because your memory isn't exact, however, we want to be close so that when you look at it, it helps you remember what he looks like. So keep that in mind.

211.EW: Ok.

AQC 212.INV: (shows sketch) Here's what I have so far.

213.EW: Mhm.

 214.INV: First of all, just the shape of his face? How's the shape of his face?

215.EW: Pretty accurate.

 216.INV: Ok, in the ballpark?

217.EW: Ahuh.

 218.INV: His hair on his head?

EW: Well the top looks ok, but I'd say there was a bit more volume on the sides.

 219.INV: Ok, you want to see more volume? Do you see how I elected keep it kind of straight and up cuz I kinda felt that's how your hand was going?

220.EW: Mhm

 221.INV: Is that the same style you want coming off the sides?

APPENDIX E

PQ   222.EW: Um yeah just feel that it's just slightly too straight. I do remember like a lock of hair just curling down like this.

PQ   223.INV: Down the back? Sides, excuse me.

224.EW: Mhm.

PQ   225.INV: Ok, so a little more weight. (drawing) I'm going to work on one side only and then you tell me if that meets your needs. (shows sketch) How's that?

226.EW: Oh, yeah.

PQ   227.INV: Is that ok?

228.EW: Mhm

OEQ   229.INV: So, I'll do the same thing on this side. Forehead. How are we doing on the forehead?
EW: I think that's pretty much how I remember it.

OEQ   230.INV: Mhm. How do the ears feel?

231.EW: Considering that I don't remember the ears, yeah.

OEQ   232.INV: His nose. How does that feel?

233.EW: Mmm, um, I'd say it was a bit more hooked maybe.

PQ   234.INV: So when you say "hooked" that's what I'm trying to give it here. So is that what you're talking about "hooked" or is there something else you're trying to think of.

235.EW: Um, so let's see…So I was looking at it sort of from a 3/4 angle, and let's see, so I guess it was - protrude more. I think it's in the ballpark though.

MQ   236.INV: Ok, so does this feel… how about this. Tell me, does this nose the way I've drawn it - what do you think it's showing for you? So if it's not protruding, what is it doing? Or not protruding enough? I don't know. So how about that? I just kind of increased the height of it.
EW: Mhm. I think that was sort of what I'm trying to say.

OEQ   237.INV: Alright, good. Ok, his mouth and his lips?

238.EW: Um yeah they look pretty accurate.

PQ   239.INV: Mhm. And then I gave him a little bit of stubble, is that ok?

240.EW: Mhm.

OEQ   241.INV: Alright. The beard. How are we doing on the beard?

242.EW: Yeah, I think that's pretty much (inaudible). Yeah, it wasn't particularly like large or short.

PQ   243.INV: Right, and then I gave him some blemishes in the skin. How does that feel?

244.EW: It feels accurate. He definitely didn't have like model skin or anything.

APPENDIX E

OEQ 245.INV: Alright, and the neck area and the shoulders?

246.EW: I think his neck was slightly more long but ...

PQ 247.INV: How about thickness?

248.EW: Thickness, yes.

OEQ 249.INV: (drawing) I lengthened it a little. Glasses? How are we doing on the glasses?

250.EW: Yeah, I feel like these are slightly - it was more shorter on the sides and slightly rounded on the bottom, but in terms of size, yes.

PQ 251.INV: Ok, bring them in just a little bit and then not as straight, more rounded?

252.EW: Yeah.

AQC 253.INV: So that's what I'm gonna do here - I'm gonna take off something like that. (drawing) And they were black.

254.EW: Yeah.

PQ 255.INV: (drawing) So you just got back from, did you go away on business, vacation?

256.EW: Oh, um a grad student and I'm studying in England.

AL 257.INV: Oh, ok.

258.EW: I came back for the holidays.

PQ 259.INV: Ok. So what are you studying?

260.EW: Archaeology.

FC 261.INV: Ok, wow. Are you going to end up back here or going to be somewhere else eventually?

262.EW: Mm well I'm hoping to come back here but I'm just on this course to getting a job in England

PQ 263.INV: Oh, really. They want you there, huh.

264.EW: It's just that the time period in what I'm studying, it's not popular in America anymore so...

ARC 265.INV: That obviously begs the question (inaudible).

266.EW: I know. Roman coins.

AL 267.INV: Oh my gosh.

268.EW: Yeah, I mean, I feel that in America now a days, they're more interested in American coins, so there are tons of people with interesting coins just not Roman.

FC 269.INV: Wow. So are you part of a team that goes out and authenticates them or actually look for them?

APPENDIX E

270. EW: Both, actually.

 271. INV: Really?

272. EW: Yeah.

 273. INV: And who do you use for, how would I say, for relying on information that a certain coin is in a certain place?

274. (Discusses coins/career….)

Topic 5

 275. INV: Alright I'm gonna show you the sketch one more time. When you look at it, I want you to ask yourself, "Does it remind me of him?"

276. EW: Ok.

 277. INV: If there's something you want me to change or adjust, just let me know and we'll take care of it, otherwise we should be pretty…

278. Areas like you said the glasses that are black. The next time you see this, if you ever see it again, will be very black. I don't need you to stick around for me to really make it black.

279. EW: Ok.

 280. INV: But it will definitely be much darker than it was, so just keep that in mind. (drawing) (shows sketch) Does that remind you of him?

281. EW: Yeah, it does.

 282. INV: In the ballpark?

283. EW: Mhm.

 284. INV: Any other changes?

285. EW: Not that I can think of.

286. INV: Good. Very good. Alright so the next thing that will happen is if MVPD finds somebody that matches this description, they may contact you about viewing a photo lineup so just keep that in mind. They may contact you for that. Ok, you have my business card. I'll walk you out.

287. EW: Ok.

INTERVIEW ENDS

481

APPENDIX E

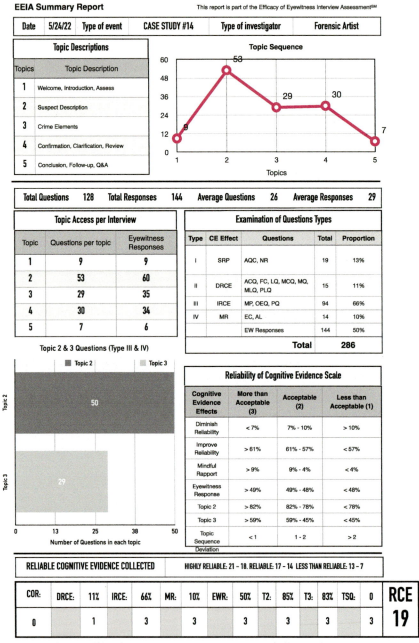

APPENDIX E

CASE STUDY #15

This section includes: a. Coded transcript, and b. EEIA summary report. For complete EEIA reports for case studies 6 through 15 go to www.mindfulinterviews.com/CaseStudies.

Each case study was evaluated and prepared for EEIA processing. Every attempt was made to standardize the evaluation and coding process for every case study. Any errors in coding, calculations, or assignment of RCE score, should be directed to the author. All of the transcripts were anonymized for instructional purposes, any resemblance to specific investigations is purely coincidental. The crime types and agencies are listed for informational purposes and to give the reader an idea of the variety of cases used in applying *The Mindful Interview Method*.

EYEWITNESS INTERVIEW ANALYSIS (EIA)
CONFIDENTIAL TRANSCRIPT REVIEW

Date of transcript review: May 17, 2022

Crime type: Attempted kidnapping

Notes: Because the eyewitness responded "No" to my QQ I needed to determine whether we would continue the interview or not. The topic sequences (1, 3, 2) I access at this early stage of the interview is merely a way for me to assure him that the interview is something he can complete. By the time I get to question 101 I have determined that the eyewitness should be able to complete the interview session, and he agrees.

Topic 1

 1. INV: Alright, and what was your first name again?

2. EW: Michael

 3. INV: Michael, ok. Alright, do you know why you're here?

4. EW: Yes.

 5. INV: Ok, good. And so if you saw this guy again, would you recognize him?

6. EW: No.

 7. INV: You wouldn't? And how come?

8. EW: Well I was in a panic mode and I, when I was running, I looked back for like a second or two and I just kept running.

 9. INV: Ok, so what about, so did this happen during the day or at night?

10. EW: During the day.

 11. INV: During the day? After school?

12. EW: Yes.

 13. INV: Oh, ok. And is this your school? Where you're at?

14. EW: Yeah.

APPENDIX E

PQ 15. INV: Ok. And were you with somebody?

16. EW: No.

MQ 17. INV: And is that normal for you? After school?

18. EW: Yeah.

PQ 19. INV: And how far from school to home? I mean, is that where you were going?

20. EW: Yeah, well I walk to my grandma's and then my dad picks me up.

PQ 21. INV: Oh, ok. And how far is your grandma's place?

22. EW: Not too far. Just 5 minutes away.

AL 23. INV: Oh, ok. That's nice.

24. EW: From the school, it's 5 minutes away.

PQ 25. INV: And she's always there?

26. EW: Yeah. Sometimes she's not, like she has to pick up my brother first.

OEQ 27. INV: Ah, ok. So how do you get into her place if she's not there?

28. EW: Um, there's a key under the stairs and it goes to the front door.

PQ 29. INV: Oh, ok. So you know all that?

30. EW: Yeah.

PQ 31. INV: So, what grade are you in?

32. EW: Twelfth.

PQ 33. INV: What school is this?

34. EW: Westbrook High School

OEQ 35. INV: Westbrook? Oh, ok. So has anything like this ever happened to you before?

36. EW: No.

MQ 37. INV: And why do you think this happened to you that day? How long ago did this happen?

38. EW: On Thursday.

UP 39. INV: Oh, this Thursday?

40. EW: Yes.

OEQ 41. INV: So why do you think his happened to you?

42. EW: I just wasn't expecting it and that's when he came up behind me.

PQ 43. INV: How do you know it was a he?

44. EW: I saw his hair when I looked back.

Topic 3

AQC 45. INV: Ok. So, why don't you tell me what was going on right before. So from the time you got out of school and then you're walking. Start from there.

APPENDIX E

46. EW: I had my hood on and my earbuds in and I saw this guy in his car and it didn't look like his car was started or not. It looks like he was on his phone and I took out my earbud to itch my ear and that's when I heard a car door and that's when he grabbed me. And then I was getting my right arm free and elbow him in the face and that's when he let go of his grip. And then while I was running, I looked back and his, he was bleeding and he was crouched down and I saw his car trunk open.

PQ 47. INV: And then what happened?

48. EW: And then I just kept on running.

PQ 49. INV: And then what happened?

50. EW: That was it.

OEQ 51. INV: You ended up where?

52. EW: At my grandmas.

PQ 53. INV: Who called the police?

54. EW: My mom said the school did.

PQ 55. INV: Why did they call the police?

56. EW: Well I think yesterday my mom called them.

PQ 57. INV: OH, Friday.

58. EW: Yeah.

PQ 59. INV: So not the day it happened.

60. EW: Yeah.

PQ 61. INV: Ok, so your mom called the school and told them what had happened to you?

62. EW: Mhm

PQ 63. INV: And then they called the police.

64. EW: Yeah.

NR 65. INV: Got it. So let's back up. So you say you're walking home to your grandmother's, right?

66. EW: Yeah.

OEQ 67. INV: And you said you have your headphones on, your hoodie, and you see somebody in a car. Why do you notice that person in the car?

68. EW: He was waiting for someone to respond to his text or something, I don't really know.

MCQ 69. INV: Mhm. Is he on the right of you or the left of you, in front of you?

70. EW: His car was on the right and he was inside on the left side - the driver's side.

PQ 71. INV: So are you on a sidewalk and he's to the right of you?

72. EW: Mhm. And his car is facing this way.

PQ 73. INV: Oh, ok. And so what's to the left of you? If he's to the right of you, what's to the left of you?

APPENDIX E

74. EW: Um just trees and plants and what not.

NR 75. INV: Ok. And then he's parked facing you and he's on the driver's side which is the other side of the car?

76. EW: Yeah.

PQ 77. INV: Uhuh, and you see him, you're going forward and you see him. What do you see about him?

78. EW: Um that he looks like he was about to get out of his car and open his trunk and what not.

Topic 2

OEQ 79. INV: Mhm. So how old do you think he was?

80. EW: Mid-40s.

PQ 81. INV: Mhm. And you said you thought he was texting?

82. EW: Yeah. He was looking down, so I thought he was on his phone.

OEQ 83. INV: Ok. And have you ever seen him before?

84. EW: No.

OEQ 85. INV: No? So how did he comb his hair?

86. EW: It's kinda wavy.

MP 87. INV: Kinda wavy? Long, short, medium?

88. EW: Short to me.

PQ 89. INV: Mhm. And did he have any facial hair?

90. EW: No.

OEQ 91. INV: And did you say his race? What did you say his race was?

92. EW: Light skinned. White.

MQ 93. INV: White. You think he's white, ok. And then no facial hair. In his 40s. What about the look in his face. What was that like?

94. EW: I don't know. I didn't really get to see it.

PQ 95. INV: You said you saw him - you saw his hair, you saw no facial features.

96. EW: Yeah, he was covering his nose and his mouth…

AQC 97. INV: No, no, no, I'm talking about before. Remember you saw him, you're walking, you see him. You think he might be texting. He's kinda doing this back and forth. You also say you think he might be opening his trunk. So there's a moment there where I think you have an idea, a snapshot of what he might look like. That's kinda what I'm doing here. That's all I'm doing. I'm just trying to get a sketch of somebody. It's never going to be exact because your memory isn't exact.

98. EW: Mhm

 99. INV: But we want to get it close enough so that when you see it, you go, "Alright, now that I think about it, that kinda reminds me of him." Do you understand?

100. EW: Yeah.

Topic 1

 101. INV: So that's kinda what I'm trying to get at with this sketch. I think that you can do it cuz it sounds like you saw him face-forward for a little bit, and sometimes it's just seconds, that's all we need. So let me ask you the questions. I'm gonna kinda draw along, and then you just tell me what kinda pops in your head, ok?

102. EW: Yeah.

 103. INV: Now, the way this works, since we're dealing with memory. It's a lot easier if you close your eyes because when you close your eyes, you're able to think back, your able to kinda relax, and then you think of that person in the car and you kind of take yourself back to what was going on on Thursday. Kinda the music you were listening to, the way the weather was, and then you just kind of hear my question, then you just kinda go, "Ok, that's what I see because here's my picture and it's nice and, it may not be super clear, but it's enough where you can go, "Ok." Because you already said he was a man, you already said he was in his 40s, and you said he was white, so that's good. You just keep hanging onto that image and then as I ask you questions, if you remember, you kind of access your memory and look at his face and then you say to yourself, "Ok, this is what I remember." Or if you don't remember something, you say, "I'm trying, but I don't remember that part." And that's ok. Alright. Now I may ask you another question about that same thing just to see if that helps, but if you don't remember, you don't remember. Ok? You want to try it?

104. EW: Sure.

Topic 2

 105. INV: Alright, good. So do me a favor - go ahead and close your eyes. Give me a nice deep breath and we'll begin. Give me another deep breath. Very good. So first of all, his race. What was his race again?

106. EW: White.

 107. INV: Good. His age range?

487

APPENDIX E

108.EW: mid 40s

OEQ 109.INV: Very good. His body build overall. His body - what was that like?

110.EW: Um kinda skinny like me.

OEQ 111.INV: Ok, skinny. Good. When you think about the shape of his face, what kind of shape does it make?

112.EW: I don't know.

PQ 113.INV: So some people, you have an idea of face shapes, right?

114.EW: Mhm.

FC 115.INV: So was his face shape kind of unusual or just kind of normal?

116.EW: Kind of normal.

MQ 117.INV: Good. That's what I like. Tell me about his hair, how he combs it, the color, things like that. The length.

118.EW: It's wavy and it's short to medium.

OEQ 119.INV: Mhm. Very good. And thinking back on his face, how would you say he combs his hair?

120.EW: I don't know.

MQ 121.INV: So are we thinking that he may - does he comb it away from his face, on his face, forward, back, messy, neat? You know, anything you can think of.

122.EW: Probably back and forth.

PQ 123.INV: Ok, very good. And the color again?

124.EW: Black.

MP 125.INV: It was black hair?

126.EW: Mhm

OEQ 127.INV: What about his ears? What are they like?

128.EW: They looked similar to mine

PQ 129.INV: Mhm. Was he wearing any earrings?

130.EW: No.

OEQ 131.INV: Tell me about his forehead. What is that like?

132.EW: Um, kinda rounded.

OEQ 133.INV: Kinda rounded. Very good. Tell me about his nose. What is that like?

APPENDIX E

134. EW: I don't remember.

MQ 135. INV: Ok. And then what about facial features? I mean, excuse me, facial hair. That's what I meant to say.

136. EW: I don't know if he had facial hair or not.

OEQ 137. INV: Ok. Talk about his mouth and his lips.

138. EW: When I last saw him, it was bloody.

PQ 139. INV: Mhm. So I'm thinking about the time you saw him, he was in the car, kinda before all this stuff. How do you know he was the same guy that grabbed you?

140. EW: I, when I was walking by, I saw his hair and his ears and head...

PQ 141. INV: And you think it's the same guy?

142. EW: Yeah.

FC 143. INV: Ok, good. So any mustache or beard or anything like that?

144. EW: No.

OEQ 145. INV: What was his attitude like when you saw him in the car?

146. EW: Kinda mad a little bit.

MP 147. INV: Kinda mad? Why do you think he was mad at you?

148. EW: I think he thought I was the perfect victim for a kidnapping.

OEQ 149. INV: Mhm. What about his chin? What is that like?

150. EW: I don't know.

OEQ 151. INV: Mhm. What kind of clothes was he wearing?

152. EW: Just a white t-shirt and some pants, I didn't see the color.

OEQ 153. INV: What kind of car was it?

154. EW: Alls I know it was a black 4-door sedan.

FC 155. INV: Black 4-door sedan. Clean looking, dirty looking?

156. EW: Clean.

OEQ 157. INV: Clean? What about his skin color?

158. EW: Tannish.

OEQ 159. INV: Ok. Now think about this, just kinda focus on - you're doing really well - focus on the time you saw him in the car, you notice him and now think about the look in his eyes. The look that he gave you even for a split second. What was that like?

APPENDIX E

160.EW: Hostile.

MCQ 161.INV: Hostile? Ok. And think about his eyes. We're they big eyes, small eyes, medium eyes, average eye?

162.EW: I don't know.

PQ 163.INV: What made them hostile?

164.EW: I have not idea.

PQ 165.INV: What is hostile to you?

166.EW: Hatred, like he hates me and other people.

OEQ 167.INV: Uhuh. And what would you say the color of his eyes were?

168.EW: I didn't get a real look at them.

FC 169.INV: Were they dark or light?

170.EW: Kinda light.

MP 171.INV: Kinda light?

172.EW: Mhm

OEQ 173.INV: What were you listening to? What music were you listening to?

174.EW: Hard rock.

FC 175.INV: Hard rock? Pretty loud or not too loud?

176.EW: Full blast.

PQ 177.INV: Ok. What was the band?

178.EW: Umm, I don't know if it's a band or not but his name is Disturbed.

OEQ 179.INV: Mhm. Has anything like this ever happened to you before?

180.EW: No.

OEQ 181.INV: What about his eyebrows? What are they like?

182.EW: Kinda thin, a little bit.

PQ 183.INV: Mhm. Anybody see this guy do this to you?

184.EW: No.

FC 185.INV: (drawing) Any scars or marks on his face?

186.EW: I don't think so.

OEQ 187.INV: What's the one feature you remember the most about this guy's face?

APPENDIX E

PQ 188.EW: Um just that he looked bloody.

PQ 189.INV: Mhm. And this is after you saw him in the car?

190.EW: Mhm

FC 191.INV: Lot of blood? Little blood?

192.EW: Lots.

PQ 193.INV: Who taught you that move?

194.EW: My father taught me how to fight and all that.

PQ 195.INV: Mhm. Do you practice?

196.EW: No.

MP 197.INV: No?

198.EW: No.

MQ 199.INV: So do you practice at home? Does he teach you at home?

200.EW: He used to but I now know the moves of self-defense.

FC 201.INV: Oh ok. Is it a kind of martial arts or no?

202.EW: No.

PQ 203.INV: What do you call it?

204.EW: I don't know.

MCQ 205.INV: Did this guy look clean, dirty, average looking?

206.EW: Clean.

MP 207.INV: Clean?

208.EW: Mhm

Topic 3

AQC 209.INV: Ok, you can open your eyes. Now what I want you to do is I want you to tell me, again, what happened. I want you to tell me what you were doing prior to seeing this guy and then kinda walk me through everything that happened, all the way up until you get to your grandmother's house, ok?

210.EW: I got out of class a little bit late because my teacher kept all of my classmates and including me because they were talking when they weren't supposed to and when I got out there was barely almost anyone there.

MP 211.INV: There was hardly anybody there?

491

APPENDIX E

      212. EW: Yeah

[PQ] 213. INV: You mean outside in the school grounds?

      214. EW: Yeah.

[OEQ] 215. INV: What time was that?

      216. EW: 3:15 ish.

[PQ] 217. INV: Mhm and then what happened?

      218. EW: Then I put my earbuds in full blast and then I was walking, I crossed the street and then I...

[PQ] 219. INV: What street are you on?

      220. EW: I don't really know the street name. It's near Westbrook.

[PQ] 221. INV: Is this the street you go to all the time?

      222. EW: Yeah.

[PQ] 223. INV: Mhm and then?

      224. EW: And then I see a (inaudible) I saw the guy in a car about two car lengths away and I kinda looked down for a bit and he gave me that look...

[MP] 225. INV: What was that look?

      226. EW: He was hostile and wanted to kill someone.

[PQ] 227. INV: Really?

      228. EW: Mhm.

[PQ] 229. INV: And then?

      230. EW: And that's when I felt my ear itch and I took it out to itch and that's when I heard a car door and I didn't notice until, I heard it and then I (inaudible) and that's when he grabbed me and I said, "Let me go. Let me go." Twice, and then that's when I got my right arm free and then I elbowed him.

[PQ] 231. INV: Where did you elbow him?

      232. EW: In the face where the nose and mouth are.

[PQ] 233. INV: Mhm and then?

      234. EW: And then he let out a scream of agony and I went running and I looked back and I saw his (inaudible) was down over his face.

[PQ] 235. INV: With the trunk open?

APPENDIX E

236. EW: Yeah.

[PQ] 237. INV: And then?

EW: And that's when I just ran to my grandma's and then I didn't tell her yet.

[PQ] 238. INV: You didn't tell who?

239. EW: My grandma yet cuz I didn't want her to freak out.

[MP] INV: You think she'd freak out?

240. EW: Yeah.

[PQ] 241. INV: And then.

242. EW: I waited for (inaudible) that's when my dad came and he was talking to my grandma and that's when I told them both.

[PQ] 243. INV: You told them what had happened?

244. EW: Yeah.

[PQ] 245. INV: And what'd they say?

246. EW: They were all, "No way!"

[MQ] 247. INV: And then? Why'd they say no way?

248. EW: The never heard this happen to a family member before.

[PQ] 249. INV: Mhm. And then what happened?

250. EW: That's all I remember.

[PQ] 251. INV: Nobody talked about it anymore?

252. EW: Yeah, we did for a bit and then talking about it to me for 2 1/2 straight days.

[PQ] 253. INV: Talking to you about it?

254. EW: Yeah, and how it's going on the news and everywhere.

[PQ] 255. INV: It was on the news?

256. EW: It was on Facebook first. The incident that happened to me.

[PQ] 257. INV: How did people find out on Facebook?

258. EW: I told the Officer…

[PQ] 259. INV: Oh, this is the next day when you tell the police?

260. EW: Yeah. Yesterday it was on Facebook first. I don't know how (inaudible).

[OEQ] 261. INV: Mhm. And what are people saying on Facebook?

493

APPENDIX E

262.EW: I don't know. That's all my dad showed me. (inaudible)

PQ 263.INV: Mhm. So did you get hurt?

264.EW: Hurt?

AL 265.INV: Mhm.

266.EW: No.

PQ 267.INV: What about the blood on you? Cuz you said you bloodied him. Was it on your shirt?

268.EW: No. Not at all.

MP 269.INV: No?

270.EW: As soon as I yelled at him, that's when he let go.

PQ 271.INV: Oh, and then he bled after?

272.EW: Yeah.

PQ 273.INV: Oh. Have you ever used that move before?

274.EW: No.

DEQ 275.INV: So what kind of car was it again?

276.EW: Um a black 4-door sedan.

PQ 277.INV: What was the make?

278.EW: Ford.

PQ 279.INV: What year?

280.EW: 2000s - 2005ish

Topic 4

AQC 281.INV: Alright, I'm gonna show you the sketch. When you look at the sketch, I don't need you to tell me whether it looks like him or not. Not just yet. What I want you to do is I want you to do is just look at the sketch, see what I've been doing. After you look at it for a few seconds, I want you to just go ahead and answer to the best of your knowledge. Most people don't remember everything in great detail, however most people tend to remember a lot especially when you're here and focused on the questions. I just want you to tell me whether we're in the ballpark or whether you want me to make some changes. Ok? Here's what I have so far. (shows sketch) First of all, just the shape of the face? How's the shape of the face?
EW: Normal.

MQ 282.INV: Mhm. That's ok? That's what I want to know. Are we in the ballpark? Are we ok?

APPENDIX E

283.EW: I think we are.

OEQ 284.INV: Ok, good. The hair on this head?

285.EW: Mhm.

MQ 286.INV: Something like that but color, are we ok or does it need to be darker/lighter? Are we ok?

287.EW: That's alright.

OEQ 288.INV: Good. The ears?

289.EW: That's alright?

OEQ 290.INV: Good. And the forehead?

291.EW: Normal.

OEQ 292.INV: Mhm. The nose?

293.EW: A bit off.

PQ 294.INV: Mhm. What do you want to do to it?

295.EW: Um(inaudible)

MQ 296.INV: Ok. Well a bit off. A bit off which way? I don't get it. You need to help me with that.

297.EW: Actually, that's fine.

OEQ 298.INV: Ok, good. The mouth and the lips?

299.EW: Um fine.

OEQ 300.INV: Mhm. And the chin and the cheeks?

301.EW: Good.

OEQ 302.INV: Good. And then, I'm sorry about this - it's just the paper, see that right there? Don't worry about that. The neck area. How's that?

303.EW: Good.

PQ 304.INV: And then he's wearing a white t-shirt.

305.EW: Mhm

OEQ 306.INV: And then his eyes. How are we doing on his eyes?

307.EW: A bit bluish.

FC 308.INV: Mhm. We're dealing with black and white here, so do you want it a little darker or lighter?

309.EW: Darker.

PQ 310.INV: Ok, good. Very good. (drawing) How's that?

495

APPENDIX E

311.EW: Good.

OEQ 312.INV: Overall his age, how are we doing on his age?

313.EW: Good.

OEQ 314.INV: Good. Anything else you want to change?

315.EW: Nope.

MQ 316.INV: Any tattoos, scars or marks?

317.EW: No.

OEQ 318.INV: (drawing) So was there anybody around when this happened?

319.EW: No-one was around.

OEQ 320.INV: No? Have you seen that car since?

321.EW: No.

PQ 322.INV: (drawing) What did he say when he grabbed you?

323.EW: He didn't say a word.

PQ 324.INV: No?

325.EW: Mhmn.

PQ 326.INV: What did he have on his hands?

327.EW: As far as I know, blood.

PQ 328.INV: Mhm. No I'm saying before, when he grabbed you.

329.EW: I didn't get to see his hands.

OEQ 330.INV: Mhm (drawing) And I think I already asked you, but has this ever happened to you before?

331.EW: No.

PQ 332.INV: Do you know of anyone else it's happened to?

333.EW: No.

PQ 334.INV: Why do you think he had his trunk open?

335.EW: I don't know but I did see a couple bags…

MP 336.INV: A couple bags? What kind of bags?

337.EW: Like briefcase and moving bag.

MP 338.INV: Briefcase and moving bag?

339.EW: Some sort of bag.

APPENDIX E

PQ 340.INV: And so what color was the bag?

341.EW: Black.

PQ 342.INV: So you could see inside the trunk?

343.EW: Mhm

NR 344.INV: So he grabs you, you say he doesn't say anything, you elbow him, him releases and you look back and what do you see when you look back?

345.EW: He's crouched down, his trunk is open.

PQ 346.INV: He's crunched down and his trunk is open. And then what?

347.EW: I see blood on his hands…

PQ 348.INV: On his hands, yeah you said he was covering, kind of, was he saying anything then?

349.EW: No.

MQ 350.INV: No. So are you running away or are you walking? Are you standing there. What's going on.

351.EW: I looked back while I was running.

PLQ 352.INV: Mhm, so when you looked back at him, so you're seeing him and his car facing you, right?

353.EW: Yeah, when I was walking by.

NR 354.INV: Right, when you're walking by, the car is facing you, so when you turn back…

355.EW: The car is facing the opposite way.

PQ 356.INV: Ah, so you see the trunk open.

357.EW: Yeah.

FC 358.INV: Was the trunk already open before or after?

359.EW: I don't remember.

PR 360.INV: Because I think you said your music is on but you hear the car door open.

361.EW: Mhm.

PQ 362.INV: So when he grabs you, where's the car?

363.EW: Um a few inches away from us.

PQ 364.INV: Is it right there?

365.EW: When he grabbed me, he was like right where the door is.

497

APPENDIX E

PQ 366.INV: Back here?

367.EW: Yeah.

PLQ 368.INV: Oh, ok, maybe ten feet away or so.

369.EW: Mhm.

Topic 5

AQC 370.INV: (drawing) Ok, I'm gonna show you the sketch one more time. I want you to ask yourself, does it remind you of him. If it does, just let me know. If there's something else you want me to change, let me know and I'll take care of it. Ok? (shows sketch)

371.EW: That reminds me of him.

PQ 372.INV: Ok. Want to make any changes?

373.EW: Nope.

PQ 374.INV: Ok. Very good. And the initials to your name?

375.EW: TL

AQC 376.INV: Alright. Thank you so much for being here and I will, I'm going to walk you out one second here. Hang on.

INTERVIEW ENDS

APPENDIX E

EEIA Summary Report
This report is part of the Efficacy of Eyewitness Interview Assessment℠

Date	5/24/22	Type of event	CASE STUDY #15	Type of investigator	Forensic Artist

Topic Descriptions

Topics	Topic Description
1	Welcome, Introduction, Assess
2	Suspect Description
3	Crime Elements
4	Confirmation, Clarification, Review
5	Conclusion, Follow-up, Q&A

Topic Sequence (values by topic order shown on chart): 22, 18, 11, 2, 44, 36, 45, 4

Total Questions	178	Total Responses	187	Average Questions	36	Average Responses	37

Topic Access per Interview

Topic	Questions per topic	Eyewitness Responses
1	22	24
2	55	63
3	52	54
4	45	43
5	4	3

Examination of Questions Types

Type	CE Effect	Questions	Total	Proportion
I	SRP	AQC, NR	13	7%
II	DRCE	ACQ, FC, LQ, MCQ, MQ, MLQ, PLQ	29	16%
III	IRCE	MP, OEQ, PQ	136	76%
IV	MR	EC, AL	2	1%
		EW Responses	187	51%
		Total	**367**	

Topic 2 & 3 Questions (Type III & IV)
- Topic 2: 40
- Topic 3: 47

Reliability of Cognitive Evidence Scale

Cognitive Evidence Effects	More than Acceptable (3)	Acceptable (2)	Less than Acceptable (1)
Diminish Reliability	< 7%	7% - 10%	> 10%
Improve Reliability	> 61%	61% - 57%	< 57%
Mindful Rapport	> 9%	9% - 4%	< 4%
Eyewitness Response	> 49%	49% - 48%	< 48%
Topic 2	> 82%	82% - 78%	< 78%
Topic 3	> 59%	59% - 45%	< 45%
Topic Sequence Deviation	< 1	1 - 2	> 2

RELIABLE COGNITIVE EVIDENCE COLLECTED
HIGHLY RELIABLE: 21 – 18. RELIABLE: 17 – 14 LESS THAN RELIABLE: 13 – 7

COR:	DRCE:	16%	IRCE:	76%	MR:	1%	EWR:	51%	T2:	73%	T3:	89%	TSQ:	2	RCE
0		1		3		1		3		1		3		2	**14**

Confidence of Recollection (COR): 0 = Confidence is affirmed; -1 = Confidence is questionable; -2 = Confidence is unreliable

BIBLIOGRAPHY

Ainsworth, P. B. (1981). Incident Perception by British Police Officers. *Law and Human Behavior*, Vol. 5(2–3), 231–236. https://doi.org/10.1007/BF01044766

Bailey, C. A. (2018). *A Guide to Qualitative Field Research* (3rd ed.). Sage, London.

Bikel, O. (Producer). (2010). The Confessions [Television series episode]. Frontline. Retrieved from https://www.pbs.org/wgbh/pages/frontline/the-confessions/interviews/

Brennan Center for Justice. (2019). Brennan Center for Justice at New York University Law School. https://www.brennancenter.org/sites/default/files/Retention_and_Release_1.pdf

Brief for Innocence Network as Amicus Curiae supporting Defendant, Oregon v Lawson, 239 or App 363, 244 P3d 860 (2010) no. S059234), (no. A132640), (no. 03CR146FE).

Chabris, C. & Simons, D. (2010). *The Invisible Gorilla: And Other Ways Our Intuitions Deceive Us*. Crown Publishers/Random House, New York, NY.

Chiao, J. Y. (2017). Cultural Neuroscience of Compassion and Empathy. In *The Oxford Handbook of Compassion Science*. Ed. Seppala, E. M., Simon-Thomas, E., Brown, S. L., Worline, M. C., Cameron, C. D. & Doty, J. R. Oxford University Press, New York, NY, pp. 147–157.

Chiesa, A., Calati, R. & Serreti, A. (2011). Cognitive Mechanisms of Mindfulness: A Test of Current Models. *Clinical Psychology Review*, Vol. 31(3), 449–464. https://doi.org/10.1016/j.cpr.2010.11.003

Chodron, P. (2002). *The Places That Scare You*. Shabhala Publications, Inc, Boulder, CO.

Chopra, D. (1994). *The Seven Spiritual Laws of Success: A Pocketbook Guide to Fulfilling Your Dreams*. Amber-Allen Publishing, San Rafael, CA.

Commission on Peace Officer Standards and Training. (2021). Retrieved from http://www.post.ca.gov/status-of-current-legislation

Creswell, J. D. & Lindsay, E. K. (2014). How Does Mindfulness Training Affect Health? A Mindfulness Stress Buffering Account. *Current Directions in Psychological Science*, Vol. 23(6), 401–407. https://doi.org/10.1177/0963721414547415

Crime Data Explorer. (2022). *Trend of Violent Crime from 2010 to 2020*. FBI Uniform Code Reporting Program. Department of Justice. https://crime-data-explorer.app.cloud.gov/pages/explorer/crime/crime-trend

Davis, M. H. (2017). Empathy, Compassion, and Social Relationships. In *The Oxford Handbook of Compassion Science*. Ed. Seppala, E. M., Simon-Thomas, E., Brown, S. L., Worline, M. C., Cameron, C. D. & Doty, J. R. Oxford University Press, New York, NY, pp. 299–315.

Dirks, S. (Producer) & Lewis, S. (Host) (2021). *On Our Watch* [Podcast]. KQED, podcast. Retrieved from: https://www.npr.org/transcripts/1000175441

Doyle, J. M., Dysart, J. E., Loftus, E. F. & Newirth, K. A. (2019). *Eyewitness Testimony Civil and Criminal* (6th ed.). Bender & Company, New York.

Doyle, J. M., Dysart, J. E., Loftus, E. F. & Newirth, K. A. (2020). *Eyewitness Testimony Civil and Criminal* (6th ed.). Bender & Company, New York.

Drigas, A. & Karyotaki, M. (2018). Mindfulness Skills Training & Assessment and Intelligence. *International Journal of Recent Contributions from Engineering, Science & IT*, Vol. 6(3). https://doi.org/10.3991/ijes.v6i3.9248

English, D. & Kuzel, M. (2014). Reliability of Eyewitness Reports to a Major Aviation Accident. *International Journal of Aviation, Aeronautics, and Aerospace*, Vol. 1(4), Article 9. https://doi.org/10.15394/ijaaa.2014.1040

Eyewitness Identification Reform. https://innocenceproject.org/eyewitness-identification-reform/

FBI. (2021). Law Enforcement Employees Data, 1960–2020 [Data set] FBI Uniform Crime Reporting Program. Crime Data Explorer. https://crime-data-explorer.app.cloud.gov/pages/downloads

FBI. (2021). *Trend of Violent Crime from 2009 to 2019*. Crime Data Explorer. FBI Uniform Code Reporting Program. Department of Justice. https://cde.ucr.cjis.gov/LATEST/webapp/#/pages/explorer/crime/crime-trend

FBIa. (2020). *FBI, Full-time Law Enforcement Employees*. Retrieved from https://cde.ucr.cjis.gov/LATEST/webapp/#/pages/le/pe

Fisher, R. P. & Geiselman, R. E. (1992). *Memory Enhancing Techniques for Investigative Interviewing: The Cognitive Interview*. Charles Thomas Publisher, Springfield, IL.

Fisher, R. P. & Schrieber, N. (2007). Chapter 2 – Interview Protocols to Improve Eyewitness Memory. In The Handbook of Eyewitness Psychology, Vol 1. Memory for Events (1st ed.). Ed. Toglia, et al., Psychology Press, pp. 53–56. https://doi.org/10.4324/9781315086309

Fisher, R. P. & Schrieber, N. (2019). Interview protocols for improving eyewitness memory. In *The Handbook of Eyewitness Psychology, Volume 1, Memory for Events*. Ed, Toglia, M. P., Read, J. D., Ross, D. F. & Lindsay, C. L. Taylor & Francis, New York, NY, pp. 53–80.

Foster & Freeman. (n.d.). Detecting Latent Fingermarks; Can *We Really Develop Marks* without *Chemical Agents*? Retrieved 6/23/2022, http://www.fosterfreeman.com/webinars.html

Fulero, S. M. (2009). System and Estimator Variables in Eyewitness Identification: A Review. In *Psychological Expertise in Court*. Vol. 2. First Ed. Eds. Lieberman, J. D. & Krauss, D. A. Routledge, London, UK.

Galef, J. (2021). *The Scout Mindset: Why Some People See Things Clearly and Others Don't*. Piatkus, Hatchette.

Genova, L. (2021). *Remember, The Science of Memory and the Art of Forgetting*. Harmony Books, New York, NY.

Goldin, P. R. & Jazzier, H. (2017). The Compassion Cultivation Training (CCT) Program. In *The Oxford Handbook of Compassion Science*. Ed. Seppala, E. M., Simon-Thomas, E., Brown, S. L., Worline, M. C., Cameron, C. D. & Doty, J. R. Oxford University Press, New York, NY, pp. 237–245.

Government Training Agency. (2021). https://www.govtraining.com/wellness-stress-management/

Griffiths, A. (2008). *An Examination into the Efficacy of Police Advanced Investigative Interview Training?* (Doctoral dissertation, University of Portsmouth).

Gross, S. R. & Shaffer, M. (2012). *Exonerations in the United States, 1989–2012 Report by the National Registry of Exonerations*. https://www.law.umich.edu/special/exoneration/Documents/exonerations_us_1989_2012_full_report.pdf

Hahn, T.N. (2005). *Keeping the Peace*. Mindfulness and Public Service. Berkeley, CA. Parallax Press. https://www.ncjrs.gov/nij/eyewitness/procedures_intrv.html

Innocence Project. (2022a). DNA Exonerations in the United States, Fast Facts. Retrieved from: https://innocenceproject.org/dna-exonerations-in-the-united-states/

Innocence Project. (2022b). The Cases: Steven Barnes, Time Served: 20 Years. Retrieved from: http://www.innocenceproject.org/steven-barnes. Accessed 4/7/2022.

International Association for Identification. (2017). Certification Program Operations Manual. FCMB-01-2020-C7, Originated 2017, revised 5/31/2022. 61 pages.

International Association for Identification (IAI). (2023). Forensic Certification Management Board, International Association for Identification. Certification Program Operations Manual. [Forensic Art Certification Established 1995]. Retrieved from https://www.theiai.org/docs/01_Ops_Manual_FCMB-01-2020-C11_1_3_2023.pdf

Interrogate. (2021). In *Oxford Dictionary of English*. Retrieved from https://www-oed-com.libaccess.sjlibrary.org/view/Entry/98260?rskey=4r63fp&result=3#eid

Jaquet-Chiffelle, D. & Casey, E. (2021). A Formalized Model of the Trace. *Forensic Science International*, Vol. 327. https://doi.org/10.1016/j.forsciint.2021.110941

Johnson, M. K., Hashtroudi, S. & Lindsay, D. S. (1993). Source Monitoring. *Psychological Bulletin*, Vol. 114(1), 3–28. American Psychological Association, Inc.

Kabatt-Zinn, J. (1994). *Wherever You Go, There You Are: Mindfulness Meditation in Everyday Life.* Hyperion, New York.
Kabat-Zinn, J. (1990). *Full Catastrophe Living: Using the Wisdom of Your Body and Mind to Face Stress, Pain, and Illness.* Bantam Books, New York.
Kahneman, D. (2011). *Thinking Fast and Slow.* Farrar, Straus & Giroux, New York, p. 35.
Kahneman, D., Sibony, O. & Sunstein, C. R. (2021). *Noise: A Flaw in Human Judgment.* Little Brown Spark, New York.
Kahneman, D., Sibony, O. & Sunstein, C. R. (2021). *Noise: A Human Flaw in Judgment.* Hatchette Book Group, New York, NY.
Klein, C., DeRouin, R. E. & Salas, E. (2006). Uncovering Workplace Interpersonal Skills: A Review, Framework, and Research Agenda. In *International Review of Industrial and Organizational Psychology. Vol. 21.* Ed. Hodgkinson, G. P. & Ford, J. K.. Wiley and Sons, New York, pp. 80–126. https://www.ncbi.nlm.nih.gov/books/NBK84226/table/ch3.t1/?report=objectonly
Köhnken, G., Milne, R., Memon, A. & Bull, R. (1999). The Cognitive Interview: A Meta-analysis. *Psychology, Crime and Law,* (5), 3–38. doi: 10.1080/10683169908414991
Kolts, R.L. (2012). *The Compassionate Mind Approach to Working with Your Anger: Using Compassion-Focused Therapy.* Constable & Robinson, London.
Lane, S. M. & Houston, K. A. (2021). *Understanding Eyewitness Memory: Theory and Applications.* New York University Press.
Langer, E.J. (2014). *Mindfulness (25th Anniversary Edition).* Da Capo Press, Philadelphia, PA.
Lartey, J. & Li, W. (2022). As Murders Spiked, Police Solved About Half in 2020. Marshall Project, Analysis. https://www.themarshallproject.org/2022/01/12/as-murders-spiked-police-solved-about-half-in-2020
Laughery, K. R., Alexander, J. F. & Lane, A. B. (1971). Recognition of Human Faces: Effects of Target Exposure Time, Target Position, Pose Position, and Type of Photograph. *Journal of Applied Psychology,* Vol. 55, 477.
Loftus, E., Doyle, J. M., Dysart, J. E. & Newirth, K. A. (2019). *Eyewitness Testimony: Civil and Criminal* (6th ed.). Matthew Bender & Company, Danvers, MA.
Loftus, E. F. (1996). *Eyewitness Testimony.* Harvard University Press, Cambridge, MA.
MacDonald, S., Snook, B. & Milne, R. (2017). Witness Interview Training: A Field Evaluation. *Journal of Police and Criminal Psychology,* Vol. 32(1). https://doi.org/10.1007/s11896-016-9197-6
Masao, A. (1987, March 22–25). Transformation in Buddhism. Paper presented at the second Buddhist-Christian Theological Encounter at Vancouver School of Theology, Vancouver, British Columbia, Canada. Retrieved from https://www.jstor.org/stable/1390230
Memon, A., Holley, A., Milne, R., Koehnken, G. & Bull, R. (1994). Towards Understanding the Effects of Interviewer Training in Evaluating the Cognitive Interview. *Applied Cognitive Psychology,* Vol. 8(7), 641–659.
Memon, A., Mastroberardino, S. & Fraser, J. (2008). Munsterberg's Legacy: What Does Eyewitness Research Tell Us About the Reliability off Eyewitness Testimony?. *Applied Cognitive Psychology,* Vol. 22, 841–851. John Wiley & Sons, Ltd.
Miller, M. T. & Massey, P. (2016). *The Crime Scene, A Visual Guide.* Academic Press, Elsevier Inc., London, New York, Oxford.
Milne, R. & Bull, R. (1999). Investigative Interviewing: Psychology and Practice. John Wiley & Sons, Ltd, Chichester, West Sussex.
Mistek, E., Fikiet, M. A., Khandasammy, S. R. & Lednev, I. K. (2019). Toward Locard's Exchange Principle: Recent Developments in Forensic Trace Evidence Analysis. *Analytical Chemistry,* Vol. 91, 637–654. pubs.acs.org/ac
Mitchell, S. (1988). *Tao te Ching: A New English Version* (Translation). HarperCollins Publishers, New York, NY.

Morin, R. & Mercer, A. (2017). A *Closer Look* at *Police Officers Who Have Fired* their *Weapon* on *Duty*. Pew Research Center. Retrieved 7/10/2022, https://www.pewresearch.org/fact-tank/2017/02/08/a-closer-look-at-police-officers-who-have-fired-their-weapon-on-duty/

National Institute of Justice. (1999). Eyewitness Evidence: A Guide for Law Enforcement [Office of Justice Programs Publication No. 178240] U.S. Department of Justice. https://www.ojp.gov/pdffiles1/nij/178240.pdf

National Institute of Justice. (2019). Exonerations Resulting from NIJ Postconviction DNA Testing Funding. https://nij.ojp.gov/topics/articles/exonerations-resulting-nij-postconviction-dna-testing-funding#list-of-exonerations

National Police Improvement Agency. (2009). Principles of Investigative Interviewing (NPIA). *National Interview Strategy*. Retrieved from http://www.acpo.police.uk/documents/crime/2009/200901CRINSIO1.pdf

Neff, K. & Germer, C. (2017). Self-Compassion and Psychological Well-Being. In *The Oxford Handbook of Compassion Science*. Ed. Seppala, E. M., Simon-Thomas, E., Brown, S. L., Worline, M. C., Cameron, C. D. & Doty, J. R. Oxford University Press, New York, NY, pp. 371–385.

Nordell, J. (2021). *The End of Bias: A Beginning; The Science and Practice of Overcoming Unconscious Bias*. Metropolitan Books-Henry Holt. New York, NY.

O'Brien, B. (2009). Prime Suspect: An Examination of Factors that Aggravate and Counteract Confirmation Bias in Criminal Investigations. *Psychology, Public Policy, and Law*, Vol. 15(4), 315–334. https://doi.org/10.1037/a0017881

Oregon v Lawson. (2012). Supreme Court of Oregon [Filed November 29, 2012]. CC 03CR1469FE; CA A132640; SC S059234. Appendix (pp. 53–79).

Oregon v. Lawson, US Supreme Court of Oregon. Douglas County Circuit Court Case No. 03CR1469FE Court of Appeals No. A132640 Supreme Court No. S059234. Amicus Brief-Oregon case (p. 8, pph. 2).

Panneerchelvam, S. & Norazmi, M. N. (2003). Forensic DNA Profiling and Database. *Malaysian Journal of Medical Sciences*, Vol. 10(2), 20–26. PMID: 23386793; PMCID: PMC3561883.

Pirsig, R. M. (1974). *Zen and the Art of Motorcycle Maintenance*. New York, NY. HarperCollins Publishers.

Public Safety Officers Procedural Bill of Rights Act. (1976). California Legislative Information, Government Code, Title, 1, Division 4 Public Officers and Employees (Chapter 9.7, 3300, Ch. 465). Retrieved from https://leginfo.legislature.ca.gov/faces/codes_displayText.xhtml?lawCode=GOV&division=4.&title=1.&part=&chapter=9.7.&article=

Roediger III, H. L. & McDermott, K. B. (1995). Creating False Memories: Remembering Words Not Presented in Lists. *Journal of Experimental Psychology: Learning, Memory, and Cognition*, Vol. 21(4), 803–814. American Psychological Association, Inc.

Sartre, J. (2007). *Nausea*. Alexander, L. (translator), New Directions Publisher.

SB494, Law Enforcement: Training §13519.11 (2021). https://leginfo.legislature.ca.gov/faces/billTextClient.xhtml?bill_id=202120220SB494

Shepherd, E. & Griffiths, A. (2013). *Investigative Interviewing, the Conversation Management Approach* (2nd ed.). Oxford University Press, New York, NY.

Skulmowski, A. & Xu, K. M. (2022). Understanding Cognitive Load in Digital and Online Learning: A New Perspective on Extraneous Cognitive Load. *Educational Psychology Review*, Vol. 34(1), 171–196. https://doi.org/10.1007/s10648-021-09624-7.

Smith, J. & Weisman, A. (2010). *The Beginner's Guide to Insight Meditation (Revised Edition)*. Wisdom Publications, Boston, MA.

Taylor, K.T. (2001). *Forensic Art and Illustration*. CRC Press, Boca Raton, FL.

Tirch, D., Silberstein, L. R., & Kolts, R. L. (2016). *Buddhist Psychology and Cognitive-Behavioral Therapy: A Clinician's Guide*. New York, NY. The Guilford Press.

The California Reporting Project. (2022). https://projects.scpr.org/california-reporting-project/

The Effects of Delay on Long-Term Memory. (2007). *Handbook of Eyewitness Psychology, Memory for Events*. Ed. Lindsay, R. C., Read, J. D., Ross, D. F., Toglia, M. P. Lauren Erlbaum Associates, London, p. 135.

The National Registry of Exonerations. (2022). *2021 Annual Report*. A Project of the University of California Irvine Newkirk Center for Science & Society, University of Michigan Law School, and Michigan State University College of law. Retrieved from: https://www.law.umich.edu/special/exoneration/Documents/NRE%20Annual%20Report%202021.pdf

The National Registry of Exonerations. (n.d.). http://www.law.umich.edu/special/exoneration/Pages/Exonerations-in-the-United-States-Map.aspx. Accessed 1/20/22.

Trejos, T., Koch, S. & Mehltretter, A. (2020). Scientific Foundations and Current State of Trace Evidence—A Review. *Forensic Chemistry*, Vol. 18, 100223. Elsevier.

Tversky, A. & Kahneman, D. (1973). Availability: A Heuristic for Judging Frequency and Probability. *Cognitive Psychology*, Vol. 5(2), 207–232. https://doi.org/10.1016/0010-0285(73)90033-9

USA Facts. (2020). *Police Departments in the US: Explained*. Retrieved 7/11/2022, https://usafacts.org/articles/police-departments-explained/?utm_source=google&utm_medium=cpc&utm_campaign=ND-JusticeDefense&gclid=Cj0KCQjwlK-WBhDjARIsAO2sErS0Ez3R1GrYvlRE1BJcErcP5vu8wjPSofyodCTNyYMg1-27Yb6333saAkNNEALw_wcB

USDOJ. (2016). State and Local Law Enforcement Training Academies, 2013. Office of Justice Programs, Bureau of Justice Statistics [July 2016, NCJ 249784].

Vera Institue. (2022). Vera Arrest Trends [Victimizations, How common are victimizations, and how often are they reported to law enforcement?]. https://arresttrends.vera.org/victimizations

Voss, C. & Raz, T. (2016). *Never Split the Difference, Negotiating As If Your Life Depended On It*. Harper Collins, New York.

Walsh, D. & Bull, R. (2013). The Investigation and Investigative Interviewing of Benefit Fraud Suspects in the UK: Historical and Contemporary Perspectives. In *Applied Issues in Investigative Interviewing, Eyewitness*. Ed. B. S. Cooper, et al. Springer Science + Business Media. New York, NY.

Watson, C. D. (2017). The Empathy-Altruism Hypothesis: What and so What? In *The Oxford Handbook of Compassion Science*. Ed. Seppala, E. M., Simon-Thomas, E., Brown, S. L., Worline, M. C., Cameron, C. D. & Doty, J. R. Oxford University Press, New York, NY, pp. 27–40.

Webb, S. (2008). Cop Armed with a Pencil, San Jose Police Artist Shows Uncanny Knack for Drawing Suspects. *San Jose Mercury News*. September 7, 2008.

Weize, E. & Zaki, J. (2017). Empathy-Building Interventions: A Review of Existing Work and Suggestions for Future Directions. In *The Oxford Handbook of Compassion Science*. Ed. Seppala, E. M., Simon-Thomas, E., Brown, S. L., Worline, M. C., Cameron, C. D. & Doty, J. R.. Oxford University Press, New York, NY, pp. 205–217.

Wells, G. L. (1978). Applied Eyewitness-Testimony Research: System Variables and Estimator Variables. *Journal of Personality and Social Psychology*, Vol. 36(12), 1546–1557. https://doi.org/10.1037/0022-3514.36.12.1546.

Wells, G. L. (2011). *Perry vs. New Hampshire: Reflections on the Oral Arguments of November 2 2011*. The Way Back Machine. https://web.archive.org/web/20120501202016/http://www.psychology.iastate.edu/~glwells/Wells_articles_pdf/Perry_vs_New_Hampshire_-_Gary_Wells.pdf.

Wells, G. L., Lindsay, R. C. L. & Tousignant, J.P. (1980). Effects of Expert Psychological Advice on Human Performance in Judging the Validity of Eyewitness Testimony. *Law and Human Behavior*, Vol. 4(4), 275–285.

Wells, G. L. & Olson, E. A. (2005). Building Face Composites Can Harm Lineup Performance. *Journal of Experimental Psychology: Applied*, Vol. 11(3), 147–156.

Wells, G. L. & Seelau, E. P. (1995). Eyewitness Identification: Psychological Research and Legal Policy on Lineups. *Psychology, Public Policy, and Law*, Vol. 1(4), 765–791. https://doi.org/10.1037/1076-8971.1.4.765

Wells, G. L., Small, M., Penrod, S., Malpass, R. S., Fulero, S. M. & Brimacombe, C. A. E. (1998). Eyewitness Identification Procedures: Recommendations for Lineups and Photospreads. *Law and Human Behavior*, Vol. 22(6), 603–647. https://doi.org/10.1023/A:1025750605807

BIBLIOGRAPHY

Wise, R. A., Sartori, G., Magnussen, S. & Safer, M. A. (2014). An Examination of the Causes and Solutions to Eyewitness Error. *Frontiers in Psychiatry*, Vol. 5(102). https://doi.org/10.3389/fpsyt.2014.00102

Zamora, G. (2018). *What If Forensic Artists Are Wrong?* [Video file]. Retrieved from https://www.youtube.com/watch?v=h_Z2ArYmsuc

INDEX

Note: Page numbers followed by f and t indicate material in figures and tables respectively

Accusatory comment or question (ACQ), 165, 263t
Active listening (AL), 165, 188, 206, 263t
Administrative question or comment (AQC), 165, 206, 237, 263t
The Approach, 18, 117, 118, 128–133, 131t
Art of policing, 7–9
Attempted kidnapping
    Eyewitness Interview Assessment Summary Report, 371f
    transcript review, 353–371

Bath Inn sign, 23

Case study transcript review, 279–499
    attempted kidnapping, 353–371, 483–499
    civil case, 372–380
    home invasion, 381–400
    indecent exposure, 444–456, 457–468, 469–482
    robbery, 401–418, 423–435, 436–443
    suspicious person, trespassing, 419–422
CCT, *see* Compassion Cultivation Training
CI, *see* Cognitive interview
Civil case
    Efficacy of Eyewitness Interview Assessment Summary Report, 380f
    transcript review, 372–380
Cognitive evidence, 12–13
    accountability, 32–33
    Confidence of Recollection (COR), 21–22
    culprit and eyewitness, 17, 18f
    DRM experiment, 31, 31f
    estimator variables, 25, 25t
    experiments and practitioners, 30–32
    eyewitness memory, 20, 24
    facial feature, 28
    facial hair, 27
    forensic artists, 28, 29
    guidance on eyewitness interviews, 18–19
    latent fingerprints, 20f
    light beard, 27
    reliable/unreliable, 24
    sketch created without simple manipulation, 29f
    straight edge with simple manipulation, 28, 28f
    system variables, 25–26, 25t
    TIATI, 27
Cognitive interview (CI)
    eyewitness interview, 118–119, 118t
    framework, 121
    Mindful Interview Method (MIM), 119–120, 120t
    technique, 13, 85
Cognitive sketch, 19
    analysis, 81f, 113f
    interviews, 19
    from recollection, 59f
Commission on Peace Office Standards and Training (POST), 47
Compassion Cultivation Training (CCT) program, 87
Complexity interview, 212–228
    body language, 212
    cognitive sketch of subject, 228f
    crime event details, 212
    details confirmation, 212
    Eyewitness Interview Assessment Summary Report, 229, 230f
    RCE score, 228f
    suspect description, 212
Confidence of Recollection (COR), 21–22, 27, 28, 31, 76, 86, 95, 103, 105, 120, 122, 125, 129, 132, 133, 158, 161, 162t, 164, 169, 193, 199, 200, 213, 234, 266t, 283, 301, 308, 318, 338
Confidential transcript review
    cooperative eyewitness, 301–303
    eyewitness interview, noise of, 283–296
    first mindful interview, 308–313
    interview complexity, 318–333
    mock interview, 338–351
Conversation management approach, 127–129, 128t
Cooperative eyewitness
    confidential transcript review, 301–303
    denial of circumstances, 194

INDEX

EEIA, 298–303
  efficacy of, 195–196, 197f
  EIA, 301–303
  eyewitness interview assessments, 195–196, 197f
  hiding behind imperfect knowledge, 194
  RCE score, 195f
COR, *see* Confidence of Recollection
Court testimony, 17
COVID-19, 232, 249
Crime Scene Investigators (CSIs), 19

Department of Justice (DOJ), 259, 260f
Detective mind
  be mindful, 42
  cognitive evidence, 35
  drug money, 37
  eyewitness interview, 36–38, 46–47
  heuristics for, 44
  Hispanic, 38
  mental activities, 36
  serial robbery case, 40–41
  surfer-type jacket, 41
  suspect's facial description, 38
Diminish reliability of cognitive evidence (DRCE), 158, 169, 170, 208, 229, 255, 263t, 264t, 265t, 274t
  benchmark scale, 274t
  maximum proficiency scores, 274t
DNA exonerations, 4
DOJ, *see* Department of Justice
The Dove Real Beauty Sketches, 11
Do you know why you are here? (DYKWYAH), 3, 95, 101, 107, 120, 263t, 266t

Efficacy of Eyewitness Interview Assessment (EEIA), 5, 175
  cooperative eyewitness, 298–303
  eyewitness interview, noise of, 280–296
  first mindful interview, 305–313
  interview complexity, 315–333
  mock interview, 335–351
  summary report, 280–499
Efficacy of Eyewitness Interview Assessment Summary Report
  attempted kidnapping, 371f, 499f
  civil case, 380f
  efficacy of, 191f, 197f
  first mindful interview, 208, 209f
  home invasion, 400f
  indecent exposure, 456f, 468f, 482f
  interview of complexity, 229, 230f
  mock interview, 256f
  robbery, 418f, 435f, 443f
  suspicious person, trespassing, 422f
Empathetic comment/concern (EC), 165, 206, 263t
Empathetic strategy
  establishing rapport, 85–86
  integrating empathy and compassion, 87–89
End of Bias, 55
Enhancing investigative process, 9–10
EW Interview Analysis (EIA), 283
  cooperative eyewitness, 301–303
  eyewitness interview, noise of, 283–296
  first mindful interview, 308–313
  interview complexity, 318–333
  mock interview, 335–351
EWR, *see* Eyewitness Response
Eyewitness
  centre stage interviews, 10–11
  cognitive evidence, 5
  court testimony, 17
  day-in and day-out process of meeting, 24
  forensic artists, 26
  interview guidance, 18–19
  interview techniques, 5
  investigators interviewing, 30
  memory and testimony, 4
  memory works, 24
  real beauty, 11
  system variables, 25–26, 25t
  violent crime, 5
Eyewitness interview
  approach, 130
  cognitive interview, 118–119, 118t
  cognitive sketch of subject, 228f
  conversation management approach, 127–129, 128t
  efficacy in, 199
  element of the crime, 122
  embracing the positives, 133
  forensic art, 139–141
  forensic artist, 118
  framework for interviewing, 117–118
  GEMAC mnemonic, 131t
  investigating paradigm, 118
  investigators, 130–131
  judgmental approach, 131–132
  lack of awareness, 231

lack of efficacy, 231
lack of understanding, 143–144
law enforcement personnel, 141–143, 142t
mirror probe, 124
mock interview, 254, 255
narrative recall *vs.* suspect description, 122
open-ended narration phase, 122
PEACE framework, 132
POST learning, 137
probing images and concept codes, 122–125
rapport building, 120–121
RESPONSE mnemonic, 129, 129t
review and closing phases, 126–127
robbery suspect, 123f, 126f
scrutinizing, 145–147
supplemental training for certain officers, 144–145
training, 136–139, 137t
triggers, 129–130
type courses, 146t
Eyewitness interview, noise of
  closed-ended questions, 181
  Conduct Unbecoming, 176–189
  confidential transcript review, 283–296
  EEIA, 280–296
  efficacy of, 189–190, 191f
  EIA, 283–296
  eyewitness interview assessments, 189–190, 191f
  leading question (LQ), 188–189
  mirror probe questions (MPs), 176, 177, 181
  multiple leading question (MLQ), 181, 188
  open-ended question (OEQ), 176, 177, 181, 188
  RCE score, 189
  re-inspection, 188
  summary report, 191f
Eyewitness Response (EWR)
  benchmark scale, 274t
  maximum proficiency scores, 274t
Eyewitness Testimony, 30

Field Training Officer (FTO), 7, 8, 40, 46, 54, 142
First mindful interview, 199–208
  confidential transcript review, 308–313
  EEIA, 305–313
  EIA, 308–313
  Eyewitness Interview Assessment Summary Report, 208, 209f
  RCE score, 208f
Force-choice (FC), 165, 169, 264t

Forensic art, 4, 8, 9, 11, 12, 44–46, 74, 79, 95, 114, 139–141, 149–150, 156–158, 260
Forensic Art and Illustration, 259
Forensic art indexing, 269–275
  benchmark scale, 274t
  forensic art cases, 273t
  maximum proficiency scores, 274t
  non-forensic art cases, 272t
  random forensic art interviews, 270t
Forensic artists, 28, 29
Frontal cortex, 12
Full Catastrophe Living, 55

Giants' logo, 3
The Golden Rule, 19
Government Training Agency (GTA), 53
The *Guide*, 70t

The *Handbook of Eyewitness Psychology, Vol. 1, Memory for Events*, 233
Home invasion
  Eyewitness Interview Assessment Summary Report, 400f
  transcript review, 381–399

Improve reliability of cognitive evidence (IRCE), 168, 169, 206, 263t–265t
  benchmark scale, 274t
  maximum proficiency scores, 274t
Improve the reliability of cognitive evidence (IRCE), 158, 169, 206
Indecent exposure
  Efficacy of Eyewitness Interview Assessment Summary Report, 456f, 468f, 482f
  transcript review, 444–455, 457–467, 469–481
Innocence Network, 19
Intergovernmental Training and Development Center (ITDC), 53
Interrogations
  eyewitness memory like trace evidence, 77–78
  interviewing eyewitness, 75–77
  objective perspective, 79–80
  qualifying question, 76
  sketch analysis evaluation, 80t, 81f
  stay with interview process, 82–83
  suspicious tools, 78–79
  unreliable eyewitness, 80–82
Interview complexity
  confidential transcript review, 318–333

EEIA, 315–333
EIA, 318–333
Interviewing eyewitnesses
    breaking habits, 48–49
    forensic artist, 44–46
    interviews and interrogations, 43–44
    investigative heuristic, 44
    practicing active listening, 47
    qualitative research, 46–47
    qualitative researcher reviews, 49
    semi-structured interview, 47–48
    unstructured conversations, 46
Investigative process, enhancing, 9–10
The Invisible Gorilla, 37

Keeping the Peace: Mindfulness and Public Service, 56

Leading question (LQ), 264t

MCQ, *see* Multiple-choice question
MIM, *see* Mindful Interview Method
Mindful Interview Method (MIM)
    analysis, 112–114
    cognitive evidence, 102–103
    cognitive interview, 119–120, 120t
    comments and questions, 263–266
    composite sketch, 260
    conclusion section, 103–104
    discipline of, 93, 94f
    essence of, 38
    expectations and future research, 259–262
    FBI facial identification, 45f
    focus of topic sequence, 106t
    highlights of guide, 260f
    identifying the culprit, 261f
    intentional listening standard, 98–99
    interrogations, 44
    interview framework, 4
    mindful format, 106t
    mindful reset, 58, 95–97
    mirror probe questions, 100–102
    overview, 93
    practice session, 105–112
    principles, 94–95
    probing framework, 97–98, 98t
    qualifying question, 21
    sample script, 267–268
    suspect's facial description, 38
Mindfulness
    awareness, 57, 59–60
    benefits of practicing, 61
    cognitive scientists, 51
    driving mindfully, 54
    interview the eyewitness, 56–57
    investigator, 51
    opportunities, 53–54
    pay attention, 57–58
    paying close attention, 54
    practice as investigators, 89
    practicing being present, 55–56
    spiritual laws of success, 52–53
Mindfulness-Based Stress Reduction (MBSR), 87
Mindful of the innocent
    case studies, 72–74
    eyewitness interviews, 73
    Innocence Project, 67–68
    mindful of DNA, 65–67, 66t
    misidentifications and wrongful convictions, 73
    reforms, 68–71
    reliable eyewitness evidence, 69, 70t
    transparency and adherence, 71
Mindful rapport (MR), 265t
    benchmark scale, 274t
    maximum proficiency scores, 274t
Mirror probe (MP), 99, 100, 108, 109, 111–113, 124, 165, 176, 204, 206, 218, 231, 238, 240, 241, 247, 264t
Misidentifications and wrongful convictions, 13, 73
MLQ, *see* Multiple leading questions
Mock interview, 231–254
    confidential transcript review, 338–351
    EEIA, 335–351
    EIA, 338–352
    Efficacy of Eyewitness Interview Assessment Summary Report, 256f
    eyewitness interview assessment, 254, 255
    mock robbery victim, 232f
    RCE score, 254f
MRP, *see* Mindful rapport
Multiple-choice question (MCQ), 165, 169, 264t
Multiple leading questions (MLQ), 165, 181, 188, 264t
Multiple questions (MQ), 165, 237, 264t

Narrative review (NR), 165, 245, 247, 265t
National Institute of Justice, 66, 66t, 260

The National Institute of Justice (NIJ) booklet, 25–26
National Institute of Justice Information, 66t
Noise, A Flaw in Human Judgment, 39
Noise measurement
    cognitive evidence, 153–154, 153t
    COR evaluation, 162t
    data collection, 157–161
    EEIA process, 161–162
    EEIA summary report, 168f, 170
    eyewitness interview assessment process, 163f
    eyewitness performance, 153
    forensic art workshop, 149–150
    forensic sketch interviews, 156t
    interviewer performance, 154–155
    investigations, 152–153
    law enforcement, 163–164
    mindful interview, 155–156
    narrative report, 171
    Question Category matrix, 164–165, 166t
    reliability of cognitive evidence, 169–170, 172f
    reliability scale changes, 171
    routine eyewitness interview, 155t
    shadow sketching, 150–152, 151f
    system variables, 171–172
    Topic Access section, 165–169, 167t
    transcript and coding exchanges, 164
Non-forensic artists, 61, 199, 228

On Our Watch, 175, 193
Open-ended question (OEQ), 165, 231, 265t
Oregon v. Lawson, 19

The Places That Scare You, 55
Police artist, 5, 7, 8, 10, 13, 24, 52–54, 75, 117, 135, 140, 150, 259
Probing leading question (PLQ), 165, 181, 265t
Probing question (PQ), 165, 265t, 268

Qualifying question (QQ), 128, 129, 162, 200

Reliability of cognitive evidence (RCE) score, 112, 189
    benchmark scale, 274t
    case studies, 277t–278t
    complexity interview, 228f
    cooperative eyewitness, 195f
    eyewitness interview, noise of, 189
    first mindful interview, 207f
    may affect, 266t
    mock interview, 254f
    no effect on, 263t, 265t, 266t
Reliability score, 79, 81, 158, 161, 172
Reliable eyewitness evidence, 69, 70t
robbery
    Efficacy of Eyewitness Interview Assessment Summary Report, 418f, 435f, 443f
    transcript review, 401–417, 423–434, 436–442
Robbery crime report, 38

The Scout Mindset, 39
The Seven Spiritual Laws of Success, 52
Shadow sketching, 150–152, 151f
Standard rapport (SRP), 266t
Students and eyewitness interviews, 11–12
Suspicious person, trespassing
    Efficacy of Eyewitness Interview Assessment Summary Report, 422f
    transcript review, 419–421

That Is All There Is (TIATI), 22, 26, 27, 33, 43, 83, 95, 102, 113, 124, 130, 204, 207, 211, 215, 239, 242, 244, 266t
TIATI, *see* That Is All There Is
Topic sequence deviations, benchmark scale, 158, 274t

Uniform Crime Reporting (UCR) Program, 135, 136, 136f, 144, 260